ALTERNATE
CHANNELS

ALTERNATE

CHANNELS:

THE UNCENSORED STORY OF GAY AND

LESBIAN IMAGES ON RADIO AND TELEVISION

STEVEN CAPSUTO

BALLANTINE BOOKS

NEW YORK

A Ballantine Book
The Ballantine Publishing Group

www.randomhouse.com

Library of Congress Card Number: 00-104495

ISBN: 0-345-41243-5

Cover photos: (left) © Ellen Denuto; (right) © The Special Photographers Co. Both courtesy of Photonica

Text design by Ann Gold

Manufactured in the United States of America

First Edition: July 2000

10 9 8 7 6 5 4 3 2 1

TO MY PARENTS,
for teaching their children about love and tolerance at an early age . . .
and for letting us stay up to watch the "good" TV shows

TO MY BELOVED PARTNER, ED FERRY,
without whom my life—and this book—would be less complete

Contents

FOREWORD

Alternate Channels began in 1987, while I was a volunteer with Gay & Lesbian Peer Counseling of Philadelphia. Many of the phone-in clients were gay or bisexual teenagers who had internalized so much of society's prejudice that they were contemplating suicide. "What do you think gay people are like?" we would ask them. Their invariable response: "I only know what I see on TV." The consistency of that reply amazed me, because television was such a gay-friendly medium during my own teenage years. In the late 1970s, I had done what these young people were doing: I had scoured the media for clues about gay adults' lives. Could gay people be happy? Did they have friends? Could they find jobs? Did their families still talk to them? I found most of the answers I needed in TV talk shows, newscasts, and episodes of prime-time series like *All in the Family*, *Maude*, *Lou Grant*, *Barney Miller*, and *Soap*. These programs showed me responsible, productive, everyday lesbians and gay men who reflected a range of professions, personalities, lifestyles, and political views. TV taught me something vital that our school curricula had neglected to mention: that there were other people in the world like me. But by the late 1980s, when our young counseling clients were desperate for role models, television's message had changed.

By the third time I heard a shaky, young voice say, "I only know what I see on TV," my stomach was churning. I wondered what they had seen that could make them feel so hopeless. I also wondered about previous generations. What must it have been like to grow up "queer" amid the media images of the 1930s or the 1950s? What social changes must it have taken to bring about those gay-positive portrayals that I remembered from the 1970s? And what—if anything—was being done in the 1980s to bring back some of that fairness? At the time, no books addressed these issues in a comprehensive way. So in 1989, I decided to write one.

A little research revealed that those gay-friendly shows of the late 1970s were an oasis in the desert. If I had been born just a few years earlier or later, my teenage quest for role models would have exposed me to the most rancid and slanderous stereotypes. For example, in the fall 1974 TV season, six prime-time dramas portrayed lesbian, gay, bisexual, or transgender characters. *All* were rapists, child molesters, or murderers. On popular variety hours and game shows, the mere mention of homosexuality was treated as a cause for hysterical laughter. Gay organizations of the mid 1970s built strong consulting relationships with the TV networks and studios in response to such portrayals. In the mid 1980s, though, these relationships decayed almost completely, which explained some of what we were hearing in the counseling center. With that background in mind, I initially set out to write a scathing exposé of television's antigay bias. In the 1990s, though, the TV networks' attitude toward homosexuality improved dramatically, and so the focus of this book changed. As a result, *Alternate Channels* evolved into something far more balanced and useful: It became a case history of how—in the course of one generation—a marginalized minority group was able to completely reverse its media image through the use of protests, negotiations, positive reinforcement, and occasional threats. The proven techniques described in these chapters can easily be readapted by almost any segment of society experiencing problems with mainstream media representation.

Like other underrepresented groups, gay and bisexual people always longed to "see themselves in the picture." To be sure, there are some individuals who do not want their lives "cheapened" on commercialized, prepackaged TV. But on the whole, sexual-minority people are as fascinated with the medium as any other part of the population. For decades, gay viewers had to content themselves with mentally translating heterosexual stories and relating to them as best they could. Or they would half jokingly read queerness into characters on such mainstream shows as *I Love Lucy*, *Batman*, *The Odd Couple*, *Sesame Street*, *The Flintstones*, *Star Trek*, and *The Beverly Hillbillies*. Describing this phenomenon, lesbian humorist Yvonne Zipter quipped: "[T]here simply were no lesbians on TV. Therefore, we had to make them up: Betty and Wilma, Lucy and Ethel, Miss Hathaway, Alice from *The Brady Bunch*. Obviously, judging from the above cast of characters, we were a desperate people."[1] When gay and bisexual viewers did recognize their lives on screen, even for a moment, the reaction was strong. Amanda Donohoe's lips touched Michelle Greene's for two seconds in a 1991 *L.A. Law* episode, touted as the first lesbian kiss on TV. Phones buzzed. People mailed videotapes back and forth across the continent. Many hosted *L.A. Law* parties to watch and rewatch that nervous kiss. For three years, various neighbors would borrow my tape of the show. The impact of that two-second kiss, even three years later, reflected how inadequate the portrayals were during the intervening three thousand hours of programming. But by 1994, interest in those two seconds of film had diminished as more compelling and engaging portrayals reached the home screen.

All told, some fifty network series of the 1990s had gay or bisexual recurring roles—more than twice the combined total for all previous decades. There were so many likable, sympathetic characters that the occasional killer-queer stereotype could slip past without a breath of protest from gay groups. The late 1990s even brought two sitcoms with openly gay title roles: *Ellen*, whose protagonist came out as a lesbian in 1997, and *Will & Grace*, about the friendship between a gay man and a straight woman. *Spin City*, *Dawson's Creek*, and other ensemble shows now present gay characters as "one of the gang"—as full plot participants rather than as an "issue of the week." In recent years, the media also have given unprecedented coverage to that relatively new phenomenon, the openly lesbian or gay celebrity. Of course, even today, there is room for improvement. At this writing, lesbians have again vanished from prime time. Almost all of the gay regular characters on the broadcasting networks are young, white, and male. Depictions of same-sex couples are rare. But even with these limitations, things are better than they were in 1990, and far better than the near invisibility of the 1950s and 1960s.

The issue goes beyond the mere frequency of depictions. Those young people who only knew what they saw on TV had access to televised images, but the images were selective and narrow. Some of the counseling clients described seeing news footage of Gay Pride parades that showed *only* "men in dresses," "lesbians on motorcycles," and people in S&M gear. Others cited fictional TV characters whose lives seemed stunted and unfulfilled when compared to the straight characters around them. Still others saw homosexuality as a freakish subject, only suitable to the sideshow atmosphere of certain daytime talk shows. And most of the callers accepted the media's implication that gay men in the late 1980s were busy with just one activity: dying of AIDS. These young people had used television's cues as yardsticks to measure their own worth and their future prospects. This sort of response to the media is not unique to sexual-minority youth. Much has been written about TV's portrayal of ethnic and cultural minorities, and its historically negative impact on the self-esteem of young people in those groups. Distorted images of gay lives have a similar effect on lesbian, gay, and bisexual youth. But unlike children in most minorities, whose family and friends can serve as role models, gay youth historically had only stereotypes to tell them who they were. In 1989, a federal study of teen suicide estimated that one-third of such deaths in the United States were gay teenagers who had learned self-hatred from many sources, including the media.[2] That report—and later, more specific studies of gay youth—confirmed what we were seeing in Philadelphia: that visibility, role models, and fair broadcast depictions were too important to dismiss as just a luxury.

A full decade into this project, I continue to marvel at the enormous influence of this medium. In the early 1990s, I was astounded by the impact of round-the-clock news coverage about gays in the military— how it brought home to the public some basic concepts that the gay civil rights movement had been trying to communicate for years. In 1997, I was amazed at the strong emotions (pro and con) that surrounded the coming out of Ellen DeGeneres and her TV character. And today, I am amazed at the casualness with which gay characters and out-of-the-closet celebrities turn up on the small screen. Again and again, television's gay and bisexual images have had subtle but profound effects on American society—not only on gay youth, but also on families, workplace environments, attitudes toward hate crimes, and discourse about civil rights. There is every indication that this influence will continue in one form or another for many years. To understand where TV portrayals of same-sex attraction are headed, it is crucial to know what images appeared in the past, where they came from, and how they were discussed and challenged in each era. *Alternate Channels* explores the nature of those depictions and—more important—reveals how they got on the air in the first place.

ABBREVIATIONS KEY

A great many organizations play a role in this story. To keep their abbreviations from running together into a confusing alphabet soup of initials, here is a quick reference guide:

ACT UP	—	AIDS Coalition to Unleash Power
AFA	—	American Family Association
AGLA	—	Alliance for Gay and Lesbian Artists
CBTV	—	Coalition for Better Television
CLeaR-TV	—	Christian Leaders for Responsible Television
DOB	—	Daughters of Bilitis
GAA	—	Gay Activists Alliance
GLAAD	—	Gay & Lesbian Alliance Against Defamation
GLF	—	Gay Liberation Front
GMTF	—	Gay Media Task Force
MSNY	—	Mattachine Society of New York
NGLTF	—	National Gay and Lesbian Task Force
NGTF	—	National Gay Task Force (old name for NGLTF)
QN	—	Queer Nation

INTRODUCTION

[In the 1950s, I was] overwhelmed with a sense of my abnormality; I had no idea there were millions of other teenagers going through the very same thing. Everywhere, in the newspapers and magazines, on radio and TV, in the movies, there wasn't the slightest affirmation of homosexuality.
　　　　—Gay author/activist Allen Young, recalling his teenage years[1]

When I came out to one of my best friends [in the early 1990s], she was just, like, "Well that happened on *90210.*" She was, like, "I don't care."
　　　　—A lesbian teenager on a TV talk show[2]

In America, broadcasting wields a power once reserved for religion: the power to tell people what is real. The social norms embedded in television shows have the capacity to shape public thought as much as any preacher, politician, or journalist. Even fictional shows—prime-time comedies and dramas—convey strong messages about what is normal, good, strange, or dangerous. Regardless of whether the messages are explicit or implicit, many viewers come to accept them as common knowledge after hearing them repeated night after night. As propagandists know, people tend to internalize the ideas they hear most often, and Americans tune in to their favorite TV shows very often indeed. The A. C. Nielsen Company estimates that U.S. households average around seven hours of television viewing *per day*. With that much access to the public, TV can marginalize topics or legitimize them, inspiring sympathy or scorn toward issues and people. Its images of gay and bisexual lives are especially influential since so many viewers believe they do not

1

personally know anyone who is gay.[3] For some of these viewers, TV is a principal source of information on the subject.

The television networks spent forty years, from the mid 1950s to the mid 1990s, treating homosexuality as if it were a brand-new, cutting-edge "contemporary theme." Starting in the late 1960s, the networks often inserted gay content into the premieres of new shows to prove how topical and daring the series would be. Later episodes of these shows, however, almost never incorporated gay content. This desire to appear innovative—but not *too* innovative—has long been a part of commercial television. To compete for ratings and advertising dollars, the networks must present shows that are novel enough to pique the public's interest. But programs must not push the envelope too hard, or they will scare away potential viewers. Walking that fine line of public taste is very tricky where gay content is concerned. At this writing, public attitudes toward homosexuality are thoroughly divided. National surveys by the Gallup Organization suggest that four-fifths of Americans now consider antigay job discrimination wrong, but most Americans also still consider homosexuality immoral.[4] Commercial TV therefore tries to negotiate that paradoxical middle ground between tolerance and acceptance.

If some series now tend more toward the "acceptance" side of that continuum, it is because TV writers and producers are generally more gay-friendly than the public. Given their work environment, many people in TV's creative side have friends and colleagues who are openly gay or bisexual. Even the straightest of TV writers usually has some inkling of the issues that sexual minorities face. Writers' motivations for creating likable gay roles vary. Sometimes, the impetus is political—a sense that promoting tolerance is the socially responsible thing to do. But just as often, those who have gay friends or who are gay themselves are just heeding the old maxim, "Write what you know": they are drawing on events in the lives of the people around them. Network executives, who must keep an eye on the Nielsen ratings and profit margins, often feel the need to rein in some producers' enthusiasm for gay content. How much leeway a producer is given in these cases depends not only on the show's Nielsens, but also on what is happening in the broader political context of current events. Gay-themed scripts have been approved most frequently during periods when gay issues were receiving heavy news coverage. The nature of those news stories and the ways that prime time echoed them varied widely from decade to decade.

A QUICK TIMELINE

Sexual-minority images on the air date all the way back to television's prehistory, when radio comedy and drama held a hallowed place in popular culture. When network broadcasting began in the 1920s, it was, like the cinema before it, a very morally conservative medium. Homosexuality, at that time, was generally considered so filthy, so warped, so unmentionably dangerous that even *anti*gay speeches were banned from the airwaves. From the 1930s to 1950s, gay imagery reached radio listeners implicitly, mostly in the form of swishy male comic-relief roles. So long as no one actually *said* that a sissy character was homosexual, the network censors allowed him on the air. Sometimes a radio script might refer mockingly to same-sex attraction, or a male radio villain might seem all the more sinister because of his effeminate air. But mostly, when it came to same-sex desire, there was silence. When famous novels, plays, and historical events were adapted for broadcast, gay content was censored out. These same guidelines held true on early TV, amid network rules that forbade scripts about "sex abnormalities." Only in the mid 1950s, in televised news stories and talk shows, did the commercial networks begin using concrete words like "homosexual" on the air. This social problem of homosexuality could be mentioned *only* in nonfictional shows, and only rarely. Gay fictional characters were years away, and bisexual roles were even further in the future.

Broadcasting did not operate in a vacuum. In most areas of American society, gay people were every bit as invisible as they were on TV and radio. Homosexual sex was a crime in every state of the Union. Public revelation often meant disgrace, loss of employment, jail time, or involuntary subjection to psychiatric procedures. In the 1950s and early 1960s, the public imagination also linked homosexuality with communism. Amid police harassment and mass arrests of patrons in gay bars, antigay harassment of many sorts became increasingly common. To protect themselves, gay people generally kept a low profile during this period.

Homosexuality remained virtually invisible on television through the mid 1960s, except for a few neurotic and/or violent lesbian roles around 1962. As mainstream movie theaters began screening low-key gay content, homosexual references became permissible on television. The practical effect of this liberalization, however, was to bring in antigay material. In the mid 1960s, smirking references to male homosexuality became a frequent feature of comedy programs and game shows. During the same era, a few dramas portrayed straight men who were falsely accused of homosexuality: these men faced harrowing discrimination until they could clear themselves of that hideous charge. No gay characters appeared on-screen. In short, as far as TV's entertainment shows were concerned, homosexuals were strange, unseen beings who presumably existed somewhere off-camera, and whose mere mention was cause for snickering or terror. There had always been gritty, issue-oriented shows on TV, but even these did not dare address homosexuality directly. Those conventions, however, were about to change.

Around 1967, TV sponsors started clamoring for shows that might appeal to urban, college-educated young adults. TV executives responded with topical programs that dealt with the youth counterculture, the antiwar movement, racial conflicts, the Sexual Revolution, feminism, and countless once taboo issues. In their quest to cash in on social controversies, some producers experimented with different ways to safely incorporate gay content into existing TV genres. Certain patterns quickly emerged, and continued unchanged into the 1980s. Most of the gay characters were white men in their twenties or thirties. When a lesbian did appear, she typically was carrying a smoking gun or bloodied knife. Other acceptable roles for a lesbian were as a victim of violence (often at the hands of other lesbians) and as a woman mourning her lover's death. As these descriptions suggest, gay women seldom appeared in comedies. By contrast, gay men were considered *very* funny, especially in the 1960s and 1970s. Regardless of gender, gay roles generally were one-shot guest appearances: gay regulars were such an oddity that those few who did appear became the subject of news reports. On commercial TV, gay roles almost never turned up in period pieces or in science fiction: sexual deviance was presented as a uniquely twentieth-century phenomenon.

TV script writers of the early 1970s finally settled on two main genres of "gay script": the "coming out" script, in which a show's regulars learn to tolerate a gay guest character, and the "queer monster" script, in which the sexual-minority guest roles are killers or child molesters. The monster approach soon became the norm. From fall 1973 to summer 1975, lesbian and gay characters seldom appeared as doctors, detectives, or other problem solvers. Instead, viewers tuned in to shows like the *Police Woman* episode "Flowers of Evil," which portrayed a trio of murderous lesbians who ran around killing old women. Or viewers heard kindly Marcus Welby, M.D., describe homosexuality as a grievous but treatable ailment, more worrisome than diabetes or alcoholism.

Gay organizations protested the portrayals bitterly. When their attempts at polite negotiation went nowhere, some activists tried more confrontational and colorful tactics to get the TV industry's attention. Network vice presidents eventually decided to compromise with the more polite, professional negotiators, rather than continue to be annoyed by the radical, direct action groups. Over the years, this two-pronged approach— using both polite tactics and raucous, "in your face" protests—has often worked better than either tactic has by itself. By spring 1975, after months of lobbying and meetings, all three networks promised to avoid stereotypes when portraying gay characters, just as they theoretically did when depicting ethnic and religious minorities. The networks also adopted a practice that NBC had used sporadically since 1973: gay-themed scripts would be run past openly gay consultants to increase the shows' believability, and as a way to spot stereotypes before filming. The Gay Media Task Force (the most frequent source of gay-script consulting) encouraged a balance between "good" and "bad" characters—"a gay cop for every gay robber." This arrangement turned TV portrayals around so quickly that the *Washington Post* heralded 1976 as television's "Year of the Gay." Visibility increased still further in the late 1970s, amid massive news coverage of antigay crusades by the still coalescing Religious Right. With gay civil rights in the headlines almost daily, TV dramas, too, began dealing with antigay prejudice as a civil rights issue. Noble lesbian and gay characters went to court to fight discrimination in a half-dozen shows. The old-style gay killers and rapists were replaced by characters so uniformly squeaky-clean that they were scarcely believable.

The late 1970s and early 1980s brought the first hit shows with prominent gay male regulars. The characters were self-accepting, law-abiding citizens. But the limits of commercial TV meant that these "gay" men spent more time romantically involved with women (whom they hugged and kissed) than with their boyfriends (whom they did not). Then, in 1981, the networks pulled back almost completely from gay content and from other controversial subjects. Network executives looked at recent events, and decided that the country had taken a morally conservative turn, especially on gay issues. Ronald Reagan and a host of conservative candidates had swept the 1980 elections with strong backing from Reverend Jerry Falwell and his influential organization, the Moral Majority. Religious Right groups—an impressive political force in 1981—were threatening to boycott sponsors of "immoral" TV shows, and the networks capitulated to their demands.

Starting in 1982, the networks had yet another reason to think that audiences would avoid shows with gay content: news coverage of the mysterious AIDS epidemic led to widespread fear and hatred toward gay and bisexual people. There was a brief resurgence of gay content in the 1984–85 TV season, but the antigay backlash inspired by fear of AIDS kept many proposed shows off the air. The networks were especially skittish about portrayals of gay and bisexual *men* (whom the public blamed for spreading AIDS). One side effect of the pullback was that lesbian roles finally achieved greater visibility, even in sitcoms. However, because the gay community was preoccupied with AIDS-related survival issues in the 1980s, activists did not have time to maintain pressure on the networks. The media negotiating mechanisms that were set up in the 1970s soon fell apart. Big-time gay media advocacy toward the commercial networks did not reemerge until around 1989, when the Gay & Lesbian Alliance Against Defamation (GLAAD) began getting national attention.

Sexual-minority roles began appearing on television again in large numbers in the early 1990s. Some of the top-rated shows of the decade included gay or bisexual regulars, seen week after week as an ongoing part of life. The portrayals diversified, not only in the characters' demographics (more women, people of color, teenagers) but also in the types of stories where they could appear: period pieces, cartoons, wholesome "family" dramas, Christmas stories, and so on. And, as previously noted, several series since 1997 have since portrayed lesbians or gay men in central leading roles.

This increased visibility still operates within firm limits, even as we approach the seventy-fifth anniversary of network broadcasting. Although television has achieved a reasonable level of casual inclusiveness toward gay male characters, bisexual roles remain rare. Lesbian images—plentiful for a couple of years in the mid 1990s—are fading fast. Racial diversity among gay and bisexual characters is again minimal. Perhaps most important, proposed portrayals of even minimal same-sex affection still make network executives squirm mightily.

THE POLITICS OF VISIBILITY AND DESIRE

In the 1970s and 1980s, lesbian and gay roles fell into two main categories: violent sociopaths and saintly victims of prejudice. The "bad gays" were easy to spot: they were the ones with a sex drive. "Good gays" were almost asexual: Except for a few recurring roles, they usually did not date anyone of their own sex, form a relationship, or seem to even *know* other gay people. Gay villains, on the other hand, were seen leering at people of the same sex, could have long-term relationships, and were physically affectionate with their partners on-screen. It is no coincidence that the first passionate same-sex kisses in prime time involved murderers. "Good" gay couples—a rarity—were desexualized. Compared to the gay villains (and to TV's straight couples), these "good" duos' relationships seemed cold: they lacked physical contact, emotional strength, and durability. Only since the mid 1990s have nonsociopathic gay roles been allowed to display a moderate level of physical affection on the small screen.

Achieving even this limited visibility has required a constant struggle. No matter how bizarre or bland the portrayals, shows with sexual-minority themes attract controversy. Since the late 1970s, the loudest opinions on this subject generally have come from antigay organizations on the Religious Right and from national gay groups. Although they are on opposite sides in the war over gay visibility, both camps have borrowed tried-and-true methods from ethnic and racial minorities, which in turn drew on other, earlier social change movements.[5] The Religious Right and the gay activists have also taken advantage of each other's marginalized status in mass culture: each group portrays the other as a small band of noisy, extremist malcontents. Amid all the posturing and propaganda, it is easy to forget that each side is working from a set of sincere, deeply held beliefs.

For conservative Christian groups like the American Family Association (AFA), the presence of gay characters on TV is a shining example of all that is wrong with "man-centered" (as opposed to "God-centered") morality. Such organizations hold that moral relativism is destroying America. They point to increased violence in the streets, teenage pregnancies, and other ills they attribute to a move away from Christian biblical absolutes—absolutes which they believe are the only thing that can hold society together. They fear that their children will grow up in a chaotic world without values, kindness, or respect. Before the advent of broadcasting, religious fundamentalists could raise their offspring in a comparatively closed environment. Radio and TV, however, brought alien, worldly concepts right into the home. Some religious conservatives see television as contributing to society's problems by teaching young people that morality should be flexible. In recent years, groups like the AFA and the Christian Leaders for Responsible Television (CLeaR-TV) have tried to win back some of that original parental control. Since they consider few transgressions more heinous than homosexuality, the elimination of sexual-minority content from TV has become one of their key rallying points. These Religious Right media-watch groups often contrast the networks' sympathetic gay roles against TV's frequent portrayal of conservative Christians as hypocrites, bigots, or serial killers.

Organizations like the Gay & Lesbian Alliance Against Defamation, meanwhile, are resolute in their efforts to protect their communities' tenuous, newly won freedom. They say that the media have historically underrepresented and maligned gay and bisexual people. Particularly in the early 1990s, some organizations cited rising statistics about antigay violence, which they attributed, in part, to a callous society trained by biased media images. GLAAD and other groups have argued that there ought to be likable, dignified, sexual-minority roles on TV because, quite simply, such people are a part of everyday life. Many nonactivist gay and bisexual viewers also feel strongly about seeing their lives reflected on TV, but for them the issue is more personal than political. Some talk fondly or bitterly of the first time they watched a gay-themed TV show with their family. Many who came of age in less gay-friendly times recall an adolescence without role models, since everything in the media reinforced the notion of universal heterosexuality. In their 1972 book, *Sappho Was a Right-On Woman*, Sidney Abbot and Barbara Love wrote:

> Lesbians are [told] by society as a whole, by the media—especially
> television—that women love men. This is not only omnipresent, it seems

fixed, final . . . Consider the loneliness and pain of participating in a culture that absolutely refuses to recognize your existence.[6]

Film historian Vito Russo echoed this in 1986:

> We go to the movies to see ourselves. Motion pictures in America have been a reflection of the way we see our country and our people. So when you go to the movies and you don't find yourself up there, it really comes home to you in a double sense that you're an alien in your own culture.[7]

These are the main reasons why gay organizations and individuals have so persistently praised the media's recent progress toward gay inclusiveness, and are working so hard to improve things further.

ABOUT THE TEXT

Alternate Channels documents the history of gay and bisexual content in national entertainment shows from the 1930s through 1990s. It examines radio from 1930 to 1952, and television from 1948 to 2000. The material is organized chronologically into brief vignettes. Prime-time broadcast comedies and dramas are the main focus, but there is some discussion of newscasts, talk shows, daytime serials, and other genres, as well as brief glimpses of cable TV programming. For context, there is some discussion of transsexual characters, though these have been extremely uncommon on network television. The text often refers to "sexual minorities," a term that properly includes lesbians, gay men, bisexuals, and transsexual (or transgender) people. Given the shortage of prime-time transsexual images, the book's discussions of "sexual minorities" will, in practice, usually focus on homosexuality and bisexuality.

I define "lesbian characters" and "gay characters" as ones who express feelings of attraction for people of their own sex. "Bisexual characters" reflect romantic or sexual interest in both men and women. No other criteria apply. Except in passing, we will not discuss characters like the butch woman carpenter, Ralph, from *Green Acres*; nor fussy Uncle Arthur from *Bewitched*; nor plain Jane Hathaway from *The Beverly Hillbillies*; nor high-strung Dr. Smith from *Lost in Space*. We will not probe the psyche of the neighbor, Monroe, from *Too Close for Comfort*, even though he gave off an undeniably gay "vibe." Nor will we ponder the sexual and political leanings of Tinky Winky, the handbag-toting purple imp from the *Teletubbies*, whom some Religious Right leaders consider part of a scheme to promote acceptance of gay men among toddlers. Such characters do require discussion in another forum, because viewers' perceptions of them illustrate forcefully the power of stereotyping.[8]

When I refer to "the shows studied for this book," I mean the more than 4,300 relevant broadcasts about which I compiled notes in my research database. For approximately 1,200 of these, my information came directly from broadcast recordings, dating from 1933 to 2000. For another 100 shows, I was able to study production scripts, program transcripts, backstage memos, or network censors' reports. Other data came from interviews with people who worked on the programs, and from published reviews, *TV Guide* listings, and the work of earlier historians. Some of my best sources have been Religious Right media-watch newsletters, which document gay-themed telecasts far more assiduously than does any gay organization. Plot summaries in the *Journal of the American Family Association* have proven particularly accurate, though of course thoroughly biased against gay-friendly content.

Except in stock phrases such as "lesbian and gay," "gay" means both men *and* women in this book. I use the terms "lesbians" and "gay women" interchangeably. In the later portions of the text, I sometimes use contractions and abbreviations like "lesbigay" (for "lesbian, bisexual, and gay"), "GLB" ("gay, lesbian, and bisexual"), and "GLBT" ("gay, lesbian, bisexual, and transgendered"). Though a bit colloquial, they reflect the era being discussed, and they make for faster reading than constantly repeating "lesbians, gay men, bisexual men and women, and transgendered persons" multiple times on the same page. The terms "homophobic" and "heterosexist" (which I dislike for a variety of linguistic and political reasons) do crop up occasionally where no other terms seemed to work. In my view, their meanings are very specific. As the suffix "-phobia" suggests, homophobia is active prejudice based on an irrational fear of gay people. Since not all antigay prejudice is rooted in such fear, not all antigay prejudice really qualifies as "homophobic." Heterosexism, a tangentially related term, refers to society's pervasive, unthinking, and often well-meant assumption either that everyone is straight or that gayness is an inherently pitiable and inferior condition.

FUTURE DIRECTIONS

At this writing, during the 1999–2000 television season, it is fashionable to talk about the supposed proliferation of "queer" roles on TV. But in truth, the head count of GLBT characters is no longer all that impressive. In fact, during the current TV season, there are weeks when one can find more portrayals of vampires in prime time than of gay people.

Making predictions is always a potentially embarrassing pursuit, but current trends do offer some hints of what may be in store. The number of televised sexual-minority images seems likely to increase over the next ten years, as TV converges with Internet technologies, allowing for high quality video-on-demand. This will make niche-market programming—including unapologetically gay-inclusive shows—more affordable and more profitable. Mass-market TV shows may react in either of two divergent ways: either (as happened during the rise of cable TV) the broadcast networks will make their own programming more daring to compete with the frank, niche-market shows, or else they will go back to television's traditional common denominator—stories about straight, white Christians. Only time will tell.

It is especially hard to predict what role sexual-minority media activists will play in all this. During four decades of activism, gay and bisexual people have often wondered if television portrayals were really improving, and whether the media-watch groups really served any useful purpose. Especially before *Ellen*, some people believed—as gay journalist John Mitzel wrote in 1992—that most changes in TV's depictions since 1972 were merely cosmetic.[9] Some now argue that society has progressed so far that all GLB activism is obsolete. Others think, as I do, that things *have* improved, but that those insufficient changes have made gay and bisexual people a bit complacent. As society moves farther from the "bad old days," it becomes harder to remember what it is that the antigay activists want to bring back. And with time, the sexual-minority communities also forget their own victories and how they achieved them.

This book, I hope, will serve as a reminder, a reminiscence, a useful context in which to understand future media images. I hope it will also add to a broader understanding of how mainstream broadcasters have attempted to make peace with historically marginalized segments of society.

IN THE BEGINNING . . .

Early Radio

Radio is dedicated to God . . . When you switch on your receiving set, you may sit back in perfect confidence that no manner of diabolic doctrine, from atheism to zymology, will afflict your ears.

—*Mitchell Dawson, "Censorship in the Air," 1934*[1]

Fashion photographer Russell Paxton was a rampaging queen who threw fits at the drop of a designer hat. "I've taken pictures of beautiful males," he gushed after one photo shoot, "but this one is the end—the absolute *end*! Oh, I tell you he's *godlike*!" Russell arrived on ABC Radio in 1947 when *The Theatre Guild on the Air* presented Moss Hart's play "Lady in the Dark." As on Broadway, the play featured this supporting character, an openly gay photographer. *Theatre Guild* was a prestigious series known for breaking taboos. Its writers toned down this play for radio, but somehow convinced ABC to allow Russell explicitly gay lines like "He's a *beautiful* hunk of man!"[2] As played on radio by Keene Crockett, he was a stereotypical, childish, self-centered whiner, but he was also a first. From the start of network radio in the 1920s until 1952, *Theatre Guild*'s "Lady in the Dark" was the only known broadcast to include an explicitly homosexual character. This shortage of gay roles was hardly surprising. At the time, homosexuality was officially considered a sex crime and a sign of profound depravity. It was, therefore, unfit for early radio.

Radio's moral standards *had* to be strict. Unlike theater or film or vaudeville, radio signals reached into every home that had a receiver.

Children, women, and old people might be listening (so the argument went), and society had a duty to protect them from shocking, tasteless broadcasts. This medium, where toothpaste was once considered too "personal" a product to advertise—this medium where married, heterosexual characters seldom did more than kiss—was not ready or willing to acknowledge sexual deviates.[3]

Besides being immoral, any mention of homosexuality could have meant financial ruin for broadcasters. Angry sponsors and the United States government had closed stations over less controversial subjects. Homosexuality was so taboo that even *anti*gay comments were dangerous. In 1930, the Federal Radio Commission (FRC) decided not to relicense station KVEP in Portland, Oregon. The FRC cited numerous "obscene, indecent, and profane" utterances that the station had allegedly broadcast, including antihomosexual remarks by a local politician, Robert G. Duncan. As commentator Carroll O'Meara observed in *The Forum* magazine in 1940, ". . . radio's unwritten code can be summed up about as follows: *Nothing shall be broadcast which might embarrass, offend, or disgust any decent parents or their children seated at the dinner table in mixed company . . ."[4]

Writers who adapted plays and novels for radio broadcast routinely straightened or neutered gay characters.[5] Newscasters ignored stories involving "sex perversion."[6] Censors rewrote or banned suggestive popular songs. In 1946, columnist John Crosby reported in the New York *Herald-Tribune*:

> [Cole] Porter's sophisticated lyrics have been a headache for the song-clearance departments of radio networks for years . . . The broadcasters took a long, long look at "My Heart Belongs to Daddy" before it was allowed on the air. Then, for obscure reasons of their own, they decided young ladies could sing it but young men couldn't . . .[7]

Lesbians and gay men looked in the mirror of the mass media and saw no faces like their own. When an image did flicker briefly into view—usually in the print media—the view was grotesque. "The sex pervert," *Newsweek* reported in 1949, ". . . is too often regarded as merely a 'queer' person who never hurts anyone but himself. Then the mangled form of some victim focuses public attention on the degenerate's work." Gay-themed books and plays ended in "recovery" (conversion to heterosexuality) or suicide. A comparatively liberal 1947 article in *Collier's* magazine urged mandatory "treatment" of gay adolescents. It described a New York project that "cured" homosexuals before their deviance could lead to harsher crimes, like child molestation, arson, and murder.[8] Even these sensationalist articles avoided lesbianism, a subject that combined two taboos: homosexuality, and the idea of women as active, autonomous sexual beings.

Radio's avoidance of gay themes made sense in that climate. There had been a few exceptions, though. One night in 1933, a San Francisco station began airing a performance of Rae Bourbon's gay drag revue "Boys Will Be Girls," live from Tait's Café. The risqué production was cut short quickly, and listeners heard the local police raiding the café to close down this illegal "pansy show." On the major radio networks, a handful of early-1930s' broadcasts included more low-key homosexual jokes, usually without legal problems. These vaudevillian routines based their humor on the assumption that all people were straight. In an episode of the Marx Brothers' *Flywheel, Shyster and Flywheel*, Groucho and Chico stow away on a ship. A ship's officer identifies himself to Groucho as the bos'n's mate. "You're his mate?" asks Groucho. "Well, I hope you are very happy together. Give my regards to the bos'n." Other programs used antigay prejudice to get laughs, as did a 1933 *Rudy Vallee Show*:

> WOMAN: Mother says I'm too young to have company. What would
> you do if you went out with a young fella and he tried to kiss you?
> MAN: *(warily)* Look, I don't go out with fellas who try to kiss me.[9]

Such jokes soon disappeared. In the late 1930s, the networks restricted all sexually suggestive humor in an attempt to avoid proposed government censorship. Under the new industry guidelines, radio comedians limited their "homo" gags to oblique sissy jokes and occasional "radio drag." Though drag is primarily visual, it had a close cousin on radio. On a 1939 *Jack Benny Program*—a typical example— men play the catty, female leads in a spoof of the movie *The Women*. In preliminary dialogue, they complain about having to wear dresses and makeup for the skit, but they use their regular male voices throughout the routine. As a result, they sound like *very* bitchy queens. ("That hussy! I could scratch her eyes out! . . . Phyllis, you say one more word . . . and I'll slap the rouge right off your face. And *then* will those bags show!")[10]

From the early 1930s to the mid 1940s, *Myrt and Marge*, a popular soap opera about theater folk, featured what may have been the first implicitly gay regular character on the air. Ray Hedge plays Clarence Tiffingtuffer, a fretful, nervous, effeminate young costume designer who is a close, loyal friend of the title characters. As with other comic-relief "fairy" characters, Clarence's sexuality is conveyed indirectly, through broad stereotypes. He is snide, snitty, egotistical, and sometimes infantile—though this is less obvious when he is talking with the two heroines. The scripts often present Clarence in feminine terms. Awaiting the arrival of new costumes he has designed, he exclaims, "I'm as jumpy as a bride!" Almost lisping, he assures the chorus women that their outfits will be "simply gorgeous. *Simply* gorgeous! I'd love to try one on myself!" Clarence addresses other males as "my dear man"—unless they are authority figures who are inconveniencing him, in which case they become "You brute!" He is unquestionably, as *Radioland* magazine called him, a "thithy." And when it comes to bitchy repartee, he can dish with the best of them. "I don't mean to be catty," he confides before ripping into someone, "*but* . . ." At the height of the censorship crackdown in the late 1930s, *Myrt and Marge* seemed to tone him down slightly. But by the mid 1940s, Clarence was back in full flame.[11]

On network radio, the eight years between the 1938–39 crackdowns and *Theatre Guild*'s Russell were mostly years of "clean" entertainment shows sprinkled between war news and public affairs programs. The postwar years, however, brought an intense sexualization of American culture. One of the most visible symbols of this attitude toward sex was Dr. Alfred Kinsey's Institute for Sex Research. Kinsey's famous report on male sexuality appeared in January 1948 amid extensive media hype. The report's findings caused shock and moral indignation, particularly its assertion that homosexuality was far more common among American men than most people had believed. Smirking allusions to male homosexuality proliferated on radio within three weeks of the report's release. The change in radio scripts may have been a response to the

Kinsey report. But in some ways, both the report and the radio gags were reflections of a broader shift in sexual attitudes.

On January 10, a Sam Spade mystery on *Suspense* featured swishy, comic-relief characters who sobbed hysterically at the least provocation. The script hints that Spade's effeminate male client, Larry LaVerne, finds the detective *terribly* attractive: "Why, Mr. Spade," LaVerne pants on getting his first glimpse of the tall, handsome investigator. "You are a *pleasant* surprise, a *pleasant* surprise *indeed!*" The show also suggests that the two bickering villains are a couple. "Why on earth do I stay with him?!" one thief weeps, complaining of his long-time companion.[12] Delicate, nervous males like these got laughs on many types of shows. They were ambiguous characters whom a naive listener might easily perceive as straight. Innuendo reigned. Like *Theatre Guild*'s Russell and *Suspense*'s overemotional queens, radio's implicitly gay men were portrayed as unstable, unimportant, and very comical.

Meanwhile, dozens of comedy shows joked about the seemingly ridiculous idea of two men being married to, or in love with, each other.[13] The new banter was mostly innocuous and reflected no real acknowledgment of gay people. For instance, on *The Burns and Allen Show*, George Burns thinks he hears his wife at the door:

SOUND: *Doorknock*
GEORGE: Come in, Sweetheart.
SOUND: *Door opens*
BILL: *(enters)* Thank you, Honey.
 Audience laughs
BILL: . . . Why this sudden affection?
GEORGE: I took you for my wife.
BILL: Not that I remember.
 Audience laughs[14]

Radio jokes almost never paired women with women. Series of the 1940s produced no implicit lesbian characters to parallel the male sissy. The closest radio came to presenting stereotyped "bulldykes" were characters who were not gay at all. Supposedly grotesque butch women turned up on several comedy shows, but mostly as "man-crazy girls" whose plainness thwarted their search for the right man. Some, like the "lady wrestler" on *The Phil Harris–Alice Faye Show* and Sweetie-Face Wimple on *Fibber McGee and Molly*, were asexual hulks who did not know their own strength.[15] Among attractive, young woman characters, the main pastime was husband hunting. Lesbian listeners heard no echoes of themselves on the air.

The main exception was NBC's *The Big Show*, a ninety-minute all-star variety series hosted by "the glamorous, unpredictable Tallulah Bankhead," as she was introduced each week. By 1950, when her radio show premiered, the once-great stage actress had become something of a self-parody. Her sexual orientation had been the subject of wide-spread speculation for years (biographers usually suggest she was both bisexual and promiscuous) and she had a devoted gay male following. The comedy writers behind *The Big Show*, including Goodman Ace and Selma Diamond, wrote material that played off of Bankhead's unmentionable but supposedly scandalous sexual past. Other running gags included her increasingly masculine appearance as she approached old age, and her insistence that she had no need for a husband. Her sidekick, Meredith Willson, often called her "Miss Bankhead, sir." Guests on the show often referred to Bankhead in masculine terms. One week, comedian Fred Allen quipped, "Tallulah Bankhead? Oh, *him*!" On another episode, guest Groucho Marx told Tallulah, "For lo these many years, I've admired you, man and boy. You were a *cute* boy . . ." The writers sometimes even allowed her the sort of mistaken-identity humor usually reserved for men. On one episode, guests Joan Davis and Judy Holliday try to convince Tallulah to chase men as they do. They finally get her to phone Allen and try to pick him up. When the phone is answered, Bankhead unwittingly hits on Allen's wife. The studio audience, which almost always included a large number of gay men, howled with delight. But to keep things safely ambiguous, the writers followed these gags with reminders that their star still had an eye for muscular, young men.[16]

Network censors frustrated any radio writer who tried to adapt serious literature that even mentioned homosexuality. Introducing a Sunday broadcast of highlights from *A Streetcar Named Desire*, the president of the New York Drama Critics Circle apologized that they could not present the scenes as written. "The Sabbath being the Sabbath," he told listeners, "and the radio being the radio, *A Streetcar Named Desire* is not an easy drama to present on the air of a Sunday afternoon . . ." He expressed hope that the censored version would "not be too inhibited or diluted to suggest the full strength and power of [the play] when it is seen onstage." The broadcast included the scenes in which Blanche discusses her late husband, but all mention of his male lover vanished.[17] Numerous works underwent similar cosmetic surgery. Acclaimed plays like *The Captive* and *Tea and Sympathy* could not be broadcast at all because they made "perversion" too central a theme.

As television stole radio's ratings in the late 1940s, radio censorship decreased. At least one series seemed to include a gay regular, though the scripts never came right out and said so. That series was *Candy Matson*, a show about a sexy "girl detective." Produced and set in San Francisco, it aired from 1949 to 1951 on NBC Radio's West Coast stations. Candy's sidekick is a witty, effete San Franciscan photographer named Rembrandt Watson. He is a recovering alcoholic and as radio historian John Dunning put it, "not much in the down-and-dirty department, being something of a creampuff." Candy and Rembrandt's relationship has all the hallmarks of "the typical" gay man–straight woman friendship. He is her friend and confidant and, she explains, "He's been like a mother to me many, many times."[18]

More blatant references turned up on comedy/variety shows. A 1950 *Bing Crosby Show* from San Francisco includes a tongue-in-cheek, mock wedding between Crosby and Bob Hope, with Judy Garland officiating:

> HOPE: [It's] too beautiful to just stand here, Bing. Shall we dance?
> CROSBY: Well, I'm game. But what'll we do with Judy?
> GARLAND: Well, you boys go ahead. I'll stay here by the light switch in case the Law breaks in.

The program also continues the previous week's skit about Hope and Crosby selling the sponsor's product as cigarette girls in drag:

> HOPE: You mean I have to be a cigarette girl at Ciro's?!
> CROSBY: What're you beefin' about? I'm working the Mocambo.

HOPE: Holy smoke! Are you Carlotta?! . . .

CROSBY: My black curls fooled you, didn't they? . . .

HOPE: You must have had those curls glued on real tight. We had quite a tussle . . .

CROSBY: I did enjoy slapping your face . . . And incidentally, I'll thank you to return my garter.

HOPE: I may as well. All the snap's gone out of it.

Crosby and Hope got away with this because they were major stars with long-standing heterosexual credentials. Aside from the remark about "the Law" breaking up same-sex dancing (a common occurrence at the time), this was safe absurdism. Hope often used this kind of humor to vary his perennial skirt-chasing routine. Its practical effect was to reinforce the idea of homosexuality as "other" and to reinscribe heterosexuality as normal.[19] Male homosexuality was seen as terribly funny.

By contrast, starting in 1952, scripts usually depicted lesbians as leading violent lives. From the 1950s through the 1980s, most lesbian characters on radio and TV dramas were portrayed as either killers or corpses. Gay men could be funny; lesbians could only be dangerous or tragic. The U.S. networks' first known lesbian character died of strangulation in her only scene on a 1952 broadcast of *The Black Museum*, a radio crime anthology from England. Based on a true case, the episode "The Brass Button" certainly *seemed* to be about an antilesbian killing. The writers could not say that, of course, so they used euphemisms like "not interested in men," "living that strange and unnatural kind of way," "had no men friends," and "a boyfriend would have been too ordinary for her." A local vicar tells police he has long suspected that Jeanette Morgan would end badly, though listeners knew from her one scene that she was charming if eccentric. The vicar explains that despite Jeanette's unnamed faults, her killer must be punished. In the end, the soldier who killed her is found guilty. The jury rightly concludes he had heard gossip about Jeanette, then sought her out and made advances. When she resisted, he strangled her. The clearest suggestion of lesbianism comes from Jeanette herself, who tells the soldier, "Get away. When you found out so much about me, you might also have found out that I'm not interested in *men*—least of all soldiers." Radio's first lesbian survived just over 90 seconds.[20] British radio toyed with implicitly queer characters throughout the 1950s, so it is not surprising that U.S. radio's first lesbian was imported. This broadcast's veiled references marked the outer limits of what American radio was prepared to allow.

Radio writers did not invent the idea of comic sissies or tragic lesbians. Those conventions had long histories in fiction and the stage. As an audio medium, radio could go only so far in reiterating those stereotypes. Also, because of taboos, radio performers had to make queer characters *sound* gay without *saying* they were. Television added ·a whole new dimension: women could look menacingly male and men could use the swishy physicalizations that had drawn laughter in vaudeville a generation earlier.

APPLE PIE, BUXOM BLONDES, AND WIMPY WRESTLERS

Early Television

> Respect is maintained for the sanctity of marriage . . . ; Illicit sex relations are not treated as commendable; Sex crimes and abnormalities are generally unacceptable as program material; . . . Criminality shall be presented as undesirable and unsympathetic.
> —*Television Code of the National Association of Radio and Television Broadcasters (NARTB), which was incorporated into all of the networks' policy books, 1954*[1]

TV producer Milt Josefsberg has recalled that around 1950, numerous gay men gave up production jobs in the New York theater and migrated west to Hollywood's television colony. "Every TV show had at least one homosexual on its staff," Josefsberg said. "It was fashionable to have a token homo." The era's scandal magazines put a less positive spin on this: they implied that theater and broadcasting were controlled by a kind of "lavender" mafia.[2] But even if gay men were visible to their colleagues behind the cameras, the reality of gay lives found no concrete expression on-screen.

Early network TV promoted marriage, the nuclear family, and traditional gender roles. Sitcoms like *Father Knows Best* and *The Adventures of Ozzie and Harriet* celebrated the white, suburban, American family, offering it as the pinnacle of human existence. Whatever social problems viewers faced in real life, they knew that such issues would not intrude upon the idealized world of these escapist shows. Television treated heterosexual marriage as humanity's only natural goal, the only route to happiness. Characters expressed pity for the perennially single. Divorced characters were rare. Most of these were bitter and unhappy until the story reunited them with their ex-spouse or engaged them to someone else.[3] Even commercials sold marriage, implying that any woman who did not devote her life to pleasing her husband and children was a failure.

Once wed, TV suggested, a woman became incapable of anything other than housework. TV depicted single women and widows as competent workers, but any married woman who wanted a job outside the house was a "wacky" incompetent. In sitcoms like *I Love Lucy*, even an intelligent wife like Ethel Mertz could not hold down the simplest of jobs. Reinforcing the rigid gender roles of the 1950s, these shows also suggested that married men could not iron a shirt without burning it, nor cook without destroying the kitchen.[4]

Early television banned even hints of same-gender dating. The paranoia reached such a peak that NBC dropped the word "gay" (meaning "happy") from a sitcom title after two episodes in 1950; apparently, they feared viewers would mistake the leads for lesbians. The sitcom was *Young and Gay*, based on the popular novel *Our Hearts Were Young and Gay*. NBC changed the title to *The Girls* in January 1950 without public explanation. Retitling a series was rare, and usually accompanied a change in format, cast, or network.[5] None of these applied to *Young and Gay*. Amid growing awareness that "gay" could mean more than "frolicsome," NBC probably thought *Young and Gay* was a dangerous title for a series about two Bryn Mawr alumnae sharing a Greenwich Village apartment.

TV—like radio, vaudeville, and minstrelsy—thrived on stock characters. Television's clichés included the happy, wise black maid; the scheming, wacky housewife; the addled, breadwinning husband; and the scrupulously honest cowboy—all of whom seemed to be Christian or, in very rare cases, Jewish. Each reflected cherished myths about race, gender, class, and religion. Together, they suggested the existence of an America with no contradictions—a society where straight, white, middle-class Christians ruled benevolently and other people stayed gladly in the background. Another stock character, the "sissy," reflected a cherished myth about gay men: it reduced them to giddy incompetents. Television followed the lead of earlier entertainments by reinforcing the weak public image of minorities. Like the happy, singing slave characters in blackface minstrel shows, TV's sissies were funny, childlike, silly, impractical, impulsive, and powerless. Although the networks forbade mentioning homosexuality, the ubiquitous sissy combined so many stereotypes that viewers recognized him anyway.

TV reflected a cherished myth about lesbians, too: the myth that they did not exist. Of course, many people *knew* that lesbians existed in the 1950s, but it was an awareness tinged with distaste. Some of the public outcry over Kinsey's report on female sexuality reflected that attitude, as did the proliferation of lesbian pulp novels—which stores displayed next to women's prison novels and other genres considered inherently sensationalist. A lesbian allusion even crops up in a wild "gag episode" of the radio soap opera *The Guiding Light*, recorded by the cast as a gift to writer/producer Irna Phillips. The not-for-broadcast recording uses every taboo the cast could think of, including four-letter words, a depiction of child abuse, and a mock commercial advocating use of the sponsor's detergent as a douche. At one point, a promiscuous character tries to figure out when she became pregnant. She says that it could not have happened in April, because "I went with girls in April."[6] But lesbian characters—even implicit ones—generally did not appear in actual broadcasts.

Television's first major "queer" character was wrestler Gorgeous George, one of the biggest video stars of the late 1940s. Although off-camera he was, by all accounts, straight, in the ring he swished and preened. George played the villain: audiences booed when he entered, and cheered when he lost—which he usually did. His entrances were legendary. First, a dapper valet sprayed the ring with perfume. Organ music played while George minced around the arena in one of his eighty hand-embroidered silk robes. Men in the crowd jeered, hissed, blew kisses, and called "Yoo-hoo!" On one occasion when George bowed, the announcer cracked, "I'm surprised it's not a curtsy." The valet would remove "Georgie pins" from the hulking wrestler's marcelled hair and George would toss the pins daintily to fans. If a referee touched The Gorgeous One, the valet dusted the spot and sprayed the ref. Between falls, George admired himself in a mirror and primped his luxuriant blond curls. George played his queeny image to the hilt. In what was surely someone's idea of a joke, he even appeared on a broadcast of the women's audience-participation show *Queen for a Day*. His persona in the ring was that of a stereotypical, self-absorbed gay man, and viewers flocked to TV sets week after week to see him take a beating. On the rare occasions when he won a match, audiences booed and jeered. When he lost, the sight of the defeated sissy, with his expensive coiffure reduced to a sweat-drenched wreck, generated raucous applause.[7]

Other wrestlers, hoping to imitate George's financial success, created effeminate characters.[8] "Swish wrestlers" soon were legion, prompting antigay crusader Arthur Guy Matthews to write in 1957:

> TV wrestling shows openly display homosexuals or deliberately feminized men behaving like homosexuals. The responsible commission should ban such characters from the wrestling field until they cut their hair and stop wiggling their hips and throwing kisses to men. Those who are really homosexuals and not just putting on a show, should be permanently banned and the wrestling promoters arrested and fined. I love wrestling and have wrestled myself. It is a wonderful sport. I have to grit my teeth each time I see a "queer" wrestler on my TV screen. I am sure there are millions of Americans who feel the same way.[9]

Most video "pansies" were fictional characters on comedy and variety shows. Sissy characters were safe objects of ridicule who had no friends, relatives, or romantic partners. They were portrayed outside the sacred nuclear family, thus outside TV's ideal of humanity. The only family ever ascribed to them was an overbearing mother. Unconnected to other members of society, TV sissies held jobs considered unessential—"women's work" by 1950s standards: they were secretaries, florists, ham actors, numerologists, and decorators. Most were one-shot guest roles. Audiences could laugh at a sissy, secure in the knowledge he was no one they knew or needed. By separating implicitly gay characters from the viewer's life, they remained nonthreatening. As a result, gay men saw themselves on television only through the distorted lens of comic stereotypes.

A 1953 episode of Ann Sothern's sitcom *Private Secretary* was typical. Actor Franklin Pangborn, famous for portraying sissies in the movies, plays an effeminate secretary who gave up dreams of being an interior decorator because he was too delicate for that profession. "I bruise easily," Mr. Hollis explains, "and when you have to hang drapes, you've got to climb ladders." With his white gloves clutched in one hand, his dapper wardrobe, his dark walking stick, and a perpetual pout, Hollis was every cartoonist's vision of the male homosexual. Even here, though, an "innocent" viewer might just think him an eccentric, funny man who longed to meet the right woman. He says nothing to suggest heterosexuality *or* homosexuality.[10]

A better-known ambiguous role was comedian Ernie Kovacs's purse-lipped, lisping poet, Percy Dovetonsils, who began regular TV appearances around 1951. Percy is wealthy, giddy, and seems more asexual than anything else. Many reviewers called Percy a "sissy." An NBC press release just called him "strange." He turns up in almost every Kovacs show, reading silly verse on a set representing his Greenwich Village penthouse. Percy came closest to saying he was gay one week when he lifted the plastic flower from a drink and began plucking petals, reciting, "He loves me, he loves me not . . ." Again, "innocent" viewers could think he was jokingly imitating schoolgirls, who were more likely than boys to engage in the petal-plucking ritual. Kovacs also played an effeminate, presumably gay Hollywood film star named Rock Mississippi (the name was a spoof of Rock Hudson). Mississippi swished, wore long false eyelashes, and spoke in effusive, gushing tones.[11]

On other variety hours, straight male characters mistakenly kissed each other, then reacted with disgust, humiliation, or violence. For instance, at the end of a soap opera spoof on *The Steve Allen Show* in 1958, a man tries to kiss his wife but accidentally kisses the policeman who is handcuffed to her. The humor comes from both men's embarrassment.[12] Studio audiences usually laughed uncomfortably at such gags. These skits, like the old vaudeville sketches on which they were based, portrayed repulsion and anger as the only responses to affection between men. This was no malicious media conspiracy: just unthinking reflections of the era's "obvious" truths.

THE QUEERING OF
AMERICAN TV
Television: 1953–1959

I doubt if my mother ever heard the word homosexuality or would have known what it meant. It seems we have come far when we are even disposed to discuss it.
—*TV talk show host Fannie Hurst, 1958*[1]

The 1952 and 1954 Television Codes' ban on "sex abnormalities" began eroding immediately. Two things paved the way for more open depictions of gay people: one was transsexualism, and the other was comedians' tendency to ad lib on live shows. The "new" topics—sex change and homosexuality—appeared first on news and talk shows, then entertainment shows. These broadcasts usually reinforced traditional ideals of heterosexuality. Even so, official and unofficial censors fought to keep the topics off the air from the start.

Transsexual Christine Jorgensen came back from Denmark as a woman in February 1953 amid much media hype. Television had banned homosexuality, but there were no clear rules yet on the new phenomenon of sex-change surgery. Talk shows and print reporters pounced, discussing Jorgensen so extensively that nightclub comedians only had to mention the word "Denmark" to get laughs. By breaking gender taboos, these discussions and Jorgensen's on-camera appearances broke trail for shows on homosexuality. Broadcast executives learned they could stretch the "sex abnormalities" rule without tragic consequences. This freedom spread quickly to network variety shows, where censors began allowing "Denmark" jokes. An early example appeared on *The Jack Benny Show*. Benny and guest Bob Hope play hunters carrying a dead tiger to their campsite. The script apparently contained one vague Denmark joke. But because the show aired live, Hope could push the boundaries by improvising lines that CBS might never have approved:

> BENNY: Here we are in Africa with a tiger. Everybody knows there are no tigers in Africa . . .
>
> HOPE: You sure?
>
> BENNY: I'm positive.
>
> HOPE: Okay. *(Turns the tiger around. On the other side, it is a leopard.)*
>
> BENNY: Hey! *(Examines both sides of the animal, then looks at the audience.)* He must have gone to a veterinarian in Denmark. *Audience—huge laugh and applause.*
>
> HOPE: I wondered why he had his hand on his hip when I shot him. *(Benny stares at Hope in shock, slowly loses concentration and laughs, swatting Hope's arm.)*
>
> HOPE: *(just as Benny regains his composure)* Oh look, he has his claws manicured.
>
> *(Benny, still laughing, looks worriedly at Hope.)*
>
> HOPE: Don't point. I know the line.[2]

At the same time, two political movements were under way that would soon expand television's treatment of homosexuality beyond derisive comedy. In the early 1950s, the Mattachine Society, a homosexual support group, was gaining adherents on the West Coast. Meanwhile, in 1950, Congress launched a campaign to remove homosexuals from government jobs. The chairman of the Republican National Committee announced that "perverts" in government were "perhaps as dangerous as the actual communists."[3] These two movements—pro-gay and antigay—grew up side by side, each generating more and more press from 1950 to 1954. The government investigations peaked in 1954 with the nationally televised Army–McCarthy hearings. By then, two other gay groups had formed in California: the Daughters of Bilitis (DOB, a lesbian group) and ONE, Inc.[4] The Mattachine Society began mailing press releases to publicize its efforts. For the first time, mainstream media knew where to find politically active, openly gay speakers. A few mainstream periodicals devoted long articles to sexual deviance, but no broadcasters were biting. Then, just as the Army–McCarthy hearings were beginning, *Confidential File*, Los Angeles's top-rated local television talk show, devoted a half-hour program to the subject. It was, apparently, the first TV or radio panel on homosexuality.[5]

Confidential File reveled in topics usually considered too controversial for television. Introducing the 1954 gay-themed telecast, host Paul Coates explained:

> According to Kinsey's estimates, there are about 200,000 homosexuals in the Los Angeles area . . . We're going to talk about these people tonight and about the problem they present to the community at large. You'll hear from a psychiatrist, a police official, and a homosexual.

Inviting a homosexual, especially a Mattachine officer, was daring: by prevailing standards, the Mattachine was a bunch of lonely subversives and communists who advocated perversion. The young gay man appeared only in profile and used a pseudonym, "Curtis White." White discussed the impact of antigay prejudice and said he believed that society and homosexuals could one day coexist in mutual respect. After the medical and police experts had their say, Coates showed silent film footage of a Mattachine discussion group. He expressed surprise at White's willingness to appear on TV:

> COATES: I'd like to ask you, does your family know that you're—a homosexual?
>
> WHITE: They didn't until tonight.
>
> COATES: Do you think they're likely to learn about your homosexuality as a result of this program?
>
> WHITE: I'm almost certain they will. And I'm quite certain that I will probably lose my job as a result of the program, too.
>
> COATES: Well, then may I ask why you agreed to appear on this program?
>
> WHITE: I hope that through this means I can be of some use to someone other than myself.

The overall presentation suggested that homosexuality was sinister. *ONE* magazine noted:

> Films of the Mattachine discussion group . . . revealed nothing but a group of men and women drinking coffee, eating cookies and chatting amiably in a homey living room. But Alfred Hitchcock–like shots of this commonplace scene managed to give it a suspicious character.

A year later, the *New York Times* would voice similar concerns about another sensationalized Paul Coates film on homosexuality. Certainly, the 1954 *Confidential File* was a large step forward—from nothing to something. For most viewers, however, the Mattachine rhetoric probably carried little weight alongside testimony by an M.D. and a vice-squad officer. White lost his job the next day, which chilled other activists' willingness to go public. Only a few thousand people saw that local broadcast.[6]

What ultimately brought the subject of homosexuality into living rooms nationwide was the Army–McCarthy hearings. Networks gave full live coverage (and nightly "highlights") of Senator Joseph McCarthy's face-off with the U.S. Army starting in April 1954. The hearings culminated McCarthy's crusade against alleged communists, "perverts," and other perceived security threats in federal jobs. From April to June, more than thirty million viewers saw him bully his way through seemingly endless charges of subversion and immorality in the Armed Forces. Both the Army and McCarthy made accusations of homosexuality to discredit their opponents: an Army lawyer insinuated that McCarthy's chief counsel, Roy Cohn, was a "fairy," and McCarthy repeatedly accused the Army of tolerating homosexuals at an unnamed military base. (Several senators promptly proclaimed that the tainted base—wherever it might be—could not *possibly* be in their home states.)[7] The daily broadcasts of these hearings set a precedent for news and entertainment shows alike. When gay-themed shows and talk shows were proposed thereafter, network executives could no longer claim, "We've never dealt with homosexuality on the air."

The first known TV drama with an openly gay character aired four months later: a TV production of the musical, *Lady in the Dark*. On

Broadway in 1941, Danny Kaye had played the gay character, Russell, as a bitchy queen with wrists aflailing. In the 1947 and 1950 radio productions of the play, Keene Crockett's characterization was nearly as broad. But the 1954 TV adaptation portrays photographer Russell Paxton as likable, even charming. He is a stereotype, but no caricature. The telecast keeps more of the character's gay dialogue than the radio play did, and lets audiences actually *see* Russell fawn over the sexy actor he is photographing. Actor Carleton Carpenter, who played Russell on TV, is gay himself, which may explain why his performance avoids stereotypes. In the early 1950s, Carpenter had acted in MGM movie musicals. Like Rock Hudson, with whom he often socialized, Carpenter participated in publicity stunts to convince the public of his "manhood." MGM even sent him on a well-publicized hunting trip. "I hated guns," Carpenter recalled in 1985, "but it was very macho." NBC censors and the sponsor, Oldsmobile, considered *Lady in the Dark* so prestigious that they let many rules slide. NBC approved unusually strong language (casual uses of "hell" and "sex") and a likable gay character.[8]

Between the McCarthy newscasts, the "Denmark" jokes, and *Lady in the Dark*, the Television Code's "abnormalities" clause had weakened noticeably. This erosion of taboos paved the way for television's first serious discussions of homosexuality and homosexuals.

A dozen U.S. talk show broadcasts focused on homosexuality from 1955 to 1959. Several factors made broadcasters more willing to address the forbidden subject. Lesbians and gay men were starting to gain self-awareness, and heterosexuals began to realize (often with alarm) that people they knew might be "abnormal." Gay magazines' circulation increased—especially publications such as *ONE* magazine, *The Ladder* (published by the Daughters of Bilitis), and *The Mattachine Review*—though none would ever approach the circulation of late-twentieth-century gay publications. Branch chapters of the Mattachine Society and DOB sprang up in the 1950s and started sending press kits to the media. Coincidentally, the FCC was pressuring stations to produce more local talk shows. Gay groups were mailing news releases just when broadcasters were desperate for topics. The shows' scramble for novel issues worried *New York Times* critic Jack Gould:

Because [Mike] Wallace has touched on matters infrequently discussed on the air—effeminacy in particular—some rather envious gentlemen on the fringe of [broadcasting] apparently believe they can garner impressive ratings by going further.

Predicting the rise of tabloid TV three decades before it materialized, Gould said that even responsible discussions of such topics could lead talk shows down a slippery slope toward becoming "peephole journalism . . . a video variation on *Confidential* magazine."[9]

Most of these gay-themed broadcasts of the 1950s were local debates between conservative "experts" ("Homosexuals are sick/evil/ criminal") and liberal "experts" ("Homosexuality is a tragic affliction; let's be nice to them"). These aired in Detroit, Los Angeles, and New York.[10] Since homosexuality was a crime, a disease, and a sin, producers held that the most qualified panelists were criminologists, vice-squad police, lawyers, psychiatrists, sociologists, and theologians. Gay male child molesters were a popular topic, and *Confidential File* aired a grim, nationally syndicated documentary about them in 1955.[11] The reflection that gay viewers saw in the mainstream media was still terrifying.

Religious pressure groups contributed to the rarity and biases of these programs, as did stations' senior managers. The experiences of two New York broadcasters reveal the impact of antigay pressure. Historian Richard Heffner and novelist Fannie Hurst hosted TV interview shows on different stations in New York City during the 1950s. Each devoted several discussions to homosexuality. Both faced censorship attempts, though with different results.

The era's most in-depth TV survey of homosexuality aired on Heffner's *The Open Mind* on the NBC station, WRCA-TV. Heffner scheduled three shows on the subject during the 1956–57 season. Consistent with the era's focus on outside experts, none of the broadcasts had openly gay guests. The first show featured a lawyer, a minister, and a psychologist. They favored more lenient sex laws and agreed that homosexuals' biggest problems came from the pressures of a rejecting society. The trio spent part of the show discussing gay male child molesters. After this first broadcast, word spread backstage that the

Catholic church was trying to block the two remaining shows. In 1991, Heffner recalled:

> I received word from the station manager that Cardinal Spellman had called [NBC founder] David Sarnoff's office and had protested violently against this series on homosexuality, and had said—and all of this is from my memory and from hearsay—that if they didn't take it off the air, the Archdiocese was going to sue for the revocation of the station's license at the next license-renewal period. And so they were scared, of course . . .
>
> I was told that [NBC's] publicity vice president had called to find out what this thing was—this *Open Mind*—and this series on homosexuality . . . But much to the credit of the broadcasters, even in those early days, he said all he wanted to make sure was that I was a responsible person and knew what I was doing, that I was careful, that I was fair. And by the end of the day they had satisfied themselves that that was the case and nothing further happened. So there was no pressure on me— except that as a young fellow just into broadcasting really, I had to be concerned. But I was very pleased, for all that was said about the timidity of broadcasters.

Heffner, who at this writing still hosts *The Open Mind* as a local show in New York, said that the series' purpose is to shed light on vital, seldom-explored issues. The first gay-themed show accomplished that: it caused a stir in the industry (even *Variety* reviewed it) and in the gay community (*The Ladder* printed a detailed summary and organizations played tapes at meetings). The second and third broadcasts aired on schedule. A doctor on the second show said that fathers should divert effeminacy in boys by offering masculine examples: "Take him to a ball game," he suggested. On the third broadcast, anthropologist Margaret Mead and sociologist/journalist Max Lerner discussed gender roles and antihomosexual prejudice.[12] A mixed bag from the homophile standpoint, the shows gave reasoned airing to a long-censored topic. Outside pressure had failed.

Fannie Hurst's series *Showcase* was less fortunate. She scheduled one program on male homosexuality and another on lesbianism for March 1958. Lester Wolf moderated the male panel, which included two psychologists and an anonymous Mattachine member. The next day, Hurst and a panel of women were in the studio just before airtime when WABD-TV management ordered them not to discuss lesbians. Hurst was furious. She started and ended the show with impassioned speeches on censorship. Without mentioning the taboo subject, Hurst apologized that she had been ordered not to proceed with the planned program. "After the high plateau reached yesterday," she said, "the *station* feels we are a little premature." Instead, the guests discussed handwriting analysis. *The Ladder*'s reviewer likened the station's decision to Nazism: "I swear, as I was dropping my pencil, I truly did see the stenciled letters swim before my eyes—VERBOTEN." Del Martin and Phyllis Lyon, founders of the Daughters of Bilitis, recall that censorship of lesbian themes was common. "Somehow," Lyon says, discussing lesbians "was much more frightening for them than to have a gay man on. They were terrified."[13]

Hurst, however, was not terrified. She insisted the media could and should fight antigay prejudice. Broadcasters, she said, were too prudish, and gay organizations too scared of publicity. "[The Mattachine's] attitude is good," she told the group's 1958 convention, "but you must reach the people . . . in their own idiom . . . through TV, magazines, and the newspapers." After repeated clashes with WABD, Hurst took her show to the more liberal WNTA-TV, New York's Channel 13. A year after *Showcase*'s first gay panel, producer Art Arnold contacted the Mattachine Society of New York and asked them to help plan at least three shows. Hurst was to moderate panels on various aspects of homosexuality, including sociology, psychology, the homophile movement, and homosexual youth. Channel 13's management knew they were getting controversy with Hurst, but this was probably more than they expected. WNTA canceled *Showcase* after the second Mattachine-planned broadcast, a discussion of teenage homosexuality titled "Problems of the Teenager Who Doesn't Fit," which aired April 28, 1959. Two months later, the *New York Mattachine Newsletter* reported that neither Hurst nor the Society knew if the gay shows were "the direct cause of her summary dismissal."[14]

After trade publications like *Variety* described the local interviews and after gay public-policy controversies appeared in the press, a few creators of entertainment shows tried to use gay themes. Comedians had some limited freedom to use the topic for cheap laughs, but writers of drama continued to hit roadblocks. From 1955 to 1959, prime-time social-issue dramas explored changing ideas of womanhood and manhood. Still, only vague, passing comments acknowledged nonheterosexuals. Even the series *Medic*, which presented controversial dramas about menopause, cocaine, electroshock therapy, sterility, cesarean operations (shown on-screen), and nuclear war, reportedly could not get approval for a proposed script about homosexuality.[15] (Given the series' format, the suppressed episode presumably would have portrayed homosexuality as the disease of the week.)

Networks and sponsors occasionally approved topical, gay-themed skits on variety shows. In some ways, they resembled radio skits of the early 1950s. A 1959 *Steve Allen Show* on NBC-TV alluded whimsically to recent British gay scandals. The skit features Tom Poston, who plays a TV news show's travel correspondent. During Poston's report from Scotland, anchorman Allen asks about the kilt he is wearing:

ALLEN: Don't your knees get cold?
POSTON: No, but they do get a lot of compliments. I haven't had to pay for a drink since I've been here. (*Audience laughs.*)
ALLEN: Now cut that out.
POSTON: A Duke proposed to me last night.
ALLEN: That's ridiculous.
POSTON: That's what his parents tried to tell him. (*More audience laughter.*)
ALLEN: Forget about the Duke, please.
POSTON: Well, it ain't gonna be easy. We're engaged, you know. (*Primps effeminately. Audience laughs.*)[16]

Homosexuality was still alien, comical, seen always through heterosexuals' eyes. Gays were "them." Straights were "us."

The growth of public radio and TV brought the first breakthroughs in giving gay people their own voice on the air. Pacifica Radio, a listener-supported chain, produced several programs with gay male panelists. In 1958 and 1959, Pacifica stations in Berkeley, Los Angeles, and New York aired and repeated a two-hour special titled *The Homosexual in*

Our Society. It featured homophile activists, the mother of a gay man, and gay-friendly lawyers, psychologists, and sociologists. The eloquent, unapologetic symposium debunked myths and talked of homosexuals as an oppressed minority. It drew a generally positive response from station members, was first runner-up for a statewide broadcasting award, and a transcript was sold in book form.[17] In retrospect, Pacifica's pro-gay broadcasts and a few daring commercial radio shows foreshadowed the more open radio and TV programming of the next two decades.

IMAGE UNDER CONSTRUCTION
Radio and Television: 1960–1963

If we issue a statement saying that homosexuality "must not be considered an illness," [we'll look like] those marijuana smokers who organize for the sole purpose of saying, "We are not criminals." They look like a bunch of jackasses . . .
> —*A delegate to the National Planning Conference of Homophile Organizations, 1966*[1]

Gay visibility in American society had increased by 1959. This higher profile created the illusion that "deviance" was spreading. Amid public fear that homosexuality was on the rise, police stepped up raids, arresting people in gay bars, restaurants, and cruising areas. Sex-control laws ("sodomy" laws) existed in all fifty states, and the authorities began enforcing them more strictly against homosexuals. The 1959 San Francisco mayoral race centered largely on "the gay bar problem." Universities purged known lesbians and gay men from their enrollment and staff. During 1959 and 1960, the New York State Liquor Authority closed almost every gay bar in Manhattan.[2] Meanwhile, gay-baiting spread to the most seemingly innocuous of TV shows.

On early-1960s television, even children's series humorously taught that violence was an appropriate response to affection between men. Viewers laughed at an episode of *Walt Disney Presents* in which animated hero Goofy kept mistakenly kissing men. One of the men is a brawny sailor, Goofy's boatmate in an amusement park Tunnel of Love. When their boat emerges into the light, each character realizes he has been kissing a man. The sailor's bashing of Goofy is the scene's comic climax.[3] Live-action film and TV comedies had used similar routines for years, with the basher usually snarling, "Why, I oughtta . . . !" In some cartoon series, male characters would kiss other males to degrade or humiliate them. Recipients of such kisses react furiously, but all males react to female kisses with sparks of ecstasy.[4] The message to a new generation was that for one man to kiss another was disgusting, but queer-bashing was good, clean fun. As in the 1950s, this was no malicious conspiracy: just unthinking reflections of "obvious" truths.

In response to these raids, purges, and media portrayals, homophiles devised strategies to improve their public image. There was little consensus about what approach to take: activists agreed only that, in the end, they needed to win over the law, the clergy, and the psychiatrists. The activists' diverse solutions would affect the image of gay people in the mass media for years. Publicity plans fell into two camps: the conservative/appeasement camp, and the liberal/civil rights camp. Two extreme examples illustrate the range of tactics tried: the Mattachine Society's appearance on a public TV documentary, and Randy Wicker's approach to getting a gay panel on WBAI radio.

Antigay psychiatrists like Dr. Edmund Bergler dominated gay-themed discussions on talk shows in the early 1960s, claiming that homosexuals were mentally ill. The doctors considered gay people's supposed sickness as a given: instead of proving the allegation, they jumped right to seeking causes. "A homosexual," Bergler told radio listeners in 1961, "is a man who acquired in early childhood the unconscious wish, or tendency, to be mistreated by a woman."[5] The more progressive doctors said homosexuals could not be "cured" but could learn to adapt to their "handicap." Such therapists had spoken at Daughters of Bilitis meetings and national Mattachine conventions, and these conservative homophile groups began recommending them to radio and TV producers. ONE, Inc. and the Mattachine Society of Washington (MSW) rejected that approach as too apologetic. They compared homophiles' plight to that of America's black population; they insisted that homosexuality was neither sick nor immoral, and instead advocated immediate, full equality.[6]

Conservative Mattachine and DOB leaders in California and New York argued that challenging Law, God, *and* science all at the same time would hurt the new movement's credibility. The groups joined liberal psychiatrists in touting homosexuality as an incurable, minor mental illness. They hoped to convince lawmakers and clergy that it was wrong to punish sick people for harmless, compulsive sexual behavior—as long as it was between consenting adults. A few dissenters, like Randy Wicker, split from the large groups to carry out aggressive personal campaigns. Others, like Barbara Gittings, incurred the wrath of their colleagues by vocally opposing sickness-theory tactics.[7]

The movement's neurosis-peddling worked, at times, winning support from unlikely outsiders. When two leading clergymen appeared on a public TV documentary and encouraged an end to sodomy laws, they used the sickness theory as their primary justification. That 1961 special, *The Rejected*,[8] gave homosexuality a human, upbeat face, but relied heavily on mainstream academics as on-screen speakers. This first national, gay-positive telecast originated in 1960 when an independent producer began pitching a program idea called *The Gay Ones*. John Reavis was a publicist and writer/producer apparently unaffiliated with the homophile movement. Reavis's program proposal reveals how difficult an issue homosexuality was for broadcasters in the early 1960s:

> Since this is about as delicate a subject as can be treated by television, the program might open with a statement by the station manager, or someone of like stature, explaining why the station is presenting a program of this nature, on a subject repugnant to much if not all of the viewing audience. The explanation would be, in brief, that the public's lack of knowledge . . . is so great, and the numbers of people involved is so huge, that increased understanding of the condition and its social ramifications is at least desirable.

Commercial stations and sponsors refused the proposal. Around January 1961, KQED-TV San Francisco bought the show for National Educational Television (NET) under the new title, *The Rejected*. On-camera participants included anthropologist Margaret Mead, Mattachine board members, and renowned lawyers, psychiatrists, clergy, and civil rights experts.[9]

The special debuted in San Francisco in September and later aired on almost forty NET stations. Broadcasters, activists, and reviewers—gay and straight—applauded the program. Conservative homophile leaders praised panelists Rabbi Alvin Fine and Bishop James Pike, both of whom espoused the sickness model of homosexuality on the show. Pike, a reasonably well known religious broadcaster of the era, said that "A homosexual is like anyone else with an illness and should be cared for as such . . ." He held that this compulsive condition did not necessarily mark a person as evil, because "without freedom, there cannot be counted a sin." Mainstream journalists seemed most taken with the show's Mattachine panel, which included national president Harold Call, executive secretary Donald Lucas, and treasurer Les Fisher. The corporate-looking Mattachines explained that "the 'swish' or the 'queen' represents a small minority within the whole homosexual grouping." They never questioned the experts' charges of sickness. Harold Call and his colleagues represented themselves as polished, average Joes, which contrasted sharply with the image most outsiders had of the organization.

KQED reportedly received "several hundred letters" about the show within a week of its debut airing, 97 percent of them favorable. *The Rejected* was good publicity for the movement. As other stations ran the program, new supporters wrote to the Mattachine Society in unprecedented numbers. Pan Graphic Press, a print shop owned by Mattachine members, reportedly received almost four hundred transcript requests within a week of the first San Francisco broadcast. By commercial television standards, these numbers seem low; for the fledgling educational TV system, it was strong audience response.[10]

Some gay leaders preferred a more confrontational, less apologetic stance than the one that gay organizers expressed in *The Rejected*. Unlike the national boards of the Mattachine and the DOB, Dr. Franklin Kameny opposed catering to "experts" if they considered homosexuality inferior. Kameny, the charismatic president of the Mattachine Society of Washington, D.C., had lost his federal job as an astronomer in the 1950s. He gained prominence by suing the U.S. government for discrimination and pushing the matter to the Supreme Court, which refused the case. This forceful speaker, who advocated emulating the black civil rights movement, made his first TV appearances in the early sixties. Like the conservatives, he encouraged activists to project a corporate image, but he rejected any hint that homosexuality was undesirable. Within a few years, he would be one of the movement's most visible representatives.[11]

Randy Wicker was a different breed of rebel: one who promoted gay visibility through brash publicity. In the fifties, he had ruffled Mattachine feathers by broadly advertising the otherwise discreet Mattachine Society of New York (MSNY). He not only distributed leaflets in the antipolitical atmosphere of gay bars, but also attracted a largely straight audience of three hundred people to one MSNY event after hanging posters around the city. His efforts to publicize that lecture attracted more people than the hall could hold and more straights than the closeted members cared to face. Wicker's media career began in 1962 when he heard a rerun of *The Homosexual in Our Society* on WBAI-FM. The part he heard was a sympathetic conversation among ostensibly straight lawyers and therapists. Despite the show's liberal bent, he decided to demand equal time for the "*real* experts"— homosexuals. MSNY leaders disliked aggressive tactics, so Wicker gathered fellow rebels, named himself publicity director of "The Homosexual League of New York," printed business cards, and started knocking on doors. His public relations background and student experience as a white ally in the black civil rights movement made him a natural. He first contacted Dick Ellman, WBAI's public affairs director. In 1991, Wicker recalled:

> I said, "Why in the world do you have these jerks on? Why don't you let the *real* experts talk? These people don't know what they are talking about." There was no relationship between what I'd heard on the air and what I saw in my own private life in the gay bars and people that I met. So Dick Ellman said, "Well, get together a panel," which I did. 'BAI was really very open.

Ellman moderated a one-hour, unscripted conversation among eight culturally and economically diverse gay men, including Wicker. All had heard of the Mattachine, but only Wicker knew specifics about the movement. Unlike the gay panel on *The Rejected*, they discussed cruising, bars, sex, gay subculture, police raids, and other topics that, in this public forum, shocked veteran organizers. "The Mattachine tries to present a good 'corporate image' of the homosexual," Wicker explained in 1963, "to show that he's an ordinary citizen and all that. Well, there are also a lot of parties, fun, and promiscuity . . . I want to be able to sit on the fence and throw things at both sides." *Live and Let Live* first aired in 1962 on WBAI and on Pacifica stations in Los Angeles and Berkeley. Upon request, Pacifica also supplied the show to educational stations in Illinois and Delaware.[12]

Listener-supported radio seldom attracted wide publicity or large audiences. Still, the premise of *Live and Let Live*—homosexuals speaking for and about themselves—was so strange that the mainstream press gave the show and Wicker national attention. The New York *Journal-American* broke the story a week in advance. Their columnist Jack O'Brien lambasted WBAI for giving in to an "arrogant, card-carrying swish." "We've heard of silly situations in broadcasting," he wrote, "but FM station WBAI wins our top prize for scraping the sickly barrel-bottom." Armed with that clipping and his Homosexual League business card, Wicker set out to notify any periodicals still unaware of his show. *Variety* gave it an advance write-up, and reviews appeared in the *New York Times*, *Herald-Tribune*, and *Newsweek*. With a combined readership in the millions, these publications raised the issue of homosexuality uncritically to a far greater audience than did the show. A liberal/leftist satire magazine, *The Realist*, broadened the audience further by serializing a complete transcript of *Live and Let Live*. Radio and TV shows invited Wicker to appear on panels. He and his ad hoc committee of envelope-stuffers had demolished barriers. Male homosexuality, at least, was a hot topic.[13]

THE INVISIBLE LESBIAN

Television: 1960–1966

The word "homosexual" is being thrown around as never before in the mass media, but almost always it refers to the male of the species . . . The male homosexual has become socially "visible," but the lesbian is the invisible woman.

—*L.E.E. in* The Ladder, *1965[1]*

The Daughters of Bilitis prepared its press package carefully: brochures, articles, back issues of *The Ladder*, and an explanatory cover letter. A Daughter was going on TV, and the DOB wanted to give the show's moderator as much information as possible. Airtime: the broadcast light goes on and host Louie Lomax fires the first question at DOB cofounder Phyllis Lyon. "How," he asks, "are lesbians different physically from other women?" According to Lyon, he was not playing devil's advocate; he sounded serious.[2] America was just starting to re-examine its myths about gay people. Broadcasters had stopped obsessing about gay male child molesters, but still had wildly inaccurate ideas about lesbians.

The media mentioned lesbians very rarely, usually as an afterthought to reports about gay men. Talk show emcee Paul Coates hosted what was probably the first national TV interview with an open lesbian. Coates's syndicated series devoted a broadcast to the 1962 Daughters of Bilitis convention in Hollywood. As usual, the DOB had sent press releases to local media several weeks before the event. Panelists on the show included "Terry" (president-elect of DOB, Los Angeles) and Dr. Fred J. Goldstein (a psychologist who spoke at the event). Terry said the organization chose her to appear on TV because, being self-employed, she was "less vulnerable." She gave background on the Daughters, their convention, and recent controversies over the legality of lesbian and gay bars. Such broadcasts' impact on individual listeners was astounding. Women who had never told anyone of their lesbianism wrote or phoned the DOB, some telling their life story.[3] Each time local DOB members appeared on radio or TV around the country, membership increased.

Television's strongest influence on the public's ideas, however, came from prime-time comedies and dramas: even the least popular prime-time series usually drew more viewers than did daytime or late-night talk shows. Two network dramas dealt with lesbians in the early sixties: an episode of ABC's *The Asphalt Jungle* presented a rifle-toting, implicitly lesbian sniper in 1961. And an episode of NBC's *The Eleventh Hour*—a short-lived dramatic series about mental-health professionals—depicted a neurotic, paranoid, mean-tempered lesbian mental patient in 1963.

The Eleventh Hour script was arguably the networks' first serious treatment of homosexuality. Kathryn Hayes guest stars as temperamental actress Hallie Lambert, whose tantrums are causing dissent among the cast of a play. At first, it seems a straightforward persecution complex: she is convinced that her director (Beverly Garland) hates her. The series' Freudian-therapist male hero finally discovers that Hallie is in love with the director and has channeled her denial and confusion into hostility. *The Ladder*'s Robin Richards wrote:

> [The script] dealt frankly with Lesbianism, on an adolescent level and in sophomoric language and platitudes . . . Beverly Garland as the director did the only good job of acting . . . The only good angle was that Hallie has a so-so happy ending instead of being dragged to the nut hatch. May programs on this series improve or cease.

NBC canceled the series in 1964 amid low ratings and tepid reviews.[4]

It is hard to know why a major network suddenly approved this first TV drama about lesbianism. It may be significant that the approval and production came shortly after the acclaimed lesbian-themed film *The Children's Hour* debuted in theaters. This episode of *The Eleventh*

Hour was apparently the last national prime-time telecast to acknowledge lesbians for five years. The networks' near-blackout on lesbian imagery may explain why local talk shows that dared broach the subject generated so many positive letters and phone calls from gay women: the local panels were the only source of affirmation available for many, many women in the audience.

Some producers deliberately avoided lesbian issues. For instance, in an early outline for NET's *The Rejected*, producer John Reavis discouraged inclusion of a lesbian panel. His reasons were typical of the era:

> First, the repugnance—or desire not to think about the problem—is even greater in society than that towards the problem of Gay men. Second, the number of persons involved is much smaller . . .[5]

Society hated to discuss female sexuality. When Kinsey's report on women appeared in 1953, with its observations about both heterosexuality and homosexuality, public fury was more rabid than it had been against his report on men. Judging from articles written at the time, much of the anger masked the message, "Hey, that's my sister/wife/daughter you're talking about!" Women were not supposed to have sexual needs. And lesbianism, in particular, forced a male-centered society to contemplate the threatening idea of a woman who did not need a man.

The lack of lesbian visibility on interview shows was also due, in part, to the shortage of gay women willing to face TV cameras. Where a small number of male Mattachine leaders were willing to be interviewed, the Daughters of Bilitis had no such corps of interview subjects. In 1961, not even members of DOB's national board felt they could appear on television in their home cities.[6] By 1962, DOB's California chapters had set up an exchange program: San Francisco members traveled to appear on Los Angeles shows and vice versa. DOB tried similar exchanges in other regions when a few local shows around the country began discussing female homosexuality.[7]

The only "out" lesbians on national TV from 1964 to 1966 appeared fleetingly in news footage of homophile protests. These brief, infrequent newscasts probably had little impact on the public.

GETTING GAYER

Television: 1963–1969

What's ruining television today are those big productions—the fairies who come in here and sing with the big balloons. It's the fairies who are going to ruin show business.   —*Jack Paar on* The Jack Paar Show, *circa 1964*[1]

Humorist Fred Allen once remarked, "Imitation is the sincerest form of television." Via imitation, television's handling of gay issues spread from one local talk show in 1954 to a dozen in the late 1950s. From 1961 to 1963, at least twenty-five local radio and TV broadcasts dealt with the subject, many drawing strong ratings. A core group of homophile speakers traveled around the United States making broadcast appearances. Educational stations reran *The Rejected* in 1963 and 1964. Soon afterward, gay references crept slowly into prime-time and late-night network shows. As before, the references to homosexuality focused almost exclusively on men.

Many pioneering efforts during this period were canceled before they could air. In early 1964, for example, CBS's flagship station in New York spent over $15,000 producing a documentary on homosexuality before network management decided to kill it. CBS News soon announced that *it* was producing a one-hour prime-time documentary on gay men, ballyhooed as the first network effort of its kind.[2] Following suit, NBC News told the New York Mattachine Society in July that they might consider filming a report on the subject. The same week, the New York *Herald-Tribune* reported that ABC's new late-night talk show starring Les Crane was considering taping a program on homosexuality. None of the shows actually aired that year. The CBS News documentary became an on-again, off-again cause célèbre, not broadcast until 1967. NBC's vague inquiries came to nothing. ABC's late-night *Les Crane Show* taped an interview with Randy Wicker and a sexologist, but several affiliates threatened to drop the series if it ran. ABC postponed the segment indefinitely. In 1965, CBS bought the rights to Otto Preminger's acclaimed movie *Advise and Consent*. The network planned to censor references to the protagonist's homosexual past and to cut a scene set in a gay bar. Preminger deemed the cuts too extensive and exercised his option to withdraw broadcast rights.[3]

Broadcasters have long insisted on "balance" in presenting controversial issues, yet allusions to gay men were never positive and seldom serious. Sometimes, the humor carried an edge of sarcastic homophobia. Just as often, the mere fact of homosexuality *was* the joke. These gags had an innocence reminiscent of children telling a story they think is dirty: the enjoyment came not from malice, but from the fun of mentioning a taboo subject in public. Comedians revived old routines, such as men spitting after accidentally kissing each other.[4]

In 1964 and 1965, network executives were increasingly aware of homosexuality as an important "social problem." Trade publications told them that CBS was still filming its documentary. A ten-part, nationally syndicated radio series called *Homosexual: A New Minority* aired in numerous markets.[5] Gay panelists became more prevalent on local talk shows. ABC's evening news covered homosexual rights demonstrations.[6] The growing visibility allowed entertainment programs to be bolder, though they still would not present openly gay characters. Allusions to homosexuality (mostly male-focused and negative) flourished on comedy shows. Activists were not offended: most took the jokes as a sign that TV was becoming "gayer."[7] The major homophile magazines never criticized this humor.[8]

By 1965, for the first time, TV comedy was acknowledging homosexuals in more concrete terms than before. A 1965 issue of *The Ladder* reported:

> Johnny Carson, emcee of the "Tonight" show, told about . . . ticker-tape parades in New York. When a hero moves along Wall Street, Johnny

explained, executives throw memoranda out the windows; when he moves on to Greenwich Village, executives there throw kisses.

On a 1966 variety show, stand-up comic Joan Rivers cheerfully quips, "Two of us just got married in my family: an old maid cousin and me. *(worried smile)* Not to each other! But . . . it's hard to meet [men] in the business because everybody you meet is either married or a dancer." *The Ladder*'s editor at the time, Barbara Gittings, recalls that many homophiles were grateful if a celebrity talked about them at all, even derisively, as long as it was not out-and-out abuse.[9]

Despite the activists' neutral response, the new gags had a mocking edge. Queer jokes on TV in the 1950s had been absurdist humor, which never acknowledged the actual existence of homosexuals. Now, in the 1960s, the jokes were clearly about a real group of people. Scripts made it clear that something was wrong with those people. Gay one-liners showed up on unlikely, escapist series. On *The Flying Nun*, Sister Sixto (Shelley Morrison, later of *Will & Grace*) panics when she thinks she sees two men necking:

SR. BERTRILLE: Look at that!
SR. SIXTO: *(shocked)* I don't think Reverend Mother would want I should look.

Sixto expresses bemused relief when she realizes that one of the men is really a woman in disguise. On a Christmas episode of *The Monkees*, the boys make coy faces and flick limp wrists while caroling, "Don we now our *gay* apparel."

One week on *The Munsters*, Herman plans to drink an Instant Disguise potion to become a suave playboy. He is shocked that the "Man About Town" flasks include one marked "Mr. Clean" (a character from commercials for a cleaning product). Grandpa assures him, "He's a big swinger when he's not making commercials. Don't let that earring fool you." A long, canned laugh follows. Herman uses one of the potions, and Grandpa drinks another to become a beautiful woman. Herman's reaction to the "woman" alternates between hormonal attraction and self-disgust at the knowledge it is his father-in-law. More canned laughter.

Several storylines on *The Dick Van Dyke Show* include throw-away gags where characters mistakenly think one of the regulars is gay (such as a scene in which a janitor thinks that Van Dyke's character is hitting on him). The spy spoof series *Get Smart* is a gold mine of gay references.[10] To most viewers, the jokes were harmless and funny. Still, no positive messages balanced the dozens of implicit or explicit negative ones.

Early-sixties TV shows, like their predecessors, seldom challenged social conventions. Forces of Law and Order were trustworthy. Stars were white. Male heroes rescued helpless women. Around 1965, however, a new type of show gained favor. In a multidecade survey of entertainment shows, the research team of Lichter, Lichter and Rothman found that programs questioning the status quo first attained popularity and longevity in the mid 1960s. As the "opening wedge of coming change," they cited *The Fugitive* (1963–67), about a doctor mistakenly pursued by police who thought he had killed his wife. "While fleeing the law," they noted, "this fugitive saw a vast array of corruption, evil and inequity in 'proper' society." They noted the increasingly respectable and independent roles given to black characters *(I Spy, Mission: Impossible)* and women *(Honey West* and *The Avengers)*. Television, they noted, began as an agent of social control, and, by the mid 1970s, developed into an instrument of social change. Producers sensed a growing freedom. In 1965, *ONE* magazine reported:

> The producers of the sensationally successful TV shows, *The Defenders* and *The Doctors and The Nurses*, said their success is because they're not afraid of controversial subjects and they've covered about everything but homosexuality, "and sooner or later we'll hit that."

That production company already came close the previous year in the series *The Nurses* (an earlier version of *The Doctors and The Nurses*). In an episode called "Nurse is a Feminine Noun," hospital workers tease and, in so many words, gay-bait a burly, straight male nurse because he is in a "women's" profession.[11]

The shift to socially relevant entertainment began in earnest during 1967 and 1968. Previously, the networks had sought to maximize audience size by offending as few people as possible. In selling advertising, networks were in the business of ensuring the highest possible Nielsen ratings: the more heads in the audience, the more the networks could charge for commercials. In 1967, that strategy began to change. Marketing executives started to wonder about affluent subgroups within the Nielsens. (The A. C. Nielsen Company would begin offering detailed demographic analyses a few years later.) Many sponsors began to focus in on "target audiences" that had more disposable income. Teenagers and young adults were a lucrative market, so network programming departments began creating topical "hip" comedies and gritty, urban, social-issue dramas. For a time, there was great tension between two factions within the networks: censors sought to protect family viewing, but the program schedulers wanted to titillate the money-spending youth market. The censors eventually lost. Amid the new freedom, CBS finally aired its report on male homosexuals.

7

DESIRE UNDER
THE POTTED PALMS

Television: 1967

> The dilemma of the homosexual: Told by the medical profession he is sick, by the law that he's a criminal. Shunned by employers, rejected by heterosexual society. Incapable of a fulfilling relationship with a woman or, for that matter, with a man. At the center of his life, he remains anonymous.
>
> —*Mike Wallace, summarizing at the end of* CBS Reports:
> *"The Homosexuals," 1967*[1]

The nineteen-year-old sailor had left his girlfriend on the beach and headed for a nearby men's room for anonymous sex. A camera crew filmed his arrest for CBS News as the young man, near tears, lamented, "for life I'll be wrecked by this . . ." Renowned psychiatrist Charles Socarides commented, "The whole idea of saying 'the happy homosexual' is to again create a mythology about the nature of homosexuality." A depressive homosexual—hiding in the shadows behind a potted plant—rambled about how mentally sick he was. Some readers will recognize these as "highlights" from the much-touted, long-delayed *CBS Reports*: "The Homosexuals," hosted by Mike Wallace. The show sandwiched brief attempts at "balance" between thick slices of sleaze and Freudianism. It was the first gay-themed program to reach a wide audience, and stands as an infamous landmark in gay TV history. Its tortuous evolution from bare outline to finished production exemplifies the problems producers faced in getting sexual-minority topics into prime time in the 1960s.

The original outline that CBS approved in 1964 was even more lurid than the final film. After producer Bill Peters and his crew learned more about the subject, they decided to include happy, self-accepting gay men as well as self-loathing ones. Principal filming occurred from the fall of 1964 through early 1965. In March 1965, the gay magazine *Drum* reported that CBS had postponed the show: "One of the reasons for the delay is the production presents the view of the homophile organizations and does not give much emphasis to the sickness position . . ." Peters sent a detailed memo to CBS News president Fred Friendly around July, listing proposed revisions. Friendly approved it enthusiastically, and production was on again.[2]

Peters added more footage of sickness-theory psychotherapists and some last-minute scenes of the 1965 East Coast Homophile Organizations (ECHO) convention. The network approved the show and slated it for spring of 1966. Then, Fred Friendly resigned from CBS News in a dispute over an unrelated matter. His replacement, Dick Salant, and CBS's chief of specials, Bill Leonard, questioned the gay film's "taste" and it went back into limbo. Around April 1966, Peters announced he had reworked the documentary to the satisfaction of network brass. He promptly left to take a job with ABC. CBS News boasted that it had a bold, exciting documentary in Peters's show and scheduled it for the fall. All seemed well until network executives rewatched the film shortly before the planned airdate. Now they thought it was *too* cold and unsympathetic. CBS brought in a new producer, Harry Morgan, to salvage its investment. *Variety* noted, "There are those at CBS News who believe the project would have been scrapped entirely except for too much press exposure." Peters's film had relied on documentary footage of bars, hustlers, cruising areas, the ECHO convention, and homophile pickets. Woven through the film were scenes of "five homosexuals who had never met before in a living room discussing their problems." Only about ten minutes of Peters's show survived in Morgan's version.[3]

Morgan and reporter Mike Wallace filmed positive interviews to give the report a more human face and to balance the existing material. Mattachine activist Jack Nichols ("Warren Adkins" on the show) recently recalled that "Mike Wallace took me aside after the taping and told me that while I'd answered his questions, he didn't feel I believed what I, myself, was saying." Wallace believed firmly that homosexuality was a mental disorder that led to promiscuity and unhappiness. "That was—God help us—what our understanding was of the homosexual lifestyle a mere twenty-five years ago," Wallace said in 1992, "because nobody was out of the closet and because that's what we heard from doctors . . . I should have known better. Two of my best friends at that time were homosexual and they had been living together forever."[4] In February 1967, CBS executives decided that the self-accepting homosexuals made too strong an impression. Morgan's staff reedited two interviews to make the men sound less happy. The show aired in that form on March 7, 1967. One of the reedited interviewees threatened to sue CBS for misrepresentation but decided not to. The other man lodged a formal complaint of fraud and withdrew his release, which prevented reruns of the documentary.[5]

CBS had planned to be first in exploiting the new subject in prime time, but the delays let NET scoop them twice: in fall of 1966, the educational stations ran a British TV documentary about homosexuals, and in February 1967 they showed the first of many gay panel discussions which would appear on *The David Susskind Show*. By then, most people had forgotten about the 1961 documentary, *The Rejected*, and critics praised the Susskind broadcast as an American breakthrough. Best known for this intelligent talk series, Susskind was also a producer of prestigious dramas for TV. In 1967, his company was developing a police series for ABC called *N.Y.P.D.* Each week, it was to dramatize a different, seldom-televised urban problem. Susskind believed that homosexuality was an illness.[6] Despite that belief, or perhaps because of it, the topic of the cop show's first episode was homophobia and antigay blackmail.

BREAKTHROUGH—
FOR MEN ONLY
Television: 1967–1969

> You have an extravagant idea of the grapevine, lieutenant. Just because I'm
> homosexual, that doesn't mean I know every other one in the country . . . [You
> want] information about Huntington Weems? About an area of human activity
> feared and abominated by our pluralistic, moralistic, straighter-than-thou—
> forgive the expression—body politic? . . . They do their own secret things and
> call it "having a little fun," and what someone else does they call "perversion."
> —*"Charles Spad" (played by John Harkins), television's first*
> *self-identified homosexual character, on* N.Y.P.D., *1967[1]*

The youth counterculture continued to grow and become more politicized throughout the late 1960s. But on network TV, only two comedy
series were trying to speak to the new generation: *The Smothers Brothers
Comedy Hour* (CBS) and *Rowan and Martin's Laugh-In* (NBC). Both
shows critiqued politicians, bigotry, pollution, the Vietnam War, and
sexual mores. Since controversy was "in," network publicists sent out
press releases enumerating censorship battles and reminding everyone
how "hip" the shows were. *Life* magazine reported:

> Over in Smothersville . . . every bleep [is] money in the Nielsen bank.
> Newsmen were dutifully informed when it was reluctantly decided that
> Ronald Reagan could not be called "a known heterosexual" on the
> grounds that too many people would not understand what the word actu-
> ally meant.

NBC assigned a full-time censor to *Laugh-In*. Unlike Tom and Dick Smothers, who had a clear political vision, *Laugh-In* randomly tossed daring topics at the viewer. One never knew where hosts Dan Rowan and Dick Martin really stood on the issues. *Laugh-In* thrived on coy queer humor. The 1968 premiere introduced "the toast of Greenwich Village," a long-haired singer named Tiny Tim. His onstage appearance and behavior were exaggeratedly effeminate and campy. On his *Laugh-In* debut, Tim sang "A Tisket, A Tasket" in falsetto while Martin made shocked faces; at the same time, the caption "Lassie Is a Boy" flitted across the screen. Referring to Tim's supposed homosexuality, Rowan said, "Well, it kept him out of the service." Martin replied, "I bet the *Army* burned *his* draft card." Tiny Tim made frequent appearances on *Laugh-In* during its early years. The series' debut also poked fun at recently published rumors of a gay scandal in the cabinet of California governor Ronald Reagan.[2]

Nearly every week from 1968 to 1973, *Laugh-In* made jokes about gay men's increased visibility. When the government considered "legalizing homosexuals," guest Carol Channing remarked, "Oh, darn! Now I'll have to take mine down to City Hall and register them." A man sang a ditty called "You Don't Have to be Happy to be Gay." Comedian Alan Sues played an array of lovable sissies on the show, including his famous sportscaster, "Big Al"—a silly queen who called every report a "Featurette!," rolled his eyes comically, and tinkled his trademark bell. "Oooh!" Big Al would moan, "I *love* my tinkle!" Because *Laugh-In* ranked in the Nielsens' Top Ten for years, its frequent references helped expose millions of viewers to the once-unmentionable topic.[3]

Television's new focus on social change strongly affected dramatic scripts as well. ABC, CBS, and NET presented at least five gay-themed dramas in 1967 and 1968: the premiere of *N.Y.P.D.* (ABC), a *CBS Playhouse* (CBS), a production of Harold Pinter's *The Dwarfs* (NET), an episode of *Judd, for the Defense* (ABC), and a slightly trimmed version of *Advise and Consent* (CBS). Nothing so explicit had aired since NBC's *Eleventh Hour* in 1963. Of the new dramas, only the *N.Y.P.D.* debut drew immediate attention from the gay press. Activists noticed this show not because it dealt with homosexuality, but because it dealt with antigay harassment and gay people's quest for self-esteem.

It presented successful, diverse gay characters, and drew parallels between antigay prejudice and racism.[4]

In that 1967 show, an extortion ring poses as cops to blackmail closeted gay men. Police investigate the death of one victim, who committed suicide in a hotel bathtub rather than face exposure. He was a middle-class husband and father whom the Navy had discharged for "homosexual tendencies" in World War II. Early in the episode, a detective visits Charles Spad, a homophile activist, to see if he has heard anything about blackmailers. Spad is a successful business executive who travels the country making speeches about equality for homosexuals. For the first time, a television character says the words "I'm homosexual." Much of the episode focuses on a closeted gay construction worker (played by James Broderick) whom the criminals are blackmailing. Police catch the extortionists by having the youngest of the three detectives go undercover cruising in a bar. In the end, the straight black cop encourages Broderick's character to come out of the closet; he says it is always best to be one's self, no matter what the majority thinks. The positive, affirming message was unprecedented for primetime TV. *N.Y.P.D.* was unusual in that the series presented gay people as everyday members of society: several later episodes featured respectable, implicitly gay male characters—responsible citizens who helped the police fight crime.[5]

Film critic Judith Crist dubbed 1968 "the year of the Third Sex" in cinema, a proclamation she discussed at length on NBC's *Today* show.[6] That year brought more lesbian, gay, and bisexual visibility in film and onstage than ever before. Most of the plots depicted a queer character's spiritual or physical destruction—usually both. Movie theaters were showing *The Killing of Sister George*, *The Sergeant*, *The Fox*, *The Detective*, *Les Biches*, *Reflections in a Golden Eye*, and a dozen other films with dead or unhappy homosexual or bisexual characters. Pitiful gays were also turning up onstage. *The Boys in the Band*, Mart Crowley's "comedy" about a gay birthday party, was one of the most talked-about plays in the New York theater. *The Boys in the Band* gave a freak-show peek into the witty, neurotic world of self-hating, middleclass New York gays.

Unlike their film counterparts, most television writers avoided sensationalizing the topic. They even showed restraint when gay characters appeared in an otherwise sordid plot. *CBS Playhouse*'s gay entry was "Secrets," a drama by playwright Tad Mosel. Paul Bogart, later known for his work on *All in the Family*, directed it. "Secrets" deals with a woman on trial for trying to kill her illegitimate, drug-addicted son after learning of his homosexuality. A sympathetic supporting character (played by Barry Nelson) also seems to be secretly gay. Many critics hated the show: Bob Williams of the *New York Post* dismissed its message as "[merely] that everybody is entitled to some secrets, including a homosexual . . ." But the New York *Daily News* praised it at length.[7]

By 1969, much had changed in society and on television. The Sexual Revolution had hit full force. Women's Liberation was promoting the "radical notion that women are human beings."[8] Students staged militant protests against the Vietnam War. Hippies and Flower Children were spreading a message of peace and love; many of them linked this message to promiscuity, drugs, and fighting The Establishment. In many places, racial tensions had escalated into rioting. TV was changing, too. *Laugh-In* was a firm hit. Social-change dramas were the norm. ABC had financed two pilots for the daring comedy/drama *Those Were the Days*, which, retitled *All in the Family*, would soon explore many of those divisive issues on another network.

TV networks began letting writers sensationalize homosexuality in 1969, when NBC's *The Bold Ones* and ABC's *N.Y.P.D.* aired dramas about murderous homosexuals.[9] This echoed the way Hollywood films had consistently portrayed homosexuals as killers or victims.[10] Lesbian media activist Ginny Vida recalled this era vividly when she testified at a congressional hearing in 1976:

Until just a couple of years ago, the only gay men to be found on network television were a breed of closet Stepin Fetchits, who traded on the hilarious potential of that great American hallucination, the "sissy." Then, the big breakthrough came, and gay men, labeled as such, were allowed to be not only comic sissies, but hysterical drunkards ridden with guilt, cowardly murderers who burst into tears on the witness stand . . .[11]

Broadcasters thought that it did not matter how TV portrayed gay people, since this was the one minority that had never organized to fight the networks. But gay militancy was about to explode.

The first militant action was unplanned: for three days in June 1969, a diverse group of "queers" rioted in New York after a police raid on the Stonewall Inn, a gay bar in Greenwich Village. The riots' aftershocks quickly reshaped the gay movement. That protest, originally called "The Sheridan Square Riots," soon became famous as "Stonewall."

9

NETWORKS MEET THE
GAY MILITANTS
Television: 1970

Now we've got something else to worry about: Sissy Power. I want to tell you, their leaders are really tough: they wear leather panty hose. You know, the Gay Liberation had a big parade in New York, and they floated down the avenue like Macy's Thanksgiving balloons. I'm not sure where the parade was. I think it was over in Queens.　　　　　　　　　　　　　*—Bob Hope, NBC-TV, 1970*[1]

Gay activism became a highly visible, if unpopular, part of America during 1970. That year, the mass media often reported on gay issues and protests. Mainstream bookstores carried writings by and about homosexuals. Movie theaters ran the film version of *The Boys in the Band*, hyped as the "most frank" major-release film ever about gays. Throughout the year, articles, sermons, and phone-in radio shows regularly discussed the supposed increase in homosexuality. The media also debated whether the lesbianism of noted feminists like Kate Millett jeopardized the integrity of the Women's Liberation Movement. Although much of the discussion was sensationalized, at least gay and bisexual people could be mentioned in public.

The events following Stonewall inspired the formation of dozens of militant organizations, known collectively as the Gay Liberation Movement. These groups were strongest in Los Angeles, San Francisco, and New York City, near TV network headquarters on both coasts. The groups fell roughly into two camps: revolutionaries and reformers.

The revolutionaries expected massive social upheaval in their lifetime;

59

as a result, they focused on restructuring society. Their stock-in-trade was civil disobedience and grassroots consciousness-raising, not negotiating with The Establishment. The mass media, from this perspective, was a lost cause—a mouthpiece of the oppressive military-industrial complex. Revolutionaries frequently quoted jazz artist Gil Scott-Heron's pronouncement, "The Revolution Will Not Be Televised." These activists occasionally protested against employment discrimination by the TV networks, and tried to attract news coverage for gay protests. But they seldom bothered to challenge the content of entertainment programs.

Unlike the revolutionaries, reformers hoped to sell the idea of gay civil rights to society's existing authorities. They negotiated with police, clergy, television programmers, and others who held sway in the dominant culture. In this way, they were similar to the earlier homophile groups. But unlike most of their homophile predecessors, these new reformers often used civil disobedience to gain access to policy makers. Negotiation was usually the ultimate goal of a reformist "zap."

Where the two schools of thought agreed—and differed from most earlier homophile groups—was on the importance of coming out. Both camps considered gay visibility a primary tool of self-liberation and public education. As John D'Emilio wrote in his landmark history, *Sexual Politics, Sexual Communities*:

Throughout the 1950s and 1960s, leaders of the homophile cause had in effect extended their coming out to the public sphere through their work in the movement. But only rarely did they counsel lesbians and homosexuals at large to follow their example, and when they did, homophile activists presented it as a selfless step taken for the benefit of others. Gay liberationists, on the other hand, recast coming out as a profoundly political act that could offer enormous personal benefits to an individual. The open avowal of one's sexual identity, whether at work, at school, at home, or before television cameras, symbolized the shedding of the self-hatred that gay men and women internalized, and consequently it promised an immediate improvement in one's life. To come out of the "closet" quintessentially expressed the fusion of the personal and the political that the radicalism of the late 1960s exalted.[2]

Though many gays remained closeted in the early 1970s, thousands of others stopped hiding. In the mid 1960s, there had been about twenty homophile organizations in the United States and a couple hundred activists, most of whom knew one another. By December 1970, gay political organizations existed not only in large, liberal, coastal cities, but also in repressive strongholds such as Utah. The idea of coming out was seen as central to ending gay invisibility, and from there, ending antigay oppression. But how to get the word out? How could the movement reach the masses and increase gay visibility quickly? The reformist groups, at least, considered TV—especially variety shows and talk shows—to be a logical pressure point.

The first coordinated gay protest against a TV network involved employment discrimination, and so attracted both the revolutionaries and the reformers. It began on January 16, 1970, when one hundred people stood in the pouring rain to picket ABC-owned KGO-TV. The San Francisco station had fired a gay employee, news writer/editor Leo Laurence. As *The Ladder* succinctly explained, "Their charge is simply that he is homosexual, and he admits it." More to the point, Laurence was active in the Gay Liberation Movement. The picketing was generally uneventful, except when police arrested two young men who were chanting, "Suck cock—beat the draft!" In a demonstration of support for the fired employee, activists in New York picketed ABC-TV headquarters. Los Angeles's newly organized Gay Lib group sent a written protest to ABC's West Coast management.[3]

Most TV protests were centered in New York, where the networks' top executives worked. Manhattan's first Gay Lib group was the anarchic, revolutionary Gay Liberation Front (GLF), founded in 1969. Later that year, other New Yorkers formed the Gay Activists Alliance (GAA), which offered more structure than GLF and more militancy than the Mattachine. GAA focused much of its energy on the media: it immediately established a Publicity Committee, headed by Arthur Bell. Six to eight of them met weekly in his apartment, creating cross-indexed files of reporters, media outlets, and gay-rights groups. "We . . . broke it down so that each of us would be responsible for the feeding of information to one segment of the list," Bell later recalled. "We initiated news releases and discussed future actions to spread the Gay Activists name."[4] GAA drew the most media attention with its attempts to elicit a gay-rights statement from Mayor John Lindsay. When New York's mayor refused to meet with them, the group started confronting him at public events. They shouted questions about the police's frequent bar raids, or asked his views on antigay discrimination. When that failed, they tried more extreme tactics. Lindsay's evasions led to the first Gay Lib disruption of a TV show.

GAA planned an indoor showdown where the mayor could not easily leave: they would confront him during taping of his local TV talk show, *With Mayor Lindsay*. Their tactics in this "zap" would become a staple of gay media activism. Dozens of GAA members wrote for tickets to the April 19 program so they could thoroughly infiltrate the studio. The day of the taping, forty protesters met early to rehearse questions. They practiced how and when to chant, when to applaud, and when to stamp their feet. The TV studio seated only about one-hundred-twenty, so a third of the audience were activists. Taping began. Lindsay had just settled into a chat about ecology with guest Arthur Godfrey when—zap!—Arthur Evans lunged to his feet. "Mr. Mayor," he demanded, "what are you doing to end job discrimination against homosexuals?" Bell recalled:

> The mayor tugs his ear. Arthur Godfrey fidgets like mad, and a loud eruption takes place in the audience. A stampede of stamping feet. Voices everywhere: "Answer the question, answer the question." Someone yells, "Are you in favor of repeal of the sodomy laws?" The TV cameras stop rolling. [Evans] is pulled out of sight by a security guard . . . The program continues . . . Interruptions soon take the form of a ritual. Godfrey or Lindsay makes a statement on ecology, the statement is picked up by a Gay Activists Alliance person and thrown back at Lindsay in gay terms . . . On noise pollution the mayor says, "If you're stuck in a traffic jam, it's illegal to blow your horn," and another member comments, "It's illegal in New York to blow anything," and leaves the studio to much stamping and applauding.[5]

The show aired that night with the interruptions meticulously edited out. Ten days later, GAA met with Deputy Mayor Aurelio. The zap had succeeded.

Shortly thereafter, gay groups began to apply similar pressure to network talk shows, then comedies and dramas. All three networks heard from the gay liberationists regularly in 1970—usually from reformers who encouraged more balanced on-air depictions of gay men. Each network responded in its own way: ABC was indifferent, CBS progressive, and NBC blatantly abusive. All three eventually aired shows that acknowledged the existence of gay men that year, but continued to ignore lesbians.

Around the time of the Lindsay TV zap, viewers in several states complained to ABC about its *Dick Cavett Show*. The viewers said Cavett's guests often made antigay remarks on the program, and that ABC never presented opposing views as required by the FCC's Fairness Doctrine. Later that spring, GAA phoned Cavett's director to request equal time, without success. Around May, comedian Mort Sahl appeared on the series with his usual tirade about how homosexuals were enemies of civilization. GAA contacted Cavett's director again, now firmly demanding rebuttal time. The director agreed to interview possible panelists. According to Bell, she met with GAA twice, promised she would get back to them, but never called. A likely reason is what Cavett has called "constant and bewildering" pressure from ABC to "get big names" rather than big issues.[6]

CBS, by contrast, wanted big issues: big, gritty ones that TV usually shunned. In the late sixties, CBS had built its success on rural sitcoms like *Green Acres* and *The Beverly Hillbillies*. They drew high overall ratings, but not the money-spending viewers whom advertisers hoped to reach. CBS wanted a richer, more sophisticated audience. In March 1970, the network announced that the fall season would tackle controversial subjects, dramatizing individuals' attempts to change society. That summer, the hit CBS series *Medical Center* began preparing a script about antigay job discrimination. *TV Guide* said the episode would have been "unthinkable even last year." ABC's new president, Elton Rule, soon announced plans similar to CBS's: he said that in the 1970s, the networks had a responsibility to dramatize "contemporary problems and their possible solutions."[7] "Relevance" was the new industry buzzword by September. As a result, the fall season brought unprecedented acknowledgment of gay lives.

The season's biggest innovation arrived with the *Medical Center* episode of September 23: it was the first of TV's now-familiar tales about a likable gay person battling discrimination. The plot concerns a brilliant researcher working on a cancer cure. Anonymous, obscene letters to coworkers at the hospital brand him a homosexual. His liberal colleagues say they consider him innocent until proven guilty—but clearly equate homosexuality with "guilt." For twenty minutes, the researcher seems to be a victimized straight man; then, just before a commercial, he becomes the second character in TV history to self-identify as a "homosexual." Coworkers begin a campaign to end his career, but in the end, a fine physician keeps his job. The show pleasantly surprised many gay people, despite some concerns that the gay character seemed unhappy about his condition.[8]

Even some "family" shows acknowledged society's growing tolerance of homosexuality: they drew humor from the resultant culture shock. One such series was CBS's *Mary Tyler Moore Show*, a hit sitcom set in a TV newsroom. One week, a male regular, Murray, substitutes as host of an interview program. Due to an editing error, the final broadcast of this show-within-a-show implies that he and a male guest are going out for a romantic evening. At the end of the episode, Murray is upset because no viewers have phoned to comment on his week of broadcasts:

> MURRAY: This is my last day of filling in for Ted and nobody even
>   bothered to call.
> LOU: *(Arm over Murray's shoulder)* We had a lot of calls after your
>   appearance on *Scrutiny* with Eric Matthews.
> MURRAY: *(Hopefully)* You did? Well, why didn't you tell me, Lou?
> MARY: Er, we—we didn't think you'd really want to know.
> MURRAY: Sure I want to know, Mary. What kind of calls did we get?
>   *(Pause)*
> LOU: A lot of people wanted to know how your dinner date with Eric
>   turned out.[9]

The gag mixes old-style mistaken-identity humor with a new reality: some viewers of the fictitious station are as interested in the happiness of a gay newscaster as they would be in that of a straight newscaster. Activists praised CBS and contrasted it favorably with NBC's and ABC's perceived homophobia.

The complaints against NBC had merit. Almost all gay references on that network in 1970 were negative, often aggressively so. The network's only gay-themed drama that year was a rerun of a *Bold Ones* episode in which a gay killer frames his boss for murder. In the fall, NBC escalated its attacks via alarmist newscasts and derisive comedy. *NBC Nightly News* reported on a Gay Liberation Front plan to take over Alpine County, California. GLF had recommended that gays gain political clout by moving en masse to one place—Alpine County—to establish an electoral majority. Neither CBS nor ABC bothered with the story, but NBC related it in harrowing terms. Coverage focused on opponents' rage: it gave airtime to a county supervisor, who likened the GLF to Nazis; a social worker, who said that gay people were a menace to children; and the local sheriff, who threatened violence. No GLF representatives were interviewed, nor were the group's goals or plans explained. This was the only story about the gay community that NBC's evening news covered in 1970.[10]

That year, veteran TV writer Robert Collins was asked to submit scripts for NBC's *The Bold Ones*:

> The second show I proposed concerned itself with the question of whether a homosexual in government was, by the fact of his homosexuality, a possible security risk. The producer was willing in this case—but because the treatment of the homosexual in my story was sympathetic and he was portrayed as neither nance nor psychopath, and I refused to treat him as such, the network refused the story.[11]

NBC did let *The Bold Ones* present a gay killer in government in 1969 and a neurotic, fickle lesbian in 1972; Collins suggests that only positive portrayals were taboo, which is easy to believe given NBC's gay-themed broadcasts of the early 1970s.

Antigay gags on NBC grew more mean-spirited in the fall of 1970. "Hairdresser" jokes abounded. Comedians like Carson and Hope openly mocked Gay Lib, much as they derided the Women's Liberation Movement. *Laugh-In* delivered hip one-liners poking fun at gay men throughout the fall. Its October 19 spoof of Mafia films drew laughter with the killing of a tutu-clad gay mobster: the punch line remarked how long he and his executioner held an offstage "kiss of death."[12] The name "Bruce" had a reputation as stereotypically gay:

Carson, Hope, and *Laugh-In* launched a barrage of jokes about swishy, cowardly, gay men called "Bruce." The name appealed to comedians partly because it ended with an "S" sound, which they would lisp. "Bruce" or "Brucie" became television's composite target for homophobia. A few of the NBC gags were gentler than that. In a skit on *The Dean Martin Show*, a computer dating service mistakenly matches up Dean Martin with guest Frank Sinatra. They meet in a park, each expecting to find a young woman. "No offense, fella," Martin says, "but I think there's been some mistake." (He lisps the last two words.) Sinatra cracks: "Either that or we've been using Liberace's computer." The scene ends with Martin, Sinatra, and a group of policemen tangoing around the park on their way to a police ball.[13] But most gay jokes on NBC in 1970 were harsher than that.

NBC's November *Bob Hope Special* contained an all-out assault on "Sissy Power." Regarding the Alpine County takeover, Hope speculated that GLF's town sheriff would have worn "boots, chaps, buckskin jacket—and pearls"; GLF riot police would have sprayed protestors "with Chanel No. 5" instead of mace. "You know," Hope continued, "they tried to hold a convention, but the building was too close to the railroad tracks. A train whistle blew, and the whole thing turned into a dance!" In late 1970, *The Advocate*, a gay newspaper, printed several letters suggesting a boycott of Hope's sponsor,[14] however, the movement lacked the national cohesion to orchestrate a boycott. Local, focused protests were more successful. In New York, GAA targeted ABC and Dick Cavett.

GAA publicity chair Arthur Bell had kept reminding Cavett's producer and director all summer that his group wanted equal airtime. When no response came, GAA planned a Lindsay-style zap against *The Dick Cavett Show*. Members wrote for tickets to the October 27 taping. Fifty activists planned to blow whistles ten minutes into the show, while ten others would leap onstage to confront Cavett. By the target evening, Cavett had heard that "gay libbers" planned to stack his audience. As the activists waited to enter, the show's staff was watching TV reports about GAA's disruptive zap against *Harper's* magazine that afternoon. Cavett's staff discussed the matter briefly, then ushers asked the activists to identify themselves. Cavett was ready to schedule a gay panel.

A month later—the Friday after Thanksgiving—two GAA members and a representative of the Mattachine Society of New York (MSNY) joined guests James Earl Jones and Phyllis Diller in front of the cameras. Cavett gave a typically glib introduction: "This subject still upsets some people," he warned, "so we will try to discuss it reasonably. But if it's going to give you apoplexy, for heaven's sake don't watch." What followed was forty minutes of rational discussion featuring GAA's Marty Robinson and Arthur Evans, joined later by MSNY president Dick Leitsch. For perhaps the first time, a panel of gay activists was addressing a national audience via commercial TV. After the show, some members of the studio audience waited outside to beat up the GAA men. ABC staff escorted the activists through a maze of hallways to another exit.[15]

Years later, Cavett would recall:

> They were quite effective as guests, I thought, reasoned and self-possessed, considering the pressures they must have been under. I did think that they and their companions made a rather excessive show backstage of kissing each other on the mouth . . .

He said "the usual number" of irate viewers wrote to say the gay panel had alienated them and they would never watch the show again. Bell took the negative reactions and the threat of violence philosophically: "I guess," he wrote, "that meant the show was a success." GAA chronicler Donn Teal considered the *Cavett* broadcast "the Gay Activists' ultimate coup."[16]

Predictably, some activists were less enthusiastic. They considered media acceptance a bourgeois, superficial pursuit that cheapened the movement's message. Analyzing the *Cavett* broadcast in the newspaper *Gay Sunshine*, Morgan Pinney observed:

> What they said was the simple I'm-a-human-being-too stuff but they could have said anything, rapped the most eloquent political line, or said absolutely nothing, and achieved the same results. The media surrounding them was so overpowering as to negate anything they said . . . The commercials and the level of talk on TV creates such a phony world, and no mere thirty-minute guest appearance can counteract that. . . . All the media can offer us is co-option . . .[17]

Lesbians, at least, did not need to fear being co-opted in 1970. The closest a network came to mentioning them in prime time that year was in late December. A public TV documentary about Gertrude Stein, *When This You See, Remember Me,* often mentioned her long friendship with Alice B. Toklas. However, it identified Toklas only as Stein's live-in "secretary."[18] By the end of 1970, GAA was one of a handful of gay organizations committed to media activism, and even they had not focused on the lack of lesbian images. GAA's publicity flyer for that December's "Mediazap Dance" listed male-focused grievances as it proclaimed GAA's new rallying cry: "Out of the closets and into view— MEDIA PENETRATION!"[19]

10

SIX SCRIPTING EXPERIMENTS

Television: 1971–1973

Television is an invention that permits you to be entertained in your living room
by people you wouldn't have in your home.   —*David Frost, 1971*[1]

Appealing to a mass audience was difficult in the early 1970s, an era of
social dissent and political polarization. The rise of "relevance TV"
forced the networks to seek a new balance between familiar themes
and innovation: bland shows lost ratings, but challenging too many
assumptions alienated viewers. So TV writers developed *new* clichés to
present the unfamiliar in safe, predictable ways. "There is almost no
subject we can't do now," an NBC executive told *Variety*. "It's all in the
treatment."[2] As part of this process, the early seventies brought intense
experimentation in the content and form of lesbian- and gay-themed
scripts. In hindsight, the broadcasts may seem tame and apologetic, but
tremendous caution was necessary in these experiments. Popular
thinking in the early 1970s defined "gay" solely as a set of forbidden sex
acts. Libraries and newspaper indexes catalogued gay-themed writings
under subject headings such as "sex" and "sex perversion." Network
executives claimed that the mere hint of gayness in a show constituted
"adult subject matter" or "discussing sex" on television.

Many early experiments involved mistaken identities: straight characters mistaken for gay and vice versa. America had started to realize that
gay people could look like everyone else. Writers now used this surprising fact in stories. New reverse-stereotypes emerged. Lesbians, on the
rare occasions when they did appear, were unhappy and angst-ridden,

but conformed to traditional ideals of womanly beauty. The new gay male cliché was the "macho" man who astonished everyone by coming out. Mistaken identity scripts emphasized the difference between sexual orientation and gender-role behavior.

The change in focus was particularly noticeable on *Laugh-In*. Starting in 1971, the show presented gravel-voiced gangsters, tough cowboys, and surly soldiers whose gayness surprised audiences. Viewers laughed at the imagined incongruity of "manly" gay men. Tony Curtis appeared in a brilliant skit about gays in the military, which hinged on keeping the audience guessing who was gay. Another sketch had a cowboy in the Old West unknowingly enter a gay saloon.[3] All of these comedic references were male; lesbians, deemed more threatening than funny, appeared only in dramas.

One way that producers helped straight viewers feel secure during gay-themed shows was by casting familiar actors—usually ones who had played a heterosexual role on a weekly series. Almost every gay character from these years was a familiar face. But the shows' most important shared trait was the heterosexual viewpoint: they were shows *about* gay people but clearly *for* straight audiences. TV executives said that the new gay programming reflected society's pluralism, and the networks often touted the shows as sensitive, tasteful, groundbreaking, unusual, and courageous. Richard Gollance, writing in *Out* magazine in 1973, pointed out how the hype exposed the limits of the networks' inclusiveness:

> When homosexuality is considered a "sensitive" subject and an author "courageous" for dealing with it, we are being told that it is unpleasant (unless dealt with obliquely), foreign, and needy of special "sensitivity," and the plot becomes a test for the audience's broad-mindedness and tolerance, instead of a story about people.[4]

In an industry where continued employment depends on ratings, even the most gay-friendly broadcasters made concessions to market forces and to society's basic prejudices.

A close study of the era's scripting experiments reveals that the forces at work in the early 1970s shaped later depictions of gay characters. Some pressure for change came from within the television industry, some from the gay community, and some from the changing mores of American culture. The following pages examine six scripting experiments that illustrate how television tried to fit this "new" topic into existing entertainment formats. The shows will be examined in chronological order, from February 1971 to February 1973, with emphasis on each program's plot, innovations, and background.

EXPERIMENT #1:
ALL IN THE FAMILY
"Judging Books by Covers"[5]
February 9, 1971—CBS
(situation comedy)

Plot

Archie Bunker squawks when his daughter and her husband invite an effeminate male friend to visit. Archie, who believes it is easy to spot a homosexual, complains that "Sweetie-Pie Roger . . . is as queer as a four-dollar bill." It turns out Roger is straight, but one of Archie's athletic, middle-aged drinking buddies is gay. Archie refuses to believe it. The script presents Archie's prejudice as ridiculous and irrational.

Innovations

The script established a sitcom formula for depicting gay characters that would remain the norm from 1971 to 1976.

- A series regular learns a longtime friend is gay.
- The gay man or lesbian is single, attractive, and "straight-acting"; if male, he is an ex–football player.
- There is no mention of other gay people with whom the gay character is friendly.
- The script teaches, "You can't spot a gay person just by looking."
- It preaches tolerance, if not acceptance.
- The gay character and the series regular are on good terms by the end.
- Despite their long friendship, the gay character never appears again.

On most shows, the disappearance of gay characters after one episode let a series preach tolerance without ever having to show it or sustain a commitment to it. This formula provided the commercial balance programmers needed: it piqued the interest of jaded viewers and appeased gay libbers, but avoided the outcry that an ongoing positive role might have attracted. Not having gay regulars also improved a show's marketability in post-network syndication. As before, gay people were a "them," not part of an "us."

Background

All in the Family defined the social-reform sitcom genre. Today, the series is a familiar classic; in 1971, it was revolutionary. Previous hit comedies like *Leave It To Beaver* and *The Beverly Hillbillies* had offered cheerful escapism. On TV, "nontraditional family" had meant *The Brady Bunch*. Noting this long, bland tradition, CBS president Bob Wood described the impact of *All in the Family* as "like breaking peanut brittle with a ball peen hammer."[6] It offended many with its politics, but it topped the Nielsens within a year and inspired a throng of imitators.

The show had an unorthodox hero and setting: Archie Bunker was a working-class bigot who lived in an urban, racially mixed neighborhood. The Bunkers were no jolly TV family: they shouted insults while arguing about politics, religion, and sex. Creator/producer Norman Lear found humor and pathos in topics like homophobia, racism, corruption, bureaucracy, murder, rape, illness, and adultery. Some conservative viewers complained that the show had a liberal bias, and that sitcoms had no business advocating a viewpoint. Lear replied that those older shows which had failed to address cultural diversity or social issues *did* put forth a political view:

> There was nothing but white bread and contentment in the 1960s' American situation comedy. What about *that* point-of-view-by-omission? There was nothing I thought we could ever say or do that would be as total as the point-of-view-by-omission of all of those shows of the sixties.[7]

Gay references were frequent from the start. For instance, Archie complained that the younger generation trusted all kinds of "revolutionaries and hippies and queers." Episode 5, "Judging Books by Covers," took mistaken identity to an extreme: it presented an effeminate straight man *and* an athletic gay man. The episode drew both positive and negative reactions. Perhaps the most interesting complaint came from then-President Richard Nixon: he asked why the writers made a "good man" like Archie Bunker look foolish at the story's end.[8] *All in the Family* earned a fortune and much prestige during its first year. Suddenly, issue-oriented humor was hot, and other comedies and comedy/dramas introduced gay guest characters.[9]

EXPERIMENT #2:
ROOM 222
"What Is a Man?"[10]
December 3, 1971—ABC
(comedy/drama)

Plot

Students harrass sixteen-year-old Howard (a guest character, played by Frederick Herrick) when they become convinced he is gay. Howard is artistic, unathletic, shy, and never dates. When he plays a woman convincingly in Shakespeare's *Twelfth Night*, other boys exchange knowing glances. Classmates Steve and Mark taunt Howard and warn Howard's friends not to spend time with him. Howard's best friend, series regular Bernie, shies away. A crowd gathers to watch Howard find the word FAG painted on his locker.

Howard damages his health and his grades trying to fit others' ideal of "manhood." But after informal counseling from a sympathetic teacher, he finally begins to develop confidence. In front of other students, he tells Mark off. Mark decks him, trying to provoke a fight. Howard refuses to throw a punch:

> HOWARD: I want to know if by putting me down, it makes you all feel like men. I want to know if writing "fag" on my locker is your standard for guts. . . . Do you think I would play the girl's part in a play if I were really trying to hide what you say I am? . . . And even if you *could* make something of it—what about you? I notice

you guys on the football field when you win a game—all over each other . . . Suppose people picked up on that and made something of it . . . What would you say? "Oh, that's different. That's *sport*." *(pause)* Well . . . It's what anybody wants to make of it! I'm not so sure what a man is, but I do know what he isn't. And that's you.

Innovations

This script followed most of the conventions the *All in the Family* episode established, right down to the longtime friend who never appears again. But it added two new plot formulas.

Room 222 broke ground in depicting schoolyard homophobia and its impact on young people's mental health, safety, and ability to get an education. It also pioneered a form of ambiguous "balance," which soon became a standard way to sell gay TV scripts about youth: liberal characters criticize homophobia, but at the last minute it becomes unclear whether the targeted character is really gay. Howard's final monologue underscores the episode's theses: that there are as many types of "manhood" as there are men, that rumors are dangerous, that gender-role behavior is distinct from sexual orientation, and that being oneself is much healthier than trying to fit a mold.

Background

Room 222 debuted in 1969, early in the networks' drive for "relevance." It was set in a racially integrated urban high school. When the series moved from 8:00 to a later time slot in 1971, ABC began allowing more controversial plots. That year, writer Don Balluck and the show's story editor considered an episode about a student who suffers merciless persecution. The story would show how harrassment can affect a teenager's prospects for success and happiness. Eventually, they agreed that Balluck would write about a boy victimized by antigay prejudice.

In the sociopolitical climate of 1971, Balluck knew he must balance the script carefully. To maximize marketability, he borrowed a plot device from film and theater: the persecution of a "gay-acting" male who is really straight (as in the 1950s drama, *Tea and Sympathy*). Balluck recalled in 1993:

The only reason we could do the story was that it turned out the kid was straight. I have vivid memories of how homosexuals were treated when I was in high school, and I saw some terrible things happen, mostly psychological. But the networks, by and large, were and still are cowards: it's a pose when they do controversial issues because they know exactly what they can exploit and what they can't, and when and how much.[11]

Howard's heterosexuality may have seemed clear on paper, but the filmed performance left room for doubt. On-screen, Howard seemed unsure of his sexuality.[12] Ambiguous endings became a hallmark of gay TV drama, particularly in stories about adolescents. The market probably would not have tolerated a more direct story about gay teens in 1971. No prime-time comedy or drama was to depict an explicitly gay high-school student until 1977 *(Alexander: The Other Side of Dawn)*, and after that apparently not again until 1984 *(Ellis Island)*. In 1979, CBS's *The White Shadow* aired an episode that covered essentially the same ground as the *Room 222* story; the main difference was that the possibly gay teenager was a star basketball player (played by Peter Horton).[13] Taken together, early shows about schoolyard homophobia sent the message that antigay harassment was a problem particularly when it mistakenly victimized "normal" kids. The networks left lesbian and gay youth as a faceless abstraction.

EXPERIMENT #3:
THE CORNER BAR
summer 1972—ABC
(situation comedy)

Plot

Like *All in the Family*, this series had a working-class setting: a run-down bar. *The Corner Bar*'s regulars were comic stock characters—a stereotyped Jew, a doddering drunkard, a wrist-flicking homosexual, and a two-dimensional bigot. *Newsweek* described the flamboyant gay character, played by Vincent Schiavelli:

Many of the one-liners are directed at the show's only original character, a swishy . . . designer named Peter Panama. Determined to spruce up his establishment for the arrival of a campaigning congressman, [owner] Harry suggests to Peter: "Maybe you could put a splint on your wrist." At another point, Peter tries to upgrade the patrons' tastes in TV programs by lisping: "Couldn't we switch to Channel 6? Julia Child is stuffing a wild duck."

One week, Peter describes a recent party he attended that was full of weirdos: all married couples. Peter delivers his lines with an exaggeratedly "gay" speech pattern and a caricatured swish of the hand.[14]

Innovations

The Corner Bar was the first series with an openly gay regular character. This, by itself, was so unusual that the character had to stick to familiar ground: old sissy stereotypes. Shows like *All in the Family*, with only gay *guest* characters, could ask audiences to rethink ideas of manhood once or twice a year; but a regular visitor had to be much less threatening. Even in the 1970s, the era of the "macho" televised gay male, gay regulars were laughable, often ineffectual men whom viewers could identify as having a "problem." The sissy-regular trend continued with *Hot l Baltimore* (1975), *The Nancy Walker Show* (1976), and early episodes of *Barney Miller* (1975).

The Corner Bar was also probably the first prime-time series whose producer agreed to negotiate with gay libbers after they complained about his show. Gay Activists Alliance president Rich Wandel had called Peter "the worst stereotype of a gay person I've ever seen" and vowed action. In response, producer Alan King agreed to "redirect" the character if ABC bought *The Corner Bar* for the fall.[15] The series, however, ended in August. When it returned for another summer run in 1973, most of the old characters were gone, including Peter.

Background

By 1972, the networks were using homosexuality as a selling point. In promoting its fall season, even reactionary NBC announced a lesbian-themed episode of *The Bold Ones*, and an episode of *Emergency* in which a man thinks that his son may be gay.[16]

ABC had a head start: it had emphasized gay content while presenting its summer lineup to a meeting of affiliates in May 1972. After that meeting, *Variety* reported:

> Trigger-happy trendspotters could be predicting a swing to homosexual comedy and drama.
>
> A scene from . . . *The Corner Bar* features a male character with exaggerated femme gestures and intonation . . .
>
> In a preview of another summer show, *Wow*, Phyllis Diller [says] with a leer that the "fairies" like the show . . .
>
> In his presentation on ABC's daytime programming, ABC daytime veepee Michael Eisner noted that the soap operas aren't what they used to be. These days, he said, "John loves Mary who loves Bruce—who may love John."[17]

No gay characters would appear in soap operas for years, but the choice of previews proved that ABC considered gay men highly marketable, perhaps as evidence of how liberal the network was. That tolerance, however, operated within narrow limits.

By the time *The Corner Bar* debuted, ABC's senior offices were abuzz with talk of homosexuality. Network executives debated what amounts and types of gay-themed programming were acceptable.

Vice presidents argued about whether the public saw *The Odd Couple* as gay lovers. ABC's market research showed that some viewers considered Felix gay, and disliked him as a result. At least one network vice president blamed this perception for *The Odd Couple*'s poor ratings. Ultimately, ABC decided that this sitcom had an image problem and could never do a gay episode. According to costar Tony Randall:

> They wouldn't let us do a show on homosexuality. On the "fear of flying" one, it was originally supposed to be that we got on a gay-lib flight. But they wouldn't let us use it, so we made it a parachute-jumping flight, and that was funnier.
>
> We had a script where Oscar was doing an article on homosexuality in sports, and I come across the article in his desk and I think he's writing about *himself*. We had the wonderful line, "Gee, if it was either of us, you'd think it would be *me*!"

Finally, producer Garry Marshall and the production crew got fed up with the censors' close scrutiny. "Just to make them crazy," he said, "we would send them film clips of homosexual scenes we would make up." The not-for-broadcast scenes showed Felix and Oscar hugging and kissing. "It infuriated them," Marshall recalled.[18]

But elsewhere at ABC, Standards and Practices was reviewing the lesbian-themed season premiere of *Owen Marshall, Counselor at Law*. Around the same time, outside consultants were reviewing an ABC TV-movie script about a gay father coming out to his teenage son.

As usual, ABC was dead last in the Nielsen ratings. It could afford to take some risks.

EXPERIMENT #4:
OWEN MARSHALL, COUNSELOR AT LAW
"Words of Summer"[19]
September 14, 1972—ABC
(drama)

Plot

Collegiate diving champ Ann Glover (Meredith Baxter), is accused of trying to molest a fifteen-year-old girl.

A prosecutor tries to prove that Ann is gay, and thus probably guilty. He calls as a witness Ann's college roommate, Meg Dayton, an unhappy, semicloseted lesbian who writes for a newspaper called *The 12th Letter*. (" 'L' for 'Lesbos' " the prosecutor explains, adding that "mythologically speaking," Lesbos was once "an all-girl island.") Meg tells of her two years as Ann's roommate, and describes the hurtful things their dormitory neighbors said about both women. "Even though I don't flaunt this," she says of her lesbianism, "the kids seemed to guess pretty quickly." She offered to move out, but Ann stuck by her friend.

At the story's end, we learn that teenage Ardis—the alleged victim—had a crush on Ann and panicked: no one had ever told Ardis that such feelings are normal. She made up the molestation story because she thought Ann did not like her anymore. A therapist assures Ardis that such crushes are common and that they do not really mean anything.

Innovations

Meg was the first self-identified lesbian character on a prime-time network show. Compared to previous pseudolesbians—on *The Asphalt Jungle* and *The Eleventh Hour*—she was amazingly stable. After all, she was neither a sniper nor a mental patient. Meg was the youngest gay character to have appeared in a TV drama—about twenty years old—and the first to state that her orientation was firmly in place when she was a teenager: "I am what I am, Mr. Marshall," she testifies. "I guess I always have been." But despite acknowledgment that gay people could be likable, there was still no indication that they could be happy; and while Meg said she had been a lesbian youth, the script reassured the audience that no such unhappy future awaited young Ardis.

Background

Screenwriter Edward DeBlasio, who had written scripts for impressive dramatic shows such as *The Defenders*, considered legal drama his forte. In 1972, he was writing for *Marcus Welby, M.D.*, but had been trying to get his foot in the door at the same producer's *Owen Marshall* series for some time. This was the fourth *Owen Marshall* story he pitched, and the first that sold. He says he got the idea of writing about a woman athlete after reading about Babe Didrikson Zaharias—the star athlete who had excelled at so many different sports in the 1930s and 1940s. When he originally pitched the idea in a story conference, he described Ann as husky, strong, and slightly masculine. The producers asked, "Can't she be pretty?" He was so happy to have the sale that he conceded the one point and Ann became a more feminine, girl-next-door type. "It was early in my career," DeBlasio recalled in 1997, "and I probably would have said yes to anything." It was the only substantial change requested by the producers or ABC from initial pitch to broadcast.[20]

Like other shows of the era, this series cast familiar performers in its "gay episode." Kristina Holland (who played Meg) had just finished a three-year run as Tina, the lovable secretary on *The Courtship of Eddie's Father*. And by this episode's airdate, CBS was awash with ads touting Meredith Baxter (who played Ann) as Bridget in the new sitcom, *Bridget Loves Bernie*. The *Owen Marshall* episode had a talented cast, and the cleverly plotted script kept audiences guessing where the story would end up.

The diverse reactions to the episode indicate much about the status of lesbian characters on television in the early 1970s. Some reviews, such as one in the *Hollywood Reporter*, praised the script. But writing in *Variety*, another critic felt the handling of the lesbian angle was not daring enough:

> *Owen Marshall* took a look at lesbianism in its season opener and didn't see much ... The one attempted look at the life and times of a femme homosexual was a brief soliloquy by a minor character who gave the expected speech about how hard it is to be out of step with community sexual mores. So much for "the new daring" on television this season ...[21]

By contrast, many gay women were thrilled. It was the first time they had seen their lives reflected on TV in a vaguely familiar, nonviolent way.[22]

EXPERIMENT #5:
THAT CERTAIN SUMMER[23]
November 1, 1972—ABC
(TV movie/drama)

Easily the most important, influential, gay-themed TV drama of the 1970s, *That Certain Summer* deserves particularly close examination.

Plot

ABC's press release boiled it down to one sentence: *"That Certain Summer is the story of a divorced man whose failure to discuss his homosexuality with his family makes it necessary for him to explain his lifestyle to his fourteen-year-old son."*[24]

Doug Salter (Hal Holbrook) is a semicloseted divorcé. His ex-wife,

Janet (Hope Lange), knew he was gay when they married; she had thought she could change him. Every summer, their son Nick (Scott Jacoby) visits Doug in San Francisco. But this year, things are different: Doug has a live-in lover (Martin Sheen), and hiding their homosexuality will be difficult. Doug is in his mid forties, part of the discreet pre-Stonewall generation. He thinks Nick is too young to handle information about homosexuality—especially his dad's. Doug's thirtyish lover, Gary, thinks they should come out to Nick. "He's a bright boy," Gary says. "He picks up on things." There is a lot for Nick to pick up on: although Gary has moved out for the duration of the son's visit, Doug and Gary's home is filled with evidence of two people sharing a life.

As Nick pieces things together, he becomes scared and confused. From the adults' secrecy, he knows that something unmentionable and wrong is going on. He has questions that no one seems willing to answer. Nick runs away and spends the day wandering around the Bay Area, as the three adults—Janet, Gary, and Doug—try to find him. After Nick reappears that evening, father and son go for a walk in the woods. Doug explains that he and Gary have "a kind of a marriage." The scene is darkly lit, with the two characters often obscured by trees. Throughout, Nick looks away from his father and seems about to cry. Doug's usually firm voice quavers and hesitates:

DOUG: Do you know what the word "homosexual" means? (*Nick begins to walk away. Doug gently takes his arm. Nick pulls away but stops walking.*) Nick, come on, look at me. Keep the door open. Do you know what it means?

NICK: I think so.

DOUG: You probably heard about it in school or in the streets. Well that's just one side: put-downs and jokes. A lot of people—most people, I guess, think it's wrong. They say it's a sickness. They say it's something that has to be cured. I don't know. I do know it isn't easy. If I had a choice, it's not something I'd pick for myself. But it's the only way I can live. Gary and I have a kind of a marriage. We—

NICK: (*Anguished*) I don't want to talk about it.

DOUG: Nick. We love each other. . . .

Nick runs back to the house. As Nick and Janet prepare to leave for Los Angeles, the boy refuses to even say good-bye to his father. The film ends with a dejected Doug watching home movies from Nick's childhood, showing the father and son enjoying each other's company.

Innovations

Critics hailed *That Certain Summer* as a "landmark," a "breakthrough." Even now, articles surveying the history of gay images on TV often start with this film. It was the first network drama to depict a stable, same-gender couple; the first to depict a gay parent; and the first gay-themed show to win an Emmy. Entertainment trade publications wrote about it extensively, as did fan magazines, medical journals, and just about every periodical but *Sports Illustrated*. Almost thirty years later, much of the show looks stilted and apologetic. But for years, *That Certain Summer* symbolized television's new frankness. *Variety*'s TV critic, Les Brown, used *That Certain Summer* as the lead example in a 1972 article about television's changing morality. At the May 1973 ABC affiliates meeting, ABC-TV president Walter A. Schwartz pointed to *That Certain Summer* as proof that the network was "progressive."[25]

Background

The idea for *That Certain Summer* reportedly originated in 1971 when writers Richard Levinson and William Link learned that a gay male colleague had sons from an earlier marriage. In a 1980 essay, Levinson and Link wrote that the situation intrigued them. Did the sons know that their father was gay? Did Dad's lover stick around during the sons' visits? How did the children react? The writers found themselves thinking of the situation's dramatic potential:

> . . . given the realities of television, we assumed it would have to be written as a short story, or play, or a book. Homosexuality, not yet quite a political cause and anathema to many Americans, was simply too threatening to be the stuff of TV drama.[26]

Levinson and Link had a proven track record in many genres of TV writing. They had cowritten award-winning, controversial telefilms like

My Sweet Charlie and created popular entertainments like the series *Columbo*. Networks actively sought their ideas. When they casually mentioned the gay father idea to an NBC executive, he rejected it outright—hardly surprising from the network whose comedians specialized in "fairy" jokes. But Barry Diller, in charge of ABC's new TV-movie division, encouraged them to develop the idea.

The writers deliberately created the characters in stark contrast to the hairdressers and hustlers who populated most gay-themed Hollywood films: Doug and Gary would be "the nice men next door, or down the block," members of the "upper middle class." According to Levinson and Link, Diller "told us there would be corporate problems because of the nature of the project, but he assured us he was fully behind it . . ." The problems became apparent in the first script review notes from the department of Standards and Practices. The censors were most concerned about the script's use of the word "love" in reference to the male couple, and objected to any hint of physical affection. A sampling of their demands follows:

> page 8, scene 23: I don't think your story needs any visual subtleties, such as "the unmade king-size bed" to make its point.
>
> page 51, scene 108: Gary puts his arm on Doug's shoulder. This must be nothing more than "casual" as described.
>
> page 72, scene 166: It will be preferable that the line "But to me it's just . . . another way of loving" be deleted or in some manner modified. Perhaps ". . . another way of living." And the line "we love each other" will need to be said in some other way, less explicit.

After many long meetings between the writers and the network, the line "we love each other" was approved. Some of the censors' cuts led to ridiculous moments on screen. In one scene, the script called for a male couple to walk past Gary, Doug, and Nick, holding hands. But in the broadcast version, the extras run past *not* holding hands, and the audience is left baffled or amused when Doug gripes, "I don't like public displays."

The Standards and Practices people said that the writers needed to insert some antigay dialog for balance—perhaps by adding an "Archie

Bunker-type" cop character. Instead, Levinson and Link decided to give Gary a pseudo-liberal brother-in-law, whose "enlightened" comments could not mask his prejudiced assumptions. The writers also added the line in which Doug says that maybe homosexuals *are* sick, but that there is nothing he can do about it. It was this speech that most offended gay activists during the prebroadcast test screenings. Many gay viewers also said that the gay characters were "too straight."

More damning than the sickness monologue was the couple's lack of physical affection. This is most problematic in the final scene. Doug, reeling from his son's rejection, sits on the stairs, fighting back tears. Gary tries to comfort him. Logically, the scene requires physical contact— a comforting arm over the shoulders at the very least. But since this was the first mass-market, gay-positive telefilm, the portrayal was made as unthreatening as possible. Gary kneels on the landing above and talks briefly to the back of his distraught lover's head. Then Gary strolls off to work, touching Doug's shoulder for a second as he walks past. They never look at each other in this scene. Doug weeps. Imagine if a TV-movie presented the same scenario with a straight husband and wife who never seemed to touch each other, even at a time of such great emotional pain. What conclusions would viewers rightly draw about the health, lovingness, and value of that marriage? But for a first effort, the film is remarkably well made.

Aside from script changes, the network's principal demands had to do with casting: ABC wanted recognizable film or TV stars in the three adult leads. Many noted actors wanted nothing to do with the film, fearing its effect on their careers. Hal Holbrook finally accepted the role of Doug over objections from his agent. Martin Sheen, who had played a gay character on TV in 1971 (a cab driver, murdered by his lover in an episode of *Dan August*)[27] apparently accepted with little hesitation. In a 1985 press conference to promote another TV movie, Sheen said that despite having played every sort of criminal on film, no role garnered him more hate mail than his playing a likable gay man in *That Certain Summer*.[28] As filming was about to begin, the producers still had not been able to find a name actress to play Janet. Hope Lange's casting was a lucky fluke: one of the scriptwriters ran into her in a grocery store and mentioned the project, and she was interested.

To defuse possible advance protests, ABC prescreened the film for a wide range of groups: religious leaders, gay libbers, college students, the American Civil Liberties Union, disc jockeys, and parents' media-watch organizations. These people then went home and wrote articles about the film for trade papers, organizational newsletters, and mainstream media. The screenings generated tremendous advance publicity. ABC press packets described the show in detail, hoping to allay public fears about potential "sexual" content. At least one affiliate, WEAT-TV in West Palm Beach, Florida, chose not to air the film. In Atlanta, WQXI-TV moved it from 8:30 P.M. to a late-night slot.[29]

GAA president Rich Wandel wrote to ABC expressing both praise and concern: "We commend the ABC television network and Universal Pictures for taking a significant if tentative step in the right direction . . . We applaud the efforts of the writers and directors to smash the appalling TV stereotypes of gay men, and to treat homosexual characters with sympathetic respect." However, he questioned the network's treating homosexuality as if it were a debatable, controversial subject. He wrote that GAA would have preferred an ending in which someone directly challenged the son's prejudice. Wandel wrote, "We object when bigotry—even that of a fourteen-year-old boy—is left unresolved in a melodrama which, if it dealt with any other minority group, would be resolved four-squarely for justice."[30]

Like many firsts, *That Certain Summer* was tame, but it blazed a trail for other, less cautious shows. ABC's risk in airing it paid off in ratings and prestige: the film overwhelmingly won the evening's Nielsen wars (per *Variety*, it marked ABC's "first Wednesday-night win in a long time for regular programming")[31] and was nominated for eight Emmys. Martin Sheen, opposed to awards on principle, asked that his nomination be withdrawn. In May 1973, Scott Jacoby won a Supporting Actor Emmy for his performance as the son. *That Certain Summer* proved to television executives that the public and the critics were open to well-made, serious shows about gay people.

EXPERIMENT #6:
AN AMERICAN FAMILY[32]
January–March 1973, PBS
(cinema verité)

Plot

A forerunner of MTV's *The Real World*, this was the first national series built around real people who let film crews document their lives daily for months. It is not, strictly, a "scripting experiment," but the producers had great control over the final storyline: they edited more than three hundred hours of film down into this twelve-hour exercise in voyeurism.[33]

The subjects were the Loud family, seven middle-class suburbanites in California. During the show's weekly, one-hour installments, America saw the parents' marriage break up and watched the children's lives evolve. The eldest son, twenty-year-old Lance, was openly gay. Viewers saw him try on his sisters' makeup, move to New York's Chelsea neighborhood above Greenwich Village, and wear leather togs and blue lipstick. Young viewers found an antihero in Lance. This was the era of androgynous pop stars, when men like Alice Cooper and David Bowie dressed unisex, wore makeup, and told the press about their supposed bisexuality. Lance fit the era's sensitive-young-rebel image: he wore long, hippie hair; he refused to work; and he lived in the infamous Chelsea Hotel where Andy Warhol had filmed *Chelsea Girls*. In episode two, Lance's mother, Pat, visits him in New York. The camera follows as they tour the city and attend a joyous drag show at the La Mama Experimental Theatre Company.

Innovations

Anthropologist Margaret Mead theorized that *An American Family* "may be as important for our time as were the invention of drama and the novel for earlier generations: a new way to help people understand themselves." It certainly captured viewers' imaginations. Touted as the most expensive documentary ever made, it drew PBS's highest ratings to that date for an American-produced show. It was a Nielsen oddity. In Boston, for instance, the premiere drew a 10 share, (i.e., ten percent of the TV sets that were on during that time slot were tuned to *An American Family*). Such numbers were unheard-of for public TV. Critic Frank Rich has cited *An American Family* as the first TV series to regularly show American viewers a gay man—someone familiar whom they could visit week after week rather than a guest character who vanished after one appearance. This serial amplification was further played out in print and broadcast interviews with Lance.

Background

Filmmaker Craig Gilbert, who produced *Margaret Mead's New Guinea Journal*, decided to turn a similar anthropological eye toward a family in the U.S.—preferably a family with opinionated teenagers in fad-ridden California. He hit pay dirt with the Louds. With two assistants, he filmed their lives from June to December 1971, and spent much of 1972 winnowing it down to the three-month series that aired in 1973. Through editing and exploitative publicity, the Louds' story became a look at the unexplored underside of the American Dream. Nationally placed print ads showed a photo of the wholesome-looking family under the headline, "Would You Live Next Door to the Louds?" In 1991, Lance Loud recalled, "The series' producer had once told us it would be 'the greatest home movie in the world.'" But after the ads hit, Lance said, "Even the Louds began to wonder if they'd want to live next door to the Louds."

Magazine and newspaper commentators in 1973 wondered what sort of family would allow filmmakers to invade their privacy for seven months, letting the entire world watch humiliating personal moments. Some wondered whether Pat and Bill Loud's marriage would have broken up if the cameras had not been there. Several of the Louds gave TV interviews on popular programs like *The Dick Cavett Show* to answer some of these questions. Most of Lance's public discussions about his sexual orientation occurred in interviews to promote the show, rather than on *An American Family* itself. As he noted in a later episode of the documentary, his sexuality was not something his family could discuss openly.

Stephanie Harrington wrote in the *New York Times*, "you find yourself sticking with the Louds with the same compulsion that draws you back day after day to your favorite soap opera." Her review of the second episode raises many of the same issues that other commentators took away from it:

> You watch Pat visit her oldest son . . . , see her meet his friends (some, like Holly Woodlawn, in drag) . . . and wonder . . . that not once do they utter the word "homosexual." Of course, this might be admirable if it represented a sophisticated and understanding acceptance of reality by Lance's parents. But it doesn't. They simply refuse to acknowledge the reality. In the end the silence is shattering.[34]

In the 1990s, Lance Loud parlayed his twelve hours of fame and his writing skills into a job as a columnist for *The Advocate*. He had a small speaking role as a gay man in the 1993 miniseries *Armistead Maupin's "Tales of the City."*

TO ZAP OR NOT TO ZAP?

The Rise of Gay Media Activism: 1973–1974

> We were really *into* confrontation. We were angry. It was the early days of the movement, and there were a lot of street demonstrations and other confrontational tactics. We got a lot of pleasure out of it. It was very therapeutic.
> —*Activist Ginny Vida, recalling GAA's and LFL's early-1970s media zaps, 1991*[1]

Lesbian and gay media advocates learned much from ethnic minorities' experiences with broadcasters. There are practical differences between racism and homophobia, but many of the weapons to combat them are similar. In both cases, activists fought against stereotyped images in the broadcast media, citing the power of entertainment shows to promote intolerance. In both cases, small, single-issue organizations formed national coalitions and national mailing lists in an attempt to present a united grassroots front. The media-watch achievements of the NAACP, Justicia, and other ethnic organizations had already helped network executives to understand the harmful impact of broadcast stereotypes. As a result, lesbian and gay negotiators were not starting from square one.

By 1973, the TV networks had formal policies to limit demeaning portrayals of ethnic minorities. Gay Liberation groups wanted the same consideration. In January, the Gay Activists Alliance's new president, Dr. Bruce Voeller, and the group's News and Media Relations chief, Ron Gold, set concrete goals for TV activism. They would write to producers and network executives, explain GAA's concerns about recent programs, and request meetings with industry decision makers. GAA would try to draw a parallel between racism and homophobia. If letter writing failed, they would use boycotts, picketing, sit-ins, and the threat of future disruptions to gain meetings with TV executives. The ultimate goal was for the networks to ban, in writing, any "slighting or offensive references" to gay people. Voeller wrote to each network's head of program standards, citing the "recent rash of antihomosexual remarks, jokes and characterizations" on network TV. He said that GAA did not want censorship; it just wanted the networks to expand existing policies on minority portrayals to include sexual orientation:

> We have no objections . . . to humorous remarks or skits dealing with homosexuality and depiction of homosexual characters on television . . . But sniggering "fag" and "dyke" jokes won't do, nor will the suggestion that the mere fact of homosexuality is hilarious. In short, we do not object to jokes that deal with our lives—but our lives themselves are not a joke!

GAA praised recent skits on *Burns and Schreiber* comedy specials: one in which a father accepted his openly gay son, and another that satirically depicted a gay man harassing straights in a bar. GAA also liked a *Mary Tyler Moore Show* episode which casually revealed that Phyllis's brother was gay.[2]

GAA was especially concerned about the casual, antigay comments that peppered late-night talk shows. In 1971, Johnny Carson's fag jokes had led to unproductive GAA negotiations with *Tonight Show* producer Fred de Cordova and a letter-writing campaign to NBC.[3] In January 1973, during the first week of ABC's *Jack Paar Tonite*, GAA found that host Paar uttered an average of five antigay jokes per show. For instance, he had described ballet as "the fairies' baseball." Paar was the same talk show host who had proclaimed on his 1960s' series, "It's the fairies who are going to ruin show business." In mid-January, Voeller wrote to Paar requesting airtime for GAA to rebut his comments. "In the course of a single week," Voeller wrote, "you have managed to offend and infuriate twenty million American citizens with a barrage of antihomosexual jokes and innuendoes. This is to put you on notice that you will have to stop." Again, GAA emphasized parallels between racism and antigay prejudice, asking that Paar apply the same broadcast standards to gays as he did to other oppressed minorities. In February, the *New York Times* printed a letter to the editor from Voeller, outlining GAA's concerns about Paar; Voeller cited antiracist comments Paar had made in a recent *Times* interview, and contrasted them with Paar's fairy jokes. By then, Paar had offered GAA representatives an appearance on his March 8 show.[4] Voeller and Gold also wrote to Dick Cavett, asking him to challenge guests' homophobic remarks on *his* talk show. Here, too, GAA equated the dignity of gay people with that of racial and ethnic minorities. *Variety* reported: "Giving Cavett credit for being 'obviously uncomfortable on [these] occasions,' Voeller urged . . . positive action . . . 'You'd be quick to cut off anyone who was fast with nigger or kike jokes, wouldn't you?' "[5]

New York was the hub of gay media activism in the early 1970s, but California, with its longer history of gay organizing, was quickly catching up. On the West Coast, television activism centered in Los Angeles's Gay Community Services Center, where board president Morris Kight devoted much of his energy to negotiating with local stations. Other West Coast gay leaders participated more tangentially in media activism—people like Reverend Troy Perry, founder of Metropolitan Community Churches, and Joe Gruber, coordinator of Gay Youth of Los Angeles.[6] While New York organizers had the advantage of being in the same city as the networks' top executives, the Los Angeles activists were closer to TV production centers and creative personnel.

People working in the television industry, especially closeted gay men and lesbians, often smuggled scripts to activists while shows were in production. In 1972, according to screenwriters Levinson and Link, their script for *That Certain Summer* found its way to "several gay coalitions."[7] Around January 1973, someone secretly gave gay groups the script to an upcoming episode of *Marcus Welby, M.D.* That drama, "The Other Martin Loring," deals with an ostensibly heterosexual, married man who consults Dr. Welby about diabetes, depression, alcoholism, and homosexual tendencies. Welby seems most worried about the last problem, calling it "a serious illness" curable through psychotherapy. Dr. Welby tells Martin to resist his homosexual urges so that "you'll deserve the respect of your son."[8]

GAA fired off a letter to ABC's Standards and Practices department objecting to the *Welby* script. The letter emphasized the importance of responsible media portrayals, given the scarcity of gay-themed shows: "[G]ay people in our society are where blacks were not so many years ago, just emerging from media invisibility. Greater caution is needed at present to avoid giving offense."[9] Voeller and Gold knew that *Marcus Welby, M.D.* was one of TV's top-rated dramas; its antigay message would reach millions. On February 13, GAA representatives, including Gold, met with Grace Johnson, ABC's Standards and Practices vice president. She cited *That Certain Summer* as proof of the network's sympathy toward homosexuals, and mentioned a letter from a young gay man who had decided against suicide after seeing the TV movie. A GAA negotiator asked how ABC would feel when some teenager did commit suicide after seeing "The Other Martin Loring." Johnson finally agreed to consider asking Universal Television to reedit the episode. She also said that ABC might negotiate with gay leaders to create guidelines for gay-themed broadcasts.[10]

Two days later, ABC announced that *Marcus Welby, M.D.* would air "The Other Martin Loring" on February 20, as scheduled. The announcement did not mention reediting. Since negotiations had failed, GAA authorized a zap for the next day. It would be Gay Liberation's first civil disobedience against a major TV network. At 3 P.M. on February 16, some thirty irate protesters converged on the ABC building in New York. They burst into the top two floors—the executive suite—where they commandeered the phones and occupied the chairman and president's offices. Bill Bahlman, a teenager when he participated in the ABC zap, recalled in 1991 that surprise was a key element:

> You want to scare them and make them feel your wrath, but you also want to keep a degree of control so they don't think that you're going to throw a bomb. We charge into the offices and someone shouts, "Give me a 'G'!" And everyone yells, "G!" "Give me an 'A'!" "A!" "Give me a 'Y'!" "Y!" Until you spell out "GAY POWER." That burst of sound is *loud*. I've got a loud voice. Most members of GAA had loud, powerful voices. Believe me, you can get receptionists and secretaries and office staff so stunned by this loud, booming burst of sound coming into their nice, little, quiet offices that you've got a few seconds to do anything you want, including charge right in.

GAA distributed leaflets during the zap, denouncing Dr. Welby as "a quack and a bigot":

> Does Welby give his patient sound medical advice? Does he tell him not to be uptight, that he's in the same boat with twenty million American citizens who know how to be happy and gay? No. Instead Welby congratulates him for resisting his feelings.

An ABC senior manager offered to meet with two GAA representatives if the others left first. Gold refused, promising that his colleagues would sit quietly for the duration of the meeting. ABC called in the police. Approximately twenty-five protesters left the building, and police arrested the remaining six. GAA told reporters that, during the sit-in, they had answered phone calls from such noted mental health professionals as the American Psychiatric Association's vice president, Dr. Judd Marmor, who had called to encourage ABC to cancel the show.[11]

In Los Angeles, Morris Kight and others planned demonstrations for the episode's broadcast date. The morning of February 20, twenty-five picketers gathered in front of the Los Angeles County Medical Association. They carried placards that read MARCUS WELBY, WITCH DOCTOR; WELBY'S QUEER! BUT I'M GAY; and MARTIN LORING — WE LOVE YOU, GAY BROTHER. The Medical Association often provided consultants for TV's medical dramas, including *Welby*. During the two-hour picket, activists urged the Medical Association to pressure the networks for a more enlightened attitude toward gay people. As they marched, protesters branded Welby a "quack doctor": "Quack! Quack! Quack!" they chanted. Organizers used the event to advocate a nationwide gay boycott of *Welby* sponsors. Afterward, Medical Association representatives met with demonstrators and promised to file a complaint with ABC about the *Welby* story. Several protesters moved the picketing to ABC's Los Angeles headquarters, but executives refused to meet with them or let them in the building. Ultimately, the proposed boycott came to nothing, since there was no effective way to spread the word.[12]

One of Gay Lib's main obstacles in 1973 was a lack of cohesion. There was no national organization to distribute information. There were no large, national gay mailing lists for publicizing political actions or for direct-mail fund-raising. This lack of coordination gave the TV networks an easy way to avoid dealing with gay negotiators. When New York activists explained their concerns to network executives in Manhattan, the executives would say that program content was a creative issue decided in Hollywood; meanwhile, in California, TV producers and network censors told activists that policies about minorities were the realm of the New York executives.

Because communication among activists was erratic, the *Welby* protesters in Los Angeles did not know that ABC had already announced a compromise in New York: the network agreed to delete two lines of Martin Loring's dialogue. One line had him describe his homosexual feelings as "degrading and loathsome"; in the other, he said his sexual urges made "my whole life a cheap, hollow fraud." The *New York Times* reported that GAA, "an organization of militant homosexuals," would have preferred deletion of Dr. Welby's " 'offensive and obnoxious' " lines, which treated homosexuality as an illness. ABC executives, tired of being caught in the middle, urged *Welby*'s executive producer to meet directly with gay leaders. After those negotiations, activist Newton Deiter later recalled, "We were assured that this [kind of program] would not happen again." It was an empty promise.[13]

Gay media activism increasingly grabbed headlines throughout 1973, though it remained scattershot and uncoordinated. Individuals often engaged in civil disobedience without formal approval from Gay Lib organizations. In terms of press coverage, the most visible "guerilla" activist was Mark Segal. He was best known for chaining himself to heavy objects: TV cameras, tables, historic monuments, and public buildings. Daily papers around the country reported Segal's stunts, and his protests against TV shows rated bemused coverage in *Variety*.[14] He was a hero to many young, angry gay activists, who called him "Prince Valiant" and "The Gay Crusader." Some assimilationist gays had less flattering names for him. Many dismissed him as a shameless self-promoter, more interested in personal publicity than changing the world. But whatever anyone thought about him, Segal deserves some credit for helping to keep a spotlight on TV's gay portrayals throughout the mid 1970s.

In 1972, Segal and a male friend were bodily ejected from the taping of a television dance show in New Jersey. They had been dancing together. Later that week, he and some friends, calling themselves the Gay Raiders, stormed the station's *Action News* studio in Philadelphia during a live telecast. In March 1973, Segal flew to Los Angeles to protest antigay humor on Johnny Carson's *Tonight Show*. During a *Tonight* taping in early March, he jumped up from his seat in the audience, shouted, "*The Tonight Show* oppresses gay people!", ran down the aisle and handcuffed himself to a railing that separated the audience from the stage. NBC removed Segal and Carson's exchange from the videotape. Guards cut him loose and NBC refused to press charges. The next night, Carson told viewers that a protester had disrupted his previous taping. "You've heard of the Chicago Seven?" Carson reportedly asked. "Well this was the Burbank One." A week later, Segal and Mike Walters (an L.A. Community Services Center volunteer) were arrested in the lobby of NBC's Burbank studios; Segal had handcuffed himself to a table and said he would not leave unless they met with Joseph Cunneff, executive producer of *The Tonight Show*. That meeting never materialized. Segal and his Gay Raiders struck again in May: he handcuffed himself to a camera during a taping of *The Mike Douglas Show*, a daytime series that had canceled a discussion of Gay Liberation.[15]

Individuals like Segal and local groups like GAA and the L.A. Community Center could do only so much. The need for a coordinated, nationwide effort grew increasingly clear. By May 1973, GAA was using national gay periodicals to broaden its efforts. The magazines asked readers to send media-watch reports to "Complaints" c/o GAA's New York post office box.[16] The efforts by some GAA leaders to nationalize and professionalize the movement led to a schism within GAA. Most of the members favored grassroots action over what Bruce Voeller was proposing: a gay civil rights agency patterned after the NAACP, complete with a paid staff, board of directors, and "respectable" lobbyists. This ideological split led to the creation of the National Gay Task Force (NGTF), which was originally based in Manhattan. Voeller and Gold left their positions in GAA to assume the equivalent titles in NGTF: executive director and communications director. NGTF's first chairman was Dr. Howard J. Brown, former New York City Health Commissioner. Brown announced NGTF's formation in an October 15 news conference. Nine days later, NGTF told reporters that gay groups were launching nationwide protests against NBC, largely in response to two *Sanford and Son* episodes that used homosexuality for cheap laughs.[17]

The independent Gay Raider, Mark Segal, traveled to Washington, D.C., later that month. On October 26, he disrupted a live newscast on NBC's *Today* show. As usual, viewers heard little of his comments, as the camera cut away instantly. But cohost Barbara Walters interviewed him off-camera, then returned to the studio to tell viewers the rationale behind the zap: displeasure over the treatment of gays in NBC entertainment shows. The same week, four representatives of NGTF ("a group unconnected with the Gay Raiders," *Variety* assured its readers) met with NBC Programming and Program Standards executives. They discussed the most recent *Sanford and Son* episode and Johnny Carson's frequent fairy jokes. Per *Variety*:

> After the meeting, an official of the web sent a wire to the press saying that NBC representatives "expressed their understanding of the Task Force position and acknowledged that improvements could be made. These will include continuing liaison with the Task Force, other representatives of the gay community and knowledgeable professionals for consulting purposes where necessary."[18]

Meanwhile, in Los Angeles, Morris Kight, Pat Rocco, and others were forming an organization that would permanently change the power dynamic between gays and the media.

12

THE NEGOTIATORS

Television: 1973–1974

. . . what the public really loathes in homosexuality is not the thing itself but
having to think about it.   —*E. M. Forster, 1960*[1]

The Gay Media Task Force (GMTF) began meeting informally as a
committee of the Los Angeles Gay Community Services Center in
1973. GMTF's purpose was to negotiate with the local media, with network executives, and TV and movie producers. Throughout the mid
1970s, GMTF and the National Gay Task Force worked in tandem—
GMTF negotiating with the people who made the shows on the West
Coast and NGTF dealing with network executives in New York. The
two task forces worked together so closely that many in the TV industry
thought they were one organization called The Gay Task Force.

NGTF publications often asserted that their organization cofounded
the Gay Media Task Force, and they implied that Ron Gold was an initial driving force behind GMTF.[2] Gold did fly to Los Angeles in
November 1973, after GMTF began meeting, to attend a planning session to draft demands to present to the networks. Many who attended
that meeting had worked in the television industry for years. Gold's
experience was less direct, as a negotiator (in GAA) and sometime
writer for *Variety*. In New York's activist circles, Gold was very well
known. People valued his talent for persuasive writing so highly that
they were forever asking him to draft or ghostwrite an article, a speech,
a letter, or an ad. At this West Coast meeting, however, Gold was an

outsider, eyed with suspicion. Some of his suggestions carried weight, but his cockiness and his infamous temper did not endear him to some West Coast organizers. In New York, Gold had dealt mostly with corporate network executives, not their Californian counterparts on TV's creative side. To some Los Angeles activists, he seemed to advocate an unnecessarily conservative, apologetic, middle-class image. For his part, he doubted whether the L.A. activists' more confrontational plans would convince anyone of anything. Gold favored low-key negotiating within the system. To him, picketing and civil disobedience were a last resort.

In the NGTF newsletter of May 1974, Gold described his preferred tactics. By the time he wrote this, GMTF and NGTF had each won concessions from the mass media.

> At the beginning of our media battle there was only one way to get attention to our cause or make complaints—To "zap" the villains. Now, and we like to think it's a result of our efforts, there are two ways. Sometimes we still need to zap, but more often all that's required is to write a letter of complaint, point [out] something inaccurate or abusive about gays that's appeared on the air or in print, and ask for a meeting.
>
> . . . These meetings have seldom spent much time on the subject of the complaint. Since we pick our first shots carefully, they almost always agree we're right and promise not to do it again. The discussions soon get on to the things they've been missing that are real news, by their own lights; to the subjects they haven't thought of for drama or talk shows . . . Usually they buy a few of these ideas and promise to follow through on them. And then we get on to the last step, establishment of a steady means of communication for further suggestions and complaints: a means of making sure that promises are fulfilled.[3]

At the 1973 GMTF planning meeting, some of the more radical West Coast activists interpreted Gold's confidence as condescension. In a 1991 interview, Jim Kepner recalled that several of the Californians believed that Gold was determined "to show us benighted West Coast people how we should go about doing this." According to Kepner, Gold "was probably competent, but a lot of us just didn't want to hear it." Given the diverse politics of the participants, it is amazing that the meeting produced any kind of consensus. Even among themselves, members of the Los Angeles contingent held a wide range of political views, from social revolutionaries to negotiators and reformers.[4] The meeting's attendees finally did agree on an eight-point platform. This one-page document became the unofficial Constitution and Bible of gay media activists for the next decade. Negotiators distributed copies to the press and gave the document to TV network executives, scriptwriters, producers, and directors at every opportunity. Mimeographed copies were on hand at negotiating sessions. The document read:

GAY MEDIA TASK FORCE PLATFORM

1. Homosexuality isn't funny. Sometimes, of course, anything can be a source of humor. But the lives of 20,000,000 Americans are not a joke.
2. Fag, faggot, dyke, queer, lezzie, homo, fairy, mary, pansy, sissy, etc., are terms of abuse. If you don't want to insult, the words are gay, lesbian and homosexual. This doesn't mean that nobody on film can use a dirty word, but if you have general rules about the use of "kike," "wop," "spic," and "nigger," use them for "dyke," "fag," et al.
3. That's it, use the same rules you have for other minorities. For example, if bigots don't usually get away with it if they hate Catholics, they can't get away with it if they hate gays. To put it another way, the rights and dignities of homosexuals are not a "controversial" issue.
4. Stereotypical people do exist, but if such a minority of any group receives exclusive media exposure, that's bigotry. Until a broad spectrum of the gay community has been stressed on film, and the stereotypes are put in perspective, the use of stereotypes is damaging.
5. Homosexuality is a natural variant of human sexuality. It is not an illness, nor is it a "problem" for the vast majority of gays who are pleased and happy to be what they are. If all blacks (or Jews, Irish, Chicanos, etc.) were presented as anguished, oddball or insane, blacks (etc.) would be angry. Gays are angry.
6. If you are doing a drama, comedy, talk show or whatever about homosexuality or gay characters, you have an obligation to do your homework and to free yourself of the myths.

7. There is a wide variety of available themes concerning the place of homosexuality in contemporary society and the range of gay relationships and lifestyles, and many of these can provide viable entertainment for a broad public. Gay people do not want to return to media invisibility.

8. A permanent board of consultants, consisting of gay women and men (including knowledgeable professionals in a variety of fields) is now available to the industry. But there are gay people all around you in your job. It's up to you to provide the climate in which they feel free to speak out.[5]

During the fall of 1973, GMTF and NGTF met with the program-standards chiefs of all three networks. At the same time, GMTF began cultivating friendships with closeted gay and bisexual people in the TV industry. Such contacts were easy to make. In these early days, when GMTF was still a good-sized group, most of its members were media professionals in Los Angeles and Hollywood. In a 1976 article, a GMTF leader wrote, "Our major sources of information to this day are these people actively employed within the industry and closeted about their own gayness, who provide us with the overwhelming majority of the confidential information we receive."[6]

Jack Petry, NBC's West Coast head of Program Standards, took the gay groups' suggestions to heart, but with reservations. He agreed to censor Johnny Carson's disparaging comments, for example, but felt that comic sissy characters were not really about homosexuality. He continued to permit prissy characters like Sammy Davis, Jr.'s Little Lord Fauntleroy. Right after NBC's meetings with NGTF and GMTF, Screen Gems sent Petry's office a *Police Story* script for approval. It dealt with a closeted, cross-dressing, fiftyish homosexual who strangles and butchers young gay men who reject his sexual advances. The dialogue suggests that one gay character "got that way" because of his overbearing mother. According to *Lesbian Tide* magazine, the original version of the script depicts "a hustler, several uptight nellies, and an unhappy Lesbian couple, not to mention four passive heterosexual women who smiled for their men and did what they were told."[7] Petry returned the script to Screen Gems, citing its potential to offend gays. At Petry's suggestion, Screen Gems sent the script to GMTF for input.

Eight members of GMTF met with Screen Gems' vice president Arthur Frankl and *Police Story* producer Stanley Kallis. GMTF representatives at the meeting included psychologist Newton Deiter, who soon would emerge as the organization's leader and chief spokesperson. Filmmaker Pat Rocco and other GMTF negotiators explained in detail the problems with the script. They recommended specific plot changes and dialogue that would make the episode more acceptable. The producers sent the changes to Don Engels, who had written the original script, with orders to incorporate them. Kallis agreed to hire a consultant from GMTF. The task force provided two technical advisers for the price of one: a man (Newt Deiter) and a woman (named Country). The two participated in the script revision and attended the filming to ensure accuracy and believability. Deiter told *The Advocate* that in their consulting work, he and Country walked a fine line:

> We hope to avoid the "Superfag" approach, and [the first rewrite of the *Police Story* script] was overdone on *our* side. So Country and I sat down with Kallis and went through it line by line in order to restore a little conflict. It's important, you see, that while we're winning these battles with the media, that we also show our responsibility and sense of entertainment.[8]

The revised *Police Story* episode, "The Ripper," aired in February 1974. It marked the first time a network show was completely revamped with the cooperation of a gay organization. In the broadcast version, two police detectives investigate a series of antigay butcher-knife killings. One cop is gay-friendly, the other highly prejudiced against gay people. During the investigation, they meet many lesbians and gay men—some single, some in couples. The killer turns out to be an embittered man who never accepted his son's gayness. The son and the son's lover have died in a car crash, and the father blames the gay community. He exacts revenge by strangling and then butchering young gay men. By the end of the show, the antigay cop (Darren McGavin) has seen that most of his stereotypes about homosexuality were false, though the script avoids any forced, artificial "conversion" from homophobia.[9] Producer Kallis was impressed with Deiter's judgment, and continued to use him as a script consultant on gay issues for more than a decade.

Several producers regularly consulted gay organizations about male characters in 1973 and 1974. Men's issues dominated gay media activism, and most gay people negotiating with the networks were men. Television professionals and the activists tended to ignore the minimal and negative portrayal of lesbians. This was particularly true in New York at GAA. As early as 1972, women in GAA's Lesbian Liberation Committee (LLC) complained that GAA was neglecting women's issues and hindering lesbian empowerment. In spring 1973, LLC became an independent organization called Lesbian Feminist Liberation (LFL). It became involved in media activism that fall, after members saw a *Bold Ones* episode in which a young nurse was "rescued" from lesbianism by having sex with a man. Like GAA before it, LFL's first TV zap involved a talk show: They disrupted a *Dick Cavett Show* interview with antifeminist, antilesbian author George Gilder. GAA planned no zap at all. LFL decided to plant twenty-five activists in the audience. Two women would request permission to speak. If Cavett let them, they would read a prepared statement and present Gilder with an urn of ashes, representing the women who had died at the hands of the male supremacism he advocated. If Cavett did not let them speak, all twenty-five LFL members in the audience would storm the stage in waves. The organization established a bail fund, since they knew they could be arrested.

Longtime LFL organizer Ginny Vida recalled that it was easy to find participants for the group's zaps. It was the early seventies, and confrontational tactics were in the air. "The women, in a way, were angrier than the men," she said, "because we were getting hit as women and as lesbians both. The women were real angry."[10] The *Cavett* zap went off beautifully. The prepared statement was broadcast nationwide. Cavett placed the urn on the floor between him and Gilder. Elaine Lafferty, one of the women who presented the urn, told *The Advocate*:

> We waited until Gilder said he didn't think women should be aggressive before we made our move. Then we stood up and asked permission to speak. The ushers tried to quiet us down, but Cavett said, "I know I might be creating a precedent, but I'll let them speak." So we got up onstage and read our statement . . . I admit there was some fear about doing it, but we

felt it was time to zap the media and we trusted our own strength. We're glad we did it. Safety isn't as important as results.

The prepared statement described the ways in which sexism promotes violence against women. They told Cavett's viewers about a lesbian who was burned to death by three men in Boston that same month. In summing up, they vowed "to confront and disarm the attitudes and institutions that attempt to limit" women's right to be fully realized individuals.[11]

By year's end, LFL claimed two hundred members. Some men and women in GAA felt that there was no need for a separate women's organization. LFL spokesperson Susan Meyer disagreed. She said that one of LFL's main goals was to "end lesbian invisibility." She explained that until 1974, lesbians were all but excluded from dialog with the media. For instance:

When we called NBC to protest, they'd always call the National Gay Task Force instead of us. They've never dealt directly with us. Neither have the press. Whenever there's a demonstration that includes men, the press always runs to the men for comment, never talking to us.[12]

LFL had to zap several more times before broadcasters started taking them seriously. Only in late 1974 would the group briefly find itself on the media's "A-list" of gay representatives.

By late 1973, zaps by individuals were giving way to negotiating and protests by organizations. December of that year saw one of the last great, publicity-generating private actions. On December 7, Mark Segal phoned a producer at *The CBS Evening News*. Segal used an assumed name and claimed to be a reporter for a college newspaper. CBS granted him and a colleague, Harry Langhorne, permission to attend a live newscast and see anchorman Walter Cronkite in action.[13] Ten minutes into the newscast, as Cronkite was describing Henry Kissinger's security entourage, Segal pulled a large, yellow sign out of his briefcase. He ran between Cronkite and the camera shouting, "Gay people are protesting CBS's policies! . . ." Viewers caught a glimpse of the hand-lettered poster: GAYS PROTEST CBS PREJUDICE. Technicians rushed the stage to grab Segal. Then the picture went blank. When the image returned a few seconds later, Segal had vanished and shouting was heard off-camera. The usually-serious Cronkite, with a look of amused bafflement on his face, gave a play-by-play:

> Well—a rather interesting development in the studio here: a protest demonstration right in the middle of CBS News' studio. Maybe we'll find out what it was all about in a moment. We'll go on with the news, at any rate. With security precautions heavier than those provided President Nixon—*(chuckling)* and perhaps with some we could use around here— Secretary of State Kissinger is in London now . . .

Later in the show, Cronkite told viewers, "That interruption of our broadcast a moment ago was by a member of something called Gay Raiders—an organization protesting, he said, CBS's alleged defamation of homosexuals on entertainment programs."[14]

Zaps like these reflected the tactics of an outsider group with whom few, if any, decision makers were willing to negotiate. Society had constructed gays' outsider status on three pillars: scorn from the clergy, the judgment of the law, and condemnation from the medical community. One of those pillars toppled in December 1973 when the American Psychiatric Association (APA) deleted "Homosexuality" from the list of illnesses in its *Diagnostic and Statistical Manual of Psychiatric Disorders*. This gave the gay civil rights movement an influential ally in the APA. NGTF urged the APA to publicize the decision in a press conference, and Ron Gold organized a media blitz. He contacted the editors and TV news directors who had promised to cover lesbian and gay news. Here, he said, was a big story.

Politicians and media executives seemed more willing to meet with gay groups once homosexuals were no longer officially psychopaths. NGTF's emphasis on negotiating began to eclipse zaps and picketing. During this period, there were clashes between (and within) gay organizations over which approach to use. In March 1974, NGTF learned that GAA was planning a big demonstration outside CBS headquarters in New York. The GAA picket had support from a dozen organizations in four states. Morris Kight had phoned to ask that GAA also include West Coast concerns in its demands to CBS.

NGTF's Ron Gold tried to convince GAA to call off the protest, saying it could jeopardize secret negotiations with CBS. When that failed, he asked local organizations to boycott the protest. But people were furious over recent gay portrayals on *M∗A∗S∗H*, *The Carol Burnett Show*, and *Kojak*, as well as CBS Radio's refusal to grant rebuttal time in response to an antigay editorial. Two hundred protesters gathered in subfreezing weather to wave signs, chant slogans, and face off with New York City police in front of CBS headquarters. Within a week, GAA president Morty Manford had his own meetings with CBS executives.[15]

With the TV industry hearing regularly from a variety of gay mediawatch groups, a sense of cooperation began to emerge between gays and broadcasters. That spring, CBS announced that it would submit future gay-themed scripts to GMTF for input. ABC and NBC already had similar policies.[16] Network executives began to question scripts that bought into the old stereotypes. All seemed to be going smoothly until August, when David Victor and *Marcus Welby, M.D.* struck again.

PHYSICIAN, HEAL THYSELF!

Television: 1974

It is clear why gay groups found the program offensive. [The show] comes out solidly for intolerance.   —Washington Post *TV critic John Carmody, 1974*[1]

Homosexual child molestation was a hot topic in the mid 1970s. Network newscasters and other mainstream journalists gave frequent coverage to the "Houston Child Murders." The case involved two Texas men accused of having sex with and killing twenty-seven young boys and male teenagers. Televised reports covered the discovery of the crimes, then the investigation, then the trial. After so much media attention, the subject was bound to turn up in TV dramas.

Marcus Welby, M.D. creator David Victor got ABC's approval for a child molestation story in summer 1974. Eugene Price drafted an episode about a fourteen-year-old boy who had been raped by a male teacher. ABC sent the script, titled "The Outrage," to the National Gay Task Force (NGTF) for approval and suggestions. NGTF urged ABC to scrap the episode. That was not the kind of input ABC wanted, so the project continued.[2]

In 1974, TV executives apparently still doubted that lesbians and gay men were organized enough to fight back. Despite progress in negotiations the previous year, by September 1974, NBC had approved a *Police Woman* episode about lesbians who kill and rob old women; ABC had accepted a *Harry O* script about a deadly gay male couple; ABC had approved the *Marcus Welby, M.D.* child-rape story; NBC's *Born*

Innocent, a TV movie with a lesbian rape scene, was ready to air; and PBS had bought an episode of the British series *Upstairs, Downstairs* in which the family's former footman axe-murders his male lover. Every sexual minority character in a network drama that fall was a violent criminal. *The Streets of San Francisco* even had an episode about a female impersonator (John Davidson)—presumably straight—who kills while dressed as a 1940s film diva.[3] By September 1, however, gay organizations still only knew about the *Welby* episode.

NGTF spread the word about the show by mail and through the gay media. Loretta Lotman of the Boston organization Gay Media Action agreed to coordinate a national campaign against "The Outrage" while negotiating with Boston's ABC station, WCVB. She mailed the script and tactical instructions to groups around the country. NGTF president Bruce Voeller spoke in several cities to launch local initiatives. The most successful local campaign—organized by Philadelphia's Gay Media Project—involved almost every gay organization in that part of the country, plus nongay groups that had supported Philadelphia's gay civil rights bill. By September 6, ABC had ordered minor script changes, including an explanation by Welby that the rape had "nothing to do with homosexuality," that pedophiles were "often married," and that the perpetrator in this case was "terribly, terribly ill—a psychotic." ABC deleted some—not all—references to the boy's violated "manhood." As in the original script, Dr. Welby cautioned, "This man, whoever he is, won't stop with your boy. He'll go after other children. It's their pattern."[4]

NGTF argued that the script was misleading. Pedophilia, they said, was almost exclusively heterosexual. ABC stood by its script. The task force said that typical pedophilia would involve a younger child; activists argued that a show about a teenage victim would too closely resemble straightforward homosexual rape. ABC stood by its script. Gay rights groups appealed to the network's civic duty, citing the potential impact on pending gay rights legislation.[5] ABC told Victor to film the minimally revised script and scheduled it to air October 8.

The *Welby* battle became one of public relations and political ploys. The network answered the *Welby* protest mail with a form letter claiming that gay leaders had approved the script changes. In response, gay leaders asserted that *no* gay organization or national leader had approved any part of "The Outrage." Activists shifted attention to sponsors and local affiliates, hoping they, in turn, would pressure ABC. Ad agencies and stations were bombarded with letters ranging in tone from rational to apoplectic. NGTF approached ABC again, this time with support from the American Psychiatric Association and the United Federation of Teachers. The Gay Activists Alliance in New York lobbied *Welby*'s regular advertisers, which led to sponsor defections.[6] The lost advertising was not necessarily a pro-gay political statement: sponsors sometimes ask networks not to run their ads during controversial shows, regardless of the advertisers' personal views on the subject. They seldom want their product associated with *any* side of an explosive issue.[7]

Wherever possible, activists met with local station officials. In Philadelphia and Boston, broadcasters agreed to preview "The Outrage" with representatives of gay media-watch groups. The first victory came on September 25 when WPVI-TV, Philadelphia, announced it had canceled the episode. The station's director of advertising and public affairs, the Reverend Father H. Francis Hines, issued a statement that read, in part:

> It appears to us . . . that integral to the author's original premise is a false stereotype of homosexuals as persons who pursue and sexually assault young boys. While it is clear that the producers have earnestly attempted to alter the effects of this unfortunate premise, it is equally clear that they have not succeeded.

ABC hurriedly offered the show to independent stations in Philadelphia. Despite potential profit, they refused it.[8]

Opponents of "The Outrage" campaigned up to the airdate. In the end, six stations and most of the original sponsors rejected the episode. The Philadelphia and Boston cancellations clearly resulted from gay pressure. After negotiations, WMAL-TV in Washington, D.C., agreed to precede and follow the show with a disclaimer. Stations in Lafayette, Louisiana, and Springfield, Massachusetts, reportedly canceled the show out of a belief that any dramatic treatment of man-boy rape was unfit for prime time. Between lost ad revenue and lowered ratings from affiliate dropouts, the network lost a great deal of money.[9] Looking back on the victory, Loretta Lotman wrote:

> The single greatest change in the struggle for good gay representation in media has taken place in the minds of gay people themselves. Until the *Marcus Welby* protest snowballed, no one, not even we, thought gays could muster that much strength. By working together on a national level, we produced the largest, most coordinated action in the history of the gay movement.[10]

ABC kept insisting that the script was about a child molester, not a homosexual. But *Marcus Welby*'s creator/producer apparently saw it differently. In an interview for the 1983 book *The Producer's Medium*, David Victor listed the controversial topics that his shows had treated. In this list, he describes "The Outrage" as "the story of a homosexual rape."[11]

The battle over "The Outrage" had little immediate impact on ABC. Two nights after the *Welby* broadcast, the network aired an episode of the detective series *Harry O* titled "Coinage of the Realm." According to the *Los Angeles Times*, it involved:

> a homosexual team of killers (finely played by David Dukes and Granville Van Duesen). When one of these gay men is fatally shot, the other cuddles his bloody head in his arms and weeps in a very tender scene. There were no [gay liberation] protests.[12]

That was the silence between storms.

KILLER-DYKE SYNDROME

Television: 1974

I met the three women who run the place. I'm not sure you'd fit in there. One of them looks like she ought to be driving a diesel truck. The other two were pretty much the same—maybe a little more discreet.

—*"Sergeant Bill Crowley" (Earl Holliman)*
to the title character on Police Woman, *1974¹*

If ABC responded slowly, NBC was taking no chances. On October 10, two days after ABC's costly *Marcus Welby* broadcast, NBC withdrew an already-approved *Police Woman* episode for reediting. The drama, titled "Flowers of Evil," deals with three deadly lesbians—Mame, Gladys, and Janet—who run a nursing home. *Lesbian Tide* magazine aptly described them as "the Butch, the Bitch, and the Femme."² This murderous trio starves and drugs their elderly residents, steals their money, then kills them. The ringleader, Mame, is a growling, scowling, swaggering, crude-talking, racist ex–Marine nurse—an austere bulldyke who wears men's shirts and puffs bitterly on little black cigarettes while leading sweet old women to their deaths. The most likable gang member is the most traditionally feminine-looking: Janet, portrayed as a young innocent led astray by older lesbians. Angie Dickinson plays the series' hero, Sergeant Suzanne "Pepper" Anderson, who infiltrates the operation by masquerading as a sexually available lesbian nurse. "Flowers of Evil" would eventually provoke more persistent gay protests than any TV show before or since. The fallout from it would lead to the networks' and producers' increased cooperation with gay consultants.

In announcing NBC's decision to recut the episode, a network spokesperson cited the show's "somewhat sensationalized and insensitive" treatment of lesbians. He added that the move had nothing to do with pressure from gay groups. David Gerber, in charge of production at Columbia Pictures Television, told reporters he was "surprised and upset" at the network's decision. After all, Gerber said, the script was based on a true case, whose investigating officer had written the first draft. And, Gerber argued, "we also have shows where the criminals are straight."[3] But whether other shows portrayed straight criminals was beside the point. The real issue was that TV almost never portrayed gay women who were *not* criminals. In that context, "Flowers of Evil" was irresponsible and offensive. NGTF hastily mobilized the informal media-watch network it had established during the *Welby* controversy. Gay and feminist organizations on both coasts demanded that NBC permanently shelve the show. No amount of editing, they maintained, could redeem yet another drama about violent lesbians.

The episode changed considerably between its filming and the broadcast date. The initial edits removed only "meaningful glances" and touching of hands. After seeing the revised version, NBC's corporate chiefs in New York decided it was still potentially offensive. They ordered the producers to remove all explicit references to lesbianism, hoping that this would assuage gay activists. But the edits just made matters worse. Sergeant Crowley's "diesel truck" crack was allowed to remain, since it did not contain the word "lesbian." But Sergeant Anderson's comeback ("If you mean to say lesbian, say lesbian") was deleted. Even without the word "lesbian," and even without the shot of Gladys licking her lips over Sergeant Anderson's figure, the killers were still clearly gay. What viewer could possibly mistake Mame—that mind-boggling aggregation of stereotypes—for a heterosexual? Besides, in the final, tear-jerking interrogation scene, Sergeant Anderson still acknowledged Janet and Gladys's relationship of "ten, twelve years." The same scene also still included Anderson's recollections of her beloved college roommate, whose closeted existence had nearly destroyed her. (A reference to the roommate's attempted suicide was excised).[4]

Faye Spain, who played Mame, discussed the show with a reporter from United Press International (UPI) that fall. She said the producers ordered her to chop her hair short, bind her breasts, and speak in the deepest, harshest rasp she could summon. "I had to change my walk," she told UPI, "and make all my gestures more masculine. I've never played anyone less attractive." She speculated that gay groups had not mounted *Welby*-style protests because word about the show had spread only a few weeks before the scheduled broadcast date. The NGTF *Action Report* confirms this: "NBC received less flak [than ABC], at least in advance, mostly because we got hard information about the content of the show only a few days before airtime." During the 1974 *Welby* controversy, NGTF had sent action kits to almost every gay group in the country. In the *Police Woman* case, "phone calls to some key cities were the most we could do to alert the movement."5

NBC announced that the supposedly *de*-lesbianized episode was to air November 15. At the last minute, they ran it a week earlier. At a Los Angeles protest the day of the broadcast, lesbian organizer Gudrun Fonfa told the press, "It is infuriating to see the powerful media structure take it upon themselves to totally misrepresent our lives. All they have to do is come to us and ask what it means to be a woman who cares about other women."6 Drastic action was needed.

Eleven days after the broadcast, at 10:30 A.M., occupying forces from Lesbian Feminist Liberation synchronized their watches. Five pairs of women entered NBC headquarters in New York at fifteen-minute intervals, taking elevators to different floors, then walking downstairs to a stairwell door near the department of Program Standards and Practices. An LFL member had taped the second-floor door lock open that morning. As a fail-safe, Stevye Knowles and her three children rode an elevator directly to the second floor. She told the guard she was meeting her husband for lunch. No one tried to stop her. The women and children entered vice president Herminio Traviesas's office at noon and asked to see him. His secretary said he would be away for another week. "We'll wait," came the reply. Outside, on the sidewalk below, some seventy-five women from feminist organizations gathered to protest against the *Police Woman* episode. Some distributed leaflets to passersby. Elected officials spoke at the rally and sent messages of support.

Traviesas, who was at a network meeting in Jamaica, booked an early plane for New York. The sit-in came as a surprise to him, since NBC president Robert Howard and five NBC vice presidents had met with representatives of a dozen gay groups earlier that week.[7] After that contentious meeting, the lesbian and gay negotiators said they were cautiously optimistic about the network's future cooperation. However, Traviesas, who had promised that the *Police Woman* episode would not be about lesbians, was conspicuously absent from that session. And NBC had yet to agree not to rerun "Flowers of Evil." With the sit-in in Traviesas's office, LFL hoped to get his attention and the network's. LFL also hoped to solidify its position as a strong lesbian voice in the until-recently male-dominated realm of gay activism. From Jamaica, Traviesas gave orders for NBC to feed the overnight protesters and bring them a color TV to watch.

The next morning, Knowles's children and five of the women left the office. Knowles stayed behind with the others. With TV news cameras rolling, the youngsters waved to her, crying, "Mommy, Mommy, we love you." By then, the press, radio, and three independent television stations had picked up the story. Hoping to provoke arrests, four lesbians walked onto the balcony outside Traviesas's office and unfurled a two-story-high red, white, and blue banner that read, LESBIANS PROTEST NBC. They and the picketers on 50th Street began chanting, "NBC works against lesbians," and "Lesbians are sitting in." Bystanders, NBC employees, and workers in nearby buildings craned their necks to see the spectacle.[8]

For years, the mass media's antilesbian biases had had a devastating effect on the lives of gay women. Lesbian activists were determined to return the favor, and to demand a change in broadcast representations. Slowly, they and other groups were succeeding. During the next year, direct action protesters played "bad cop" to the negotiators' "good cop." TV executives knew they could either negotiate or face zaps, so they chose negotiation. By spring 1975, ABC and NBC agreed not to rerun the controversial 1974 episodes of *Marcus Welby, M.D.* and *Police Woman*.[9]

Loretta Lotman became NGTF's media director that year. In June, she traveled to Los Angeles to meet with media executives and strengthen the relationship between NGTF and GMTF. Afterward,

NGTF set up the Gay Media Action Network (G-MAN)—a national phone tree and mailing list—to quickly mobilize lobbying and letter-writing campaigns to the media. G-MAN alerts and regional coalition-building strengthened the position of gay media activists as a powerful lobby.[10]

After an intense year of negotiations, Lotman resigned and returned to Boston. Her successor, Ginny Vida, set out to ensure that the two *Marcus Welby* episodes would never rerun in syndication. She wrote to Hal Cranton in the New York office of the syndicator, MCA Television, outlining objections to "The Other Martin Loring" and "The Outrage." MCA-TV vice president Ernest B. Goodman wrote back in a letter widely quoted in the press. He argued at length that neither episode dealt with homosexuals, and that therefore neither was of legitimate concern to NGTF. He warned of the dangers to free communication that "militant minority groups" pose when they try to influence program content. He went on to assert:

> If, as you indicate, there are twenty million homosexuals in America, then there must be at least one hundred eighty million heterosexuals. To our knowledge, not one heterosexual has ever pressured us or attempted to dictate program content.[11]

Even beyond his silly assertion that straight people never object to TV shows, his core argument was unsound. Where portrayals of heterosexual criminals were balanced by thousands of law-abiding heterosexual characters, there was no such balance among sexual-minority roles at the time. Despite Goodman's protests, the two *Marcus Welby* episodes were reportedly withdrawn. Separately, the *Police Woman* episode was removed from syndication and remains out of circulation at this writing. (It can be viewed in New York and Los Angeles at the Museum of Television and Radio.)

One theme in Goodman's letter, however, was used by many television executives. He argued that preventing writers from depicting homosexuality negatively denied freedom of communication "to an overwhelming majority" of Americans. Goodman said that if viewers did not like what was on TV, they should change channels.

THE RIGHTS OF THE MAJORITY

Antigay Religious Organizing and the
Broadcast Media: 1972–1975

> I have a plan that I believe is from God, a plan that can change the media, can change the entertainment world . . . I expect in the next two years to see a dramatic revolution in this area.
>
> —*Evangelical activist Bill Bright, President and Founder of Campus Crusade for Christ, ca. 1975*[1]

Just as gay media activism grew out of the fight for gay civil rights, so *anti*gay media activism evolved from religious movements that sought to punish and discourage homosexuality. Since the 1970s, antigay conservative Christians have led the crusade to ban positive lesbigay images from television. The heads of these pressure groups are usually fundamentalist ministers, such as Pat Robertson, Jerry Falwell, and Donald Wildmon. Their multi-issue organizations helped elect New Right politicians like Senator Jesse Helms in the 1970s and 1980s, and the groups regularly coordinate strategies with powerful elected officials. Given fundamentalists' long history of shunning politics (and given politicians' long-standing desire not to be associated with the popular negative stereotypes of fundamentalism), this religious activism surprised many political analysts in the 1970s and early 1980s.

Television was a ripe target for fundamentalists and evangelicals because broadcasting—like their other nightmare, secular public-school curricula—indoctrinated children with "nonbiblical" ideas. In 1972, a Virginia-based ministry, the Society for the Christian Commonwealth, organized a group called Stop Immorality on TV (SITV). SITV contacted clergy around the country, encouraging them to give sermons about televised immorality. The group circulated television action kits nationwide. Preprinted postcards urged NBC's chairman to cancel *Laugh-In* and *The Dean Martin Show*—shows which "make a mockery of traditional American moral standards." That fall, SITV joined other religious groups to send CBS seven thousand letters protesting an episode of *Maude* in which the title character had an abortion. A rerun of that episode, shortly after the Supreme Court's 1973 *Roe v. Wade* ruling legalized abortion, drew seventeen thousand more protest letters.[2]

These crusaders and the gay activists often assaulted the same shows. Where gay groups worried about the *content* of lesbian- and gay-themed broadcasts, groups like Stop Immorality on TV considered the shows' mere *existence* inappropriate. For instance, SITV encouraged protests against ABC simply because *Owen Marshall, Counselor at Law* had "dealt with lesbian seduction." The TV movie *That Certain Summer* attracted angry mail from fundamentalist Christians (who considered it antibiblical propaganda) *and* complaints from some gay activists (who objected to the ending). In 1973, an SITV mailing complained, "Recent episodes on *The Bold Ones* and *Marcus Welby, M.D.* have shown homosexuality in a favorable light." Gay Libbers deemed those same shows hopelessly *anti*gay. Other antigay media-watch groups, like Clean Up TV (CUTV) in Joplin, Missouri, used similar tactics. Founded in 1975, CUTV spread its activist message through an evangelical radio series, *Revival Fires*, heard Sunday mornings on fifty-five stations. Its supporters reportedly included singers Dale Evans, Pat Boone, and Dean Jones. Another group, Morality in Media, worked to keep ABC from airing the film *Midnight Cowboy*, even with the network's plans to eliminate twenty-three minutes of sexual content. *Variety* reported that Morality in Media "has recommended boycotts of sponsors in unapproved shows before, and that's the kind of action companies take to the hills over."[3]

Not until the 1980s would TV's "promotion" of homosexuality become a primary focus of groups like the National Federation for Decency. But the increasingly sympathetic portrayal of gay characters in the mid 1970s did give these organizations cause for worry. In 1975, producer Norman Lear added salt to the wound when he launched the sitcom *Hot l Baltimore*. It focused on the social outcasts who lived in a fleabag hotel in Maryland. The female lead was a prostitute. The only stable, long-term couple in the place were George and Gordon, a pair of bickering, fiftysomething queens. In one episode, they break up over George's desire to attend law school. The other residents help bring them back together. The series' reliance on sexual innuendo and the inclusion of prostitutes and homosexuals angered the watchdogs of morality. Many local stations dropped *Hot l Baltimore* because of the risqué content. The show's Nielsen ratings were respectable, but they hardly reached the heights that networks expected from a Norman Lear production. ABC canceled the series after thirteen episodes. Christian media-watch groups claimed a moral victory.[4]

But like the early-1970s' gay groups, these conservative Christian reformers of the mid 1970s had little immediate impact with their scattershot efforts. To get results, they needed cohesive national organizing. In 1974, a group of conservative Christians in the Washington, D.C., area set out to create that cohesion, working under the belief that they represented America's great disenfranchised majority. By the end of 1974, they had grand plans to reshape America's identity, from government to popular culture. Their well-funded organizations, including the Christian Embassy and Third Century Publishing, joined forces with existing groups like Campus Crusade for Christ and the Christian Freedom Foundation to politicize the faithful. According to Rus Walton, the new movement's chief spokesman, their goal was to "rebuild the Republic as it was when first founded—a 'Christian Republic.'" They planned to create an environment in which "real Christians" would take an interest in politics, run for office, and be elected by other "real Christians." These men mostly came from outside the evangelical and fundamentalist world. But some prominent clergy and religious broadcasters within that world were also moving toward political action. Even the syndicated TV series *The 700 Club*— sort of a Christian *Tonight Show*—began edging into the political topics that would later become its mainstay. As conservative Christian TV shows attained ever-wider national distribution, they provided a national platform that helped the new hybrid religious/political movement reach and politicize its target audience.

The movement had to do more than just interest born-again Christians in politics. The Religious Right needed allies in the major political parties. At the time, American popular ideals held that religion and politics were an undemocratic combination. Candidates would need a new, compelling reason to woo evangelical and fundamentalist ministers and their flocks. That incentive materialized, in part, with the Federal Election Campaign Act of 1974. It limited to $1,000 the money a candidate could accept from any one donor. The secular New Right needed to increase its donor base quickly, so it reached out to the fledgling Religious Right. Richard Viguerie, the leading conservative direct-mail fund-raiser and a pioneer in the use of computers to market activism, predicted, "The next real major area of growth for the conservative ideology and philosophy [will be] among evangelical people. I would be surprised if in [1976] you did not see a massive effort to involve them, using direct mail and other fund-raising techniques."[5]

Even before the Religious Right's political movement really took off, there was already a nonsectarian movement afoot to clean up television, a movement the Religious Right would eventually coopt and supplant. This was the political drive by parents' groups, which led to the "Family Hour" policies of the mid 1970s. As part of that trend, the networks were about to ban homosexual characters from most of prime time.

THE FAMILY HOUR

Television: 1975–1976

Parents who wrote letters of protest [about televised sex and violence] a decade ago need to watch only one week of television in 1973 to see that . . . the abuses of yesteryear . . . have multiplied now and arrive before our eyes in color.
—*TV critic Paul Molloy, 1973*[1]

In the early 1970s, parents' organizations expressed concern about the growing violence and sex on TV. Random bloodshed, sexual innuendo, and exposed female skin had become staples of prime time. Even more baffling to these media-watch groups was the networks' trend toward scheduling issue-oriented shows at early hours when children controlled the dial. Historically, television had run mostly "family-oriented" programming from 8 to 9 P.M. In fall 1972, *Variety* expressed surprise that the networks had scheduled "adult-tinged" shows like *Maude* and *M*A*S*H* in the early evening, while placing shows "with great appeal to youngsters," like *The Julie Andrews Hour* and *The New Bill Cosby Show*, at 10 P.M.[2] Some network executives opposed the trend, as did many executives at affiliate stations.

The networks received stacks of mail complaining about their relaxed standards. Some parents said that no matter how conscientiously they monitored their children's TV habits, the networks were making it impossible for them to make responsible viewing choices. Newspapers and magazines devoted countless articles to the controversy. In a *New York Times* essay, psychologist Dr. Joyce Brothers advocated a rating system similar to the one used by movie theaters—an approach that television would, in fact, adopt a generation later. In describing how TV could emotionally scar children, Dr. Brothers wrote about a little boy who had seen the *Marcus Welby* child-rape episode. The boy's mother had told her, "He's been afraid of grown men, even his teacher, ever since he saw a man rape a boy on the *Marcus Welby* show. I'm very careful of what I let him watch. Nothing on *Marcus Welby* has ever upset him before."[3]

CBS-TV president Bob Wood defended the adult themes, saying it was what the public wanted. A Gallup poll confirmed Wood's perception: it said that only 20 percent of viewers disapproved of controversial topics in entertainment shows. Gallup said that younger, better-educated, more affluent viewers (the main target audience for advertisers) were most likely to approve of controversy. This survey was prompted by public outcry over the abortion episode of *Maude* and a controversial dramatic special, *Sticks and Bones,* about a blinded Vietnam veteran.[4]

The industry largely ignored complaints about sexual and violent content, so some concerned organizations began to lobby the FCC and Congress. In 1974, the Senate Subcommittee on Communications, headed by Senator John O. Pastore (D-R.I.), held hearings in anticipation of a planned government crackdown on "inappropriate" programming. The TV movie that most directly inspired this was *Born Innocent*, one of several mid-1970s dramas that depicted same-sex prison rapes. This one was especially disturbing: just inches off screen, a girl in her early teens (Linda Blair) is violated with a mop handle by other girls in a juvenile detention center. The camera alternates between her face and a shot of the girl who is moving the Jonny Mop in and out. After hearing testimony about such envelope-pushing broadcasts, Senator Pastore ordered the FCC to draft detailed recommendations about how to clean up television. Congress had created the FCC and had full oversight authority over the commission, so congressional demands for information were not unusual.

For years, the Communications subcommittee had tried to convince the networks to cut back on portrayals of sex and violence, but it was hard to be persuasive with a tiny budget and a support staff of one. With the reorganization of its parent committee, the subcommittee suddenly had money and a team of lawyers. FCC chairman Richard

Wiley, under pressure from Congress and some network affiliates, met with top executives from the three commercial networks. He said the FCC and Congress would use any legal means to regulate TV's excesses, including the FCC's power not to renew stations' licenses. Wiley said the networks and local stations should institute self-regulation to avoid government action.[5]

In January, CBS president Arthur Taylor publicly announced three new network policies:

- A "Family Viewing" hour starting at 8 P.M. (7 P.M. Central Time).
- On-air warnings before Family Hour shows that represented an exception to the "appropriate-for-family-viewing" rule.
- Warnings when shows later in the evening "might be disturbing to a significant portion of the adult audience."

Taylor publicly asked the National Association of Broadcasters, local stations, and the other networks to codify the same policies and end their stalemate with the government. NBC and ABC jumped on the bandwagon amid praise from Pastore and Wiley. However, the NAB and many independent stations resisted what they saw as federal censorship. *Variety,* too, strongly opposed the Family Hour, commenting, "The biggest problem now is that the three networks in public are in agreement, and Wiley and Pastore approve. The first broadcaster to point out that the king isn't wearing any clothes may incur a good deal of royal displeasure." In February 1975, the NAB's Television Code Review Board voted 6 to 1 to adopt CBS's idea. The NAB's board of directors overwhelmingly approved the proposal in April, saying that it would go into effect in the fall. Without any official legislation by Congress, the Family Hour had become the law of the land.

Each network and government agency had a different idea of "family viewing." Did the mere mention that a character was gay, or having an extramarital affair, constitute "sex on television"? Everyone involved agreed that it was best not to set definitions in stone yet. Surely, each network's guidelines would develop organically over time.[6]

By May 1975, producers and writers began to realize the Family Hour's implications. Shows already produced for the fall season, such as the much-touted NBC sitcom *Fay* (about a divorcée who begins dating and having sex again), would have to be scrapped or heavily censored. ABC vice president Alfred Schneider told writer/producer Danny Arnold that his 8 P.M. series *Barney Miller* could no longer depict gays or prostitutes. This was a tall order for a sitcom set in a police station in Greenwich Village. Loretta Lotman of the National Gay Task Force met with executives of all three networks in June 1975. One executive told her that he considered any gay content inadmissable during the Family Hour. Even the word "gay," itself, was suspect. Mary Tyler Moore Enterprises had to fight CBS censors for permission to use the word in an episode of *Phyllis*, slated to air at 8:30 P.M. CBS wanted the word "gay" replaced with a wrist gesture. The network finally relented in August.[7]

Before approval of the Family Hour, *Barney Miller* had introduced a semiregular character named Marty—a gay male purse snatcher. When the first Marty scripts were written, in late 1974, ABC worried that the swishy character would offend gay viewers. This was just after the second *Marcus Welby* fiasco, and ABC wanted to avoid another run-in with angry gay libbers. Danny Arnold phoned Newt Deiter at the Gay Media Task Force and got his approval on the script. ABC agreed and the episode aired.[8] Despite GMTF's approval, the character did offend many gay viewers. Deiter took their complaints to Arnold and the two men agreed on a solution: Marty would no longer be a criminal, and he would be given a lover, Darryl. The episode introducing Darryl would deal with antigay harassment and blackmail. It would also depict a nonstereotypical gay cop. Danny Arnold was excited about the idea: the script could be funny and poignant. It offered great opportunities for character development among the regulars. Then came the Family Hour and ABC lowered the boom on gay characters.

The Family Hour battle over *Barney Miller* grew volatile. Arnold and ABC's Schneider engaged in much fist-banging and name-calling in private meetings and on the set in front of the cast and crew. In September, Arnold decided to ignore ABC's edict and began preproduction on the blackmail episode. Meanwhile, ABC aired the Oscar-winning film *Cabaret*, minus its entire bisexual plotline. By September 26, the scheduled tape date for the *Barney Miller* episode, ABC still refused to approve its gay content. At a cost of roughly $100,000, Danny Arnold taped the banned show and sent it to ABC's New York headquarters. A week later, he had approval for this one exception.[9] Apparently, the only other ABC show to depict a gay character that season, even outside the Family Hour, aired the same night that the *Barney Miller* episode was taped. The TV movie *Death Scream* focuses on the murder of a lesbian. Her lover (played by Tina Louise) is a suspect. It aired at 9 P.M. NBC and CBS allowed gay characters after 9 P.M., but these were rare. The Family Hour had a chilling effect on gay people's right to be served equally by the public airwaves.

In 1976, the family-viewing controversy heated up further. The Writers Guild of America West sued the three networks, the FCC, and the NAB, to prohibit enforcement of the Family Hour. When the initial decision went against the Writers Guild, NGTF offered to file an amicus brief for the appeal. *Variety* quoted NGTF's new media director Ginny Vida as saying, "The reason for the NGTF interest is its suspicion, confirmed by testimony at the 'Family Hour' trial, that gay characters and relationships are being systematically and deliberately excluded from network shows aired during the early evening hours." During Congressional hearings about the Family Hour, Vida testified that "We think it is not only immoral but illegal for the industry, mandated to serve the needs of the public, to fail to serve our needs." She said, in part:

> On programs directed to children and in the so-called Family Viewing Hours, there are still no gay people. Why is that? Because, the people at the networks tell each other, parents think that gay people are synonymous with violence and with sex.
>
> No wonder, we answer, that parents think we are violent, considering the stuff they have been served up in adult viewing hours.
>
> "But what about the sex?" they ask each other in the corridors at the networks. "Surely, if it is called homosexuality, how can it not be about sex?"
>
> Our answer, of course, is to ask the same question about heterosexuality. The truth is that pictures of two homosexuals, two women or two men, kissing each other tenderly on the lips are no more and no less about sex than what heterosexuals are seen doing in full view of everybody in family viewing time. The truth is that stories about two young women or men discovering love and regard for each other are not about explicit sex,

and stories about lesbians or gay men coming out to their parents are not about sex at all . . .

Gay people do care about morality. We think, for instance, that just as it was immoral to foster prejudice and discrimination by pretending to the children of America that there were no black people, no real people who were Jews, Mexicans, or Poles, it is immoral to foster prejudice and discrimination by pretending to the children of America that there are no real people who are gay.

We think that just as it was immoral to provide no role models for America's black children to look at television and say, "Yes. That is just like me," it is immoral to provide no models for the children that all of us millions of gay women and men once were, children who sit by their sets with their families and hope for a sign that there is someone about whom they can say, "Yes. That is just like me."[10]

The Family Hour also raised financial concerns: it was costing the networks money. Viewership from 8 to 9 P.M. dropped noticeably as soon as the networks sanitized their early-evening shows. Of the six network series canceled in the first month of the season, five had been airing during the Family Hour.[11] By fall 1976, enforcement of the early-evening policy had begun to wane. On November 4, a U.S. District judge ruled that the process by which the Family Hour was created violated the First Amendment. The 223-page decision said that broadcasters were free to institute any program guidelines they wanted, but that the NAB's existing Family Hour policy was essentially government censorship and must not be enforced.[12] Networks and the NAB did not challenge the decision. Their appealing this far showed Congress and the FCC that broadcasters had acted in good faith.

Conservative media activists, having lost this battle, began organizing on a national level.

17

BATTLE LINES

Television: 1975–1977

The Year of the Gay on television.
    —TV Guide *and* The Washington
       Post's *description of 1976*[1]

The Year of the Evangelicals.
    —Newsweek's *assessment of*
       the same year[2]

Unprecedented numbers of gay people came out of the closet—or were forced out—in the mid 1970s. And for the first time, the mass media gave some positive visibility to openly gay public figures. During 1975 and 1976, journalists focused in on three men whose gayness was considered incongruous with their macho personalities: a Vietnam veteran who had won medals in active combat; a man who had saved a U.S. president's life; and a former professional football player. Less often (but more than in the past), the media also interviewed lesbians who defied stereotypes, such as a politician from New England and a suburban mother from the South.

In 1975, Air Force Technical Sergeant Leonard Matlovich came out to his superiors and requested permission to stay in the military as an openly gay man. The story of this queer but exemplary soldier and his legal battle fascinated the American media. From May to October alone, Matlovich was the subject of at least twenty-seven network news reports, many of which let him speak on-camera. The September 8 edition of *Time* magazine ran a cover photo of Matlovich in uniform with the headline: "I AM A HOMOSEXUAL": THE GAY DRIVE FOR ACCEPTANCE. Later that year, the national media reported that Oliver Sipple—the burly ex-Marine who had saved President Ford from an attempted assassination—was a closet homosexual. That public revelation destroyed his relationship with his family and caused many friends to abandon him. Sipple filed an unsuccessful invasion-of-privacy suit against the newspaper that first betrayed his secret, thus, ironically, calling still more media attention to his sexuality. By year's end, ex–NFL football player David Kopay had come out in interviews and a published autobiography. Local and network news featured his story, and he appeared on interview programs such as Tom Snyder's late-night *Tomorrow* show.[3]

In the six months that saw those twenty-seven network reports about Sgt. Matlovich, only two network news stories focused specifically on lesbians: NBC's early-morning news magazine, the *Today* show, presented a filmed report from Ft. Devens, Massachusetts, where two open lesbians were fighting to stay in the Women's Army Corps; and in October, on *The CBS Evening News*, Walter Cronkite delivered a two-sentence report about the National Organization for Women's resolution in favor of lesbians' rights. That was all. Talk shows, however, did let lesbians speak for and about themselves. Elaine Noble, an open lesbian recently elected to the Massachusetts state legislature, appeared on *Tomorrow* along with two other lesbian-rights advocates, Sally Gearhart and Eleanor Cooper. Noble also appeared on other programs, such as the *David Susskind Show*. Meanwhile, Mary Jo Risher, a lesbian mother from Texas who was fighting for custody of her son, appeared on *The Phil Donahue Show*, *Consenting Adults*, *The Lou Gordon Show*, and *Tomorrow*.[4]

Visible gay and bisexual faces were no longer limited to far-out hippies and psychedelic rock stars. In the wake of these telecasts, and after heavy lobbying of the media by gay activists, prime-time scriptwriters also ran with the subject. During fall of 1976, the networks broadcast more than fifteen gay-themed scripts, most of them coming-out dramas. One series, *The Nancy Walker Show*, even had a gay male regular character. An editorial in the *Phoenix Gazette* observed, " 'Tis the season, apparently, to be gay on television. Nearly every show, new or old, is featuring a homosexual situation of one sort or another." The editorial called the explosion of gay characters a "sad fad on television" that most viewers surely would find "offensive, or at least quickly unfunny and boring." The same month, syndicated columnist Nicholas von Hoffman wrote, "You can hardly dial around on prime time without clicking on to some actor explaining to a disappointed, would-be girlfriend that he's gay." Von Hoffman poked fun at the uniformly liberal, preachy quality of these broadcasts.[5] Despite the shows' pleas for tolerance, the new wave of scripts still held the subject at arm's length. Most of them constructed homosexuality as a lack of interest in someone of the other gender, not the ability to love someone of the same gender.

None of this happened in a vacuum. Gay themes abounded in the popular culture of 1976. At the movies, there was *The Ritz*, *The Rocky Horror Picture Show*, *Norman . . . Is That You?*, *Ode to Billy Joe*, and supporting characters in *Car Wash*, *Murder by Death*, *The Man Who Fell to Earth*, and other films. On the comic strip pages, *Doonesbury* introduced a gay character who comes out to a woman who wants to marry him. The disco music scene was brimming with homosexual overtones and undertones. Pop singer/songwriter Elton John came out as bisexual. On Broadway, *A Chorus Line* swept the musical categories at the Tony Awards. But the change was most noticeable in television that fall. Nineteen seventy-six was, as some TV critics called it, the "Year of the Gay." This sudden growth in televised images grew out of events in the summer of 1976, when the Gay Media Task Force and the National Gay Task Force held intensive negotiations with some of television's top producers.

One series that used extensive input from GMTF was *Snip*, slated to air on NBC starting in fall 1976. In this sitcom, a straight hairdresser (David Brenner) lives and works with his ex-wife (Lesley Ann Warren) in Cape Cod. Their best friend is Michael (Walter Wonderman), a high-strung, frizzy-haired gay haircutter. Michael is a fully integrated member of the cast, around whom some plotlines revolve. One episode, "Out of the Closet and Into the Fire," deals with Michael's decision to come out to his mother. James Komack produced the series. Just before the start of the fall season, ABC and NBC redesigned their announced prime-time schedules. *Snip* got lost in the shuffle and was never broadcast in the U.S. The produced episodes reportedly aired in Australia to positive reviews in the late 1970s.[6]

Notable images that did reach the American airwaves that fall included a gay male regular—the secretary, Terry (Ken Olfson)—on ABC's *The Nancy Walker Show*. Terry was a campy queen with a strange habit of spelling words O-U-T. ("S-I-L-L-Y," observed an NGTF newsletter.) Another sitcom, *All's Fair*, revealed that its male lead's ex-wife was a lesbian. And *Mary Hartman, Mary Hartman* featured a gay male couple who share a house near Mary's home. Each of these three series came from one of Norman Lear's production companies: Tandem Productions or T.A.T. Communications. In two December 1976 episodes of the drama *Executive Suite*, a closeted lesbian fought for child custody after leaving her abusive husband. (A truck ran her over before there was time for a verdict.) And amid the craze over United States history that accompanied the nation's Bicentennial, CBS's *American Parade* anthology dramatized Walt Whitman's relationship with Peter Doyle. Rip Torn played Whitman, with Brad Davis as Doyle.[7]

But if 1976 was the Year of the Gay in television, it was also the Year of the Born-Again Christian in politics and society. In the mid 1970s, the Christian Right made every effort to supplant the old *Elmer Gantry* stereotype—the image of the hypocritical preacher who preys on the gullible masses—with a more likable, human image. Around 1976, Bill Bright and a group of professional publicists created a barrage of T-shirts and bumper stickers emblazoned with the sign of the Cross that proclaimed, "I found it!" In national TV commercials for another religious organization, athletes, singers, and other celebrities said that the most important thing in their lives was "my personal relationship with God." Jimmy Carter's 1976 presidential campaign speeches often mentioned that he was a born-again Christian. Political analysts credited evangelicals with Carter's growing popularity in the polls. In October, *Newsweek* proclaimed 1976 "The Year of the Evangelicals."

That December, during the Christmas holidays, a United Methodist pastor in Southaven, Mississippi, was watching TV with his children early one evening. His reaction to what he saw led the Rev. Donald E. Wildmon to become one of the most visible and perhaps one of the most effective conservative Christian media activists. That evening, he has often recalled, he and his children could not find one program without sex, violence, or profanity. One show explicitly depicted adultery. Another included profane language, and a third showed a man being savagely beaten with a hammer. Each time, Wildmon reacted "as I had been taught" and asked a child to change the station. Finally he gave up and told one of the children to turn the set off.

> As I sat in my den that night, I became angry. I had been disturbed by the deterioration of morals I had witnessed in the media and society during the previous twenty-five years. This was accompanied by a dramatic rise in crime, a proliferation of pornography, increasingly explicit sexual lyrics in music, increasing numbers of broken homes, a rise in drug and alcohol use among the youth, and various other negative factors. . . .
>
> Realizing that these changes were being brought into the sanctity of my home, I decided I could and would no longer remain silent. I decided to do something, even though at the time I had no idea what that something would be.

He organized friends and family to monitor TV shows and keep tallies of sexual and violent content. In early 1977, he announced "Turn Off Television" weeks in nearby communities, but these early efforts had little impact; in one town, the Homes Using TV index actually increased. Wildmon realized that lobbying the mass media required more time than his ministerial duties allowed. So in June, he resigned his job and moved his family to Tupelo, Mississippi, where he founded the National Federation for Decency (NFD). Since the late 1970s, Wildmon has been a leading voice in opposing gay content on television.[8]

By late 1976, the embryonic Religious Right still lacked a central rallying issue. It would need two or three causes that could evoke a gut reaction from conservative Catholics, fundamentalists, and nonfundamentalist evangelicals alike. Many issues were tried. Early fund-raising drives built around abortion brought in large sums of money, but the movement continued to seek an issue with even greater emotional appeal. The solution became evident in a flash in January 1977. In Miami, Florida, the Dade County Commission had banned discrimination on the basis of sexual orientation—including discrimination against gay schoolteachers. Rousing fundamentalists to political rage had usually required a controversy over public education, such as the teaching of evolution or the banning of organized prayer from the schools. The Miami controversy had all the emotional appeal of any such "threat" to children. Like those previous controversies, it received massive media attention. Abortion and gay rights soon became the Religious Right's key rallying points.

In 1977, Reverend Bill Chapman led the early fight to repeal the Miami law. Singer Anita Bryant—a former Miss Oklahoma who, by the mid 1970s, was best known for her orange juice commercials—belonged to Chapman's church. She listened as he sermonized about the law's implications for schoolchildren. Bryant agreed to use her fame to publicize efforts to repeal the law by public referendum. That month, she made two appearances on *The PTL Club* to promote her organization, Save Our Children. Bryant warned of the advances "militant homosexuals" had made nationwide. She urged viewers to organize against gay civil rights. In a February appearance on *The 700 Club*, she explained that her concerns were partly biblical ("the Word of God . . . says that homosexuality is an abomination") and partly democratic ("homosexual acts are illegal under Florida law and the laws of most states. The Metro Commission, nevertheless, chose to ignore the spirit of our laws and caved in to the small, vocal group of militant homosexuals"). Within weeks, Bryant was again a household name—and no longer just as a singer or a peddler of orange juice. She was both mocked and venerated: even as her legions of enemies worked against her, a poll in *Good Housekeeping* rated her as the most admired woman in America. Constant media coverage of the so-called "Bryant versus Gays" controversy moved the question of gay civil rights to the center of national discourse.[9]

Reverend Jerry Falwell of Virginia, two years before he founded the Moral Majority, was an early Bryant ally. In a televised appearance in spring 1977, he introduced Bryant to a cheering crowd of nine thousand in Miami. He congratulated her on opposing the Dade County law, which he inaccurately called an "ordinance legalizing homosexuality" (sex-control laws were a state matter, not a county one). "You don't have to be a Christian to know that what is happening in [Dade] county is vulgar and vile and dirty," Falwell said. He praised Bryant for leading this difficult fight, "Because I want to tell you, we're dealing with a vile and vicious and vulgar gang. They'd kill you as quick as look at you."[10]

The mainstream media, from journalists to comedians, held Anita Bryant up as a symbol of intolerance. She had issued press releases telling parents that "Homosexuals cannot reproduce—so they must recruit. And to freshen their ranks, they must recruit the youth of America." She expressed similar views on popular TV talk shows and newscasts. On many of the same shows, well-known actors, singers, authors, and politicians denounced her as a hatemonger. Celebrities like Norman Lear and actor Ed Asner opposed the antigay referendum in TV ads. For their part, the Bryant camp ran commercials showing a San Francisco Gay Pride parade while an announcer intoned:

Men hugging other men, cavorting with little boys, wearing dresses and makeup. The same people who turned San Francisco into a hotbed of homosexuality want to do the same thing to Dade County. On June 7, vote for the human rights of your children. Vote for repeal of Metro's dangerous homosexual ordinance.

In June, Dade County voters repealed the civil rights ordinance. They thus guaranteed their neighbors the right to discriminate against gays in jobs, housing, and public accommodations. After that victory, Bryant promised to make her antigay campaign a national one.[11]

Network television made Bryant a frequent butt of topical jokes in 1977. *Saturday Night Live*'s "Weekend Update" reported that she had had intercourse in the middle of a shopping mall to promote heterosexuality. On the *Tonight Show*, Johnny Carson bashed Bryant almost nightly. One night, he said that the great New York power outage of 1977 could not have been an Act of God because "Anita Bryant would never have given Him time off." *Laugh-In '77* depicted Miami cops in drag singing "I Enjoy Being a Girl" and proclaiming, "We love you, Anita!" On the same show, guest host Bette Davis quipped:

Anita Bryant [has] . . . won her court suit to force Florida orange growers to cover their navels and quit pinching the fruit. The fruit was not available for comment . . . Meanwhile, Dale Evans has thrown her support behind Anita. The future does not look good for rodeo queens.

Carol Burnett burlesqued Bryant on her comedy hour. She played Anita as a bigoted hypocrite, too stupid to realize she is searching for antigay supporters in a gay bar. Burnett wore a corsage of oranges and carried a pitcher of juice. Some humor was more subtle. On *Maude*, homophobic Arthur visited a gay bar that his civic group wanted to close down. He drew suspicious stares from the bartender and customers when he innocently requested an orange juice. "We don't serve orange juice anymore," the bartender informed him. After a moment of confused silence, the studio audience got the joke and laughed.[12]

The backlash against Bryant's activism all but destroyed her singing career. "I've been blacklisted," she told reporters, and strong evidence suggests that this was so. The end of Bryant's stardom was fraught with ironies. Anita Bryant, who supported employers' right to discriminate, lost work because of her politics and beliefs. While mainstream concerts began eluding her, television news cameras continued to follow her through 1977 and most of 1978.

In 1978, Bryant threw her weight behind a public referendum in California: State Sen. John Briggs's Proposition 6. The so-called Briggs Initiative would have given school districts authority to fire, without recourse, any teacher who was gay or who stated, publicly or privately, that homosexuality should be tolerated. The Briggs Initiative generated as much media coverage as the Miami battle had. Advance polls predicted the results would be close to fifty-fifty. On November 7, the Briggs Initiative went down to defeat, 58 percent to 42 percent. By then, gay equality was one of the most commonly featured issues on national newscasts and prime-time entertainment shows.

18

BREAKING MURDEROUS STEREOTYPES:
LIKABLE LESBIANS, TENDER TRANSVESTITES
Television: 1973–1977

A recent episode of ABC's *Family* dealt with a topic we wouldn't normally find very appealing. The subject was lesbianism. The object, however, was humanity. And the result, in our view, was series television at its best . . . Our conclusion is that sex on television can be treated tastefully . . .

> —TV Guide *editorial about the* Family *episode,*
> *"We Love You, Miss Jessup," 1977*[1]

Television's fascination with queer criminals extended not only to lesbians but also to men in drag—some heterosexual (as in a 1965 *Alfred Hitchcock Hour*) and some implicitly or explicitly gay. Killer transvestites appeared in the TV movie *Scream, Pretty Peggy* (1973), episodes of *The Streets of San Francisco* (1974), *Police Woman* (1976), and *Charlie's Angels* (1981), and HBO's production of *Wait Until Dark* (1982), among others. As with TV's deadly lesbians, there was an implied link between the perpetrators' "otherness" and their criminal behavior. But there were also a few noncriminal depictions of gay women and cross-dressers on 1970s television. Some were minor supporting roles, such as a drag performer in a gay bar (Charles Pierce) who helped *Starsky and Hutch* capture a killer in 1977.[2] But this chapter will focus on more central guest characters.

Medical Center, typically ahead of its time, portrayed American TV's first productive, happy lesbian character: psychiatrist Annie Claymor (Lois Nettleton) in 1973. Homosexuality was still on the books as a mental illness, and what better way to challenge the sickness theory than to portray a capable, caring, stable mental-health professional who happens to be a lesbian? The episode title, "Impasse," refers to her patient's emotional troubles, and to Annie's problems with prejudiced colleagues. The title also describes the frustration of the series' male hero, Joe, who wants to date Annie. Unlike TV's previous morose lesbians, Annie Claymor has a winning personality and a sense of humor. So when Joe says that he does not believe she is gay, she replies, "Why? Because I didn't bite you on the ankle when you asked me for a date, and I let you kiss me and I enjoyed it? . . . I'm a person, I'm a woman, I'm a psychiatrist, and I am a homosexual." Activist Ginny Vida wrote that the "attractive, successful lesbian psychiatrist" was an improvement. "The character was flawed however," according to Vida, "by the psychiatrist's attempt at the end of the program to persuade a young girl that her lesbian feelings needn't be taken seriously."[3]

After the 1974 controversy over *Police Woman*, lesbian portrayals on TV improved slightly for a couple of years. In 1976, when another *Police Woman* script dealt with female homosexuality, the producers consulted the Gay Media Task Force for suggestions. In "Trial By Prejudice," the Angie Dickinson character is accused of sexually molesting a woman suspect. To get her job back, Sergeant Anderson must prove that she is heterosexual. The challenge for the show's producers was how to do this without reinforcing the impression that they were prejudiced against gay women. In the finished script, viewers meet Anderson's former college roommate, previously referred to in "Flowers of Evil." (The roommate had been in love with Anderson, who was sad not to be able to return those feelings.) In the 1976 episode, the ex-roommate is a successful business executive. Although coming out could harm her career, she testifies about her college crush and vouches for Anderson's heterosexuality.[4]

In fall 1977, during the controversy over gay teachers and the Briggs Initiative, ABC's *Family* and CBS's *All in the Family* both portrayed sympathetic lesbians who worked in education. In both scripts, the teacher had been in a relationship, but is safely single as the story begins.

The previous fall, *Family* had aired a gay male teen drama that pulled respectable Nielsens. According to producer Nigel McKeand, the network then showed "an unseemly haste" for the series to produce another such story. Newt Deiter of GMTF arranged for a lesbian schoolteacher to act as a consultant on this new episode, titled "We Love You, Miss Jessup." In this drama, teenaged Buddy Lawrence (Kristy McNichol) suddenly develops an interest in literature thanks to her dynamic new teacher, Flora Jessup (Blair Brown). Miss Jessup is a mass-media archetype of girl-next-door wholesomeness. But amid rumors that Flora is gay (true) and once seduced a minor (false), some parents want her fired. One particularly nasty classmate (Helen Hunt) gay-baits tomboy Buddy for being the "teacher's pet" of a reputed lesbian. Ultimately, Buddy becomes terrified that Flora will make a pass at her. The script shows how rumors can snowball, how mob mentality can take over before facts are known, and how all of this hurts students. The episode also acknowledges that even liberals sometimes have mixed feelings about gay people. Buddy's mother, Kate (Sada Thompson), tells her daughter, "I can't, and I don't want to, defend Miss Jessup's way of life." But she adds that people's private and professional lives are two different things. Kate says that Miss Jessup only wants her students to love learning what she loves teaching them.[5]

On *All in the Family*, the teaching angle is almost incidental. The Emmy-winning episode "Cousin Liz," finds Archie and Edith at the funeral of Edith's cousin, a teacher. There, Edith learns that Veronica, the other "old-maid schoolteacher" with whom Liz lived for a quarter century, was not just her roommate. Liz has left behind a family heirloom, a valuable silver tea service. Every day after school, Veronica and Liz took tea together from that set. Now Veronica wants to keep it, though she promises it will get back into Edith's family. Edith—ever compassionate—acknowledges Veronica as Liz's next of kin and gives her the tea set, despite Archie's orders to the contrary. When Edith refuses to take back the silver, Archie says, "You mean you're going to defy your husband?!" Edith's eyes widen in realization, and she says, "*Yeah!*" Archie vows to take Veronica to court, knowing that revealing her sexual orientation could end her teaching career. Edith protests that Archie surely does not want to take away someone's job.

ARCHIE: Who the hell wants people like that teachin' our kids? I'm sure God don't. God's sittin' in judgment.

EDITH: Well sure He is. But He's *God*. *You* ain't! *(applause)* . . .

She's all alone in the world now. And she's got nobody to take care of her, like I have . . . Archie, I can't believe you'd do anything that mean.

Rather than risk losing Edith's respect, Archie gives in.[6]

All in the Family also supplied the era's most sympathetic, three-dimensional depiction of a cross-dresser. Three episodes from 1975 to 1977 focused on Beverly LaSalle, an implicitly gay drag performer played by female impersonator Lori Shannon. Beverly first turns up in "Archie the Hero," when cabbie Archie gives "mouth-to-mouth restitution" to a tall, "classy dame" who passed out in his taxi. Having saved a life, Archie basks in his hero status. When the "dame" comes to his house to pay the cab fare plus a large tip, Archie's wife Edith (Jean Stapleton) and Beverly have a friendly chat. Edith is her usual, slightly dense self. When Beverly says, "I'm a transvestite," Edith replies, "Well you sure fooled me! I mean, you ain't got no accent at all!" Archie, who clearly finds Beverly attractive, is thrilled to see "her" alive and well. But when Beverly's wig comes off, Archie becomes rabid. In a later scene, Archie concedes that "them people" have a right to live, but adds, "It says in the Bible that a witness shall not bear falsies against thy neighbor—which is what that fag bore up against me!" Lori Shannon returned to this role in 1976's "Beverly Rides Again," in which Archie fixes a male friend up with Beverly as a practical joke.[7]

In December 1977 *All in the Family* brought back female impersonator Beverly LaSalle. Beverly had remained friendly with Edith, sending her letters from everywhere he performed. When he visits the Bunkers for Christmas, Edith gives him a scrapbook she has kept of his reviews. At dinner, Archie is thrilled to see Beverly in his everyday male garb. Later, when Beverly leaves to find a taxi, he is beaten to death by gay-bashers. Edith approaches Christmas angry at God, renouncing her faith. God, she says, cannot possibly care about the world if He would let something like this happen to one of His children. Archie, dressed as Santa, tries to cheer her.

ARCHIE: Hey, little girl. What would you like for Christmas?
EDITH: I want Beverly to be alive.
GLORIA: *(comforting her)* Oh, Ma.

EDITH: *(crying)* I can't understand it. I mean, everything was going
so good for him and then somebody had to kill him.

GLORIA: Just because he was different.[8]

In part two, which aired on Christmas Night in 1977, Archie says
that Beverly was lucky to live as long as he did. "You see it in the paper
every day: in New York, fags—that's what you call an ungendered
species. So cheer up!" Finally, Mike, the atheist, reminds Edith of all
the people who love and need her, and he helps her find her faith
again.[9]

SELLING *SOAP*

Television: 1977–1980

> The summer of 1977 may well go down in television history as the summer of
> *Soap*. Never have so many words been written about a television pilot which so
> few people have actually seen.
>
> —*Fred Silverman, president, ABC Entertainment, 1977*[1]

After much negative publicity about TV violence, the networks turned
to sex to attract viewers. "Jiggle" shows like *Charlie's Angels* and *Three's
Company* spiced up traditional TV genres by adding sexual innuendoes
and big, bouncing, braless breasts. ABC was jiggle TV's biggest practi-
tioner. This genre did worry the morality groups, but it was another
series—part of a different genre—that did more than any other show to
nationalize the Religious Right's media-watch efforts: the sitcom, *Soap*.
This prime-time spoof of daytime serials had something to offend
everyone, but ABC was determined to make it work.

Two years earlier, all three networks had rejected the comedy soap
opera *Mary Hartman, Mary Hartman*, only to kick themselves when it
did well in first-run syndication. *Soap* was ABC's second chance, and
the network did everything it could to generate advance publicity. So in
June and July, months before the fall premiere, newspapers and magazines previewed *Soap*'s plots. A middle-aged married woman and her
daughter were going to take turns in the bed of a twenty-six-year-old
tennis pro. One script would hint that he also had eyes for the older
woman's gay transvestite nephew, who was really the tennis pro's long-

lost stepbrother. The nephew would seek a sex change operation in order to stay with his NFL-quarterback boyfriend. A young woman would seduce a Jesuit priest *in church* and conceive a demonically possessed child by him. Her sister would have an affair with a married presidential candidate. Their cousin, a reluctant gangster, would work for Italian mafiosi. One of the male leads would suffer sexual impotence brought on by guilt over having killed his current wife's first husband.[2] And all of this would air at 9:30 P.M., when an estimated eighteen million children were still watching TV.[3]

Demands for *Soap*'s cancellation erupted from all sides, mostly from people who had never seen it. Some protests got little press, such as Italian American opposition to the Mafia stereotypes. The most visible complaints came from religious groups, who found the show lewd; and gay organizations, who worried about the gay/transvestite/transsexual character. With each new protest came more free publicity through news articles and published interviews. The producers generated still more press by sending reporters copies of the ABC censors' demands for script changes, thus positioning *Soap* as a free-expression cause.

ABC's announcement of *Soap* prompted thirty-two thousand letters of protest. Many were part of a campaign organized by groups like Reverend Wildmon's National Federation for Decency (NFD). But NFD, the Coalition For No Soap, and similar small groups were the least of ABC's worries. That summer, large, mainstream, religious denominations spoke out against the show. On August 31, the *New York Times* reported, "A number of religious groups around the country . . . have in recent weeks been successful in persuading advertisers—with the implied threat of a product boycott—to remove their commercials from *Soap*."[4] The press was filled with discussions of whether such boycotts constituted censorship. Was it un-American for pressure groups to deny others the right to see the show and make up their own mind? Opinions seemed evenly divided.

Gay concerns centered on the character of Jodie, and on scriptwriter Susan Harris's apparent confusion of homosexuality, transvestism, and transsexualism. Advance press coverage suggested that Jodie would be treated as one long fag joke. In July, the Philadelphia *Gay News* summarized what was then known about the character:

> . . . Mary Campbell is beleaguered by an impotent husband and a gay son who seeks a sex change operation. The boy dresses up in Mary's clothes and sings "There Is Nothing Like a Dame" before the mirror. This doesn't upset Mary nearly so much as the fact that "he looks better in that gown than I do." . . . The gay character does nothing but reinforce that old stereotype, which ABC should now realize is a tiring rehash.[5]

Three years earlier, a cross-dressing gay character whom others call a "fruit" would have led to zaps, picketing, and sit-ins. But the movement's tactics had changed. Corporate-looking activists now sat quietly with less-corporate-looking TV executives to discuss scripts. In May, after seeing scripts of the first two *Soap* episodes, Newt Deiter wrote to Tom Kersey, the head of ABC's Broadcast Standards and Practices office in Hollywood. Kersey had consulted Deiter often since 1975, so each had a sense of the other's priorities. Deiter understood the need for *Soap* to be irreverent, and prefaced his suggestions by saying that GMTF was not asking for a Superfag. His goal, he said, was "balance." (This contradicted Ginny Vida's demands to Kersey's superiors in New York: NGTF wanted zero tolerance for gay clichés until society no longer held such stereotypes.) Deiter said that, judging from the two-part pilot, Jodie seemed to be "a physically attractive 'wimp' " who never speaks up to defend himself—"the butt of everyone's humor."

Deiter made concrete suggestions:

> My proposal is that in the next episode to be filmed, "Jodie" first of all discards the idea of being a transsexual and, instead, becomes an up-front and somewhat militant Gay Liberationist. The advantages are several. The characterizations and slurs that are so much a part of the show could then remain except "Jodie" would be answering back in kind. That could possibly result in his emerging as an even stronger character, and I am not sure that that is the sort of thing the producer has in mind.

Deiter also included a veiled threat:

> . . . [S]hould the character remain as shown in episodes one and two, there will undoubtedly be substantial backlash reaction from the Gay community nationally. At this point, the matter need not go in that direc-

tion, since by letting our constituency know of the character's future development, we should be able to assist aborting any protest.[6]

In July, NGTF used its Gay Media Action Network to prepare for all manner of protests: letter writing, negotiations with local stations, sponsor boycotts, and picketing. ABC also heard from the International Union of Gay Athletes, which described itself as "an organization of gay and bisexual varsity athletes with affiliates on university campuses around the world." The athletes' union said it was working with other gay groups to unleash "massive demonstrations" against ABC in the fall. A press release, distributed by wire, quoted the group's senior officer, Richard Raymond: "Until these mythical stereotypes are laid to rest once and for all, people like Anita Bryant will exploit them to deny us fundamental rights."

Deiter and a representative of the athletes' group met with ABC executives and *Soap* producer Paul Junger Witt. GMTF, NGTF, and the International Union of Gay Athletes were displeased to learn that Jodie's scenes in the pilot were not among those reshot for broadcast. However, they came away assured that Jodie would drop the sex-change idea, develop a relationship with a nonstereotypical pro-football player, and stand up to his antigay stepfather. He would also confront his brother, Danny, who was in denial about Jodie's being gay. (Whenever Jodie came out to anyone, Danny would guffaw and say, "My brother's got a great sense of humor.")[7]

These were not exactly concessions. Susan Harris had already drafted episodes containing those storylines.[8] The ABC censors' notes on these scripts included two stipulations that marked the borders of network tolerance. They were typical of all three networks' attitude, espousing tolerance of homosexuality as an abstract concept, but not true acceptance. ABC ordered that:

> In order to treat Jodie as a gay character, his portrayal must at all times be handled without "limp-wristed" actions or other negative stereotyping.

But:

> The relationship between Jodie and the football player should be handled in such a manner that explicit or intimate aspects of homosexuality are avoided entirely.[9]

In practice, that meant Jodie and Dennis could be a romantic couple but they could not touch.

The football player story line sounded promising, as did the other developments the activists learned of in the July meeting. The protests, it seemed, could be put on hold. But to appease the "morality" groups, ABC's spin-control experts were frantically scrutinizing *Soap* scripts and plot outlines, looking for moral lessons. Via closed-circuit TV, ABC's programming chief Fred Silverman gave a fervent speech to the affiliate stations' staffs, promising that *Soap* was not "immoral." He cited many examples in which characters would suffer because of their misbehavior. One promise infuriated NGTF. "Jodie, the homosexual man," said Silverman, "is going to meet a girl and find out there are other values worth considering." Immediately, the protests were back on.[10]

As the premiere date approached, anti-*Soap* outrage continued to boil and bubble from all sides. The National Federation for Decency sponsored demonstrations against the series in fifteen cities. A leader of NFD, San Diego, told the press, "*Soap* is not entertainment. It is dirt. It is moral degradation and filth." Meanwhile, the National Gay Task Force asked its members to contact local ABC stations and demand an advance screening of the show, which had already been done for some church groups. If the station agreed to the screening, activists were to point out (scene by scene) what concerned them, explain why, and urge the station not to carry *Soap*. NGTF also took out a full-page ad in *Variety*, headlined, WHY ONE OF THE LARGEST AD AGENCIES IN THE WORLD WILL NOT LET ITS CLIENTS SPONSOR "SOAP." Drafted by Ron Gold, it outlined the stereotypes the show presented and encouraged people to write to Fred Silverman demanding the show's cancellation.[11]

Soap debuted on September 13. The first two episodes were far less polished than the rest of the first season, but audiences took to *Soap* immediately. It became the top-rated new series of the season. Most of the protests subsided after the first month, when viewers had a chance to see what a well-written, craftily performed satire it was. Jodie, played by comedian Billy Crystal, turned out to be sweet, proud, basically non-stereotypical, and very open about his gayness. Many isolated gay and bisexual teenage viewers embraced him as a role model. By episode four, viewers learned that Jodie's planned sex change was a last-ditch effort to stay with his boyfriend. As promised, episode eight included a sweet scene in which Jodie convinces his brother Danny to accept Jodie's gayness.[12]

Soap was the first hit series where a gay regular played a central role week after week. The scripts reflected a clear understanding that there were gay people watching the show; early dialog included inside jokes, such as allusions to gay men's supposed obsession with Bette Midler and Barbra Streisand. In November, the series got rid of the sex-change story line: Jodie, in the hospital for the operation, instead attempts suicide when Dennis dumps him. After recovering, Jodie seems stronger and more in control of his life.[13]

Fred Silverman's "moral" plot twist did materialize. Jodie does meet "a girl." Their first meeting was typical of the banter that writer Harris often gave Jodie:

CAROL: *You're* the suicidal homosexual?!

JODIE: Do we have mutual friends?

CAROL: Oh—no. No. . . . uh—I mean—

JODIE: Well what did you expect? That I'd be in a dress with a noose around my neck?

CAROL: I'm sorry. I guess what threw me is, you're just so adorable.

JODIE: *(after a pause, as Danny and others look at Jodie expectantly; he smiles)* Most suicidal homosexuals *are*.

During a one-night stand, he and Carol conceive a child, Wendy, for whom they will engage in a typically soap-operatic custody battle. The court case—an end-of-season cliff-hanger—is resolved in Jodie's favor in the 1980 fall season premiere. He thus became the first TV regular to raise a child as an openly gay parent.[14]

In its first seasons, *Soap* drew strong ratings partly because of the controversy, partly because of the show's quality, and partly because it aired immediately after *Three's Company*, one of the most popular shows on television. *Three's Company*, like the British show on which it was based, told the story of a horny, young straight man who must pretend to be gay so that his conservative landlord will let him share an apartment with two women friends. The show was steeped in sexual double entendres but no one ever seemed to have sex (unlike *Soap*, where bed hopping was chronic). The gay angle was one of *Three's*

Company's central running jokes. The male lead, Jack (John Ritter), is forever pretending to flirt with obnoxious studs who make unwanted advances toward his roommates. True to the show's slapstick style, each would-be Romeo does a comic "take," then quickly backs away. Landlord Stanley Roper (Norman Fell) frequently gay-baits Jack, which gets laughs because viewers know that Roper is dead wrong. "We're just having fun," Ritter told reporters. "We don't want to offend anyone. A gay from New York told a friend of mine we were making fun of homosexuals. That's the last thing we want to do. It's foolish to make fun of it."[15] Apparently, there were no formal protests from the major gay organizations, who surely realized that the scripts were mocking the landlord's prejudice.

Soap drew respectable ratings throughout its run. However, the *Los Angeles Times* later quoted ABC Entertainment president Lewis Erlicht as saying the network had trouble getting sponsors for it, eventually selling time at reduced rates. "We lost $3 million a year on *Soap* because advertisers wouldn't support it," he said. The 1985 *Times* article speculates that ABC stuck with the show for four seasons "to prove that it wouldn't be intimidated by outside pressure."[16]

Both *Soap* and *Three's Company* remained on the air into the 1980s. After the summer of 1977, nothing further was heard from the International Union of Gay Athletes. A *TV Guide* article later revealed that the organization was an "inspired bluff," consisting of "four rank-and-file members and a fictitious leader."[17]

THE YEARS OF THE QUEERS
Television: 1977–1980

We are everywhere!
—*Slogan from the Lesbian and Gay
March on Washington, 1979*

Anita Bryant and Senator John Briggs accomplished what Gay Liberation alone could not: By unashamedly promoting discrimination, they
helped to redefine homosexuality as a civil rights issue and turned it
into an everyday topic of discussion. Prime-time scripts reflected this
change. Gay rights issues—employment discrimination, child custody,
couples' rights, and antigay violence and harassment—became familiar
TV fare through shows like *All in the Family*, *WKRP in Cincinnati*, *The
White Shadow*, *Barney Miller*, and *Lou Grant*. Gay activists, sometimes
portrayed as lawyers or political candidates, were guest characters on
Starsky and Hutch, *The Associates*, and other shows. TV movies dramatized recent headlines about gay people who had fought for their rights,
among them *A Question of Love* (about a lesbian fighting for child custody) and *Sergeant Matlovich vs. the U.S. Air Force* (about discrimination in the military).[1]

A *Question of Love* evolved, in part, from a meeting that National
Gay Task Force leaders had with ABC in March 1977. NGTF's Ginny
Vida requested the meeting after *The Streets of San Francisco* depicted
a lesbian college student who stabs her lover's best friend to death for
fear that the friends might run off together. ("I didn't mean to kill her,"
she weeps when confessing. "I only meant to scar her. She was so

pretty . . .") Richard Gitter, ABC's vice president for Standards and Practices, told NGTF that ABC sometimes presents bad gay people and sometimes good ones, just as they do with heterosexuals. "You'll just have to trust our judgment," he said. Vida retorted that as far as she could remember, this was the first time ABC had *ever* depicted lesbians, and it was a tired, negative stereotype. The fact that the episode had been written and approved at all, she said, reflected "stereotypic notions of lesbians." Vida wanted positive lesbian portrayals—not "balanced" but out-and-out positive—and she wanted them immediately.[2]

She assured ABC's programming staff that positive, dramatic stories about lesbians could appeal to a general audience. She told them about Mary Jo Risher and Ann Forman, a lesbian couple in Texas, who had gone to court because Mary Jo's ex-husband wanted custody of their young son. Mary Jo was, by all accounts, a caring mother. The child wanted to stay with her. The ex-husband had admitted to cheating on his new wife with a teenage girl and paying for the girl's abortion. But the court ruled that Mary Jo's lesbian relationship made her a less fit parent and gave custody to the father. Having shared that story, Vida moved on to other topics and that seemed the end of the matter. By 1978, Doubleday had published Risher's autobiography, and there was talk of a TV movie. That spring, William Blinn wrote *A Purely Legal Matter*, an ABC telefilm based on her case. Blinn excerpted the court scenes from the original transcripts, changing the names, and created scenes depicting the Risher/Forman family's happy home life. The project attracted an outstanding cast, including Gena Rowlands, Jane Alexander, Bonnie Bedelia, Ned Beatty, and Clu Gulager. ABC censors asked for dozens of script cuts, most of which Blinn convinced them to retract. He won the battle to have young Billy tell his mother's lover that he wanted to stay with them. But ABC prevailed regarding a key stage direction. Blinn had written:

> Linda Rae resumes drying Barbara's hair. Barbara reaches back and touches Linda Rae's hand, bringing it slowly and softly to her lips. Linda Rae smooths out some of the moist tangles in Barbara's hair, gently, nicely.

Standards and Practices wanted the hand-kissing out. A copy of the script in the Gay Media Task Force files has a note in the margin:

"Shoot both ways, with and without." In the final cut, a compromise, Barbara holds Linda Rae's hand to her cheek. The film aired in November to rave reviews under the new title, *A Question of Love.*[3]

Bryant's and Briggs's campaigns also inspired numerous story lines about lesbian and gay teachers, including scripts for *All in the Family*, *Mulligan's Stew*, *Family*, *Watch Your Mouth*, and *The Baxters.*[4] News coverage about discrimination against gay police led to a string of gay cop TV dramas from 1977 to 1981, including praiseworthy episodes of *The Streets of San Francisco*, *Starsky and Hutch*, *Lou Grant*, *Trapper John, M.D.*, and a yearlong story arc on *Barney Miller.*[5] All of the scripts advocated tolerance toward gay employees, even in these traditionally homophobic professions.

Some early-1977 scripts were revised that summer to incorporate these topical themes. In April, Tom Bagen wrote a *Starsky and Hutch* episode, "Death in a Different Place," about a married cop, John Brody, who is posthumously outed as gay. In the original draft, Brody had been in a secret, long-term relationship with a closeted journalist. They broke up when the journalist came out and opened a gay newspaper. But the script was thoroughly rewritten four months later, as production began for the fall season. By then, newscasts were covering the debates over gay teachers and gay police. In the new script, John's secret lover, Peter, is a schoolteacher who lost his job because of his homosexuality. Peter becomes involved in gay rights and runs for office as an openly gay candidate (which Harvey Milk was then doing in real life in the same city). The couple broke up because the police officer (played by game show host Art Fleming), a husband and father, could not go public. In the original draft, City Hall had pressured the police to soft-pedal the case since the primary suspect was another cop. The rewrite was more topical: It focuses on the plight of gay police who have to hide in the closet. The title character's boss explains: "The department is under a lot of pressure these days to let gays on the force. No one's anxious to reveal that one of the department's finest may have been a homosexual." Unlike the original draft, the final version establishes that the late officer was a decorated, exemplary cop who once saved Starsky's life. At Newt Deiter's request, most of the seedy suspects were no longer identified as gay.[6]

Some producers and writers had mixed feelings about the task force.

They were glad to hear an insider's views of gay life, but some found that negotiating with GMTF could involve "interminable phone calls" about issues that the TV people considered trifling. At least two prime-time producers decided that the process was too intrusive, and they vowed to avoid all gay content in the future.[7] Even some people who worked well with Deiter had questions about the amount of power the networks gave him. Allan Burns, a writer for *Lou Grant*, said that the networks required consultation with GMTF no matter how "remotely gay" a script's content was. Nigel McKeand, producer of *Family*, said that in prime time, "no one can (whether you believe this or not) say that, for instance, homosexuality is infantile, and it is an absurd way to lead your life, and it's an arrested development."[8] Sitcom producer James Komack, who had a strong working relationship with the task force, said that gays had become "the most powerful lobby in the enter-tainment business"—more influential than blacks or women's libera-tionists or any cultural or racial group. "If you don't have the approval of the Gay Media Task Force," he said, "you don't go on the air. The networks are terrified of them." Komack conceded that GMTF's sugges-tions had improved the shows for which he consulted them, but he found the networks' general deference to pressure groups bewildering.[9]

At the decade's end, the networks were suppressing antigay mes-sages almost as assiduously as they once promoted them. Almost the only gay plots on the networks were ones whose message was that sexual orientation—an innate, unchangeable trait—had no negative bearing on a person's morality, loyalty, or honesty. A *TV Guide* article described a 1979 seminar where a panel of network officials boasted that TV could present *any* issue, given a sufficiently tasteful script. But veteran TV writer Ernest Kinoy ("a man of impeccably liberal creden-tials" the article noted) was able to dream up one plot that the execu-tives all agreed could *not* air at that time: the story of a man whose family is upset when he announces that he is gay, and who decides to seek psychiatric treatment to change his sexual behavior.[10]

Barney Miller offers an example of just how quickly things changed. In 1975, the gay couple Marty and Darryl had effeminate mannerisms and speech, and dressed in bizarre clothing. To borrow a line from a later series, they "walked with a lisp." In that first season, viewers knew little about either character, and they were the only gay recurring roles on the show. But by the 1979–1980 season, *Barney Miller* was offering a broader range of gay male types. Darryl—now sporting a suit and tie—looked and sounded more mainstream, though Marty remained a very funny, over-the-top queen. That season, the series added a third recurring gay role: Officer Zitelli, whose sexual orientation was known only to Barney Miller and to the show's viewers. Early in the season, Zitelli wrote an anonymous letter to Internal Affairs saying he was a gay officer and that the New York Police Department needed to stop discriminating. Viewers watched him stand silently by as colleagues made comments about "fruits" and as a zealous Internal Affairs investigator tried to rout out the queer cop. Zitelli's story peaked during an episode in which gay dad Darryl steals his seven-year-old son back from his ex-wife. As Darryl's argument with his child's mother escalates, the former Mrs. Driscoll turns to Captain Miller. "You're a policeman," she says. "You *know* how these people are." In front of his coworkers, Zitelli glares at her and announces, "*I'm* gay!" Although GMTF apparently was not consulted on this script, the show follows guidelines that Deiter and producer Danny Arnold discussed years earlier: Comic-sissy stereotypes like Marty were fine—such people do exist—but there needed to be other images to go with them.[11]

By 1979, after two years of "gay rights" news, Anita Bryant jokes, *Soap,* the Briggs Initiative, gay-themed documentaries, and after reports about the assassination of openly gay politician Harvey Milk, the mere mention of lesbian and gay issues was no longer considered shocking. In fact, gay imagery was influencing mainstream popular culture in some surprising ways. Recordings by The Village People sold in the millions as straight kids danced to implicitly gay songs like "San Francisco," "Y.M.C.A.," "Macho Man," and "In the Navy." The Village People made appearances on *American Bandstand* and other mainstream shows, wearing their trademark macho-camp costumes: They dressed as a cowboy, an S/M leatherman, a Native American warrior, a construction worker, and other male archetypes. Almost every article and review mentioned the group's origins as a gay novelty act, so the public was very much in on the joke. In 1979, NBC Entertainment planned a *Village People* variety special, with a possible weekly series to follow if it drew strong ratings. The group became so successful that they came in for kidding on satire shows: on *Saturday Night Live,* a gay music combo called "The Village Persons" sang "Bend Over, Chuck Berry."[12]

At neighborhood cinemas, *The Rocky Horror Picture Show*—that campy celebration of glitz, hedonism, and sexual nonconformity—was in its heyday as a midnight movie ritual. Teenage filmgoers from farms to major cities dressed as the movie's polysexual cross-dressers, threw props toward the screen at preordained moments, yelled kinky dialog, danced and sang to the same film they had seen the previous weekend, the weekend before, and the weekend before that. For many sexual-minority teens and others who did not fit into society, the film's anthem, "Don't Dream it, Be it!" seemed a benediction of their right to be themselves. Around the same time, the French film farce *La Cage aux Folles*—about a middle-aged, butch/femme male couple—became a surprise hit. It reportedly earned more money in U.S. theaters than any foreign film before it.

Had gays become a marketable product, or at least a lucrative market to target? TV executives, always on the watch for program ideas, gave that question serious thought. Most years, ABC, CBS, and NBC had no gay- or bisexual-themed series in development; on a good year, there might have been two. But in 1979 and early 1980, the commercial networks considered at least six such shows, three of which had gay leads. By the end of 1980, none of these had aired in series form, though most were strong concepts. The six contenders were:

BEANE'S OF BOSTON

Beane's was an American version of the bawdy, slapstick British comedy, *Are You Being Served?*, then in its seventh year on the BBC but still unknown in the United States. Comedy veterans Charlotte Rae, Alan Sues, Tom Poston, and John Hillerman were to star as department store workers, under the guidance of producer Garry Marshall. One of Paramount Television's sitcom geniuses, Marshall had proven his skill with hits like *The Odd Couple*, *Happy Days*, *Laverne & Shirley*, and *Mork & Mindy*. One of the biggest problems with *Beane's*, according to several accounts, was actor Alan Sues, formerly the resident sissy on *Laugh-In*. In the *Beane's* pilot, Sues played department-store clerk George Humphreys as an unsubtle, shrill fag—an "eye-popping . . . screaming homosexual to end all such portrayals" according to *Variety's* review. His performance lacked the charm of John Inman, who played the much-beloved Wilburforce Humphreys in the show's English and Australian incarnations. When the pilot aired in May 1979, NGTF duly wrote to CBS and accused the show of homophobia, sexism, and ageism. The pilot got decent reviews, but it relied on broad stock characters at a time when the networks were trying to get away from stereotypes. It never became a series.[13]

ADAM AND YVES

Danny Arnold loved *La Cage aux Folles*. After seeing the film, the writer/producer toyed with the idea of a sitcom about a similar butch/femme male couple who had been together for years. It was a revolutionary idea. No U.S. series had ever centered on an openly gay protagonist, much less a gay couple. *Adam and Yves* was a great title, too, with resonances of a then-famous antigay slogan, "God created Adam and Eve, not Adam and Steve." Riding high on the success of *Barney Miller*, Arnold pitched the idea to ABC. In fall 1979, ABC Entertainment president Anthony Thomopoulos ordered a pilot script. But when ABC announced the project to the press five months later, Arnold still had not written a word. He could not think of any tasteful way to develop and sustain the premise without repetition and clichés. "It was going to be too tough to get the writers," he recalled in 1992, "and it was going to be too monumental a job to keep it on a high level of quality week after week." Any series about a gay couple would also need careful media relations, and more publicity and spin control than even *Soap* had required. Arnold did not have the staff to pull it off. He got caught up in other projects and finally announced he had dropped *Adam and Yves*. The two film sequels to *La Cage aux Folles* proved him right: the premise does *not* sustain well over multiple episodes. Although *Adam and Yves* went inactive in 1980, it lived on for years in newsletters from American Christian Cause, the National Federation for Decency, the Coalition for Better Television, and other antigay media-watch groups who implied that ABC might reactivate the project at any moment. By January 1982, ABC had received over one hundred thousand letters protesting this nonexistent show. In the mid 1980s, ABC was still getting hate mail about *Adam and Yves*, begging the network not to pick it up.[14]

CAGES

CBS had been earning huge profits since early 1979 with a strange concept: *Dallas*, a nighttime soap opera that had shot into the Nielsen ratings' Top Five. Previously, common wisdom held that serials were for daytime. The networks had experimented with prime-time soaps in the 1960s and mid 1970s, but *Dallas*'s phenomenal success ensured the genre's future. In late 1979, ABC desperately wanted a nighttime serial to compete with *Dallas*, so they turned to Lorimar, the company behind the CBS hit. ABC paid Lorimar for an American version of the popular Australian soap, *Prisoner: Cell Block H,* set in a women's penitentiary. The Australian series had pulled strong Nielsens when it ran locally in Los Angeles and New York. *Prisoner*'s ensemble originally included an angry, young, street-tough dyke named Frankie Doyle, and later seasons brought still more lesbian characters. ABC broadcast the *Cages* pilot in June 1980 under the title *Willow B: Women in Prison*, but never picked up the series.[15]

OIL

Oil was another ABC attempt to out-Dallas *Dallas*. This prime-time serial was meant to focus on an obscenely wealthy oil magnate and his scheming, backstabbing family and colleagues. On that level, it sounds *exactly* like *Dallas*, but *Oil* creators Esther and Richard Shapiro envisioned a more sweeping, romantic fantasy about corruption, opulent wealth, class conflict, and dark secrets—sort of *Peyton Place* meets *Dallas* meets *Upstairs, Downstairs*. If all went as planned, it would draw a younger, richer, more sophisticated, and larger audience than *Dallas*. The two-hour pilot script ends with the conservative, homophobic patriarch confronting his liberal son, Steven, about the son's homosexuality.[16] This series eventually aired from 1981 to 1989 under the title *Dynasty*, and will be discussed in later chapters. The gay character was slated to develop an interest in women, causing him much confusion (and, when the plotline finally did air, confusing much of the show's huge audience). Through it all Steven was to be identified as a "homosexual" who dates women, never as "bisexual."

IT JUST SO HAPPENS AND *BROTHERS*

The most progressive gay-themed projects of 1980 were two remarkably similar sitcoms: *It Just So Happens* (under consideration at NBC) and *Brothers* (at ABC).

NBC optioned *It Just So Happens* in late 1979 or early 1980, and was still considering it in June 1980 when the network submitted the pilot script to Newt Deiter. Ten-Four Productions had pitched the show as a twist on *The Odd Couple*: Tony, a lovable, laid-back, sloppy, gay veterinarian in a California beach town, invites his recently separated, uptight, straight brother to live with him. Brother Donald is a very tidy ex–baseball player from New England. Tony's best friends include his neighbor Larry, who is Tony's ex-lover, and a heterosexual veterinary assistant, Kim. They and a host of bohemian Californian neighbors, straight and gay, were to spend the series trying to get Donald to loosen up.[17] Rick Podell and Mike Preminger's script was as warm, funny, and tight as anyone could ask for. NBC turned down the show, reportedly, because the dialog handled Tony's gayness too matter-of-factly. That July, CBS aired a different version of the script, minus all gay content. In this heterosexual version, also by Podell and Preminger, the protagonists are adopted brothers who have been separated for years: The tidy one is a working-class New York Jew who moves into the California bachelor pad of his brother—a sloppy, Irish American lawyer.[18] The premise is cute, but far less believable than the gay/straight pairing.

While NBC pondered *It Just So Happens*, ABC seriously considered an equally strong sitcom called *Brothers*, which had much going for it. The idea came from writer/producer Ed Weinberger, famous for his work on *The Mary Tyler Moore Show*, *Taxi*, and other hit sitcoms. Weinberger and Paramount producer Gary Nardino (himself a former

ABC programming executive) pitched the idea to Marcy Carsey, the vice president in charge of sitcom development for ABC. Based on an oral submission of the concept, Carsey commissioned a script. Weinberger assigned the project to Emmy-winning staff writer David Lloyd. The pilot script introduces three brothers: one gay (the youngest), and two straight. The gay brother, Cliff, and the middle brother, Joe, share an apartment. Cliff is fresh out of the closet, uncertain of himself. Writer Lloyd planned for the audience to go through the coming-out process with Cliff and his family. Joe, who is a single father and ex-football player, owns a restaurant. The eldest brother, Lou, is a grand comic creation: a burly, macho, working-class guy who utters the sort of addled lines that Hollywood once reserved for bubbleheaded, blond women. Cliff's best friend, Donald, is arguably the funniest character in the script: an emotionally strong, compassionate queen with an acid wit. The proposed regulars also include Joe's teenage daughter, Penny, and a wisecracking waitress, Kelly.

Despite some support for the script at ABC, the network never picked up *Brothers*. Paramount and Nardino would later resurrect Lloyd's script for Showtime cable.[19]

So with four possible sitcoms, two dramatic series, and a *Village People* variety special all in the works, what went wrong in 1979 and 1980? With all three networks developing gay-themed projects, why did only *Dynasty* materialize? Partly, it was business as usual. The networks consider hundreds of series ideas every year, most of which go nowhere. *Dynasty* had an inside track since its cocreator, Esther Shapiro, was an ex-ABC executive with a guaranteed development deal. It also seemed like the right show at the right time: The Reagan presidency brought with it a renewed fascination with conspicuous consumption and extreme wealth.[20]

But a more pervasive social change was also at work, which explains why so many gay-themed projects were dropped. By 1980, journalists were reporting a drastic shift toward conservatism in America's attitudes toward sex and morality. Fundamentalist and evangelical Christian organizations had grown into a powerful political force. According to *Forbes* magazine, TV preachers grossed $600 million in 1979—twice as much as they had in 1977 and twelve times their income in 1969. Much of the support seemed to result from their new political focus and the use of controversial issues in fund-raising pleas.[21]

Amid the media deluge about the Religious Right's growing clout, TV executives assumed that a massive change had occurred in public taste—an assumption that the November elections seemed to confirm. By year's end, the networks were backing away from scripts about sex, violence, and liberal causes. For example, in October 1980, CBS had approved a gay-themed *Trapper John, M.D.* script called "Straight and Narrow," by Barbara Hammer Avedon and Christopher Haun. It dealt with the shooting of a gay cop during a Gay Pride parade. According to Haun, CBS seemed comfortable with the story at first. "The only resistance to the script that I'm aware of," Haun recalls, "came just before it was to be filmed—which followed by a week or so Ronald Reagan's right-wing landslide. Suddenly, the network was nervous."[22]

The *Trapper John* episode was one of the last major gay-themed dramas to air for years. After the elections, word went out in Hollywood that the networks no longer wanted liberal social change scripts (à la *Lou Grant*), nor gratuitously sexy scripts *(Three's Company)*, nor GLBT scripts of any stripe. Established series could stay on the air, but new projects of this sort were out of the question.

SERMONS AND *SIDNEY*

Television: 1979–1981

I resent that a small cadre of creative and/or production people among the three networks will decide what 200 million Americans watch on television, and then scream "censorship" if a significant number of those Americans wish to have some say in the programming of those networks.

—*Reverend Jerry Falwell, 1981*[1]

The political New Right and the new Religious Right enjoyed a four-year courtship before they finally wed in 1979. That year, Reverend Jerry Falwell founded his famous organization, The Moral Majority, which he committed to electing allies into the White House and congress. The same year, a lobbying group, Christian Voice, opened a Washington, D.C., office from which to influence current officeholders. Falwell had been active in Anita Bryant's antigay campaign, and Christian Voice evolved out of Bryant's mailing lists and those of the Briggs Initiative. As a result, the New Religious Right had no shortage of antigay crusaders. Television quickly became this movement's main vehicle to attract and inform followers.

In the late 1970s and early 1980s, satellite distribution of TV shows became cheaper. Reverend Pat Robertson had experimented with satellites as early as 1977, when he leased a transponder on RCA's Satcom I. This gave cable TV companies throughout North America access to his Christian Broadcasting Network and its flagship show, *The 700 Club*. In 1979, RCA announced that a relay channel on its soon-to-be-launched Satcom III had been leased exclusively to religious programs. Although Satcom III failed just after takeoff, the religious shows were soon beamed throughout the hemisphere via another satellite service, subleased by RCA. Thanks to satellites and the growth of cable TV, it was more affordable than ever for preachers like Robertson and Falwell to "narrowcast"—that is, target a special-interest audience spread over a huge geographic area. In 1980, Robertson added a news commentary and political-action segment to his show—a public manifestation of a shift that was already taking place behind the scenes in much of the conservative Christian world.[2]

By summer 1980, Falwell and the Moral Majority held center stage in mainstream news reports, editorials, and political speeches. Anyone whom Falwell embraced as an ally became newsworthy, and some reporters started calling him "Jerry, the Kingmaker." Falwell and his colleagues heralded a "return to traditional family values." His "Clean Up America" crusade bolstered his mailing lists and raised funds through scare-tactic publications about abortionists, homosexual pederasts, pornographers, and man-hating feminists. By then, he was publicly supporting Ronald Reagan for president. Falwell said he liked that Reagan not only favored laws to promote biblical sexual values, but also advocated teaching creationism in public-school science classes. Since Falwell's followers had actively funded the Reagan campaign, the Republican party invited Falwell to play a key role in drafting its 1980 platform. By inauguration day, the "family values" movement had the attention of one of the world's most powerful leaders, and he owed them.

In the early 1980s, TV preachers spearheaded a multimillion-dollar campaign to crush homosexuality. Falwell's *Old-Time Gospel Hour* printed "Declarations of War" against homosexuals and other demonic scourges upon the land (abortion, pornography, and socialism)—suitable for framing and available to viewers for a donation.[3] Falwell's mailings about homosexuality brought in more money than his mailings about any other issue, so he ordered more of the same. Other Religious Right organizers also jumped on the antigay bandwagon. The gay civil rights movement, whose only large, national organization (NGTF) earned $266,871 in 1979, was under attack by a $600 million-a-year publicity machine with its own radio and TV outlets.[4]

Over a two-year period, homosexuality became the most frequently cited social "problem" in TV preachers' sermons and funding pleas.[5] In nationally syndicated telecasts, Falwell, James Robison, Charles Sustar, Bob Jones, and others railed against queers with greater frequency and vehemence than they did against murder, drugs, rape, genocide, pornography, atheism, communism, or even that old standby, abortion. Falwell used the "slippery slope" school of rhetoric in opposing gay-rights legislation. "What's next?", he would ask. "Imagine giving child molesters and rapists special preference in the law because they, too, have a bizarre sexual preference." Robison called homosexuality "a perversion of the highest order," comparable to prostitution and drug addiction, and he quoted articles from the tabloid *National Enquirer* as proof that gay men often attack each other and molest little boys. Robison called the murders of San Francisco Mayor George Moscone and City Supervisor Harvey Milk examples of divine retribution against tolerance of homosexuality. One station, WFAA-TV in Dallas, canceled its local airings of *James Robison Presents* following a gay group's complaints. The station manager told Robison that his one-sided broadcasts raised too many Fairness Doctrine issues. Robison filed a complaint with the FCC to have his show reinstated, but lost. Another preacher, Charles Sustar, also gave antigay sermons so vitriolic that some stations dropped his show or, in one case, preempted it to let a lesbian minister rebut his accusations.[6]

But while preachers often spoke out against homosexuality and gay rights, most had not yet begun lobbying against gay TV characters. Until late 1980, Falwell and company paid scant attention to prime-time TV. In a lengthy 1980 article explaining the Moral Majority's goals, Falwell barely mentions mainstream entertainment at all.[7] But after conquering Washington in November, he felt ready for a new project: his Moral Majority would take on the networks and demand that prime-time comedies and dramas reflect the importance of "Judeo-Christian" values.

On December 3, 1980 Falwell met with advisers to discuss the project, among them Reverend Donald Wildmon. Since 1977, Wildmon had battled the networks over prime-time immorality as head of the National Federation for Decency. When the networks did not respond to his negotiating attempts, Wildmon decided to hit them in the one place they were bound to notice—the profit line—through sponsor

boycotts. But his followers were too few to implement this plan effectively. When Falwell took an interest in prime time, Wildmon saw his
chance to get enough volunteers, money, and participants for a first-
rate national boycott.[8] Falwell's support catapulted the Mississippi
preacher into the public eye. Wildmon, whose previous press coverage
was limited to local newspapers and occasional scoffing mentions in
Variety, became a subject of national journalism.

In February 1981, Wildmon unveiled the Coalition for Better
Television (CBTV). By then, he had two hundred churches and
community groups on board, mostly thanks to Falwell's mailing lists.
Reporters informed the public that four thousand CBTV volunteers
would monitor prime time for three months in search of sex, violence,
and profanity. (Homosexuality counted as "sex.") Wildmon explained
that monitoring would continue until June, at which point boycotts
would begin. Falwell did not share Wildmon's enthusiasm for boycotts.
He told reporters he hoped that negotiating with the TV industry
would solve the problem. Wildmon treated the boycotts as a foregone
conclusion.[9]

Television remained on the Moral Majority's agenda for most of
1981. When Falwell's right-hand man, Tim LaHaye, wrote a position
piece on TV's "anti-Christian" decline that year, homosexuality topped
his list of prime-time sins: "A medium that once featured family-
oriented programming," he wrote, "now makes jokes about homosexuality, incest, wife-swapping, and depravity." Falwell publicly lashed
out at Norman Lear, the producer of *All in the Family*, *Maude*, *One
Day at a Time*, and *Mary Hartman, Mary Hartman*. According to Falwell, Lear was "the Number 1 enemy of the American Family," whose
liberal shows had set an amoral trend. (More likely, Falwell was angry
at Lear for a more recent project. Lear had just launched a well-funded
civil liberties group, People for the American Way, to battle the Religious Right.) As for CBTV, Reverend Wildmon gave frequent interviews in which he used the same rhetoric that he has since the 1970s:
"All television is educational," he said in 1981. "I am concerned about
what it is teaching."[10]

By spring 1981, the television industry was afire with talk of the Religious Right's assault. The Coalition for Better Television's three-month
monitoring period had begun, and Reverend Wildmon sent letters

to suspect sponsors, warning that it was not too late to get off the June boycott list. All three networks' senior executives insisted that they were not worried about the threatened boycotts. But for people who were not worried, they spent an awful lot of time telling print and TV reporters how *un*worried they were. When pressed, several network chiefs admitted that sponsors were defecting from controversial shows in unprecedented numbers, apparently in response to Religious Right pressure.[11]

Donald Wildmon was especially upset about a newly announced NBC sitcom, *Love, Sidney,* slated to star Tony Randall as a middle-aged, Jewish, New York homosexual. From a Religious Right perspective, the show's premise sounded immoral: lonely, gay Sidney finds new meaning in life after he invites a vivacious sexually active nineteen-year-old, Laurie, into his home; together, they lovingly raise the bastard baby she conceived during an affair with a married man. Wildmon supplemented his general campaigns with a special crusade against this series. He threatened boycotts and demonstrations. He phoned NBC, whose spokespeople told him not to prejudge the show: They predicted that, unlikely as it sounded, the show would not offend CBTV. Wildmon sent a round of *Sidney*-specific letters to potential sponsors. He contacted the news media and offered to grant interviews about *Love, Sidney.* Claiming victory for keeping ABC's *Adam and Yves* off the air, Wildmon told reporters, "Networks make a mistake when they try to legitimate a homosexual lifestyle."[12] Given the resurgence of conservatism and sponsors' growing caution, he hoped that advertisers had begun to see America as a basically moral, God-fearing nation. Many journalists pointed out that the anti-*Sidney* protesters knew virtually nothing about the show. The Religious Right's focus on *Love, Sidney* proved hasty. The show's bare-bones plot summary sounded radical, but the program itself espoused extremely conservative moral values.

A friend of Tony Randall's had first sent him the *Sidney* story in early 1979. Randall thought the premise tremendously original and began to nurture it as a possible TV movie. Throughout 1980, he worked on it with Warner Bros. Television and scriptwriter Oliver Hailey. By fall, all three networks had rejected it. "It couldn't possibly be because of the homosexuality," Randall told *The Advocate*, "because television has done shows before on the subject." Finally, Randall persuaded NBC president Fred Silverman to buy the comedy/drama for him.[13] By March, the film was complete and NBC was trying to sell Randall on a weekly sitcom version. Getting him to agree would be a coup. Randall, a popular TV star since the 1950s, had appeared in such highly rated shows as *Mr. Peepers* and *The Odd Couple*. In 1978, he had publicly sworn off series television, but he agreed to appear in *Love, Sidney* on three conditions: that Warner Bros. and NBC give him complete creative control, that the show be produced in New York, and that Warner Bros. provide startup money for Randall's dream project, a classic repertory theater in New York. With those terms met, Randall signed on and NBC shelved the TV movie to air in the fall with the series.[14]

In many ways, Sidney was the sort of character the Religious Right said it wanted. In the TV movie, Randall's character goes to great lengths to thwart Laurie's plans for an abortion—finally confronting her in the lobby of the clinic and offering to raise the baby himself. What he really wants out of life, he says, is a family. Prudish, meddlesome Sidney is a stereotypical "Jewish mother" type, much like his own late and oppressive mother, Yetta. His conservatism and possessiveness were apparently what made his former lover, Martin, walk out of his life. Burned by that experience, Sidney became celibate and reclusive. He still misses Martin and prominently displays his photo in his huge apartment.[15] Randall said that Sidney's homosexuality was an important part of the backstory. He said it helped to explain why Sidney felt so cut off from the world, and it actually made the show *more* moral: as a celibate homosexual, Sidney's intentions toward Laurie could not be misconstrued. Religious Right activists who worried that *Sidney* would teach small children about homosexuality had nothing to fear. The title character's sexual orientation, clear to most adults, was communicated in terms that no youngster would be likely to understand.

The TV movie, *Sidney Shorr: A Girl's Best Friend*, wrapped production just as news broke about Reverend Wildmon and his Coalition for Better Television. By May, when the networks unveiled their fall seasons, CBTV had grown to three hundred organizations, still including the influential Moral Majority. The networks' new fall lineups differed greatly from those of recent years: there were no new "jiggle" shows, no sex comedies, not even on ABC. Instead, they served up cozy sitcoms, bloodless action shows, and a western. ABC-TV President Fred Pierce explained the new rationale at the annual affiliates meeting:

> Our new schedule . . . reflects something important that is happening in the country right now. There's an evolving mood based on a renewal of traditional values: home and family, courage and honesty, respect for authority and teamwork.[16]

When NBC announced its schedule, reporters asked the network executives about *Love, Sidney*, which had been in the headlines for months.

In the new social climate, NBC tried to expunge Sidney's (already soft-pedaled) homosexuality. Among themselves, some NBC executives said that homosexuality had been "overexposed" on television in recent years—that it was "played out" as a dramatic subject. In June, Newt Deiter appeared on the *Today* show and criticized NBC's blackout on gay characters:

> In the hinterlands—in Wyoming, Wisconsin, Massachusetts, little towns— there are young gay men and gay women who have never seen a positive role model: people who are successful, who are achievers, who make something of themselves *and* are also gay . . .
>
> Last year, NBC made a film that yet to air: *Sidney Shorr* starring Tony Randall. In the film, the character is clearly identified as homosexual. Now it's turned into a sitcom and, magically, NBC has discovered a half-hour cure for homosexuality.

Deiter said that the network must have felt the subject was worth portraying or Sidney would not have been homosexual in the first place. "Obviously," he said, "somebody upstairs in this building caved in to pressure." At the annual fall press tour, NBC Entertainment President Brandon Tartikoff (Fred Silverman's protégé) confirmed that Sidney Shorr would still be a homosexual in the pilot, but not in the series. Meanwhile, in another room, executive producer George Eckstein and actor Randall were telling reporters that every episode of the series would treat Sidney's homosexuality "exactly as it was in the film": undeniably there, but incidental to the plot.[17]

NBC officials admitted that they had received several thousand letters of protest against the as yet unproduced series. Tartikoff said the

Moral Majority and CBTV had nothing to do with the decision to neuter Sidney. However, a remarkable coincidence happened. The week after Wildmon called off his boycott (saying that television had begun to clean up its act), NBC's new chairman, Grant Tinker, quietly decided that *Love, Sidney* would deal with Sidney's homosexuality much as the film did. As Randall promised, almost every episode did allude, very obliquely, to Sidney's homosexuality. ("I love a man who's hard to get," says a woman who wants to date Sidney. "In that case," replies Laurie, "you're in for a marvelous evening.")[18] The only significant change in tone came from a change in cast: Lorna Patterson, who played Laurie in the film, was unavailable, so Swoosie Kurtz took over the role. Kurtz's Laurie was less flaky, more of an intelligent wit. This warm comedy/drama premiered to rave reviews. It focused on these two adults and the little girl—Patti (Kaleena Kiff)—whom they love. Typical episodes dealt with everyday issues that face any family, though there were also some issue-of-the-week episodes about such topics as teenage runaways.

Laurie earns her living as a soap opera actress, which allows the show to lampoon television's handling of sexual minorities. Few reviewers of *Love, Sidney* have mentioned Laurie's role as "Gloria Trenell," the home-wrecking bisexual nymphomaniac on the show-within-a-show, *As Thus We Are.* If *Love, Sidney* absurdly dodged its protagonist's sexual orientation, the *As Thus We Are* segments satirized television's potential to grotesquely exploit sexual-minority characters. Gloria is a send-up of daytime TV's glamorous femmes fatales. First Gloria woos a woman away from her husband, then dumps her—even though the woman financed a rescue mission to bring Gloria back from the Amazon jungle after a plane crash. Late in the run, Laurie learns that her character is to have a sex-change operation, and she will play a man, "George Trenell." Laurie patterns George after Sidney, who begins demanding script changes. It provides the perfect context for the weekly coy reminder of Sidney's homosexuality:

> LAURIE: George Trenell may dress, walk, talk like Sidney Shorr, but he's *not* Sidney Shorr. Yesterday, George rushed into a burning building to save the life of a dog. Now would Sidney Shorr do that?

SIDNEY: Yes! Even though I'm afraid of dogs.

LAURIE: Would Sidney Shorr land a 747 after the pilot's had a heart attack?

SIDNEY: Yes!

LAURIE: *(with a glint in her eye)* Would Sidney Shorr go out with a beautiful woman?

SIDNEY: *(a pause, then . . .)* No, but I haven't had a sex change.[19]

Sidney was allowed a romance in only one episode near the end of the series. In a "very special" one-hour broadcast, Sidney starts to fall for a woman coworker named Alison. The relationship seems to be going well, but Sidney is conflicted because of—well, you know, that thing he can't mention outright on the show. In a tear-filled scene toward the end of the episode, he breaks up with her, staring all the while at his ex-lover's photo. Alison, not understanding why she has been dumped, asks: "Who was the big love of your life that did this to you, that left you for dead? Well, whoever it was, I'll hate her for the rest of my life." Sidney finally manages to say, "Don't hate—that person." To bring things back into alignment and finish on an upbeat note, the episode ends after Laurie and Patti return home, with Sidney happily nestled between them, joking, on the living-room couch.[20]

During the run of *Love, Sidney*, Reverend Wildmon's credibility as a menace to advertisers took a nosedive. As long as he merely *threatened* to organize boycotts but never actually held one, his threat had power: No one knew for sure whether he could or could not dent major sponsors' profits. But in March 1982, his Coalition for Better Television finally went through with a boycott. Their original plan was to target sponsors of "anti-Christian" shows. They hoped to use a $2 million grant from the Moral Majority to publicize the names of advertisers, their subsidiaries, and products. In late 1981, however, Reverend Falwell withdrew the offer of funds, again expressing a distaste for coercive tactics. With a tighter budget, Wildmon chose an easier target. On March 4, he announced a national boycott of NBC-TV (which he said was, by a small margin, the most anti-Christian network) and its parent company, the financially shaky RCA. Wildmon said he had support from eighteen hundred churches and organizations. Four weeks into the boycott, several NBC shows, including *Love, Sidney*, showed ratings increases, not losses. RCA's second quarter 1982 earnings showed a rise of 2.5 percent. Profits for the third quarter, which included much of the boycott period, were up by $152 million over the same period in 1981.[21] Wildmon insisted that the ratings and financial results were taken out of context and indicated little, especially since 1981 had been a bad year for RCA. Regardless, Wildmon's name dropped out of the headlines for the next five years.

THE INSIDERS

Television: 1980–1983

[A] break in ideology, strategy, communication, and vision polarized the gay and lesbian movement in the late 1970s and early 1980s. The grassroots gay movement fought antigay repeal efforts, protested police harassment, countered homophobic media coverage, and picketed antigay films . . . ; the national movement focused on establishing its presence in Washington.

—*Urvashi Vaid, former executive director, National Gay and Lesbian Task Force, 1995[1]*

In an era of neckties, corporate clones, and conformity, the grassroots model of gay activism got competition from lesbians and gay men who were—or wanted to be—insiders. These included political insiders and show business insiders, both of whom influenced TV's portrayal of sexual minorities. Reagan-era gay yuppies ("guppies") sought to professionalize the movement on two fronts: through national civil rights groups run by paid staffs (usually with a focus on government), and through trade associations (gay lawyers' groups, gay journalists' associations, and so on). Corporate attire became the new uniform for activism, which was increasingly a sit-and-negotiate type of activity.

In early-1980s America, protests and militancy were widely considered boring, whiny, and passé, as journalists heralded the death of 1960s idealism and 1970s activism. Even college students, usually the last bastion of social criticism, protested little. Given the spirit of the times, the professionalized gay groups used positive reinforcement, such as awards or political donations, to encourage gay-friendly behavior. Appropriately, early-1980s television reflected the gay civil rights movement's new suit-and-tie image.

Where gay-themed documentaries of the 1970s had been very personal, anecdotal, slice-of-life affairs,[2] early-1980s broadcasts focused on lobbying groups and the gay vote. The shows' narrators reported with surprise that politicians had begun accepting gay money and offering favors to gay organizations. Would the trend continue? Would activists' vision of gay voting blocs materialize? Reporter Harry Reasoner, introducing a 1980 *CBS Reports* special, commented: "For someone of my generation, it sounds a bit preposterous. Political power for homosexuals? But those predictions are coming true." The prospect seemed to worry him.[3]

The shift in news coverage reflected a change in gay political tactics. Openly gay women and men were participating in party politics in unprecedented numbers, mostly in the Democratic party. NGTF encouraged its members to try to get onto statewide nominating committees. The payoff for all this hard work was most visible at the 1980 Democratic National Convention. The previous Democratic convention, in 1976, had included only four openly lesbian or gay delegates; in 1980, there were reportedly seventy-seven, representing more than twenty states.[4] The 1980 convention was the first to approve a gay civil rights plank in its campaign platform, after failed attempts in 1972 and 1976. Another growing strategy involved campaign donations: starting in the late 1970s, certain activists invested heavily in gay political action committees (PACs).

Someone at CBS noticed the gay involvement in party politics and dispatched two news producers to San Francisco, one of the few places where candidates felt a need to woo the gay vote. CBS's Grace Diekhaus and George Crile arrived in June to work on an hour-long documentary about gay influence in the 1979 mayoral election. If they wanted a typical picture of gay politics in San Francisco, their timing could not have been worse. They got there just after a mob of gay San Franciscans had gone on a violent rampage, trapping police and elected officials inside City Hall, smashing windows on city property, and setting fire to police cars. The "White Night" riot followed the conviction of ex-politician Dan White, who had assassinated Harvey Milk and gay-friendly Mayor George Moscone. The straight, white jury convicted

White of voluntary manslaughter—not, as many hoped, first-degree murder. The court sentenced him to less than eight years in prison, with a possibility of parole in five. ("Sara Jane Moore got life for *missing* Gerald Ford," noted one observer.) News coverage showed that some San Francisco police sympathized with ex-cop White, which heightened decades-old tensions between the city's police and gays. To many activists, recent events proved that police and the courts still considered gay people and their allies expendable. After a peaceful daytime protest, gay rage exploded into rioting. A group of police responded that night with a spree of random gay-bashings on Castro Street. A few weeks later, activist Cleve Jones gave CBS News producers Diekhaus and Crile their first tour of the Castro. When they arrived, local TV stations were still replaying and reanalyzing the violence. All of this informed the producers' subsequent coverage of the 1979 mayoral election.

Their film, "Gay Power, Gay Politics," aired on *CBS Reports* in April 1980 as that series' second gay-themed documentary. CBS publicized it as "a case history of how homosexuals became the new power brokers in San Francisco's recent mayoral election." Two weeks before the broadcast, a CBS press release promoting the show revealed that the special would stray from its announced topic into gratuitously sexual areas.

> San Francisco homosexuals are not willing to stay in their bars. The broadcast demonstrates how gays are attacking traditional values, and frightening heterosexuals with such proposals as a "demystification program" for the schools to teach children about homosexuality as a normal lifestyle.
>
> The broadcast points to a recent Kinsey study reporting that the average San Francisco gay man has had sexual encounters with at least five hundred different men; to "gloryholes," places where gay men go for anonymous sex; and to a thirty-seven-acre park in the heart of the city comandeered by gay men for public sex.[5]

What viewers saw on April 26 was a biased, hour-long attempt to discredit the new suit-and-tie activists who openly courted and influenced political candidates. A good documentary might have found solid ways to link the sexual topics to the election. But "Gay Power, Gay Politics" linked them through unsupported innuendo, hinting broadly that gay men were a physical threat to both children and adults.

"Gay Power, Gay Politics" makes its case mostly through editing. It shows civilized-looking gay PAC events, explains the legal protections that gay San Franciscans enjoy, and touches on a proposed gay-inclusive school curriculum; it then intercuts these with footage of sadomasochism, nudity at a Gay Freedom Day parade, cruising, a wild Halloween drag party, and an interview with children who have seen men having sex in Buena Vista Park. Footage of the 1979 National March on Washington for Lesbian and Gay Rights frames the report, showing a massive sea of GLBT faces. After showing part of a speech from the march, anchor Harry Reasoner promises that viewers will witness "the birth of a political movement and the troubling questions it raises for the eighties, not only for San Francisco, but for other cities throughout the country." Through juxtaposition, the film repeatedly and implicitly links the wildness of 1970s San Francisco with the national goals of the gay civil rights movement. Presumably, the "troubling" issues for viewers in "other cities" are meant to include the implicit question, "Will gay-rights laws cause such horrors to spread to *my* town?" The show never quite explains the supposed connection between Dianne Feinstein's mayoral campaign and private, consenting S&M. Nor does it mention that the S&M sequence was filmed in a club patronized almost exclusively by heterosexuals. The show's most gaping omission concerns the demographics of the gay people seen on-camera: CBS's gay San Francisco contains almost no lesbians, working-class people, or people of color. What emerges is a story about privileged, promiscuous, middle-class white men scrambling for special rights to "absolute sexual freedom," a phrase the show repeats several times. Footage of the White Night riot hints at how far gay men will go to achieve that "absolute sexual freedom."

Two months after the broadcast, San Francisco journalist Randy Alfred, in conjunction with NGTF and the San Francisco Board of Supervisors, filed a complaint against the show with the National News Council. In September, the Council found that the broadcast was misleading and had violated journalistic ethics on several counts.[6] Viewed as a whole, "Gay Power, Gay Politics" looks like a longer version of the antigay commercials that Anita Bryant used to run in Miami.

In 1980, leaders of the Gay Rights National Lobby organized the first national committee to raise funds for gay-friendly candidates: the Human Rights Campaign Fund (HRCF). Like the local election committees, HRCF used time-honored fund-raising methods. It held cocktail parties, issued direct-mail solicitations, produced a fund-raising video narrated by a TV star (Mike Farrell from *M**A*S*H), and finally, in September 1982, held an expensive, formal-dress awards dinner at New York's Waldorf-Astoria Hotel. Politicians who lent their names to the dinner committee included senators Alan Cranston, Edward Kennedy, Daniel Patrick Moynahan, Paul Tsongas, and Paul Weicker. Former Vice President Walter Mondale gave the keynote address. Those famous names attracted the attention of CBS's and ABC's news departments. ABC's *Nightline* profiled Gene Ulrich, the openly gay mayor of Bunceton, Missouri—a town whose small population (four hundred nineteen) was religious enough to keep three churches busy on Sundays. The show credited gays as a key swing vote for recent elections in Los Angeles, San Francisco, Philadelphia, and Washington, D.C. In at least one big-city primary, the report indicated, HRCF had been the largest single donor to the winning candidate. Politicians reciprocated by addressing discrimination issues and by naming openly gay people to government posts. But none of the politicians whom HRCF supported was willing to appear on *Nightline* to discuss the matter. Nor were any of those who had lent their support to the HRCF dinner. ABC News' political director, Hal Bruno, dismissed so-called "Gay Power" as a fragmentary phenomenon that might, or might not, become national at some future date.[7]

The National Gay Task Force, too, became more of a professionalized civil rights agency in the 1980s. It narrowed its focus to legislation and public policy, minimizing its involvement in entertainment consulting. Ginny Vida and Ron Gold resigned from NGTF in 1979. In 1980, NGTF redefined the role of its media director, making it primarily a liaison to the news media. Amid legislative attacks, assaults from the Religious Right, news coverage of a "homosexual serial killer" (John Wayne Gacy), and early "outings" (tennis star Billie Jean King, and various congressmen, years before the term "outing" was used in this context), NGTF focused its energy on bare essentials. Especially once AIDS hit the headlines, having a liaison to reporters, it seemed, was more urgent than negotiating about TV sitcoms. Within a few years, NGTF would evolve into a professional public policy agency, change its name to the National Gay and Lesbian Task Force, and relocate to the nation's capital.

By the time Vida left NGTF, Newt Deiter's Gay Media Task Force was essentially a one-man operation, and he was beginning to drift toward retirement. The networks continued to consult Deiter regularly until 1981. Thereafter, he served as an independent consultant to a few major production companies. Around 1987, he retired from activism to pursue other interests. The need for his skills was less dire by the 1980s. In the 1970s, when almost all gay people in entertainment were closeted, GMTF's "agents in place" had smuggled Deiter inside information. He had then passed their concerns along to TV executives who, as likely as not, did not know any other openly gay people. But by the early 1980s in California's production community, straights knew more about gay people.

Many series had openly gay and/or lesbian staff members. While actors still could not afford to be out of the closet, TV writers and technicians had more flexibility. Straight writers, producers, and directors often used gay friends and colleagues as a sounding board to see if portrayals rang true or were potentially offensive. In publicity interviews, writers of many gay-friendly shows often mentioned gay and lesbian friends. Stu Silver, who cowrote *Soap*, was also head writer for the groundbreaking cable sitcom *Brothers* in the mid 1980s; in published interviews, he mentioned having close friends who happened to be gay, including his son's godfather.[8] Some of television's most interesting gay-themed scripts came from writers who were gay or had gay friends. One popular drama series[9] had two principal writing teams: one team consisted of a lesbian and a straight woman with whom she had written for years; the other consisted of a gay man and a close straight woman friend. The series produced several remarkable episodes about sexual-minority characters. And during the five-year run of *Brothers*, that sitcom always had gay male and/or lesbian staffers.[10] Most early-1980s producers interviewed for this book proudly stated that their shows did not need to consult gay media organizations because they had the advice and judgment of lesbian or gay colleagues or relatives.

A *Taxi* episode exemplifies how everyday gay people in the industry can have an impact. In late 1980, the series produced an episode in which cabbie Elaine Nardo (Marilu Henner) falls for a guest character, Kirk (John David Carson), a nice man she meets at a bar. The twist: Kirk is the first openly bisexual character to appear on an American network series. (Previously, one had appeared in a syndicated show. Annie "Tippytoes" Wylie was a recurring role on the 1976–77 season of *Mary Hartman, Mary Hartman*.) Kirk likes Elaine, but never meant to get involved with her. When he first approached her, he was really after her friend Tony (Tony Danza). When Tony learns about this, he asks advice from a coworker, the foreign-accented emigré Latka (Andy Kaufman). Latka tells Tony that bisexuals are "very popular in my country." Tony is shocked. "Almost everybody have them," Latka explains, "and one of our favorite sports is racing them. And when we are not using them, we have special racks where we chain them up at night." Not *bicycles*, Tony explains, "I'm talking about *bisexuals*." Latka replies, "So am I." In the end, *Taxi*'s lead character, Alex (Judd Hirsch), meets Kirk at a gay bar to tell him that Tony is not interested. Alex winds up having a grand time dancing at the bar and wins a dance contest.[11]

The script is absent from the files of the Gay Media Task Force because the producers got their gay consulting in-house. Instead of going to Deiter, they sought advice from Don Draper, Hirsch's openly gay personal assistant. They asked him about the "look" of the gay bar, the extras, and their costumes. In some ways, he was a fine choice: he knew more about the insides of New York gay bars than most of his coworkers. But the Kirk plot made him uncomfortable because Draper distrusted people who identified themselves as bisexual. "That's my own prejudice," he explained, "and my own problem." Working with set designer Tommy Getz, Draper helped make the bar set brighter and less "squalid," eliminating posters from old Broadway dramas and campy horror films, replacing them with mirrors, antiques, and prints. When only six extras answered the casting call, the show got a waiver from the actors' union and told Draper to find everyday gay men to populate the pivotal bar scene. At a coming-out support group that week, Draper announced that he needed fifteen men by two o'clock the next day. "Who doesn't?" someone piped up. At a bar that night, Draper found himself in an odd position for someone whose secretarial duties usually found him behind a typewriter. In an *Advocate* interview, he mused, "How often do you get to go into the Motherlode, walk up to somebody, and say, 'Hey, you want to be in the movies?'—and actually be able to deliver!"[12]

For producers who did not have the luxury of openly gay consultants on staff, there was always the Alliance for Gay Artists—a textbook case of a grassroots gay organization that professionalized itself and changed its mission in the early 1980s. Founded in 1979 as the Gay Actors Rap, it was originally an informal, low-profile support group in Los Angeles, open only to professional actors. Several months after the group began meeting, it admitted technicians, producers, and others on the production side of television, film, and theater. The Gay Actors Rap became the Alliance of Gay Artists (AGA), but it was still essentially a discussion group about coming-out and employment issues. Since actors usually need to resell themselves every few weeks—and since what they are selling is, in large part, an image—they tended to be more closeted than the nonactors in AGA. As more business and technical staff joined, the rap session component became less prominent. In 1981, several nonactor members, among them Chris Uszler, led an effort to change the organization's name and purpose. Instead of a secretive group who met to discuss their own concerns, they proposed turning AGA into a high-profile trade association. Goals might include promoting fair hiring practices, informing gay people in the industry of upcoming projects, and encouraging unbiased media portrayals.

Active Hollywood professionals could not afford to use confrontational tactics like picketing. Instead, the proposal to restructure AGA suggested establishing negotiations with show business executives and distributing annual awards to honor nonstereotyped depictions in plays, films, and TV. The most controversial suggestion involved changing the group's name from the Alliance *of* Gay Artists to the Alliance *for* Gay Artists. Some original members saw this as a concession to internalized homophobia and a betrayal of the group's purpose. But many saw it as a way to network with allies: by being *for* gays rather than *of* gays, the organization could invite powerful, well-known straight or closeted people in the industry to join. The group approved the proposed changes in 1981, and a number of early members left in protest.[13]

The first AGA Awards were presented privately with little fanfare in 1981. The *Taxi* episode was among the winners. By October 1982, when AGA distributed its second annual awards, the group had gone thoroughly public. The awards ceremony packed four hundred people into the three-hundred-fifty-seat L.A. Stage Company theater in Hollywood. It was emceed by actors from two Top-25 TV shows: Lynn Redgrave of *House Calls* and Gregory Harrison of *Trapper John, M.D.* TV recipients included *Love, Sidney*, for depicting "episodic TV's first homosexual hero." Robert Preston lent excitement and respectability to the proceedings by paying his own airfare to accept an award for his performance in the movie *Victor/Victoria*.[14]

Over the next year, representatives of AGA began meeting with network executives, writers, and producers, much as NGTF and the Gay Media Task Force had in the past. Since AGA members all worked in the industry, their recommendations reflected an understanding of the realities and limitations of show business. "When we have had a meeting with executives at NBC," said then chairperson Uszler in 1983, "there were five of us and five people from the network sitting around a conference table. And I don't think anyone just walking in could have picked the AGA people out from the NBC people." "I don't know if that's true," laughed AGA board member Josh Schiowitz. "We were the ones wearing ties."[15]

AGA's 1983 awards ceremony, too big for the L.A. Stage Company, moved to the larger Huntington Hartford Theater in Hollywood. Rita Moreno and Robert Preston cohosted. Stars who agreed to serve as presenters included Eileen Brennan, Ted Danson (star of the sitcom *Cheers*, which won an award that night), Alex Karras (who had played a gay bodyguard in *Victor/Victoria*), Burt Lancaster, and Lynn Redgrave. TV honorees included *Dynasty*, *Donahue*, and actor Richard Thomas for his role in the PBS *American Playhouse* presentation, *Fifth of July*. By the mid 1980s, the networks and the press treated AGA as *the* voice of gay people in show business.

In 1984, the group added the word "Lesbian" to its name, becoming the Alliance for Gay and Lesbian Artists (AGLA).[16] Some networks and producers arranged advance screenings of gay-positive shows for the group in the mid 1980s. The screenings were designed to court AGLA awards and to help AGLA generate advance press for the shows. The awards ceremonies, which always drew high-profile talent, continued until 1988. At that point, many of AGLA's leaders redirected their energy into AIDS organizations. (The group would disband formally a few years later.)[17] For AGLA, as for many gay organizations of the 1980s, the decision to go mainstream had paid off. However, it had done so at the cost of the group's original grassroots mission. In AGLA's case, the benefit may well have outweighed the cost.

THE HOLLYWOOD TOUCH

Television: 1981–1983

Now he plays the field. Asked what kind of girls he likes best, he grinned and replied, "I'm not a bit fussy, just so they're girls."
— *Newspaper interview with Rock Hudson, 1955[1]*

Television programmers spent the early 1980s trying to figure out what the 1980 election indicated about America's tastes. With an older, conservative Hollywood couple in the White House, some TV executives reasoned that the public wanted glossy, nostalgic reflections of 1950s Hollywood. First, the networks tried law-and-order dramas that reflected a clear line between good and evil, and that starred stern but fatherly Hollywood icons of the past. These shows pulled dismal Nielsens and vanished. The networks had misread the Republican landslide slightly. The public was not hungry for remakes of 1950s and 1960s TV shows starring he-men stars from that era. Instead, many viewers apparently were nostalgic for the kind of old-style Hollywood elegance, glamor, and prosperity that the Reagans symbolized.

By 1982, as that lesson sunk in, the look and feel of prime time changed radically. Gone were the brash, colorful, revealing 1970s clothes. Gone, too, were the leering, hormonal humor, the gratuitous car chases, and the electronic "wocka-wocka" music that had underscored everything from shoot-'em-ups like *SWAT* to teen-angst dramas like *James at 15*. As American fashion and politics shifted to the right, TV viewers became fascinated by the extremely wealthy. By 1983, prime-time soaps *Dallas* and *Dynasty* ruled the Nielsens, with settings that were far from the working-class urban neighborhoods of earlier hits like *All in the Family*, *Sanford and Son*, and *Chico and the Man*. Mansions, chauffeurs, stables, opulent jewelry, expensive champagne, tuxedos, and $5,000 Nolan Miller gowns replaced the 1970s sitcoms' row homes, junkyards, discount beer, worn-out trousers, and housecoats.

The growing fascination with millionaires and big business played out in weekly soap operas and soapy TV movies and miniseries about the ultrarich. The underlying philosophy of it all seemed to be "Thou *shalt* covet . . . Thou shalt covet thy neighbor's spouse, thy neighbor's oil field, thy neighbor's modeling career, thy neighbor's spouse's evil look-alike . . ." Where 1970s characters had worried about social change and gasoline rationing, the clans on *Dallas* and *Dynasty* worried about keeping control of multimillion-dollar petroleum companies. Prime time's new darlings schemed, backbit, and made each other miserable. It was fun, and millions of viewers scheduled their lives around the weekly adventures of the Ewings and Carringtons.

Dynasty differed from the 1970s issue-oriented shows in another important way. In *Dynasty*, oil baron Blake Carrington's patriarchal power is the immovable center. As Jostein Gripsrud observes in his scholarly book *The Dynasty Years*, it hardly matters that he is challenged by rival oil companies; by his idealistic, bisexual son; and by a parade of scheming foreigners, chief among them his British ex-wife, Alexis. Viewers may have enjoyed seeing these challenges, but they were secure in the knowledge that American industry and Blake's authority would prevail.[2]

In terms of gay visibility, *Dynasty* was the most influential show of the 1980s, thanks to its openly homosexual (or bisexual, depending on the year) regular, Steven Carrington. Writers Esther and Richard Shapiro understood what makes soap operas tick: basic, unresolvable conflicts that can be played out over years and years of episodes. Right from the pilot episode, they set up conflicts between Steven (Al Corley) and his conservative, antigay father, Blake (John Forsythe), who is accustomed to controlling everyone in his mansion. Steven also reflects Esther Shapiro's taste for social issues and her interest in the impact of gender-based prejudice. Esther has described herself and her husband as "liberal," albeit, in her case, "a *conservative* liberal."[3]

Early episodes establish that Steven is not just sensitive, but can also hold his own in a brawl. He gets a job on an oil rig run by his father's business rival, Matthew Blaisdel. Steven befriends Matthew's wife, Claudia (Pamela Bellwood), and she and Steven become clandestine lovers—his first sexual experience with a woman.[4] He apparently likes it: For the next six years, Steven is torn between his love of men and his love of two women—Claudia and Sammy Jo (Heather Locklear). Given the networks' general aversion to bisexuality, it is ironic that the sexual-minority character seen by the most viewers worldwide was, at least in practice, bisexual.

The producers insisted publicly that Steven was not a bisexual, but a homosexual who got involved with women. A statement from the Shapiros in early 1984 affirmed that "Steven Carrington has not gone straight. He was, is, and always will be gay." In spring 1984, coexecutive producer Aaron Spelling promised, "The gay integrity of the character will be carried out next season. Steven's gay relationship is not over by a long shot." Years after the series ended, Spelling said that Steven had been a confused homosexual who got married, then realized he was "truly gay and living a lie." Since many gay men have gotten married and then decided it was a bad idea, Spelling says, this was a legitimate story to explore. Whether he was homosexual (as the producers claim) or bisexual (as the episodes themselves suggest), the scripts often gave Steven occasion to defend his feelings for men. "Okay, I'm in love with a man," he tells his spoiled sister in an early episode, "and you're married to a man you don't love. Now you tell me something, Fallon: Which one is worse? Which one is more immoral?!" Early episodes emphasize his homosexuality, even as he explores his attraction to Claudia. Coworkers on the oil rig harass him because they perceive him as gay. Some violently assault him. A more compassionate colleague drags him to a brothel to "fix" his "problem."[5]

Steven's boyfriend Ted makes his first on-camera appearance in a February 1981 episode. Three weeks later, Fallon (Pamela Sue Martin) secretly goes to meet Ted at an airport and begs him to give up Steven. She assures Ted that the relationship would cost Steven "everything"— his father's respect, his wealth, his power. Fallon tries to convey the antigay prejudice inherent in being Blake Carrington's son: "Steven comes from a world where culls, cripples, and homosexuals are taken out behind the barn and slaughtered," she explains. Ted asks if she has ever really loved anyone—loved someone more than her own life. The answer, apparently, is no.[6] Despite Fallon's entreaties, he does see Steven and asks him to return to New York.

Ted and Steven's reunion posed a problem for scriptwriter Edward DeBlasio. In this first season, the Shapiros wrote a skeletal outline for each episode. DeBlasio was responsible for turning it into a full script. He recalls that Richard Shapiro wrote just four words about the tender scene between Steven and Ted: "Steven, Ted: Love Scene." How, DeBlasio wondered, could he write a love scene between two men that ABC would allow on the air? ABC's Standards and Practices department was *almost* comfortable with Steven's homosexuality, as long as Steven did not show physical affection for a man. According to Spelling, ABC made it clear that anything resembling a kiss was out of the question. "They didn't give us any problems," said Spelling, "as long as there was no kissing. Tony Thomopoulos was president of ABC at the time, and he had great vision. He didn't let the Broadcast Standards department interfere."[7] Still, to keep the network and sponsors happy, even minor physical affection between gay men, such as a hug, was handled gingerly and unnaturally. This was nothing new at ABC. *Soap* had faced this dilemma, which it resolved by having "gay" regular Jodie spend most of the series romantically involved with women.[8]

"So I know they can't touch," writer DeBlasio recalled in 1997. "That was a rule. You could pat him on the shoulder, but that was it: no holding hands or hands through the hair or—the kind of thing that you would want to do for two people who had been lovers and still have this attraction." For the Ted/Steven reunion, he knew he wanted a romantic, honest, sweet scene that showed Steven and Ted's genuine affection for each other. He finally hit on the idea of having them play a game they had played in college, quoting lines of love poetry to each other. If they could not cuddle, they would make love verbally, through the poems. For 1981, it was heady stuff, but their idyll was short-lived. In the next episode, buckling to family pressure, Steven breaks off his relationship with Ted. As they share an awkward good-bye embrace, Blake shows up, misreads the situation, attacks Ted, and throws him to the ground. Ted strikes his head and dies. This was one of the few things the Shapiros had planned from the beginning: they knew that the first season would end with Blake on trial for murder. The court finds Blake guilty of manslaughter, but he serves little time in jail. Thereafter, the show's writers had Steven waffle between Claudia and Sammy Jo, finally marrying the latter.[9]

Like Billy Crystal of *Soap*,[10] heterosexual actor Al Corley received some public harassment for playing a gay regular. He also drew attention from some women fans who wanted to "reform" him. What seemed to surprise Corley most were the letters from gay and bisexual men, which made up almost half of his fan mail. "I get a lot of mail from young guys who say they've never admitted it before but they have homosexual feelings," he said. "I really feel sorry for these teenagers who can't communicate with anyone but an actor." After increasingly public disagreements with Corley over his character's development, the writers had Steven vanish in spring 1982, with plans to bring him back, recast, around the middle of the 1982–83 season. In the interim, wife Sammy Jo bore Steven's son. In a late-1982 episode, word reached Blake that Steven was in Indonesia where, in December, an exploding oil rig blew his face off. After extensive plastic surgery, he looked remarkably like Jack Coleman—the actor who replaced Corley.[11]

In outlining the second season, new head writers Eileen and Robert Pollock transformed the struggling show. What had been a serious, male-focused serial about class struggle became a more stylish, playful hit that focused on strong, manipulative women in flamboyant, high-fashion outfits. More and more, *Dynasty* looked like a camp take on the lavish "women's films" of the 1940s and 1950s. "We found," Esther Shapiro said, "that the audience wasn't very interested in the oil workers' stories. But people were just fascinated by what was going on inside that castle."[12] The Pollocks, veteran daytime soap writers, came up with the idea of adding a "superbitch" villainess: the wicked, elegantly campy Alexis Carrington (Joan Collins)—Blake's first wife and the mother of Fallon and Steven. Alexis first appeared in fall 1981 as a witness against Blake in the murder trial. She quickly became the show's most famous character, whom many fans assumed had been there from the start.

When the Pollocks wrote their "Bible" for the 1982–83 season, they planned to eliminate Steven's heterosexual love interests. After the first three episodes, the always unstable Claudia was supposed to be shipped off to a sanitarium, and Sammy Jo was supposed to return for just one episode. They planned for Steven to realize that he was gay, not bisexual. They outlined a story arc in which he would get custody of his son and become an openly gay father, over objections from Blake.[13] But by the time Steven returned to *Dynasty*'s fictional Denver, the real world was in an uproar over AIDS. Alarmist news reports talked of "innocent victims" and transmission of AIDS to heterosexuals. The public developed a terror of this disease and feared the homosexuals with whom they inseparably associated it.

Dynasty's any-topic-goes atmosphere did not extend to the truly depressing. Esther Shapiro acknowledged that certain subjects were off-limits: cancer, for instance, or incest, or child molestation.[14] AIDS clearly fits in the same category, and any open treatment of homosexuality in 1983 could not help but bring AIDS into viewers' minds. *Dynasty* was escapist entertainment, and its fans did not tune in to see things that genuinely frightened them in everyday life. As AIDS-phobia fueled antigay violence and discrimination, and as some heterosexuals— including many doctors—feared even being near gay people, *Dynasty*'s writers rescued Claudia from her sanitarium and married Steven off to her.[15] Steven and Claudia were portrayed as a couple very much in love for the next two years.

Soap opera creator/producer Agnes Nixon, the reigning monarch of daytime drama, had her own theories about why gay couples almost never turned up in TV serials. The main problem, she said, was that the story inevitably would have to turn ugly:

> I don't think one can win. You can't do such a story the way you could do it in a play or a movie. It really doesn't lend itself to the soap opera form. For instance, *That Certain Summer* was a wonderful movie. But the continuation of it in the serial form would be very difficult because in this long form we should have to present people against as well as for the gay community. It just seems to me a very difficult topic to tackle. But I'm still thinking about it.[16]

A groundbreaking 1983 lesbian story arc on her *All My Children*— daytime TV's first ongoing depiction of an openly gay character— avoided depicting homophobia by having child psychologist Lynn Carson (Donna Pescow), in town for just a few months. During that time, only two locals find out she is gay. One is a troubled young mother who comes to rely on Lynn as a friend and adviser. The sensitive, well-handled story line ends at Christmas, with Lynn moving back to her hometown to reconcile with her estranged lover.[17] Popular soap opera lore states that Lynn was written out due to negative audience response. But, in fact, ABC had announced up front that Pescow would appear for just eight weeks, since she had another professional commitment to meet.[18]

While homosexuality was a tough topic to address in a series *regular* circa 1983, the same was not true for gay *guest* characters on *Dynasty*-inspired dramas about rich, glamorous heterosexuals. While gay male regulars were allowed to date women or no one at all, gay guest characters could be homosexual in practice. As Samir Hachem noted in *The Advocate*, gay TV characters were either "tentatively present or tentatively gay."[19] One place where they were tentatively present was in glossy, big-budget miniseries that focused on high fashion, high emotion, and strong women who achieve wealth and influence. Based on novels by the likes of Judith Krantz, they were invariably about a plucky, young, down-on-her-luck woman who fights her way to the top of the fashion or entertainment industry. Ultimately, she finds a handsome, strong, kind, wealthy Mr. Right (following a long relationship with Mr. Very Wrong).

Gay men are almost always trusted confidants to the leading lady. Examples include *Scruples* (1980), *Paper Dolls* (a 1982 TV movie and a 1984 series), *Bare Essence* (a 1982 miniseries, and 1983 series), and the ridiculous miniseries *Sins* (1986, overlong nonsense with Joan Collins as a French publisher whose black, gay confidant helps her stop a vengeful ex-Nazi from destroying her fashion magazine).[20] The gay men in these films are usually makeup artists, hairdressers, fashion photographers, or clothing designers. Gay characters, including cosmeticians, also turned up in the script for the 1983 Spelling/Cramer TV movie *The Making of a Male Model*. This film reversed the genders of the clichéd fashion-industry films, telling of a simple country boy's rise to the top in the world of fashion modeling. It also capitalized on the new "beefcake" trend—the media's craze for sexualizing the male body much as it had long objectified women.[21]

Lesbianism was also visible in TV's tales of wealth (though, as usual, it was less visible than male homosexuality). The stories usually linked a basically heterosexual woman with a confirmed lesbian. On *Dallas*, J. R. Ewing (Larry Hagman) was determined to break up his brother's marriage, so he faked evidence that sister-in-law Pam had a lesbian lover and was working in the sex industry: He hired an ex-prostitute, Leanne (Veronica Hamel), to renew her friendship with Pam and trick her into a compromising position. Then he had photographers take pictures of them undressing together. Hagman called it J.R.'s "most dastardly deed that year."[22]

In the high-fashion miniseries *Jacqueline Susann's "Valley of the Dolls"—1981*, French artiste Vivienne helps Jennifer, her model, get off drugs and clean up her life. Jennifer (Veronica Hamel again) is essentially straight, but an emotional bond forms between them. They begin a romantic and sexual relationship, and Jennifer moves into Vivienne's home in Paris for several months. But Jennifer becomes uncomfortable when friends start to comment on their relationship. As Jennifer looks at her face in Vivienne's paintings, she realizes that she does not look content in any of them. "I know I haven't made you happy," Vivienne concedes. "That's disappointed me, 'cause I love you. But until tonight, I thought I had at least made you capable of coping." They part on fond terms, and Jennifer returns to the United States and heterosexuality.[23] Another "plucky-girl" miniseries about the clothing industry, *Scruples*, includes gay men, a bisexual man, and the ultimate March–December lesbian couple, played by teenybopper Kim Cattrall and 1940s film icon Gene Tierney.

The glossy series *Hotel*, (coproduced, like *Dynasty*, by Aaron Spelling), presented celebrity guest stars in romantic dramas in the elegant surroundings of a luxurious San Francisco hotel. Hollywood legends Bette Davis (in the premiere) and Anne Baxter (after Davis fell ill) starred as the owner and manager. Guest stars were chosen to appeal to a variety of age groups. *Hotel* finished its first season ninth in the Nielsens, and remained in the Top 25 for years. Although it had no openly gay regular roles, *Hotel* usually included gay-themed stories once or twice per season. Of *Hotel*'s seven gay-themed scripts, two dealt with lesbians, four with gay men, and one with a straight teenager whose father mistakenly fears that the lad is gay.[24]

One of *Hotel*'s first episodes in 1983, "Faith, Hope and Charity," featured a lesbian playwright (Carol Lynley). She shares a room with her old college roommate (Barbara Parkins) the night her new play debuts in San Francisco. After both women consume much alcohol, the playwright comes out to her old friend and professes her love for her. The old roomie panics, retires to the hotel bar, and promptly beds the first sleazy stud who hits on her. When she returns to the room in the morning, repentant, she finds that her lesbian friend has just spent the night with the woman who led their aerobics class the previous day. Although neither friend was happy about having sex with someone they did not love, the playwright had enjoyed herself more. As a dramatist, she said, "I have a good imagination."

Television's imitation of all things Hollywood was a promising sign for gay content. As cable and VCRs continued to deflate the big networks' Nielsens, broadcasters desperately copied trends from the movies in a bid to win back viewers. In the fall of 1982 alone, every network had a knockoff of the summer blockbuster *Raiders of the Lost Ark*, and several shows echoed the hit movie *Time Bandits*. Adventure films were not the only Hollywood trend that year. Mainstream movies were giving unusual prominence to gender-bending roles and GLBT themes. The hit comedy *Tootsie* starred Dustin Hoffman as an out-of-work actor who dons a dress and becomes a popular actress. In part, *Tootsie*'s message was that love is not limited by such things as gender. The Robin Williams comedy/drama *The World According to Garp*—twenty-first in box-office receipts that year—featured a fine, multilayered performance by John Lithgow as a male-to-female transsexual, Roberta Muldoon. Only slightly behind *Garp* in profits was *Victor/Victoria*, a musical whose leading lady (Julie Andrews) masquerades as a female impersonator. ("A woman pretending to be a man pretending to be a woman?!") The film's male lead is a charming, not-too-stereotypical gay man (Robert Preston) who "gets the boy" at the end. By midyear, some cinemas were showing out-and-out gay and lesbian love stories, including *Making Love* and *Personal Best*. These were not blockbusters, but they did attract significant mass-media attention. ("Tonight on *20/20*: Hollywood comes out of the closet with different kinds of love stories . . .")[25]

Television's penchant for imitation kicked in on cue. Representatives from Aaron Spelling Productions met with network executives about several TV movie scripts—written by successful, acclaimed writers—about young men who were coming out to their families. Marstar Productions sold ABC-TV on a telefilm based on the coming-out novel *Consenting Adult*, by Laura Z. Hobson. HBO cable announced plans for a weekly series based on Armistead Maupin's GLBT-inclusive novel, *Tales of the City*. Gay viewers seemed to have reason for optimism. That optimism, however, was premature.

BACKLASH

Television: 1982–1985

I don't think AIDS is the reason for an antigay backlash. I think it's the excuse. These are not new bigots. These are old bigots who feel a new permission to be more vocal because of AIDS.
                                                                 —*Vito Russo, 1990[1]*

"Faggots aren't allowed to look at my ass while I'm onstage," says Eddie Murphy, maneuvering his leather-clad backside to be visible to as few members of the huge studio audience as possible. The audience cheers wildly. It is 1983, and the twenty-two-year-old comedian from *Saturday Night Live* is starring in his first stand-up comedy special, *Delirious,* on HBO cable. Soon, Murphy will incorporate a broadly played, high-strung, swishy, gay hairdresser character into his repertoire on *Saturday Night Live*, but it will be tame compared to the blatant gay-baiting of *Delirious*. "I'm afraid of gay people," he tells his HBO audience. "Petrified. I have nightmares about gay people." Why? "That new AIDS shit . . . It petrifies me 'cause girls be hanging out with them. And one night they could be in the club having fun with their gay friend and give 'em a little kiss and go home with AIDS on their lips." The studio audience whoops, laughs, and applauds.[2] It is laughter of recognition—recognition of a fear that was more epidemic in 1983 than the medical condition that triggered it. It was fear of a "controversial new disease" as one TV listing called it, an ailment that seemed 100 percent fatal and whose agent of transmission doctors had yet to identify. HBO's famous lack of censorship cut both ways: here it gave a public forum to the sort of panicked AIDS/fag jokes that had been making the rounds for months in bars, frat houses, office cafeterias, schoolyards, and private homes.

By May 1983, much of the public found it impossible to distinguish the word "AIDS" from the word "gay." The fear of AIDS turned into a widespread, absolute terror of gay people. Over the previous year, the emaciated figures of "AIDS victims" (as they were then called) were a familiar sight on evening newscasts. Many viewers watched these reports with the same detachment they usually reserved for documentaries about starving orphans in faraway lands. That detachment turned to fear as reports of babies with AIDS and other "innocent victims" rolled in. The fear increased exponentially with each new indication that AIDS was spreading beyond gay men and users of illegal intravenous drugs. The fear increased in April 1983 when the *CBS Evening News* reported that people receiving blood transfusions were at risk for AIDS. It increased in May when several networks reported that AIDS had reached epidemic proportions in New York. And, in particular, it zoomed in May and June amid numerous reports about transmission of the disease through heterosexual sex—a topic which seemed to suddenly make the syndrome more newsworthy. No one knew exactly how this illness was transmitted, and so imaginations ran wild. From May to August 1983, the public terror of AIDS and fear of being near gay people were the subject of many national telecasts.[3] Pat Buchanan summarized and propagated that fear in his May 24 newspaper column: He called homosexuals "a community that is a common carrier of dangerous, communicable ... diseases," and described AIDS as "nature's revenge." "The poor homosexuals," Buchanan wrote, "they have declared war on nature and nature is exacting an awful retribution."[4]

News and talk shows documented AIDS-phobia in many forms that summer. They told of doctors, social workers, and others in the helping professions who routinely turned away clients who had AIDS. Some doctors refused to help anyone they suspected of homosexuality. Average people heard the stories and wondered if these doctors, who seemed petrified of contagion, knew more than they were telling. Some gay community leaders admitted that even *they* no longer shook hands with gay acquaintances or shared others' drinking glasses.[5] It was at the height of this panic that HBO taped its Eddie Murphy special, which may explain, though not excuse, the monolog and his audience's enthusiasm for it.

On most fronts, television had recovered from the imagined threat of conservative boycotts. TV scripts about promiscuity and violence returned, but gay characters made no such comeback. Several TV writers and producers interviewed for this book theorized that AIDS scared the networks and sponsors away from stories about gays. "It's a commercial entertainment industry," one said (asking that his name not be used), adding that viewers do not want to be reminded of a spreading, deadly plague that "scares the hell out of them" daily. Ed DeBlasio, who cowrote many dozens of *Dynasty* scripts, says he assumed that concern over AIDS was one reason why the producers had Steven Carrington go straight. As critic Frank Rich noted, that character's year-to-year plot fluctuations "became the first reliable index of how much homogenized homosexuality was acceptable to a large public, and what was still off-limits." AIDS played a role: Steven was involved with women during major public panics over AIDS (in 1983 after the first reports of infected heterosexuals, and in late 1985 following the announcement of Rock Hudson's illness) and Steven dated men during calmer periods (1981, early 1985, 1986–87). "AIDS scared a world," DeBlasio said. "Why wouldn't it scare a show?"[6] Similar concerns put the brakes on HBO's planned *Tales of the City* series.

In summer 1982, at the height of press coverage about Hollywood's gay love stories, Home Box Office cable had announced plans to start producing original comedies and dramas. Until then, HBO had attracted subscribers primarily by running recent Hollywood movies—uncut, uncensored, and uninterrupted by commercials. Hoping to create the first major cable sitcom, HBO bought video rights to the first two *Tales of the City* novels: witty, colorful, episodic stories about the eccentric residents of a boardinghouse on San Francisco's Russian Hill. The tenants—a mix of straights, gays, and bisexuals—are watched over by landlady Anna Madrigal, a motherly, middle-aged transsexual who doles out marijuana joints as if they were cookies. It was perfect material for a weekly cable sitcom, making full use of HBO's biggest draw: a level of creative freedom and sexual frankness that broadcast sponsors and censors forbade.

Tales of the City began preproduction in the fall of 1982 for a proposed 1983 debut. Richard Kramer wrote a pilot script, which he described as a *"Mary Tyler Moore* for the '80s: Here were these stories of this simple, Midwestern girl, Mary Ann Singleton, and her wacky misadventures in this crazy city." But like *Dynasty*'s proposed gay story line, HBO's *Tales* fell victim to the AIDS epidemic and changing social values. Reportedly, scripting problems were the main snag. HBO had planned to set the series in the present, but the novels' nonjudgmental celebration of promiscuity and homosexuality, and their casual attitude toward marijuana, seemed out of place in the 1980s. Taming the stories would have gone against HBO's carefully cultivated reputation for uncensored content, and would have destroyed the very values that made the books appealing to begin with. The other option, filming the stories as a period comedy, would not work either. Maupin's first two novels took place circa 1977; as a general rule, new TV series are set in the present or at least fifteen years in the past. No one wants to see a period piece set five years ago. After several abortive attempts to update the stories, plans for a video *Tales of the City* went on a ten-year hiatus.[7]

The link between AIDS and the hot-button issue of homosexuality meant that few social institutions and few individuals could treat the syndrome on its merits as a medical crisis. Some saw it as an uncomfortable topic to be avoided, some saw it as divine punishment, and some as a political tool to use against the gay civil rights movement. Sooner or later, anything that controversial was sure to become fodder for TV scripts, but it would take years and extremely cautious handling.

The prospect of AIDS dramas was a public relations nightmare for the networks, placing them in a no-win situation with both gay and antigay activists. If the networks were to depict representative AIDS stories—predominantly among gay and bisexual male characters—right-wingers would accuse them of trying to win sympathy for homosexuals, while the gay community would accuse the networks of promoting homophobia by reinforcing the idea that "gay = AIDS" and "AIDS = gay." If shows focused primarily on straight characters, gay activists would accuse them of denying the real struggles of the gay community, while antigay groups (along with gays) would accuse television of creating a false view of AIDS. Instead, the networks chose to deal with AIDS exclusively in news and discussion shows. They got angry letters anyway, accusing them of shirking a responsibility to raise public consciousness through prime-time scripts.

NBC had a reputation in the early 1980s for gritty, issue-oriented programming. This network had an AIDS-drama TV movie in development as early as summer 1983. Various delays put it through more than a dozen rewrites, several sets of writers and directors, and tight scrutiny by physicians and network censors. It eventually aired more than two years later under the title *An Early Frost*. In the meantime, NBC's acclaimed but (as yet) low-rated medical drama *St. Elsewhere* was developing a script called "AIDS and Comfort." It depicted a popular city councilman—a married man with a young son—who is diagnosed with AIDS. This sensitive story dramatizes many of the real-life situations that AIDS brought about: A gay or bisexual man who must simultaneously tell his family about his illness and his sexual orientation; the symptoms of AIDS; doctors and other hospital staff who refuse to go near the case; a shortage of blood products because people irrationally fear that *giving* blood puts them at risk; and vandalism and graffiti motivated by fear of AIDS. The story aired that December as a Christmas episode. Two and half years after CNN's first 1981 news report about Kaposi's sarcoma, TV finally had a first prime-time drama about a gay or bisexual man with AIDS.[8] The next gay-themed AIDS dramas would not air until late 1985 on the cable sitcom *Brothers* and CBS's *Trapper John, M.D.*

The 1983–84 season generally avoided contemporary stories about young, sexually active gay or bisexual men. But gay characters were still of interest as a means to prove a show's topicality. In fact, AIDS made homosexuality more topical than ever. Indirectly, the epidemic brought about a diversification of queer characters on TV. For one thing, lesbian characters showed up more often. The lesbian story on *All My Children* from October to December 1983 was originally supposed to be about a gay man. The official reason for the change was that the writers hoped to break new ground, and *Dynasty* had already "done" gay men.[9] This explanation is entirely plausible, but the timing of the change raises questions: The character became a lesbian just after news broke about contaminated blood supplies.

There were still a few contexts where stories about gay men were acceptable. For example, some shows aired stories about gay men, but set in a period before AIDS and before the Sexual Revolution. In the 1984 miniseries, *Celebrity*, Joseph Bottoms plays a closeted, Rock Hudson–type athlete-turned-Hollywood-idol. He is eventually murdered by an old friend, a homophobic religious fanatic with a messianic complex. Bottoms's character is sexually active, but *Celebrity* is safely set in the 1950s and 1960s.[10]

Contemporary gay characters would eventually peek their heads back into prime time in the mid 1980s, with the advent of a comparatively new genre: semiserialized dramas with large, diverse, ensemble casts, and a taste for controversy.

THE COPS

Television: 1981–1984

The ideal piece of programming for selling things, I suppose, lulls you into a pleasant sense of well-being, and that's what some of the most successful people in this business have done. There's nothing wrong with that, but they're entrepreneurs, not artists. That's not what I want to do.

—*Steven Bochco, cocreator of* Hill Street Blues, *1986[1]*

While ABC and CBS played safe with formula shows, canceling anything that did not grab high Nielsens quickly, NBC was taking chances and innovating. NBC had little choice. Ratings were low, money was tight, and the network had few backup shows waiting in the wings. In an era when most ABC and CBS shows had six or thirteen weeks to sink or swim, NBC president Grant Tinker and head programmer Brandon Tartikoff nurtured well-written, high-quality, topical shows. Tinker's predecessor and Tartikoff's former boss, Fred Silverman, had started the trend in 1981 when he renewed the low-rated *Hill Street Blues*. Innovative shows can take time to develop a following, so Tinker and Tartikoff kept renewing series like *Hill Street Blues*, *Cheers*, *St. Elsewhere*, and *Family Ties* year after year, trying them in different time slots until they found an audience. As they renewed the shows, the network ordered subtle changes: NBC required the serialized *Hill Street* to wrap up at least one plotline per week; ordered MTM Productions to repaint the run-down hospital on *St. Elsewhere* in brighter colors and required them to boost the patients' survival rate.[2]

Hill Street Blues broke new ground and set the standard for shows to come—not just 1980s shows like *Cagney & Lacey*, *St. Elsewhere*, and *L.A. Law*, but also their 1990s descendants such as *E.R.* and *NYPD Blue*. *Hill Street* had an almost documentary feel, created by using handheld movie cameras, complex ambient sound patterns, and a huge ensemble cast that floated in and out of story lines. It brought a cinematic feel to TV. In these tales, Good did not always triumph over Evil. In fact, the line between Good and Evil was often blurry. *Hill Street Blues* pushed boundaries not just in form, but also in content, by increasing prime time's level of sex and violence.

Hill Street debuted in January 1981 to critical acclaim and dismal Nielsens. In September, this series that almost no one had seen won four Emmys, including awards for acting, writing, and Outstanding Drama Series. Thereafter, it developed a following. In November, it aired the first of over a dozen episodes that would focus on sexual-minority characters. Over the years, *Hill Street* would present gay heroes including, in 1986 and 1987, Kate McBride, a recurring lesbian cop played by Lindsay Crouse. It also presented less-heroic characters such as the cowardly gay informant, Eddie Gregg, played by Charles Levin from 1982 to 1986. Eddie was a well-meaning, drug-addicted prostitute. Tough cop Mick Belker's ongoing friendship with Eddie was apparently there to humanize the Belker character.

Meanwhile, at CBS, another group of groundbreakers introduced television's first buddy drama about two policewomen, *Cagney & Lacey*. Writers Barbara Hammer Avedon and Barbara Corday had been pitching this feminist cop story in various formats since 1974, when they envisioned it as a gender reversal satire for theatrical release. In the late 1970s and early 1980s, they and producer Barney Rosenzweig pitched the idea to all three networks. By the time the characters made it to CBS in a TV movie starring Tyne Daly and Loretta Swit, the story was a thought-provoking crime drama. This was an unusual film for commercial TV, focusing on a close, supportive friendship between two working women who were tough, capable, undercover officers—neither sex objects nor damsels in distress. The organized feminist movement generated advance publicity for the film through magazines like *Ms.* The TV movie drew strong ratings when it aired in October 1981.

In late 1981 and early 1982, feminism enjoyed a resurgence as a topical subject as the Equal Rights Amendment neared its final vote in Congress. In fall 1981, CBS ordered six episodes of *Cagney & Lacey*. Since Swit was still committed to *M*A*S*H*, the producers hired Meg Foster to costar with Daly in the series, set to debut in spring 1982. At the same time, ABC bought a weekly sitcom based on the feminist hit movie comedy, *9 to 5*, also for spring 1982.

From the start, the producers of *Cagney & Lacey* faced conflicts with CBS over the show's tone and image. Queer-baiting played a role in those conflicts for four reasons. First, films and shows about same-sex buddy duos have always inspired queer jokes and gay subtextual readings, from *Butch Cassidy and the Sundance Kid* to *Batman* and *The Odd Couple*; from *Young and Gay* to *The Lucy Show*; from *Starsky and Hutch* to *Sesame Street*'s Ernie and Bert. Second, at least one CBS casting executive objected to hiring Foster, whom he believed was a lesbian, a troublemaker, and not talented enough to carry a series. Third, feminists and women who do not devote their lives to turning men's heads have long been "accused" of lesbianism—a ploy intended to keep would-be feminists in line. And finally, in interviews around the debut of *Cagney & Lacey*, Foster said that the best film role of her career was that of a lesbian who marries a gay man in 1978's *A Different Story*. It was just a matter of time before the word "dykes" echoed through CBS's corridors of power.

In one of television's all-time worst scheduling moves, CBS and ABC scheduled the only two feminist shows on the air—*Cagney & Lacey* and *9 to 5*—opposite each other on Thursdays, splitting their target audience and guaranteeing both shows poor Nielsens. Some fans presumed deliberate bad faith: This way, the theory went, the men who ran the networks could say they had tried feminist shows and there was no audience for them. In late April, CBS moved *Cagney & Lacey* to Sundays, where it delivered a whopping 34 share—more than one-third of all available viewers in its time slot. As the ERA vote deadline neared, CBS said it would renew *Cagney & Lacey* only if Rosenzweig fired Meg Foster and if the writers reconceived Chris Cagney as feminine, dressy, rich, and less overtly feminist. Harvey Shephard, CBS's West Coast senior vice president for programming, said that audience research indicated that "the characterizations of both Cagney and Lacey were too tough and there was not enough contrast between these two partners." *TV Guide* quoted another CBS manager (reportedly the casting executive who had objected to hiring Foster) as saying, "These women on *Cagney & Lacey* seemed more intent on fighting the system than doing police work. We perceived them as dykes."[3]

After the ERA died in Congress that summer, both networks muzzled their shows' feminism. Some people interpreted the failure of the ERA as proof that feminists lacked broad-based public support. When *Cagney & Lacey* and *9 to 5* returned in the fall of 1982, they portrayed male chauvinism as a personal defect that afflicted certain individual men—much as television usually portrays homophobia as a personal prejudice rather than an institutionalized problem. Despite the show's makeover (and a boosted wardrobe budget for the new Cagney, Sharon Gless), *Cagney & Lacey* remained gritty and still tackled issues that made network executives squirm.

Like *The Odd Couple* before it, *Cagney & Lacey*'s "image problem" meant that gay-themed scripts would be difficult to get past the network, especially in the early years when the show's survival was far from secure. This was not NBC: CBS had little patience with low-rated shows, no matter how much the critics praised them. In 1982, the writers managed to get approval for a script about a straight cop who suffers homophobic discrimination. His colleagues mistakenly think he is gay after a nude photo of him appears in a gay porn magazine.[4] (In later years, *Cagney & Lacey* would acknowledge that Cagney's brother is gay, and would occasionally portray a gay male neighbor of one of the leads.)

When most other TV shows were backing away from gay male content, NBC's *Hill Street Blues* confronted homophobic violence and workplace discrimination head-on. It launched the fall 1983 season with a drama about a massacre in a gay bar near the station house. Like the gay-cop episode of *Trapper John, M.D.*, it portrays the gay community as politically active and vocal: Activists are pressuring Captain Furillo (Daniel J. Travanti) to find out who is responsible for this and other recent antigay violence. But there is little Furillo can do. The only surviving witness, an off-duty officer who was in the bar at the time, refuses to testify because it would mean coming out.[5]

"PRIME TIME COMES TO TERMS WITH GAY ROLES"[1]

Television: 1984–1985

> How do the networks fight back against cable? We can't do it by putting on more sex and violence, but we can probe the social issues that haven't been explored.
>
> —*Perry Lafferty, an NBC senior vice president (and, later that year, producer of* An Early Frost*), 1985*[2]

The 1984–1985 season was a turning point for network television. It was the year when NBC's Thursday lineup (*Cosby, Family Ties, Cheers, Night Court*, and *Hill Street Blues*) became a national institution, pulling NBC out of the Nielsen basement in which it had skulked for nine years. It was the year when situation comedies began a comeback after critics had written them off as a dying format.[3] It was the year when issue-oriented TV movies and original miniseries became big business. And it was the year when gay characters made an abrupt, unmistakable return to prime time. Each of these changes was tied, directly or indirectly, to the competition between pay-TV and the Big Three networks.

The "custody battle" for viewers between cable and broadcast TV intensified as both media prepared for the 1984–85 season. Broadcast networks were busy courting the profitable eighteen- to-thirty-nine-year-old market. In the 1960s and 1970s, there had been no easy way for sponsors to buy that young audience in a concentrated dose. But in 1983, advertisers realized that the new cable music network, MTV, was attracting young viewers in large numbers. Hollywood movies had already jumped on the MTV bandwagon with pop/musical films like *Flashdance* and *Footloose*. For the 1984–85 season, the broadcast networks incorporated MTV-style rock videos into several series, including a cop drama (*Miami Vice*) and a sitcom about a rock band (*Dreams*). ABC also used hit songs from MTV as background music in a soap opera about teenage fashion models (*Paper Dolls*). ABC hoped to lure the cable station's young viewers back to broadcast fare. NBC's *The A Team* even built an episode ("Cowboy George") around openly gay MTV icon Boy George.

Cable's stock-in-trade was sex, violence, and controversy. What the networks could sell to compete was the 1980s itself: topical shows about hippies who had yuppie, Reaganite children (*Family Ties*); serials about understaffed police precincts and underfunded hospitals, reeling from recent budget cuts (*Hill Street Blues*, *St. Elsewhere*); a sitcom that belatedly reflected America's black middle class (*Cosby*); shows that reflected the increased integration of gay people into society; shows about the social and sexual politics of the Reagan years; and dramas that reflected the latest medical concerns, such as breast cancer and AIDS. NBC's Tartikoff said the trick was to push the envelope just enough to attract viewers, but not far enough to scare off sponsors.[4]

As always, sexual minorities were a handy way to prove how contemporary and cutting edge a show was. The return of gay characters was sudden: There had been no prime-time series with gay characters recurring during the 1983–84 season. Even *Dynasty*'s Steven had apparently "gone straight." By contrast, the 1984–85 season had five series with regular or recurring gay or bisexual male roles. Two of the shows were on Showtime cable, two on ABC, and one on NBC. In addition, NBC had funded and aired a pilot for a family sitcom, *All Together Now,* whose leads included a twentysomething male couple. NBC also had approved plans for a regular character on *St. Elsewhere* to have a lesbian relationship that fall. But just depicting GLBT characters was not enough anymore; that had been done. To seem novel, the new characters had to be more diverse in gender, age, and race, or had to serve a different function within the script than previous gay characters had. "I think the country has grown up some," said sitcom writer Susan Harris in 1985. She noted that in 1977, "In certain cities, *Soap* couldn't be shown before 11:30 at night. Now it's being shown in syndication at 5:30 and 7:30 in the evening and nobody cares. So things have changed."[5]

Not only did the quantity of GLBT characters on TV jump during the 1984–1985 season, but the characters turned up in the most unlikely of series (a gay couple on *The Love Boat*?), and sometimes were even at the center of a story. In an interview with *USA Today*, Newt Deiter praised the new shows. He said that until 1984, "basically what you've seen on TV has been reactive characterizations: someone reacts to the fact that a person is gay or lesbian. This is the first year you will see interactive characterizations, where we're not a problem, but are whole people."[6] It was also the first season in which some heterosexual characters, for various reasons, found it in their best interest to be perceived as gay. Of course, *Three's Company* had done this before, but these 1980s scripts used this plot device to make a social point. These plots reversed the standard coming-out formula by showing heterosexuals how hard it would be to hide *their* sexual orientation. Such shows point out that sexuality is not just something one can "leave in the bedroom."

The three main areas to consider in examining the 1984–85 TV season are: the advent of made-for-cable sitcoms in the fall of 1984, all of which included gay content; gay guest characters on the broadcast networks; and broadcast series that included gay regulars and recurring characters.

CABLE SITCOMS

By late 1983, the premium cable channel Showtime was well into the business of producing original series, from sketch comedies (*Bizarre,* 1980–85) to children's fare (*Faerie Tale Theater,* 1982–87), to literate drama (*The Paper Chase,* 1983–86). In 1983, Showtime's head of programming, Peter Chernin, went looking for weekly sitcoms. The network's senior management hoped that original comedies would distinguish Showtime from other premium channels (which mostly ran theatrically released movies) and attract more subscribers. Cable subscriptions were still expanding in 1983, but the growth rate had slowed. To draw more viewers away from broadcast TV, the first pay-TV sitcoms would have to be funny and, most important, include content that broadcast TV could not touch. One sitcom that Showtime bought was *Steambath*, based on a controversial stage play that had already been seen on television in 1973 on PBS's *Hollywood Television Theater*. Both the play and the series portrayed God as a lewd, hard-cussing Puerto Rican janitor (played by José Perez on both PBS and Showtime) who held court for the newly dead in a steambath, an antechamber to the Next World. Regulars include two gay chorus boys—supporting characters who serve as comic relief, singing Broadway tunes to punctuate the action. (In the premiere, the couple sings "I've Got Rhythm," punching the lyric, "I've got my man, who could ask for anything more?") *Steambath* debuted in August 1984 for a brief, undistinguished run.[7]

Showtime's most successful original, prime-time show was the previously mentioned sitcom *Brothers*, which ABC had recently rejected. This was the first TV series with an openly gay protagonist (the closeted *Love, Sidney* notwithstanding), and the first show to include two gay leading characters: twentysomething boy-next-door Cliff (Paul Regina) and his strong-queen best friend Donald (Philip Charles MacKenzie, playing the show's most capable, "together" character). *Brothers* ran from 1984 to 1989, through one hundred fifteen episodes. For a production team used to dodging network censors, cable was a pleasant change of pace. In 1997, *Brothers* producer Gary Nardino—the former head of Paramount TV—recalled:

> [Showtime was] considerably more liberal in every aspect of creativity and show production than was our experience in the years past at networks. I can't remember them giving us any of that kind of bluenose attitude at all. When we decided we had to have our gay brother character kiss someone who was attracted to him, we had no trouble with that; we did that. We had him involved with people from time to time. And we had an *outrageously* gay character, Donald . . .[8]
>
> Within a year of its 1984 debut, *Brothers* was Showtime's most highly rated regular offering.

HBO's quest for an original sitcom was finally fulfilled with the December 1984 premiere of *1st and Ten*, a bawdy series about a woman (Delta Burke) who owns a professional football team. In the premiere, she gets the team in a divorce settlement after her husband runs off with one of his players. The series ran into the 1990s, though gay content did not appear regularly.

Because of their "controversial" cable sensibilities, both *Brothers* and *1st and Ten* have proven almost impossible to resell in syndication, though *Brothers* has been seen in reruns in Philadelphia (where it takes place), Las Vegas, and several foreign countries.

GUEST CHARACTERS ON BROADCAST TV

On the broadcast networks that season, old-fashioned coming-out episodes turned up on series where no one would have expected any gay content at all. A prime example was the "Frat Brothers Forever" story on *The Love Boat* in October 1984. This heterosexist series had flirted with gay content once before in 1980: In "Strange Honeymoon," a man (Al Corley, pre-*Dynasty*) jilts his bride and shares his intended honeymoon cruise with his brother. The running joke is that everyone on board thinks they are a gay couple.[9] But by 1984, tastes had changed. The exotic fantasy/escape genre was on the rocks, supplanted by more reality-based shows. In the gay-themed episode, a long-term male couple tries to enjoy a much-deserved vacation. The older partner, Buzz (Roy Thinnes) recognizes the ship's doctor (Bernie Koppell) as an old fraternity buddy from college. To avoid risking Doc's rejection, the gay couple awkwardly stay in the closet, posing as cousins. Doc and Buzz make fools of themselves partying and chasing women as they did when they were twenty, each trying to impress the other with his stamina. The show hits all the "right" political points about why life in the closet is unhealthy. Thinnes plays the coming-out scene with a bit more shame than the script seems to call for, making Doc's non-rejection seem more magnanimous than it probably should. But that *The Love Boat* hosted a same-sex couple at all was amazing.[10]

The 1984–85 season offered more women protagonists than TV presented in 1982 and 1983. Following a massive letter-writing campaign from fans, CBS brought back *Cagney & Lacey* in March 1984 and renewed it for the fall 1984 season. Other 1984–85 shows about women included newcomers *Jessica*, *Kate and Allie*, *Murder, She Wrote*, *Paper Dolls*, and *Partners in Crime*. All were mainstream, commercial shows, a few of them sexually exploitative. The sitcom *Kate and Allie* was impressive, not just because it was a well-made comedy, but also for portraying two straight single mothers who had set up a household and considered themselves a family. Commercial television had seldom portrayed two divorced women who were surviving on their own. On previous shows of this sort, such as *The Lucy Show*, the women had been zany widows who needed copious male advice to survive.

Kate and Allie (Susan Saint James and Jane Curtin) share an apartment in New York's Greenwich Village, though somehow they almost never see gay people there. An early episode, which the show's writers have cited as one of their favorites, involves their landlady—a fiftyish lesbian—and her lover of eight years. "No *that's* not the breakthrough," reported *TV Guide*'s "Grapevine" column. "Turns out that the landlady's lover is (gulp) a grandmother!" The point of the episode was: what makes a family? Initially, when the landlady learns that "two families" are living in the one-family apartment, she doubles the rent. Out of desperation, Kate and Allie tell her they are a gay couple. Allie hates this approach ("I refuse to live *Three's Company!*"), but affordable apartments are scarce in Manhattan. After they lie to the landlady, she comes out to them and introduces her lover. The older couple takes Kate and Allie under their wing, trying to help them through the coming-out process and offering to introduce them around the community. The series' leads feel guilty deceiving their new friends, but they cannot afford to come out as straight. The script turns around situations that many closeted gay people face every day to avoid losing a job or a home: Kate and Allie have to concoct lie after lie, avoid talking about boyfriends and ex-spouses, and remember what lies they have already told. After several wacky attempts to conceal their heterosexuality, they are accidentally outed when the landlady overhears a conversation between them. The episode ends with the two pairs agreeing that a family is defined by love alone. Kate and Allie's friendship with the lesbian couple, now grounded in honesty, seems strong, and they all go off to a dance at the Lesbian & Gay Community Services Center.[11] Although the script seems to set up the lesbian couple as possible recurring characters, they never appear again during the remaining four years of the series.

Guest shot coming-out tales that season included a November 1984 episode of *Hotel*, in which a woman learns that her husband, a sports-caster, is gay. A month later, the sitcom *Night Court* had its resident sexist jerk, Dan (John Larroquette), get stuck in an elevator for several hours with a gay man (Jack Riley). True to the genre, Dan grudgingly learns to respect the man, who turns out to be just as callous and money-grubbing as Dan. On the adventure series *Hot Pursuit*, the leads (a married fugitive couple) befriend another straight couple who are guest characters. The wife in the second couple falls in love with the show's leading lady.[12]

In November 1984, *St. Elsewhere* began a story arc involving a les-bian guest character, Dr. Chris Holt (Caroline McWilliams). A visiting leukemia specialist, she becomes fast friends with series regular Dr. Annie Cavanero (Cynthia Sikes). The original plan was for the two to become romantically involved for several episodes. The scripts were supposed to explore what happens when Cavanero, who has always been attracted to men, falls for a woman. It might have been the sort of new, interesting story line that NBC was trying to cultivate that year. But actress Sikes, not anxious to act in that subplot, reportedly talked the producers out of it. Instead, the story became a good but conven-tional friend-comes-out-then-vanishes plot.[13]

Several TV movies and specials depicted same-sex couples that season. In November, the trashy CBS miniseries *Ellis Island* showed a love affair between spoiled teenager Vanessa Ogden (Kate Burton) and an eccentric art dealer, Una Marbury (Cherie Lunghi). It was one of few commercial shows pre-1990 to depict homosexuality in a historic context: This plot was set in Greenwich Village circa 1913. Vanessa's stepmother (Faye Dunaway) offers Una $15,000 to sign a contract promising never to see the girl again. Una delivers a passionate monolog about the love the two women share—"a love that surpasses understanding." The stepmother ups the ante to $20,000. Una answers, "I'll get my pen."[14]

The most groundbreaking gay-themed TV movie of the season aired in February 1985: ABC's *Consenting Adult*. Based on Laura Z. Hobson's 1975 novel, it stars Marlo Thomas and Martin Sheen as dis-traught, suburban parents who have trouble accepting that their twenty-year-old son, Jeff (Barry Tubb), is gay. In every other way, Jeff is the perfect son: polite, a college scholar, a champion athlete. The mother, Tess, hopes for a medical cure. The father, Ken, wounded to the core by Jeff's revelation, tells Tess, "If it's true, it'll stay true." Ken struggles with health problems throughout the film, and dies without ever reconciling with his son face-to-face. Instead, he leaves behind a note saying that he loves Jeff and is proud of him. Tess finally realizes that if she wants to be part of her son's life, she should start soon, since no one knows how long their life will be. In the final scene, she phones Jeff and invites him to bring his lover, Stuart, home for Christmas.

Ray Aghayan had bought the screen rights to *Consenting Adult* as soon as the book came out. In the late 1970s and early 1980s, with help from others, he tried unsuccessfully to sell it as a theatrical film, then as a TV movie. Especially in the early 1980s, gay TV movies were hard to sell. In 1983, when that chill ended, Eileen Burk of ABC's movie division snapped up the project. ABC had previously rejected *Consenting Adult* at least twice. "I think times are a little different," Aghayan said in 1985, "and there were different people at ABC."[15]

The film is a bit safe. Like the book, it is clearly the mother's story, not the gay son's. The family fits TV's "ideal" archetype: white, suburban, and upper-middle class. But in some ways *Consenting Adult* broke new ground. That Jeff has a boyfriend whom he actually *touches* is a breakthrough all by itself. Opinions varied as to which aspect of the film was most innovative. The *St. Paul Pioneer Press* said that what distinguished *Consenting Adult* was that in previous TV shows, "gay characters rarely have seemed like people you were likely to know personally or care about." One reporter said it was provocative of ABC to show a scene where Jeff is clearly about to have his first sexual experience with a man. But Marlo Thomas, who played Tess, offered a different take:

> [We already know] that homosexuals have sex. What we don't accept is that they have love. A much more . . . daring scene is when Jeff tells his mother how he feels about his love for a man. Or when Jeff and his lover express tenderness toward each other. Those . . . are the most groundbreaking scenes.[16]

ABC scheduled *Consenting Adult* during February sweeps, a sign of confidence in the film's ratings potential. The network generated publicity by sending out hundreds of press kits and arranging media interviews with Marlo Thomas and Martin Sheen. Many of the write-ups got the title wrong, pluralizing and sexualizing it as *Consenting Adults*, an error that also occurs in more recent articles that mention this film. The show drew strong Nielsens, opening the door for other gay-positive projects. Reviews were generally good, though the *Charlotte Observer* thought the project was too generic and familiar to be groundbreaking. "What if the same plot had been set in a ghetto," asked staff writer Lawrence Toppman, "where homosexuality might be punished with beatings rather than ostracism? What if these blandly comfortable WASPs had been replaced by blacks or Hispanics or Orientals . . . ?" Why, in short, were almost all gay characters on TV middle-class to wealthy white men, many of whom lived in "houses with pillared porticos and circular driveways"?[17]

Issue-oriented TV movies drew strong ratings in the mid 1980s, and some sponsors actually started clamoring to be associated with controversial films. So the networks went overboard buying the rights to potentially incendiary books and plays. In mid 1985, ABC Circle Films (who produced *Consenting Adult*) optioned the book *Lesbian Nuns: Breaking the Silence*, a collection of autobiographical essays published by Naiad Press.[18] It was one of Naiad's most popular nonfiction titles, and was the subject of many talk-show discussions over the years. However, a prime-time dramatization of it surely would have generated intense hostility from traditional Catholics and other religious groups. Even in the mid 1980s, it is doubtful that it could have found sponsors. It was never filmed.

THE REGULARS

In April, *TV Guide* previewed the 1984–85 season's roster of gay male characters. GAY CHARACTERS ALMOST ROUTINE predicted the headline. A month later, *USA Today* and other periodicals ran similar articles. Readers learned that in the upcoming season, the writers of *Dynasty* would "revert" Steven to homosexuality, that Showtime had picked up *Brothers*, and that two proposed new sitcoms—*All Together Now* and *Dreams*—would have recurring gay characters.[19] That fall, *Brothers* broke new ground left and right, but it did so on premium cable where comparatively few viewers would notice. Despite the optimistic newspaper articles, TV's gay regulars were still nowhere in sight that fall: *Dynasty*'s Steven seemed committed to saving his heterosexual marriage; NBC never picked up *All Together Now*; and no gay regulars were prominent in CBS's short-lived *Dreams*.

But the winter and spring of 1985 were another story. In January, a few weeks before ABC's *Consenting Adult*, NBC debuted the series *Sara*. This ensemble sitcom from the producers of *Family Ties* was set in a yuppie San Francisco law firm. Bronson Pinchot played the gay regular, lawyer Dennis Kemper, a full-fledged member of the ensemble. Starting in April, ABC ran *Hail to the Chief*, a serialized sitcom from the producers of *Soap*. It starred Patty Duke as the first woman president of the United States, with Joel Brooks as her longtime friend and bodyguard, a gay man named Randy. And on *Dynasty*, Steven had a new beau, Luke.

Sara starred an impressive cast of relative unknowns, including Geena Davis, Alfre Woodard, Bronson Pinchot, and Bill Maher. Pinchot's Dennis is a well-dressed, likable, slightly high-strung guy, part of a firm of struggling young attorneys. He is a bit of a stereotype, easily distracted from urgent matters by the sight of attractive clothing or interesting lighting. But he is a caring person, always willing to go out of his way for a friend. In his day, he was also a rarity: a gay male regular who was actually attracted to men, and was never seen dating women. His homosexuality is referred to often. (In one episode, he explains: "My parents decided to tell me the truth about Santa Claus, the Easter Bunny, and the birds and the bees all on the same day. I bought two out of three.") Like the other characters on the show, Dennis is tired of being single. One week, a woman hits on him, and he kindly tells her that he is gay. "I don't believe this. You guys are all *over* the place!" she exclaims as she walks away. Dennis looks around and forlornly asks, "*Where?*" Even if it is unclear why Dennis is single, we *know* why the women he works with are alone: straight bachelors are at a premium in this version of San Francisco. In the premiere, Roz (Woodard) tries to entice Sara (Davis) to join her at a party after work. "There'll be heterosexual men there," Roz promises. "We're having them flown in from the Midwest."[20] The show received good reviews, but had the bad fortune to be scheduled opposite *Dynasty*, the most popular show on TV. *Sara* vanished after six months, though NBC reran it in prime time during 1988.

ABC's crude *Hail to the Chief* came from the same sharp-edged writer and producers as *Soap* and *Benson*. It boasted a cast of known talents: Patty Duke, Ted Bessell, Herschel Bernardi, and Dick Shawn. With that pedigree, it should have been funnier. Creator Susan Harris blamed network censorship for removing the most biting, topical segments. What remains is sophomoric bedroom humor, racial and ethnic slurs, and overcooked, unsympathetic characters, interspersed with rare moments of political satire. It clicks along well enough when President Julia Mansfield is on-screen—a tribute, perhaps, to Patty Duke's acting. Julia's scenes with her mother (Maxine Stuart) and with the gay bodyguard Randy are among the few signs of real character development on this series. Randy fits into the gay-man-as-confidant/problem-solver mold. He is a big, hulking tough guy, but sensitive and bit a of a mincer when he is alone with Julia. One story arc involves a nuclear terrorist who threatens to blow up the world. Julia and Randy sit up late on what may be their last night alive. Throwing their diets to the wind, they eat Oreos and ice cream in a leisurely fashion, and speak about how much their friendship means to each of them. He says that when he came out a few years earlier, she was the only friend who still treated him the same as before. Throughout the series, he uses humor to lighten the burden that Julia carries as President. *Hail to the Chief* debuted with respectable Nielsens, but they slid downhill as each unfunny episode caused more viewers to abandon ship. ABC mercifully dropped the axe after seven weeks. Susan Harris swore that this would be her last sitcom, but by summer 1985 she was hard at work on a sitcom pilot called *The Golden Girls*. It was originally supposed to focus on three older women who share a house with their gay, live-in houseboy.[21]

Meanwhile, high atop the Nielsen charts, *Dynasty*'s Steven Carrington seemed to be coming out of his heterosexual phase. He and his new boyfriend Luke Fuller (William Campbell, later known as Billy Campbell) met in late 1984. The next spring, Steven asked Luke to join him at his half sister's wedding to a European prince. Steven and Luke planned to move in together, make a life for themselves, and raise

Steven's young son. A month later, as the cast gathered in the fictional realm of Moldavia, audiences wondered what cliff-hanger could possibly top the previous season finales. The answer came in the form of machine-gun fire: as the bride and groom kissed, Moldavian revolutionaries crashed through the windows, shooting randomly. The episode ended in a blood-spattered, artsy tableau, with all the regulars lying motionless on the chapel floor. ("It was a fairy-tale terrorist attack," said coexecutive producer Esther Shapiro. "It was beautifully shot, like a Goya painting.") When the smoke cleared in fall of 1985, the only two casualties were Luke and another secondary character. Like Steven's first boyfriend, Luke met a sudden, violent ending, even as Steven's heterosexual love interests lived on and on. This time, Steven at least had the dignity of a tearful farewell at Luke's deathbed. All the series principals attended Luke's lengthy funeral, where Steven gave the eulogy. Choking back tears, he told the gathered mourners:

> I thought I had to keep my relationship with Luke a secret. But to Luke's great credit, he wouldn't let me do that. He knows that love doesn't grow in a closet: it needs air . . . Luke had the imagination to envision life as it might be, and the courage to live it as if it were that way. I loved him very much, and I'll carry him with me always.[22]

Times had changed, but not enough to allow a gay couple a happy ending. In 1969, a gay guest columnist in the *New York Times* wrote an article about gay characters in films, titled "Why Can't 'We' Live Happily Ever After, Too?"[23] Sixteen years later, it was still a good question. And, of course, the media's evolving awareness of AIDS would only aggravate the situation.

THE *FROST* REPORT

Television: 1983–1985

This is not a "gay movie": it is a family tragedy. Anyone in a family will want to see this. I think people are interested. It's like a terrible accident: people want to turn away, but cannot. I don't think they should turn away.

—*Daniel Lipman, cowriter of* An Early Frost
quoted in the Omaha World Herald, *1985*[1]

An Early Frost, the first TV movie to focus on AIDS, took over two years to research and write, surviving fourteen grueling drafts. (Three or four rewrites is typical for a TV movie.) In some ways, this drama had much to recommend it. When it aired in 1985, it offered the most naturalistic portrayal of a loving, same-sex couple that had ever appeared on American commercial TV. In a time when so many people knew so little about AIDS, the film gave twenty million viewers sound medical information and a plea for compassion. For nine years, it remained the highest-rated TV drama ever to focus on the epidemic.[2] The film boasted a brilliant cast: Aidan Quinn, Gena Rowlands, Ben Gazzara, Sylvia Sidney, and John Glover, among others. NBC treated this as a prestige piece, and every aspect displays tremendous thought and care. It makes a good case study because more backstage information is available about this show than any other gay-themed broadcast of the mid 1980s.

Despite outstanding ratings, cheers from reviewers, an Emmy, eight Emmy nominations, and an AGLA Media Award, not everyone was thrilled with *An Early Frost*. In 1985, many activists found the movie too pat, too safe, too apologetic, too manipulative, too little, and far too late. Four years, thirteen thousand AIDS cases, and seven thousand deaths into the epidemic, with no effective treatment in sight, there was ample cause for cynicism. Some activists joked that, given the film's clichéd white-picket-fence family, NBC should have called it *Norman Rockwell Does AIDS*. A lot of history contributed to this cynicism: the history of gay rights in the 1980s, the history of the government's reaction to gay people and AIDS, and the history of this film's press coverage as its airdate approached. With nothing to compare the show to, it was easy to hold it to optimistically high standards. In retrospect, compared with most of the bland, hollow AIDS TV dramas that have followed, *An Early Frost* is impressive. So was its timing: by the film's airdate in November 1985, AIDS was again major headline news.

On July 25, 1985, a spokesperson for actor Rock Hudson confirmed rumors that the star had AIDS and was gravely ill. The news struck a chord with the public. Reporters latched onto the story, refusing to let it go. AIDS: A STAR LEGITIMIZES IT read a typical headline.[3] Many in the gay community were dismayed that after so many years, after so many deaths, it took the demise of a closeted gay actor to bring home the reality of AIDS to the broader public. At last, Acquired Immune Deficiency Syndrome had a "poster child." There was an outpouring of sympathy for Hudson on some fronts, and the news convinced many people to get more information about AIDS. But a groundswell of antigay hostility was also gathering. The day Hudson died and for several days afterward, understaffed AIDS hotlines were deluged with requests for information. During those same days, countless gay individuals, organizations, and businesses were targets of death threats, harassment, vandalism, or violence. The specifics varied, but the two leitmotifs of the harassment were "You're gonna die of AIDS like Rock Hudson" and "We're gonna kill you fags 'cause you've made us have to worry about AIDS." The National Gay and Lesbian Task Force documented a steady increase in antigay violence and discrimination in the late 1980s, much of it linked to fear or anger about AIDS.

From August to November 1985, the news media seemed unable to go a day without talking about AIDS, Hudson, and the fear of transmission to heterosexuals. Reporters wondered aloud whether Hudson might have jeopardized the health of actress Linda Evans when they kissed on *Dynasty*. Evans seemed unconcerned, but other performers called their agents or lawyers to see if they could get out of love scenes. In response, the Screen Actors Guild adopted a policy that put kissing in the same category as risky stunt work, like jumping off rooftops. Newspapers in most major cities wrote that actors who were gay or had AIDS were forced to lie if they wanted work. (Gay actors had *always* felt a need to be closeted, but in 1985 it became newsworthy.) Some articles were historical overviews of Hollywood's arranged marriages, "beard" dates, publicity stunts, bribes, and blackmail. AIDS exacerbated the problem for gay actors. Some producers feared contagion, or worried what would happen to production costs if an actor suddenly became too sick to finish a project. Even as AIDS and fear of AIDS spread, ex-actor Ronald Reagan, the Leader of the Free World, had made only one public mention of the health crisis: in September, he made a plea for compassion toward schoolchildren with HIV. Federal spending on AIDS research remained low.

Network dramas were far behind the news media in acknowledging AIDS. By late 1985, when, for the second time on a prime-time drama, a gay man with AIDS appeared, more than one hundred twenty news reports, documentaries, and talk shows about AIDS had aired nationally.[4] On October 23, Showtime's *Brothers* aired an episode called "The Stranger." The episode focuses on one of Joe's old pro-football buddies, who had come out in an earlier episode. Now he returns with the news that he has AIDS and has quit his team. The series regulars initially are afraid to be in the same room with him, but they overcome their fear.[5] This sensitive story drew applause from the critics and nary a complaint from viewers. But then, this was a premium cable channel: no household received it without ordering it. Anyone offended by *Brothers'* gay content probably had stopped watching long before this episode. On November 10, CBS's medical drama *Trapper John, M.D.* developed one of its new regulars, Nurse Libby Kegler (Lorna Luft), with a story about the epidemic. She is devastated to learn that one of her former boyfriends is bisexual and has AIDS.[6] Dozens of newspaper articles mentioned these episodes of *Brothers* and *Trapper John* briefly, but only as sidelines to coverage of the main event: the long-awaited *An Early Frost*, which aired November 11.

Perry Lafferty originated this TV movie in late 1982 or early 1983, when he was NBC's West Coast senior vice president for programs, the second-in-command under Brandon Tartikoff. Doctor friends of Lafferty's first called his attention to articles about AIDS before it was big news. In several interviews, he said that these epidemiologists "convinced me they had statistical proof to show that it doubled every year." Here was an idea for a TV movie about an issue that no other network had touched. Lafferty decided to drop AIDS into the lap of "a straight-arrow family . . . and have them find out almost simultaneously that [their son] was gay and had this disease." He spent several days meeting with other NBC brass, pitching the idea to one person at a time, before the network approved it. The sales department worried that advertisers would stay away; Lafferty promised that the sales staff could have the film four weeks early to screen for sponsors. NBC senior managers and the Broadcast Standards department were also hesitant. "Mostly," Lafferty recalled, "they were concerned that we would present a fair picture of the homosexual community, that it wouldn't be loaded in their favor or against them; that we wouldn't have any technical inaccuracies about the disease, and that we wouldn't send the American public into a panic."[7]

In early 1983, Lafferty hired the first writer, Sherman Yellen, who had done excellent work for PBS's *The Adams Chronicles*. By April 1984, he was replaced by the writing team of Ron Cowen and Daniel Lipman. Together, this duo had written for *Family*, *Emerald Point N.A.S.*, and *Knots Landing*, and later created NBC's crisis-a-minute serial, *Sisters*. From the beginning, they shared Lafferty's vision of the film as a drama about a family. But the writers could not accept NBC's premise that the lead character—close to age thirty, in a two-year relationship—would not be out to his parents. So they asked some doctors about their patients. The doctors said that at least half of their gay patients with AIDS had not come out to their families.[8]

The film's interminable delays and tribulations were more typical of a major-release film than a 100-minute TV movie. Midyear, the first producer quit and Lafferty himself took over. His vision for the film was a bit different, so the first three drafts of the script became obsolete and a new set of rewrites began. Cowen and Lipman spent much of the summer meeting with AIDS patients in Santa Monica Hospital, where the writers made repeated visits to a British film director who spent his final months there. They also worked closely with an immunologist who specialized in AIDS, and a psychologist whose patients included many HIV-positive gay men. In later interviews to promote the film, Cowen and Lipman talked about their own initial ignorance about AIDS, and their fear of shaking hands with a patient during their first visit.[9]

NBC finally approved a script and scheduled production to start in June of 1985. By then, ABC had already aired *Consenting Adult* to impressive ratings. In the spring and summer of 1985, all three networks received TV movie proposals that told coming-out stories about young gay men, but which added AIDS to the *Consenting Adult* model. Executives at CBS and ABC knew that NBC had just such a project in the pipeline, so they held off buying anything.[10] All of this was before Rock Hudson's illness hit the news in July.

Lafferty hired John Erman, a prolific television director whose credits date back to the 1960s, to film *An Early Frost*. By July, they had hired a name cast—the surest way to sell a film about an unpleasant subject. Since *An Early Frost* has no prolog, the cast list is the first thing the audience sees. It may have been enough to keep some viewers from changing channels.

The public interest in AIDS, due to Rock Hudson's illness, accelerated the production schedule. Originally, NBC had scheduled the film to air in January 1986. But just as rehearsals began, the Hudson story broke. Since NBC brass saw a potential for huge ratings, they moved the show earlier, to the November Nielsen sweeps. During preproduction and production, the script continued to evolve. Aidan Quinn and director Erman visited a filmmaker who was hospitalized with complications from AIDS in New York that summer. His stories about living with AIDS gave them still more dialog for the script, which then went back to NBC for reapproval. Meanwhile, a scene written in 1984, with the mother going to the library to read up on this obscure disease, was cut: by August 1985, everyone knew what AIDS was. Instead, it was decided that Kay would take a magazine off her nightstand—a fake, prop magazine with an AIDS cover story. By the week they shot the scene, no dummy prop was needed: the epidemic was the cover story of both *Time* and *Newsweek*.[11]

The film never shows Michael's decline and death, but treats it as inevitable—probably within two years, a doctor says. The script emphasizes medical facts and the diversity of people who have AIDS. In one scene, a doctor lists all the permutations of patients he has seen dead or dying: a mother and her newborn daughter; a straight couple where the husband was a hemophiliac; and of course, gay men. The audience sees a hospital support group for men with AIDS: Phil—a straight, married man, got the virus from a prostitute; Victor—a frail, wry, flamboyant queen with thinning hair, is alone because his friends and family had abandoned him; another man, the only African American in sight, lost his job when his boss found out about his illness; and a young man with Kaposi's sarcoma lesions on his face, perhaps twenty years old, breaks down and cries because every time he makes friends with someone on the ward, they die.[12]

Victor (John Glover) uses humor to get through his daily medical trials: At one time or another, he has survived almost every conceivable infection. Glover, too, visited people who had AIDS to prepare for his role. "I felt guilty about it at first," he said, "because it was for some kind of play, you know, a movie. I was pumping them." One of the four men he spent time with was a doctor with full-blown AIDS. He explained to Glover what was happening inside his body, both physically and emotionally. "It was very frightening," Glover said. "It is not an easy death. I hadn't realized how painful and how devastating it is."[13] In the film, Victor and Michael become friends. When Michael's mother, Kay, finds out that everyone in Victor's life has abandoned him, she vows that her son will not die alone. Victor's experience steels her resolve as she confronts her husband (who seems more bothered by Michael's homosexuality than his HIV status) and Michael's pregnant sister (who is afraid to be in a room with him). When Kay tells Nick about Victor, she adds firmly, "That is not going to happen to our son. Not to Michael." Victor's death serves as a reminder of what awaits the Perfect Son.

The portrayal of the gay couple's relationship is unusually up-front by 1980s TV standards. (It did not approach the naturalism of independent cinema, but it was a step in that direction.) In an early scene, before the audience officially knows that Michael is gay, he is seen asleep in his bed. A hand enters the shot and playfully flicks Michael's ear. He stirs. More tweaking: Michael's lover is waking him up for work. This is the first time we meet Peter, a preppy who refurbishes furniture for a living in Chicago. They share a huge duplex apartment. The two do not just recite lines that *say* they are in love: they interact and talk like a couple. They smile spontaneously when they look into each other's eyes. There is even a variation on one of TV's classic spousal scenes: Michael, half-naked, shaves, as Peter sits on the counter—rather closer than a good friend or a brother would. They just come off as two men in love. In the course of the film, their relationship is strained almost to the point of breaking. Peter is angry over Michael's closeted existence: Michael spends time with Peter's family and friends, but Michael's family and coworkers are not allowed to know Peter exists. "When are they going to have the great honor of knowing who you are?" Peter asks. "After you're dead?" Michael, in turn, is furious to learn that Peter cheated on him with a stranger during one of Michael's many business trips:

> PETER: I'm sorry, Michael.
> MICHAEL: *You're* sorry, and *I* have AIDS. All this time I thought we were safe. Because we had each other, we'd be protected. I could have gotten this because of you!
> PETER: We don't know that.
> MICHAEL: Then how else? How else?!

Michael was—as Newt Deiter used to say—a Superfag: a rich, white, successful, gorgeous lawyer in his twenties who had also been a champion athlete in high school. In trying to prove that AIDS can happen even in the "best" of families, NBC revealed much about the industry's ideas of "best."

To protect its sweeps-time investment, NBC made a concerted publicity push for *An Early Frost*. The network sent out two hundred thousand study guides to schools, social service agencies, and community groups.[14] NBC scheduled prescreenings for the press, AIDS groups, and gay organizations. The week of the broadcast, NBC's news shows ran special reports on AIDS. Many gay activists were prejudiced against the film by advance news reports (in the *New York Times* and elsewhere) that NBC had censored out a line in which Michael's grandmother says she thinks his boyfriend is nice.[15] Some gay people were also put off by all the advance publicity for the film, which frantically emphasized that *An Early Frost* was not "about" homosexuals or AIDS, but rather about people in a family—as if these concepts were mutually exclusive.

In hindsight, *An Early Frost* is a better than average TV movie. The script draws its characters carefully, with great emotional depth. It is still a bit too pat to swallow whole, but no one was doing anything better at the time. As the ink was drying on the preview articles, which were legion, television's knack for imitation was already kicking in. Before the film could air, writers for several series were already outlining potential "AIDS episodes" that would air starting in early 1986.

AIDS AS AN "ISSUE OF THE WEEK"

Television: 1985–1989

On TV, AIDS is primarily a disease of middle-class white children, who get it from blood transfusions, and secondarily of middle-class white heterosexuals, who get it from prostitutes, and middle-class white homosexuals, who get it from a single lover who committed a single indiscretion.
—*Editorial*, San Jose Mercury News, *1988*[1]

Most AIDS dramas of the mid and late 1980s were "message" scripts. The main messages were "Be nice to people with AIDS" and "Protect yourself from HIV." The first shows were emotional, interpersonal dramas: characters learn that they have AIDS, and people in their lives react. These scripts emphasize medical facts and compassion, and remind viewers that any sort of person can get HIV and AIDS. Common lessons include the importance of condoms; that it is safe to touch a person who has AIDS; that people *need* to be touched; and that HIV is a virus, not a punishment from God. Later, writers found other ways to work AIDS into plots: stories condemning the antigay backlash of violence and discrimination; legal dramas, often involving mercy killings or job discrimination; and a few shows that chose more inflammatory tactics to scare viewers into protecting themselves.

There were several dramas about families torn apart by the news that an adult child was gay and HIV-positive. These families eventually reconcile, reassuring the viewer that the HIV-positive character will have someone to take care of him. None of these broadcasts showed how the community was caring for its own through individual efforts and through a massive network of gay social service agencies, educational programs, health-care centers, and advocacy groups. As media scholar Larry Gross observed, the networks' vision of the epidemic "falsely suggests that gay people with AIDS are alone and abandoned, unless and until they are taken back into the bosom of their family."[2]

Two weeks after Rock Hudson died, writer James Fritzhand of *Hotel* finished a detailed episode proposal that he called "Scapegoats." It would be the first drama about a person with AIDS to air after NBC's much-vaunted *An Early Frost*. One story line in the episode follows Frank, a recently divorced, homophobic bartender at the hotel—a guest character who is diagnosed with AIDS. He works every day with Joel, a young gay waiter, whom he harrasses and gay-baits. But beneath their verbal sparring is a tenuous mutual respect. When Frank is diagnosed, he accuses Joel of somehow giving him AIDS. Despite Frank's antigay epithets, Joel is almost the only person who sticks by Frank in his time of need. (Here again is TV's gay reverse stereotype of the mid 1980s: the saintly, altruistic gay character, a compensation for the networks' past sins.) Frank later learns that he contracted HIV from a blood transfusion. This revelation reunites him with his wife and child, who suspected that he was gay or a drug addict. The episode aired in January 1986, with Ken Kercheval (of *Dallas*) as Frank. Joel was played by Leigh McCloskey (formerly of *Dallas*, and who had played a bisexual hustler in two 1970s TV movies: *Dawn* and *Alexander*).[3]

NBC's trio of intense semiserials—*St. Elsewhere*, *Hill Street Blues*, and *L.A. Law*—all ran AIDS stories later that year. On *St. Elsewhere*, a promiscuous heterosexual, Dr. Caldwell (Mark Harmon), is diagnosed with AIDS. His colleagues ponder their own unsafe behaviors as Caldwell tries to remember all the women he has slept with. He leaves the series the next week, after almost three years as a regular. On *Hill Street*, Mick Belker's gay snitch, Eddie (Charles Levin), returns just long enough to say a tearful good-bye and die of AIDS in a tiny, run-down apartment. (During Eddie's absence, Levin played the gay houseboy, Coco, in the 1985 pilot of *The Golden Girls*. Coco was supposed to be a regular, but he was axed after the premiere when the producers decided to focus exclusively on the female leads.) Meanwhile, on *L.A. Law*, Deputy D.A. Grace Van Owen (Susan Dey) is forced to prosecute a young gay man with AIDS, charged with the mercy killing of his gravely ill lover. After the man's conviction, Van Owen wants him to know that she understands why he did it, but that the law is the law. In the following episode, she gives his attorney grounds for a retrial—a move that gets her assigned to night court as a punishment.[4]

TV still treated AIDS as an issue of the week: the message about safer sex was given, then life went on as before. If anything, casual sexual references on 1980s television had increased because the networks, losing profits to other media, had "downsized" their censorship departments. Until then, gay media advocacy groups had remained conciliatory and, from the networks' standpoint, reasonable to deal with.

Militant, grassroots, in-your-face activism made a comeback in March 1987 with the formation of ACT UP. The moment seemed right for a return to raucous, strident protests. As the number of AIDS cases soared, research dollars remained scarce and the Food and Drug Administration delayed in approving treatments. Antigay violence was on the rise, apparently in response to AIDS-phobia. Just a few months earlier, the U.S. Supreme Court had ruled (in *Bower v. Hardwick*) that the constitutional right to privacy did not extend to homosexuals. These new developments fit in with preexisting, long-term trends. For example, gay people were still considered criminals in twenty-four states, and federal laws still banned gay foreigners from entering the country. Taking all of this evidence together, ACT UP said that gay people and people with AIDS were under siege by a hostile government and a prejudiced society. Many ACT UP organizers held that federal inaction on AIDS was an act of deliberate genocide. They believed that the only solution was to call attention to the crisis and get large numbers of people involved in as vocal a way as possible. ACT UP encouraged people to "get in touch" with their rage and channel it into direct action protests. The tactics—part anarchic activism, part primal-scream therapy—resembled ones used a generation earlier by groups like GLF and GAA. (In 1991, ACT UP would return to the scene of the Gay Raiders' crime: eighteen years after Mark Segal disrupted Walter Cronkite's *CBS Evening News*, ACT UP would do the same for Cronkite's successor, Dan Rather.)[5]

ACT UP's signature stickers—a black circle with a pink triangle and the slogan SILENCE=DEATH—appeared all over the Greater New York area in the late 1980s. Then they spread across the continent and beyond.

The stickers showed up on banks, on U.S. mailboxes, government buildings, subways, park benches, doorknobs of Catholic churches—anyplace a reminder seemed appropriate. ACT UP's chapters staged numerous "die-ins," in which hundreds of protesters feigned death in front of government buildings.

Anger over *Bower v. Hardwick*, government inaction on AIDS, and the new wave of antigay prejudice led to the 1987 March on Washington for Lesbian and Gay Rights. The demonstration was held in October, eight years after the first large gay march on the capital. As in 1979, the organizers' main demand was for a federal antidiscrimination law, though now the discrimination was not based just on sexual orientation but also on HIV status. At the end of the day, organizers estimated the turnout at eight hundred thousand. (The National Park Service said two hundred thousand; D.C. Metro Police reportedly said five hundred thousand, which seemed more likely.) Whatever the head count, it was huge. The mainstream press, especially the glossy news weeklies, ignored the march. Broadcast coverage was slightly better, though NBC somehow missed the gay-rights angle and reported it as an AIDS protest. ABC's *Nightline*, ever a source of intelligent journalism, was one of the few that got it right. *Nightline*'s first broadcast after the march examined how AIDS-era homophobia had refocused and intensified the gay community's struggle for equality.[6]

Things were changing behind the TV cameras, too. During the summer of 1987, the industry began responding to pressure from both the left and the right to treat sex less casually on TV because of AIDS. In news releases and interviews, network executives promised more depictions of fidelity and said that scripts would include references to condoms. The daytime soaps, previously hip-deep in hormones, would be less steamy: they would place more emphasis on sex in committed relationships. CBS and producer Barney Rosenzweig announced that on *Cagney & Lacey*, Cagney would reevaluate her promiscuity in light of AIDS. Rosenzweig said it was a tough issue to work into the story line, but that he was not proud of the example the series had set in that sexually dangerous era. Ted Harbert, ABC's vice president for motion pictures, said that scripts about AIDS were all well and good, but "it's more important for us to treat the issue of responsible relationships and safe sex on an ongoing basis." NBC's Broadcast Standards chief,

Maurie Goodman, said his network had rejected several scripts that treated AIDS exploitatively. However, he was proud to announce that "at least a dozen episodes" of NBC shows had "used the word prophylactic or condom" during the 1986–87 season. Goodman predicted even more such references for 1987–88. It was announced that even *The Golden Girls*, which thrived on libidinous innuendo, would rein in its sex-positive punch lines.[7]

The AIDS-phobia that the gay and AIDS communities had been describing for years was suddenly becoming more visible in the news media. The latest targets of harassment and violence were no longer just people who had gotten AIDS through taboo sex or illegal drugs: now they included children, who were considered more sympathetic and photogenic. In Arcadia, Florida, the Rays, a family with three HIV-positive hemophiliac sons, were forced to move when someone burned down their house in 1987. This followed a year of death threats, several changes of residence, and a court order allowing their little boys to attend public school. Network reporters swooped into the small town and offered yet another series of emotional, picture-perfect stories about "innocent victims" of AIDS who had been targets of provincial prejudice.[8] Reports about children with AIDS also got regional attention in several states as alarmed neighbors demanded that schools bar HIV-positive students.

AIDS-related homophobia was hard to miss in the less censored areas of TV comedy. In a 1987 *HBO–On Location* special, rant comedian Sam Kinison blew off steam about AIDS and the gay men he blamed for it. He demanded to know how a man could possibly look at "another guy's hairy ass and fall in love." Kinison lisped: "Yes, I knew it would come along. They told me I was a fool to dream . . . I've had a lot of guys' smelly balls on my face, but this is love!" He told his cheering audience that he would have thought the threat of AIDS would be enough to straighten out any man who ever fantasized about gay sex:

> It wasn't like they were being encouraged in their cause [even before AIDS], you know. But AIDS is really—Oh, man! Thanks, guys, for giving us the Black Plague of the '80s! . . . I sit around with that extra thirty, forty dollars in my pocket and go, "Now . . . [Do I] give this so they're gonna can find a cure for AIDS, or keep cablevision and all the movie channels?" . . .

Sorry, guys. You know, maybe if I had a second income with a little more cash, but I need my tittie channels.[9]

As the fall approached, more and more producers went to the networks with scripts about people with AIDS. *St. Elsewhere,* which NBC had canceled, then resurrected, committed itself to a season-long story arc about the epidemic. It would include an abandoned HIV-positive baby, a gay couple who appear in at least four episodes, and a homophobic doctor who jabs himself with a contaminated needle. On *Designing Women,* a young neighbor would reveal that he is gay and has AIDS. On the cop comedy/drama *Hooperman,* the title character (John Ritter) would exchange himself for hostages held by an HIV-positive prison inmate.[10]

Television's messages about AIDS and gay people varied, depending on who was writing, producing, and directing. A creative team's personal experiences with AIDS, naturally enough, played a role. The *Designing Women* episode is a clear example. Linda Bloodworth-Thomason was a prolific writer and producer of topical, pointed sitcoms that often explored controversial subjects. She has strong liberal political views, which she does not disguise in her scripts. Most or all of her series have been GLBT-inclusive: in addition to occasional sexual-minority characters, casual references in other episodes remind viewers that these shows take place in a universe that includes gay, bisexual, and transgender people.

In November 1986, eight weeks after the premiere of *Designing Women,* Bloodworth-Thomason's mother died of complications related to AIDS, which she contracted from a blood transfusion. During her mother's final months, Linda and her husband, coproducer Harry Thomason, learned about the medical and social realities of AIDS: the progression of the disease, the types of prejudice and fear that could move the uninformed masses, the connections between AIDS-phobia and homophobia, and the ways in which people vented their fear by placing blame. Bloodworth-Thomason overheard many hateful and ignorant remarks in hospital waiting rooms and hallways. But one comment drilled into her consciousness—a comment that many gay people remember hearing (or seeing on bathroom walls) in the 1980s: "The good thing about AIDS is that it's killing all the right people."

When she began writing the second season of *Designing Women*, she used what she had seen, heard, and felt, and channeled it into an episode she called "Killing All the Right People." She could have taken the easy way out in writing an "AIDS episode." She could have done what three daytime soap operas and several prime-time shows did that season: portray a heterosexual woman who got AIDS from a male partner or from a transfusion. Surely, it would have hit closer to home for her, given her mother's history. But to critique the prejudice behind most AIDS-phobia in the United States, she wrote about religious judgmentalism, homophobia, irrational fear of contagion, and how those attitudes hindered attempts to halt the spread of AIDS.[11] Impressively, she worked it all in between punch lines without resorting to gallows humor.

The episode tells two stories. One involves Mary Jo (Annie Potts), whose child's high school is debating whether to distribute condoms to students. Mary Jo is the only parent willing to prepare a speech in favor of condoms for the next PTA meeting. Opposing her is Carolyn, a caricature of a sugary, perky, "perfect" housewife. The episode's other story—in a convenient TV coincidence—involves a gay neighbor in his twenties, Kendall (Tony Goldwyn), who has AIDS. Together with the Designing Women, he redesigns a room at a local funeral parlor that will be donated for use in ceremonies for indigent and abandoned people who have died of AIDS.[12]

The new Fox network, which entered the prime-time race in 1987, featured one of the era's few political, social issue drama series: *21 Jump Street*. This slick, MTV-generation show followed the adventures of young undercover cops who could pass for high-school or college students. The series was designed to get adolescent viewers thinking about the difficult, gray areas of moral issues. In November 1987, *21 Jump Street* aired a story about serial gay-bashings near a military academy.[13] Three months later, the series presented a tale about an HIV-positive teenager whose neighbors want him out of their high school. This thoughtful, moving hour contains some elements of the Ray case from Florida. In the show, sixteen-year-old Harley Poolish (Philip Tanzini) has received death threats and is attending his fifth school in two months, during which time his family has moved twice.

The script also echoes the experience of a more famous boy with AIDS, Ryan White. Like the Rays, White was a hemophiliac who picked up the virus through a transfusion. White won the right to attend school in his Indiana town, and later became an AIDS educator and media celebrity.

As the *Jump Street* episode begins, Detective Hanson (Johnny Depp) is assigned to protect Harley and make sure that no one interferes with the court order allowing him in school. Though Harley's image and personality are different from Ryan White's (Harley's look can best be described as proto-grunge), most viewers probably thought the show was cribbing White's story. But midway through the episode, writer Patrick Hasburgh (who cocreated the series) turns the Ryan White story on its head. Detective Hanson tries to puzzle out how a hemophiliac like Harley could afford to participate in athletics and race motorcycles. The boy reveals that he is actually gay, and that the hemophilia story was a ruse invented by his ashamed father. Harley explains that when the media started focusing on his case, his father "had to tell 'em *something*." The word "gay" is never used, this being a show with young viewers. Instead, the boy tells Hanson his father "is kinda like the Anita Bryant of the hardware business and—well—I'm not." Anyone who understood it, understood it. Anyone too young to remember Anita Bryant remained uncontaminated by the knowledge that there was such thing as a homosexual. The most questionable part of the scene is a line where Harley implies that the only ways to get AIDS are blood transfusions, sharing needles, and gay sex. No one challenges this, and the question of heterosexual transmission is nowhere in the episode, even though a subplot focuses on the heterosexual misadventures of one of Hanson's colleagues. At the end of the episode, Depp appears out of character, still looking very MTVish, to introduce a message about AIDS from the U.S. Assistant Secretary for Health and from Surgeon General C. Everett Koop.[14]

As previously mentioned, television usually sexualized GLBT characters only if they were serial killers. It has also been noted that bisexual characters are exceedingly rare. In 1988, TV writer Steven Zito blended those ingredients into television's ultimate sexualized, killer-queer bogeyman. The series was *Midnight Caller*, a stylish, violent drama about Jack Killian (Gary Cole), an ex-cop who hosts a late-night, call-in radio show in San Francisco. In the episode, "After It Happened," Killian finds out that his ex-girlfriend, Tina (Kay Lenz), has AIDS. She contracted HIV and became pregnant during a one-night stand with a man she met in a bar. Killian helps her search for the man to let him know he has HIV and to include him in the decision of whether to abort the fetus. The man, Mike Barnes, turns out to be a promiscuous bisexual who knows he has HIV and is deliberately infecting as many women and men as he can in the time he has left. Characters include Mike Barnes's ailing male lover, whom he has abandoned. This cautionary tale about unprotected, casual sex reinforces widespread negative stereotypes about bisexual men and about people with AIDS. All of the HIV-positive characters just assume that they got the virus from Mike, a logic leap that no one challenges. TV's sole purpose for finally putting bisexual male characters on-screen seemed to be as a conduit for bringing AIDS into the heterosexual world. The script originally ended with one of Mike's female victims cornering him in an alley and shooting him dead. That script was leaked to AIDS activists and gay newspapers in mid-October, leading to the most militant, disruptive gay media activism in almost a decade. Activists demanded a complete rewrite, arguing that the episode would promote violence against GLBT people and people with AIDS.

Midnight Caller had not yet debuted when protesters made national news by interfering with the filming of the episode in San Francisco. In nearby San Jose, the *Mercury News* called the week of protests "the biggest television fury ever seen here." As filming began, producers found themselves negotiating with local activists, NBC executives, and the mayor's office over this script. The producers refused to change the ending. In response, ACT UP held its first major demonstration in San Francisco on October 20: Sixty protesters from ACT UP and other groups shut down the outdoor filming by blowing whistles, yelling, clapping, and chanting.[15] These were tactics that had gone by the wayside in the early 1980s. The last time activists had disrupted a filming session this way was probably in 1979, when gay New Yorkers interrupted the production of the Lorimar movie, *Cruising*. *Midnight Caller* was produced by the same company.

Timothy Wolfred, executive director of the San Francisco AIDS

Foundation, blasted this "sleazy" episode as exploitative. The series' executive producer, Bob Singer, saw the story as a compassionate warning not to trust everyone sexually. "The hero says that the murder is absolutely the wrong solution," he said. "No one watching it could think we were condoning this by any stretch of the imagination." But Singer and Lorimar were in an awkward position. The series was set in San Francisco, where they hoped to produce the show for years to come. That meant they needed the goodwill of the locals to get permission to film on location and avoid future protests; and the goodwill of City Hall, for legal permits. Singer and Zito did not seem out-and-out hostile; they just did not grasp the broader implications of the episode.

Three groups—the San Francisco AIDS Foundation, ACT UP, and Mobilization Against AIDS—spearheaded the campaign for rewrites. Negotiators suggested making the Mike Barnes character unaware of his HIV status and showing his struggles to alter his behavior and act responsibly—as, they argued, most San Franciscans were doing. Singer said he would not change Mike nor his violent death, but he asked the AIDS organizations for other input to flesh out the script. The activists shared their concerns, but vowed to disrupt filming if the deliberate infections and the murder remained in the script. On Monday, October 24, Lorimar got a temporary restraining order that barred two of the organizations from coming within one hundred feet of the shoot or causing noisy disruptions. Activists announced that they would be there anyway. The day of the court order, Singer made a minor change: The woman would still kill Mike, but the audience would see her arrested for it. Tuesday afternoon, Singer announced that the killing would come out entirely: The show's hero would stop the shooting, and Mike would escape into the night when the gun went off, presumably to continue his sexual killing spree. The decision was the result of much "soul-searching," Singer said. By then, word had spread among San Francisco's newly energized direct action activists. That night—the same night when NBC aired the series premiere of *Midnight Caller*—three hundred demonstrators violated the court order and gathered outside Lipps Tavern. Protesters again brought whistles and chanted "ACT UP! Fight back! Fight AIDS!" while the Lorimar crew tried to film.[16]

NBC broadcast the episode on December 2, 1988. A few lines of dialog may have been concessions agreed to in the negotiations, such as when a bartender in a gay bar says that his policy is to "eighty-six irresponsible cruisers" like Mike. "We've had too many friends die," he explains. But one of the most troubling aspects of the script—the character of Mike Barnes—remained. The day of the broadcast, activists demonstrated outside NBC affiliates' buildings in several cities. The episode got mediocre reviews, generally on the grounds of its perceived irresponsibility and how far it fell from the most common ways that heterosexual women got AIDS. But once the story pulled away from Mike Barnes, the dramatic elements clicked, and actress Lenz won an Emmy for her performance.

The next year, *Midnight Caller* did a follow-up story about Tina. This time, Zito and Lenz met with representatives of the three AIDS organizations. They interviewed people in AIDS hospices as Zito planned the script, a process which reportedly took five months. In the sequel, aired in November 1989, some straight women whom Mike Barnes infected form a support group and go on the radio to raise consciousness about AIDS. This episode scored high marks from almost every reviewer, for both accuracy and drama. It was also one of the few "AIDS dramas" to show a death scene—a tender farewell between Killian and his former girlfriend.[17]

EDGING TOWARD DIVERSITY

Television: 1986–1990

TEE: Lorraine, you *are* a lesbian. A dyke, a lezbo, a butch—all those names that
   boy was callin' you . . . Why can't you just accept it?
LORRAINE: I have accepted it! I've accepted it all my life! I lost my *family*
   because of that, but it doesn't make me any different from anybody else in
   this world!
TEE: It makes you damn different. . . . As long as *they* own the whole damn
   world, it's them and us, and that spells *different*.
   —*An African American lesbian couple of the 1960s in*
   The Women of Brewster Place, *1989[1]*

Until the mid 1980s, sexual-minority characters generally shared certain traits. They were almost always gay or lesbian (rather than bisexual
or transgendered), white (even on *Sanford and Son*, where white characters were few and conspicuous), single, had no gay friends, were
middle-class, and were in their twenties or thirties. Lesbian characters
were rare and, as we have seen, often violent. Starting in 1986, however, the GLBT images on-screen began to diversify. There were
coming-out tales about gay high schoolers. Couples and *slightly* older
characters appeared. Lesbian visibility increased, including more characters who were not killers. A well-publicized TV movie focused on
a bisexual protagonist. Dramas included transsexual and transvestite
characters, and no longer just for comic relief. On a very limited basis,
even some racial diversity began to appear among GLBT roles.

   Most significant in broadening the racial spectrum was the highly unusual two-part TV movie, *The Women of Brewster Place*. The film portrayed the well-developed relationship of a black, lesbian couple (Lonette McKee and Paula Kelly). Much of the film's second night focused on their stay in Brewster Place. This production was note-worthy, and not just because it drew strong ratings: it depicted likable lesbians, a physically affectionate same-sex couple, black gay charac-ters, and acknowledged that gay people existed before Stonewall. It was unusual in the wider scheme of things, too: it was almost the only TV drama of the 1980s to focus on strong friendships among African American women.

Oprah Winfrey produced and starred in the film, which was based on the book by Gloria Naylor and was directed by Donna Deitch (*Desert Hearts*). Set in a run-down tenement in an unnamed city around 1967, it focuses on seven black women whose lives are made miserable by selfish, irresponsible, cruel black men. (To mitigate this, the TV adaptation gives larger roles to two of the book's minor charac-ters, responsible black men.) The film's central symbol is a brick wall that blocks out the sun and separates this poor neighborhood from the rest of the city. In a film where most heterosexual relationships are abu-sive, brief, and/or dysfunctional, longtime lovers Lorraine and Tee (Lonette McKee and Paula Kelly) are the best-developed, most stable romantic couple.

When they are home alone, they are playful and clearly in love. Lor-raine, a teacher, lost her last job when her sexual orientation became known. She and Tee have moved house twice to escape prejudice. When this middle-class couple first arrives, their new neighbor, gossipy old Miss Sophie (Olivia Cole) predicts, "It's gone be trouble . . . them two." There will, indeed, be trouble, though Miss Sophie herself will stir up most of it. Sophie quickly realizes that the new tenants are "that way," and she becomes obsessed with having them thrown out of the building. The only neighbors who show kindness to Lorraine are Kiswana (a young black activist who grew up in the suburbs) and Ben (the elderly handyman who treats Lorraine like a daughter). Besides Miss Sophie, Lorraine's principal nemesis is C. C. Baker, a thug who threatens her with violence and calls her "lezbo," "butch," and "freak." In scene after scene, we see the affable couple worn down by the scorn and fear of neighbors. In the final scene, gang leader C. C. pulls a switchblade and rapes Lorraine in a dark alley. Kindly Ben finds her moaning, bloodied, crazed. She wobbles to her feet, shouting that she wants no one to come near her. Ben tries to calm her down. Lorraine grabs a heavy wooden beam and starts swinging it wildly, knocking Ben to the ground. He falls against the brick wall, just below camera range. Lorraine, wild-eyed, trembling, and crying, batters his head with the post. In Naylor's original book, Lorraine kills him. In the film, his face is not covered as medics load him into an ambulance, leaving his fate deliberately ambiguous. (Given Winfrey and Deitch's history of lesbian-positive media work, the change was probably made to avoid TV's killer-lesbian stereotype.) Tee climbs into Lorraine's ambulance and the last image viewers see of them is a tight embrace. The attacks inspire the residents of Brewster Place to take matters into their own hands: as a rainstorm drenches them, they find a crowbar and scraps of piping, which they use to tear a large hole in the brick wall.[2]

When ABC reran *The Women of Brewster Place* in 1990, Winfrey appeared in a commercial, dressed as her character from the film, Mattie. "I'm real proud to announce that Mattie Michael, along with her old friends and quite a few new ones, will be back on Brewster Place as a weekly series," she said.[3] *Brewster Place* ran for two months on ABC. Miss Sophie, nasty as ever, was a regular. But this revamped Brewster Place had no room for Lorraine or Tee. It was unfortunate, because the characters could have filled a void: they were just about the only black gay or bisexual women in prime-time fiction before 1995.

Before 1986, few programs had depicted GLBT people of color at all. Of the shows studied for this book, only four from before 1980 include nonwhite/Anglo sexual-minority characters: the TV movie *Cage Without a Key* (1975), which portrays a black, lesbian teenager in a juvenile detention center, who nobly sacrifices her life to save that of the film's heroine—a wrongly imprisoned white girl (Susan Dey of *The Partridge Family*); an episode of *Police Story* (1977) that centered on a teenage Chicana lesbian street gang; an episode of *The Jeffersons* (1977) that featured an old Navy buddy of George Jefferson's—a black woman who used to be a man; and an episode of the sitcom *Sanford Arms* (1977), which portrayed a black, gay male attorney (Lisle Wilson) whom a straight male regular (also African American) learns to call "friend."[4] No Asian characters and no more Latinos appear in the shows studied for this book until the 1990s. Three black gay men showed up in rapid succession during 1980 and 1981. After that, there was nothing until 1986.[5]

Partly, this reflected television's general underrepresentation of minority characters. It also represented the networks' desire not to risk offending more than one minority at a time: Certain African American leaders considered homosexuality a white European vice that was weakening black families. Such leaders have often objected to black gay characters. In the mid and late 1980s, as more gay African Americans came out of the closet (or, like many other people, were forced out by AIDS),[6] black gay visibility in the media increased. At the same time, as antigay violence and discrimination became more blatant, several renowned black civil rights leaders, such as Jesse Jackson and Coretta Scott King, threw their support behind equality for gay people.[7] These changes probably helped improve the networks' receptiveness to these characters.

The late 1980s brought six black GLBT characters, including the ones in *The Women of Brewster Place*. In 1986, the Joan Collins miniseries *Sins* portrayed a black, sexually active fashion photographer (William Allen Young) as a major supporting role. The same year, a black transvestite prostitute made a brief appearance on *Hill Street Blues*. On the John Ritter cop series *Hooperman*, starting late in the 1987–88 season, there was a recurring character named Rudy (Rod Gist), a tall, heavyset, middle-aged drag queen who lived in Hooperman's apartment building. On *Dear John*, Cleavon Little guest-starred as a new member of John's singles support group, who falls in love with John (Judd Hirsch).[8]

The age range of sexual-minority roles also broadened during these years. While most of the expansion happened among gay teen roles, one series—*The Golden Girls*—offered a guest character who was in her mid or late forties—rather older than the norm for such roles. In this well-written, fondly remembered episode, Dorothy (Bea Arthur) has invited her old college friend, Jean (Lois Nettleton), to visit. Even before Jean arrives, Dorothy's elderly mother, Sophia, expresses tolerance toward lesbianism. "Jean is a nice person," says Sophia. "She happens to like girls instead of guys. Some people like cats instead of dogs.

Frankly, I'd rather live with a lesbian than a cat. Unless a lesbian sheds—that I don't know." Viewers learn that Jean is mourning the loss of her beloved Pat, who died a year ago. Dorothy's friends, Rose and Blanche, assume that Pat was Jean's husband, and Dorothy does not correct them. Jean is down-to-earth, earnest, likable, and fits right in with the Golden Girls. She becomes fast friends with Rose (Betty White), who is also a widow and, like Jean, grew up on a dairy farm. The two women spend whole days together, laughing and crying, sometimes talking about what it is like to lose a spouse. Jean does not come out to Rose, who seems too naive to understand. Instead, Jean decides to cut her visit short. "I haven't met anyone as good and decent as Rose since Pat died," Jean tells Dorothy, "and I think I'm in love." Rose eventually finds out why Jean is planning to leave early. Rose says that if she were gay, she would feel very honored to have someone like Jean care about her, and that Jean is welcome to stay if their friendship can be enough for her. They hug, still friends. Predictably, however, Jean never reappears on *The Golden Girls*. In the late 1980s, media scholar Marguerite Moritz interviewed the NBC censor in charge of this show. Moritz reported that the network had demanded only one change in the script. Near the beginning of the story, Jean was supposed to tell Dorothy, "If you think [your friends] are sophisticated enough, let's tell them." NBC's Warren Ashley objected to the word "sophisticated." The line, he said, "might be demeaning to anyone who disapproves of that lifestyle. It's like saying if you don't approve of homosexuality, you are not sophisticated." In the broadcast version, Jean says, "If you think they can handle it, I'd just as soon tell them."[9]

Although the networks generally kept away from bisexual and transsexual characters until the 1990s, 1986 brought some diversification in this area, too. The portrayals were few, but for the first time they were protagonists. In April, ABC ran the TV movie *My Two Loves*, about a widow (Mariette Hartley) who discovers her bisexuality when she falls in love with a man and a woman and must choose between them. In May, Vanessa Redgrave starred in the CBS movie *Second Serve* based on the life of transsexual tennis star Renée Richards. (Richards made headlines in the mid 1970s during controversies over whether she should be allowed to compete in women's tournaments.) And in fall 1986, the first two episodes of *L.A. Law* featured a transsexual secretary who speaks at the memorial service for a recently deceased partner of the firm. In a moving eulogy, she posthumously outs the man as gay and outs herself as his transsexual best friend, perhaps his lover. Her main functions in the script seem to be 1) to let viewers know that this will be a series where the unexpected can happen, and 2) to establish up front how narrow-minded and judgmental one of the regulars is, by having him fire her. Among the prime-time shows studied, it had been more than five years since the most recent bisexual character (*Taxi,* 1980) or transsexual character (*WKRP in Cincinnati,* 1980).[10] The next portrayals in both categories were still years away: 1986 was an oasis.

Another big change was that gay youth issues were beginning to get attention, especially on teen-targeted shows whose advisory committees included school counselors. In the early and mid 1980s, some high school educators began to suspect that GLBT youth had much higher suicide and dropout rates than the general population. Various studies consistently confirmed this, and such research circulated widely in liberal educational circles. Researchers unsuccessfully tried to have their findings included in the Reagan administration's much-vaunted 1983 report, *A Nation at Risk,* intended as a blueprint for educational reform. At the time, however, "condoning" homosexuality was deemed an "antifamily" stance, so the studies languished. By 1985, many educators had read similar research, and began advocating change. As usual, the issue first reached TV via newscasts and talk shows. In parts of the New York City school system, the problem of physical safety for sexual-minority youth was so extreme that the school board and an outside agency were cosponsoring a special school where gay dropouts could finish their education. In early and mid 1985, reports about the controversial Harvey Milk School appeared on *ABC World News Tonight* and *CBS Evening News*, while debates about the school appeared on *Donahue, CBS Morning News,* PBS's *MacNeil-Lehrer News Hour,* and other shows. The media attention further raised the issue of gay youth support services in educational circles, leading to more research. In 1988, the National Education Association passed a resolution urging schools to institute supportive counseling programs for gay, bisexual, and questioning students.

From fall 1986 through 1990, at least seven TV dramas portrayed lesbigay or questioning teenagers—again, mostly on programs whose content was influenced by school counselors. In keeping with the research, the scripts generally showed how antigay prejudice can lead gay teenagers to depression. The stories suggest that even a modicum of support from family and friends can solve most of the problem. Dramas dealing with gay youth were more frequent than ever before, and also had a different focus. Back in the 1970s and early 1980s, TV stories had shown young people asking, "Might I be gay?" Starting in 1986, most of the dramas focused on young people who knew they were gay and were wondering—implicitly or explicitly— "What is my place in the world? Where do I fit in? Will I have any friends? What can my future be?" These characters are idealized archetypes: particularly in the shows from 1986 to 1990, the boys are championship athletes and the girls work on the school newspaper or yearbook. A quick comparison of these new shows with their predecessors reveals how TV's construction of adolescent sexuality had changed.

For clarity, the gay-youth dramas from before the summer of 1986 will be referred to as the "earlier" shows and those from that summer onward will be called the "later" shows. Of the earlier shows, which number about a dozen, only a third depict teenagers who seem sure of their sexual orientation; of the later shows, almost all portray youths who know they are gay or lesbian, even if they are not initially happy about it. Just one later show (*Degrassi Junior High,* a Canadian import on PBS) depicts a character who is completely unsure of her sexual orientation. Her confusion is understandable: she is only around twelve years old, the youngest character ever to be the focus of such a TV drama.[11] The first two new-style gay-youth dramas almost certainly had input from professional educators: one was a Scholastic coproduction seen on HBO, and the other a *CBS Schoolbreak Special.*

In 1986, Scholastic Productions released a fifty-minute teen coming-out drama, *The Truth About Alex.* In the film, a high school boy, Brad (Scott Baio) learns that his closest friend, Alex (Peter Spence), is gay.

The two are star players on their school's winning football team, though Alex's true passion is classical piano. Alex's homosexuality becomes public knowledge after a truck driver makes a pass at him in a gas station men's room. Alex is just there to use the toilet and rejects the man, who beats him up and spits on him. On his way out, the truck driver tells the station attendant that *Alex* had made a pass at *him*. Brad encourages Alex to press charges, and cannot figure out why his friend is just willing to accept a beating. The reason, naturally, is that Alex is secretly gay, a fact that soon becomes common knowledge. Brad stands by Alex, becoming a target of homophobia himself when people assume they are a couple. Brad crosses his coach, his girlfriend, and his own father to be a loyal best friend. The film had its U.S. TV debut in February 1987 on HBO's *Family Playhouse*. It is one of the only TV dramas about a gay teen who is self-assured and secure in his identity from the start, and whose parents accept him when they find out. It was not a typical "Oh, God, I might be queer" youth story.[12]

The next month, a *CBS Schoolbreak Special* trod what would become the more traveled route in "What If I'm Gay?" The drama is well thought out, right down to the "teaser" before the broadcast. By using alternate footage with different camera angles, the preview suggests that the gay character will be shy, brainy Alan. The drama's first act continues setting him up as the gay character: unlike his jock-hero friends Kirk and Todd, Alan is unathletic and does not have a girlfriend. Kirk and Todd make antigay comments, which Alan challenges. Kirk harasses Alan about his weird taste in clothes, music, and his lack of interest in sports. Then the show surprises the viewer when Alan finds a gay porn magazine in Todd's bedroom while Kirk is there. This outs Todd and creates a rift between Todd and his lifelong best buddy Kirk. Todd finally finds the self-respect and confidence to confront Kirk's prejudice, thanks to the friendship of Alan, Alan's new girlfriend, some other friends, and advice from a guidance counselor (Ed Marinaro). Todd and Kirk call a truce, though they are no longer friends. A repeat broadcast in 1990 drew advance protest from several religious groups. In Birmingham, Alabama, over three hundred callers demanded the rerun's cancellation because, they said, the show never says that homosexuality is wrong and never discusses heterosexual alternatives supposedly available to Todd. The station aired the show despite the protests.[13] "What If I'm Gay?" later reran many times on cable's *HBO Family Playhouse*, but without the clever, misleading preview scenes.

The series *21 Jump Street* presented the era's only commercial TV drama about a young lesbian (rather than a gay teenage boy). In the 1990 episode "Change of Heart," a lesbian student is disconsolate after her favorite teacher, also a lesbian, is killed. The teacher had been a role model for young Megan—her only image of a successful, basically happy gay person. The episode shows how the support system to which teenagers are supposed to be able to turn—personified in a well-meaning but ignorant guidance counselor—is pushing her toward self-destruction by alternately pathologizing and dismissing her sexual orientation. Megan's self-esteem, never that high to begin with, goes into a tailspin as every aspect of the educational system conspires to deny her very existence. She becomes depressive and drinks heavily, yet no one will let her talk through her problems, since that would mean acknowledging that she might be gay. This was a remarkable script for its time: it did not just say that there was a great need for support services, but it pointed to the existence of institutional problems that had the potential to kill young people. Late in the episode, Megan confronts her late teacher's closeted lover: the school's married vice principal, whose husband turns out to be the murderer. Megan asks the vice principal how she can teach honesty while living a lie. The older woman says that she has been lying for so long that she can no longer afford to stop, but that Megan has a chance for a happier life if she chooses to live honestly from the start.

Other youth stories appeared on *21 Jump Street* (1987, Fox: the AIDS-discrimination episode); *Bronx Zoo* (1988, NBC: a high school teacher tries to dissuade a closeted male student from marrying a girl and using her as a cover); and *Degrassi Junior High* (1989, PBS: a student struggles to accept his gay older brother—an all-star athlete, of course). In every case, the newer dramas depicted "average," gender-conformist white youth who, on the surface, looked and acted like their peers. Portrayals of racially diverse GLBT youth characters would have to wait until the mid 1990s.

Not only did sexual-minority characters' demographics become more diverse during this period, but so did the types of stories in which they could appear. Scripts addressed couples' rights, gay parenting, queer-bashing, and gays in the military. Some shows casually included guest characters whose GLBT status was incidental, and was not treated as a social issue. Gay characters also turned up in genres where they were previously ignored. For example, the new *Twilight Zone* depicted a gay man (a comparatively small role) who dies, is unjustly sent to Hell, and is rescued and sent to Heaven.[14] With so many different types of guest characters on screen, the time was ripe for the reemergence of gay and lesbian recurring roles.

REGULAR VISITORS

Television: 1986–1990

Now, David, we have a Tenants' Association meeting. There's an undesirable couple trying to get into the building, and we want to be there to support them.
—*William Manchester (Sam McMurray), half of the gay couple on* The Tracey Ullman Show, *1990¹*

TV's tendency to shunt gay characters into one-shot guest roles marginalized gay images for decades. The remarkable growth of GLB regulars, which became most noticeable in the 1990s, actually began in the mid 1980s. Some of the characters had been around for years, like Steven on *Dynasty* or Donald and Cliff on *Brothers*. One of the regulars in 1988 and 1989 appeared on a daytime soap: Brian Starcher played Hank Elliot, a squeaky-clean, athletic-looking designer of women's clothing, on *As the World Turns*. The other GLB recurring roles were new prime-time characters, such as the stereotyped assistant, Jules (Richard Frank), in the sitcom *Anything But Love*. Between 1986 and 1989, at least a dozen series had gay or lesbian recurring roles.

On *Hill Street Blues*, Lindsay Crouse first appeared as Officer Kate McBride in March 1986.² The next week, she was at the center of a scandal. The same basic plot had appeared on other shows before: a female suspect falsely accuses a woman cop of sexual harassment. McBride appeared in at least three other episodes over the next year, which made her an interesting but underused recurring character. She is never reduced to just "the lesbian cop": subsequent scripts focus on other aspects of her personality. She has been on the force for over four years. She makes good and bad judgment calls, like other characters on the series. In a January 1987 episode, scripted by Crouse's husband, playwright David Mamet, McBride is forced to shoot an armed robber. Shaken by her first killing, McBride turns to one of the series regulars, Detective Buntz (Dennis Franz), who counsels her through the experience. In March 1987, near the end of the series' run, McBride attends an awards ceremony, which dredges up painful memories of her father's death.[3] Kate is just a good cop who happens to be a lesbian.

Gay recurring characters got more frequent exposure on Fox's *The Tracey Ullman Show*, a sketch-comedy series built around chameleon-like actress/singer Ullman. She played hundreds of characters over the three-year run, showing off her brilliant sense of comedy and sharp ear for dialect. In at least ten skits from 1987 to 1990, regular cast members Dan Castellaneta and Sam McMurray played David and William, a Manhattan couple who are raising David's adolescent daughter, Francesca. British Ullman, then in her mid-twenties, submerges herself completely in the persona of an idealistic American girl, around age fourteen. There is a refreshing joy and affection among the three characters: amid all the punch lines and gags, they come off as a family that has lived together for years, respect one another, and love being together. The male couple are a bit of a gay-yuppie stereotype—William lisps and is a compulsive housecleaner—but eminently likable and a lot of fun. Avoiding the preachiness of some shows, Ullman's writers simply create their characters and tell stories about them.

Francesca's debut, seven weeks into the series, finds David and William giving her advice before her first date. "I remember *my* first date," says William. "I was a typical high school kid: boy-crazy." He sits on Francesca's bed and David puts his arms around him. This is the first time the audience realizes that Frannie is being raised by two men, and the line gets a big laugh. When her date, Martin, arrives (a classmate played by a teenage actor), Francesca invites him into the apartment to meet her folks. The audience laughs in anticipation. "This is my dad," she says. Martin and David exchange greetings. "And this is my William," Frannie adds. William waves.

MARTIN: *(with growing trepidation)* I get it. You guys live together—like *The Odd Couple*? *(tries to make a joke)* Which one of you is Felix?

DAVID AND WILLIAM: *(in unison)* Both of us.

Later that year, Frannie enters an essay contest about "What Family Means to Me." Her teacher wants her to omit her parents' gender. Francesca leaves it in and wins the contest, thanks to a gay judge. In later episodes, the family survives Frannie's first job (aired during the 1987 March on Washington), a visit from her resentful mom (Julie Kavner), a slumber party, and the dads' disapproval when Francesa falls for an older boy. Averaging about ten minutes, each skit usually occupies half an *Ullman* broadcast. David and William appear alone in at least one sketch: in "Flesh and Desire," they bicker over vegetarianism. But they are most entertaining when interacting with their inquisitive daughter.[4]

As the 1987–88 season approached, TV critics predicted that the season's defining trait would be half-hour "dramedies"—light dramas with no laugh track. As it happened, the genre never attracted much of an audience, and only a handful of these shows were renewed. One that did make it through a full second season was *Hooperman*, an offbeat cop show starring John Ritter, and created by Steven Bochco and Terry Louise Fisher. Detective Harry Hooperman (Ritter) divides his time among police work, a girlfriend, and being landlord of a run-down San Francisco apartment building full of eccentric tenants. The series is part rough-and-tumble crime drama, part whimsy. Two young officers work with Hooperman: openly gay Rick Silardi (Joseph Gian) and openly straight Maureen "Mo" DeMott (Sydney Walsh). Between shoot-outs, Mo's goal in life is to bed her attractive gay partner. As originally conceived, this was to be the central trait of their relationship, high-lighted in ABC's press packet for the first season. This plotline made some mainstream reviewers uncomfortable. They did not object to Rick's gayness, but rather to the idea that a straight woman in San Francisco at the height of the AIDS crisis might *want* to bed a gay man.

In addition to its gay regular (Rick) and a recurring character (drag queen tenant Rudy), gay men occasionally appear as guest roles on

Hooperman. This distinguishes it from other series set in San Francisco. As early as 1908, Xavier Mayne described San Francisco as one of America's "homosexual capitals." Since the 1940s, the Bay Area has been home to increasingly visible gay communities. Nonetheless, a viewer would never know that from watching the dozens of TV series set there. In the 1970s, when *The Streets of San Francisco* was popular, some people jokingly called it *The Straights of San Francisco*, since that is who constituted the overwhelming bulk of its characters. *Hooperman* was an exception. However, like most gay characters then on TV, Rick Silardi is hopelessly single.[5]

That problem did not plague the first lesbian regular in a prime-time drama, Marilyn McGrath (Gail Strickland) on ABC's *Heartbeat*. Sara Davidson, the writer who created her, is best known for two books: *Loose Change* (1977), a novel about the women's movement in the 1960s; and *Rock Hudson: His Story* (1986), a best-selling "as-told-to" biography published after Hudson's death. In Davidson's television work, series about women doctors are a dominant theme: in the mid 1980s she wrote for *Jessie*, about a police psychiatrist, and in the 1990s she coproduced and frequently scripted *Dr. Quinn, Medicine Woman*. Around 1987, Davidson created *Heartbeat*, a sudsy drama about a women's medical practice. Gail Strickland said that after hearing Davidson describe all the regulars, she asked for the role of nurse-practitioner Marilyn because she liked her idealism, directness, and sense of humor. One reporter asked if she was worried about being stereotyped. Strickland said that after playing many mean characters, "If I'm typecast as a woman as nice as this, I wouldn't mind that at all."[6]

In *Heartbeat*'s backstory, the Women's Medical Arts center was founded by three old friends: gynecologist Joanne Springsteen (Kate Mulgrew), surgeon Eve Autrey (Laura Johnson), and Marilyn. Tired of the medical establishment's ideas about treating women patients, they dreamed of founding their own clinic. Years before, they sat on a beach and toasted that dream. Now, in the two-hour premiere, they assemble a team of women and men who share their vision. As ABC publicists put it, these are "Doctors Who Give a Damn." ABC's ad sales department was glad to have a show that targeted women consumers, a coveted market. The network ordered six episodes for spring 1988. After minor retooling and an eight-month hiatus, the show returned with new episodes for thirteen weeks in 1989.

Marilyn is a well-developed character whose friends and colleagues knew she was gay long before the story begins. There is no big coming-out scene, no dramatic plea for tolerance. Coexecutive producer George Eckstein (formerly of *Love, Sidney*) said that Marilyn's homosexuality is simply "a given." He said the scripts generally "wouldn't comment on it any more than we would comment on a character being black or Jewish." The other characters treat Marilyn's longtime partner, Patti (Gina Hecht), much as they treat one another's straight spouses.[7]

Viewers did not meet Patti until the last two episodes of the initial six—a two-part story built around the wedding of Marilyn's daughter (Hallie Todd, of *Brothers*). "We wanted people to see [Marilyn] as a terrific person first," said Davidson, "then to find out she has a private life that at its core is no different from anyone else's."[8] The few conflicts that involve Marilyn's gayness are interpersonal issues with new friends or estranged relatives. The scripts never mention more practical questions, such as whether the financially strapped couple can put Patti on Marilyn's insurance.

Heartbeat was a paradox, a soapy melodrama about feminists: It depicted the women's resourcefulness, emotional strength, and basic humanity in confronting life's challenges, but the show's sudsy format played into nonfeminist assumptions about women viewers. It had all the emotional manipulation and visual tidiness of a 1960s daytime soap, even when the stories seemed to require a grittier approach. (The lack of grit might be explained by the participation of executive producers who were better known for glossy fare like *Dynasty*, notably Esther Shapiro and Aaron Spelling.) The show's attitude toward lesbianism is equally paradoxical. The straight characters seem perfectly comfortable with Marilyn and Patti, but the camera, the blocking, and the writing hold the couple at arm's length, which sends the viewer conflicting signals.

ABC's censors did not want Patti and Marilyn to touch in any kind of affectionate way. This put the writers in an awkward position, since they wanted some degree of believability. Judging from the finished product, the agreed-upon solution was to keep the women's hands busy. So Patti pays bills while Marilyn brushes her teeth. Or Marilyn prepares lasagna while Patti grates cheese. In one emotional scene, when it looks as though they might actually clasp hands, Patti instead hands Marilyn oven mitts.[9] They could bicker like other couples on the show, but ABC was not comfortable with viewers' seeing them make up afterward. *Heartbeat* got mixed reviews and spent its second season scheduled opposite NBC's ratings juggernaut *L.A. Law*. Against that kind of competition, *Heartbeat* flatlined in the Nielsens and vanished.

Starting in spring 1989, ABC's *thirtysomething* was supposed to add a gay male regular. The series, created by Marshall Herskovitz and Edward Zwick, is a drama about seven friends who, though well past their teens, are still coming of age. These glib, upwardly mobile baby boomers have reached a point where they must make tough choices and compromises: marriage versus independence, commercial success versus integrity, honesty versus protecting the people they care about.[10] They talk about these dilemmas incessantly and sometimes wrestle with them in whimsical fantasy dream sequences. Some viewers embraced *thirtysomething* as a leisurely study of confused, unfulfilled, basically good folks. Others dismissed it as a bunch of slow, whiny stories about "skinny white people from Hell."[11] For viewers who clicked with the characters, the series became a Tuesday night tradition. The show ran for four years on ABC, winning eight major-category Emmys and garnering awards from gay organizations such as GLAAD. However, it never attracted enough of a mass audience to guarantee a long run.

Herskovitz acknowledged that the absence of gay characters in a show about college-educated, liberal Philadelphians in creative professions was "conspicuous." In summer 1988, after the first season, the producers announced plans to add a gay regular: Russell, a friend of an existing regular, photographer Melissa Steadman (Melanie Mayron). The writers planned to treat him just like any member of the ensemble. "We have strong interest in people of all circumstances," Herskovitz told reporters in September 1988. Russell was going to have relationships. "It would be ridiculous," Herskovitz said, "to introduce a character and be afraid to explore any aspect of his life." But while the character would be sexual, his sexuality would not be his defining feature.[12] Richard Kramer, the third member of the series' creative trio, created Russell. The character debuted early in the second season of *thirtysomething*. He would have been the fourth gay regular on a network series that season—if only he had become a regular. Played by David Marshall Grant, a versatile stage and film actor, Russell is a painter who lectures in contemporary art at the University of Pennsylvania. In the episode "Trust Me," he and Melissa meet at a wedding and bond instantly. They have a similar sense of humor, similar self-doubts, a quirky outlook on life, and—it is hard to tell, since viewers do not yet know that he is gay—*maybe* he is interested in Melissa romantically. She seems uncharacteristically relaxed as he makes flirty comments and makes wisecracks about the bride's nose job. When Melissa visits his home later that week, she listens as he takes a devastating phone call. Obviously shaken, he makes a halfhearted joke: "You know what they say about guys like me: we know how to dance and we know how to die." He has just learned that a friend has AIDS. This is how Russell comes out to Melissa. (When Richard Kramer wrote "Trust Me," Kramer's closest friend, thirty-six-year-old film producer David Bombyk, was suffering through the final stages of AIDS. The epidemic was very much on Kramer's mind and frequently appears in his scripts.)[13] Russell tells Melissa he hopes she did not get the wrong idea since he is "pretty open" and was not trying to lead her on. They also talk about AIDS, and how he tries not to let it make him too afraid.[14]

With help from Herskovitz and Zwick, Kramer drafted a year's worth of plot for the new character. They planned for Russell and Melissa to develop an intense friendship, spending so much time together that neither could pursue a love relationship. Since both fear intimacy, they would use each other as a crutch and an excuse to avoid commitment. Kramer planned for Russell to appear in a few episodes during season two. Then, in season three, he was supposed to appear in six out of twenty-four episodes.[15] It did not work out that way. Russell appeared in just two episodes of season two, both in January 1989. Then Kramer and the other writers got caught up in telling stories about the preexisting regulars. Kramer drafted some material for Russell, but he was not happy with how it turned out. By the third season, when Kramer was ready to incorporate the character more fully, actor Grant was knee-deep in other projects,[16] including two Mel Gibson films produced overseas. After Russell's initial appearances in early 1989, he resurfaced for two episodes in November, then one last time

in 1990.[17] That year, *The Advocate* quoted Kramer as saying, "I think
we sort of blew it with Russell the second year by giving him only those
two shows. We have too many stories to tell, and we should have had
him in the original bunch [of characters] for it to have been good."[18]

During a break between projects in fall 1989, Grant filmed one of
thirtysomething's most controversial episodes. "Strangers" was widely
debated in the press and was the target of canceled advertising. The
reason: It showed two men talking in bed—*not* touching each other,
mind you—after sex. According to Kramer, when he and Herskovitz
and Zwick brainstormed ideas for this script,

> we all agreed . . . that the radical approach to material like this was not to
> sensationalize it . . . I remember Marshall saying, "Let's go into Russell's
> bedroom just like we go into Hope and Michael's"; I also remember Ed
> saying, "Just make sure Russell's not there at the time."

The episode has Melissa and her cousin, Michael, fix Russell up with
one of Michael's coworkers, Peter (Peter Frechette, in his first *thirtysomething* appearance). Russell and Peter get together for dinner. A
later scene finds them side by side in Russell's bed, their bare chests
visible above the cover, looking very relaxed. Peter lights a cigarette,
hastily saying that he plans to quit soon. They talk about their youth
(each tried to deny his sexuality in high school, dating "the requi-
site" Asian musician girlfriend), their coming out, and friends who have
died of AIDS. At the end of the conversation, they smile at each other
again. (The stage direction that originally ended the scene—"They
move closer, into each other's arms"—fell victim to the censor's
pencil.) Peter appeared in five additional episodes, eventually testing
HIV-positive in one of the series' final installments. The principal
writer for that episode was Paul Monette, the noted AIDS activist and
openly gay, openly HIV-positive literary figure whose later works focus
almost exclusively on AIDS issues. Monette's lover, an NBC West
Coast casting manager, died of complications from AIDS later that
year.[19]

Even with the physical affection cut from "Strangers," sponsors
balked, canceling (according to ABC) $1.5 million in advertising. ABC
censors and sales executives bandied that figure around often circa

1990–91, as leverage to remove sexual content of all sorts from shows. All three networks shied away from sexual material in the late 1980s and early 1990s anyway, but publicity about the *thirtysomething* pull-outs intensified matters. Few viewers had a chance to see "Strangers." It originally aired on election night, 1989, and was wholly or partly preempted in many cities. In New York, the episode aired well after midnight.

The other gay regular of the 1980s was Richard Stratford (Tony Careiro), an affable, insecure assistant professor of English on the CBS sitcom *Doctor, Doctor* (1989–91). Richard lives downstairs from his older brother, the boisterous leading character Dr. Mike Stratford (Matt Frewer, of *Max Headroom* fame). The brothers are completely at ease with each other and engage in comfortable banter. The show focuses on the group medical practice where Mike works. So while Richard participates in the story lines almost every week, viewers generally see his life only insofar as it overlaps with Mike's or the other doctors'. Like most characters on the show, he has a horrific track record at dating: Richard is a nice guy who keeps getting involved with self-centered jerks. Usually this is only referred to, though in a 1990 episode, he dates the practice's insufferable new administrative assistant, Charles (guest star Charles Rocket). Another recurring character on the show—an obnoxious, HIV-positive TV personality named Hugh Persons (Brian George)—was also gay.[20]

Of course, while all these regulars and recurring roles were appearing, guest characters continued to turn up on other shows. Some of them were truly a horror. On a 1986 episode of *Hunter* ("From San Francisco, With Love"), dysfunctional gay women Valerie and Casey bump off Casey's husband and stepson to get at $8 million. Even when this troubled couple embraces (as they are allowed to do, being killers and all), their faces show obvious contempt for each other.[21] Three years later, with lesbian characters still rare on television, NBC ran a disturbing episode of *Unsub*. This crime-drama series portrays investigations into serial killings. One string of grisly mutilation murders appears to be motivated by homophobia, until evidence suggests that the victims were straight men. There *is* a gay tie-in, however: the killer is a man-hating lesbian cop who cuts off her victims' genitals and keeps them in her freezer as trophies.[22] However, such nightmarish stereotypes were finally sharing the screen with other, less extreme images that appeared on a more regular basis.

In the last year of the 1980s, at least eight series had recurring sexual-minority characters: *Anything But Love; As the World Turns; Brothers; Doctor, Doctor; Heartbeat; Hooperman; thirtysomething;* and *The Tracey Ullman Show*. Things were looking up. Only when compared to shows of the 1990s do the limitations of these 1980s characters emerge—including many limitations we have noted in other contexts. Except for cable's *Brothers*, none of the 1980s regulars was a series protagonist. None was bisexual or transgendered. All were white, ablebodied, and "good-looking" by mass media standards. Except for Marilyn on *Heartbeat*, all were men in their twenties or early thirties—usually single, usually middle-class. Considering the vast diversity of GLBT people, TV was still painting on a microscopic canvas.

31

WELCOME TO THE QUEER '90s
Television: 1989–1991

I've been trying to get a gay series on TV for years. And what's hysterical is what bothers the networks—and we won't mention names—is not the gay sex. They love the sex jokes. It's the gay politics. They don't want to hear that maybe there are gay people who don't like heterosexuals. They don't wanna hear that.

—Actor/playwright Harvey Fierstein, 1991[1]

The 1990s brought unprecedented growth of sexual-minority images throughout American culture. Singers, athletes, writers, and legislators came out, as did a former speechwriter for antigay televangelists. Top-selling magazines ran well-publicized cover stories about lesbian and gay issues. Comic-book heroes in Marvel and DC publications came out in the 1990s. So did longtime characters in the comic strips "For Better or for Worse" and "Doonesbury." The term "homophobia," which had been an in-word in the gay community since the 1970s, entered the American vernacular in the 1990s as part of the standard liberal litany of social prejudices ("sexism, racism, religious intolerance, homophobia . . ."). It was the first decade in which, during a presidential election, most of the viable candidates openly courted the gay vote. It was the first decade when gay issues were mainstream enough that a sitting U.S. president agreed to serve as the keynote speaker at a gay civil rights event. There were some notable setbacks, of course: reports of antigay violence reached new highs in the early 1990s, and referenda in several states turned antigay discrimination into an inalienable right. But even among many people who opposed homosexuality, there was a growing understanding that sexual orientation—whatever moral issues one might associate with it—was not a matter of choice: that the choices lay in what one did with that orientation and how others reacted to it.

Television both mirrored and fueled that explosion of visibility. Some fifty network series in the 1990s had gay or bisexual recurring roles. As mentioned earlier, this was more than twice the combined total for all previous decades. Gay news stories and openly gay celebrities also held the TV cameras' attention at the end of the twentieth century. It was the decade of Queer Nation, "outing," *Roseanne,* "Don't Ask, Don't Tell," k.d. lang, Melissa Etheridge, the 1993 March on Washington, "lesbian chic," *The Real World, Northern Exposure,* RuPaul, Greg Louganis, *Friends, Ellen,* and *Will & Grace.* It was the decade when, for two years, reporters gave round-the-clock coverage to the debate over whether the U.S. military should stop its expulsion of gay service members. Televised sexual-minority images were not just more numerous, but also more diverse. Shows portrayed lesbians more often and more realistically. Gay youth and senior citizens appeared more often. As TV characters in general become more diverse racially and ethnically in the first half of the decade, viewers saw more black and Latino gay characters. Gay Asian characters, still rare, appeared as minor roles in a few shows.

In an almost unprecedented move, several series in the 1990s casually incorporated gay or bisexual regulars whose sexuality was not made an issue. Where earlier shows had required that an antagonist spout antigay rhetoric which others could rebut, 1990s characters' sexual orientation was often just there, without comment. At most, gay characters' straight friends might go through an adjustment period, but the straight characters now treated this discomfort as their own problem. Religious Right groups loudly denounced such portrayals as proof of liberal Hollywood's "normalization" of perversion. Most important, gay characters in the 1990s could date, have long-term relationships, kiss, and, on rare occasions, have a sex life. In a marked contrast from the 1970s, GLB recurring roles now appeared on some of the top-rated series on television.

A great many interwoven threads contributed to the revival of GLBT images. To understand how these images came about, one must look at both the "big picture" and the individual threads of the story. This chapter will look at the backstage politics of the early 1990s, the antigay backlash's effect on sponsors, and the gay movement's return to media activism. The next chapter will offer an "aerial view" of on-screen images from 1991 to 1993, with emphasis on shows with strong Nielsens. Later chapters will deal with a variety of themes: the further diversification of GLBT characters and narratives, "lesbian chic," the role of gay-friendly broadcasts in the battle over PBS funding, and TV's portrayal of affectionate same-sex couples. The final chapters will celebrate major landmarks since 1995, and offer predictions for the new millennium.

Looking back on all of this diversity and mainstreaming, it is easy to forget that at the start of that decade, changes of this magnitude seemed inconceivable. The 1990s began with a freeze-out on lesbian, gay, and bisexual characters on TV. At the same time, Hollywood motion pictures were featuring some of the most viciously antigay stereotyping ever to appear on film. Movie scripts that included homicidal GLBT roles—*Basic Instinct*, *The Silence of the Lambs*, *JFK*, and so on—were allowed to reach the screen more or less intact, even as scripts with sympathetic gay roles were rejected or "de-gayed." The developments in other media were equally disheartening. Several major recording companies, for instance, were distributing songs and comedy routines that advocated antigay violence, sometimes explicitly.

The crisis of media representation circa 1990 had its roots in the 1980s. During the early years of AIDS, gay media activism atrophied. Of necessity, many gay people spent the 1980s concentrating on survival, on promoting the development and availability of medical care, on encouraging safer-sex education, on supporting their friends, and on grieving. The epidemic had claimed some of the movement's most dynamic, effective leaders of the 1970s and 1980s. With such emergencies at hand, gay organizations appropriately put show business activism on the back burner. ACT UP and the Gay & Lesbian Alliance Against Defamation targeted television on occasion in the 1980s, but the resources were not there to address GLBT portrayals in a persistent fashion. By 1989, the former friendly relations with the broadcast networks were in decay. Many of the television executives who used to meet with Ginny Vida or Newt Deiter in the 1970s had since retired or changed jobs. There were few gay media activists around to meet with these executives' successors. In any case, the new network vice presidents had other issues to worry about. Responding to pressure from the Religious Right, several multimillion-dollar sponsors were threatening to pull funding from shows that made "exploitative" use of sex and violence.

In 1989 and 1990, the American Family Association (AFA) and Christian Leaders for Responsible Television (CLeaR-TV) had their first notable successes in scaring sponsors away from specific shows. In an atypical move, several major advertisers acknowledged publicly that they had been swayed by the Religious Right's letter-writing campaigns. It was an ideal time for CLeaR-TV to influence programming. Advertisers were already receiving an unusually large number of complaints from viewers about the content of TV shows. Every network had broadcasts that blatantly stretched the industry's traditional boundaries of taste: sexual situations, nudity, gore, and "gross-out" humor were on the rise in prime time. This reflected the increased competition for viewers: the traditional Big Three networks were losing market share not only to local stations and cable and VCRs, but also to the increasingly successful Fox TV. The major networks relaxed their program content in hope of luring viewers back.

Other factors contributed to the loosening of broadcast standards. A 1988 federal court decision had curtailed the FCC's jurisdiction over "indecent" (but "nonobscene") content after 10:00 P.M.[2] Corporate "downsizing" meant the networks had fewer censors to enforce program standards policies—policies that had, in any case, become more lax as part of that competition for viewers.[3] Staff reductions in advertising meant that ad agencies had fewer people to enforce their clients' advertising guidelines. Commercials were showing up on series that seemed like a bad fit for the products. Toys "R" Us spots appeared during steamy episodes of *thirtysomething*. Several companies with family-friendly images found that their ads were supporting the scatological sex comedy *Married . . . With Children*—a bawdy send-up of TV's "happy-family" sitcoms.

In January 1989, Reverend Wildmon's umbrella organization, CLeaR-TV, made another attempt to organize national boycotts. Again they announced a monitoring period, after which the sponsors of the most offensive shows would be shunned. Conditions were right for a boycott. The networks were anxious to bolster their family image to counterbalance negative press about the new, crude shows. Although many of the complaints came from individual viewers and dealt with clearly exploitative broadcasts, Wildmon's organizations did most of the direct negotiating with sponsors. This meant that opposition to gay-friendly programming got strong emphasis in the bargaining sessions and in news coverage.

In March 1989, the *New York Times* heralded the new age of advertising pullouts with a front-page story headlined A MOTHER IS HEARD AS SPONSORS ABANDON A TV HIT. It told of Terry Rakolta, a mother of four from an upscale suburb of Detroit. By writing letters to forty-five sponsors—so the story went—she had single-handedly convinced Procter & Gamble, McDonald's, Tambrands, and Kimberly-Clark to stop advertising on Fox's *Married . . . With Children*. The *Times* said she was "appalled" at the sitcom's "sexual innuendo and treatment of women, particularly its references to homosexuality . . ." That night, Rakolta was a guest on ABC News's *Nightline*, where she said she hoped to meet shortly with leaders of Concerned Women for America and the AFA to throw her support behind national boycotts. Journalists quickly went looking for more established sources, to find out what sorts of shows boycotters were targeting. Again, they focused on Wildmon, who was having some success at the time. After campaigns by his AFA, several advertisers publicly disassociated themselves from *Saturday Night Live*, pulling millions of dollars' worth of ads. At least one *SNL* sponsor, Domino's Pizza, acknowledged AFA's role in convincing them to cancel their sponsorship. Quotations from Wildmon appeared in many—probably most—major daily newspapers and in glossy newsweeklies. In July, Wildmon announced one-year boycotts of Mennen and Clorox, saying his group would spend $2 million to publicize the campaign.[4]

Under pressure, major sponsors ordered their ad agencies to prescreen shows on an episode-by-episode basis, and withdraw ads from inappropriate broadcasts. Usually, anything remotely controversial was considered suspect. Gay-themed shows were hard hit. ABC's TV movie docudrama *Rock Hudson* had had trouble finding sponsors to begin

with. In January 1990, two companies that had placed numerous commercials in the film—Chesebrough-Pond's and Johnson & Johnson—
dropped out after learning that the script would directly acknowledge
Hudson's homosexuality. ABC resold the ad time at a discount. With
echoes of ABC's $1.5 million *thirtysomething* deficit ringing in their
ears, network executives saw the *Rock Hudson* ad losses as a sign. ABC's
vice president for Movies and Miniseries, Allen Sabinson, acknowledged
that in commercial TV, "the subject of homosexuality may be a greater
taboo at this time." Just after the *Hudson* defections, NBC dropped two
projects that had been repeatedly mentioned in the press: its own film
about Hudson's life, and a long-touted miniseries based on Randy
Shilts's political history of AIDS in the 1980s, *And the Band Played On*.
The latter had been in development for two years, promoted as a prestige drama being adapted by Emmy winner John Gay. The cancellation
of *And the Band Played On* hinged not just on sponsorship—though
that was an essential factor—but also on concerns over the original
book's politics. Shilts had excoriated the Reagan administration for allowing thousands of deaths to occur amid the government's homophobic
inaction on AIDS. Network executives were uneasy about presenting
such a controversial thesis. The day that NBC dropped the project,
HBO cable grabbed up the video rights to Shilts's book.[5]

TV executives initially said that the AFA/CLeaR-TV campaign was
having no effect on network decisions. But by early 1990, the change in
program policies was unmistakable. NBC boosted the size of its Broadcast Standards staff from fifteen people back up to its early-1980s level
of twenty-five. Networks ordered that shows be completed further
ahead of airtime to accommodate sponsors' beefed-up prescreenings.
NBC's Brandon Tartikoff noted that sponsors had begun to "look at
everything in greater numbers," and that prescreening involved "more
people at the [ad] agency than ever before." That summer, ABC's
Sabinson said that sensationalist TV movies would no longer be approved at that network: instead, scripts would have to pass a "moral
litmus test."[6]

ABC announced that it would exclude the "Strangers" episode of
thirtysomething from the summer repeat cycle. Although gay organizations and *TV Guide* criticized that decision, ABC Entertainment
president Robert Iger said that "the sponsors are the ones who should

really get the pressure." He said ABC had lost $14 million in pulled advertising over morality issues during the previous season. Nine million of that was from TV movies. The 1989 *thirtysomething* episode accounted for around 30 percent of the losses in regular programming. ABC was not the only network to face large ad deficits. During the fall of 1990, NBC reportedly lost over $1 million due to canceled ads on two episodes of *Law and Order*. One of those episodes dealt with an openly gay AIDS activist (Peter Frechette) involved in the mercy killings of gay men in the later stages of AIDS. Its portrayal of a militant gay protest made it one of the first TV episodes to depict a gay-rights demonstration (a full quarter century after the first homophile picketing, and two decades after the first wave of Gay Lib zaps). Shortly after, NBC postponed a gay/AIDS-themed episode of *Lifestories*. When it finally aired in a later time slot, it was only partially sponsored, and cost the network a reported half-million dollars.[7] In December, ABC announced that it, once again, had lost ad revenue over a *thirtysomething* broadcast involving Russell and Peter—$500,000 this time.

Director John Erman, then at work on the TV movie *Our Sons* (an AIDS drama about the mothers of a gay male couple), said it was amazing that a network was backing his film. "It's the worst time to do a movie that concerns AIDS. . . . People are more afraid of homosexuality than ever before. There are so many more angry people out there now." In a 1991 interview, Harvey Fierstein told how quickly the market had dried up. "I was hired last year to write the first openly gay sitcom," he said. "I wrote it and they called me and said they loved it but couldn't put it on the air—because who would they sell their advertising time to?" He said that CBS executives told him they were put off by the amount of money ABC reportedly lost on the *thirtysomething* "Strangers" episode.[8] By February 1991, the number of series with gay or lesbian recurring characters on the Big Three networks had dropped to zero. On Fox, the only recurring characters were two very funny but stereotyped, woman-hating gay men—the swishy, black snap-divas, Blaine and Antoine—who dished out attitude on the African American comedy series *In Living Color*. It was a different world from the one in which, during 1989, at least eight network shows had presented lesbian or gay recurring roles.

With gay media images becoming rarer (on TV) and more abusive (in Hollywood films and recorded music), the organized GLBT communities threw their support behind media activism with renewed energy. As in the past, the approaches of different gay groups were a study in contrasts. The remainder of this chapter will examine the comparatively "professionalized" activism of the Gay & Lesbian Alliance Against Defamation, contrasted with the more militant approach of early-1990s Queer activists. It will also look at the concessions that their tandem assault wrung from the entertainment industry.

GLAAD

The main organization working to improve portrayals of gay characters in the 1990s was the Gay & Lesbian Alliance Against Defamation (GLAAD, pronounced "glad"). Originally called the Gay & Lesbian Anti-Defamation League, GLAAD began as a small, local, direct action and negotiating group in New York City. It was founded in 1985 by a circle of lesbian and gay writer/activists who included Vito Russo, Jewelle Gomez, Larry Kramer, Arnie Kantrowitz, Marcia Pally, and Darrell Yates Rist, and veteran New York activists, including Jim Owles and Marty Robinson. The impetus for its formation was a series of articles and editorials in the *New York Post*, which had been using the public's fear of AIDS as an excuse to continue spreading alarmist, misleading myths about gay people.

GLAAD's "cultural advocacy" mission was unique. Unlike the National Gay & Lesbian Task Force or the Human Rights Campaign Fund, GLAAD did not focus on public policy or government. Instead, it examined the treatment of lesbians and gay men across American culture—from employment practices to definitions of "homosexuality" in dictionaries, from pop music to school curricula, from radio "shock jocks" to the classified listings in phone books. GLAAD also differed from earlier media-focused gay groups like the Gay Media Task Force and the Alliance for Gay and Lesbian Artists. Those had been small outfits that worked alone, with minimal outreach to the general gay populace. By contrast, GLAAD quickly became a national membership organization that tried to keep the broader sexual-minority communities and their allies aware of current issues.

The group's first major actions were raucous, confrontational demonstrations in the tradition of the Gay Activists Alliance. GLAAD's initial tactics foreshadowed later direct action groups that would grow up in New York City from the mid 1980s to early 1990s—organizations like the Lavender Hill Mob, ACT UP, and Queer Nation. GLAAD's zap-action squad, "The Swift and Terrible Retribution Committee," kept busy for a year or two. GLAAD organized rowdy demonstrations at the *New York Post* and ABC-TV. After the Supreme Court's *Bower v. Hardwick* decision, GLAAD branched out and coordinated mass protests at the Statue of Liberty and the American Bar Association. But once ACT UP formed in early 1987, GLAAD's street protesters jumped ship, moving into the more urgent field of AIDS activism. With its pool of New York–based zappers running dry, GLAAD reinvented itself as a more sedate, structured agency with a stronger focus on negotiation and letter-writing campaigns. Former Wall Street attorney Craig Davidson (previously a GLAAD volunteer) became its first executive director and first paid employee. The revamped group began publishing *The GLAAD Bulletin*, a bimonthly newsletter that bore the slogan: "The only way to destroy homophobia is to confront it." Entertainment lawyer Richard Jennings cofounded a second chapter in Los Angeles, echoing the bicoastal approach to media advocacy that had succeeded in the 1970s. GLAAD soon became a frequent news source for gay periodicals and community-based radio and cable shows.

In January 1989, just before news of the sponsor defections broke, GLAAD won its first concession from a famous show business figure: it convinced Bob Hope to make a public-service announcement denouncing antigay violence. The TV ad was an apology of sorts: GLAAD/ New York's assistant director Karin Schwartz had contacted Hope's production company to challenge his recent use of the word "fag" on *The Tonight Show*. She told them of the devastating impact that antigay prejudice was having in the 1980s. This was during a national wave of gay-bashings, when a series of brutal antigay assaults in New York City made national news. In the thirty-second PSA, Hope said:

> I'm proud to live in this great, free country. I'm proud of our commitment to free speech—and I'm proud of our country's commitment to protecting the rights of its citizens to work and live free from bigotry and violence.

That's why I was amazed to discover that many people die each year in antigay attacks and thousands more are left scarred, emotionally and physically. Bigotry has no place in this great nation, and violence has no place in this world. But it happens. Prejudice hurts—kills. Please don't be a part of it—by your words or by your deeds. Thank you.

Hope's cooperation was a coup for GLAAD. Schwartz observed that his well-known Republicanism made him an especially effective spokesperson against gay-bashing: "[he] takes [the issue] out of the partisan political sphere to a purely moral ground where all violence is wrong—and un-American!" GLAAD members encouraged their local TV channels to run the ad. Few TV stations would air it, though, since it was not produced by the Ad Council (the nonprofit agency that produced most national public-service announcements seen on U.S. TV). Mostly, the Hope ad ran on gay cable shows whose audiences already knew that gay-bashing was a problem. Nevertheless, the ad did have an impact. Gay organizations in Washington, D.C., and New York State used the tape in lobbying for laws related to antigay violence. The ad also was the subject of a report on the nationally syndicated TV show *Entertainment Tonight*. Meanwhile, GLAAD representatives showed the Hope tape when they visited other organizations in search of support. People reasoned that if GLAAD could get a conservative star like Bob Hope for its PSA, the group obviously knew how to negotiate with the media establishment. The approach that GLAAD used with Hope would become a frequent strategy: contact the management of celebrities who had made antigay remarks, and suggest an opportunity for them to do something prosocial to prove that they were not prejudiced.[9]

GLAAD had its first taste of mainstream visibility in 1990. The organization made headlines when it faced off with CBS News's resident curmudgeon, Andrew A. Rooney, whose weekly commentary "A Few Minutes with Andy Rooney" had appeared on the top-rated *60 Minutes* since 1978. Since at least 1980, Rooney had been making comments, both in press conferences and as a newspaper columnist, that some people considered antigay. Activists usually let his comments pass without reaction, partly because he worded them as personal opinions. For instance, in 1989 he wrote: "I feel the same way about homosexuals as I do about cigarette smokers. I wouldn't want to spend much time in a small room with one but they don't bother me otherwise." Two months later, CBS gave Rooney a year-end special called *1989: A Year with Andy Rooney*. In the special, he went beyond opinion. Through a mix of bad journalism and sloppy research, he unthinkingly rehashed the tired notion that gay men are unstable murderers, unfit for high-pressure jobs. He repeated as fact a widely reported rumor that journalists and Navy investigators had raised, then discarded as baseless in mid 1989. Rooney told his viewers that an explosion aboard the U.S.S. *Iowa*, in which forty-seven sailors had died, had been an act of "murder and suicide by a lovesick homosexual for his companion on board." Later in the special, Rooney observed: "There was some recognition in 1989 of the fact that many of the ills that kill us are self-induced: too much alcohol, too much food, homosexual unions, cigarettes. They're all known to lead quite often to premature death." In listing homosexuality with things that are inherently harmful to the body, he spread misinformation about how AIDS was transmitted and propounded the myth that GAY=AIDS and AIDS=GAY.

In February 1990, GLAAD targeted CBS News president David Burke with a letter-writing campaign about the Rooney special. Members were told to specify clearly what bothered them about it. Meanwhile, Michelangelo Signorile—the features editor at *OutWeek* magazine, and a proponent of more militant tactics than GLAAD's—published Rooney's and Burke's office phone numbers with an order to "ZAP CBS!" "Call Rooney directly," Signorile urged, ". . . and tell him what a bigoted shithead he is. Then you can call his boss . . . and tell him what an asshole he is for not firing Rooney immediately."

GLAAD representatives met with CBS News executives on February 6, just as GLAAD's and Signorile's contrasting pressure campaigns were beginning. Burke agreed to let GLAAD distribute literature about gay issues to all CBS News staff, but he refused to fire Rooney. By then, Rooney had generated more controversy. Anxious not to be seen as a bigot (and, he said, to avoid losing what gay friends he still had), Rooney wrote an open letter to *The Advocate* and granted that magazine a phone interview. The interview article, published with the letter, attributed antigay and racist comments to Rooney, who later said he was misquoted. Most major news outlets reported on this, quoting both the *Advocate* article and Rooney. Many quoted Rooney's letter, in which he had written: "Do I find the practice of one man introducing his penis into the anus of another repugnant? I do. Is it ethically or morally wrong and abnormal behavior? It seems so to me, but I can't say why, and if a person can't say what he thinks, he probably doesn't have a thought, so I'll settle for thinking it's merely bad taste." Throughout the controversy, there was a steady stream of faxes and phone calls between GLAAD/New York and Burke's office.

On February 8, Burke suspended Rooney without pay for three months, and issued a statement saying that "CBS News cannot tolerate such remarks or anything that approximates such comments since they in no way reflect the views of this organization." Burke refused to say if it was the alleged comments about blacks, the comments about gays, or both that prompted the suspension. Newspapers quoted unnamed CBS insiders who said the suspension had more to do with Rooney's having sent the letter without running it past his superiors or CBS spin doctors. (A revised version of the letter, faxed from CBS News's northeast bureau on February 1, omitted the discussion of anal sex.)

In the short run, the dispute backfired on GLAAD and CBS. The public largely saw Rooney's unpaid leave as liberal censorship run amok. CBS was inundated with letters, faxes, and phone calls censuring them for allowing a pressure group to cost someone his job just for expressing an "opinion." The network commuted Rooney's suspension after a month. He returned to 60 Minutes with a commentary that sought to prove he was not a racist. In passing, he also made a brief, almost-apology to gay men, whose lives, he said, he hoped he had not made more difficult. In the long run, the controversy benefited GLAAD. It gave them a foot in the door at a major network, and brought news coverage. This boosted the group's visibility and legitimacy among many gay people, and meant that when GLAAD contacted media outlets in the future, some decision makers had at least heard of them.[10]

Throughout coverage of the Rooney controversy, GLAAD worked hard to ensure that the publicity would continue. They told reporters about the upcoming first annual GLAAD Media Awards, scheduled for April 1990. GLAAD leaders knew that award presentations get more news coverage if they take place in a prominent locale and include speeches by famous people. GLAAD focused on getting both. The April 29 ceremony, in the Tower Suite atop the Time-Life Building in

Manhattan, began with introductory remarks and congratulations by New York's Mayor David Dinkins. The emcee was TV talk show legend Phil Donahue, who also accepted GLAAD's Media Person of the Year award. Presenters included former *That Girl* star Marlo Thomas (star of 1985's *Consenting Adult* and wife of emcee Donahue). Awards went to *Newsweek*, the *New York Times*, and other print media. Television honorees included *As the World Turns; Doctor, Doctor;* and PBS's *AIDS Quarterly.*

Having built small amounts of credibility within the industry, GLAAD turned up its own pressure on sponsors. In the past, antigay groups had held the upper hand in negotiating with advertisers. Groups like AFA could go to a company and say, in effect, "We know you don't want controversy. If you sponsor this show, we'll publicize that your 'family-friendly' company promotes perversion, corrupts children, and undermines the family." In the 1990s, for the first time, organizations like GLAAD could successfully turn that tactic around. Gay activists could say, in essence: "If you systematically *remove* commercials from shows that portray gay people fairly, we will let the public know that you are prejudiced against a large part of the population—that you have a vendetta against gay people." This sometimes worked in the 1990s because there was starting to be a social stigma attached to antigay prejudice. For the first time, a generation of adults had grown up aware of a gay-rights movement, and had heard sexual orientation discussed as a civil rights issue. People who had been in their late teens during Anita Bryant's campaign were now in their thirties, and many had openly gay friends, relatives, or coworkers. Some gay people of the Stonewall generation, in their forties by 1990, had risen into policy-making jobs, or they were in a position to raise issues with influential people. Thanks to recently published and rather skewed market research, gay people were starting to be perceived as a disproportionately affluent and knowledgeable (hence desirable) consumer population.

Generally, an advertiser's initial replies to AFA and GLAAD were just vague enough that each side could claim a partial victory. However, AFA's goals were broad, not limited to gay issues. Since GLAAD's interests were more focused, its demands were more specific and easier to measure. GLAAD was also more media savvy. Thus, the gay organization often had the last word. Most companies wanted to be seen as supporting "family values" in at least a nebulous sort of way, but they also did not want to be seen as homophobic—as enemies of a large chunk of the buying public. In September 1989, GLAAD/New York lodged a protest with the corporate management of Wendy's Restaurants. Following recent AFA complaints, Wendy's had issued a statement to the effect that its sponsorship of an *L.A. Law* episode with possibly gay characters was "inappropriate." According to GLAAD, after its own negotiations with the restaurant chain, Wendy's formally apologized to the gay community, calling its earlier apology to AFA a "mistake." GLAAD apparently hoped for something equally decisive from Toys "R" Us. The toy store chain had pulled its ads from *thirtysomething* because of the episode that showed Russell and Peter's postcoital conversation. Toys "R" Us president Robert Nakasone issued a clarification regarding *thirtysomething*. He said his firm "has nothing against gay and lesbian people," and that the withdrawal from *thirtysomething* and other shows was motivated purely by their adult content, whether gay or straight. But he would not go so far as to say that there might be gay content that was not also "adult content."[11]

GLAAD got a break in its next campaign when Wildmon targeted Burger King over eighteen supposedly offensive broadcasts, including NBC's miniseries *People Like Us*. CLeaR-TV and AFA's stated objection to this show was that it "developed the homosexual relationship between Hubert and Juanito, portraying the homosexual lovers as caring, sensitive, rational men while Hubert's antihomosexual mother is cold, uncaring, and vindictive." They also objected to the program's portrayal of a movie star who campaigns to raise money for AIDS research, much as Elizabeth Taylor was famous for doing in real life.

Burger King's corporate executives quickly met with AFA and promised to run print ads proclaiming support for "traditional American values" on TV. Wildmon called off the boycott, claiming victory. A Burger King spokesperson told reporters, "It must be stressed that Burger King Corp. did not change its principles of its media buying policies as a result of the boycott." She added the standard, transparent denial, stating that the ads were not a concession to CLeaR-TV but a way to clear up any public confusion that the threat of a boycott had caused. In the context of the CLeaR-TV boycotts and the recent sponsor defections, Burger King's large ads in over five hundred U.S.

newspapers sent a clear message to networks and TV writers that this major corporation would be very selective in buying TV ad time.

Wildmon's campaign against the fast-food chain soon proved to be a miscalculation, however. The wording of his groups' complaints, and the prosaic things to which they objected (such as portrayal of a separated husband and wife who have sex and then reconcile) sounded judgmental and petty to many people who did not share CLeaR-TV's particular worldview. Certainly, the description of Burger King as the "leading sponsor of sex, violence, and profanity" on TV sounded overwrought. Wildmon's complaint that "a major part of the plot [in *People Like Us*] included a movie star committed to raising funds for AIDS research" proved especially damaging. GLAAD reprinted that comment in letters to sponsors and networks, in newsletters and other mailings, along with AFA's aforementioned other complaints about this show. GLAAD usually followed those excerpts with the sentence, "That's a *direct quote* describing what the AFA found offensive!"

Several GLAAD chapters asked Burger King to clarify whether it considered gay characters alone sufficient grounds to avoid advertising on a show. The company's executive vice president for marketing wrote to GLAAD/San Francisco Bay Area to say that Burger King would not discriminate in advertising on the basis of gay content. Further, he said he had personally contacted the company's ad agency to emphasize this. He added that if Burger King had realized that "traditional values" was an antigay buzzword, the print ads would have been worded differently. GLAAD promptly summarized the interaction with Burger King in a news release, which it used as a tool to convince networks that major sponsors *would* consider advertising on gay-themed shows.[12] The organization set about obtaining similar letters and assurances from other prominent advertisers to use the same way.

In fall 1990, GLAAD reached out to show business executives directly through full-page ads in industry trade papers. The second ad, in the October 3 issue of *Hollywood Reporter*, focused on television. Its headline asked: WHERE ARE THE GAY AND LESBIAN CHARACTERS THIS SEASON? The ad generated phone calls from people involved in several TV series. In late 1990 and 1991, GLAAD/Los Angeles provided script consultants for four or five TV projects, including episodes of *The Golden Girls* and *Dear John*.[13] During 1991 and 1992, GLAAD ran workshops for creative personnel and corporate managers in several TV-related companies, and distributed copies of *The GLAAD Media Guide* to key industry professionals.

By fall 1991, at least twelve GLAAD chapters had formed in seven states and Washington, D.C.[14] The *Washington Blade* reported that GLAAD/New York alone had "more than eight thousand members, a full-time staff of three, and an annual budget of about $5,000."[15] GLAAD's ascendancy was sudden, considering that two years earlier almost no one had heard of it, and considering that it received virtually no mainstream news coverage before 1990. The chapters built alliances with local gay organizations, wrote action-alert columns for gay periodicals, published newsletters, engaged in letter-writing campaigns, and negotiated with media outlets and other businesses. Although the chapters operated independently and often focused on regional concerns, they were able to create swift, united responses to national issues as well. This could happen because several GLAAD chapters were coordinating national campaigns through a pioneering use of computers. Years before home use of computer modems became widespread, GLAAD became one of the first gay groups to use E-mail, online news releases, and electronic document libraries as an organizing tool.[16] As a result, the networks and film studios began receiving letters and phone calls from gay people and their allies in far-flung parts of the country, putting forth similar and convincing arguments.

Much of GLAAD's national work shifted to a focus on Hollywood movies by 1991. News coverage of this activism further opened up dialog between GLAAD and the major studios, most of which also produced prime-time TV shows. During this period, the mainstream media began to treat GLAAD as *the* gay spokesgroup for media issues. But GLAAD, with its newly professionalized tactics, did not turn the tide alone. While GLAAD was quietly growing and expanding, an explosion of militant Queer activist organizations helped to redefine homophobia as a problem that Hollywood professionals—gay and nongay—had a responsibility to confront. The Queer revolution was a radical departure from GLAAD's then-current "civil" approach, and a complete detour from recent patterns of gay activism.

OUTING AND THE QUEER REVOLUTION

From the 1950s to the 1980s, the word "queer" was almost universally considered an antigay slur. "Queer Theory" was not yet the name of an academic discipline. The letter "Q" (as in the title of the 1990s magazine *NYQ*) did not yet denote GLBT content. Most gay activism in the 1980s had been designed to convince the establishment that gay people were *not* "queer"—that they were essentially like everybody else. Edgy militancy in the 1980s had been associated with the life-and-death struggle of AIDS activism, not general gay civil rights work.

The AIDS Coalition To Unleash Power—ACT UP—celebrated its third anniversary in 1990. ACT UP was, by then, well established in most major U.S. cities, in many college towns, and had spawned sister organizations in other countries. Especially in Manhattan, Los Angeles, and San Francisco, it was no longer unusual to round a corner and find a hundred or more AIDS protesters gathered on an almost daily basis, shouting themselves hoarse with such slogans as "Needle use won't go away! Change your fucking laws today!" ACT UP's early successes revealed the power of direct action protest to a new generation of organizers. In New York City during the spring of 1990, some ACT UP members set out to reapply those militant techniques to GLBT rights, including issues of fair media representation. These activists had taken to calling themselves "queers," an attempt to take away the old slur's power by turning it into a badge of pride. Leaders of the new, radical organization Queer Nation (QN) argued that polite tactics *never* would win gay equality, nor stem the tide of premature gay deaths caused by AIDS, queer-bashers, and public indifference. Their central assumption seemed to be that straight people—even gay-friendly liberals— were ultimately apathetic about the safety of queers, and that only militancy, threats, and fear would bring about meaningful change. The QN movement spread quickly. It appealed mostly to teenagers and young adults, though it also attracted some older activists. Within two years, variations on the group's "We're here, we're queer" chant could be heard wherever there was a large gay demonstration. Their actions had a certain underlying playfulness and theatricality, but also—always—a sense of menace, an implicit threat that violence might follow if solutions could not be found within "the system."

This approach and the more civil methods were not mutually exclusive. Many activists volunteered for both the "polite" groups and the radical ones at the same time. In Atlanta, for example, the local coordinators for both GLAAD and Queer Nation were more or less the same people, and their membership overlapped considerably.[17] In and around Hollywood, there were several Queer groups, including an organization known as Out in Film. Some of these groups' membership overlapped with GLAAD/Los Angeles. Though the new militants did not focus on specific TV shows as often as GLAAD did, their shocking, abrasive tactics contributed to an atmosphere that forced Hollywood to reexamine its attitudes toward both homosexuality and AIDS, on-screen and off.

The format of QN's zaps was nothing new. When the Los Angeles chapter disrupted a 1990 taping of *The Arsenio Hall Show*, the scene looked much like an old Gay Activists Alliance or Gay Raiders action.[18] The new Queer groups differed from previous activists mainly in their philosophy toward privacy. As late as the 1980s, there was still a generally accepted privacy code in the gay community, even in large, liberal cities. The movement for gay equality had long held that everyone had the right to choose where, when, and to whom they would come out. Some new Queer activists agreed with that idea as applied to private citizens, but not for public figures. They said that if the sexual orientation of *straight* celebrities was not too "private" to mention on gossip shows like *Entertainment Tonight*, then homosexuality should be treated the same way. They argued that "outing" (as *Time* dubbed the practice) would have been irresponsible in more homophobic times, but that the gay-rights movement had created an environment in which it was safer to come out. Proponents of outing noted that respectable news outlets had always been willing to report on the homosexuality of people they wanted to discredit—politically unpopular figures such as Roy Cohn, or killers, or pedophiles—even as reporters compromised their journalistic integrity to knowingly portray gay stars and politicians as straight. This double standard, the Queer activists argued, implied that homosexuality was sick and shameful. Opponents of outing said that the double standard was a pragmatic acknowledgment that careers and families could be destroyed if people were forced out of the closet.

In the entertainment industry, where homosexuality was well known and widespread, gayness was, indeed, treated as a dirty secret. Activists knew that homophobic films often starred closeted gay actors working under closeted gay producers handled by gay publicists. At a time when antigay scapegoating and violence were on the rise, Queer activists said that these gay celebrities had a responsibility to come out and speak out. It was also generally known that HIV-positive people in Hollywood were also unemployable. Numerous actors forwent medical care rather than file medical forms and risk having their HIV status become known. Privately, many TV and film executives deplored Hollywood's homophobia and AIDS-phobia. But they worried that if they spoke out on these subjects, people might assume that they were gay. From the militant Queer perspective, this meant that the Hollywood closet was the enemy: celebrities' *fear* of being seen as gay and/or HIV positive was what fueled the conspiracy of silence and let homophobia flourish unchallenged in that influential city. If stars' and producers' homosexuality became public knowledge, Queer activists reasoned, no one would have anything to lose by taking a public stand against prejudice. This was a radical notion. Most established, mainstream gay organizations considered it an appalling breach of the movement's traditional commitment to privacy rights.

By May, it seemed as though every TV interview with an openly gay person included the question, "What do you think of 'outing'?" Many outers on both coasts targeted Fox TV mogul Barry Diller, who they said was a closeted gay man who fed homophobic notions by not coming out. They also said he was not taking a public enough stand against homophobic and AIDS-phobic job discrimination in Hollywood. The most famous or infamous outer of all was Michelangelo Signorile of *OutWeek* magazine, who had a taste for colorful, four-letter words and SCREAMING CAPITAL LETTERS. He reserved special ire for David Geffen, the almost-billionaire producer of films and records, whom the media tended to portray as a straight bachelor. Signorile and many others said that Geffen (who has since come out) was profiting from the blood of his own people by publishing recordings by gay-baiting singers and comedians. Signorile called on him to use his influence to facilitate the production and distribution of gay-positive TV shows and films. Some believed that if Geffen would only come out, it would make all the difference for gay images and gay workers in show business. Geffen was the target of phone zaps, street demonstrations, and even, reportedly, death threats.[19]

After widespread GLAAD and Queer activist protests against films like *Basic Instinct* and *The Silence of the Lambs*, rumors circulated that Queer groups might disrupt the next Academy Awards telecast and read off a list of closeted megastars and film directors. If nothing else, Queer activists knew how to keep people talking—and reporting— about GLBT issues. By redefining the political center, the militants also made groups like GLAAD look more moderate, and provided an incentive for the people who had power in Hollywood to sit down and negotiate with the more corporate, GLAAD-style organizers.

THE CONCESSIONS

Through a combination of negotiations by GLAAD, threats and harassment by Queer groups, grassroots letter writing, and backstage work within the industry, a return to gay visibility began in 1991. In February, a regular TV character on *L.A. Law* came out as bisexual and kissed another woman on-camera. David Geffen came out as bisexual in an interview for the March 1991 issue of *Vanity Fair*. (He would later take to calling himself gay.) In spring 1991, *Roseanne* and *Northern Exposure*—both in the Nielsen Top 20—introduced openly gay male couples as recurring characters.

Meanwhile, *The Arsenio Hall Show*—which Queer activists had publicly accused of gay-baiting humor and of never presenting openly gay guests—invited Harvey Fierstein to appear in an extended conversation with Hall. Fierstein and Hall kept the studio audience laughing as they traded one-liners. Hall then encouraged tolerance of gay people and gave his take on the Queer Nation complaints against his show: He said the people who heckled him six months earlier "didn't realize that that night they might have been looking at some homosexual guests. It's just some homosexuals don't want to be introduced as *(announcer voice)* 'Balladeer and *homosexual*, here is . . .' You know." Fierstein talked about media stereotypes, outing, the closet, and why society's prejudices made gay people in entertainment afraid to live more openly. "Sometimes I feel like I am *theeee* homosexual," he told Hall. "It's like I'm the only one that I ever see on TV."[20]

The first big step toward turning gay equality into an acceptable cause in Hollywood had already taken place. A few weeks before that *Arsenio Hall Show*, while San Franciscan activists were busy disrupting the filming of *Basic Instinct*, prominent Hollywood lawyer Alan Hergott was sending letters to many of the top show business executives. Hergott, who was openly gay, asked them to lend their names as honorary cohosts of an August fund-raiser for the National Gay & Lesbian Task Force. Hergott and his lover, Curt Shepard (an NGLTF board member), saw this as a chance for Hollywood leaders to prove they were not homophobic while supporting an organization in which Hergott believed. As Hollywood's industry leaders pondered the invitation, the press was starting to pay attention to gay organizations' accusations of media bias and job discrimination. Articles in daily papers, show business trade journals, and gay periodicals echoed these concerns. Los Angeles newsstands were displaying magazines with such cover stories as *The Advocate*'s "Homophobia in Hollywood" and *L.A. Weekly*'s "The Hollywood Closet."

There were other well-publicized pressure campaigns and some gay-friendly media images that spring and summer. Chapters of the international gay science fiction fan club, The Gaylaxians, wrote letters and confronted producers of *Star Trek: The Next Generation* at science fiction conventions. They asked why every character in the series' utopian, prejudice-free United Federation of Planets seemed to be heterosexual. That summer, GLAAD and other gay organizations received letters of commitment from producers of several TV series—including *Star Trek*—promising that their shows would deal with gay issues in a positive way.[21] Unexpected bits of gay inclusiveness on television that summer included a July episode of Fox's *Beverly Hills 90210*, which briefly portrayed a teenage boy who thinks he might be gay.[22]

By then, Hergott's $250-per-ticket, three-hundred-seat garden party for NGLTF was sold out, and there was a waiting list. Although Hollywood was known for its glittering AIDS fund-raisers, this was apparently the first time the industry had gotten behind a gay-rights benefit. According to the event's sponsors, the garden party raised more than $80,000 for the task force, not counting last-minute donations. More important than the dollar amount was the prominence of the people who supported this historic benefit. Industry chiefs who attended and/or lent their names to this event included Diller and Geffen, along with CEOs, chairmen, directors, presidents, and senior vice presidents of ABC, CBS, NBC, Columbia Pictures, MCA/Universal, MGM/Pathé, Orion Pictures, Paramount, TriStar, 20th Century Fox, Walt Disney Studios, Disney/Touchstone, Warner Bros., and the leading talent agencies—CAA, ICM, Triad, and William Morris. Attendees included famous producers (Bernie Brillstein, Lorne Michaels), directors (Joel Schumacher), and actors (Bruce Davison, Tom Hanks, Anjelica Huston, Carol Kane, Judith Light, Jimmy Smits, Alfre Woodard, and others).

The *Los Angeles Times*, which ran several articles about the event, reported that "two industry executives refused interviews and photographs, saying they had received hate mail and threats" following advance reports about the fund-raiser. ICM president Jim Wiatt told the *Times* that he, too, had received "a couple of threatening phone calls this week from people. That's why it's important to really step forward and be accountable for the things we believe in." Hergott said that even he was pleasantly surprised at the level of support from corporate senior managers. "I have been keenly aware that many gays and lesbians feel Hollywood is an unsafe place to work," he said. "My experience has been a positive one, as an openly gay man, so I wanted to make a point of asking the employers to support a gay civil rights organization, hoping to send a message to gays and lesbians in the industry." The message was a muted one, especially since the organizers and some attendees had tried to avoid publicity about the benefit. Besides, Hollywood's "glitterati" attend all sorts of benefits without necessarily internalizing the causes behind the parties. Much of the Los Angeles gay community saw this as a one-shot deal, designed to counteract the negative press.

As it happened, one of the most powerful executives present, Barry Diller, *was* willing to speak out. "I'm hopeful," he told a reporter, "that this will send a clear signal to anybody who believes that this is a subject that the entertainment industry is *not* interested in."[23] Few people knew that Diller was already working on a project to address gay issues and AIDS-phobia in Hollywood on an ongoing basis. Shortly before the NGLTF benefit, he and MCA president Sid Sheinberg had talked about forming an industry-funded organization to promote fair employment practices regarding sexual orientation, and to make it safe and easier for HIV-positive employees to seek medical care. As they envisioned it, the organization would also encourage more balanced on-screen portrayals of gay characters and people with AIDS. Both men had long been supportive of fair portrayals on TV: in 1972, Diller was the ABC-TV vice president who shepherded *That Certain Summer* through the obstacle course of network approval, while Sheinberg had supported the project from his position at Universal Television. In 1990s interviews, Sheinberg has said that he and his wife had a great many gay friends in the industry, and had seen the ways double standards and discrimination had played out. At a gay fund-raising event that year, Diller met Richard Jennings, the executive director of GLAAD/Los Angeles. Over the following weeks, Sheinberg and Diller worked with GLAAD/Los Angeles and AIDS Project/Los Angeles (APLA) to decide what needs the new organization should address.

That fall, amid massive negative press about Hollywood's discrimination against HIV-positive workers, six thousand people packed the Universal Amphitheater for the industry's big, annual benefit for APLA. From the stage, Sheinberg announced that he and Barry Diller were committing $125,000 to found Hollywood Supports, an industry agency designed to battle AIDS prejudice and homophobia in show business. Sheinberg proclaimed from the stage, "Homophobia in Hollywood will no longer be tolerated." Within a month, more than ninety founding members had signed up, including a large number of filmdom's most famous executives and directors. Hollywood Supports worked closely with GLAAD and APLA to design workshops about gay and HIV issues in the workplace. For some industry leaders, it was apparently the first time they had held a serious conversation about these topics.[24] The patterns of media discrimination had been blatant enough in recent years that it was possible to point out the trends and win people over in these workshops.

In TV scripts, 1991 and 1992 brought more and better-developed gay characters, a combined result of all of the trends discussed in this chapter. By midyear, there were lesbian, gay, and bisexual recurring roles on some of TV's top-rated shows. By fall 1991, the advertiser pull-outs appeared to be over. Gay-themed episodes of popular series were attracting good ratings and full advertiser sponsorship. Eighteen months later, gay issues seemed to be everywhere. In 1992, *Entertainment Weekly* listed GLAAD as one of the one hundred most powerful forces in Hollywood.[25] That was an exaggeration, of course, but that the editors listed GLAAD at all reflected how quickly the organized gay community was building friendships and credibility in the entertainment industry.

RATINGS AND REGULARS, CANDIDATES AND STARS

Television: 1991–1993

It's great to be here because it's the 1990s and it's hip to be queer and I'm a biiiiig dyke! Yes I am! I'm a big one! And that's okay . . .

—Comedian Lea Delaria, in a stand-up comedy routine on The Arsenio Hall Show, *1993[1]*

Television is a fiercely imitative medium. The networks seem most open to approving GLB content under two circumstances: when gay issues loom large in the news (making the subject topical), or when an existing show with gay characters is pulling strong Nielsens (making it commercially appealing). From 1991 to 1993, the combination of highly rated gay-friendly shows, pervasive coverage of gay news, and the visibility of gay celebrities—with help from the lobbying work of GLAAD and Hollywood Supports—reversed the networks' pullback from gay and bisexual content. Those years brought the first new slivers of visibility that made possible a full-scale renaissance of sexual-minority characters later in the decade.

By mid 1991, two hit series, *L.A. Law* and *Roseanne*, had sexual-minority regulars. Other shows, such as *Northern Exposure*, quickly followed with gay recurring roles. These shows' continued high Nielsens proved that GLB content was compatible with commercial success.

Attention from the news media provided the other ingredient needed to spur on the new inclusiveness. From 1992 to 1995, homosexuality was topical in the mainstream media in a way it had not been since Anita Bryant's 1977 crusade. A string of news stories—the coming out of such celebrities as k.d. lang, gay-rights controversies in the 1992 elections, the 1993 March on Washington, and (most important) endless reports about gays in the military—introduced the issue of homosexuality to audiences on a daily basis. News reports and panel discussions of these filled more airtime than all of the GLB fictional characters combined. Together, the fiction and nonfiction broadcasts helped dull the veneer of strangeness through which much of the public viewed GLB people. By the fall of 1993, a full year into heavy news coverage about the military, hearing the word "gay" on TV was becoming an unremarkable experience.

The networks' love of topicality meant that they were willing to approve comedy and drama scripts containing gay themes in unprecedented numbers during this period. The head count of GLB regular characters on network comedies and dramas increased from five in 1991 to over twenty in 1995. Moreover, in terms of their potential to influence the public, these 1990s regulars had an edge over their predecessors: this time, the public was watching. In earlier decades, gay regulars were not only marginal within a show's plot, but most of the shows on which they appeared were marginal as well. In the 1990s, however, many of these characters were on series in the Nielsen Top 25.

The first 1991 series to break the de facto ban on GLB regulars was *L.A. Law*, a prestigious show that by then had ten major-category Emmys to its credit.[2] Part soap opera and part legal drama, it was entering the second half of its fifth season as 1991 began. At that time, three of *L.A. Law*'s most popular actors—Susan Dey, Harry Hamlin, and Jimmy Smits—were contemplating leaving the show. To flesh out the cast, coproducer David E. Kelley and the show's staff had added three new regulars—young, maverick lawyers who stood out from the series' usual corporate stuffed shirts. One newcomer was Cara Jean "C. J." Lamb, a sexually adventurous bisexual attorney played by British actress Amanda Donohoe.

L.A. Law had a long history of exploring sexual-minority issues. The gay and transgender plots from *L.A. Law*'s earliest seasons have already been mentioned in previous chapters. More recently, in a spring 1990 script, a closeted gay police hero had sued the gay journalist who "outed" him. That fall, new supervising producer Patricia Green wrote a sensitive episode suggested by the celebrated real-life court case of Sharon Kowalsky, who had suffered severe injuries and brain damage in a car accident. Kowalsky's parents denied that their daughter was a lesbian and tried to keep Sharon away from her live-in lover, Karen Thompson. The *L.A. Law* adaptation focuses on a gay male couple, one of whom suffers from the degenerative disease ALS (i.e., Lou Gehrig's disease) and can no longer communicate. A judge rules that the man's parents, not his lover, should have custody, since the couple are not legally related, and the partner cannot prove that the disabled man would rather stay with him. In late 1990, GLAAD asked its members to write letters of praise for these gay male episodes, and to ask for stories about gay women as well.[3]

Amanda Donohoe's character had already joined the cast, but was not yet out of the closet. When the producers cast Donohoe, she was almost unknown in America. In England, she already had a cult following thanks to her roles as sensuous, scarcely clad, usually kinky women in such movies as *Castaway* and *Lair of the White Worm*. She was a popular photo subject for the British tabloids, and one magazine reportedly nicknamed her "Amanda 'I'll Bare My Breasts in Any Movie' Donohoe." Her left-of-center politics were common fodder for the British press, which quoted her disdainful views on organized religion, Prime Minister Thatcher, corporate greed, pollution, and prudery. Her first *L.A. Law* episodes in fall 1990 had established C. J. as a similarly outspoken idealist who was willing to stretch the law if a strong principle was involved. A shrewd courtroom tactician, C. J. also stands out from her colleagues because of her clothes, which are fun, funky, and sexy. Producer Kelley wrote C. J.'s most famous episode, "He's a Crowd"—famous not for its main plot (about a killer with multiple personalities) but for a scene in which C. J. kisses coworker Abby Perkins (longtime regular Michele Greene). Those two seconds of film would be mentioned in almost every news story about *L.A. Law* for the next six months.

Though Abby was an *L.A. Law* regular from the beginning, she had been a secondary role: a bright, young lawyer who had survived a marriage to an abusive alcoholic. Abby considered herself heterosexual—and as far as the audience knew, so was C. J. In this episode, aired

February 7, C. J. and Abby dine together to celebrate winning a big case, and they find they have much in common. In the parking lot outside the restaurant, they look at each other and hug. Then C. J. gives Abby a sisterly peck on the lips. After a pause, they both lean in for a gentler, longer buss. It's tender, it's sweet, and brief. Then Abby nervously drives off as C. J. stares after her. The episode established C. J. as the first openly bisexual (or as she put it, "flexible") regular on network TV, and the only GLBT regular on any series at the time. During 1991 and 1992, C. J. would be seen in serial relationships with men and with women.

GLAAD praised the "historic smooch," which the press played up as TV's "first lesbian kiss." It was not really a "lesbian" kiss, since the scene had a bisexual woman kissing a basically straight friend. It was not even a first: 21 Jump Street had done something similar the previous year, but without the media attention.[4] That L.A. Law kiss between friends passed swiftly into gay community lore. People held house parties to watch videos of the episode, often using a copy of a copy of a tape that some distant acquaintance had the foresight to record. For straight friends of gay viewers, it was probably baffling that this minor scene should seem like such a revelation. But for many gay viewers, it was the first time they had ever seen their love reflected, however remotely, in the nation's most influential medium. Accustomed to total starvation, they savored this tasty crumb.

The kiss was also held up again and again by both gay and straight media as a benchmark of how far portrayals had progressed. NBC reported receiving only about eighty-five phone calls about the story line that night, of which just over half were negative. NBC's vice president for Corporate and Media Relations, Susan Binford, confirmed that some sponsors had pulled ads from this episode (a familiar occurrence for L.A. Law). "Plenty of other advertisers were willing to come in on that episode," she said, "but at a reduced rate. We will go to the wall for certain things," Binford explained. "But we're also a business: if we wake up one day and have no sponsors, we're in trouble." Patricia Green, an L.A. Law producer at the time of the kiss, dismissed the sponsors' concerns. "There are probably twenty-five million gay people out there," she said, "all of whom have friends and relatives and loved ones. That is so many more people than those . . . who are liable to be offended by it that, to us, the advertiser saying 'We lose business' is irrelevant. It's a perception, not a fact."[5]

The same month as C. J.'s famous kiss, Roseanne Barr—the star and coproducer of TV's most popular series, *Roseanne*—announced that her ABC sitcom would add at least one gay character "very soon." "I want it to be a natural thing," she said in a February interview. "I want to show that gay characters aren't freaky, aren't weird, aren't all dying of AIDS." If anyone could convince a network to allow gay regulars in 1991, Roseanne Barr was that person. *Roseanne* had been in the Nielsen Top Two since 1988, so she could afford to make demands. In fact, she was famous for making them. In her show's first two years, she fired or scared away producers and head writers who she felt did not understand women or poor people, and who were not taking the show in the direction she wanted. The show was based on the stand-up comedy she had been doing for years, she insisted. She was not about to sit still as some stranger told her what her character, Roseanne Conner, would and would not do. On the set and in production offices, she browbeat producers, cursed, threatened people with violence. Entertainment reporters described some of these skirmishes, and indicated that Roseanne was—to use a polite phrase—difficult to work with. (Roseanne's second autobiography elaborates on these confrontations. She says, for example, that she threatened her new manager with a pair of scissors after the manager told crew members to take orders from the producers and directors, not from Roseanne.)

In the early planning stages of her sitcom, there was talk of giving her character a lesbian sister, patterned after Barr's openly gay sister, Geraldine—then serving as her personal assistant, manager, publicist, and confidante. Actually, this plan was discussed mostly in private, between the Barr sisters. They hoped that if the show became a big enough success, they could become its producers and lobby to have the protagonist's sister, Jackie, come out. They planned to treat Jackie the same as any other character, except that anyone she dated or moved in with would, incidentally, be a woman. By early 1990, however, Roseanne Barr's relationship with her sister was becoming strained, as Geraldine constantly expressed her distrust of Roseanne's new husband, Tom Arnold.

That year, ABC and Carsey-Werner Productions were anxious to keep the profitable series in production. Hoping to relax the bitter backstage atmosphere, they granted Roseanne and Tom creative control of *Roseanne*. When Tom Arnold, not Geraldine, was made a coexecutive producer, the Barr sisters' relationship became even more tense. Roseanne soon fired Geraldine from the show, and before long they stopped speaking to each other. Nonetheless, Roseanne continued to talk about the idea of having Jackie come out as a lesbian. In a 1992 interview, Roseanne announced that it would happen soon. Ultimately, however, nothing would come of it except for a passing reference in the show's final episode, in 1997.

In spring 1991, when gay regulars were rare, Roseanne insisted that her series should introduce a male couple. On the show, Roseanne Conner found herself out of work anyway, so the writers gave her a job that their star knew firsthand: waitress. Producer Roseanne Barr pushed hard for permission to make her character's crusty new boss, Leon (Martin Mull), openly gay—perhaps a gay father, like Barr's real-life brother. If the network would not buy that, she had other ideas, such as having a buddy of the husband's, a plumber, come out. The idea of adding a gay character, she emphasized, was her own. "Once the network gives you their ideas, forget it, because the characters end up being so stereotypical." Leon was established for two episodes before his gayness came up. He was the sort of "average-acting" character whose sexual orientation no one would question if he did not come out explicitly. In his third appearance—broadcast April 20, 1991—he is seen turning down advances from a beautiful woman. At the episode's end, a man named Jerry (Michael Des Barres) picks him up at work, and it becomes obvious that they are a couple. News reports indicated that the characters would continue to appear in the fall season.

Roseanne's contributions to gay visibility on 1990s TV were vital and inestimable. Between 1991 and 1997, her show would casually portray more recurring same-sex couples and more concurrent GLB regular characters than any other American network series, before or since. These supporting characters' sexual orientation was integrated into the plot as a nonissue. There were no politicized tales of job discrimination. There were no coming-out stories about long-lost friends who vanished after one episode. Instead, *Roseanne* simply acknowledged that the key people in her character's world included lesbians, gay men, and bisexual people who interacted freely with their straight neighbors (some of whom occasionally expressed antigay sentiments). Reacting to these GLB characters, Religious Right newsletters said that Roseanne Barr had a political agenda. They were right. From the time she became a stand-up comic in the early 1980s, Barr worked against show business's marginalization of women, the working class, fat people, and gay people. She belonged to most of those groups herself. Although Barr identified herself as straight, she had spent much time around gay relatives, friends, and coworkers. She was annoyed that the only gay references she heard in mainstream comedy were crude, antigay remarks from certain male comedians.[6]

Back at NBC, both positive and negative mail was arriving in connection with *L.A. Law*'s Abby/C. J. flirtation. Much of the positive mail was generated by GLAAD's national letter-writing campaign. The show's writers later said that viewers' feedback was far more supportive than they expected. So amid rumors that actress Michele Greene was lobbying against continuing the story line, the writers had her character, Abby, ask C. J. out on a date in a late-April episode. The two women have dinner at C. J.'s apartment, laugh, swap stories about their teenage years, and leaf through C. J.'s photo album. As filmed, the scene leaves open the possibility of developing the relationship further. "They shot it one way to leave it up in the air," Greene recalled, "and then we got a rewrite three days later. They said, 'No, we're going to drop this story line. We're not going to continue it.' And we re-shot the second half of the scene to close the door on it." C. J.'s dialog in the grafted-on shots seems unmotivated. C. J. says that Abby is clearly not ready for a relationship—which *could* be gleaned from Abby's nervousness—but then C. J. suddenly accuses Abby of being a horrible friend—which comes out of nowhere. "You can consider yourself two things," C. J. tells Abby: "Dumped, and relieved." In the season finale, after years of struggle, Abby finally becomes a partner in the law firm.

In late spring, the writers began drafting the fall 1991 scripts with the assumption that Abby would be there. In a June newspaper interview, new executive producer Patricia Green said the show would continue to explore the ambiguous relationship between C. J. and Abby. "I don't want to lose that side of C. J.," she said, "and I don't want to write off their relationship. It's C. J.'s closest at the firm, and it makes Abby more interesting." Two weeks later, Michele Greene announced she was leaving the series. "My five years on *L.A. Law* were just terrific," she said, "but it's time I start thinking about the next step in my career." She said the Abby/C. J. plot was not the reason for her departure. "I want to try other things," she said, "and I want to move in other directions."[7] That spring, after five years on the show's production team, writer/producer David Kelley left to develop a new show, *Picket Fences*, for which he would soon write a similar "lesbian kiss" episode. The new *L.A. Law* writing team would try to develop C. J.'s love life off and on for another year, though the results were not nearly as interesting.

The third and final series to introduce recurring sexual-minority characters in 1991 was CBS's *Northern Exposure*, a quirky comedy/drama set in Alaska. Although it was a big hit that year, it had begun life as a little-watched summer series in 1990. Joshua Brand and John Falsey, the same duo who created *St. Elsewhere*, created and produced it.

Northern Exposure had casually acknowledged the existence of gay people right from its premiere, even if gay characters did not appear on-screen until May 1991. The series takes place in Cicely, Alaska, a remote, rural outpost with a population under nine hundred. The open-minded townspeople—a mix of Native Americans and whites—view cultural and personal differences nonjudgmentally. In the pilot episode, the town's new doctor, Joel, an uptight New Yorker, is welcomed by Maurice Minnifield (Barry Corbin). Maurice, a fiftyish ex-astronaut, has bought up fifteen thousand acres nearby, and plans to turn Cicely into a tourist haven. He proudly shows Joel the sparse, weathered, wooden structures of Main Street. "This is it," Maurice says, "This is Cicely. She and Roslyn founded the town ninety-seven years ago. Rumor and innuendo notwithstanding, they were just good friends." He directs Joel's attention to the "Roslyn's Cafe" mural and explains: "A hippie passing through painted that picture on the wall. He was so high on the weed that he forgot the apostrophe *S*. I had to squeeze that in myself."[8] Each week, the opening credits end with a moose walking past the mural, which reads ROSLYN'S CAFE: AN OASIS. References to the town's founding mothers and their loving relationship show up periodically throughout the five-year series, often sending Maurice into a rage.

The oft-mentioned backstory of the town's founding by intrepid lesbians circa 1900 actually developed by chance. While Brand was directing the pilot, he noticed that a big, colorful mural for the Roslyn Cafe kept showing up on-camera. "Roslyn Cafe" was a sensible name for a restaurant in Roslyn, Washington, where the series was filmed. But it was an odd name for a restaurant in Cicely, Alaska. He had the sign modified to read "Roslyn's Cafe." "I was standing there," Brand later recalled, "and I said, 'Well, let's put an apostrophe S up there, and say that the town was founded by Roslyn and Cicely, who were these two lesbian lovers. . . .' "9

The story of Cicely and Roslyn was not the only forum through which *Northern Exposure* treated gay issues. Early episodes in 1990 developed Maurice's conflicting traits: homophobia and honor, greed and generosity, sensitivity and callousness, violence and the desire to be seen as a man of culture. In episode two, Maurice, who owns the local radio station, beats up and fires a radio personality who has read homoerotic poems by Walt Whitman on the air. Maurice temporarily takes over the man's time slot with his own idea of wholesome entertainment: Broadway tunes of the 1940s and 1950s. He leads off with a Cole Porter song—the unstated irony being that show tunes are often considered stereotypically gay, and that Cole Porter, like Walt Whitman, was homosexual. The townspeople hate the show tunes, and Maurice reluctantly reinstates the original deejay, "Chris-in-the-Morning" Stevens (series regular John Corbett).10

When *Northern Exposure* returned for a second trial run in April 1991, its new writer/producers included the husband-and-wife team of Diane Frolov and Andrew Schneider—Berkeley alumni who had lived in the gay-friendly San Francisco area for years. One of their first *Northern Exposure* scripts, "Slow Dance," introduces new recurring characters: a gay couple, Ron and Erick (Doug Ballard and Don McManus), who move to Cicely to open a bed-and-breakfast. To buy a property for their new venture, they must do business with landowner Maurice, who hits it off with them instantly. Ron and Erick share his love of Broadway music, antiques, and gourmet cooking. Maurice knows that their inn will advance his dream of exploiting the town for tourism. Ron and Erick, who had worried that they might not be accepted in their new hometown, are relieved to find a kindred spirit in Maurice. Only after the couple holds hands in front of him does their dinner host realize they are gay. A furious Maurice unsuccessfully tries to back out of the real estate deal. He slowly realizes that the hobbies that he thought marked him as cultured could also be read as signs of being gay. Maurice wonders how his neighbors perceive him. As the episode ends, Ron and Erick are integrated into the community in a romantic scene where the town's couples slow dance at the local bar. The camera neither emphasizes nor deemphasizes the men: The scene puts them on a par with the town's other lovers, and visually suggests their new neighbors' casual acceptance of them.[11]

From their first appearance, Ron and Erick are clearly men with a history, not just cardboard cutout characters. They talk about how and when they first met, their friends back home, what businesses they have operated together, and why they want to be innkeepers. Their interaction and body language exude a level of comfort with each other that is believable in a couple who have been together for seven years. Ron and/or Erick would appear in six more episodes from 1992 to 1995, almost all of them written by Frolov and Schneider.

As promised, the television regulars who came out in early 1991 continued to appear in fall 1991, though *Roseanne* made far better use of Leon than *L.A. Law* made of C. J. Without David Kelley at the helm, the writing and plotting on *L.A. Law* suffered. Its ratings began to sink and reviewers savaged the new scripts. The writers seemed unsure how to handle C. J.'s personal life. Several months into the season, an episode cowritten by Patricia Green finally did something interesting with C. J. In this script, titled "The Nut Before Christmas," C. J. brings the law firm a case involving a divorced woman who is battling her ex-husband over child custody. The ex-husband—who had been an irresponsible, verbally abusive, neglectful alcoholic during their marriage—has stopped drinking and says he is ready to be a responsible parent. He has learned that his wife was involved with another woman—C. J.—during their marriage. He plans to use that information against her in court. In this episode, viewers finally learn something of

C. J.'s past: for years, she and the lesbian mother in this case were in an intense relationship. C. J., who is wonderful around children, had been an important stabilizing influence in the children's lives. As the marriage was dissolving, C. J. and her lover broke up and got back together several times. Although the women were in love, C. J. felt she could not promise the long-term stability the children deserved, so she left. The episode leaves open the possibility that the two women will get back together.[12]

It was an interesting story, but C. J. was given little else to do that season. Amanda Donohoe resigned from the series that spring. When *L.A. Law* returned in fall 1992, a lead character explained that C. J. had quit the firm so she could join a professional golf tour. Thereafter, *L.A. Law*'s gay-themed scripts took bizarre turns away from reality—such as when a straight male regular, Douglas, uses an experimental aphrodisiac cologne in an attempt to seduce his ex-girlfriend. He mistakenly uses the bottle that attracts men and much supposed hilarity ensues. It hardly mattered by then: almost no one was watching.[13]

Leon, the cynical boss on *Roseanne*, fared much better than C. J. during the 1991–92 season. He appeared in at least ten episodes, some of which built subplots around events in his life. Viewers saw Roseanne intervene in a marital squabble between Leon and Steven (as Jerry was now inexplicably called) over whether Steven should move out during a visit from Leon's mother. Leon's mother knows that her son is gay, but he believes she cannot handle seeing him and Steven together. "My mother is a seventy-year-old woman," he says. "She was uncomfortable with Mary Martin as Peter Pan." Steven has gone along with this unwillingly for years, but he wants a chance to know his partner's family. Roseanne sides with Steven, to Leon's annoyance. "Roseanne," Leon says, "did it ever occur to you, even for one moment, to stay out of this?" "Yeah," she replies, "but by then it was way too late." Steven prevails, and he gets more than he bargained for: an overbearing mother-in-law who tries to micromanage the couple's household. The script, cowritten by openly lesbian stand-up comic Maxine Lapiduss and actor Martin Mull, develops Leon and Steven's relationship, positing Roseanne as a complication in *their* life rather than the other way around.[14]

With sexual-minority roles breaking new ground left and right, many gay viewers pinned high hopes on Fox's recently announced serial, *Melrose Place*. Advance publicity for this spin-off of *Beverly Hills 90210* said the cast would include a young gay man named Matt Fielding (Doug Savant)—an idealistic social worker who counsels teenagers in a halfway house. The Fox network and Aaron Spelling Productions had strong track records on gay content, so it seemed likely that *Melrose* would be able to examine unapologetically the romantic ups and downs of this single, gay man. The debut episode in 1992, however, foreshadowed just how marginal Matt would be during the first few seasons. In the ninety-minute premiere, aside from the opening credits, Matt was given just ninety seconds of screen time.[15] He scarcely appeared again until episode four, after which he was a minor player in everyone else's life. Matt was the show's conscience, a sounding board for his straight neighbors' woes. He was also the only character who generally could not find a date on a Saturday night. This was ridiculous, considering that the series takes place in West Hollywood, one of the gayest cities on the planet. If anything, one might expect his straight neighbors to have trouble finding mates nearby.

The creator/producer of *Melrose Place*, Darren Star, said he wanted to develop viewers' sympathy for Matt for a few months without showing his love life. After a suitable waiting period, he expected to turn Matt into a more well-rounded character.[16] The Fox network, however, repeatedly rejected proposals to explore Matt's life. His dating could be mentioned in passing, but could not be shown.

Finding story lines for Matt became trickier starting in 1993, when the once low-key (and low-rated) series changed genres and became a lust-filled soap opera. Fox and the producers could not agree on how to fit Matt into the new format. A steady boyfriend was out of the question: Fox executives still did not want Matt to be seen dating, and the point of revamping the show was to *de*stabilize its couples. Most of the characters became shallow, selfish connivers. The writers could, conceivably, have had Matt become as self-absorbed as his neighbors. But even if they could have gotten Fox's approval to show him in the same sorts of abusive relationships as everyone else, such a depiction clearly would have been branded an antigay stereotype. So it was decided that, for the moment, Matt would remain saintly, celibate, and on the sidelines. Only amid the cultural changes of the mid 1990s would Fox finally let Matt have his own story lines, and let the writers start to tarnish his altar boy image. But that is another story for another chapter.

As important as fictional prime-time characters can be, it was the new media visibility of real-life gay people in the early 1990s that did the most to change public discourse about sexual orientation. The 1990s proved something that gay organizers had theorized about since at least the 1950s: the transformative power of visibility—the power of real-life gay people talking openly about their lives. In the 1980s, gay issues and openly gay people seldom had appeared on the news except in reports about AIDS. That changed dramatically in the 1990s. Coverage of outing set the stage, but the big flashpoints for visibility all evolved from issues in the 1992 elections.

Traditionally, gay issues played no noticeable role in presidential campaigns, but a convergence of events put gay rights front and center on TV news and in the candidates' electoral strategies in late 1991 and 1992. Conservative churches were promoting referenda in several states to make discrimination against gays into a basic right by banning any mention of sexual orientation in antidiscrimination laws. Newscasts and TV talk shows focused on Oregon and Colorado, where antigay measures seemed certain to get on the ballot and had a good chance of passing. Other broadcasts dealt with governmental attempts to suppress the federal *Youth Suicide* study, and in many cases profiled support programs for at-risk GLBT youth. In the wake of the Gulf War, there were countless news stories about gay soldiers—including war veterans—who were being expelled from the military.

With the founding of Hollywood Supports, gay equality was also the issue du jour in Hollywood, where liberal political candidates usually counted on raising stacks of money and picking up celebrity endorsements. Not only was the film capital focusing on gay issues, but the town's weathiest potential donor, David Geffen, had just come out of the closet. That fall, candidate Bill Clinton contacted his old friend David Mixner, a gay activist, fund-raiser, and business consultant in Los Angeles. Clinton wanted him to take a senior position in his campaign, to help with general planning and drum up support among gay voters and donors. Mixner had known Clinton since their days in the antiwar movement of the late 1960s. He wanted to believe the candidate's claims of gay-friendliness. However, gay Californians were in a restive mood over civil rights just then, and very skeptical of politicians' goodwill. The state's governor, Pete Wilson, had just vetoed an antidiscrimination law that he had promised to sign. Mixner told Clinton he would join his campaign team only if the candidate took a strong public stance in favor of gay equality. Clinton did (as did most liberal Democrats in the race), and Mixner accepted the job.

Gay civil rights became a prominently reported issue at the major parties' 1992 conventions. Diversity—ethnic and otherwise—was a hallmark of the Democratic convention, seen on TV by over thirty-three million viewers. The cameras often picked up shots of conventioneers carrying signs that identified them as gays for Clinton. Two openly gay speakers addressed the crowd: San Francisco City Supervisor Roberta Achtenberg, who spoke on behalf of Clinton's platform committee, and Bob Hattoy, a campaign staffer who told about living with HIV. In presenting the proposed platform, Achtenberg identified herself as someone who—as a woman, a lesbian, a mother, and a Jew—had felt excluded and attacked by the Reagan and Bush administrations. The platform she presented incorporated Clinton's promises of increased funding for AIDS research and promises regarding lesbians' and gay men's civil rights.[17]

Gay issues figured prominently in televised portions of the Republican convention, too: homosexuality was portrayed as evidence that America's "family values" were in decay. The Republican nominee, incumbent George Bush, was one of the more moderate leading Republican voices on this issue. Bush was on record as saying that antigay discrimination was unjust, but should remain legal. The Republican platform reaffirmed the military ban, urged a ban on adoption and foster parenting by gay couples, and said that gay people posed a moral threat to children. The platform praised the Boy Scouts of America for barring gay teenagers from membership and gay adults from employment. In the platform and in speeches, Republican leaders said that antigay discrimination should be a basic right of landlords, employers, educators, and providers of public accommodations. In one of the convention's most anticipated speeches, defeated candidate Pat Buchanan lambasted Bill and Hillary Clinton for consorting with "radical" feminists and homosexuals, which he said put them on the wrong side in the "religious war . . . for the soul of America," a war for the soul of "God's country." He added that traditional Christian and Jewish beliefs should be the yardstick for public policy.[18]

For many voters, this exclusionary rhetoric overshadowed the party's stands on other issues. Some political analysts credited Buchanan with scaring undecided voters over to the Clinton camp. (His speech also influenced TV scripts. On *Murphy Brown*, a character at a political event in Washington quips, "Pat Buchanan's here circulating a petition to change the name of our species to 'hetero sapiens.' ")[19] After seeing the negative public response to Buchanan's speech and the media coverage of the antigay referenda, Religious Right groups organized conferences to refocus their antigay message, couching it in less confrontational language. Meanwhile, moderate Republicans set out to wrest control of the party away from the Religious Right.

Clinton's victory seemed to mark a cultural turning point for gay Americans. His inaugural celebrations and first term proved to be even more gay-inclusive than the campaign. He would go on to appoint over one hundred openly gay people to federal posts. However, these acts of inclusiveness did not generate nearly as much debate as a plan he had announced in fall 1992. In a press conference that fall, the president-elect reaffirmed his campaign promise to end the military's longtime prohibition on "homosexuals." A storm of controversy ensued. Faced with unwavering opposition from Congress, from the Joint Chiefs of Staff, and from some segments of the public, Clinton would ultimately back down and seek a compromise. Clinton and Congress would eventually agree on the so-called "Don't Ask, Don't Tell" military policy, almost indistinguishable from the regulation it replaced except that officers were no longer supposed to ask about soldiers' or recruits' orientation. Many gay leaders—including Mixner—branded Clinton as a traitor and turned against him.

The massive media coverage of the military issue between fall of 1992 and summer of 1993 was what changed—perhaps permanently— the way Americans viewed and talked about sexual orientation. Over the course of just eight months, the Big Three networks aired more than four hundred news stories and interviews about gays in the military.[20] PBS, CNN, C-SPAN, and nationally syndicated talk shows also gave it top story attention, as did Jerry Falwell's and Pat Robertson's religious programs. At the height of the coverage, one could turn on the TV at almost any hour of the day or night and, on some channel, find a patriotic, once-honored soldier who was being forced out because of homosexuality, or find a general, admiral, activist, preacher, or politician speaking for or against the ban. Though there was widespread disagreement within some liberal gay circles as to the morality of military service, it was a smart strategic move for the gay civil rights movement to highlight the struggle of gay service members. The parade of well-spoken gay cadets and soldiers, some of whom were facing expulsion *because* they had come out on TV, did more to dispel stereotypes than any fictional TV characters could. Most of the old, persistent antigay myths assumed that homosexuals were inherently undisciplined, childish, and self-absorbed—that on some subconscious level, people "became" gay to avoid such responsibilities as marriage and parenting. The military issue put forward a very different public face for homosexuality: these real-life gay people on TV were not just asking for rights, but for responsibilities—for the chance to risk their lives in a profession that requires selflessness, bravery, responsibility, and self-discipline. People like Margarethe Cammermeyer, Keith Meinhold, Joseph Steffan, Tracy Thorne, and Joseph Zuñiga had the positive evaluations, certificates, commendations, and/or medals to prove they not only *could* do the job well, but *had* done it well.

By the time the media abandoned the issue, society had changed. The words "homophobe" and "homophobia"—for better or worse—had entered mainstream American usage. Even people who were morally opposed to homosexuality seemed to have grasped that sexual attractions were not chosen the way someone chooses an ice-cream flavor, and that gay people could be as trustworthy and hardworking as anyone else. Gay people and issues, seen in the light of day, seemed slightly more mainstream.

Another major media phenomenon that influenced attitudes during this era was the advent of the "gay celebrity"—those lesbians and gay men who could be counted on to discuss gay issues on talk shows and variety shows in addition to discussing the fields for which they were best known—usually show business, sports, or government. By the end of 1993, it was common for talk shows to pull together entire panels of such celebrities, something that would have been impossible just three years earlier. Some of these gay people were already famous, such as Czech-born tennis legend Martina Navratilova. She had been open about her lesbian relationships since 1981, just after she secured her United States citizenship. She first became a political spokesperson for gay causes in 1992, after Colorado's antigay referendum passed. In reaction to the California civil rights veto, vintage sitcom actors Dick Sargent (of *Bewitched*) and Sheila James Kuehl (of *The Many Loves of Dobie Gillis*) began appearing on talk shows together as openly gay panelists in fall 1991. On shows like *Entertainment Tonight*, *Good Morning, America*, and CNN's *Sonya Live*, they talked about the Hollywood closet, relationships, civil rights, the healthiness of living honestly, and gay teenagers' need for role models. News reports in the 1990s also mentioned the now open homosexuality of other celebrities from decades past, such as 1960s Disney teen actor Tommy Kirk and 1950s *Superman* sidekick Jack Larsen (both of whom had led openly gay lives for many years without much media attention).

Other celebrities came out in a variety of forums. Music megastar k.d. lang first talked of her lesbianism openly in a 1992 *Advocate* interview, apparently marking the first time that a current, successful North American performer risked coming out. In January 1993, while lang was onstage at the gay Triangle Ball of the Clinton inaugural, rock star Melissa Etheridge took the microphone and came out. Caught up in the excitement of Clinton's victory, Etheridge proclaimed her lesbianism impulsively, not stopping to think that TV cameras and reporters would capture the moment. She later said it was a completely freeing experience. Others who came out between 1992 and 1995 included the singing duo The Indigo Girls, Olympic diving champion Greg Louganis, and sitcom actors Amanda Bearse (Marcy on *Married . . . With Children*) and Dan Butler (the ravenously heterosexual Bulldog on *Frasier*). Comedians who had worked mostly in gay venues also began getting invitations to appear on mainstream TV programs—performers such as Jaffe Cohen, Lea Delaria, Kate Clinton, Bob Smith, and Suzanne Westenhoefer. Harvey Fierstein began getting more prime-time acting work, and appearing on more late-night talk shows. Magazines and newspapers were putting gay celebrities and gay issues on their covers. Between the celebrities and the soldiers, gay people seemed to be everywhere in the mass media.

What the public was seeing on TV was also, in most cases, happening in their own lives: people around them were coming out. Workers were forming gay employees' associations to lobby for job equity and domestic partner benefits, often with support from organized labor. Since gay issues were a leading topic of the day, there were more opportunities than usual for people to come out to their families and neighbors, or at least to live openly and let others draw their own conclusions. Within the GLBT communities, long-marginalized groups—lesbians, people of color, senior citizens, bisexuals, and transgendered people—were beginning to assert their voices more effectively, demanding inclusion in the movement's goals.

Amid all of the diversification of real-life GLBT images in the media, fictional sexual-minority characters would explode across the prime-time TV schedule from 1992 to 1995 in such large numbers that it is impossible to document them all. TV's old, narrowly defined profile of The Homosexual was giving way to a more inclusive, pervasive sense that gay people had always existed, came from every background, and could fit into any genre of TV programming.

BRANCHING OUT

Television: 1990–1998

PATTY: You think there's anybody in this world who truly believes they're
  beautiful?
GRAHAM: Umm . . . RuPaul.
  —*The teenage protagonist's parents on* My So-Called Life, 1994[1]

In the 1990s, television's GLBT imagery stopped being *quite* so dominated by pictures of white, gay men aged twenty-three to thirty-nine.
While a later chapter will focus on the growth of lesbian visibility in the
1990s, this chapter concentrates on how the range of allowable images
broadened in terms of race and age, and in the greater visibility of
bisexual and transgender people. This new openness accompanied a
broadening of the types of shows that offered these images.

Few moments encapsulated all of this diversification better than a
guest appearance by an elegant, black, middle-aged, transgendered
cabaret artist on PBS's *This Old House* in 1996. The interview was
unusual, first of all, because this series was not known for its celebrity
guests. But in a broadcast from Savannah, Georgia, there she was in all
her Southern glory: the toast of that city's gay bar circuit, The Lady
Chablis, as immortalized in the bestselling book *Midnight in the
Garden of Good and Evil*. Unlike most guests on *This Old House*, she
did not demonstrate roofing techniques, reframe a door, or install a
bathroom sink. Instead, she was introduced as one of the great, gracious ladies of Savannah, and was asked to talk briefly about the town
and its people.[2] Television viewers familiar with the book already knew

The Lady Chablis. Others furrowed their brows and tried to figure out what an apparent female impersonator was doing on *This Old House*. That a home-construction show chose to chat with The Grand Empress of Savannah is one of the more unlikely examples of how the nature and context of GLBT images were starting to branch out.

During 1990, as previously noted, the most prominent gay recurring roles on television were two African American men: *In Living Color*'s giddy, entertaining, and jaw-droppingly stereotypical Blaine and Antoine (Damon Wayans and David Alan Grier). This finger-snapping duo doled out attitude and cultural criticism in the show's "Men on . . ." skits: "Men on Art," "Men on Books," "Men on Fitness," and so on. *In Living Color* was one of several minority-focused shows that Fox put on the air in the early 1990s. The young network was not yet large enough to compete effectively with the Big Three for mass-market audiences, so it pursued the underserved African American market with such shows as *Roc* (a black domestic sitcom), and *True Colors* (sort of an interracial *Brady Bunch*), and the irreverent sketch comedy series *In Living Color*.

Blaine and Antoine debuted in the show's 1990 premiere. Their theme song, "It's Raining Men," played as an announcer introduced their "public-access" show, "Men on Film." The studio audience screamed with laughter at these outrageous, swishy snap-divas. Not television's typical "politically correct" gay roles, Blaine and Antoine referred to women as "fish," and thought *The Karate Kid Part III* would have been a better film if it had focused on "the special friendship between a mature, masculine, older man and a tender, ripening, consenting young man." ("I think America is ready for that," Blaine explains. Antoine replies, "I know *I* am.") Sometimes, a film's title alone was enough to win their endorsement, as with *Great Balls of Fire*. Their rating system was simple. If they liked a movie—in other words, if it featured muscular, shirtless men—they would wave their arms dramatically and snap their fingers twice, giving it "Two snaps up!" According to a GLAAD newsletter, by 1991, this flamboyant gesture was being imitated everywhere from gay bars to New York Mets games.

Their misogyny was always evident. Any film (or book, sculpture, etc.) that featured women earned a two-word review: "*Hated* it!"

According to Blaine and Antoine, women such as the title characters on *Roseanne* and *The Golden Girls* were "what made us this way." One week, Blaine was shocked to learn that, despite her first name, actress Glenn Close was *not* a man in drag. On hearing this, Blaine daintily clasped his fingers to his chest and gasped: "Clutch the pearls! What a *sneaky* thing to *do*!!" Blaine and Antoine appeared on *In Living Color* about once a month—usually at the end of the show, since they were a tough act to follow. They quickly became two of the series' most popular characters, and Fox compiled their appearances into several prime-time "Men on . . ." specials.

Like television's first white gay regulars a generation earlier, these first black gay recurring roles entered the medium in the form of broad, comical sissies. These characters reflected, in a less offensive form, the sort of gay stereotypes that had been common in the late 1980s on HBO's black-targeted stand-up comedy specials, and on that cable channel's weekly series, *Def Comedy Jam*. Indeed, even before Damon Wayans was signed to appear on *In Living Color*, he caught the attention of the Gay & Lesbian Alliance Against Defamation with some broadly stereotyped gay characters he played on HBO specials. On one show, according to GLAAD, he portrayed an effeminate, lisping gay man who is attacked by gay-bashers and winds up deriving sexual pleasure from the beating. Some black comedians were, of course, performing more gay-friendly humor in the 1980s and early 1990s, but no one was inviting them to appear on national TV.

Part of what made the "Men on . . ." skits work was their shock value, which meant each one had to be more extreme than the last. Originally, they walked a fine line between laughing *with* gay stereotypes and laughing *at* them. As they pushed the envelope further, there were puns about gay men "bending over backwards" to help each other. There were references to such sponsors as "Jewels—the gum that explodes in your mouth." There were double entendres about Blaine and Antoine's trip to Greece: per Antoine, "It was very sad when we had to leave our soldier buddies behind." (Try saying it out loud.) By 1992, when a "Men on Football" routine aired live opposite the Super Bowl, they were doing cruder comedy—insinuating, for example, that actor Richard Gere had carnal knowledge of a gerbil. Their costumes, too, became more outlandish. For a "Men on Vacation" skit, Blaine wore a colorful print blouse, a see-through lavender skirt with lavender bikini briefs, open-toed clogs, and a fruit-salad hat.

Not surprisingly, Blaine and Antoine were extremely controversial in the gay community. On one hand, many gay viewers embraced these skits. The characters exuded what some considered an appealing self-confidence. The tightly written dialog was performed with flawless comic timing. More important, unlike the old Bob Hope or Johnny Carson sissy portrayals, Wayans and Grier threw themselves into these over-the-top roles, never breaking character to give the audience sly, sidelong glances or to distance themselves from the material. More-over, these characters did not just reflect straight people's stereotypes of gay men, but also incorporated many of the gay community's own stereotypes. Anyone who spent enough time in gay male dance clubs knew a Blaine or an Antoine. Even many solemn, dyed-in-the-wool gay media activists found themselves laughing convulsively the first time they saw one of the earlier "Men on . . ." routines. They *knew* these guys, and were surprised to see them on mainstream TV. Gay journalist Rex Wockner praised the characters as television's first "queen-positive portrayal of queens." In an *OutWeek* interview, Betty "Brandy" Randolph, coowner of a large, black gay nightclub, said that whenever Blaine and Antoine were on TV, everything in her club would stop so that everyone could enjoy these characters' latest outrageous antics.

But even if the characters' surface traits looked familiar, the things they said reinforced the persistent clichés that so many people already believed about gay men—and especially about gay black men: that they were petty, vain, effeminate, bitchy, hedonistic, superficial woman-haters who advocated sex with adolescent boys. It was all very comical, but it was broadcast into a vacuum. The public had almost never seen gay black images on television before, and at the peak of the sponsor pullbacks, there were few gay characters of any color to balance out these stereotypes. A commonly heard reaction in gay venues at the time was that it was fine for gay people to laugh at these skits, but that in the absence of other visibility, it was unfortunate that straight people were seeing them. As late as 1992, gay opinions toward *In Living Color* were deeply divided. When the San Francisco chapter of GLAAD polled its members about media issues that year, no question drew more passionate responses than one about *In Living Color*. Roughly half the respondents said that GLAAD needed to view these skits with a sense of humor. The other half branded "Men on . . ." as the most offensive, dangerous, gay stereotype then in the media. Midway through the 1992–1993 season, due to a change in the show's cast, the "Men on . . ." skits ended abruptly.[3]

Most of the other black gay visibility on broadcast television—and there was not much of it—consisted of guest appearances. For instance, two episodes of *Roc*, in 1991 and 1994, dealt with patriarch Andrew's uneasy relationship with his gay brother, Russell (Richard Roundtree). In the first gay-themed *Roc* episode, Andrew is bitter about Russell's coming out. Andrew's son, Roc, admits that he, too, is uncomfortable about having a gay relative, "But at least I'm *comfortable* about being uncomfortable—that's a big step for me!" After a long discussion, Roc tells Andrew to reconcile with Russell. "We ain't the only minority that had it rough in this country," Roc says. ". . . Face it, Pop. Things ain't gonna change. He's always gonna be your brother."[4]

The first openly gay African American regular role appeared in the short-lived 1993 sitcom *Cutters*. As on *Roc*, this character was presented as a he-man, athletic type, in broad contrast to media sissies of the *In Living Color* school. Julius Carry played Troy, a burly, black, gay former track star and two-time Olympic medalist who now works as a hairstylist. A supporting role, Troy exists mostly as a foil for the show's blustery, bigoted white, male lead.[5] In the first half of the 1990s, such parts were rare, and appeared only in short-lived, unregarded series. Not until 1996 would a strong, gay, black role appear regularly on a hit show: the sitcom *Spin City*, which a later chapter will explore.

Asian characters have been even rarer on TV than black ones, so it is no surprise that GLBT Asian roles have been virtually nonexistent. Among the shows studied, aside from an often seen but little developed Japanese-American male nurse on *ER*, the only gay role played by an Asian actor is in the 1993 cable movie, *And the Band Played On*. A central figure in this fact-based drama is San Francisco gay activist Bill Kraus (Ian McKellen). B. D. Wong plays Kraus's lover, Enrique "Kico" Govantes, who in real life is Cuban. (Any docudrama where Whoopi Goldberg and Lily Tomlin were up for the same part clearly was open to "color-blind" casting.) Wong's character has some tender scenes, but is given comparatively little screen time. Originally, Kico was supposed to have *slightly* more to do in the film: Wong and McKellen filmed a scene in which the couple kissed, but this was too much for the usually daring HBO. In a *New York Times* article, Armistead Maupin quotes McKellen as saying:

> An [HBO] executive on the set said he personally had no problem with the kiss, but it was his responsibility to see to it that his viewers—and this is a direct quote—not be grossed out. I reminded him that this film begins with a shot of dead and dying Ebola fever victims, one of whom spews blood almost directly into the camera. If the audience isn't grossed out by that, it could surely handle a little peck on the lips. . . .

The kiss did not make it into the final cut.[6]

The underrepresentation of GLBT people of color is, naturally, a subset of the media's underrepresentation of all kinds of nonwhite characters. However, no similar logic explains the traditional under-representation of gay teenagers. Here, the hesitancy reflected a then-widespread belief that everyone is "hard-wired" for heterosexuality until something goes wrong, and that seeing likable young gay charac-ters on TV might convince a teenager to "turn" homosexual. In 1990 and 1991, it was considered morally, politically, and commercially dan-gerous for a general entertainment series—as opposed to didactic fare like *Schoolbreak Specials*—to delve into the realm of teenage homo-sexuals. Even the one series that *should* have been able to air such content—Fox's high school sex-and-surf serial *Beverly Hills 90210*—was discouraged from doing so.

This series seemed the most logical place for a gay role not just because it frequently explored sexual issues (contraception, AIDS, etc.), but because Fox had aired gay-youth stories before on *21 Jump Street*. The subject also seemed like a natural because *90210* was sup-plied by one of the most gay-friendly production companies in the entire history of television: Aaron Spelling Productions. Several gay story lines were proposed. During its first two years, *90210*'s writing staff included a Texan playwright, Jordan Budde. He was, at the time, the show's only openly gay staff member. At a time when adolescent coming-out issues were in the news, Budde wanted to incorporate this issue into a script. The production company and his coworkers were excited about the idea. He was finally told to draft a script in which the show's central family, the Walshes, react to the coming out of a teenage male cousin who visits them from Minnesota. Fox executives, however, said it was too early in the new series to take the financial risk of alienating already skittish sponsors. Fox suggested that the following year might be a better time for this script. It was never filmed. Budde was not the only person who mentioned the possibility of a gay story line. In 1992, regular cast member Gabrielle Carteris said that she, too, wanted the show to present a gay-themed episode. Carteris wanted her character, Andrea, to become friendly with a woman she admires, and then learn the woman is gay. The story would focus on how Andrea reacts. This story did not materialize either. Of course, cast members do not usually originate plots for TV shows, but the point is that the shortage of gay content on this show was not because the idea simply never occurred to anyone.

During *90210*'s first three and a half years, only one two-minute scene dealt with a minor guest character's possible homosexuality. In a summer 1991 episode, promiscuous, insecure Kelly's self-esteem suffers yet another blow when a guest character, Kyle (David Lascher), resists her sexual advances at the end of a date. A few days later, he confides in her that he has never slept with anyone and is not even sure he is attracted to girls. "You mean you're gay?" Kelly asks. Kyle says he doesn't know. "I just know I wish I could have been attracted to you," he says. "My life would be a lot less confusing right now." The scene is well written and believable as far as it goes—which is not far. This dialog reappeared in a flashback a few months later when Kyle returned—this time in a story about high school athletes' abuse of steroids. Playing into the decades-old reverse stereotype of gay men, Kyle is a saintly jock with an impeccable conscience. He turns in his steroid-using teammates, causing Kelly to fear for his safety. To give the show credit, even this content was daring for 1991 and early 1992. The second Kyle episode was also one of the first times a popular series showed a (probable) gay teenager in any context other than a coming-out story. But the fact that gay-youth portrayals had to be so circumspect—even on this series—reflects what a truly threatening, almost untouchable subject this was.[7]

By mid 1992, however, the door began to open. Amid news reports about gay civil rights issues, there was also increased coverage of the federal *Youth Suicide* study. Such prominent news programs as the *Today* show and *20/20* had devoted lengthy segments to social services for gay teenagers.[8] As news of the federal study and similar research reached beyond its original audience of school counselors, it became more justifiable for entertainment shows to focus on gay teens. The main caveat was that, since the suicide studies were what gave television "permission" to air gay-youth stories, the only commercially acceptable plots mirrored the research's tales of depression, isolation, and despair. Shows could portray young people struggling with coming-out issues and facing classmates' taunts and threats. Shows could portray gay teenagers who were contemplating suicide after deciding their family and friends would never accept them. But it was rarely possible to portray a well-adjusted, self-accepting, basically happy, and functional GLBT teenager. Only the suffering of a conflicted adolescent was deemed sufficiently pitiable to win over viewers, who could then root for the character to find acceptance and self-esteem.

One of the most dramatically satisfying examples of this theme was the gay-youth story embedded in Fox's otherwise overwrought TV movie, *Doing Time on Maple Drive*. This 1992 drama deals with a moneyed suburban family in which the controlling parents set impossibly high standards of perfection and conformity, which have a destructive effect on their now-grown offspring. The youngest sibling, a twentyish college lad named Matt (William McNamara), always seemed the ideal son: considerate, a champion athlete, and an honors scholar at an Ivy League university. He is engaged to a beautiful, charming young woman from "the right sort" of family. He knows he is gay, but also knows that in his family, being out of the closet is not an option, so he plans to go through with the sham marriage. On a visit to the parents' house, however, his fiancée finds one of Matt's love letters to his ex-boyfriend. She breaks off their engagement. Rather than risk disappointing his parents, Matt drives his car off a road in a failed suicide attempt. The film dramatizes his slow realization that his sexuality is not some shameful side issue that he can ignore. He becomes the one sibling who is willing to stand up to the parents. Over time, Matt and his father (James Sikking)—a military man—feel their way toward mutual

respect and understanding. However, there is no artificial, pat ending—
no sappy hugging scene with Matt's unforgiving mother (Bibi Besch).
The mother insists that her son's sexual orientation is something Matt is
"doing to" his parents. The film was unusual in many ways. In a
medium where gay men are often portrayed as "a girl's best friend,"
Matt's best friend is a straight man his own age, with whom he shares a
platonic embrace. The film was also notable for ending with the implication that Matt may get back together with his ex-boyfriend. This was
closer than television or movies usually came to a happy ending for a
gay couple. Given the many open-ended plots, *Doing Time on Maple
Drive* felt like a busted series pilot, though it was never touted as one.
It presented, in any case, a memorable gay story line. In informal
surveys, many gay college students of the mid 1990s mentioned this
film as the one TV portrayal that most reminded them of gay people
they knew.[9]

Nevertheless, the show that did the most to break down the barriers
and demonstrate how a gay-youth story could be dealt with in a sophisticated, sensitive, credible, and ongoing manner was the daytime soap
opera *One Life to Live*. Daytime television is beyond the main scope
of this book, but this groundbreaking story deserves some attention.
From spring 1992 to early 1993, future Hollywood star Ryan Phillippe
played Billy Douglas, a high school senior struggling to come out of the
closet in the small East Coast town of Llanview. For Phillippe, then a
seventeen-year-old actor being raised in a fundamentalist Christian
community, this was a controversial role to accept. In interviews at the
time, he said that what convinced him to take it was reading about gay
teenagers' having a suicide rate three times higher than that of the general youth population. The fan letters he received from gay teenagers,
talking of their isolation and how much this story line meant to them,
reportedly reinforced his initial feeling that this was an important story
to tell.

This story on *One Life to Live* broke many conventions, some of
which prime-time television still has yet to violate. In a break from previous gay-teen characters, Billy was not a minor guest role: his story was
one of the central narratives on the show from June to August 1992,
and he continued to appear occasionally thereafter. Billy is never seen
to question or struggle with his sexuality, though he describes having

done this in the past. He is not, as most such characters are, a virgin (a trait usually required to make the gay character more sympathetic to viewers). These innovations alone would have made him a landmark character, but the serial's writers went much further. They took advantage of their five hours of airtime per week to create a more elaborate story than could be told in a one-hour prime-time weekly show. They started Billy's tale slowly by establishing him as a popular student—active in athletics, student government, and as a volunteer at an inner-city youth drop-in center. In mid June, the show revealed his homosexuality when he came out to his best friend, a straight boy who initially lashed out but was ultimately supportive.

Over the next three months, Billy's narrative intricately intersected every other story line then current on the series, especially the story of Andrew Carpenter (Wortham Krimmer), the empathetic minister at Billy's church. Although Andrew is straight, he knows what Billy is going through: Andrew's brother—a gay man who recently died of AIDS—was tormented and harrassed by their antigay father for years. The summer story arc shows how Billy, a basically normal, likable, closeted kid, is driven slowly to the brink of suicide. What nearly sends him over the edge is the outpouring of antigay comments uttered by his parents and neighbors when they mistakenly believe that the minister is a homosexual child molester. Eventually Billy comes out and realizes there are people who accept him as he is, even if his father and some classmates might not. The writers planned to wrap up his story in August, before younger viewers returned to school. There was an emotional, extended finale in which most of the series' regulars attended a display of the NAMES Project AIDS Memorial Quilt, and the minister placed a quilt panel in memory of his brother.

That was supposed to be the end of the Billy character, but there was enough viewer interest that he was brought back periodically during the school year, portrayed as a well-adjusted kid who happens to be gay. On Christmas Eve, while caroling with friends, Billy meets another gay teenager, and they begin dating. That spring, Billy was written off the show as he graduated from high school and left for college. From Billy's first appearance to his last, this was unquestionably one of the most unapologetic and credible sustained portrayals of a gay teenager ever on American television, even if the character sometimes seemed a little *too* perfect and kindhearted.[10]

Gay-youth stories made more inroads in popular culture during 1993. Cartoonist Lynn Johnston stirred up a controversy in the newspaper publishing world when her comic strip, "For Better or for Worse," dealt with the coming out of a longtime character, the teenage son's friend Lawrence. On the TV series *Doogie Howser, M.D.*, uptight college freshman Vinnie panicked after learning that his new roommate was gay. In a departure from the norm, the roommate is an easygoing, unconflicted gay man who seems more amused than wounded by Vinnie's initial reaction. On *Picket Fences*, a forlorn, lovesick, lesbian high schooler pined for a straight classmate. The last and weirdest youth-related script that year, an episode of *The Mommies*, was inspired by high-profile news reports about research that suggested a biological, inborn component to sexual orientation. In a script called "I Got the Music in Me," a man spends the entire episode trying to determine whether his nine-year-old son is gay, using such tenuous indicators as the boy's participation in marching band rather than sports.[11]

For prime-time television, the biggest breakthrough youth story debuted with the first episode of *My So-Called Life*. This intense, brilliantly written teen drama, which starred a then-unknown Claire Danes, began its nineteen-episode run in 1994. One of the core supporting roles is Rickie Vasquez, a gay high school student. Rickie is a well-developed, three-dimensional character with his own story line. The show came, notably, from Bedford Falls Productions, the company behind *thirtysomething*. Since that earlier show had trouble incorporating a gay regular in mid-series, the producers introduced Rickie as a regular in episode one. Rickie was the personification of so many people whose stories could not be told before on TV. He was the first gay teenage regular on an American series, the first gay Latino regular, and probably the first gay regular played by an openly gay actor (Wilson Cruz). In developing the character, the writers spent time talking with Cruz about his own coming-out experiences, and incorporated bits of his story into Rickie's.

Unlike TV's gay high school jock cliché, Rickie is a gender-nonconformist who is regularly beaten up at school. Rather than wearing a football jersey and hanging out on an athletic field, Rickie wears eye-liner and hangs out with female friends in the girls' lavatory. His clothing has a trendy MTV edge, as if he were perpetually on his way to a dance club. Rickie's friends obviously all know he is gay and accept it. Rickie is the only person who needs a few months to fully figure out that he is not—as he tries to convince himself—bisexual.

Like Matt on *Melrose Place*, Rickie is his show's resident idealist and moralist. (The networks consider gay characters most sympathetic when they express morally conservative, even romantic views—and of course they earn extra points if they constantly remind the audience of their celibacy.) In one of the famous girls' room scenes, the Claire Danes character, Angela, is seen hugging Rickie and lamenting the end of her first big romance. The man of her dreams has dumped her because she would not have sex with him. She says that maybe she *should* have gone to bed with the boy. "It would have been so simple," she says. Rickie looks pensive. "But maybe," he replies, "it *shouldn't* be so simple. I mean—not that I know what I'm talking about or anything, 'cause I never, you know, experienced this . . ."

The final episodes offered him still greater depth and pulled him further from TV's gay-teenager clichés. By the season's end, he had become homeless, been taken in as the foster child of a gay teacher and his partner, and formed a friendship with the show's other outsider—the awkward straight boy, Brian. The writers even let Rickie finally come out to a female friend who had a crush on him. In an outstanding episode built around a school dance, Rickie develops a crush on a male classmate named Corey, who turns out to be straight.[12]

My So-Called Life won rave reviews, support from such organizations as Viewers for Quality Television, and ratings of eleven million viewers per week. As series creator/producer Winnie Holzman pointed out, that would have constituted a hit on a smaller network like Fox, but eleven million viewers was small potatoes by ABC standards.[13] Still, because of its critical acclaim, network executives kept it on the air longer than some less well made shows with higher Nielsens. *My So-Called Life* finally built a following in postnetwork reruns on MTV cable—the ideal environment, as the show's target demographic was already watching MTV. Episodes of the show have since been sold widely on home video.

That series is an example of how context affects gay activists' responses to depictions. In the 1970s, when television's history of effeminate gay roles was a fresh memory, a role like Rickie might have elicited howls of protest. At that early date, any gay male character who wore eyeliner, dressed in colorful, showy clothes, and hung out in the girls' bathroom would have been branded a stereotype. But in the 1994–1995 season, there were more gay images in prime time than ever before, most of which avoided the oldest stereotypes. Among gay youth characters, in fact, the reverse cliché of the gay male athlete had become so overdone that activists hailed Rickie as a refreshing counterpoint—a balance to the newer stereotype. Rickie's presence, and the many narrative taboos he crossed, were further evidence that TV was beginning to recover from its traditional tunnel vision toward gay roles. It should be noted, however, that no more Latino gay regulars appeared among the shows studied. The only recurring Latino role was a saintly and doomed ambulance driver, Raul (Carlos Gomez), on the second season of *ER*. Raul made scattershot appearances through much of that season, before dying of burns he suffered while rescuing children from a fire.[14]

By 1994, youth coming-out stories were so routine and passé that they no longer had to occupy an entire episode. On *Blossom*, for instance, the coming out of a male teenage guest character was slipped casually into an episode about something else entirely. In 1995 and 1996, coming-out stories were no longer the only allowable context for gay teenagers. In an episode of the high school drama series *Matt Waters*, a Hispanic student chooses not to come out to his parents, but spends much of the episode trying to find out about the life of his late, apparently gay great-uncle, and wondering whether same-sex attraction is an inherited trait.[15] Throughout the mid and late 1990s, the bawdy, cynical sitcom *Unhappily Ever After* sporadically featured a queeny character named Barry, a schoolmate of the main family's son and daughter. Like the gay role on *My So-Called Life*, Barry was played by an openly gay actor (a stand-up comic who goes simply by the name ANT). But only in the late 1990s would there be gay teenage recurring roles on more popular shows, such as *Buffy the Vampire Slayer* and *Dawson's Creek*.

Even though there was an increase in younger gay roles, television characters did not diversify much at the other end of the age spectrum.

The usual upper age limit for gay characters did rise from about thirty-nine to somewhere in the late forties, but older GLBT people received little attention. There were at least two notable exceptions. In 1993 on HBO—where all sorts of exceptions occur—the sitcom *Dream On* had the leading man's divorced father (Paul Dooley) reveal that he is in a happy romance with another man. The father returned in another gay-themed episode a year later. In a Christmas 1995 episode of ABC's *Grace Under Fire*, the title character learns that her ex-husband's father, Emmett (Bryan Clark), is gay. He has been in a long-term relationship with another man, even while married to Grace's former mother-in-law. He swears Grace to secrecy, and says that his marriage, while sexless, is not loveless. In the next episode, Emmett dies suddenly, and his lover refuses to keep a low profile at the funeral.[16] There were very minor gay guest roles over age fifty in some of the studied shows, but nothing as significant as these. All of the characters were male.

The 1990s was also the decade when a larger number of scripts went beyond lesbian and gay into the lives of bisexual characters (usually women) and transgender people (all male-to-female, among the studied shows).

Considering that before 1990, television seldom even showed bisexual guest characters, the bi regulars on such well-established, widely viewed series as *L.A. Law* and *Roseanne* indicated that times were changing. The Amanda Donohoe character from *L.A. Law* has, of course, been discussed in depth. Sandra Bernhard's Nancy on *Roseanne* was a landmark of a different sort: she was the first frequently recurring character to come out in mid-series. For people who cared about such things, there was an added layer of interest in that Nancy was an openly bisexual character played by an openly bisexual actress.

Nancy was originally established on the show as a straight woman who married the series' obligatory sexist-pig supporting character, Arnie (Tom Arnold). In 1992, when the gay character, Leon, left temporarily, producer Roseanne Arnold was determined to keep a sexual-minority presence on the show. The writers talked about having Roseanne Conner's sister, Jackie (Laurie Metcalf), start dating Nancy. But they decided it would be funnier to have Nancy come out as a lesbian and be involved with a series of women who would be played by famous actresses. Jackie would be the character who is uncomfortable about Nancy's coming out.

Nancy came out first as a lesbian, not as bisexual. "I think I may always have been a lesbian," she says. If anything was a "phase," she maintains, it was her marriage to Arnie. For a few episodes that fall, Nancy dated Marla, played by Morgan Fairchild—an actress famous for playing glamorous, heterosexual sirens. When this icon of straight desire and sophistication appeared in the role of a small-town lesbian who works at a makeup counter, her mere presence inspired applause and laughter. When Nancy and Marla appeared in a Christmas episode that year, a newsletter from the American Family Association complained that "They behave as any 'normal' couple in love—holding hands, embracing, etc." As she explored her sexuality further, Nancy realized she was bisexual. Her bisexuality was emphasized when she dated a man briefly in 1993. The next year, however, she went back to women. She explained that she liked both sexes, but that dating men was too complicated because "birth control is such a pain." Nancy was an engaging and humorous character who was always a subject—not an object—of laughter.[17]

After *L.A. Law* and *Roseanne*, though, the floodgates did not open for bisexual characters. Apparently, the only subsequent bisexual regular in prime time was the Kyle Secor character, Detective Tim Bayliss, on NBC's *Homicide: Life on the Street*. Bayliss, who was clearly attracted to women, began exploring his attraction to men during the 1997–1998 season.[18]

As rare as bisexual roles have been, transgender characters have been even scarcer. Other than a short-lived syndicated sitcom in 1977 (*All That Glitters*, on which Linda Gray played a transsexual fashion model), none of the shows studied had a transsexual regular role. And except for a cross-dressing straight male character on *The Drew Carey Show* (beyond the scope of this book), there were no significant transvestite roles seen on an ongoing basis.

That said, there was a greater visibility of both gay-drag imagery *and* transsexual roles in the 1990s than in the past. Since in the public mind, the line between drag and transsexualism is thin, some of the new transsexual visibility may have spun off of the gender-blurring of mid-1990s "drag chic," epitomized by the increased use of drag artists in music videos and in television guest roles, and especially in the crossover success of female impersonator RuPaul—an openly gay black man who struck it rich as a cross-dressed singer/model/actor/talk show host.

Transsexual guest roles had changed considerably since the 1970s, when the most prominent appearances had been in medicalized contexts: a married vascular surgeon (Robert Reed) who wanted a sex-change operation on *Medical Center* (1975), and an East German swimming champion whose coaches did not want her to seek medical care at an American hospital on *Westside Medical* (1977).[19] The trend among transsexual guest roles in the 1990s was toward more feminine, almost glamorous male-to-female roles, all played by genetically female actresses who, in many cases, were known for their poise and beauty. With gay characters no longer packing the shock value they used to, transsexual roles became a way for a series to prove how adventuresome it was.

While white transsexual roles appeared in more narrative contexts than before, black roles appeared in the types of story lines where white transsexual characters had appeared during the 1970s and early 1980s: as a date for a straight man, and in medical dramas. In a 1994 episode of the sitcom *Evening Shade*, Diahann Carroll plays a transsexual with whom the regulars fix up the Ossie Davis character, Ponder. And on an early *ER* episode from that same year, doctors Carter and Benton treat the injuries of a depressive black preoperative transsexual. This character's story occupies much of the episode, and Dr. Carter becomes despondent after the patient commits suicide by jumping off the hospital's roof.[20]

A few of the white characters fit the traditional profiles, too. On *Chicago Hope* in 1995, Billy Kronk (Peter Berg) learned that his girl-friend, Annie (Mia Sara), was a postoperative transsexual. In a 1996 episode, Annie returns, reporting that her hormones are no longer keeping her male body traits at bay. Her newly identified medical conditions—including cancer and blood clots—mean she can no longer take estrogen. Realizing that she will no longer have any clear gender identity as a man *or* a woman, she, too, kills herself.[21]

There were, however, more unusual transsexual story lines. White male-to-female transsexual characters in the 1990s suddenly found themselves where white gay characters had been in the late 1970s: in coming-out stories and civil rights dramas. The coming-out programs include Carol Burnett's bittersweet turn as a former high school football star who meets up with her long-ago sweetheart (Swoosie Kurtz) at their thirtieth class reunion. On this 1990 broadcast of *Carol & Company*, Burnett's character, George, is clearly the episode's lead. She tries to reassure her ex-girlfriend that a part of her is still George. The Kurtz character replies, "Not the part I was hoping for." There were also several transgender civil rights dramas. On *L.A. Law* in 1991, a transsexual fashion model filed a wrongful termination suit against her former employer. Her lawyer is the ever-uptight Doug Brackman, who takes the case to make up for his callous firing of his firm's transsexual secretary a few years earlier. A Christmas episode of *Picket Fences* the next year focused on the legal battles of a transsexual music teacher who was at the center of a Church-and-State controversy. She finds herself in court for refusing to honor a ban on religious Christmas pageants in public schools. At the height of the dispute, it is revealed that she used to be a man, which leads to her firing. Since the series takes place in Wisconsin, which has strong antidiscrimination laws, she wins her job back.[22]

All of these types of demographic growth mirrored and accompanied another trend in GLBT images of the 1990s: the increasingly casual inclusion of sexual-minority content in more narrative contexts and more genres. In other words, as the next chapter will show, there was a diversification not just of *whose* stories could be told, but also *what* stories could be told, *where* they could be told, and what target audiences would see them.

WHERE NO QUEERS HAVE GONE BEFORE: CROSSING THE GENRE BARRIER

Television: 1990–1995

> My heart belongs to Roslyn, and it always will. It's difficult to explain. I feel as if she and I have known each other through many incarnations throughout the ages. Our souls are one, and I can't imagine life apart from her.
>
> —*"Cicely" (Yvonne Suhor), who, in 1908, cofounds the artists' colony that will become Cicely, Alaska, in the flashback episode of* Northern Exposure, 1992[1]

If we accept that GLBT people are full human beings, then any possible human story can be told about them, including stories that are not "about" their sexuality. It also follows that these stories can be told in virtually any dramatic situation or context. In actuality, however, until the 1990s, there were many genres where one could generally count on *not* finding sexual-minority content: period pieces, love stories (at least not among the protagonists), holiday dramas, religious stories, westerns, science fiction, cartoons, home-improvement shows, celebrity biographies, and TV commercials. But in the early and mid 1990s, GLBT content crossed over into every one of those areas—some of them many times. By the mid 1990s, the "tellable" gay story on TV was closer than ever to being defined as "any human story."

When gay people and issues reemerged into public visibility in the early 1990s, scriptwriters had to ponder again how to incorporate them into familiar TV formats. Unlike writers in previous decades, though, many TV writers in the 1990s had seen examples of GLBT content in scripts that did not treat sexual orientation as a controversial issue. The increasingly visible work of independent GLBT moviemakers—the "New Queer Cinema" movement—was beginning to incorporate GLBT protagonists into spy thrillers, love stories, screwball comedies, historical dramas, experimental films, and family dramas, in addition to the more familiar "queer narratives" (coming-out stories, dramas about street hustlers, etc.). These productions, seen both in gay film festivals and on cable TV outlets such as The Sundance Channel, showed it was possible to present sexual minorities as interacting in diverse situations. This is not to say that most or all TV writers were influenced directly by this cinema movement, but it meant that nonissue-oriented stories were "in the air" as a possible approach to gay content, in a way that they were not before.

One of the hardest barriers for gay content to cross was to appear in stories set outside the late twentieth century. The idea that gay people existed before the 1960s or might exist several centuries in the future was seen as either absurd or threatening. It was, apparently, more reassuring (and hence salable) to treat homosexuality as a "contemporary theme."

The exceptions generally aired appeared on PBS, such as the remarkable 1976 American short film, *The War Widow,* about a woman during World War I who leaves her husband and family for another woman.[2] On public TV, the gay characters who appeared in period pieces mostly were in BBC dramas, many of which PBS prefaced with disclaimers or apologies. To the degree that commercial TV in the U.S. presented gayness in historical contexts, it was usually as a humorously incongruous element in skits on satire shows like *Laugh-In* (e.g., a gay bar in the Old West) or *Saturday Night Live* (a segregated platoon of gay soldiers in the Civil War meets a segregated black platoon). In the early 1990s, however, gay history was a growing field of research, and the gay community was producing a broad literature about the gay past in preparation for the twenty-fifth anniversary of Stonewall. This interest in both academia and gay circles coincided with corporate attempts to target gay consumers. So mainstream publishing houses began offering fiction and nonfiction works about gay people who lived in earlier eras. In that environment, gay characters started to appear in network TV scripts set in the past.

At least five broadcasts from 1990 to 1993 depicted lesbians or gay men in periods ranging from the nineteenth century to the mid 1960s. The time-travel drama *Quantum Leap*, for instance, ran two such episodes: a murder mystery set in 1957, whose twist ending reveals that the deceased was in a lesbian relationship, and that her lover accidentally killed her during a quarrel; and an episode about a gay military cadet who suffers discrimination, violence, and harassment in 1964.[3] Both episodes are interesting and have their positive points. The former show even won an Edgar Award for outstanding mystery writing. All the same, it should be noted that each of these episodes is consistent with television's traditional uses of gay guest characters: the women are a murder victim and her killer (albeit an accidental killer), and a gay man is at the center of a drama that is primarily *about* gayness and homophobia.

The most important and memorable period drama, however, broke many taboos at once. Throughout the five-year run of *Northern Exposure*, there were frequent, reverent references to the lesbian couple who established the free-spirited town of Cicely, Alaska. The third-season finale rewarded longtime viewers with a flashback episode about those founders, Cicely and Roslyn (Yvonne Suhor and Jo Anderson). The episode, aired in May 1992, starts in the present. A one-hundred-eight-year-old former resident, Ned, tells the regulars about his remarkable friend and mentor, Cicely, who would have turned one hundred that week.[4] He relates how in 1908, Cicely and her companion Roslyn brought culture, philosophy, self-esteem, and a sense of purpose to what had been a miserable, violent, filthy frontier outpost. As the flashback unfolds, the sense of cooperation that the women encourage among their neighbors helps to free the town from a bullying gunman and his gang. Ned also narrates scenes showing why the town was named after his friend. The flashback continues as the gunman, angry that the townspeople no longer follow his orders, tries to kill Roslyn. Cicely, who is deathly ill with tuberculosis, throws herself in the bullet's path. After she and Roslyn exchange a few words, Cicely dies in her companion's arms. Ned recalls that at that moment, a community was born, and everyone knew that it would bear her name.[5]

Even viewers with only a passing familiarity with television could tell that this was a unique moment—either very special or very dangerous, depending on one's opinion of homosexuality. A Top 20 series was presenting a lushly filmed, richly scored, fablelike story of two women whose love for each other helps transform a lawless settlement into a utopia. This Emmy-winning episode looked more like something out of a gay film festival than a commercial TV drama. It brought an astounding number of innovations to prime time. First, it presented a lesbian love story where no character treats the couple's relationship as anything other than beautiful. Also, it depicted gay people as part of America's history. It presented a same-sex couple as the central figures in this idyllic town's mythology, in a narrative that incorporated such classical, mythic elements as lovers who are fated to be together, and a protagonist whose death leads to the creation of something great, spiritual, and lasting. If a chaste kiss on *L.A. Law* the previous year had fulfilled an unmet need in gay viewers, then *Northern Exposure*'s celebration of an eternal, preordained, same-sex love was a revelation. CBS reran the episode at least twice, just as gay issues were moving to the center of American political discourse. This was apparently the first—but not the last—commercial series episode to dramatize gay lives in such a historical context.

In September 1993, episodes of two western series—CBS's limited-run *Ned Blessing* and Fox's whimsical *Adventures of Brisco County, Jr.*—also presented gay characters in a historical setting. Like the *Northern Exposure* episode, both brought an anachronistic liberalism to the subject. The *Ned Blessing* episode takes place during Oscar Wilde's lecture tour of America. Wilde and Sheriff Blessing are kidnapped by thugs, and in a series of two-fisted adventures, each saves the other's life. Oscar Wilde's western adventures had previously been portrayed in an episode of *Have Gun Will Travel*, but his sexuality had not. In contrast, the *Ned Blessing* episode ends with a much older Sheriff Blessing writing his memoirs. He remarks that, several years after his adventure with Mr. Wilde, he heard that the author had been imprisoned for indecency. Blessing says he met many indecent men in his time, but Wilde was not one of them. Two days later, Denise Crosby guest-starred on *Brisco County, Jr.*, a series that often playfully inserted elements that were out of period. Crosby plays the sheriff of a women-only town called No Man's Land, which looks very much like a 1970s lesbian-separatist colony. Most of the episode takes place in and around this town.[6]

If there was room for gay roles in TV westerns, science fiction should have been a cinch. The genre had a huge gay following, could handle "difficult" issues well, and often portrayed utopian societies that were free of prejudice. And yet, televised science fiction proved a tough nut to crack.

As the decade began, there was only one notable American series set in the far future: the syndicated *Star Trek: The Next Generation*. If gay content was to appear in a "space opera," it would have to be this one. This seemed a logical place for it anyway: *Star Trek* was the country's largest and longest running TV science fiction franchise, whose producers prided themselves on their fearlessness and their characters' diversity. The original *Trek* series in the 1960s had dealt allegorically with such powder-keg topics as genocide, race relations, and the Vietnam War. The first sequel series, *Star Trek: The Next Generation* debuted in 1987, and was equally topical as it presented extraterrestrial metaphors for AIDS-phobia and other issues of the day.[7]

In 1991, after conversations with gay fans and gay people on his staff, *Star Trek* creator/producer Gene Roddenberry issued the following statement: "In the fifth season . . . viewers will see more of shipboard life in some episodes, which will, among other things, include gay crew members in day-to-day circumstances." He clarified, "We've established that the planet will be free of discrimination and bias by that time, so the question we'll address is what homosexuals will be like in the twenty-fourth century."[8] Less than two months later, Roddenberry died suddenly. His successors did not implement his plan. Instead, they touted an upcoming episode that would deal implicitly with homophobia, but they would not commit to depicting actual gay people as part of the ship's crew, nor among the show's guest roles. This was the opposite of Roddenberry's promise.

When the various *Trek* series portrayed same-sex attraction, it was always between women, and always something forced upon an otherwise heterosexual organism through mind control or psychic contact. In a 1990 episode of *Next Generation*, Dr. Beverly Crusher's boyfriend dies and his memories are implanted in a woman's body. Dr. Crusher has a hard time explaining to her former lover why their relationship cannot continue. Beverly sees her inability to stay with Odan as a flaw— a matter of letting physical appearance impinge on love. "Perhaps it is a human failing," Beverly tells Odan, "but we are not accustomed to these kinds of changes. . . . Perhaps, someday, our ability to love won't be so limited." Before leaving, Odan kisses Beverly's wrist as viewers had repeatedly seen the male Odan do. The episode is dramatically effective, but it also throws into sharp relief the absence of gay people from this series' vision of the future. *Star Trek: Deep Space Nine* later used this same species' body-switching to explain another piece of same-sex attraction in the famous episode "Rejoined," which we will discuss in a later chapter. In the late 1990s, yet another *Star Trek* spin-off would still be playing the same game. In an episode of *Star Trek: Voyager*, the character Seven of Nine (Jeri Ryan) suddenly tries to sexually assault a woman colleague. The script explains that Seven was possessed by the personality of a male alien whose mind she "assimilated" years earlier.[9] Gay people, per se, appeared to be extinct. Clearly, the show's post-Roddenberry producers were more willing to preach inclusiveness than to demonstrate it.

That was not the case on another science fiction series of the 1990s: *Babylon 5*. Shortly before its 1994 premiere, writer/creator J. Michael Straczynski posted the following to an online newsgroup:

> We have no intention of avoiding the gay question. We will not, however, do a "gay story," which is usually described by those [gay and bi] friends and acquaintances of mine in derogatory terms . . . à la, "fags are people too." The sense I get is that they resent the hell out of that kind of patronizing approach. The one suggestion that comes most often is, "Why not simply introduce a character, we get to know that character over the run of a season, and at some point discover, practically in passing, that this person is bi or gay . . . *don't* make a big issue out of it, just show it."
>
> And that's what we're going to do.

The character was Lieutenant Commander Susan Ivanova (Claudia Christian), one of the show's lead roles from 1994 to 1997. Two episodes from 1995 highlight that she *happens* to be attracted to women—especially one woman, with whom she has a brief affair. The show would continue to display such openness well past the mid 1990s. In a later episode, two male regulars go undercover at a resort on Mars, posing as a newlywed couple. No characters in the story consider a same-sex honeymoon couple an uncommon sight. Straczynski, who describes himself as heterosexual, explained to his fans: "I don't think Earthforce cares about sexual orientation; the reason we just set it out there without comment is that, having come through the realization of other nonhuman races . . . a little thing like sexual orientation, nobody cares about anymore." This singular example of inclusiveness received comparatively little media attention.[10]

A breakthrough in another genre—the first recurring gay role on a network cartoon series—did cause a certain amount of comment in the press. Fox's *The Simpsons* was a spin-off from *The Tracey Ullman Show*. This cartoon sitcom was the brainchild of Matt Groening, whose newspaper comic strip "Life in Hell" routinely presented gay-friendly material, including a recurring couple named Akbar and Jeff.

In 1990, during its first season, *The Simpsons* introduced the character Waylon Smithers (voice of Harry Shearer). His sexual orientation started as a quick, throwaway gag—a one-line variation on the cliché about the secretary in love with the boss. In a typically *Simpsons* twist, Smithers, a preppy, young corporate toady at a nuclear power plant, is secretly infatuated with the plant's ancient, misanthropic owner— the miserly, vaguely homophobic Montgomery Burns (also voiced by Shearer). Allusions to Smithers's crush on Burns began early in the first season: Burns, overcome with emotion, says he (platonically) loves Smithers, who pointedly replies, "The feeling is more than mutual, sir." The 1991–1992 season included at least three such remarks. It snowballed from there. In several episodes, Smithers fantasizes about Burns, imagining him flying in through a bedroom window, or jumping out of a cake naked to sing "Happy Birthday" to Smithers in the style of Marilyn Monroe. In one episode, Smithers is seen frolicking at a gay vacation spot. There were also more political references, as when he sabotages the campaign of a conservative political candidate because of the politician's views on "my choice of lifestyle." The most unexpected Smithers gag turned up in a 1992 spoof of *King Kong*. The segment finds Marge Simpson trying to join a jungle expedition led by adventurer Burns, on a ship captained by Smithers.

BURNS: *(to Marge)* Well, you'd be a welcome change of pace from the rest of these crude and uncouth sailors. *(to the captain)* What do you think, Smithers?

SMITHERS: I think women and seamen don't mix.

BURNS: We *know* what you think. *(to Marge)* Young lady, you're hired![11]

Two *Simpsons* episodes went further: they patterned central gay guest characters after the openly gay men who provided their voices: Harvey Fierstein and filmmaker John Waters. A 1990 episode finds Homer Simpson temporarily promoted to an executive position. He is given an efficient, upbeat male secretary, Karl (voice of Fierstein). Karl is implicitly gay in a low-key way, and develops what Groening called an "unrequited attraction" for Homer. In the late 1990s, the series would run a more gay-specific episode, "Homer's Phobia," with Waters as a kitsch dealer named John. That episode would be a slightly exaggerated send-up of TV's usual "coming-out" episodes, with Homer learning tolerance at the end.[12] *The Simpsons* proved to be one of the most popular and enduring comedy series of the decade. Its success paved the way for a new crop of cartoons aimed at grown-ups. In the comparatively gay-friendly environment of the mid 1990s, such animated shows as *The Tick* and *The Critic* would also introduce gay references and characters.

Some of the biggest turning points had less to do with bringing gay content *into* a genre and more to do with changing the *place* of gay content in a genre. For instance, there was little need to introduce GLBT content into talk shows or newsmagazine programs. These had long presented sexual-minority people as curiosities to explain, exploit, or justify to straight viewers. Starting in 1992, however, many PBS stations began airing *In the Life*. This series—created by, about, and for gay people—was promoted as a cross between a gay *60 Minutes* and a gay *Ed Sullivan Show*. The next year, some college and public-affairs cable stations began carrying the edgy news/talk show *Dyke TV*. Gay people who did not have cable or whose PBS stations would not carry *In the Life* had the option of subscribing to *Network Q*, a slickly produced, one-hundred-minute monthly information series distributed on VHS videotape.

No one had to make a special effort to introduce gay references into televised stand-up comedy either. They were there all along: for decades, comedy monologs expressed disparaging attitudes toward gayness, or worked under the assumption that just *alluding* to homosexuality was funny. Stand-up was one of the few areas where viciously antigay comments were not just allowed, but expected, even on shows that would never tolerate similar vicious assaults against any other group. That changed in the 1990s, as openly lesbian and gay comedians began to perform their own routines on TV—routines that alluded to homosexuality in the first person, and did not treat it as a threat. For the first time, cable outlets such as HBO and Comedy Central, and an informal network of PBS stations, ran specials built around these comedians' considerable talents. On Comedy Central's first *Out There* special in 1993, host Lea Delaria observed that it was good to see gay people telling jokes for a change, rather than being the butt of them.[13] Publicity about these shows spilled over into more mainstream venues, as these comedians began making more appearances on such programs as *The Arsenio Hall Show* and *The Tonight Show*.

Still, none of those genres was truly "the final frontier" for sexual-minority content. The most revealing shift in the relationship between commercial TV and gay people could be found in the commercials themselves. In a consumer economy, one barometer of how the media see a minority group is the way commercials acknowledge—or fail to acknowledge—that group.

In this area of broadcasting, too, gay references had existed for years. In the 1970s, commercials could include implicit gay content, but mainly in the form of campy, derisive stereotypes. Commercials of the 1970s and 1980s could also feature mistaken-identity gags, where straight male characters become worried or angry after someone apparently mistakes them for gay. Uncritical gay content was so alien to advertising that shows like *Saturday Night Live* got laughs simply by restaging familiar commercials with an infusion of gay or lesbian content. Gay comedians drew laughter with similar jokes. The idea of gay characters in a mainstream advertisement seemed absurd.

The earliest exceptions appeared on Comedy Central. The cable channel's first *Out There* special in 1993 featured what was probably the first national commercial for a gay-specific product. Along with the usual spots for cars and other familiar products, the special repeatedly ran a clever, very humorous ad for its featured sponsor, *Out* magazine. This publication continued to use Comedy Central as a way to reach a gay-friendly audience over the following months, by cosponsoring reruns of *Soap*. Other advertisers also used the *Soap* repeats to target gay-friendly viewers. The distributors of the Australian movie *The Adventures of Priscilla, Queen of the Desert*, for instance, used *Soap* as the main venue for their American television ads.

Around the same time, direct or indirect gay content also appeared in advertisements for more mainstream products. This was not long after all those marketing surveys encouraged advertisers to pursue "the gay dollar." The impact of that research appeared first in the print media. Full-page ads for major corporations' products began appearing in the glossy gay news/features magazines. The breakthrough for television advertising came in a 1994 IKEA furniture commercial. It depicts a comfy, thirtyish, middle-class male couple who buy their "first serious dining room table" from an IKEA store. The nonstereotyped pair finish each other's sentences and say they have been together for three years, ever since they met at the wedding of one partner's sister. The ad aired regionally near cities that had IKEA showrooms. The chain's ad agency placed the spot only after ten P.M. because, as an agency representative explained, "we recognize the sensitivity of the issue." Several Religious Right groups denounced the commercial, but few of them were anywhere near an IKEA store, so there was little concern over boycotts. The furniture company reaped considerable international publicity from this commercial, which the media trumpeted as a pioneering effort at inclusiveness. *New York Times* critic Frank Rich wrote of the ad, "Certainly it makes me feel better about IKEA. But I still wouldn't let that dreary table anywhere near my house." Four years later, a Virgin Cola commercial would show two men kissing and reciting wedding vows while standing on a giant bottle cap. This was one of several commercials in Virgin's "Soapbox" campaign that were refused by a number of TV stations, including some in major markets such as Los Angeles and New York.[14]

Clearly, sexual-minority content was being demarginalized in a variety of contexts and genres. Just as clearly, however, there were forces in place trying to contain that growth. In early 1994, PBS was about to push the envelope for inclusiveness further than even cable networks like HBO had dared. The result would generate the biggest gay TV controversy in more than a decade.

TELLING *TALES*

Gay Issues and the War for PBS: 1992–1995

"Mom, Michael is a homosexual."
Silence.
"He likes boys, got it? I know you've heard of it. They've got it on TV now."
—*From one of Armistead Maupin's serialized*
"Tales of the City" short stories, 1976[1]

By early 1994, television was no longer holding gay and bisexual characters quite so far at arm's length. Some writers, actors, and directors
again asked the old question: Was it time for TV to let its fictional same-
sex couples be just as caring and physically affectionate as their heterosexual counterparts? For the commercial networks, the fear of sponsor
reprisals still loomed large, but PBS and premium cable channels
seemed less susceptible to attack. Their portrayals of same-sex couples
became more realistic, matter-of-fact, and loving.

In the early 1990s, British imports seen on PBS were the main venue
for believable gay characters on American television. British television's
standards regarding sexuality have always been more relaxed than the
standards on American TV. (Common wisdom in the industry held that
American networks usually censored sex out of English shows, while
the British had to cut violence out of American shows.) Beginning with
the landmark TV film *The Naked Civil Servant* in 1976, and continuing
in the 1980s with such productions as *Brideshead Revisited*, British
programs with gay content have long delighted American public television audiences. That tradition continued in the early 1990s, when PBS

imported several English shows that depicted physical affection—even bedroom scenes—between same-sex lovers. First there was *The Lost Language of Cranes* on *Great Performances* in 1992. Based on a novel by American writer David Leavitt, it portrays a family rocked by the revelation that both father and son are gay. A month later, *Masterpiece Theater* ran *Portrait of a Marriage*, which included lesbian love scenes so candid that antigay groups branded them pornographic. (PBS offered stations the option of a toned-down version of the show.) Around the same time, some public TV stations picked up the BBC miniseries *Oranges Are Not the Only Fruit*. This alternately sweet and harrowing drama depicts a lesbian teenager's coming of age in a village dominated by Evangelical Christians. In all of these imports, the characters formed relationships, kissed, and made love, things no major American TV production had ever shown.[2] By fall 1993, PBS was advertising another frank British import, an exciting project that had been in development in various forms since the late 1970s: a miniseries based on Armistead Maupin's witty, engaging novel of life in 1976 San Francisco, *Tales of the City*.

Here was a show that did not just *tolerate* sexual minorities: it embraced and celebrated them as full-fledged, well-developed protagonists. This TV serial veers comfortably from comedy to romance, from suspense thriller to high camp. Set at the height of the sexual revolution, *Armistead Maupin's "Tales of the City"* follows its large cast of characters through myriad locales in the Bay Area: a rooming house, a bathhouse, a penthouse, a roller disco, corporate executive suites, a "fat farm," museums, churches, mansions, and singles bars. It is one of the very few programs that shows gay, straight, transgender, and bisexual characters living peacefully side by side and forming warm friendships across those sociological and sexual boundaries. Like the original book, the miniseries treats homosexuality, bisexuality, and transsexualism as nonchalantly as most TV shows treat heterosexuality.

Tales of the City was the top-rated drama to air on PBS in five years. The news media gave the show significant advance press—some of it in the form of positive reviews—and other reports followed the telecast. *Newsday*'s Frank DeCaro went so far as to call *Tales* "the *Roots* of gay-positive TV programs."[3] Many of the articles focused on the show's unusually "strong" language, its matter-of-fact approach to GLBT characters, its portrayal of casual drug use, and the use of brief nudity. The miniseries stayed in the news for months: by mid 1994, *Tales* was at the center of congressional attempts to eliminate federal funding of public broadcasting. As with several shows in 1994, the controversy surrounding *Tales* dealt partly with same-sex kissing: most of the American news reports mentioned at least one of the two scenes in which Michael (Marcus D'Amico) kisses his boyfriend Jon (William Campbell) on the lips.

Screen adaptations of Maupin's book had been in development at various film and TV studios almost since it was first published. In each case, Maupin, an openly gay writer and activist, insisted on retaining creative approval. He has said that during those eleven years, "I found that I could stop a script meeting cold with a single question: 'Will Jon and Michael be allowed to kiss?' " A proposed film version circa 1979 fell through partly because Warner Bros. reportedly wanted to drop the drug use, focus on the straight characters, and reduce Michael—one of Maupin's best-developed romantic figures—to just "the gay neighbor." The studio planned to eliminate the book's freewheeling, go-with-the-flow tone. CBS considered it as a series around 1981, but wanted the gay characters removed. Later, the already mentioned HBO *Tales of the City* sitcom fell through because the stories were too rooted in the 1970s to work in an era of AIDS panic and antidrug campaigns. But by the 1990s, enough time had passed that the stories could be presented as a period piece.[4]

Tales' mysterious landlady Anna Madrigal and her tenants—her "children," as she calls them—first appeared in serialized stories in a San Francisco newspaper in 1976. Mrs. Madrigal (played on TV by Olympia Dukakis) is a maternal, bohemian-looking woman in her fifties, who we eventually learn is a transsexual. Maupin's Everywoman is Mary Ann Singleton (Laura Linney), a wide-eyed new arrival from Cleveland. Her neighbor, Michael "Mouse" Tolliver, is a determinedly romantic young gay man from the Bible Belt. Other residents include Brian Hawkins (Paul Gross), a straight, liberal lawyer-turned-waiter; and Mona Ramsey (Chloe Webb), a drugged-out, slightly spacey 1960s throwback. Though primarily attracted to men, Mona has recently had an affair with a woman. Both on the printed page and on-screen, the characters are drawn with wit and incisiveness.

The TV version of *Tales of the City* creates an uncanny sense of place and time, recreating the Bay Area pre-AIDS, when many saw life as a huge, free-spirited party. Mary Ann's first conversation with her future landlady sets the tone for the rest of the series. "Do you have any objection to pets?" Mary Ann asks. Mrs. Madrigal smiles with a wise twinkle in her eye. "Dear," she replies expansively, "I have no objection to *anything*." As in the novel, sexual-minority issues pervade and bind the labyrinthine plotlines. Mary Ann's boss Edgar Halcyon, a married, old-money Republican, has a secret affair with Mrs. Madrigal. Edgar's son-in-law, the shifty socialite Beauchamp Day (Thomas Gibson), regularly cheats on his wife—sometimes with men in bathhouses, sometimes with women coworkers. D'Orothea (Cynda Williams) is Mona's once and future lover, a black supermodel whose dark secret is that she is really white. Clearly, *Tales of the City* was not the typical prime-time serial.

The principal ongoing love story in Maupin's first three novels is between Michael and a wealthy young gynecologist, Jon Fielding. Their romance is appropriately prominent in the TV version, and the on-screen chemistry between actors D'Amico and Campbell is great. As in an old Hollywood romantic comedy, they "meet cute": Michael inadvertently crashes into Jon at a roller skating rink, and the evening turns into their first date. Their first night together provides the most romantic, physically affectionate gay male bedroom scene that had ever been seen on American TV. They kiss briefly in this scene, and later are seen necking in Jon's convertible while waiting for a traffic light. The show's dialog, lifted almost verbatim from the novel, allows Michael a depth of development unusual in a gay TV character.

With the moving romance between Anna and Edgar, *Tales* became the first major TV drama to foreground a love story involving a transsexual, and the first to casually present a transsexual protagonist. Even after learning that Anna used to be called Andy, Edgar still finds her sexually desirable and chooses to continue their affair. There is a mystic bond between Anna and Edgar. Without being told, she can sense when he dies in the finale. In the series' final scene, Anna—famous for her home-grown marijuana—places a small cylindrical object on a newly dug grave overlooking the water. "Have fun, dear," she says. "It's Colombian."[5]

British TV's greater comfort with sexual topics, combined with its strong tradition of faithful literary adaptations, may explain why Maupin's American characters had to reach U.S. television via England. By late 1992, Britain's Channel Four had committed to an expensive, six-hour serialization of the book, to be shot in California with a mostly American cast.[6] The series would be coproduced by the British independent company Working Title in conjunction with the Los Angeles–based Propaganda Films. Maupin signed on as a coexecutive producer. After the producers rejected the first screenplay by an openly gay playwright whom Maupin had chosen, they turned to Richard Kramer for a new adaptation. Best known for his work on *thirtysomething*, Kramer had written HBO's *Tales of the City* pilot script a decade earlier. Like the *Tales* books themselves, Kramer's storytelling has often been a bit too frank for the confines of American commercial TV. He was delighted by the degree of freedom the British network allowed. *Tales* coproducer Antony Root recalled early discussions with Kramer, who was "astonished to hear us tell him that we'd lose our finance if he cut the four-letter words out or limited the gay material."[7]

Root said the greater creative freedom in Britain comes from a difference between the history of American and English TV. Until the 1960s, there *was* no nationwide commercial television in Britain, and much of television remained commercial-free in the 1990s. Root proudly told reporters that television in Britain "grows out of a tradition of public service, while America's comes from a tradition of selling goods." Even a commercial British station like Channel Four, he said, could afford to produce a high-quality, niche-audience show, while American networks needed projects with mass appeal.[8] The impact of these divergent philosophies on gay content is clear when one compares scriptwriter Kramer's straightforward, playful bedroom scene in *Tales* with the way ABC censored the gay bed scene he wrote for *thirtysomething* in 1989. Although different in tone, Kramer originally wrote both scenes with the same degree of frankness and tastefulness. Yet in the final product, the *thirtysomething* characters kept their distance from each other in bed, as if the sex they had just had was shameful. By contrast, Michael and Jon in *Tales* are clearly enjoying each other's company, the touch of each other's body, and have no regrets.

During filming, Channel Four tried to sell *Tales* to the American commercial broadcast networks, but the show was too "hot" for them. The characters' penchant for casual sex made it especially controversial in 1993, when researchers had made little progress in treating AIDS. One TV executive told Maupin and coproducer Antony Root that if *Tales* ever did air, it would have to be preceded by a health warning.[9] During the final week of shooting, PBS leased the American rights for a fraction of the asking price.

Tales of the City aired nationally on PBS in January 1994. PBS ran a disclaimer before each episode, cautioning that the series was meant to portray life as it was in a particular time and place, and that some of the content might not be suitable for all viewers. Even with that warning, and with an alternate feed of a slightly censored version of the show, several PBS stations refused to air it. Most cited their responsibility to respect local standards of decency. WTCI-TV in Chattanooga, Tennessee, advertised the show, then canceled it just before airtime. Hundreds of people had phoned WTCI that day. Although none had probably seen the show, they used talking points from fundamentalist organizations to express their disapproval. There were threats to withhold pledges, and at least one bomb threat, which may be what turned the tide. WTCI offered to set up private screenings at the station for people who wanted to see *Tales*.[10]

Because PBS's funding was largely dependent on Congress, the conservative backlash against *Tales* put public TV in a tough spot. In theory, this was precisely the sort of drama that PBS had been designed to present: intelligent, literate stories that, for whatever reasons, the commercial networks would not touch. *Tales* was also exactly the weapon that opponents of PBS had prayed for. It was an easier target than some of PBS's previous risqué imports from Britain. *Tales* was not the usual costume serial about depravity in Europe of long ago, à la *I, Claudius*. For American viewers, *Tales* hit closer to home because it takes place in the United States in the recent past. It was, as costar Laura Linney put it, "a very simple, loving, and accurate depiction of a period of time that people are not comfortable with." She noted that GLBT characters on-screen usually "are depicted with a comment placed on them. *Tales* is a story of people who are just people with no comment placed on anything one way or the other."[11]

Within weeks, the American Family Association launched a far-reaching campaign under the slogan "It's time to shut down PBS!" Reverend Wildmon asserted, "PBS can rightly be called the Homosexual Pride Taxpayer-Funded TV Network." This time, instead of lobbying the shows' corporate funders, he targeted two of public TV's biggest underwriters: the U.S. Congress and state governments. For once, his strategy was thorough and perfectly timed. On the federal level, the Corporation for Public Broadcasting's funding was coming up for renewal in 1994. AFA compiled a twelve-minute videotape, pulling together out-of-context snippets of swearing, nudity, same-sex kissing, gay bedroom scenes, and gay-friendly remarks from three recent PBS offerings: *Tales of the City*, *Tongues Untied*, and *In the Life*. (Since *Tongues Untied* featured gay people of color and *In the Life* was a regular gay-produced, gay-targeted "magazine" series, these shows were logical targets in the Religious Right's campaign.) In some states, AFA distributed the tape to every member of the state legislature. The same or similar tapes went to U.S. senators and representatives. Wildmon urged legislators to either eliminate public broadcasting or legally constrain the stations from transmitting "this filth." Accompanying the tape was AFA's detailed written analysis of *Tales of the City*. AFA also mailed its members still photos from the miniseries, showing men kissing each other and women baring their breasts.[12]

Other groups carried out similar campaigns against PBS, accusing the network of a liberal bias and a lax attitude toward morality. The protests were hypocritical in a way. For years, organizations like AFA had accused PBS of catering to a small, culturally elite audience rather than appealing to the large number of taxpayers who funded it. Now they were attacking the most popular prime-time PBS drama in years. Within ten weeks of *Tales*' first American broadcast, Georgia sliced its Public TV budget, and the Oklahoma House of Representatives passed an amendment barring funding for any show that "promotes, encourages, or casts in a favorable light homosexuality or any activity violative of the law."[13] Especially at small stations, dealing with outcry over this daring show tied up staff members and kept them from doing their day-to-day jobs. Some broadcasters had to wonder if *Tales*' high ratings were worth the threat that controversial programming seemed to pose for public broadcasting.[14]

Despite the political backlash, *Armistead Maupin's "Tales of the*

City" got rave reviews, strong Nielsens (for PBS), an Emmy nomination, and broadcasting's most prestigious honor, the George Foster Peabody award. PBS quickly entered into negotiations about cofunding a sequel. Underwriting for *More Tales of the City* seemed a foregone conclusion. Except . . .

Except that PBS could not afford to alienate Congress during deliberations over the survival of public broadcasting, and the plot of *More Tales* was even more controversial than the first book's. In addition to all of the elements that upset moral conservatives the first time around, Maupin's second novel confronts Anita Bryant–style antigay activism, focuses much of its action in a brothel, and depicts a cult of Episcopalian cannibals. That spring, PBS scratched *More Tales of the City* off its production list. GLAAD and Maupin blasted the decision as censorship, accusing PBS of buckling under to homophobic pressure.

PBS president Ervin Duggan said the decision was purely financial. He explained:

> Fully half of our remaining budget for drama would have been required to fund that sequel. So we made an economic decision. Censorship is when the cold, clammy hand of government or an outside force comes to throttle and silence free editorial choice. . . . The people who are claiming censorship and banning are disappointed authors.[15]

There was some truth to that. PBS and *American Playhouse* had paid only about $1 million for the first *Tales* series ($150,000 from PBS's drama budget, and the rest from foundation grants that *American Playhouse* pursued independently). For the sequel, Channel Four wanted the Americans to kick in anywhere from $2.5 million to $4 million. Channel Four executives said that *Tales* had been a bigger success in the United States than in Britain, and that it was reasonable for PBS to pay an amount closer to half of the sequel's $8 million tab. Without such a partnership, the British executives said, Channel Four did not have the means to produce the sequel.

In making his excuses, however, Duggan sidestepped the fact that PBS's senior management had *chosen* to remove money from the drama budget in favor of children's programming and documentaries. Their decision seemed calculated to assuage that "cold, clammy hand of government," which had reacted negatively to recent PBS broadcasts. A network trying to duck charges of liberal bias did not want to give its enemies more ammunition by funding controversial dramas. *American Playhouse,* which aired *Tales of the City,* would soon fold for lack of funds. PBS had provided $6.6 million of *American Playhouse*'s 1994 budget. Just after *Tales* aired, PBS cut its 1995 subsidy for *American Playhouse* to $2.2 million, with plans for no support at all thereafter.[16]

After PBS withdrew, Showtime cable and KQED-TV in San Francisco each expressed interest in coproducing *More Tales of the City* with Channel Four.[17] But Showtime soon backed out and Channel Four announced that the project had been scrapped. Four years later, following a coproduction agreement among Channel Four, Showtime, and Canadian TV interests, *Armistead Maupin's "More Tales of the City"* finally was released in a smaller, more tightly budgeted form. It featured only a portion of the original cast. In an interview, actress Laura Linney pointed out that while PBS was not willing to coproduce *More Tales* . . . , PBS stations were willing to use footage of the original *Tales of the City* during pledge drives to tout the network's high artistic standards. "My favorite thing now," she said, "is their ad campaign of 'If PBS doesn't do it, who will?' Well, the answer is Showtime."[18]

A KISS IS STILL A KISS

Television: 1980–1995

You know what they say, Dan. "Every time lesbians kiss, another angel gets her wings."   —*Roseanne Conner on a Christmas episode of* Roseanne, *1992*[1]

In the wake of *Tales of the City*, same-sex kissing became a topic of much backstage debate in the TV industry. Even at the turn of the twenty-first century, it remains one of the taboos that most networks will not break. The *idea* of two men or two women kissing is not what makes sponsors flee and network executives lose sleep. The big controversies occur if the kiss happens *on-camera*. Usually, just before the two characters' lips touch, the camera cuts to a straight character, who sees the kiss and reacts on behalf of the viewer. Anytime a show's writers try to violate that unwritten rule and let gay couples show affection in plain view, a media circus ensues.

Comedian Roseanne Arnold, the star and coproducer of *Roseanne*, loved a good media circus. February 1994 found her and actress Mariel Hemingway clowning on the set of *Roseanne*, rehearsing a much hyped "lesbian kiss" that ABC was threatening not to air. In this episode—titled "Don't Ask, Don't Tell"—Roseanne and her sister Jackie go to a gay bar with Nancy (Sandra Bernhard) and Nancy's new girlfriend (Hemingway). Jackie is nervous, worried that women will flirt with her. Roseanne, however, appears perfectly at ease with her lesbian pals. She makes fun of Jackie's discomfort, but then has to admit to her own hidden prejudices after the Hemingway character impulsively kisses her.

Reporters and the show's crew looked on as the actresses, scripts in hand, edged closer to rehearsing the much discussed kiss. The set, representing a small-town gay bar, was crowded with extras playing lesbian and gay couples—couples the viewers at home would barely notice thanks to cautious camera work. In a flash, Hemingway made her move, planting one on Roseanne's lips. Hemingway kept the back of her head toward the camera, as instructed, so viewers would not see anything too specific. Roseanne Arnold smiled, broke character, and ad libbed, "I guess I can't get into the army now!" The crew and ABC reporter Lynn Sherr—covering the taping for *20/20*—cracked up. Within two weeks, The Kiss would become a hot topic in newspapers, talk shows, and tabloid TV.

The relationship between *Roseanne* and ABC's Standards & Practices department had been tense for some time. Once ABC approved scripts, Arnold and her staff sometimes would revise them, record the shows, and hand over the tape with an implicit message of "take it or leave it." If ABC pushed back too hard, she would threaten to take her gold mine of a show to a competing network. Because of the series' success, ABC had let *Roseanne* casually and fully include several recurring gay and bisexual characters—four recurring roles up to that point. In a 1992 Christmas episode, ABC had even let Nancy kiss her then girlfriend, Marla, under the mistletoe. That caused only minimal fuss since the camera safely cut away just before the moment of truth. For the 1994 show, however, Roseanne Arnold felt it was essential to show the kiss so the audience would know what her character was reacting to. In theory, there was little to justify censoring the scene: a lesbian character was to kiss a straight woman, who would then grimace and wipe her mouth.

Some ABC executives, however, had misgivings. The issue was not *who* was kissed, but that the audience—and sponsors—would *see* it. If (as ABC's Robert Iger kept repeating) *thirtysomething* lost over $1 million for showing gay men not even touching, what might happen if a program showed a lesbian kiss? Arguably, such an image could have brought boycotts, preemption by local stations, and sponsor pullouts. This was a family sitcom. Would parents stop letting their children watch *Roseanne*? ABC had to raise at least some semblance of public objection.

Roseanne felt strongly about this episode—partly because of her well-known commitment to gay inclusiveness, and partly because it offered an opportunity to develop her own role. "My character thought she's really cool," she explained. But Roseanne Conner panics after the kiss, showing that "she's not as cool as she thought she was." By early February, ABC was pushing for the kiss to happen out of view. So Roseanne and Tom Arnold decided to put pressure on the network by telling reporters that ABC had rejected an upcoming episode. According to Tom, the network claimed it could lose up to $1 million in advertising if the show aired. Show business trade papers and the mainstream press carried headlines like "ROSEANNE" SHOW KILLED OVER KISS and ROSEANNE "GAY" SEGMENT NIXED.

Even if the controversy did not start out as a public-relations game, it quickly turned into one. The Arnolds invited GLAAD representatives to the taping so the group could talk to the press about the show. In interviews, the Arnolds blasted ABC's supposed cowardice. Roseanne reportedly threatened to take her series to CBS if ABC censored this episode. GLAAD took out a full-page ad in the Valentine's Day issue of *Daily Variety*, headlined ABC—DON'T BREAK AMERICA'S HEART. At the bottom, a squib explained what GLAAD was. On February 17, GLAAD hosted a press conference featuring *Roseanne*'s head writer, GLAAD's Lee Werbel, and speakers from the National Organization for Women and People for the American Way. Werbel encouraged ABC to simply "Show the episode and give the American public the freedom to judge for themselves." Now reporters knew about another source to contact: GLAAD.

ABC, meanwhile, milked the alleged controversy for every Nielsen point it could. It almost seemed as though ABC was deliberately releasing small amounts of information at a time, trying to build interest and suspense—like the cliff-hangers on a soap opera. The press obliged with ample coverage of what reporters framed as a censorship scandal. Knowing that the pervasive coverage would attract viewers, ABC scheduled the show for the final night of the February Nielsen sweeps. They even turned ABC's own news show *20/20* into an advertising tool to promote the episode. Roseanne Arnold's tell-all autobiography came out the same week, so *20/20* interviewed her about that *and* the TV kiss. Her presence boosted the sweeps numbers for *20/20*, which in turn drummed up viewers for *Roseanne*'s sweeps episode. Once it became clear the episode would air as planned, the conservative, Washington-based Media Research Center issued its own statement. The center's L. Brent Bozell lamented ABC's "spinelessness." "If they allow this scene to air," he said, "it just proves that ABC cannot stand up to the bullying tactics of Roseanne Arnold, the homosexual activists, and their liberal friends in Hollywood. . . . Once again, the values and virtues of millions of Americans are getting the shaft."

Millions of Americans disagreed. "Don't Ask, Don't Tell" was a ratings bonanza, even with two local stations refusing to air it. In the overnight Nielsens, it was the week's highest-rated show and the series' fourth highest rating for the season. A week later, on *The People's Choice Awards*, Carol Burnett presented Roseanne Arnold with a trophy. They kissed on the lips in a protracted send-up of the sitcom smooch. GLAAD/New York, meanwhile, used the *Roseanne* incident as a springboard to address other concerns with ABC. Following negotiations that spring, GLAAD reported that ABC Standards & Practices had agreed to add gay men and lesbians to the list of groups which "cannot be ridiculed or stereotyped" on ABC shows.[2]

Despite the hype and massive ratings, the scene with Hemingway was not the groundbreaking "gay kiss" it seemed. Like earlier "lesbian" kisses on TV (on *21 Jump Street*, *L.A. Law*, and *Picket Fences*), this was a kiss between a straight woman and a gay or bisexual woman. Of the previous commercial shows studied for this book, only one showed a romantic kiss between same-sex lovers: In the 1983 TV movie *Trackdown: Finding the Goodbar Killer*, a murderer kisses his lover on the lips—on-camera—before going on the run. Other male villains in dramas were allowed to make out with men just off-camera (*Guyana Tragedy*, 1980) or on-camera (*Picket Fences*, 1993).[3] Again, gay sexuality could be a joke or could be used to demonize people, but sincere same-sex affection was taboo. "Nice" gays had to be eunuchs. On *Dynasty* in the 1980s, Steven could kiss Claudia or Sammy Jo, but not Ted, Luke, or Bart. On *Heartbeat*, ABC forbade Marilyn and Patti to *dance* together, much less neck.

The networks' most important deliberations about how to depict gay couples happened between 1989 and 1997. As gay portrayals focused increasingly on couples, the question of how realistically they should

act started cropping up regularly in story conferences and meetings with censors. Generally, the response of the commercial networks
(and, less often, the premium cable channels) was that couples should
not be affectionate on-camera. So ABC removed a kiss from the 1989
"Strangers" episode of *thirtysomething*, although the producers fought
for the kiss through three drafts of the script. *The Women of Brewster
Place* managed to portray a convincingly affectionate, if tragic, lesbian
couple without an on-the-lips kiss. Instead, Lorraine calms her weeping
lover by kissing her face all *around* her mouth, that extra millimeter of
skin being the necessary safety zone to make it onto late-1980s television. Kisses between likable gay men were filmed and cut from HBO's
1993 film *And the Band Played On* and a 1994 episode of Fox's *Melrose
Place*.[4] The commercial networks' main concern was the potential for
sponsor pullouts, which is why the most straightforward portrayals of
gay affection—including kisses—have occurred where there is no
direct advertising: on PBS and on premium cable channels like HBO
and Showtime.

Why are scenes of tenderness or kissing between male lovers more
disturbing to the public than scenes suggesting loveless sex between
men would be? In our society, children are trained from an early age to
regard tenderness between males as a sign of weakness, unmanliness.
Schoolyard taunts, passed down from older children to younger ones,
teach that a boy kissing his father or holding hands with a male friend is
behavior to be punished. In practice, this form of homophobia
oppresses straight men at least as much as it does gays—such as when
straight men fear to hug other men because it is somehow "queer." As
noted earlier, even children's cartoons reinforce this norm: Bugs Bunny
and Daffy Duck kiss male enemies to humiliate and annoy them. By
early adulthood, in most cases, this lesson has been learned well.
Anyone who has attended a Human Sexuality course that includes
gay sex education films can vouch for this. Students, whether under-
graduates, medical students, or future social workers, can sit quietly
through scenes of lesbian sex, lesbians kissing, and men having oral or
anal sex. But let two men on screen smile at each other lovingly and kiss
on the lips, and an involuntary shudder goes through the lecture hall.
Both male and female students, who are trying to be mature in front of
their professor, let out impulsive cries of "Ewwwwwww! *Gross!*" These

prejudices are an undeniable reality. Even many adults who consider themselves open-minded about the *idea* of gay people get queasy when faced with the concrete reality of a same-sex kiss. It is a gut-level reaction to something unfamiliar, alien, and intimate, much like the way children react when they first see adult heterosexuals kissing. This reality informs the decisions that sponsor-dependent networks make about whether to censor on-screen affection.

While the commercial networks consistently banned this simple token of affection between gay lovers, they did permit same-sex kissing in other contexts. A straight woman could kiss a lesbian. Straight men could kiss each other as part of a comedy routine. On *The Simpsons*, a gay cartoon character (voiced by Harvey Fierstein) was allowed to kiss Homer Simpson.[5] But gay characters could not kiss *each other* unless they were murderers—and then only rarely. The viewer needed to be able to justify it as a joke or a sign of depravity—not a "real" gay kiss that might involve same-sex attraction, tenderness, or love.

These limitations closely followed the boundaries TV had placed around other types of taboo relationships in the past, such as depiction of straight interracial couples. Throughout the 1960s and early 1970s, the networks consistently removed mixed-race couples from scripts. The boyfriend on the sitcom *That Girl* was originally supposed to be part Native American. The network objected, and by airtime he had become the more white-bread Donald Hollinger. As late as 1971, ABC and Paramount repeatedly banned a proposed scene in which a black woman was supposed to have a platonic chat over drinks with a white male classmate on *The Young Lawyers*. (Over the story editor's vociferous objections, the scene was filmed with a white actress.) NBC broadcast commercial television's first interracial kiss in 1968 on *Star Trek*. The scene was allowable because telepathic aliens were *forcing* the characters to kiss. A scene in which a black woman and white man kissed of their own free will out of mutual attraction would not have been allowed. Taboo kisses can air only if they can be explained away.[6]

Twenty-seven years later, a sequel series, *Star Trek: Deep Space Nine,* aired a passionate kiss between two women. It was the longest, steamiest same-sex kiss ever on American commercial broadcast TV. The characters' eyes were closed, their mouths open, and they came back for more. But this, too, was okay because it was not a "real" lesbian kiss. The female characters were space aliens who acquire new bodies when their old ones die. This kiss was uncontroversial because, in a previous incarnation, the women had been a heterosexual couple—husband and wife.[7] The scene attracted little media attention and no discernible protests. It was a fine example of the strange plot contortions necessary to justify a same-sex kiss on television in the 1990s. As with *Star Trek*'s original interracial kiss, a plot gimmick was needed to disguise (and distort) a taboo expression of sexuality.

Another factor that made the *Deep Space Nine* script allowable was that the characters were women rather than men. In the minds of many TV executives—who are, on the whole, straight men—lesbian sensuality is sexy, but gay male sexuality is repulsive and threatening. The porn industry has long catered to straight male fantasies about lesbians; by contrast, the heterosexual market for erotic scenes of men is almost nonexistent. The generalization that straight men are turned on by lesbians, while not a universal truth, has enough basis in reality to have become a running joke in 1990s sitcoms. In the epilog to the *Roseanne* kiss episode, Roseanne's husband is initially furious that someone tried to kiss his wife. But when he learns it was a woman in a gay bar, he starts to become aroused. "What was she wearing?" he asks, trying to sound casual. As Roseanne gives details, he becomes more and more excited. But Roseanne throws cold water on his libido by also describing a muscular gay male couple who were making out at the bar. In response, an uncomfortable Dan skulks down to the kitchen for a drink. Similar gags on *Friends* and *Ellen* never failed to generate huge laughs from the studio audience.[8]

Where lesbian affection is involved, network policies have loosened considerably since 1978, when ABC would not let Jane Alexander kiss Gena Rowlands's *hand* in *A Question of Love*. The first step in that evolution came eight years later, when ABC aired commercial TV's first earnest attempt at a same-sex love story: the TV movie *My Two Loves*, about a widow just discovering her bisexuality. Four weeks into filming in 1986, costars Mariette Hartley and Lynn Redgrave had already acted out the female leads' meeting, becoming friends, falling in love, holding hands on a romantic picnic, talking about their lives, their loves, their feelings. However, on Redgrave's last day of shooting, they would play a scene that worried them, worried director Noel Black, and worried ABC's censors: a full, on-the-lips kiss. The actors focused on getting past the awkwardness of any love scene, gay or straight. The script called for the Hartley character's mother (Sada Thompson) to walk in on them during the kiss. The mother later says, "You were kissing that woman like a man!" For this accusation to make sense, Hartley and Redgrave had to play the scene much as straight couples kiss on TV. "It was a very soft, gentle, sensual kiss," Hartley told reporters after filming ended. The actors' fretting over the scene turned out to be unnecessary. As broadcast, the film used an alternate take in which Thompson enters and reacts as the lovers' mouths move toward each other, but before contact. It was played so naturalistically and timed so tightly that many viewers swear they saw the kiss. It would be another five years before the taboo was finally broken with *L.A. Law*'s famous smooch between Abby and C. J.[9]

David E. Kelley, who wrote that Abby/C. J. episode, soon went on to create CBS's award-winning, slightly surreal, small-town drama series, *Picket Fences*. Kelley wrote a spring 1993 episode called "Sugar and Spice." As in the *L.A. Law* script, the story had a straight woman share an experimental kiss with a lesbian or bisexual woman friend. Again, characters' reactions to this were central to the story, so the kiss had to be depicted somehow. Complicating matters from the network/sponsor standpoint was the age of the characters: sixteen-year-old high school girls. The script called for series regular Kimberly and her new friend Lisa to be in Kimberly's room, talking about boys, when Lisa asks if Kimberly has ever kissed another girl. They decide to try it as an experiment. CBS brass got that far in reading the script when they decided that changes were needed. They rushed to explain that they *themselves* were not offended, but they anticipated that others might be. They said the kiss should be suggested but not clearly seen. First, producers filmed the scene from above, so only the backs of heads appeared. Then the network asked Kelley to insert a fade-out before the kiss. But given television's long history of fading out just before torrid sex scenes, CBS recanted that suggestion and agreed to a compromise: the girls would pull down the blinds and kiss in the dark. Again, the problem was not the *fact* of a kiss, but that viewers and advertisers might *see* it.

Like the following year's *Roseanne* episode, this *Picket Fences* story focuses on people who think they are more liberal than they are. Kimberly's parents, Jill and Jimmy, support gay civil rights, have been honoring the gay boycott of Colorado, and are immensely sympathetic figures. Yet they flip out when they find out that their daughter has kissed a young lesbian. They wonder where they went wrong, ponder whether their adopted child might be genetically predisposed to lesbianism, and desperately try to steer her back to the joys of boy-watching. Through it all, they question their own motives, realizing that they are not—and perhaps do not want to be—as open-minded as they imagined. Of course, the Brock family has nothing to worry about: it is the seldom-seen friend, Lisa, who is a teenage lesbian. Kimberly likes boys.

This episode's kissing scene, even darkened to the point of invisibility, still worried CBS executives. This was not *L.A. Law*. *Picket Fences* averaged around eightieth in the weekly ratings and needed all the advertising support it could get. Although CBS did air the scene, some senior managers were not thrilled about it. The network's insistence on refilming and obscuring the scene reflected CBS's obvious double standard toward kissing. Just two months earlier, in another episode written by Kelley, *Picket Fences* was allowed to plainly show two men smooching in a fully lit shot. But that was acceptable because one man was Cupid, a notorious serial rapist and killer. He and his partner kiss, apparently, just before he assaults and strangles women. (The villains appear to be a bisexual man and his gay male lover, but it is never stated explicitly.) Fortunately, the poor woman he is about to kill in this episode has hidden a pen-gun inside a tampon in her purse. Just after kissing his cohort, the rapist Cupid is killed by an exploding feminine hygiene product. That episode apparently generated little or no controversy. Murder, rape, and the bisexuality of a sociopath were acceptable subjects for a family show; tenderness between two nice, young women was not.[10]

Cable stations—both premium and sponsored channels—have generally been more relaxed about such things. In March 1994, less than a week after the *Roseanne* kiss, HBO presented an original drama for teenagers about a lesbian high school student (played by Sabrina Lloyd) who plans to take her girlfriend (Kate Anthony) to the prom, unaware of how cruelly people might respond. "More Than Friends: The Coming Out of Heidi Leiter" was part of an anthology of half-hour, fact-based dramas, *Lifestories: Families in Crisis*. The real Leiter and her girlfriend had attended Leiter's senior prom in Virginia in 1991, a decision that made them targets for classmates' harassment and violence. As any teenage love story should, "More Than Friends" includes a kiss. There was virtually no public outcry against the scene. Because it was presented as a natural outgrowth of the story, the kiss itself got little attention, even when parents protested against the showing of the film in a Virginia high school. The contrast with commercial TV was obvious. Here was an on-screen kiss between two teenage lesbians in love—not thirty-year-olds, not a lesbian and a straight woman. A GLAAD newsletter noted that "unlike the half-hidden 'lesbian kiss' on a recent episode of *Roseanne*, the program features a much more loving (and more truly lesbian) kiss. . . ." Writing in the *Boston Globe*, reviewer John Koch said that this "heartfelt drama" would "certainly have been treated with more circumspection, and less emotional honesty, on network TV. The recent *Roseanne* controversy suggests how far the networks have to go before attaining the maturity of their audiences."[11]

HBO's openness came from its lack of commercial sponsors. The situation at MTV cable was different. Despite the fact that MTV did depend on sponsors, it had become one of television's most gay-inclusive networks. Its creative freedom stemmed from its niche market. Unlike the big broadcasting networks, MTV primarily attracted trendy teenagers and twentysomethings—a demographic group that ad agencies believed was more tolerant of gay content than were general audiences. The music videos that occupied much of MTV's schedule provided a steady diet of exploitative sexual imagery (mostly heterosexual), so the network's fans and sponsors were a self-selected group, not too squeamish about sexuality. MTV's original productions of the 1990s—such as *The Real World*, *Sex in the '90s*, *Hate Rock*, *MTV News Unfiltered*, and the soap opera *Undressed*—often acknowledged same-sex attraction so casually and neutrally as to be a nonissue, although they sometimes did focus on antigay prejudice as a social problem. In an unusual move, MTV even taped a same-sex episode of its fun, trashy dating game show, *Singled Out*.[12] The episode was neither more nor less playful, sexual, and superficial than the show's straight editions. It was slated to air twice on Gay Pride Day in June 1996. However, this episode's fate revealed the limits of even MTV's liberalism. Orders from high in the cable network's parent company, Viacom, were reportedly the reason why the early-evening airing was canceled. The show ran once, at 11 P.M.

MTV's inclusiveness had its greatest impact on the public in 1994, when openly gay AIDS educator Pedro Zamora became a central figure in the third season of *The Real World*. Each season, this misnamed video verité series moved a different group of attractive young strangers into a luxury home in a major city, then taped their interactions over a period of several months. According to publicity, the cameras rolled constantly except when someone was using the bathroom "or about to score." Since the participants were chosen for their contrasting backgrounds and personalities, people got on one another's nerves, tempers flew, alliances rose and fell, romances and sexual tensions came and went in this "reality-based soap opera." Except for the 1995 and 1998 seasons, it became traditional for at least one member of each group to be gay or bisexual. First, in 1992, the show spotlighted a bisexual artist named Norman, who was seen going out with future talk show host Charles Perez. The next year brought a lesbian named Beth, a devotee of social causes. But it was Pedro Zamora who made the biggest splash. Shortly after taping for *Real World III* began, he met and fell in love with Sean Sasser. Viewers saw their romance blossom, saw Pedro torn over whether to confront a housemate who made anti-gay jokes, watched Pedro speak at schools as an openly HIV-positive health advocate, and attended Pedro and Sean's union ceremony. In the wedding episode, the couple was seen holding hands and kissing more than a half-dozen times.[13]

All of these shows, including *Roseanne*, contributed to an environment where writers, producers, and directors were willing to take risks and try to make GLBT characters more believable and more fully rounded. With public opinion polls indicating greater social tolerance toward homosexuality, and amid ever-more-frank TV depictions of gay couples, Aaron Spelling Productions decided it was time to push the Fox network again for permission to develop the role of Matt on *Mel-*

rose Place. After two years as a little-seen virtual eunuch, Matt was going to show signs of a libido. It was about time: even among many of the show's straight fans, Matt's lack of a real story line had become a running joke. Like *Roseanne* and *Tales of the City*, this sexy soap opera made headlines in early 1994 because of a kissing scene, touted as American commercial TV's first romantic kiss between likable men. In the 1994 season finale, Matt was supposed to meet a man he liked at his friend Billy's wedding. Afterward, Billy would be in the apartment complex's courtyard and, to his surprise, would see his best man kissing his gay neighbor.

The actors filmed the brief good-night kiss as scripted, but Fox balked, fearing that sponsors and some affiliate stations would drop the sweeps-week episode. This network, which originally built its audience through a mixture of innovation *(The Tracey Ullman Show)* and crass, often grotesque comedy *(Married . . . With Children)*, decided that a gay male kiss was too seamy for viewers of this otherwise lusty serial. Like every installment of *Melrose Place*, this episode unflinchingly depicted all manner of perversity, so Fox could hardly have argued that family values were at stake. A tender kiss between men was considered more threatening than depicting murder, rape, adultery, firebombing, incestuous child molestation, or fag-bashers brutally kicking a gay man whom they had beaten to the ground—all of which *Melrose Place* put on-screen in the mid 1990s at 8 P.M.

What did Fox consider allowable? Where were the boundaries between tolerance and acceptance? Matt as a platonic chum and confidant—a visitor in his straight neighbors' lives—was okay. Matt as a celibate victim of gay-bashing and job discrimination was fine. Matt as an estranged son reconciling with his antigay father was also fine. Matt living with a Russian woman and her child as part of an "immigration marriage" was just dandy. But Matt could not know romantic affection. Fox had allowed same-sex kissing in the lesbian-teen episode of *21 Jump Street* in 1990, but that was, again, a lesbian kissing a straight friend on the lips. And there were big differences between *21 Jump Street* in 1990 and *Melrose Place* in 1994. The *Jump Street* episode was approved before ABC took its infamous financial bath on that *thirty-something* episode; the *Melrose Place* controversy happened afterward.

Jump Street was a relatively prestigious, issue-oriented drama for teens that was giving a serious treatment to the prevention of gay youth suicide. *Melrose Place* was a soap opera that thrived on heterosexual promiscuity and usually reduced Matt to West Hollywood scenery.

The producers urged Fox to air the episode as submitted. GLAAD bought a full-page ad in *Daily Variety* a week before the episode's airdate, headlined FOX—CENSORSHIP IS UN-AMERICAN. DON'T CENSOR THE CREATIVE COMMUNITY AND DON'T CENSOR OUR LIVES. In a news release that week, GLAAD noted:

> In the past, GLAAD has met with representatives from the Fox network to discuss lesbian and gay portrayals in programming. The network's standard response has been that it does not control the creative component and it is the individual producers who do not include stories with lesbians and gay men.

GLAAD also pointed out that there was clearly a market for gay-themed episodes, such as the *Roseanne* one that had been such a financial success. Fox refused to budge. In the censored version of the scene, viewers are allowed to see only the reaction of the heterosexual character, Billy, as he inadvertently sees the two men kiss. Once again, the viewers' gaze was safely averted just in time.[14]

"We'd have lost up to a million dollars by airing that kiss," said Sandy Grushow, president of Fox Entertainment Group. He said that a struggling show on a small network could not afford the sort of risks that *Roseanne* and top-rated ABC could. "We're in business. Yes, it's show business, but ultimately we're responsible to the bottom line. We program [only] fifteen hours a week. Our ratings aren't as high as some other networks'. We couldn't afford to take the financial hit."[15] That December, *The Advocate* ran a cover photo of Doug Savant, the actor who played Matt, with the headline: WHY CAN'T THIS MAN GET LAID? HOW A NETWORK'S FEAR OF GAY CHARACTERS KEEPS DOUG SAVANT CELIBATE ON MELROSE PLACE.[16] Coexecutive producer Aaron Spelling had seen this battle before during production of *Dynasty*, *Heartbeat*, and the TV movie *And The Band Played On*. In a 1995 autobiography, he wrote:

To think that gay lovers, men or women, do not kiss is stupid. But it's not the network that rebels against gay and lesbian characters doing what comes naturally to them, it's the sponsors. The sales department says, "Hey, I can't sell this show," and the network has a tremendous multimillion-dollar loss, so they really have no choice. It's a rotten situation, but I do think it's getting better.[17]

By the time Spelling's book hit the stores, network censorship of same-sex affection was easing up. By the mid 1990s, on very rare occasions, lesbian couples on American TV could kiss in times of stress or panic. However, during romantic scenes they were still only allowed to hug or hold hands. Gay male kissing remained taboo. In 1995, almost a half century after TV first portrayed identifiably gay characters, viewers finally got to see a same-sex TV kiss in a love story where the two characters were still alive and together at the end: the NBC TV movie docudrama *Serving in Silence: The Colonel Margarethe Cammermeyer Story*. It was part of what some reporters described as an "explosion" of lesbianism in the media during the mid 1990s, evidence of so-called "lesbian chic."

LESBIAN INVISIBILITY MEETS LESBIAN CHIC

Television: 1993–1995

It is so good to be a lesbian in the nineties! We're now like Evian water, aren't we? Trendy. Everyone wants to be seen with us. . . . But . . . I auditioned for [one New York comedy club] three times, and I did really well. And don't you know, that little worm of a manager came up to me and went, "Well, you were really good, but I don't think we can use you, 'cause we groom our people for TV and I don't think there'll ever be *lesbians* on TV." I'm like, "No lesbians on TV?! What about Wimbledon?!"

> —*Suzanne Westenhoefer on the first* Out There *special,*
> *Comedy Central cable, 1993*[1]

If you strike a match in a dark place, there is a moment before your eyes adjust when the match's dim, flickering light seems blindingly bright. Of course, it is bright only in contrast to the darkness that went before. In 1992 and 1993, American culture began allowing gay and bisexual women more visibility than ever before—which is to say, not very much. Mainstream news reporters, unaccustomed to *any* meaningful visibility for lesbians, mistook the flickering flame for a bright light. They reacted as if lesbianism had never existed before, and wrote articles that said, in essence, "Ohmigod, lesbians are *everywhere*! How did *that* happen?" Media attention to lesbians started to snowball after k.d. lang's coming out in 1992 and Melissa Etheridge's in 1993. Just after the April 1993 March on Washington, *New York* magazine put k.d. lang on its cover with the headline LESBIAN CHIC: THE BOLD, BRAVE NEW WORLD OF GAY WOMEN. That spring and summer, lesbianism was also a cover story in *Newsweek* and *Vanity Fair*. The latter ran a cover photo of lang in a barber chair in male drag, having her face shaved by swimsuit-clad "supermodel" Cindy Crawford.[2] A few weeks after the k.d. lang article, *Vogue* magazine enthused: "Not long ago, you couldn't say the word *lesbian* on television. Now everybody's gay-girl crazy."[3] Other periodicals hinted at a massive increase in lesbian visibility.

"Lesbian chic" was a media catchphrase from 1993 to 1997, though reporters disagreed on what it meant. Sometimes, it referred to the media's exploitation of lesbians as something kinky, exotic, and titillating, like the icepick-wielding *dyke fatale* in *Basic Instinct*, or the voyeuristic "lesbian" skits on Howard Stern's TV show. Or "lesbian chic" described the greater public visibility of lesbians via "out" celebrities, news coverage, and on-screen portrayals. Or "lesbian chic" meant that straight celebrities (notably Madonna) were feigning lesbianism as a fashion statement. Or it meant that stars like Whoopi Goldberg, Glenn Close, Emma Thompson, Jean Smart, and Judy Davis were now willing—even eager—to play well-written lesbian roles. Or "lesbian chic" was the media-driven notion that gay women had suddenly developed "fashion sense" and were therefore more worthy of media attention (hence all the talk-show segments about "lipstick lesbians" and "designer dykes"). The definition varied, depending who you talked to and what articles you read. Ann Northrop—a prominent gay activist who used to work for the news divisions of ABC and CBS—quipped that the media were treating lesbians like "the hula hoop of the '90s." Given all the hype, one might have thought that prime-time television was filled with titles like *My Favorite Lesbian* or *Dharma & Grace*. One might have thought that every multiplex cinema in the United States was showing films with out-and-proud lesbian protagonists. One might have thought that prejudice against lesbians had suddenly disappeared.

In fact, most of these articles were not about lesbians themselves: they were reports about the media's own supposed obsession with lesbians. On careful reading, the 1993 articles are about an "explosion" of four lesbian celebrities and a "torrent" of three magazine covers. Certainly their depiction of lesbian images as being "everywhere" was quite an exaggeration, at least as far as TV characters were concerned. At the time, exactly two prime-time regular characters were lesbians or bisexual women, both of them supporting roles. In the previous six months, there had been perhaps four new prime-time TV episodes with gay or bisexual women as guest characters (compared to a dozen with gay or bisexual men). As for fictional characters in other contexts, there were some limited-release independent films, and some exploitative images in music videos. These tentative, early advances were important: they paved the way for a radical improvement in the media's portrayal of lesbianism during the mid 1990s.

The opposite of "lesbian chic" was "lesbian invisibility," a term used widely among gay and feminist activists from the 1970s to the mid 1990s. For decades, the underrepresentation of gay women in popular culture was the subject of lectures, political essays, and activism within gay and feminist communities. Articles about it appeared in lesbian periodicals as early as the 1960s. As late as 1993, it was still a touchstone for lesbian activists and humorists. Fighting lesbian invisibility was hard, since it was also rampant in many "gay and lesbian" organizations and in the "gay and lesbian" media. Women who tried to participate in such organizations often ended up feeling outnumbered and unwelcome. A few groups, like the National Gay Task Force, did include women among their leaders almost from the start. These tended to be the more "professionalized" gay agencies that had a paid staff. Organizations that chose leaders through job interviews were more likely to have a diverse leadership than the grassroots "gay and lesbian" entities, whose predominantly male membership tended to vote other men into leadership posts.

When TV professionals met with gay negotiators before 1989, the gay representatives usually were men. (Notable exceptions included those New York–based network executives who met with women from NGTF from the mid 1970s to early 1980s.) Now and then, gay male negotiators would raise concerns about lesbian invisibility, but the media people seldom knowingly *saw* a gay woman. This made it still easier for them to think of gayness as a male phenomenon. After being frustrated in their attempts to have "lesbian and gay" groups address women's issues, many lesbian activists gave up on mixed-gender politics and joined lesbian-specific organizations instead. These groups could explain gay women's issues eloquently, but the media usually refused to meet with them. This refusal was not necessarily due to hostility toward gay women. Rather, when negotiating with a minority, TV executives preferred to deal with large umbrella groups: just one or two big gay organizations, just one or two black organizations, one or two Irish American groups, and so on. In her book *Target: Prime Time*, Kathryn Montgomery calls this "the one-voice concept," a term she says she picked up from former ABC vice president Tom Kersey.[4] The media generally considered gay men and lesbians a single minority, so the TV executives were most willing to deal with large organizations that seemed to represent both men *and* women. In most of these groups (especially the regional ones that met with local stations), it was almost impossible for women to be elected into leadership posts, so women's issues got little attention.

That changed slowly during the 1980s. During the worst years of the AIDS epidemic and the antigay backlash it inspired, gay men and lesbians learned to work together with a greater sense of trust, unity, and mutual respect. Some gay organizations and agencies revised their bylaws to require gender parity on their steering committees. In the late 1980s and early 1990s, some organizations' entrenched sexism eroded further through sheer necessity: Far fewer gay men were involved in traditional gay-rights groups due to illness, deaths, and an exodus into AIDS activism. The practical need for qualified, skilled activists meant that the exclusionary practices of the past had become untenable, so women found their leadership abilities more appreciated and welcomed. In addition, because gay men had been particularly stigmatized by AIDS, lesbians were often perceived as less threatening and more acceptable spokespeople for GLBT interests.

As women played a larger role in gay media advocacy, they made it clear that the movement's status quo on lesbian imagery was no longer acceptable. As GLAAD's longtime public affairs director Karin Schwartz wrote in 1990, just before becoming GLAAD's acting executive director:

> ...[L]esbian and gay media advocates must embrace two principles. First, we must really believe in our guts that lesbian invisibility is defamation. The reality is that lesbian invisibility contributes to lesbian-battering and to the poor self-image of lesbian youth, and it supports an antilesbian legal and legislative environment—all problems that we attribute to overt

bigotry. With this in mind, we have to attack lesbian invisibility with all the gusto with which we attack overt homophobia.

Second, we can no longer be satisfied with overviews of our community that are "gay-positive" but contain no women. In fact, I would argue that we can no longer consider these depictions to be "gay-positive" . . .[5]

With more women leaders and more diverse paid staffs, the national organizations started balancing men's issues and women's issues more evenly. And when politicians and media executives negotiated with gay groups, they were now speaking with a woman as often as with a man.

In combating lesbian invisibility, the national organizations actually had to address two issues: the rarity of lesbian images in the media, and the fact that the few lesbian images that existed often reflected narrow, tired clichés.

As late as 1991, the mainstream media did not yet consider lesbians "chic." Supermodels were not yet shaving lesbian pop stars on magazine covers. The average adolescent stock clerk in the heartland still had no idea what a "lipstick lesbian" was, because *Sally Jessy Raphael* and the other daytime talk shows had not yet aired their astonished exposés about "lesbians who are beautiful!" That year, NBC executives found nothing "chic" about a story line that the producers of the drama series *Sisters* planned for the character of Reed (Ashley Judd). A supporting character, college-aged Reed vanished early in the series to spend a summer in Paris. The producers planned for her to return in fall 1991, more sophisticated from her stay in Europe—and seriously considering the possibility that she was a lesbian. A potentially lesbian regular, especially one so young, was too radical an idea for a new series that still needed to build an audience. The era's sponsors were already expressing discomfort with gay content. No American series had *ever* portrayed a gay (or questioning) teenager as a recurring role. Until *Heartbeat* just three years earlier, there had never been a sustained openly lesbian character in prime time. NBC discouraged the proposed *Sisters* story line, saying that it was too early in the show's run. An NBC spokesperson said the network might be open to a lesbian character in later seasons (which, in fact, happened).[6] As for the vetoed Reed story line, it was replaced with one in which she dates a poor man against her mother's wishes. In 1992, when ABC's *20/20* presented a report about "Women Who Love Women," reporter Lynn Sherr could still convincingly refer to lesbians as "the invisible women."[7]

By the early 1990s, the networks were more open to the idea of lesbian visibility than they had been a decade earlier. Partly, this was a response to AIDS: As has been noted previously, since much of the public could not think "gay man" without thinking "AIDS," male homosexuality had become a subject too depressing for inclusion in escapist entertainment. So the networks began using lesbian content as proof of a show's daring, much as they had once used gay male characters.

Although many reporters seemed to think that the media emergence of lesbians in 1993 and 1994 came out of nowhere, it actually developed organically from other things that were happening in politics and the media. By the time gay organizations began working with the media to promote fair coverage of the 1993 March on Washington, women held the top executive positions at both NGLTF and GLAAD, two of the best-known national gay organizations that helped set the movement's priorities. In talking with news editors, gay media advocates now emphasized the importance of gender parity in selecting interview subjects, editing "B-roll" news footage, and choosing issues to discuss in reports about the march. GLAAD took advantage of these meetings to educate broadcasters about the historical underrepresentation and misrepresentations of lesbians in the media, and to talk about the possibility of believable lesbian TV characters.

So although the claims of "lesbian chic" were a bit exaggerated, lesbian invisibility did become less extreme in the early and mid 1990s. Most of the best-known "out" celebrities of the decade were women. Martina Navratilova, k.d. lang, Melissa Etheridge, and The Indigo Girls proved that women in certain fields could be open lesbians and still enjoy mainstream success. Lea Delaria's mid-1990s TV appearances (*The Arsenio Hall Show, Out There, The John Larroquette Show, The Drew Carey Show, Friends*) and film roles (as in *The First Wives Club*) showed that there could be a niche in the mainstream media for a very butch, outspokenly political "daddy dyke" comedian who had been out of the closet since the start of her career. With better distribution of independent cinema in the 1990s, both in movie theaters and through cable, movies by and about lesbians reached broader audiences. Soon, major-release films like *Boys on the Side* and even *The Brady Bunch Movie* also would have likable lesbian characters.

Big-league commercial TV was undergoing a minor lesbian revolution of its own. Of the shows studied for this book, only two TV episodes from 1988 had dealt with lesbianism. In 1990, there were four. In 1993, there were at least eleven. Some of the most popular series of the early and mid 1990s portrayed gay or bisexual women as recurring characters, including *L.A. Law, Roseanne, Friends, NYPD Blue, ER,* and *Mad About You.* There were also lesbian regulars on moderately well-known series such as *Sisters.*

Killer-dyke melodramas still aired occasionally in the 1990s, but even they improved. Consider CBS's 1992 docudrama about a lesbian serial killer, *Overkill: The Aileen Wuornos Story.* The TV movie subtly acknowledges Wuornos's lesbianism without sensationalizing it and without linking it to her violence (unlike most news coverage of the case, which played up the lesbian angle, even in short capsule reports). The real-life Wuornos had been in a long-term relationship with another woman. According to news reports, Wuornos was an adult survivor of child abuse, a prostitute, and a serial killer who periodically murdered her johns in brutal, bloody ways. From the standpoint of commercial TV, any life with that much tabloid potential was the perfect subject for a Nielsen sweeps-period telefilm. In contrast to previous shows in this genre, *Overkill* portrayed her relationship with Tyria as the only good, healthy aspect of her troubled life, and depicted her partner's cooperation with the police as a last-ditch attempt to get Aileen the help she obviously needed. Strong performances by Jean Smart and Park Overall gave depth to what could have been just another murderous lesbian flick. Similarly, when an episode of *Nash Bridges* included a bisexual criminal who used her sexual attractiveness to lure her prey, the script balanced things by portraying a "good lesbian" and another bisexual woman who were on the side of the law. This sort of balance was almost never seen in earlier decades. More important, depictions of violent gay and bisexual women had become the rare exception, not the rule.[8]

Far from being murderous, many of TV's lesbians in the 1990s *gave* life, as the lesbian baby boom and "turkey-baster babies" came to television. TV news shows focused on lesbian mothers and on studies about whether their children turned out as stable as other parents' kids (the consensus was yes). There were pregnant lesbian regulars or recurring characters on *Sisters*, *Friends*, and *NYPD Blue*. On *L.A. Law*, C. J. testified in her ex-lover's child custody hearing in a 1991 Christmas episode. In 1992 on *Civil Wars* (a series about divorce lawyers), a woman sued for visitation rights to her ex-lover's daughter, whom she had coparented for years. Some plots revolved around women who wanted to be pregnant but had trouble finding sperm. On the sitcom *Herman's Head*, the title character's lesbian ex-girlfriend wants his help in that department during an episode called "Sperm 'n Herman." (After much vacillating, he says no.) In the 1992 Christmas episode of *Roseanne*, Nancy tells Dan: "I want to have kids . . . I mean, I know it's early in our relationship, but, you know, I think Marla and I could get pregnant and have a baby." Dan, who is basting a turkey, asks: "Can you explain to me how you could do that, without being at all specific?" "Sure, Dan," says Nancy. "It's easy. You just get some sperm. . . ." As Dan stops squeezing the baster, drops of white liquid drip on the turkey. "*Too* specific," he says, handing her the baster and telling her to finish the job. Two years later, the new lesbian regular on *Sisters*, TV producer Norma Lear (Nora Dunn), asks a friend's husband to donate sperm so she and her girlfriend can have a baby. The baby is born early in the series' final season. On the hospital drama *Chicago Hope* in 1996, a fertility specialist learns that two of his ex-wives are a couple, and they want his help—both professional and personal—in getting one of them pregnant.[9]

Stories involving the lesbian ex-wives of male regulars have become a standard way to bring gay women into a story, both in cinema and on television. Writers use these stories to humanize, humble, or shake up these male characters, who are often very conservative, controlling, and bad at expressing emotions. Originally, such women were purely a plot device, but over time, they became more fully developed characters. The earliest lesbian ex among the shows studied was mentioned in a 1976 episode of *All's Fair*, a sitcom about a middle-aged Washington Republican (Richard Crenna) in a passionate romance with a liberal, liberated woman in her twenties (Bernadette Peters). One week, Richard painfully confesses that his wife left him for another woman, which is why he felt the need to prove his masculinity by growing a mustache.

The lesbian ex-wife in this episode is 100 percent plot device: She provides a glimpse into one of Richard's few vulnerable areas, but she is referred to only briefly and never appears on-camera. By 1991, with the "Kirk's Ex-Wife" episode of *Dear John*, the lesbian ex-wife rates a one-episode guest shot. A year later, on Linda Bloodworth-Thomason's sexy political sitcom *Hearts Afire*, a lesbian ex-wife is a major complication in the life of the show's male lead, John (John Ritter). Like *All's Fair*, *Hearts Afire* was originally about an uptight, recently divorced, male Republican in Washington, D.C., who meets and falls in love with a liberal feminist woman (played here by Markie Post). John's ex, Diandra (Julie Cobb), and her lover, Ruth (Conchata Ferrell), each rated three guest appearances over the course of the series.[10]

Lesbian ex-wives met the lesbian baby boom on *Friends*, a sitcom about six close-knit New Yorkers in their mid twenties. It debuted in 1994 as the clear-cut biggest new hit of the season. In the show's backstory, Ross Geller (David Schwimmer) had always seemed like the friend who had it all: He had married his college sweetheart, Carol (Jane Sibbett)—a smart, funny, pretty woman whom his friends adore—and he had a great job in his chosen field, paleontology. Much of the first season revolves around Ross's adjustment to Carol's having recently come out and left him for her best friend, Susan (Jessica Hecht). The lesbian ex-wife may still be a marginalized plot device, but she is a better-developed one in this case. Carol and Susan are the first credible same-sex couple sustained over time in an American series. Each time they appear, the audience learns more about their lives, their relationship, and their personalities.

In the second episode of *Friends*, Carol tells Ross that she is pregnant with his baby. The lesbian couple want him to participate in the baby's life if he wishes, though the women will have custody. This early episode establishes the relationship among the coparents—three likable people in an awkward situation. Carol loves both Susan and Ross, and both of them love her. Ross and Susan, however, cannot help verbally sniping at each other, which leaves Carol caught in the middle. In episode two, when the three meet at the hospital for Carol's first sonogram, they bicker over what to name the child. Susan wants "Helen" if the baby turns out to be a girl, but Ross disapproves: "Helen Geller? I don't think so." Carol says that is no problem, since the baby's last name will not be Geller.[11]

In incorporating Carol and Susan into Ross's narrative, the writers avoid most of the standard clichés. Ross is no repressed sexist who needs humanizing: he is vulnerable and sensitive. He and Carol are not enemies, but caring people who are slowly renegotiating the terms of their relationship. Unlike the little-seen lesbian couple on *Hearts Afire*, Carol and Susan appear in roughly a quarter of *Friends'* first season episodes, though each appearance is brief. Their life together and their coparenting with Ross often serve as a catalyst for story lines. Examples include episodes with such titles as "The One With the Birth" (near the end of season one), "The One With the Breast Milk," and a show that reflects another TV trend of the 1990s, "The One With the Lesbian Wedding."[12]

This was a breakthrough: lesbians in comedy rather than somber dramas. It is probably not coincidental that humorous references to lesbianism first became common on other TV sitcoms—especially in premiere episodes—starting in January 1995, less than four months after *Friends* zoomed to the top of the ratings. (Indeed, *every* aspect of *Friends* seemed to resonate in shows that premiered that January). Nonetheless, these supposedly "hip" gags had nothing to do with actual lesbian characters. In the first episode of *Unhappily Ever After*, for instance, an unpopular teenage boy who cannot get a date asks: "Is every girl in this school a lesbian? We're producing a nation of gym teachers!" In the premiere of *Cybill* (starring Cybill Shepherd), daughter Zoey threatens to "hold my breath till I turn into a lesbian" if Cybill scares away Zoey's new boyfriend. After meeting the older boyfriend, Cybill jokes that lesbianism might be preferable. The debut of *Women of the House*—a spin-off of *Designing Women*—features a funny-drunk character (Teri Garr) who is too soused to keep her Washington rumors straight. No matter what famous woman anyone mentions, she says she heard somewhere that the woman was a lesbian. GLAAD executive director Ellen Carton was "not entirely comfortable" with the tone of the jokes. "On the one hand," she said, "it's a step forward because we were invisible for so long. But visibility hasn't brought any understanding."[13]

After that spate of gags in the first weeks of 1995, things improved tremendously. In fact, over the course of the decade, 1995 was the only year when television came close to fulfilling the promise of "lesbian chic." The networks still were not *completely* open to lesbian roles. (CBS refused to let *Cybill* incorporate a lesbian regular into its cast.)[14] Television did, however, exhibit greater openness to such roles than ever before. Recurring portrayals of gay and bisexual women spanned the spectrum from the lowest-rated shows on TV to the highest. At the bottom of the Nielsen charts was the WB's irreverent ensemble sitcom, *Muscle*. Its regulars included an earnest, funny, recently outed newscaster, Bronwyn Jones, played by Amy Pietz. CBS's legal drama *Courthouse* sporadically portrayed a recently divorced African American judge, Rosetta Reide (Jenifer Lewis), and her more openly gay lover (Cree Summer). And, of course, two of the biggest commercial hits of 1995—*Roseanne* and the top-rated *Friends*—continued to develop their sexual-minority roles.

During that same remarkable year, an acclaimed TV movie blended a unique lesbian love story with elements of a traditional gay civil rights drama. NBC's *Serving in Silence: The Colonel Margarethe Cammermeyer Story* took an unusually romantic approach to dramatizing the autobiography of Colonel Cammermeyer, the highest-ranking person ever expelled from the U.S. military on grounds of homosexuality. Cammermeyer, who emerged as an in-demand gay spokesperson during the TV interviews about gays in the military, was a decorated army nurse who had served in Vietnam. By the early 1990s, she was one of the top administrators in the military health-care system for the state of Washington. A security interview for a promotion included a direct question about whether she was a homosexual. When she answered honestly, proceedings for her separation began, despite her twenty-six years of outstanding service. Her story caught the attention of Barbra Streisand, who signed on to coproduce the TV film. Oscar-winner Glenn Close agreed to coproduce and play the title role. *Serving in Silence* was not a typical gay-rights courtroom drama, like *A Question of Love*. Nor did it follow the lead of 1978's *Sergeant Matlovich vs. the U.S. Air Force*, which had censored out the romantic relationship that prompted the real-life Matlovich to come out in the first place. *Serving in Silence* was a full-blown love story about the relationship between

Grethe Cammermeyer and her lover, artist Diane Divelbess. The genre is served up complete with a serenade in front of a fireplace, the gift of a ring, and the first *real* on-camera, on-the-lips lesbian kiss in TV history (i.e., the characters are both lesbians and are attracted to each other). Their relationship develops over time, and is presented with a tenderness and subtlety seldom seen in TV's stories about same-sex couples. Grethe's relationship with her father and her grown children are also explored with warmth and depth. The film generally avoids formulas, though the few vocally antigay characters seem like exaggerated stock characters.

As mentioned earlier, *Serving in Silence* includes the networks' first real, on-the-lips kiss between nonmurderous, same-sex lovers who—at the film's end—are still alive and together. Firsts are always tentative: The kiss does not come during the fireplace scene, but rather at a moment when both women are suffering from tremendous stress. The kiss is more a cry for comfort than an expression of tenderness, but both it and the film in general were a huge leap forward in portraying lesbian lives with dignity and respect.[15]

Serving in Silence received much advance press because Streisand and Close were big Hollywood stars who seldom worked in television; because Cammermeyer's lover was played by the acclaimed actress Judy Davis; because the subject matter was topical; and because the love story approach was so unusual for commercial TV. Some advance protests from Religious Right groups focused on the kissing scene, but NBC left it in. The film did well in the Nielsens and won three Emmys: acting trophies for Close and Davis, and an award for Alison Cross's script. It also received nominations for direction, editing, and as Outstanding Made for Television Movie.

By the late 1990s, *Roseanne* would be off the air, and *Friends'* Carol and Susan would all but vanish from that series. Nonetheless, the precedents set by these and other shows of their era paved the way for a small number of later prominent lesbian roles. As for "lesbian chic," it burned itself out as a media catchphrase through overuse in 1997 and 1998 during the hype about the sitcom *Ellen*. By late 1998, writers were using "lesbian chic" mostly in past-tense references. By mid 1999, the phrase had pretty much passed out of use.

38

MARRY ME!

Television: 1991–1996

CLAYTON: It'll be a simple ceremony: just exchanging rings and affirming our commitment to each other in front of our friends. It's not like it's going to be a big, fancy wedding.
DOUG: Though we *are* registered at Neiman Marcus.
　　　　　　—*Blanche's brother and his lover on* The Golden Girls, *1991*[1]

Since the 1970s, as television increasingly tried to portray gay people as "just like everyone else," same-sex couples have played larger roles in more diverse types of stories. Until the 1990s, however, the wedding story—one of the most popular and engaging narratives in almost every entertainment medium—was the one arena into which it was assumed same-sex couples could never enter. Even at this writing, the very concept of gay marriage remains exceedingly controversial, one of the ever fewer topics that can inspire true moral indignation from average Americans.

Historically, homosexuality was seen as the antithesis of family, of commitment, and of marriage. In the mid–twentieth century, even many gay people felt this way. At the height of the Sexual Revolution, many gay people prided themselves in thinking that marriage—or anything like marriage—was a uniquely heterosexual pursuit that was, at its core, stifling, repellent, and bourgeois. Filmmaker John Waters has recalled that it was an era when, for many people, "[T]he good things about being gay were you didn't have to get married and you didn't have to go into the army."[2] It is a sign of how mainstream the media's gay images have become—and how mainstream the national gay organizations' political goals have become—that TV episodes involving gay weddings have become almost a cliché.

News reports about gay couples' efforts to secure legal protection for their relationships set the stage for these broadcasts. One of the firmest traditions in broadcasting is that persistent news coverage of a controversy eventually begets prime-time comedy and drama scripts. The spate of "gay marriage" episodes that began in 1991 is an excellent example of this.

We have seen how, in the days of old-time radio and early television, before legalization of gay marriage was a common topic even in gay circles, media references to same-sex nuptials were limited to a form of breezy, absurdist humor. Comedians' references to same-sex marriage got laughs precisely because the idea seemed so nonsensical: Why would a man try to marry—or even *want* to marry—another man? These jokes, performed by the likes of Bob Hope, Bing Crosby, and Groucho Marx, were predicated on the assumption that sexual attraction, couplehood, and marriage were inherently heterosexual experiences. That type of "heterosexual reversal" humor persisted in various forms for decades. For example, in the early 1970s, long before the big push for same-sex marriage, homosexual marriage was still portrayed as an absurdly funny notion. By then, the jokes tended to be swipes at Women's Liberation and other movements for social equality. In a 1972 skit on *The Dean Martin Show*, as the show's star tried to propose to a woman, a working-class man attempted to propose to Dean Martin. The disappointed suitor (played by Archie Bunker himself, Carroll O'Connor) kept insisting that Dean's refusal to marry him constituted gender discrimination.

In the 1970s, a handful of same-sex couples—in Minnesota, Colorado, Arizona, and other states—began to mount legal challenges intended to secure formal protection for their relationships. These couples' attempts to obtain marriage licenses were very much a fringe movement within gay activism, which was itself still a fringe element within American society. Nonetheless, this scattershot quest for marital protection somehow became a tiny blip in the mainstream news media and talk shows, after sympathetic clerks in a few states issued licenses to gay couples. The subject also became a blip in entertainment shows.

In its most low-key form, it consisted of scripts' casual references to long-term gay couples as "married." In 1976, to show how liberal the Bernadette Peters character was on *All's Fair*, the writers had her mention a "married couple" who live in her building: Leonard and Albert.[3]

One completely atypical script dealt directly with the questions of legalization and same-sex weddings. In 1976, inspired by a widely reported incident in Arizona, writers for the short-lived sitcom *Sirota's Court* decided to have their hero, a judge, perform prime time's first legitimate gay marriage ceremony. The series takes place in a state whose laws do not explicitly say that marriage can take place only between a man and a woman, so Judge Sirota (Michael Constantine) agrees to test the law by uniting a male couple. As in the Arizona case, the men had obtained a marriage license from a sympathetic assistant clerk. The judge warns that a higher court may invalidate the marriage. He also asks the couple to *please* shake hands, rather than kiss, when he pronounces them "man and—uh—other man." The handshake was, of course, not so much plot driven as it was a concession to the standards of 1970s television. This was apparently the only pre-1991 TV episode to focus on same-sex marriage. As gay activism around this issue went into hibernation in the late 1970s and 1980s, so did media attention to the subject.[4]

This is not to say that gay characters never stood at the altar waiting to be joined to another person in matrimony. Since the late 1970s, gay male regular characters have often found themselves in that situation, but always with women as their intended. The networks apparently think that nothing makes a gay man look more respectable than a wife and—preferably—a child. There were abortive nuptials for Jodie on *Soap,* two weddings for Steven on *Dynasty*, an "immigration wedding" between Matt and a Russian woman on *Melrose Place,* and—at the dawn of the twenty-first century—a similar "green-card wedding" for the outlandishly flamboyant Jack on *Will & Grace*. The plot devices invented to justify these weddings varied. Strangely, the most plausible explanation—bisexuality—was never posited. In contrast with these "straight" weddings, the same-sex weddings in TV scripts have usually involved guest characters or peripheral supporting roles. And again, even these kiss-free portrayals have happened only at times when news coverage of "the gay marriage controversy" was most prominent.

Between the mid 1980s and early 1990s, a handful of employers, including some liberal city governments, extended a subset of spousal benefits to the same-sex domestic partners of their employees. Such partnerships had to be exclusive and marriagelike, had to be carefully documented through a variety of financial and legal documents, and usually could be dissolved only through a process analogous to divorce. The issue of gay couples' rights began to get legal and media attention around 1990, when some couples in Hawaii began what would become a famous legal battle, and when a couple in Washington, D.C., sued that city for the right to wed. The latter couple appeared on such programs as *The Oprah Winfrey Show*, while other news and talk shows devoted segments to gay marriage. These discussions focused, appropriately, on same-sex couples' lack of legal standing. Supporters of gay marriage or domestic partnerships pointed to inequities in employment benefits, rent control laws, tax status, hospital visitation rights, marriage-related immigration laws, inheritance of property, and similar issues. Same-sex couples also began to receive positive acknowledgment in other forums. In 1990, apparently for the first time, a small number of mainstream newspapers began listing same-sex unions alongside announcements of straight engagements, weddings, and anniversaries. In a speech that year, Senator Jesse Helms said, "I was taught from boyhood to hate the sin and love the sinner . . . but these guys who are parading and demanding that they be allowed to marry and that sort of thing, they make the second part of that tough."[5]

Prime-time TV writers first developed gay marriage episodes as a genre around 1991, and it soon became the latest way to address gay issues without rehashing the shopworn formulas of the past (coming-out scripts, job discrimination stories, and so on). Because commercial television tends to personalize and depoliticize social issues, these gay marriage episodes did not generally mention the legal status of gay couples, even though this was the usual context for discussions of gay marriage in the real world. Almost without exception, the TV episodes focused on gay wedding ceremonies—or else plans for never-seen ceremonies. When a straight regular would ask why two people of the same sex would want to get married, the answers were couched in emotional terms that were considered more universally understandable than the legal equity issues. There were vague statements about love, commitment, and a desire to proclaim these in front of one's family and friends. These reasons ring true enough, but the first wave of gay marriage shows presented them in a vacuum.

The first examples, in 1991 episodes of *The Golden Girls* and *Roc*, both hinge on straight regulars' *reactions* to a gay sibling's plans for a same-sex wedding ceremony. The stories were polemics between the disapproving older regular character and a brother—a guest character who is only recently out of the closet. The debate focuses on whether such a celebration constitutes a public humiliation for the family, and whether even talking about a "gay wedding" shows disrespect for the institution of marriage. Unlike most straight television weddings, the ceremony and, to some extent, the couple are marginal to the story. Both of these episodes end in an uneasy truce between the siblings.

The Golden Girls, of course, had been a gay-friendly series right from the beginning. In a 1988 episode, "Scared Straight," Monte Markham guest starred as Clayton, the brother of series regular Blanche (Rue McClanahan). In that episode, he was single: Blanche could "accept" his homosexuality without having to deal with it in any real way. In the 1991 episode, however, Clayton is accompanied by his boyfriend, a cop named Doug. Clayton tells Blanche, "I wanted you to meet Doug for a very important reason." Clay puts his hands on his sister's upper arms and says, "Blanche, we're getting married." Blanche's dim-bulb roommate Rose pipes up, "Well, that's impossible, Clayton. Brothers can't marry sisters!" A look of terrible realization crosses Rose's face as she adds, "Oh, that's right—you're from the South!" Blanche, who always hoped Clay's interest in men was just a phase, is furious that he and Doug would do something as embarrassingly public as a wedding.

The episode's ending is typical of the new 1990s approach, distinct from the miraculous "conversions" of antigay characters in the 1970s. It acknowledges that a heterosexual can try to be happy for a gay couple, even without fully comprehending why the couple are together. Such scripts seem to say, "Even amid disapproval, keep open the lines of communication with this person about whom you obviously care deeply!" As Blanche puts it near the end of the episode, "I still can't say I understand what you're doin', but I do intend to try and respect your decision to do it. I want you to be happy."[6]

In May 1991, in between the *Golden Girls* episode and the *Roc* episode, Phil Donahue's talk show aired one of the most famous of its multitudinous gay-themed broadcasts. *Donahue* devoted an hour to a joyous, dignified wedding between a male African American couple. It was a very traditional ceremony, officiated by a black minister whose face could not be shown on-camera for fear of jeopardizing his job. The celebration included a performance by the well-known (among GLBT audiences) gay a cappella group The Flirtations. The only indignities in the broadcast followed the ceremony: angry responses from some members of the studio audience. There were also some mocking comments during the week that followed from at least one journal and such prominent comedians as Johnny Carson.[7]

In the months after the *Donahue* broadcast, TV writers were busy drafting scripts for the fall season—including the aforementioned episode of Fox's new domestic sitcom, *Roc.* In many ways, this was similar to the *Golden Girls* episode, except that here the writers hit their crusty, older regular, Andrew, with *four* troublesome revelations: that his brother Russell (Richard Roundtree) is gay, that Russell is planning to marry a man, that the man is white, and that the ceremony will take place in the house where Andrew lives. Andrew is torn between his loyalty to family—including his brother—and his inability to conceive how a proud black man like Russell could do something as degrading as marrying a white man. (Andrew cannot separate out which bothers him more: the gay angle or the interracial angle.) The basically traditional ceremony, held in the family's living room, is performed by a minister. Andrew chooses not to sit through the vows—indeed, he tries to disrupt them—but the episode ends with him and Russell hoping to eventually find common ground as brothers and to once again be as close as they used to be.[8]

Around the same time when the writers of *Roc* were drafting that episode, the producers of the sitcom *Dear John* were trying to come up with a script that would develop one of their supporting characters: Kirk (Jere Burns), a divorced, sexist womanizer. Given Kirk's defensiveness about his manhood, the producers decided the funniest option would be to bring in his ex-wife for one episode and establish that she left him for a woman. Executive producer Rod Parker often had used script consultants from the Gay Media Task Force in the 1970s, and had been happy with the results. So in 1991, he suggested that his *Dear John* staff run this draft script past GLAAD for suggestions. "We were mostly concerned with staying true to facts and not being offensive in any way," said series writer Marco Pennette. Dr. Sylvia Rhue, a board member of GLAAD/Los Angeles, made some general recommendations, such as deleting a line that called lesbianism the ex-wife's "choice." Pennette said that Rhue supplied the idea that became the script's punch line. "She was the one who told us about lesbians getting married," Pennette said, "how common it is. Her information really guided us along the way." In the broadcast version, just when Kirk seems to be overcoming his discomfort around his ex, and is forming a new friendship with her, she invites him to her upcoming (lesbian) wedding. "Are you out of your *mind*?!" Kirk asks. Then he turns to a liberal friend and adds, "Like I'm gonna be seen at *her* wedding." The friend (Judd Hirsch) gives an exasperated look as the episode ends.[9]

There were also episodes during the 1991–1992 season that used gay weddings as a background or catalyst for other types of stories. On *L.A. Law*, uptight Douglas Brackman was invited to serve as best man at an old friend's gay wedding. This was a setup for a story in which gay-bashers mistakenly attack Brackman. And on *Seinfeld*, Elaine found herself stuck in a stalled subway car on her way to be "best man" at a lesbian wedding.[10] In early 1992, however, the topics of gay weddings and gay couples' legal status dropped out of the news media, and therefore also vanished from entertainment scripts.

These subjects returned in early 1993, amid the media's intense interest in gay issues during the lead-up to the third lesbian and gay March on Washington. Shortly after the march, a decision by the Hawaiian state supreme court set the wheels in motion for gay marriage to become a much vaunted social issue of the mid 1990s. In May, the court provisionally ruled that Hawaii's refusal to marry gay couples was a form of discrimination that violated the principles of the state's constitution. The case was then put on hold to give the state attorney general time to gather more evidence.

The pending case became an obvious focal point for Religious Right rallying and mainstream media attention. For those who considered homosexuality unnatural and immoral, the Hawaiian edict was positively alarming. Because of the Full Faith and Credit clause of the United States Constitution, all fifty states might be forced to recognize Hawaii's gay marriages—if, in fact, Hawaii decided to recognize such marriages. If, as many Americans believed, marriage was the social glue that prevented chaos from erupting on earth, then any change in its definition—even a change that extended its values to a broader population—could be horribly dangerous. Several states began drafting laws to define marriage as a heterosexual institution, and asserted that they would not honor other states' same-sex unions. Within the Republican party, strategists kept an eye on how this issue was playing out in Hawaii, and began planning how to use the "protection of marriage" as a hot-button issue in the next major elections.

Amid escalating news coverage, gay marriage resurfaced in prime-time drama during the 1993–1994 season, most notably in an episode of *Northern Exposure* called "I Feel the Earth Move." This episode marks a transition between the 1991 episodes (which were about *controversies* over gay weddings) and the 1995–1996 episodes (whose characters treated same-sex weddings as essentially uncontroversial). In this *Northern Exposure* story, only one character—Maurice—mutters and sputters briefly about how Ron and Erick's wedding makes a "mockery of the covenant of marriage." Here, preparations for the wedding—and the ceremony itself—are the hour's central story line. All of the townspeople are seen pulling together to make this celebration of their friends' love a memorable, perfect occasion. It is, in most ways, a typical wedding episode of the sort one might see between heterosexual characters—right down to the obligatory scene in which one character gets cold feet and has to be talked into going through with the ceremony. The episode also shares another trait with most of the gay wedding stories of the 1995–1996 wave: the characters who get married are recurring roles, so the audience sees their union in the context of a relationship about which they already know something.

Near the end of the *Northern Exposure* episode, Chris, the town's radio announcer and philosopher, performs the ceremony. The gentle quirkiness of his dialog leavens the scene with small amounts of humor (to put otherwise uncomfortable viewers at ease) while still reflecting a sincere respect for the occasion (for those viewers who would take the ceremony seriously). With a placid smile, Chris asks such questions as, "Ron, will you have Erick to be your spouse, love him, comfort him in sickness and in health, and stick it out till the fat lady sings?" He continues, "Above you is the sun and sky, below you the ground. Like the sun, your love should be constant; like the ground, solid. You both cool with that?" The show's producers contemplated showing a brief, tasteful kiss between Ron and Erick at the end of the ceremony. But given the media's and the public's reactions to the "lesbian" kiss on *Roseanne* a couple of months earlier, the producers of *Northern Exposure* decided that a kiss would probably draw attention away from the main points of the episode: observations about love, friendship, family, and honesty. At least one sponsor and two CBS stations dropped the episode.[11]

In December 1995 and January 1996, two of television's most popular series devoted episodes to same-sex unions: *Roseanne* aired "December Bride," and *Friends* aired "The One With the Lesbian Wedding." A lesbian wedding episode of *Living Single*, "Woman to Woman," would air a few months later. These episodes depoliticized the subject. To the degree that any character is upset by these weddings, they are upset about things other than the couple's gender. On *Friends*, for instance, Ross is uncomfortable because it will be painful for him to see his ex-wife Carol marry *anyone* other than him. On *Living Single*, Max is not upset that her former college roommate is a lesbian, but that her old friend never bothered to tell her before. All three episodes seem to take it as read that homosexuality and gay weddings are morally neutral or morally positive.

The over-the-top *Roseanne* episode introduces a new recurring character—Leon's fiancé, Scott (Fred Willard), whom Leon had jilted at the altar years earlier. Producer Roseanne (who no longer used a last name) had always wanted to reunite Martin Mull with his former *Fernwood 2-Night* costar Willard and have them play her show's main gay couple. In this episode, against his better judgment, Leon agrees to let Roseanne Conner plan his wedding. She turns it into a Roseannified vision of all the tacky, kitschy things she assumes that gay grooms would want: pink flamingos, Chippendale dancers, and dueling Judy and Liza impersonators. This being *Roseanne*, the vows are thoroughly irreverent, while somehow managing to be *almost* respectful of the underlying subject matter. "You love me, right?" Leon asks Scott on the altar. Scott replies, "I love you in a way that is mystical, and eternal—and illegal in twenty states."

The most political aspect of the episode is not a comment on gay marriage, but a send-up of network television's bizarre double standard about same-sex kissing. This was the broadcasting tradition that said that shows could imply as much just-off-camera kissing as they liked, as long as none of it spilled into the visible frame. After the vows, Leon and Scott move toward each other as if to kiss, as the camera glides toward the people sitting in the pews, watching the ceremony. The straight characters react and comment on the off-camera kiss as it supposedly goes on for a good half minute. Echoing what some viewers no doubt were thinking, the character of Dan says, "And there's the kiss! I was wondering if they were gonna do it, and they're doin' it. Yeah— look at 'em go at it!" Leon's mother blissfully observes the scene. As the unseen kiss continues, Mariel Hemingway—from the previous year's much hyped "lesbian kiss" episode—plunks down behind Roseanne, grins, and says "Hi!"

On short notice—too late to make the published TV listings—ABC swapped this episode with that evening's episode of *Coach*, so that *Roseanne* would run at 9:30 rather than 8:00. Explaining the time shift for this episode, an ABC spokesperson said, "We felt the adult humor within the show was more appropriate at a later time period when there are fewer children in the audience." Journalists—who had not seen the episode, since Roseanne refused to release it in advance—wrote articles accusing ABC of antigay prejudice, and implying that the network's sole concern was to prevent children from seeing a gay wedding. But while public response to the wedding was surely one of ABC's concerns, a glance at this episode reveals more crude humor and sexual innuendo than *Roseanne* normally aired. This entertaining episode's tone was broad, crass, and exhilaratingly burlesque. Indeed, some fans theorized that producer Roseanne was bucking for a permanent shift back to her later time slot, where the censors were less prone to breathe down her neck.[12]

Around early 1996, having married Leon off to Scott, Roseanne tried to spin them off into their own series. She told ABC executives that she imagined it as a campy sitcom, with Mull and Willard as the central couple, and preferably with Don Rickles and RuPaul as the zany interracial, transgenerational gay pair next door. ABC executives reportedly told her that the idea was not feasible—that openly gay characters could appear as supporting characters on a series, but not as a show's leads. Within a few months, however, the same network was in negotiations with the producers of *Ellen* over the possibility of letting its title character step out of the closet.[13]

The *Friends* episode aired a few weeks after the *Roseanne* wedding, and is a fairly typical and well-written sitcom wedding story. It is staged far more realistically, and the processional scene is played for sentiment. Nonetheless, there are sparkling moments of comedy involving all of the show's regulars. The episode also marks a turning point in the relationship between Ross and his ex's partner, Susan. It is the first time they are seen developing a mutual respect based on each other's merits as individuals, rather than in deference to Carol or the baby. The episode features several in-joke "gay celebrity" guest appearances, which few people outside the gay community probably appreciated or even noticed. Activist Candace Gingrich played the minister who performed the ceremony, and comedian Lea Delaria played a kindly, tuxedoed butch who took an interest in series regular Phoebe. The mere fact that a show was working under the assumption that gay people were watching, and that such viewers' pleasure counted for something, was an unusual development.

The Traditional Values Coalition, of course, branded this tame episode as "shocking, appalling," and "disgusting." An NBC affiliate station in Ohio moved the episode to midnight on Sunday. A Texas station refused the episode entirely, saying it was inconsistent with "prevailing standards of good taste in our community." (This station, which normally did air *Friends*, apparently considered the sitcom's usual penis jokes and condom jokes to be good, clean family fun.) Even without a full network, it was the top-rated broadcast of the week, attracting— according to the Nielsens—almost thirty-two million viewers. Writing in the *New York Times*, David W. Dunlap noted that "the biggest news about the wedding on *Friends* was that it was almost not news at all." *USA Today* made a similar observation the day of this broadcast: "So prevalent have unexceptional and unstereotyped gay characters become in mainstream TV that even preaching about tolerance is at a minimum [in this *Friends* episode]."[14] This was one of the last of the completely depoliticized gay wedding episodes of the 1990s.

The 1995–1996 season's much-publicized gay marriage episodes coincided with the decade's most intensive and widely reported legal wrangling over the question of same-sex marriage, much of it linked to the 1996 elections. A coalition of religious activists and conservative Republicans were preparing a massive, multihour rally against gay marriage to kick off the Iowa Caucuses. The rally would be cablecast nationally in its entirety, and would feature passionate speeches or letters of support from every major Republican presidential candidate.[15] During this same period, several more state legislatures were passing preemptive measures to avoid having to recognize homosexual marriages. At the same time, in the United States Senate, a so-called "Defense of Marriage Act" was being drafted. Congress passed this bill in September 1996, institutionalizing on a federal level the principle that no state had to recognize same-sex marriages performed outside its borders. The same day, federal legislators narrowly voted down the Employment Non-Discrimination Act (ENDA), which would have banned discrimination on the basis of sexual orientation in jobs, housing, and public accommodations.

For more than a year thereafter, prime time's "gay marriage" episodes—at least on the ABC network—finally began dealing with the practical, legal, day-to-day benefits of marriage, and the pros and cons of extending these to lesbian and gay couples. On *Spin City* in the fall of 1996, two mayoral aides—a gay man and a straight woman, both regular characters—staged a conspicuous publicity stunt to call attention to the need for gay marriage, after the mayor character spoke out against legal recognition of gay couples. On *The Practice*, one of the lawyers reluctantly represented his mother in a lawsuit for marriage rights. The next summer, in the final episode of *Ellen*, Ellen Morgan and her girlfriend agreed to not have their union ceremony until it could be legally recognized.[16] Television's handling of the subject had grown and changed considerably in the course of just seven years.

In a 1990s episode of *Picket Fences*, the protagonists—a husband and wife—marvel at how different the world is from the images they remember seeing on TV when they were young. "Did you ever think," Jill asks, "[that] we'd be explaining to our kids how two men can live together as husband and wife?" "A long way from *Ozzie and Harriet*," her husband Jimmy replies, "a long way."[17]

A PRELUDE TO *ELLEN*

Television: 1993–1997

This has been an unprecedented season for positive portrayals of gay men and lesbians. We have gone beyond just identifying a character as a lesbian or a gay man to the point where the characters are multidimensional and are interwoven into each show's story lines.

> —*Tamra King, Entertainment Media Director, Gay & Lesbian Alliance Against Defamation, 1995*[1]

In the years leading up to *Ellen*, gay imagery on television became more pervasive and mainstream than in any period before or since. Increasingly, the characters were well-developed roles whose gayness was acknowledged openly as just one of many traits that made up their personality. For instance, on the hit NBC series *Mad About You*— a romantic comedy about a young married couple (Paul Reiser and Helen Hunt)—the husband's sister and her lover were more than just "the lesbian couple." Their function in the show extended well beyond the sister's coming out. Her partner was also the obstetrician who cared for the Helen Hunt character throughout her pregnancy and childbirth.[2]

As homosexuality became more topical (thanks to recent gay civil rights battles) and less frightening to the masses once AIDS-phobia decreased slightly (thanks to news of drugs that extended the average life span of people with AIDS), sexual-minority content exploded across the television schedule. The uniqueness of this period may be less obvious today than it was at the time, when the growth of GLBT visibility was unprecedented. Recall that in 1990, there were only about five series with recurring gay roles, and only one of these characters (the brother on *Doctor, Doctor*) appeared regularly. By 1993, things were not much better: of the half dozen series with recurring roles that year, only *Roseanne* and *Melrose Place* presented them with anything approaching frequency and prominence. Now consider the year 1996, during which all of the following prime-time series—several of them in the Nielsen Top Twenty-Five—offered recurring or well-developed regular sexual-minority roles: *The Crew*, *Cybill*, *ER*, *Ellen* (a male couple), *Fired Up*, *Friends*, *High Society*, *Lush Life*, *Mad About You*, *Melrose Place*, *NYPD Blue*, *Party Girl*, *Party of Five*, *Relativity*, *Roseanne*, *The Simpsons*, *Spin City*, and *Unhappily Ever After*. That year, the syndicated and USA cable series *Forever Knight* included among its regulars a bisexual woman vampire, and HBO's comedy *The Larry Sanders Show* featured an openly gay assistant played by openly gay comedian Scott Thompson. On daytime serials, *The City* presented a story arc about the outing of a secretly transsexual fashion model; a multiyear arc on *All My Children* juxtaposed the life of a gay male teacher against the story of a gay male student in the same high school. In addition, gay-positive "message" episodes were turning up in exceedingly unlikely genres—including an episode of CBS's *Touched by an Angel*, a Christian drama series about heavenly messengers and spiritual redemption.

Clearly, sexual-minority content was no longer as shocking or marginalized as it once was. This mid-1990s plateau of inclusiveness set the stage for *Ellen*, which, in turn, set the stage for *Will & Grace* and later shows with openly gay protagonists. So before we delve into how and why ABC allowed Ellen Morgan to leap from her closet, let us briefly consider a few shows that, taken together, provide a flavor for that mid-1990s heyday of inclusiveness. Many of the most gay-positive examples have already been discussed: *Roseanne*, *Friends*, *My So-Called Life*, and so on. The remaining shows are a mixed bag of the good, the bad, and the hard to categorize.

BEVERLY HILLS 90210 AND *MELROSE PLACE*

Two series that Fox forbade to emphasize gay content in the early 1990s—creator/producer Darren Star's *Beverly Hills 90210* and his spin-off series *Melrose Place*—made up for lost time in the mid 1990s.

90210 ran several brief story arcs involving lesbian or gay characters—generally in conjunction with the straight regular character Kelly, who seemed to be She-Who-Knows-Homosexuals. A few years after her friendship with gay football player Kyle was portrayed, Kelly became friends with a lesbian with whom she had been trapped in a burning building. That character, Alison (Sara Melson), appeared in a few episodes over the course of a half year. Then Kelly began volunteering at an AIDS hospice and became friends with a gay male resident (Michael Stoyanov), who died a few episodes later. There were also some sexual-minority stories involving the selfish macho-stud straight regular, Steve (Ian Ziering): he and the other guys had to decide what to do after learning their fraternity president was gay; then, in a beach-side vacation story, Steve kissed and became obsessed with a young woman who turned out to be a cross-dressed man; and in a later episode, Steve learned that his mother (a longtime recurring role played by Christina Belford) was a lesbian.

Meanwhile, back in West Hollywood, after years as a saintly eunuch, *Melrose Place*'s Matt plunged into some typically twisty Melrosian plotlines, every bit as warped as the dysfunctional relationships of his straight neighbors. First, Matt was stalked by a violent, psychotic police detective (Tom Schanley) who wanted to date him. Once it became clear that Matt and a female friend had photos of the cop beating a suspect savagely, the detective tried to kill them both. Next, Matt—who was working in a hospital while attending medical school—hooked up with a medical resident, Paul (David Beecroft), who eventually revealed that he had a wife. Paul promised Matt that he would leave his wife. Paul promised his wife that he would leave Matt. Ultimately, Paul beat his wife's skull in and successfully framed Matt for the murder.

The next season, when Matt finally was cleared of murder charges and left jail, he fell in love with a soap opera actor, Alan (Lonnie

Schuyler, seen often during the series' fourth season). That relationship seemed to be going along fine. In a "morning after" scene with the two men in bathrobes, *Melrose Place* came as close as it ever would to indicating that Matt had a sex life. Things were going so well that Alan moved into Matt's apartment. But to save his acting career, Alan felt the need to marry a lesbian coworker, and Matt dumped him. Soon, med student Matt was using amphetamines to stay up and study, which led to a drug addiction. This, in turn, segued into a domestic violence plotline, as Matt became involved with the facilitator of his substance-abuse counseling group (Greg Evigan), who had a brutally short temper.

Through all these relationships, Matt and his boyfriends *still* could not kiss, but they were finally allowed to show signs of mutual attraction and affection. Usually, they looked at each other longingly, as if they *wanted* to kiss; then they moved toward each other as if they were *going* to kiss; and then, at the last split second, they hugged instead.

In 1996 and 1997, during Matt's final full season, he had a dignified plotline in which he battled a relative over custody of his orphaned teenage niece, Chelsea. When last seen, Matt and his niece were headed for San Francisco, where he had secured work as a doctor in an AIDS clinic. A year later, it was mentioned that Matt had died in a car crash, leaving behind a diary containing revelations about all his former neighbors.

SEINFELD

Gay and bisexual content appeared often on this phenomenally popular "show about nothing." One of *Seinfeld's* most famous catchphrases— "Not that there's anything wrong with that!"—came from a gay-themed episode, "The Outing." In that classic comedy of errors, circumstances conspire to convince a reporter that stand-up comedian Jerry (Jerry Seinfeld) and his best friend George (Jason Alexander) are a couple. "We're not gay!" they keep insisting, always adding, "Not that there's anything wrong with that!"[3]

This sitcom takes place in a world where sexuality—at least the sexuality of its guest characters—is fluid, can change over time, and is a matter of what people do with their bodies rather than innate attractions. Indeed, in an early episode, Jerry theorized that the reason some men are paranoid about homosexuality is that they know that males have a weak sales resistance, and can be talked into practically anything.[4] The lead characters on the show are nonjudgmental about homosexuality, except when someone they want to date turns out to be gay.

In an episode where Elaine (Julia Louis-Dreyfus) acts as a "beard" date for a closeted gay man, she tries to convince him to "switch teams." Elaine does seduce the man, but he quickly returns to men. Elaine attributes this to men's greater familiarity with how to operate "the equipment." She explains: "Being a woman, I only really have access to the—uh—equipment—what?—maybe thirty, forty-five minutes a week. And that's on a good week. How can I be expected to have the same expertise as people who *own* this equipment, and have access to it twenty-four hours a day their entire lives?" "You can't," replies Jerry. "That's why they lose very few players."[5]

Series regular George (Jason Alexander) had better luck. In a 1993 episode, his ex-girlfriend Susan (Heidi Swedberg) takes up with another woman. (It was previously revealed that Susan's father, who is still married to her mother, once carried on a passionate affair with author John Cheever.) Susan's lesbian relationship suffers after her girlfriend sleeps with Jerry's neighbor, Cosmo Kramer (Michael Richards). In an episode in the mid 1990s, Susan reunites with George. He tells a friend that although Susan became a lesbian, "It didn't take." The writers eventually killed her off in what was meant to be the final show of the series: As George tries to figure out how to get out of his engagement to Susan, she dies from contact with the toxic glue on the envelopes of the cheap wedding invitations he insisted on buying.

CARTOONS

Until the 1990 debut of *The Simpsons*, there apparently had not been an ongoing, adult-targeted, prime-time cartoon series on the networks since *The Flintstones* in the 1960s. Americans tended to think of TV cartoons as children's fare. This was one reason why *Saturday Night*

Live's mid-1990s superhero cartoon shorts about "The Ambiguously Gay Duo" (rife with phallic imagery and sexual innuendo) inspired so much laughter: They placed adult content in what was considered a "kiddie" genre, while roasting the campy homoeroticism that some viewers read into the old 1960s *Batman* series.

Animators in the 1990s were determined to remind audiences that some cartoons were not meant for children. As ever, when a series needed to prove its sophistication or hipness, gay content was a quick fix. A running gag on ABC's (later Fox's) animated sitcom *The Critic* was that the title character's boss mistakenly thought the protagonist was gay. This series also worked lesbian and gay references into its quick cutaway fantasy gags, and its five-second spoofs of famous films and TV shows. In one episode, Jay and some children are watching an episode of *Roseanne*. On the show within a show, an animated Roseanne Conner says to her husband, "A lesbian just kissed me! Can she live in the basement?"[6]

The Simpsons continued its coy references to Waylon Smithers's sexuality throughout the 1990s (and beyond). The series' most gay-focused episode, however, was a 1997 broadcast in which the Simpson family befriended a gay male vendor of pop culture kitsch (voice of John Waters). The story finds Homer—who always seemed perfectly tolerant of gay people before—inexplicably turning homophobic for this one episode. Other than that inconsistency, the script was classic *Simpsons*, with rapid-fire gags ranging from obscure pop culture allusions to ironic paradoxes and Homer's usual blundering. At one point, Homer tells John to stop using the word "queer." "I resent *you people* using that word. That's *our* word for making fun of *you*," Homer explains. "We *need* it."[7]

Although the first season of Comedy Central's controversial cartoon *South Park* aired a few months too late to belong properly in this chapter, a late-1997 episode of the series was the ultimate satire of television's clichéd coming-out stories. This crude, cult-favorite series' fourth episode is titled "Big Gay Al's Big Gay Boat Ride." It is much like any coming-out episode, except that the household member whose gayness requires tolerance is the family dog. Sparky, now sporting a studded collar, runs around the neighborhood mounting other male dogs, as little Stan's classmates tease him over the fact that "Stan's dog's a homo!" (Or to quote the episode's most famous line, "That dog is a gay homosexual.") Stan eventually learns to accept his pet's sexuality thanks to a magical, lisping, fairylike fellow named Big Gay Al, whose sanctuary for unwanted gay pets also features an amusingly preachy amusement park ride—complete with Disneylike animatrons—that educates pet owners about the evils of homophobia. Along with the humor, the episode puts across all the standard messages of tolerance that the genre it is spoofing requires. In the tradition of literature's great satires, this episode succeeds both as a send-up *and* as a warped example of the very genre it is meant to deflate. In an unusual piece of guest-star casting, Sparky's barking and yelping were provided by George Clooney, who was then starring in the top-rated drama on television: NBC's *ER*.[8]

ER

This popular hospital drama set in Chicago premiered in September 1994. Its large, sprawling cast allowed for all sorts of characters to float in and out, both as staff members and patients. There were numerous GLBT patients, who were diverse not only in their ages and ethnicities, but also in their stories. There were also recurring gay roles.

In 1996, shortly after the series killed off its gay ambulance driver, Raul, the show introduced a new recurring role: intern Maggie Doyle (Jorja Fox). At first, the writers seemed to be setting her up as a love interest for one of the regulars, Dr. Carter (Noah Wyle). Indeed, when Jorja Fox filmed Maggie's first episodes, she had no idea that the character would turn out to be gay. Four months after Dr. Doyle's arrival, she and Carter spend an afternoon enjoying target practice at a shooting range. Carter assumes they are on a date, and is disappointed when Maggie indicates that another woman who happens to be at the range at the same time is her former girlfriend, a police officer.[9] Doyle was portrayed as a conscientious doctor who believes in honesty and doing things by the book. She would continue to appear sporadically on *ER* through the end of the 1998–1999 season. By then, the series would feature an openly gay male nurse, Yosh Takata (Gedde Watanabe), who made his first appearance in fall of 1997.

NYPD BLUE

There was much to praise in ABC's no-holds-barred saga of big-city police work. One of its few major problems was that its writers never met a tired gay cliché they did not like.

For example, the receptionist in this gritty, violent cop show is a soft-spoken, polite, effeminate gay man who is a former art dealer and amateur hairdresser. He idolizes celebrities and is an avid theater buff. And—oh yes—he typically looks as if he is about to burst into tears, which he actually does on occasion. John Irvin (Bill Brochtrup) appeared on the show intermittently starting in 1995, and would become a full-fledged regular in 1999.

In 1995, it at least *appeared* as if the show was going to balance John with a nonstereotyped lesbian character. In an episode that fall, Detective Adrianne Lesniak (Justine Miceli) told a colleague she was gay, after which rumors about her sexuality spread through the precinct. In the real world, gay TV fans also heard rumors about Lesniak, and many tuned in to watch this capable, strong, nonclichéd role. The story lasted a couple of months, and the outcome was that she was not gay at all. She simply *said* she was gay to brush off an unwanted suitor. She then briefly questioned her sexuality in light of her bad luck with men, but she decided she was straight after all.

In the fall of 1996, just after Miceli left the series, Paige Turco joined the cast as Officer Abby Sullivan, a well-developed recurring role who was definitely a lesbian: in fact, her partner Kathy (Lisa Darr, later of *Ellen*) was seen in several broadcasts. That season, a male colleague donated sperm so Abby and Kathy could become parents. This was a refreshing contrast with the old tragic-lesbian stereotypes, and made up for some of the more extreme elements of the John Irvin character. Here was a lesbian who was portrayed as a productive member of society—a cop in a stable relationship, rather than an insane killer or a murder victim. Viewers should have known it was too good to last: This was *NYPD Blue*, where endings were tragic and gay stereotypes were epidemic.

Although Abby and Kathy are responsible citizens, it turns out that Abby's former girlfriend is (surprise!) a violent lunatic lesbian who has been stalking the couple for months. Almost exactly one year after Abby's first appearance, the ex-girlfriend hires a thug to murder Kathy. For good measure, the gunman also shoots and wounds the pregnant Abby. When police interrogate the profoundly disturbed former girl-friend, she is seen as one of the most over-the-top psychotics the series ever depicted. During the interrogation she is all smiles at first, certain that this desperate act of love will win Abby back, and positive the offi-cers will realize this murder was a necessary and forgivable measure. When the grief-stricken Abby spurns her, the suspect begins gibbering insanely about how they are destined to be together. The officers drag her out, presumably to a psych ward.[10] This character could not have been more cartoonish if she frothed at the mouth and if her heels left smoking grooves in the linoleum as they dragged her away. Abby left the series immediately. In the space of this single episode, the writers managed to reduce a promising story line to the three creaky lesbian archetypes that television had deployed for decades: the bloodthirsty psychopath, the victim killed by another lesbian, and the gay woman grieving her lover's death. This aired not long after *Ellen*'s coming-out episode. Perhaps ABC felt that *Ellen* more than made up for anything *NYPD Blue* might do. Two months later, however, this cop series would again explore GLBT themes in a tale about a bisexual/transsexual ménage à trois gone murderously sour.[11]

RELATIVITY

In 1996 and 1997, ABC's *Relativity* presented one of the best-developed, most convincing, ongoing lesbian roles ever on television—a character who was multilayered and well acted, and whom the network allowed to date and kiss her girlfriend on camera.

Relativity, a seventeen-week romantic and family drama from the producers of *thirtysomething* and *My So-Called Life*, traced the ro-mance of a nice Jewish boy, Leo (David Conrad) and a nice Gentile girl, Isabel (Kimberly Williams). Rhonda Roth (Lisa Edelstein), a regu-larly seen supporting role, is Leo's insecure sister—sort of a lesbian "Woody Allen type," but more subtle than that. Rhonda seemed like someone the viewer—especially a gay viewer—might know in real life.

That realism probably owes much to the plot details and lesbian community allusions supplied by one of the show's regular writers, the noted lesbian filmmaker Jan Oxenberg.

Rhonda has a steady girlfriend in the pilot episode, but they break up by episode two. Rhonda develops a close friendship with Leo's roommate, Doug (Adam Goldberg), and they commiserate about their respective problems with women. The conversations between Rhonda and Doug add background and depth to both characters. This friendship is series television's only gay woman/straight man answer to all those gay man/straight woman friendships that so fascinate scriptwriters.

In the "earthquake episode," written by Oxenberg, Rhonda is seen on the last of a string of bad dates, after which she heads over to her brother and Doug's place to hang out and complain. There she meets a friend of Isabel's: Suzanne (Kristin Dattilo), an earthquake specialist who is inspecting Leo's and Doug's apartment for damage after a quake. This scene, in which Suzanne gently expresses interest in Rhonda, is as sweet as anything on the series. Later, to help neurotic Rhonda overcome her terror of earthquakes, Suzanne takes her back to the lab to face her fears inside an earthquake simulator. By this point, it is clear that the two are interested in each other. Before switching on the machine, the usually demure Suzanne asks breathlessly, "What intensity would you like?"[12]

And so it was that inside that earthquake simulator months before Ellen came out, and Rhonda and her winsome seismologist culminated their swift, well-acted courtship with the most unapologetic, nonexploitative, and romantic lesbian kiss ever produced for network television. (Oxenberg's script called for them to have two kissing scenes, but ABC brass said that one ten-second kiss between lesbians was quite enough groundbreaking for one episode.)[13]

This acclaimed series may not have lasted long, but it proved that a believable, solid lesbian character could be portrayed on TV without the world coming to an end.

SPIN CITY

That same season, ABC's *Spin City*—the New York City Hall sitcom starring Michael J. Fox—offered the most immediate precedent for *Ellen*: a full-fledged gay male regular who played a key role in almost every episode. He was openly, politically gay, dated men, had gay friends, and yet was never reduced to just "the gay guy." Carter Heywood (Michael Boatman) reflected an ideal balance between acknowledging a character's gayness and treating him on a par with the other members of the ensemble. No one watching the show could forget that Carter was gay—just as they could not forget that he was black—but his functions within the story lines were not tied exclusively to those traits. In most respects, he was treated just like any other regular on the show—right down to the episodes that dealt with his personal life.

Most of the premiere episode focused on Carter's arrival as a member of the mayor's public relations team. As the premiere begins, the mayor's staff cringes as a gay activist on TV—Carter—eloquently blasts the mayor's track record on gay issues, demonstrating a unique skill for political spin work. Deputy Mayor Mike Flaherty (Fox) does the only reasonable thing: he attempts to co-opt and silence the activist by hiring him. Since Carter is both gay and African American, he becomes the mayor's special liaison on minority affairs. In accepting the position, however, Carter makes clear that he will continue to speak his mind publicly. "I promise you," he tells the mayor (Barry Bostwick), "as long as you're in office, I'll be your worst nightmare." Mike assures the mayor that this is a good thing.[14]

Network television usually depoliticized and desexualized gay characters while—paradoxically—defining them solely by their sexuality. On ensemble series, gay characters were usually expected to converse about everyone else's personal life while remaining silent about their own. Carter was an exception.

Especially in the first season, Carter's presence was sometimes used as a springboard for scripts that examined sexual-minority or racial issues. For instance, when the mayor issues a statement opposing legal recognition of gay marriage, Carter and a female coworker/confidante plan an elaborate protest designed to embarrass their boss into changing his stance. Though the mayor refuses to change his position, Carter and Nikki's stunt gets press coverage for the issue. Other episodes would incorporate Carter's views on such subjects as needle-exchange programs to slow the spread of HIV.[15]

Such expressions of political passion are not unique to this character. Several of the supporting roles have causes or political priorities, and Carter's are seen as no different. However, mostly he is presented as another member of the mayor's spin-control team, and is seen doing his job and hanging out with his coworkers. Just as they talk about the things that are happening in their lives, so does Carter. Just as their various boyfriends and girlfriends are shown, so are Carter's. So far, his current and former loves have been played by such people as Isaac Mizrahi, Luke Perry, and—in a truly classic episode—Lou Diamond Phillips.

TOUCHED BY AN ANGEL

Touched by an Angel was the highest-rated show on CBS during much of the 1990s. This family-oriented religious series—a show much beloved by many conservative Christians even though its politics were a bit liberal for them—used its 1996 Christmas episode to preach tolerance of homosexuality. The episode argues that—as one of the angels, Monica (Roma Downey) says—"Nothing that God created is 'queer.'"

The episode's central plot resembles the 1985 TV movie *An Early Frost*: a gay lawyer with AIDS moves home to die in his parents' house, where his gruff, antigay father must learn to love his son again while there is still time. The innovation here was not the plotline, but the type of series on which it appeared, and the message that writer Glenn Berenbeim put into the angels' mouths. The senior angel, Tess (Della Reese), speaks directly to the gay man, Tony, who is convinced that he will go to Hell. "You have not disappointed God," she says, "because you can't surprise God. He never expected you to be anyone but who you are. You just didn't expect Him to love you, but He does." "That's not what I heard," says Tony. "What you heard," replies the angel, "were words of someone else: words of hate and confusion. But God is not the source of hate and confusion." She tells him that AIDS is a disease, not a punishment. "It *is* going to take your body," she says, "but don't let it take your soul."[16]

It did not sound all that radical, but given the context in which it aired and the audience it reached, it was one of the most revolutionary gay-themed broadcasts of that year. If anyone was looking for a sign that gay content had gone mainstream, this was it.

THE ELLEN MORGAN STORY
(OR HOW TO WIN A TOASTER OVEN)

Television: 1994–1998

Ellen DeGeneres and Anne Heche are talking about having a baby. They're worried, though, because if the baby is anything like Ellen, it's going to take much longer than nine months to come out.

—Conan O'Brien on Late Night, *1997*[1]

It was the longest tease since the days of Gypsy Rose Lee. For more than half a year, rumors circulated that Ellen Morgan, the lead character on ABC's sitcom *Ellen*, might be allowed to come out as a lesbian. Though it seems strange in hindsight, the possible coming out of one fictional TV character on a series with middling ratings was front-page news intermittently from September 1996 to April 1997, bumping more urgent stories to the insides of respected periodicals.

Star Ellen DeGeneres and her writers fed the frenzy, even though ABC had not yet decided whether to allow the proposed change. While ABC and its parent company, Disney, refused to comment, DeGeneres was appearing on talk shows to promote her new comedy CD, "Taste This." On *The Rosie O'Donnell Show*, DeGeneres joked that her TV character was going to discover that she was Lebanese during the coming season. On NBC's *Late Night*, she told Conan O'Brien that the controversy was a misunderstanding: her sitcom was just adding a male character named Les Bián. She told the same jokes on ABC's *Good Morning, America* and CBS's *The Late Show*. On *Ellen*, DeGeneres's alter ego asked her parents how they might react if she told them that her whole life had been a lie, and that she was really—*left-handed*.

Ellen jokes even turned up on other networks' sitcoms. On a Halloween episode of NBC's *NewsRadio*, just weeks after the coming-out rumors first surfaced, a male character was in drag for a costume party. When he kissed his girlfriend, they appeared to be a lesbian couple. His boss told them to stop because "this isn't *The Ellen DeGeneres Show*."[2]

When DeGeneres and her tomboyish character both finally did come out with much fanfare in April 1997, *Ellen* became the first prime-time series with an openly gay leading character and the first American network comedy or drama with a vocal, openly gay star—in a title role, no less. With its voluminous news coverage, DeGeneres's and *Ellen*'s coming out rocked American culture, setting off pervasive public debates over homosexuality and gay visibility. In its last season, *Ellen* became the most gay-centric major series up to that date, and the first to develop a same-sex romance as its central story line over the course of a season.

In the early 1990s, even before her series debuted, stand-up comic Ellen DeGeneres's lesbianism was an all-but-open secret in show business and the gay community. Rumors that she was gay had spread through the grapevine and gossip columns for years. DeGeneres had been open about her sexuality to family and close friends since the late 1970s, when she was eighteen. Publicly, she refused to discuss her personal life in interviews or in her routines. Unlike many closeted stars, however, she did not invent heterosexual romances either. It was a tenuous, stressful balance, and she had to appear upbeat and relaxed while maintaining it. "All through my career," she later recalled, "every time I was onstage, I was scared to death that the audience would find out that I was gay, 'cause I was following some guy who made dyke jokes or fag jokes and I had to stand onstage and try to act straight to fit in. And so for fifteen years doing stand-up, I was scared to death. . . ." As a child, she said, she had dreamed of being famous. Now, as an adult, she feared that if audiences or producers knew who she really was, they would stop liking her and she would lose her career. As theories about her sexuality continued to spread, she found that she was developing a huge lesbian following as she toured the nation's comedy clubs. When she saw other lesbians in the audience or after the show, she worried that they might clue people in to her secret. DeGeneres has said that when lesbian fans would greet her or call to her, a part of her mind was thinking, "You're giving it away! They're gonna figure it out! Go home!" She tried to ignore the strain inherent in constantly skirting the truth.[3]

During her years as a stand-up comic, that strain seldom showed onstage. In 1982, she won Showtime cable's "Funniest Person in America" competition. She toured the stand-up circuit in the 1980s, making occasional TV appearances. By the early 1990s, she was taping cable specials, appearing in commercials, and performing on popular network shows such as Johnny Carson's *Tonight Show*. During a solo cable special in 1993, DeGeneres said that the next day she would meet with network executives about a possible weekly sitcom. The result, *Ellen*, debuted on ABC in March 1994 under the title *These Friends of Mine*. ABC renamed it that summer to emphasize the show's strongest asset—DeGeneres—and because potential viewers were confusing *These Friends of Mine* with NBC's new comedy, *Friends*. *Ellen* is the story of Ellen Morgan, a quirky, insecure woman in her early thirties who runs a bookstore. Early episodes deal with her attempts to find a steady boyfriend and her tendency to meddle in her friends' lives. Critics agreed that DeGeneres was funny *in* the show, but that *Ellen* itself was not quite working. For two years, ABC kept changing the supporting cast, the premise, and the production staff. For a time during the 1994–1995 season, *Ellen* was the second-highest-rated comedy on American TV, just behind *Roseanne*.

DeGeneres also continued doing imaginative stand-up work during this time, much of it on high-profile award shows. She developed an almost incestuous relationship with award telecasts from 1994 to 1997, earning an Emmy Award nomination for hosting the Grammy Awards, winning an American Comedy Award for cohosting the Emmy Awards, and winning a CableACE Award for hosting the *VH1 Honors*. For her performance on *Ellen*, both she and the series received People's Choice Awards. DeGeneres seemed to have everything she said she wanted since childhood. But stardom had its disadvantages: public scrutiny meant that staying in the closet would be more grueling.

She was outed in print several times. The incidents that reached the widest readership were an unauthorized paperback biography in 1994, and a January 1996 article in *New York* magazine that was excerpted in gay newspapers internationally. The *New York* piece was a critique of how gossip columnists apply a double standard, suppressing details about gay celebrities' lives while routinely violating heterosexual stars' privacy. The writer focused on a recent squib in the usually sensation-alist New York *Daily News*:

> In a curious, coy moment of editorial discretion, the *Daily News* omitted one minor detail from a recent item on *Ellen* star Ellen DeGeneres, who was spotted "soul-kissing and pawing" a "short-haired fan" on a Wednes-day night at Nowbar. . . . What the item oddly neglected to mention: that every Wednesday the club is home to a lesbian party, "Wow Bar at Nowbar," and that the "fan" in question was a woman.[4]

While gossip writers speculated about DeGeneres's sexuality, some TV critics began to comment on her character's sexual ambiguity. In 1995, Joyce Millman of the *San Francisco Examiner* called *Ellen* "The Sitcom That Dares Not Speak Its Name." She wrote that previous heroines of single-woman sitcoms did not "throw off the, um, gender neutral vibe that Ellen Morgan does . . . *Ellen* doesn't make any sense at all, until you view it through the looking glass where the unspoken subtext becomes the main point. Then *Ellen* is transformed into one of TV's savviest, funniest, sliest shows."[5]

Through *Ellen*'s early years, ABC pressured the writers to have Ellen Morgan date more. Indeed, the second season, which empha-sized her search for a boyfriend, did better in the ratings than any other season of the series (mostly because it was in an advantageous time slot that year). DeGeneres reportedly was uncomfortable with the dating story line, despite its popularity, and felt that Ellen Morgan was not a very convincing heterosexual romantic lead. For the 1995–1996 season, some of the show's writers suggested having Ellen Morgan come out as gay. It was not a new idea. Producers had suggested a lesbian protago-nist to DeGeneres in 1993, before her sitcom began production. But she was not ready for that in 1993 nor in 1995. Even if she were ready, it seemed unlikely that ABC or the show's production company (a Disney subsidiary) would approve. Instead of coming out, starting in fall 1995, Ellen Morgan became asexual, with subtle hints that she *might* be a closet lesbian. Commenting on this obvious change in the character, the *Boston Globe*'s Frederic M. Biddle said that pseudogay characters like Ellen were proof of the problem that gay people faced in the American media: The TV networks were willing to capitalize on gay guest roles in a quest for Emmys, but were afraid to have a gay lead—even on this show, where it would make sense. What was needed, he said, was "a gay equivalent of *I Spy*," a reference to the 1960s series that had opened the door for dignified black leading characters on TV.[6]

The show's writers were at a loss for plotlines, now that their leading character was no longer identifiably heterosexual and not yet openly gay. To fill the weekly half hour, the writers had Ellen stumble into the sort of wacky, comedy-of-errors situations that tormented Lucy Carmichael (Lucille Ball) on *The Lucy Show* in the 1960s. In separate interviews, most of *Ellen*'s writer/producers agreed that this asexual phase was horribly difficult and repetitive to write. *Entertainment Weekly* quoted one of the show's writers as saying, "Can you imagine *Seinfeld* without sex? There just aren't that many driver's license stories." In a 1998 documentary, coproducer Tracy Newman said it was frustrating to have to come up with "story after story about her foot getting caught in a bucket. She wasn't dating and she also wasn't someone who was passionate about her job, so it was a very hard show to write for. And sometimes at two in the morning you'd be saying, 'Why doesn't she just come out?!' "[7]

Probably to test viewers' response, the writers began developing two recurring gay roles in 1995: Peter (Patrick Bristow) and his lover Barrett (Jack Plotnick). When Peter first appeared the previous season, he originally was written as straight. However, openly gay actor Bristow had camped the part and played off of Ellen wonderfully well. The producers decided to write him in as Ellen's new gay friend.[8] Peter and Barrett first meet at a dinner party in the classic 1995 episode, "Salad Days." They bond instantly over their mutual worship of gracious-living guru Martha Stewart, whose works they can recite from memory. Over the course of the season, the two young men exchange rings and move in together.[9] Gay male viewers' reactions to Peter and Barrett seemed to split over roughly generational lines, an indicator of how TV imagery and its impact had changed over the decades. In particular, gay men who were adolescents in the 1960s when this sort of fussy gay stereotype was the norm (obsessed with fashion, decorating, and cooking) seemed more likely to be offended. However, those who grew up watching cautiously mainstream roles on *Soap*, *Dynasty*, and *Melrose Place* tended to see Peter as refreshingly "un-P.C."

In the spring of 1996, the biggest year for gay regulars on television was just ending. DeGeneres was in therapy at the time. The strain of secrecy and self-censorship was wearing her down. She faced up to how painful it had been living in the closet all those years, always looking over her shoulder. She began to imagine how freeing—and frightening—it might be to end the rumors and come out publicly. Already stressed out from the latest round of outings, DeGeneres had something new to worry about that spring: *Ellen*'s popularity had plummeted. Once a Top Five show, it finished the season tied for thirty-ninth place. There was talk that ABC might not renew it. ABC commissioned another season with the caveat that *Ellen*'s writing needed to become more focused. The network ordered that for the 1996–1997 season, Ellen Morgan had to care about someone or something.[10]

On June 6, the usually private DeGeneres had a party at her home to which she invited the show's creative team. It was the first time most of them knew where she lived. She lifted a glass of champagne and asked for everyone's attention. "I think this year I'm gonna be coming out," she said. "What do you think if the character came out?" The writers applauded and her guests toasted the idea, unfeasible though it sounded. DeGeneres swore everyone to secrecy until she could meet with the still-merging Disney/ABC management and try to convince them that a lesbian lead could succeed without denting ABC's ratings or damaging the profits of Disney, which valued its family-friendly image.[11]

That same week, the Southern Baptist Convention was holding its annual meeting in New Orleans. With delegates representing fifteen million church members, it was the largest Protestant denomination in the United States. Their agenda included a vote on whether to boycott the Walt Disney Company and its innumerable subsidiaries, which included Touchstone Television (producer of *Ellen*) and, thanks to a recent buyout, ABC-TV. The Baptists did not know about DeGeneres's dinner party or her coming-out plans. The main reason for the proposed boycott was that the Disney Company had extended employee health benefits to same-sex domestic partners. Spokespeople for the convention argued that Walt Disney himself would have abhorred that policy. But in spite of this, and despite concerns about the content of some Disney films, they ultimately decided that Disney's transgressions were not yet grave enough to justify a direct assault.[12]

The *Ellen* creative team began secret meetings with Disney's top executives in June to discuss the fourth season. The producers wanted to use the first nine scripts to drop humorous hints about Ellen Morgan's sexuality. Ellen would go back into therapy, they said, and she would struggle with an inner secret that troubles her. Then, in November—a sweeps month—Ellen would come out to her new therapist in a funny, touching scene. During the rest of the season, the producers hoped to deal with the aftermath of her coming out: reactions from her parents, friends, and coworkers, and her personal adjustment to being openly gay. "We wanted to arc the entire season so it had some validity," executive producer Dara Savel later said.[13] At that first meeting between the *Ellen* producers and Disney executives, DeGeneres reportedly was in tears by the time she finished explaining what she wanted to do.

Given her determination to come out, Disney executives probably thought they had just two choices: cancel *Ellen*, or let the title character be gay. Popular wisdom held that American audiences would not accept an openly gay actor in a straight role. Disney CEO Michael Eisner was tentatively open to the idea of Ellen Morgan's coming out, pending the acceptability of sample scripts and assurances that her sexual orientation would not be the show's sole focus. That summer, press kits for the sitcom said that the fall episodes would include more serious elements: Ellen Morgan's parents would separate, leading her to seek professional counseling; she would reevaluate her life, and sell her bookstore to buy a house. *Entertainment Weekly*'s fall preview quoted DeGeneres as saying that in the new season, Ellen Morgan "goes on a personal journey where everything collapses around her. She finds out who she is, which is what I think the audience wants to know—*I* can't tell you who she is."[14]

One concern about Ellen's coming out was whether it would hurt Disney's chances of selling the show into syndication after the network run ended. Such reruns are where production companies hope to recoup the costs of filming a series. By mid-September, Lifetime cable—partly owned by Disney—had bought repeats of *Ellen* for more than $600,000 per episode. (As a point of reference, that year, Lifetime paid $475,000 per episode for *Chicago Hope*, FX cable paid $600,000 per episode for *The X Files*, and TNT cable paid $1.2 million per episode for *ER*.) With *Ellen* guaranteed to bring in millions of dollars in repeats, Disney had less to lose that fall than it had a few months earlier.[15]

In September, *The Hollywood Reporter* and United Press International publicized the once-secret negotiations about Ellen Morgan's sexual orientation, citing anonymous sources and an upcoming *TV Guide* article. Disney and the producers refused to comment, and Savel later said that Disney brass was furious over the "leak." The closest thing to an official confirmation came from DeGeneres's manager, Arthur Imparato. *TV Guide* quoted him as saying, "If you look hard at the whole series, there are a lot of elements over the years that could be laying groundwork for that story line." He said DeGeneres was "trying to break new ground and do something that has not been done before on television," but that what path the show would actually take was "anyone's guess."[16] Insiders told reporters that Disney had already agreed to the idea in principle. It is plausible, even likely, that the company or the producers deliberately leaked the rumor to see how the public would react. Final decisions on whether to approve the coming out could then be based on national response to the news articles.

While Disney maintained official silence, *someone* was feeding reporters information about *Ellen*. The mass media seemed fascinated with the prospect of an openly gay Ellen Morgan. The earliest coverage took the "it's-never-been-done-on-TV" tack, followed by a spate of stories that tried to guess how advertisers and ad agencies might react. *USA Today* quoted Robert Igiel of Young & Rubicam, who said he was not sure how he might advise his clients. "I'd have to see the episodes before passing judgment," he said, but warned that "advertisers are in the business of making friends for their services and products, and anything that's controversial almost by definition angers some people some of the time." Ad buyer Paul Schulman told the Associated Press that if Ellen were to find a girlfriend and "the two of them are going to the zoo together, it's not a problem. If they are in bed together, it's a problem." Most buyers interviewed for the AP piece felt that *Ellen* might lose a few cautious sponsors, but that ABC could resell the ad time easily, as had happened with the steamy, violent cop drama, *NYPD Blue*. By October, major advertisers Microsoft and Intel had confirmed that they would stick with *Ellen* regardless of the lead character's sexual orientation. Other sponsors said they would wait to see how things played out.[17]

The media's feeding frenzy over *Ellen* took many forms. DeGeneres, who has said she never wanted to be a "poster child" for gay visibility, became its cover girl instead. Over the next year, her photo would appear on the covers of major and minor periodicals, accompanied by headlines about her character's sexuality or her own. Activism was not her style. She naively hoped to stay apolitical while taking a step that most observers would consider highly political.

In September, as soon as the story about Ellen Morgan's lesbianism hit the streets, preachers, evangelists, and other conservative religious leaders denounced the show, Disney, and ABC. Disney became the bull's-eye for a torrent of letters, E-mails, faxes, phone calls, antigay speeches, pickets, televised sermons, and threats of boycott—all because one TV character *might* come out. Some of the mail was the usual God-hates-fags, dykes-must-die rhetoric. Some were reminders that it was not too late for Ellen and the Disney executives to repent and be saved. And some were personal attacks against DeGeneres, some suggesting that she would die of AIDS as punishment for her perversion.

Antigay ministers Lou Sheldon and Pat Robertson both said that DeGeneres looked pretty enough to be straight. Robertson said that she was too beautiful to convincingly play a lesbian. The Family Research Council warned that an attractive open lesbian on TV would cause children to experiment with gay sex. Reverend Donald Wildmon, still leading the American Family Association, mounted letter-writing campaigns supplemented by E-mails from visitors to the AFA's new web site. "It doesn't matter whether Disney and Touchstone keep the character straight or make her homosexual," he said, "because they have already accomplished their goal of once again shoving their 'gay is OK' philosophy into the national spotlight." Reverend Fred Phelps (who, with his congregation, is known for picketing the funerals of prominent gay people) said that *Ellen* was "a sign we're on the cusp of doom, of Sodom and Gomorrah." Robertson and Wildmon reminded sponsors about surveys that suggested that most Americans would not want to watch a show with a gay lead.[18]

Disney/ABC brass kept hinting to *Ellen*'s producers that approval of the coming-out concept was imminent, but they kept pushing back the tentative airdate. In response, the Gay & Lesbian Alliance Against Defamation and local gay groups led their own campaigns to let Disney know there was a market for gay characters. They cited the strong ratings generated by the *Roseanne* kiss episode, *Northern Exposure*'s gay wedding, and even the *Melrose Place* episode where Matt kisses a man off-camera. In all three cases, thanks to advance publicity, viewers went into the show *knowing* that there would be gay content, but they tuned in anyway. By early 1997, Disney executives were receiving boxes of waffle mix in the mail—a tongue-in-cheek campaign by some gay activists to get Disney to stop "waffling" over *Ellen*. GLAAD's national communications director, Alan Klein, explained why he thought the possibility of a gay leading character was causing such optimism in the gay community—even more so than the rumors that DeGeneres herself might come out:

> People have developed a rapport with the character, not necessarily with the actress who plays her. That's how we view television. When we think we know Ellen, we *really* know Ellen Morgan. If a celebrity comes out, people just say, "Oh, I thought so," or "Oh, I didn't know that," and go on. But if Ellen Morgan comes out, people are going to get to know a lesbian intimately, even if they don't know one in real life.[19]

GLAAD focused on lobbying major corporate advertisers, whom the Religious Right was also targeting. Klein reminded current *Ellen* sponsors that even if some people chose to boycott them, the companies would attract new customers by staying the course. GLAAD mailings asked gay people and their allies to "let Touchstone know that this groundbreaking move has your full support. Additionally, let Touchstone know that the lesbian and gay community has a long history of loyalty to advertisers who support the lesbian and gay community."[20]

The American Family Association and GLAAD each mailed their followers copies of the opposing group's action alerts. Both groups used these to frighten their constituents into writing letters by suggesting that the opposition was stronger and better organized. Members of Parents and Friends of Lesbians and Gay Men (P-FLAG) were mobilized, reportedly, by the mother of a gay actor who made occasional appearances on the show. According to alerts sent out by some P-FLAG chapters, the actor had told his mother that the show was being inundated with hate mail, and suggested that the parents' group write letters of support to ABC's chief of programming, Jamie Tarses.[21]

Barraged by gay and antigay activists, and bombarded with calls from reporters, Disney's public relations staff had little to say in response. They could only reiterate their corporate policy of not commenting on "rumors and speculation." For half a year, the battle of words continued, with near silence from ABC and Disney. Disney Television publicist Michael DiPasquale has said that he got to the point where "I was answering the phone and basically saying, 'Hello, we don't comment on rumors or speculation. Hello?' So that there was nothing we could say. We could not say *anything*. And it was maddening and it went on for months and months."[22]

The *Ellen* controversy became the news story that no one could escape. It was everywhere. ABC, Disney, and DeGeneres insinuated that they wanted the coverage to stop. They spoke as if this were an issue that the news media were creating without any encouragement from the network or the production company. But the story was getting such persistent, prominent, ongoing placement that it seemed as though a publicist somewhere might be orchestrating the whole controversy. DeGeneres herself fanned the flames with her "left-handed" and "Les Bián" gags. If the "leak" was more calculated than ABC claimed, then it was an ingenious public relations move. What better way to encourage public tolerance of an openly gay leading character than to deliberately start the controversy so far in advance that the public is bored with the idea by the time it happens?

The show's famous "clues" started with the fall season premiere. Early one morning, Ellen pads around her apartment bleary-eyed, singing "I Feel Pretty." In the middle of the first verse, where the word "gay" appears in the lyric, she discovers that her bathroom sink is broken. She sings: ". . . I feel pretty and witty and—*hey!*" Fed up with apartment life, she hires a real estate agent, Margaret, who shows her slides of available homes. In front of the projection screen, Margaret tries to entice her by doing puppet theater:

MARGARET: Just think, Ellen. This could be you, walking up to your new home. (*She makes a girl doll "walk up the steps" of the house in the slide.*)

PETER: Oh, I love this part. It's like a puppet show of your life!

MARGARET: (*produces a boy doll*) And here's your husband, coming home from work.

ELLEN: Oh, I think that puppet's in the wrong show.

The same script has references to Ellen's unfeminine wardrobe, her lack of jewelry, and the fact that she wears boxer shorts.[23]

Another episode begins with the real estate agent walking into an empty house, calling out, "Ellen? Ellen, where are you?" An interior door opens into the living room and Ellen bounds through it, proclaiming, "I was in the closet!" "It's big, isn't it?" asks the agent. "It's huge, yeah," Ellen replies, adding, "I mean, I wouldn't want to spend a lot of *time* in there. . . ."[24] Although DeGeneres had planned to use these winking references for only nine weeks, the season wore on without ABC's giving a green light for a coming-out episode. So the clues dragged on, becoming less and less subtle. Each week, the writers found another comical way for Ellen to *almost* come out. There were also frequent passing references to celebrities who were either openly gay or had become gay icons because they were widely rumored to be gay. Photos of k.d. lang appeared as set decoration, and there were allusions to The Village People, singer George Michael (who had not yet come out at that point), Jodie Foster, Rosie O'Donnell, and even Ellen DeGeneres. For Christmas, Ellen Morgan is thrilled to receive a copy of DeGeneres's new comedy CD. "Boy, Ellen DeGeneres," she says, "I love her show. Do you think the rumors are true?"[25]

In December, ABC shifted the series from its 8:00 P.M. time slot to 9:30 P.M. This solved two problems: there would be more freedom to explore "adult" themes, and *Ellen* would no longer be opposite CBS's popular *The Nanny. Ellen's* ratings rose immediately.[26] In January, ABC officially broke the silence. ABC Entertainment president Jamie Tarses acknowledged that "We are seriously considering going in the direction that everyone's speculating on. But that will be driven by creative content."[27] ABC again set and delayed tentative airdates. Business journals

speculated that the company would wait until after a Disney share-
holders meeting in February. The theory was that CEO Michael Eisner
already had enough trouble on his hands trying to justify Disney's
giving ex-president Michael Ovitz a $93 million severance package.
Eisner did not need to also deal with protests over *Ellen*.

As controversy over the series grew, so did the number of celebrity
guest appearances. In January, the *Ellen* team filmed a story where
Ellen goes to a rock and roll fantasy music camp. The episode features
performances by Queen Latifah, David Crosby, Bonnie Raitt, Aaron
Neville, and Sheryl Crow. Ellen's cousin, Spence, tells her, "This
is Rock and Roll Dream Camp. You can be anyone you want to
be . . . Melissa Etheridge, k.d. lang, Indigo Girls. . . ."[28] During filming,
DeGeneres threw in another lesbian reference that infuriated the ABC
and Disney executives who were in attendance. At the end of the show,
Ellen Morgan and others sing "Ain't Too Proud to Beg." Without
approval, DeGeneres changed the end of the song, singing "And by the
way, I'm gay! It's okay! I'm gay! I'm gay!" The audience, certain they
were witnessing the long-rumored coming-out episode, stood and
cheered. It took time to quiet them down. "That'll never go out,"
DeGeneres told the excited crowd. A small group of apoplectic ABC
executives swooped down on the producers and made clear that the
scene, as shot, could not air. (It was never intended to.) One executive
confiscated the film to make sure that pirate copies would not get into
circulation. A detailed description of the incident was quickly posted in
Ellen discussion groups on the Internet, ostensibly by a fan who was
there. DeGeneres later said she knew that ABC would never air the
footage, but she just wanted to share that moment with that studio
audience.[29]

The media hype resumed in February with news that ABC would air
a special one-hour coming-out episode on April 30, the first night of the
May sweeps.[30] The network promised that viewers would not suddenly
see Ellen Morgan kissing women. Tarses announced that Ellen would
eventually start dating, but that for the immediate future the show
would only take "baby steps." Coexecutive producer Mark Driscoll said,
"It's never going to become the lesbian dating show. I think a lot of
people are nervous about that. Ellen Morgan has always had problems
dating anyway, and that will certainly continue."[31] Reporters informed

the public that the big episode had been code-named "The Puppy Episode." The title was the producers' inside joke. The previous summer, while they were negotiating with Disney, one corporate executive suggested that giving Ellen a puppy might solve the show's problems. The producers rejected the idea, but they began referring to the coming-out story as "The Puppy Episode."

The usually relaxed atmosphere at Disney's Stage Three became tense as preparations began for the special show. On February 28, Disney security instituted a policy requiring all cast, crew, visitors, and audience members to wear Disney-issued wristbands, even to rehearsals. Everyone had to go through metal detectors when entering the studio. Similarly stringent policies were instituted to protect the secrecy of the coming-out script. During the two-week writing period, all drafts were kept in a locked safe, printed on hard-to-read red safety paper (to prevent illegal photocopying). Rejected pages were put through a shredder.[32]

It was announced that the episode would feature Laura Dern as a woman with whom Ellen falls in love, and Oprah Winfrey as Ellen's therapist-of-the-week. There would be cameos by Demi Moore, k.d. lang, Melissa Etheridge, Billy Bob Thornton, Gina Gershon, and other celebrities: a mix of gay-friendly stars and openly gay ones. The cast list and vague plot summaries got press coverage, but not as front-page news. Then on April 6, the new issue of *Time* appeared on newsstands. The cover featured a photo of DeGeneres with the headline YEP, I'M GAY.[33] Not that the news was unexpected (one publicist suggested that the headline should have read, "Duh—Hello!")[34], but there was something surprising about the concrete reality of it: DeGeneres's bright, familiar face was smiling out at the world from magazine racks around the globe, ending fifteen years of evasions. By the time "The Puppy Episode" aired on April 30, much of the American public was weary of hearing about it. After seven months of publicity, Ellen DeGeneres's and Ellen Morgan's coming out just seemed like a fact of life.

Talk of the episode's potential for strong Nielsens created a stir among antigay activists, because they saw *Ellen* as another step toward the "normalization" of homosexuality. Reverend Jerry Falwell considered the show so dangerous that he came out of retirement as a media activist to attack "Ellen DeGenerate" and to put pressure on potential advertisers.[35] "Because these are public airwaves," he said, "I think Americans who don't agree with that kind of thing should not be forced to make the effort to censor what is coming into our living rooms."[36] This was a curious notion of "public airwaves": Rather than reflecting the diversity of the public, Falwell thought the public airwaves should reflect only the views of certain people.

Prime time became dense with gay and lesbian content during the eight weeks before "The Puppy Episode" aired. *Roseanne* expanded its roster of gay recurring roles from four to five by giving Bev a girl-friend. *Suddenly Susan,* a sitcom set in the offices of a hip San Fran-cisco magazine, finally began including gay content with some degree of regularity. *NYPD Blue* began the already mentioned story arc about a lesbian cop and her lover. Amanda Bearse played a dual role on an episode of *Married . . . With Children*: in addition to her regular char-acter (superheterosexual Marcy), she also played Marcy's lesbian iden-tical cousin. USA cable ran an original biodrama about openly gay Olympic diver Greg Louganis. Most unusual, however, was the appearance of gay content in "family" shows. In an episode of *Dr. Quinn, Medicine Woman*, Walt Whitman (Donald Moffatt) visits the town and shocks the locals by his open affection for his "soul mate," Peter. The townspeople shun him until Dr. Quinn learns tolerance and tries to teach it to others—an attempt that meets with marginal success. On ABC's Friday lineup of family sitcoms, *Step by Step* had a four-year-old moppet share this revelation with her dad (Patrick Duffy):

LILY: Hi, Daddy. Guess what I learned today.

DAD: Well, what did you learn, honey?

LILY: *(big beaming smile, hands on hips)* I'm gay!

DAD: Oh. And what makes you say that?

LILY: Well, I'm a girl, and Mommy's a girl, and I love Mommy, so I'm gay!

DAD: Lily, what you're talking about here, honey, is when one girl wants to *marry* another girl. And you don't want to marry Mommy, do you?

LILY: No. Of course not. *(big grin)* I want to marry *you.*

DAD: Boy, that's a whole other conversation. . . .[37]

The week of "The Puppy Episode," DeGeneres and her family appeared on ABC news shows. As with *Roseanne*, the network used its news department as an advertising tool to boost a sitcom's numbers during a sweeps period. The day of the coming-out episode, DeGeneres also appeared on *The Oprah Winfrey Show* with her new girlfriend, actress Anne Heche.[38]

Because everyone expected high ratings, ABC was able to sell ad time at twice *Ellen*'s usual rate. It was a highly profitable, fully sponsored hour. Some of the series' regular advertisers, including Chrysler, begged off the episode, but ABC resold all of the time to major corporations. The network turned away two gay-specific ads: one from the Human Rights Campaign (HRC), and one from Olivia Cruises, a travel company that specializes in vacation packages for lesbians. The rejection of the HRC ad was appropriate: ABC consistently applied a ban on issue-oriented advocacy ads except for candidates' spots during elections. The inconsistent, often incoherent justifications given for turning away the Olivia commercial, however, carried the scent of garden-variety prejudice.[39]

Knowing there would be tremendous interest in the telecast, gay organizations created events and ads to promote both the episode and their own interests. The Human Rights Campaign offered free "Ellen Coming-Out House Party" kits. Supporters held get-togethers to watch the episode and collect money for HRC (and, less overtly, to add names to HRC's mailing lists). The HRC organizers originally expected to mail out three hundred kits. By early April they had received more than fourteen hundred requests, and they ultimately sent more than three thousand kits. The packets contained an *Ellen* trivia quiz, invitations, small posters to put up on the door of the house, and information about HRC. They also included a "Hints and Guidelines" packet with marketing suggestions to maximize turnout and convince guests to join HRC. *The Washington Post* described it as a gay twist on Tupperware parties. GLAAD held gala fund-raising parties in several cities, where they projected the show on large screens. In Birmingham, Alabama, where the ABC affiliate refused to air the episode, activists from Birmingham Pride Alabama rented a large theater and presented a community screening.[40] GLAAD helped to coordinate the event's public relations.

Many people seemed sure that after months of media saturation, the episode would be a letdown. But DeGeneres and her cowriters delivered one of the tightest hours of TV comedy in years. *Entertainment Weekly* called it "a pop-culture miracle: a media circus that lived up to its hype."[41] It was also very profitable as a sweeps-period episode, drawing ABC's highest ratings of the season except for the Academy Awards telecast.

The "Puppy" script begins with the sort of self-referential comedy that had typified the show's fourth season. Ellen's friends are in the front part of the store, waiting for Ellen to return from the back office. She is getting ready to go out to dinner with an old college friend, Richard, and is taking far too long to get herself together.

> PAIGE: (*impatient, firm, yelling toward the back office door*) Ellen, are you coming out or not?!
> JOE: Yeah, Ellen! Quit jerkin' us around and come out already!!
> ELLEN: (*pokes her head out through the office door*) What is the big deal? I've got a whole hour!

Richard, a TV reporter, wants to pursue a serious relationship with Ellen. Instead, she finds herself drawn to his producer, Susan (Laura Dern). The women have an almost identical sense of humor, say the same things at the same time, love the same music, and both tend to ramble self-consciously. Nonetheless, after learning that Susan is gay, Ellen panics. She becomes even more defensive when Susan assumes that Ellen is gay. Susan tries to put her at ease with a joke.

> ELLEN: I think I know what's going on is it's not enough for you to be gay, y'know, you've got to recruit others, y'know.
> SUSAN: Yeah, I'll have to call National Headquarters and tell them I lost you. Damn! Just one more and I would've gotten that toaster oven.
> ELLEN: (*still looking around nervously*) What is that, gay humor? Because *I don't get it*!

Ellen tells her new therapist (Winfrey) that she is in love with Susan, and recounts same-sex crushes dating all the way to her adolescence.

Later, Ellen catches up with Susan at the airport. With more pain and pathos than the character usually musters, Ellen tries to find a way to share her self-revelation. Finally, she settles on, "I guess what I'm trying to say is—I did get the joke about the toaster oven." Then Ellen tries to say it in more concrete terms. "I—I think I've realized that I am—I can't even say the word. Why can't I say the word? . . . I'm thirty-five years old. I'm so afraid to tell people. I just . . ." Ellen speaks Susan's name quietly, then leans toward her, resting her hands on a vacant airline check-in counter. She accidentally activates the public address system just as she says, "I'm gay." The words echo through the airport. The look of joy on DeGeneres's face was incredible. In the same episode Ellen Morgan also comes out to her cousin and their friends, who are supportive. Ellen and Susan do not act on their mutual attraction, however, because Susan is in a committed, long-term relationship. In the episode's surreal epilog, Melissa Etheridge shows up to congratulate Ellen and to present Susan with a brand-new toaster oven.[42]

Savel told a reporter, "It was really important to Ellen to reveal it in such a way that everybody, including middle America, was on board. That everybody saw her angst, everybody saw what she was going to go through, and that by the end, you're rooting for her."[43] As with Showtime's *Brothers* in the 1980s, and NBC's *Veronica's Closet* in the 1990s, there was a sense that viewers would be more sympathetic to a character who is struggling with his or her sexuality than to someone like *Roseanne*'s Nancy, who simply announced that she was in a relationship with a woman.

"The Puppy Episode" handily beat the usual Nielsen favorites, *ER* and *Seinfeld*, as the most-watched show of the week. It did even better in cities with large gay communities: the A. C. Nielsen Company estimated that in San Francisco, 45 percent of all households watched it. In the excitement, some journalists said it was one of the highest-rated TV shows of all time. That was an overstatement, but the episode did pull impressive numbers. The next week, the series dropped back toward its previous ratings range, attracting a still respectable 12.3 million households. That placed it between *Home Improvement* and *Walker, Texas Ranger*, and well ahead of Fox's cult favorite *The X Files*.

Ellen, which *The Boston Globe* had once found evasive, wound up becoming the "gay *I Spy*" that the *Globe* article said television needed: the show that would break the taboo and open the field to other gay protagonists. Like *I Spy*, which helped erode TV's racial barriers, the groundbreaking *Ellen* attracted both Emmy nominations and vicious hate mail. That spring, "The Puppy Episode" beat tough competition to win the Emmy for Outstanding Writing in a Comedy Series (Single Episode). It also won a Peabody Award. Anecdotal evidence from social service agencies suggests that thousands of people came out to family or friends that month, many citing *Ellen* as the catalyst. Hundreds wrote to DeGeneres thanking her and saying they wished she had been on TV when they were younger. Some young people wrote to say that she had given them hope and dissuaded them from suicide. A lesbian in her fifties said that without DeGeneres's visibility, she would never have found the courage to come out to her family, finally bringing them together in openness.[44] The letters helped to politicize DeGeneres, as she realized her show's potential to help people. The more she read and the more she heard about the show's impact, the more determined she became to present fully developed gay stories.

The antigay mail increased in June after the Southern Baptist Convention voted to boycott Disney and its subsidiaries. The nonbinding resolution cited Disney's "anti-Christian and antifamily direction." An official spokesperson cited *Ellen* as the last straw that swung the vote.[45] Not only did Disney employees receive angry letters, but as part of the boycott, some people began to send the company their Disney videos, toys, and books, saying that these were no longer welcome in their homes. Many Baptists chose not to honor the boycott, which had no apparent impact on Disney's multimillion-dollar revenues. But that such a large denomination had taken an active stand against gay content was noted by both the news media and some sponsors of prime-time shows.

When *Ellen* returned in September, the cast was the same, but almost everything else had changed. Disney brought in Tim Doyle as executive producer, replacing Savel and Driscoll. Doyle had an artist's view of writing, and a determination to push boundaries. Where Disney/ABC envisioned a show about a funny woman who happens to be gay, DeGeneres and Doyle envisioned a funny show about a gay woman. According to Doyle, he told the corporate executives his plans up front, before he accepted the job:

> Every place I went, I said, "Well, here's what I'm gonna do: I'm gonna tell this story about a gay woman looking for love. That's gonna be the show this season." And they kind of nodded and smiled and they went into this denial place. . . . And I just kept saying it. I said, "I'm only gonna take this job if I can do a show about this gay woman looking for love. That's the only thing I'm interested in. That's the only thing that makes a difference for television. . . ." They didn't believe me.

He said that the executives later acted surprised and indignant when they saw the scripts in which Ellen begins a same-sex relationship.[46] To give Disney/ABC its due, what Doyle says he promised was not exactly what he delivered. A lesbian "looking for love" probably appealed to ABC, since that implied a *single* lesbian. What Doyle and DeGeneres delivered was a lesbian who *finds* love, *makes* love (off-camera), hugs and kisses (on-camera), forms a lasting relationship, and asks her girl-friend to marry her. These were not the "baby steps" to which ABC president Robert Iger, Tarses, DeGeneres, and Eisner had supposedly agreed. Iger felt that DeGeneres and Doyle were moving too fast, far faster than public opinion could be expected to evolve.

When the supporting cast arrived to rehearse the season premiere, they found that the series and their roles in it had changed. The tone and focus were different. Now that the writers could explore Ellen's personal life, there were far fewer "B-stories" about the straight sup-porting characters. Audrey, Paige, Joe, and Spence became straight props in a gay leading character's story, much as other series used gay characters as props in straight stories. Actor Jeremy Piven (Spence) has said that on that first week back, he felt "like a kid whose parents had dropped him off at the wrong summer camp."[47]

By late October, Ellen Morgan had begun a sweet, promising, and (it turned out) long-term relationship with Laurie Manning (Lisa Darr), the mortgage broker who had helped her find financing for her house. This new character, who was raising a young daughter, was one of the best things that happened to both Ellen and *Ellen* in the final season.

Laurie originally was meant to appear on just four episodes as a woman Ellen dates briefly. However, the chemistry between Darr and DeGeneres was so good, and the character was so interesting, that she became a regular for the rest of the run.[48] Future episodes would show them meeting each other's families, going on their first vacation together, and facing Ellen's nervousness before their first sexual encounter.[49] *Ellen* seemed to be well on its way to becoming a lesbian *Mad About You*. But as production of the fall episodes progressed, the *Ellen* team began to have run-ins with ABC brass over censorship, parental guidance warnings, and content ratings.

In the mid 1990s, under pressure from Congress, the networks adopted a warning system to help parents decide what programs they should let children see. The labeling options were: TV-G (appropriate for all ages), TV-PG (parental guidance suggested), TV-14 (inappropriate for children under age fourteen), and TV-MA ("mature"—shows with graphic sex, on-camera nudity, or extreme violence—more commonly used on cable than on broadcast TV). Each network rated its own shows. In an unusual move, starting with "The Puppy Episode," ABC imposed the restrictive TV-14 rating on most episodes of *Ellen*, even as the same network gave more lenient ratings to racier episodes of other series. When *Ellen*'s "lesbian episodes" were airing in 1997 and 1998, the major networks usually assigned the TV-PG rating to comedies. In sitcoms, the networks resorted to TV-14 only for episodes that focused on sex acts, sexual bodily functions, nudity, or drug use. Examples of TV-14 broadcasts include a *Spin City* episode called "Bone Free," whose running gag has various men getting persistent, embarrassing erections in public; a *Spin City* episode in which the mayor's daughter rides through the city naked à la Lady Godiva; a *Mad About You* story about a married couple's first lovemaking session post-childbirth; and a *Friends* episode about the male characters' enjoyment of an erotic cable TV channel. In giving *Ellen* a TV-14 rating, ABC implied that any acknowledgment of lesbians' existence constituted "sexual" material.[50]

When the fall 1997 episodes of *Ellen* aired, the series earned good reviews and won its time slot most weeks, helping ABC stage a ratings comeback on Wednesday nights. The show's writers made political points while maintaining a light touch, keeping the characters funny and likable. The honeymoon between the show's producers and ABC ended in October, when ABC compounded the TV-14 rating by preceding some episodes with parental guidance warnings about "adult content." It had been ABC's practice to reserve warning announcements for shows with unusual amounts of nudity or violence, such as *NYPD Blue*. ABC almost never used them on sitcoms, no matter how lewd the jokes. And there was little lewdness about *Ellen*. The only apparent reason for the tag was that *Ellen* had a gay heroine played by a gay actress. Shortly after the advisories began, DeGeneres told *TV Guide*, "I never wanted to be an activist, but now they're turning me into one." A widely quoted *New York Times* article said that unless the warnings stopped, DeGeneres and Doyle planned to quit the show.[51]

Advisories preceded *Ellen* episodes in which Ellen hugged, kissed, or even held hands with another woman, gay or straight. But ABC did not impose a warning or a TV-14 on *Spin City* when its gay regular, Carter, kissed a straight male friend. DeGeneres noted that the only real difference was that the actors on *Spin City* were in well-publicized heterosexual marriages. When straight men on *The Drew Carey Show* performed a broadly played joke kiss, ABC aired the clip in promos at hours when children surely saw them. DeGeneres told *PrimeTime Live* that ABC was sending a clear message: "It's okay to make fun of homosexuality," she explained. "You just can't have genuine feelings and hold someone's hand. Then you get a disclaimer. But if you want to kiss a guy on the lips and wrap your leg around him and make fun of it, we're going to advertise the hell out of that." ABC president Iger said that by showing *Ellen* at all, ABC was helping society reach the point where such advisories might not be necessary. "But we're not there yet," he said. Iger said that rightly or wrongly, the episodes would upset a large number of parents, and ABC had a responsibility to warn them in advance.[52]

Parental warnings aside, ABC reluctantly let *Ellen* push the envelope on lesbian sexual content further than any show before or since. In September 1997, the *Ellen* writing team submitted a script called "Like a Virgin," built around Ellen Morgan's nervousness before her first sexual experience with a woman. In early October, Jamie Tarses phoned DeGeneres's manager to say that ABC would not approve a proposed scene that ends with Ellen leading Laurie into the bedroom.

The cast recorded the scene as written, with an unusually seductive Ellen leaving a path of flower petals for Laurie to follow into the boudoir. According to a report in the New York *Daily News*, a proposed punch line scene, never filmed, was going to show what the lovers saw when they got into the bedroom: 1960s sitcom-style twin beds occupied by a classic sitcom couple—preferably Mary Tyler Moore and Dick Van Dyke of *The Dick Van Dyke Show*. The proposed curtain line: "Hey, we were married with children and *we* never slept in the same bed!" (It is unclear whether *Ellen*'s writers came up with this, or if ABC hoped to make the seduction more palatable by turning it into a joke.) Even after the seduction was recorded, ABC brass continued to vacillate over whether the walk to the bedroom could air. The episode was broadcast in November as written, without the punch line, providing another link in the evolution of Ellen and Laurie's relationship.[53]

Some observers said that the problem with the last season was that *Ellen* had become "too gay," which supposedly made *Ellen* a "one-joke sitcom." But far from limiting the story lines, Ellen's open gayness put the series in a unique position to explore fresh material that had *never* been on American television. Even the most prosaic facts familiar to gay people were uncharted territory for TV and could be mined for laughs: newsstands that file gay news magazines in with the porn, weird reactions from hotel clerks when a couple requests one bed, references to "gaydar" (the "sixth sense" some gay people say they have for spotting other gays), or the fact that ads in gay publications sometimes sexualize *every* type of commerce.

One script from the final season was deservedly nominated for an Emmy. In "Emma," the Oscar-winning British actress Emma Thompson plays "herself" as a nervous, cocktail-swilling closet lesbian who has several deep, dark secrets. Ellen's friend Paige, who works for a film studio, gets Ellen a job as Emma's personal assistant while the actress is in town. At a celebrity party, Ellen spots Emma in a secluded corner of the room, necking with another woman. (The kiss is shown on-camera.) Afterward, in a hotel suite, Ellen tries to convince Emma that the late 1990s are a safe time for a lesbian actress to go public. "A lot has changed in the six months since *I* came out," says Ellen Morgan. Emma vows to come out that night at an awards ceremony. As she heads resolutely for the door, Emma proclaims, "Let's go terrify some Baptists!" Later, she has second thoughts for fear that the tabloids will uncover another secret that could damage her career: the elegant British actress says she is really from Dayton, Ohio. She says she learned to talk like a posh Englishwoman because she longed to play "classy roles." In a flat, drunk American accent, she tells Ellen, "I can't come out to the world tonight! You know, I can face telling them that I'm gay. Hollywood people can deal with that, but there is no 'Dayton Chic'!"[54]

In the second half of the season, however, much of the writing was mediocre—notwithstanding DeGeneres's public statements that she had finally found a writing team that was giving her what she wanted.[55] The producers seemed to be using the scripts as a form of therapy, to work through their anger toward ABC's censors and senior management. Several scripts had Ellen Morgan meet up with conservative, unimaginative broadcasting executives. DeGeneres no longer appeared to be enjoying herself, and took to trashing her bosses in interviews. The series took on an angry feel. But then, arguably, the people who made *Ellen* had cause for some anger.

DeGeneres wanted to acknowledge Ellen Morgan's sexual orientation in every episode, just as other sitcoms did with straight characters. ABC's Iger wanted her to do something more like *Seinfeld*, whose straight male lead often was involved in plots that had nothing to do with dating or relationships. ABC brass said that any episode with Laurie was a story "about" homosexuality. When the network pressured DeGeneres to do some episodes that did not mention Laurie and had no gay references, the producers decided that for one week, they would give the network exactly what it had been asking for: They would create an episode that poked fun at naive, old-fashioned sitcom fare, with Ellen apparently her old, asexual self. They came up with an awful pastiche of early-1960s TV comedies, complete with *Leave It to Beaver*–style musical bridges. The story put Ellen in a bright yellow chicken suit and got her stuck on a roof—in the chicken suit—when a ladder was taken away. Still in the chicken outfit, she crashes a neighbor's "costume party," only to realize that the "party" is a Hindu funeral. This was one of several gimmicky, high-concept episodes in the second half of the season, none of which really worked.[56]

During its controversial final season, *Ellen* remained a media icon to which other shows referred. Besides jokes by late-night talk-show hosts, there were *Ellen* gags on popular prime-time comedies. On *Just Shoot Me*, blond-haired Dennis Finch (David Spade) tried to figure out why his father thought Dennis was gay. "Is this because I look like Ellen?" he asked. A few weeks later, on the Comedy Central cable cartoon series *South Park*, the show's little boys idolized their new lesbian substitute teacher, Miss Ellen (whom a jealous little girl would eventually launch into outer space).[57]

During March of 1998, ABC put *Ellen* on hiatus to try out new sitcoms. Its replacement—the cute but vapid *Two Guys, a Girl, and a Pizza Place*—drew stronger ratings than *Ellen*'s recent episodes, so it became a regular series. ABC indefinitely shelved two remaining episodes of *Ellen* (they would air in July) and slated the season finale to air in May as the series finale. This *Ellen* special—the only *Ellen* script credited to executive producer Tim Doyle—was an hour-long diatribe about the sameness of commercial TV comedy, told in the form of a mock documentary.[58]

The problem with the final months of *Ellen* was not that it was "too gay." Rather, the producers' decision to aim their message at ABC management rather than at viewers, and the desire to prove a point rather than entertain, did as much to hasten the show's cancellation as anything else did. Obviously, TV comedy *can* make incisive observations about society while remaining funny, even when dealing with serious topics (as *All in the Family* had done with subjects like rape). But *Ellen* lacked the history, structure, and (in its last season) the staff to become that sort of show. Nor was it in a position to become a high-concept satire series on an ongoing basis. It had built its following as a character comedy constructed on wacky situations. Fans wanted *Ellen* to be light, not brooding. Toward the end of the final season, the stridency and bitterness of *Ellen*'s messages engulfed the characters' humanity and the situations' humor.

Other issues surely played a role in lowering its ratings: the producers argued that ABC had underpromoted the show, had applied discriminatory censorship and unfair use of parental warnings. Insiders at the network have indicated that there were some in senior management who hated the series and wanted to see it fail. The morale of the writers, producers, and cast surely would have been better if they could have focused on creating the show without the distraction of those problems. That could have improved the tone and quality of the end product. But as things stood, the show was simply no longer consistently funny enough to survive. *Ellen* ran for five seasons—a longer and more interesting run than most sitcoms get. In March 1998, Doyle tried to sell the series to other networks. DeGeneres has said that one network was interested, but "we decided it was time to just let it go because a lot of people wanted to move on."[59] Predictably, but incorrectly, the Religious Right claimed that the show's cancellation was due to public rejection of the character's lesbianism.

Whatever people thought about the last season of *Ellen*, the brave step taken by DeGeneres and Disney/ABC made American society a safer place in which to be openly gay—a legacy that continues at the turn of the new millennium as the series is repeated on basic cable.

DeGeneres's contributions to equality were recognized by numerous civil rights groups. In 1997, she accepted the Bill of Rights Award from the Southern California American Civil Liberties Union, for furthering "the cause of gay rights 100-fold." Accepting an award from the Los Angeles Gay and Lesbian Center the following March, she downplayed the courage it had required for her to take a stand and make a difference. "I had no idea what I was doing," she said. "If only I had known . . ."[60]

CONCLUSION

Television and Digital Multimedia—2000 and Beyond

"I only know what I see on TV."

Those words, uttered in 1987 by teenage callers to a gay crisis line where I used to volunteer, were what started me on this exploration of the history of broadcasting, of GLBT issues, of American public opinion, and of the ways that these intersect. At that time, the sexual-minority images on TV were few, and often reflected alarming stereotypes. When those young people looked at their televisions, the gay images they saw were of people they would never want to be. Many of our counseling clients thought suicide was preferable to living the sorts of lives they saw depicted on screen. Although the coming-out process is still frustrating and difficult for many people, at least the media images available to them as they seek to define themselves have improved dramatically.

When I embarked on this project in 1989, it seemed both possible and desirable for me to videotape and catalog almost every GLBT-relevant national, prime-time telecast to use as research material. The portrayals were so sparse that I could tape nearly everything that aired and still have time to go back and locate recordings of hundreds of earlier programs to cite in this book. Around 1992, my ideal of taping every gay-relevant broadcast became more difficult to meet. By mid 1993, to tape even a majority of them became impossible. And in 1995, I was finally forced to give up and resign myself to capturing only a fraction of the images. Even with multiple video recorders taping different networks at once, it was clear that I was going to miss dozens—perhaps hundreds—of relevant shows per year. Even finding out about all the shows became difficult, so numerous did they become. Compared to what went before, the networks were presenting a veritable kaleidoscope of imagery, most of it gay-friendly. Gay-themed telecasts were no longer isolated oddities to describe one by one, but a pervasive trend to view from a distance in search of patterns.

At this writing, in the year 2000, GLBT images are far more frequent and less terrifying than they were in the late 1980s. However, the heyday of "queer" TV characters is over: that heady period lasted from fall 1994 to early 1998, after which the portrayals dropped off quickly. Ongoing sexual-minority roles now are far fewer and less varied than they were just three years ago.

Television's sexual-minority images today are a mixed bag: sometimes encouraging, often disheartening. The encouraging news is that gay characters now play central, well-developed, regular roles in several popular series. The remarkable character of Carter on *Spin City* continues to be a prominent figure in that series. But the biggest breakthrough, post-*Ellen*, is a popular NBC sitcom which presents network TV's first out-and-proud gay male title character: *Will & Grace.*

This sharp-witted series is one of the most unabashedly gay-affirming programs ever on the major networks. Week in and week out, it is one of the funniest shows on television, as attested to by its critical acclaim and its recent return to the Nielsen Top 25. *Will & Grace* focuses on the intimate friendship between Will Truman (Eric McCormack)—an openly gay lawyer—and Grace Adler (Debra Messing)—a straight interior decorator. It debuted in fall 1998, on the heels of two highly profitable cinema releases that depicted similar friendships between a gay man and a straight woman: *My Best Friend's Wedding* and *The Object of My Affection.*

Will & Grace was created, coproduced, and sometimes written by Max Mutchnick ("I'm the gay one") and his writing partner, David Kohan. Although Mutchnick and Kohan are both men, they have something of a *Will & Grace* relationship. They, too, have known each other for years and speak a kind of shorthand, often finishing each other's sentences in interviews, and playing off each other as they crack jokes much like their characters'. Mutchnick is a former board member of the Gay & Lesbian Alliance Against Defamation, and says he feels strongly about there being a dignified, honorable gay male character on network television.

They originally conceived Will and Grace as supporting roles in an ensemble pilot script about several couples. But NBC's Warren Little-field thought this relationship that couldn't be consummated was the most complex, interesting one in that script, and he asked the writers to build a new pilot around them. The series' first season (and so far all of the second) was directed by sitcom legend James Burrows, who is generally credited with setting the tone for such hits as *Cheers* and *Friends*. His unerring eye for timing and physical comedy, the cast's versatility, and the scripts' sharp edge have made it one of the medium's most acclaimed recent comedies.

Will is an earnest, caring, occasionally sarcastic gay man who has just ended a long relationship. Grace, also single, has been best friends with Will since college. They know each other so well and are so dependent on each other that they seem almost psychically connected. They would be a perfect romantic couple if only they were not *both* searching for a good man. Their sidekicks—another gay man/straight woman pairing, Jack McFarland (Sean Hayes) and Karen Walker (Megan Mullally)—are the unWill and unGrace: self-absorbed, bitter, slightly hedonistic, and able to steal any scene out from under the more centered title characters. Jack and Karen have become the show's breakout comedy figures, and now occupy almost as much screen time as the protagonists.

Like most successful series, *Will & Grace* tempers its innovations with tried-and-true traditions. For example, the gay man/straight woman combination is one of the oldest, most marketable ways to sell gay content to a straight audience. In thinly veiled form, this was what the implicitly gay roles on the old-time radio dramas *Myrt and Marge* and *Candy Matson* were about: Clarence Tiffingtuffer and Rembrandt Watson were basically sounding boards for their straight, female best friends' problems. *Love, Sidney* was a slightly more open variation, with the implicitly gay man upgraded from supporting character to title role. Since the 1990s, however, the men's gayness can be acknowledged openly and fully. The Jack/Will friendship also covers familiar ground, at least on its surface. Jack is—as *USA Today* put it—"as flaming as it is possible to be on TV without setting the tube on fire." Will is the "straight-acting," responsible gay character who balances out Jack's nellie fits and keeps gay media activists from screaming "stereotype!" too loudly. It is the sort of convenient balance that was evident in early episodes of *Brothers*, where the centered, affable Cliff made it possible to have the colorful (and more amusing) queen, Donald.

The people behind *Will & Grace* have made a deliberate effort to make their political points, if any, subtly, through honestly written comedy that has a broad appeal. Director Burrows does not usually do "message shows" on any of his series: his focus and talent lie in creating solid, tight entertainment. The producers concede that Will eventually will date, and that in the second season, he will probably have at least one on-screen romantic kiss.[1] He already kissed platonic buddy Jack on-camera in early 2000. In that self-referential episode, the two men stage a protest in front of NBC headquarters over the network's supposed refusal to depict gay men kissing in a sitcom. Mutchnick and Kohan's decision about when to portray a more romantic kiss reportedly will depend on story considerations alone. The producers say there will be no target date, and no advance hype that would treat it as something out of the ordinary: it will just happen. That casual approach has worked well for episodes of several other series.[2] (For example, for all the noise that is made about television's unwillingness to show a gay man kissing another man, Fox's *That '70s Show* did precisely that with a minimum of fuss and no obvious controversy. Moreover, they did it with a cool, hip, and very likable gay teenage guest character, played by Joseph Gordon-Levitt.)[3]

One of the most important pieces of good news in 2000 is the gay regular on the WB network's prime-time teen soap opera, *Dawson's Creek*. Since early 1999, the beleaguered young people who live in Capeside have included an openly gay high schooler named Jack McPhee (Kerr Smith). On the surface, he embodies that venerable gay TV cliché, the young, intelligent, sensitive, middle-class white boy on the football team. In reality, though, he is one of the most multifaceted gay teen roles ever on TV. He is not a saint like Billy of *One Life to Live*, wonderful though that character was. And Jack has been developed in more subtle ways than *My So-Called Life*'s Rickie, mostly because *Life* was canceled after nineteen episodes, while Jack has been out of the closet on *Creek* for over a year.

Moreover, the *Dawson's Creek* role is more unpredictable than the gay men on *Spin City* and *Will & Grace*. We already *know* what will probably happen to the sitcom characters: the gay men—and Grace— will go on Dates from Hell, or get into relationships that span three or four episodes, after which they will be back where they started. But the open-ended serial format of *Dawson's Creek* means Jack's story could develop in any number of directions. Based on what viewers have seen so far, this promises to be a believable and sensitively handled plotline. Jack's story is overseen by series creator/producer Kevin Williamson, who draws on his own memories of being gay in high school. This may account for the uncanny precision with which this often sudsy series presents Jack's coming-out experiences. "As a writer, I write stories that are personal to me," Williamson said in 1999. "I'm very much gay, so it would be very hard not to include that in my work."[4] It is a sign of how times have changed that this portrayal, like those on *Will & Grace*, is taken in stride, rather than becoming the subject of boycotts and screaming headlines.

Some developments do not fit neatly under the heading of "good news" or "bad news." On NBC's *Veronica's Closet*, the executive assistant, Josh (Wallace Langham), is a regular supporting role. The running gag about him is that everyone except Josh and his fiancée knows he is gay and in denial about his sexuality. The writers and Langham keep finding witty new ways to probe the ridiculousness of his situation— such as when Josh convinces a closeted gay guest character (Scott Thompson) that it is healthier to come out than to marry a woman and cause her heartache. In other words, Josh can easily see in another man what everyone else sees in Josh. To make his willful cluelessness even more ironic, the writers see to it that Josh comes off as "gay" from every conceivable angle. His sexuality is evidenced not only by his sighing involuntarily every time a young, athletic man walks by, but also through the scripts' deployment of old gay stereotypes: Josh's fussiness, his acid wit, his impeccable wardrobe, his love of show tunes, his talent for cleaning and decorating, and his ability to whip up impromptu gourmet soufflés for breakfast without breaking a sweat. Impressively, Langham manages to portray a man with all of these characteristics without ever degenerating into an old-fashioned, vaudevillian "sissy" cliché. From one political point of view, this closeted, stereotyped character can be seen as a "cop-out" and a throwback. But from another viewpoint, Josh can easily be read as a low-key reminder that the Religious Right's suggested life path for gay people—marry someone of the opposite sex and ignore your same-sex urges—is neither as simple nor as advisable as the antigay movement suggests. Josh is, in any case, eminently likable. One hopes that he will "get a clue" before actually tying the knot with his girlfriend.⁵

There is, however, much bad news. The raw numbers of GLBT portrayals have plummeted. The racial and ethnic diversity of GLBT roles has diminished drastically. At the same time, another type of diversity has been lost: lesbian invisibility is again the norm, even as popular shows put straight women characters in lesbian situations for cheap titillation. Depictions of stable gay couples and even same-sex dating, so common in the 1990s, are again taboo.

The lack of racial and ethnic diversity is the easiest of these trends to spot. Except for Carter, a black gay man on *Spin City*, all of the current GLBT regular characters of which I am aware are white gay men. Of the recent shows studied, the only nonwhite/Anglo recurring role is Yosh, the Japanese American gay male nurse on *ER*.

Since *Ellen* went off the air in 1998, there have apparently been no regular or frequently seen lesbian portrayals on any of the six major networks. There were a few minor recurring roles, such as Maggie Doyle on *ER*. And Carol on *Friends* is good for one or two appearances per year. There were some interesting guest roles, such as a sympathetic writing teacher, Perry (Olivia d'Abo), on three episodes of *Party of Five*.⁶ But nothing currently on the air suggests that women loving women are an ongoing part of society.

The shortage of lesbian characters, however, has not stopped prime time's female regulars from kissing women on the lips on-camera. This is a throwback to the early 1990s' status quo: the straight woman who—for either plausible or exploitative reasons—suddenly finds herself sucking face with another woman under the romantic glow of the Nielsen sweeps. During the May 1999 sweeps, in a well-handled story line, Julia (Neve Campbell) on Fox's *Party of Five* impulsively kissed a lesbian friend, Perry, after breaking up with a physically abusive boyfriend. It seemed motivated, at least, by the situation: Julia was reaching out for affection from a woman with whom she felt close. In a far tackier display, two years in a row, during November sweeps, David E. Kelley dreamed up excuses for the title character on *Ally McBeal* (Calista Flockhart) to make out on-screen with female coworkers. In the 1998 episode, Ally and Georgia (Courtney Thorne-Smith) stage a passionate kiss to dissuade a man who is interested in Ally. Ally later insists that Georgia slipped her some tongue, which Georgia adamantly denies. In an episode aired a year later, the heretofore hetero Ally and Ling (Lucy Liu)—who do not even *like* each other—develop an inexplicable mutual physical attraction. They quickly give in to their overwhelming sweeps-period urge to start necking.[7] All of this seems pretty bizarre, since in real life, when two women have a really extended smooch, neither of them is usually straight. The exploitative nature of these scenes becomes clear when one realizes that similar stories are almost never told about straight *male* characters.

Some forms of diversity have fared worse than others between 1998 and early 2000.

Older gay men and lesbians—never portrayed on TV in significant number to begin with—have again vanished from view. The only recent older GLBT character that comes to mind is the sixtyish transsexual played by Olympia Dukakis in *More Tales of the City*.

Bisexual characters have been somewhat visible, but not in large numbers. The last clearly identified bisexual regular was Detective Tim Bayliss (Kyle Secor) on *Homicide: Life on the Street*. In a 1998 episode, five years into the series' run, Bayliss surprises a coworker by accepting a date with a man (Peter Gallagher) he met while investigating a case.[8] For the show's remaining year and a half, Bayliss was seen variously dating men and women. In one episode, he tells a colleague that when he is with a man, he finds himself thinking about women, and vice versa.[9]

Finally, the disappearance of recurring same-sex couples from prime time is a marked difference from the programming of the 1990s. A mere three years ago, during 1997, one could see recurring or regularly appearing lesbian couples on *Roseanne*, *Ellen*, *NYPD Blue*, and *Mad About You*; and male couples on *Roseanne*, *Ellen*, and *Melrose Place*. Today, all gay regulars are singularly single. The nearest exception is the recurring role of Javier (Ian Gomez), the title character's boss on *Felicity*.

As this book draws to a close, I must confess that researching and writing *Alternate Channels* has been a harder, more engaging task than I imagined at the outset. Much of what I found surprised me. I did not seriously expect to find much material from before 1967, much less several chapters' worth. As I gathered material for those early portions of the book, I also was dumbfounded at how closely the writings of some 1950s homophile organizers foreshadowed the politics of much later gay liberationists. The idea that people living in that decade's seemingly hopeless antigay atmosphere had the vision and courage to make waves and try to improve society is truly humbling and inspiring.

Clearly, there is still work to do, not just in Hollywood, but in society as a whole. Gay people are still officially criminals in seventeen states. Job discrimination on the basis of sexual orientation is legal in thirty-nine states. In most places, gay couples have no legal status or protection. Nevertheless, I believe it is important to pause once in a while and appreciate how far things have progressed, even while keeping one eye firmly on the future. Consider that when the research for this book began, people could be arrested for homosexuality in *half* the states of the Union. Less than forty years ago, so-called "sodomy laws" criminalized homosexual relations in all fifty states. I find it sobering to think that I was fully ten years old when, in 1975, the American Psychological Association stopped considering homosexuality a sign of mental illness. Obviously, media visibility is not a cure-all for prejudice, but past experience shows that it can go a long way toward promoting understanding.

How will GLBT visibility play out in television's future? Long-term predictions are always a hit-or-miss proposition. I am put in mind of a book of nineteenth-century essays that tried to predict what American life would be like in the 1990s. The writers conjured up an America in which live theaters largely would be replaced by a home projection system called a *tele-phote*, and in which every moderately well-off man would travel around in his own private flying dirigible.[10] One hit, one miss. So at the risk of predicting the video equivalent of personal dirigibles, I offer a few thoughts from the perspective of the second quarter of the year 2000.

The most sweeping change will be a broadening of who gets to decide what programming and images will be available to the public.

The main vehicle for this will be the next generation of the Internet, and the convergence of Internet and television technologies. This will be an extension of the types of free expression the Internet has already fostered.

In its first popular form, the Internet's World Wide Web provided an alternative to the print media. No longer did writers have to convince a newspaper editor or a publishing house to provide a platform for their views. Anyone who could afford to set up a web site could become writer, editor, and publisher all rolled into one. This process was not necessarily free of charge, but it was much cheaper than buying a printing press.

In the late 1990s, the Internet did for radio what it had previously done for publishing: provided an outlet for niche-market content. When Internet data speeds became fast enough to support digital audio, several gay-targeted Internet-only radio stations—such as PlanetOut Radio and GayBC—offered an array of gay-specific webcasts. There were talk programs, newscasts, fitness shows, spirituality features, history discussions, and deejay shows—all targeted specifically at a gay, bisexual, or transgender listenership. Delivery of these shows to a niche-market audience through traditional AM or FM technology would have been far more costly. Because many shows on these online stations remain available for playback on demand long after their original webcast date, they can reach a larger audience over a longer time period and a wider geographical area than traditional radio. This offers an added incentive for sponsors to support such programming. As a result, some of these niche shows have attracted significant sponsorship from major corporations.

At present, Internet bandwidth is not generally wide enough to support high-quality, full-motion video, though that is changing as cable modems and other high-speed connections become available for home use. Some GLBT videographers and filmmakers are already taking advantage of online distribution. One can easily imagine that by 2010, one will find several online gay TV stations—video equivalents of the radio webcasters. New technologies are also lowering the cost of shooting, editing, and distributing a TV show. In 1970, when New York's Gay Activists Alliance produced its first public-access cable documentaries, a barely portable camera/recorder set cost thousands of dollars, and broadcasting equipment cost millions. Now, however, we are approaching the point where anyone with access to a $500 cam-corder and a $1,200 computer will be able to publish their own video productions and narrowcast or microcast them to interested parties. In short, GLBT people and other niche-market audiences will no longer have to depend on the kindness of strangers if they want to see pro-gramming that acknowledges their existence.

But even if niche-market programming does grow, it remains urgently important that GLBT faces and lives continue to appear in the dominant mass media—those forms of shared entertainment that people discuss around the water cooler at work and in school lunch-rooms. The United States is already home to a diverse, pluralistic cul-ture. As new technologies cross international borders, an ever greater appreciation of pluralism is essential. If people of different back-grounds and beliefs are to live side by side with even a modicum of understanding, we all need to occasionally see each other's lives reflected on screen in a way that treats everyone as part of an "us," rather than as alien, disparate parts of a "them."

The need to see oneself reflected in the broader culture appears to be instinctive from a very young age. Most people probably do not notice this need in themselves: If they belong to a majority race, majority religion, majority sexual orientation, and are not physically dis-abled, they have seen people much like themselves on screen as far back as they can remember. For other people, though, any sort of media visibility, however fleeting, can have a visceral importance. I first became consciously aware of this while talking to those counseling clients, but people who have played gay characters on TV see it reflected every day in their fan mail. As Michael Boatman, who plays Carter on *Spin City*, noted, it is frightening how much influence this mere entertainment medium can have in the real world.

The representation of GLBT people on screen affects not only sexual-minority viewers, but their families, friends, and neighbors, all from an early age. Marta Kauffman, cocreator and coproducer of *Friends*, told an interviewer in 1996:

> We have friends—two women. They have a little girl who never got to see the show last year because it was on too late. Now that it's on at eight o'clock she got to see it. And she saw one with the two moms, and she

turned to her mother with these big eyes and said, "Mommy! A family like ours!" *That's* what we should be doing.[11]

But perhaps we do not even have to look *that* far for a reason why it is appropriate for the mass media to acknowledge the lives of sexual-minority people. Film historian Vito Russo used to tell a story about the making of the 1976 movie *The Man Who Fell to Earth*. Gay characters at that time typically were included in motion picture scripts as cheap laughs or as political symbols or as villains. In that film, however, one of the main supporting characters is, quite incidentally to the plot, gay. Baffled, actor Buck Henry asked director Nicholas Roeg, "Why is my character gay? Why am I playing a homosexual?" Roeg gave what should have been the obvious response: "Why not? There are homosexuals."[12]

NOTES

Citations of TV and radio shows refer to broadcast recordings unless otherwise noted (except for citations of ABC, CBS, and PBS news shows, which are from official transcripts).

Wherever possible, I list official titles for comedy and drama episodes. Readers who wish to build a video library of GLBT-themed shows can use these titles when searching online TV listings for upcoming reruns. Most of the old-time radio shows cited in Chapter One can be borrowed by mail from SPERDVAC (the Society for the Preservation and Encouragement of Radio Drama, Variety, and Comedy), a nonprofit organization based in Hollywood.

The following abbreviations are used throughout the notes:

Annenberg Archive Annenberg Television Script Archive, Annenberg School of Communications, University of Pennsylvania, Philadelphia. (NOTE: This valuable collection was closed indefinitely in the early 1990s. At this writing, only the following portions have been reopened: the subject index and the Agnes Nixon soap opera scripts.)

GAA Papers Gay Activists Alliance Papers, International Gay Information Center Collection, Rare Books and Manuscripts Division, New York Public Library, New York.

GMTF Records Gay Media Task Force Records, Rare and Manuscript Collections, Kroch Library, Cornell University, Ithaca, NY.

Gittings/Lahusen Tapes Audiotapes in the Barbara Gittings/Kay Tobin Lahusen Collection, Way Archives, Philadelphia.

MSNY Papers Mattachine Society of New York Papers, International Gay Information Center Collection, Rare Books and Manuscripts Division, New York Public Library, New York.

MTR Main video collection, Museum of Television and Radio, New York.

PLGTF Archives of the Philadelphia Lesbian & Gay Task Force, Philadelphia.

Testing the Limits' NBC notes Research notes about most of the gay-relevant NBC broadcasts of the 1960s and 1970s, apparently transcribed from NBC program logs; in the files of the Testing the Limits video collective, New York.

Way Archives The Gay, Lesbian, Bisexual & Transgendered Library/Archives of Philadelphia, William Way Community Center, Philadelphia.

Wicker Tapes Randolfe Hayden Wicker Videotapes, Way Archives, Philadelphia.

FOREWORD

1. Yvonne Zipter, *Ransacking the Closet* (Duluth: Spinsters Ink, 1995), p. 165.
2. Paul Gibson, "Gay Male and Lesbian Youth Suicide," in U.S. Department of Health and Human Services, *Report of the Secretary's Task Force on Youth Suicide*, vol. 3, 1989. See especially pp. 110 and 126.

INTRODUCTION

1. Allen Young, "Out of the Closets, Into the Streets," in Karla Jay and Allen Young, eds., *Out of the Closets* (New York: Jove, 1977), p. 17.
2. KYW-TV Philadelphia, *Raparound,* May 7, 1994.
3. In the most recent national Gallup survey on this subject, in 1993, 74 percent said they did not have "a coworker, friend, or relative who is openly homosexual." In a 1996 ICR poll, 44 percent said they did not know anyone who was gay or lesbian. In a 1998 Harris Poll, only 37 percent reported having a gay close friend or relative. Sources: George Gallup, Jr., *The Gallup Poll: Public Opinion 1993* (Wilmington, DE: Scholarly Resources, 1994), p. 231; "USA Snapshots: Homosexual Acquaintance," *USA Today,* September 26, 1996; *The Harris Poll* #42 for 1998, published August 19, 1998.
4. Gallup, *The Gallup Poll: Public Opinion 1993,* p. 83; George Gallup, Jr., *The Gallup Poll: Public Opinion 1998* (Wilmington, DE: Scholarly Resources, 1999), p. 89.
5. For a history of special-interest groups' television activism from the 1950s to 1980s, see Kathryn C. Montgomery, *Target: Prime Time* (New York: Oxford University Press, 1989).
6. Sidney Abbot and Barbara Love, *Sappho Was a Right-On Woman* (New York: Stein and Day, 1973), p. 37.
7. Vito Russo, interviewed by Terry Gross on National Public Radio, *Fresh Air,* April 22, 1986.
8. For instance, a dozen people in different cities have asked me if *Alternate Channels* would mention Dr. Smith (Jonathan Harris), "the gay character" from *Lost in Space*. That 1960s series never specified Smith's orientation, yet

many gay and straight viewers thought him homosexual. Like other campy, pseudo-gay characters, Smith combined many of his era's stereotypes. He was effeminate, vain, cowardly, selfish, materialistic, and a hypochondriac. Psychology in the mid 1960s saw homosexuality as "arrested development"; true to form, this middle-aged character could only relate emotionally to eleven-year-old Will Robinson. At times, Smith seemed attracted to young women, but the stereotypes convinced many viewers he was gay anyway.

9. [John] Mitzel, "The Visibility Thing," *The Guide*, March 1992.

CHAPTER 1

1. Mitchell Dawson, "Censorship in the Air," *The American Mercury*, March 1934.

2. ABC Radio, *The Theatre Guild on the Air* (aka *The United States Steel Hour*), October 19, 1947, "Lady in the Dark"; NBC Radio, *The Theatre Guild on the Air*, March 5, 1950, "Lady in the Dark" (same script, slightly different cast). Regarding this series' penchant for controversy, see John Dunning, *Tune in Yesterday* (Englewood Cliffs, N.J.: Prentice Hall, 1976), p. 598.

3. Regarding 1930s and 1940s radio censorship, see Dawson; Minna F. Kassner and Lucien Zacharoff, *Radio is Censored!* (New York: American Civil Liberties Union, 1936); Vita Lauter and Joseph H. Friend, "Radio and the Censors," *The Forum*, December 1931; Paul R. Milton, "Against the Taboos," *New York Times*, December 7, 1947; Carroll O'Meara, "Not on the Air!", *The Forum*, June 1940; Bryce Oliver, "Thought Control—American Style," *New Republic*, January 13, 1947.

4. O'Meara. Regarding the Duncan case, see Dawson.

5. Examples: CBS Radio, *The Lux Radio Theatre*, January 29, 1945, "Lady in the Dark"; Mutual Radio, *Drama Critics' Award Special*, April 4, 1948, "A Streetcar Named Desire."

6. I have been unable to locate recordings or reports of any gay-themed radio news stories from the 1930s or 1940s. Regarding journalists' tendency to suppress homosexual content during the mid–twentieth century, see Earl O. Coon, "Homosexuality in the News," *Archives of Criminal Psychodynamics*, 1957, pp. 843–865.

7. John Crosby's radio column, New York *Herald-Tribune*, August 2, 1946, in John Crosby, *Out of the Blue* (New York: Simon and Schuster, 1952), p. 279.

8. "Queer People," *Newsweek*, October 10, 1949; Howard Whitman, "The Biggest Taboo," *Collier's*, February 1947. The supposedly liberal approach described in *Collier's* was still prevalent a decade later: see "Officials Urge Compulsory Care of Homosexuals," *The Ladder*, January 1959.

9. "Rough Frisco Cops Send Pinched Boys to Women's Court," *Variety*, May 30,

1933; George Chauncey, *Gay New York* (New York: BasicBooks, 1994), p. 321; NBC Radio, *Flywheel, Shyster and Flywheel,* May 22, 1933; NBC Radio, *The Rudy Vallee Show,* November 9, 1933.

10. NBC Radio, *The Jack Benny Program,* November 27, 1939.

11. *Radioland* quotation per John Dunning, *On the Air* (New York: Oxford University Press, 1998), p. 474. Description of Clarence is based on listening to the following *Myrt and Marge* episodes. CBS episodes: January 25, 1937; February 2, 1937; February 4, 1937; September 21, 1939. First-run syndication episodes: April 2, 1946 (ep. 2); April 3, 1946 (ep. 3); April 4, 1946 (ep. 4).

12. CBS Radio, *Suspense,* January 10, 1948, "The Kandy Tooth Caper." This show brings back characters from Dashiell Hammett's original Sam Spade novel, *The Maltese Falcon,* in which most of the villains were homosexual men. In this radio sequel (not written by Hammett), Casper Gutman and Joel Cairo are clearly a couple.

13. Dozens of these one- or two-line gags showed up in prime-time comedy and variety series from 1948 to 1950. For examples from fall of 1948, hear NBC Radio, *The Phil Harris–Alice Faye Show,* October 3, 1948; NBC Radio, *The Jack Benny Program,* November 14, 1948; and NBC Radio, *The Burns and Allen Show,* November 18, 1948.

14. *Burns and Allen,* November 18, 1948.

15. NBC Radio, *The Phil Harris–Alice Faye Show,* November 27 and December 4, 1949. On *Fibber McGee and Molly*, Sweetie-Face Wimple was an off-stage character who regularly beat up her henpecked husband, Wallace "Wimp" Wimple. Wallace describes these incidents in dozens of episodes from the early and mid 1940s.

16. Lee Israel, *Miss Tallulah Bankhead* (New York: G.B. Putnam's Sons, 1972), pp. 227, 271, and 306. NBC Radio, *The Big Show* episodes from 1951: February 18, February 25, April 22, May 6.

17. Mutual Radio, *Drama Critics' Award Special,* April 4, 1948, "A Streetcar Named Desire."

18. NBC Radio—West Coast only, *Candy Matson,* October 9, 1950, "The Fort Ord Story" (aka "Murder in F-Sharp"); Dunning, *Tune in Yesterday,* p. 113.

19. CBS Radio, *The Bing Crosby Show,* October 11 and October 18, 1950, both shows with guests Bob Hope and Judy Garland. For a description of how gay dance clubs used the warning system alluded to in the show, see the interview with John Rechy in David Ehrenstein, *Open Secret* (New York: William Morrow and Company, 1998), pp. 54–55.

20. Mutual Radio, *The Black Museum,* 1952, "The Brass Button." Originally beamed to England via Radio Luxembourg, circa 1951.

CHAPTER 2

1. *The Television Code,* 2nd ed. (Washington, D.C.: The National Association of Radio and Television Broadcasters, 1954).

2. Milt Josefsberg, *The Jack Benny Show* (New Rochelle, NY: Arlington House, 1977), p. 355. By the mid 1950s, scandal magazines like *Tip Off* were running articles about what some called "the lavender casting couch." For a discussion and a sample article, see Martin Bauml Duberman, *About Time* (New York: SeaHorse, 1986), pp. 187–190.

3. This scripting practice is rooted in the *Television Code* requirement that "Divorce is not treated casually nor justified as a solution for marital problems."

4. The premise turns up on numerous domestic sitcoms of the 1950s. The most famous example is CBS-TV's *I Love Lucy,* September 15, 1952, "Job Switching."

5. See title changes documented throughout Tim Brooks and Earle Marsh, *The Complete Directory to Prime Time Network and Cable TV Shows, 1946–Present* (New York: Ballantine, 1995) and Alex McNeil, *Total Television* (New York: Penguin Books, 1991).

6. *Guiding Light* gag recording in SPERDVAC Archives.

7. "Gorgeous George is Dead at 48," *New York Times,* December 27, 1963; Joe Jares, *Whatever Happened to Gorgeous George?* (New York: Tempo/Grosset & Dunlap, 1974), p. 19; T. Perew, "Gays on TV Not the Real Thing," *The Advocate,* May 8, 1974; *Gorgeous George vs. Ilio DiPaolo,* ca. 1949, broadcast recording released on VHS by Worldwide Entertainment Marketing/BMG Music in their *Wrestling Classics* series, 1991.

8. Jares, p. 29.

9. Arthur Guy Matthews, *Is Homosexuality a Menace?* (New York: Robert M. McBride Company, 1957), p. 228. Matthews paints homosexuals as cruel, psychopathic criminals who molest children. He advocates medical treatment for this presumed illness.

10. NBC-TV, *Private Secretary* (aka *Susie*), April 5, 1953. For examples of the early-twentieth-century cartoons alluded to in the text, see Jonathan Ned Katz, *Gay/Lesbian Almanac* (New York: Harper & Row, 1983), p. 316.

11. Review by Sid Shalit, New York *Daily News,* November 14, 1954; caption on an NBC promotional photo for Kovacs's TV series (circa 1952), in Theater Collection, Free Library of Philadelphia; NBC-TV, *The NBC Comedy Hour,* January 15, 1956; NBC-TV, *The Ernie Kovacs Show,* July 9, 1956; ABC-TV, *Take a Good Look,* 1960 (undated recording released on VHS by Video Yesteryear).

Given current knowledge about Rock Hudson's sexual orientation, it may be tempting to read hidden meanings into the Rock Mississippi character. However, it is probably a straightforward parody: Rock Hudson was a symbol of virile manhood and Rock Mississippi was a spoof of effeminate actors—the exact opposite of Hudson as perceived in 1956.

12. NBC-TV, *The Steve Allen Show*, December 7, 1958.

CHAPTER 3

1. From Fannie Hurst's speech at the 1958 national convention of the Mattachine Society, quoted in "Mattachine Convention: Prognosis is Hopeful," *The Ladder*, October 1958.

2. CBS-TV, *The Jack Benny Show*, June 24, 1954, with guest Bob Hope.

3. "Perverts Called Government Peril," *New York Times*, April 19, 1950; "Wherry for Secrecy in Perversion Inquiry," *New York Times*, May 22, 1950; U.S. Senate, Committee on Expenditures in the Executive Departments, Subcommittee on Investigations, *Employment of Homosexuals and Other Sex Perverts in Government: Interim Report*, 1950.

4. Harry Hay founded the Mattachine Society in Los Angeles in 1950. "Mattachine" referred to a secret order of outlawed jester/dancers in medieval Europe. Those original Mattachines could tell unpleasant truths because they wore masks. The name was appropriate to Hay's secretive homosexual rights group: their message, too, was unpopular. In gay communities of the 1950s, "wearing the mask" was a common expression for being in the closet. Branch chapters soon opened in other major cities. The Mattachine Society published a magazine, *The Mattachine Review*, from 1955 to 1966.

Some members of a Mattachine discussion group founded the Los Angeles–based ONE, Inc. in 1952. Its initial purpose—to publish a gay news and literary magazine—soon expanded to include academic research into homosexuality. The group's academic branch, ONE Institute, continued to offer courses, seminars, and research facilities for more than forty years. Founder Dorr Legg remained ONE's director until his death in 1994. The group's principal publication was *ONE* magazine (1953–1969).

Del Martin and Phyllis Lyon founded the Daughters of Bilitis in San Francisco in 1955 to focus on the problems of the "variant" woman. DOB encouraged lesbians to try to blend into society until such time as the movement succeeded in lessening discrimination. The group's name refers to "The Songs of Bilitis," a narrative poem by Pierre Louÿs. The French poet originally claimed the work was by Bilitis, one of Sappho's contemporaries on Lesbos. The DOB published *The Ladder: A Lesbian Review* from 1956 to 1972.

5. A fascinating, often self-contradictory example of the print media's response

is Max Lerner's nine-article series, "Tragedy of the 'Gay,' " published in the *New York Post*, January 18–27, 1954.

6. KTTV-TV, Los Angeles, aired this *Confidential File* show on April 25, 1954. Quotations from the show are per audio excerpts in the 1985 documentary *Before Stonewall*. Other sources: "ONE Salutes Curtis White," *ONE*, May 1954; "Confidential File," *Daily Variety*, May 4, 1954; Curtis White [pseud.], letter to the editor, *ONE*, July 1954; Jack Gould, "TV: 'For Adults Only,' " *New York Times*, October 13, 1955; telephone interview with Jim Kepner, January 9, 1991; Edward Alwood, *Straight News* (New York: Columbia University Press, 1996), pp. 31, 43.

7. "Behind-Scenes at the Army–McCarthy Hearings," *TV Guide*, April 30, 1954; CBS-TV, *Army–McCarthy Hearings*, May 13 and June 14, 1954 (recordings in MTR). TV news footage of Joseph Welch's "fairy" comment appears in the 1968 documentary *Charge and Countercharge*.

8. NBC-TV, *Max Liebman Presents*, September 25, 1954, "Lady in the Dark"; Jerry Oppenheimer and Jack Vitek, *Idol: Rock Hudson* (New York: Villard Books, 1986), p. 41. After Hudson's death, Carpenter gave interviews about what it had been like to be a closeted gay actor in the 1950s. The hunting trip story is from such an interview: see Murray Dubin, "In Hollywood, Gays Remain in the Closet," *Philadelphia Inquirer*, August 11, 1985.

9. Jack Gould, "Tawdry Television," *New York Times*, February 3, 1957.

10. Regarding the Detroit and Los Angeles shows, see Rolland Howard, " 'Are Homosexuals Criminal?': Critique," *Mattachine Review*, October 1959; Sten Russell, "Crime Story," *The Ladder*, September 1958. The two main New York series that dealt repeatedly with gay issues, *Open Mind* and *Showcase*, are documented later in this chapter.

11. Regarding the *Confidential File* broadcast, see Gould, "TV: 'For Adults Only.' "

12. Sten Russell, "The Open Mind: A Review of Three Programs," *The Ladder*, November 1957; "Open Mind," *Variety*, August 8, 1956; interview with Richard Heffner, March 15, 1991. Information about tapes played at meetings comes from a 1965 mimeo packet, "Public Meetings Sponsored by the Mattachine Society Inc. of New York Since 1957," in MSNY Papers.

13. Lorrie Talbot and Anonymous, "A Daughter Watches T.V.," *The Ladder*, March 1958; "Mattachine Speaks Out on TV!" *New York Mattachine Newsletter*, April 1958; telephone interview with Del Martin and Phyllis Lyon, July 29, 1991. Hurst described the censorship and her reaction to it in her speech at the 1958 Mattachine convention, per the "Mattachine Convention" article cited earlier in this chapter.

14. "Mattachine Convention . . ."; "Calling Shots: Fannie Hurst Canceled from N.Y. TV Showcase," *Mattachine Review*, June 1959; T.S. [probably Tony

Segura, *Showcase*'s contact in MSNY], "Fannie Hurst's 'Showcase' Canceled," *New York Mattachine Newsletter,* June 1959. Correspondence documenting the proposed series of gay-themed *Showcase* broadcasts can be found in the MSNY Papers.

15. The Los Angeles County Medical Association, who served as the principal consultant for this series, reportedly vetoed a script about homosexuality circa spring 1955. Source: Dal McIntire, "Tangents," *ONE,* May 1955.

16. NBC-TV, *The Steve Allen Show,* April 26, 1959.

17. KFPA-FM in Berkeley first aired *The Homosexual in Our Society* on November 24, 1958. A transcript of the show appears in the July and August 1960 issues of *Mattachine Review.* Other sources: "Calling Shots: Broadcast Heard on West Coast," *Mattachine Review,* January 1959; "Awards to Pacifica Radio," in Pacifica Foundation press release, January 3, 1963, reprinted in U.S. Senate, Committee on the Judiciary, Subcommittee to Investigate the Administration of the Internal Security Act and Other Internal Security Laws, *Pacifica Foundation,* January 10, 1963, p. 70 ff. (*Pacifica Foundation Hearings* hereafter).

CHAPTER 4

1. Audio recording, Saturday evening session, National Planning Conference of Homophile Organizations, Kansas City, MO, February 1966, in Gittings/Lahusen Tapes.

2. For extensive mainstream press clippings about the 1959 San Francisco mayoral campaign, see the November 1959 issues of *The Ladder* and *Mattachine Review.* Regarding the university purges, see "Homosexual Crackdown of Dubious Value," *The Michigan Daily,* January 9, 1960 (reprinted in *Mattachine Review,* May 1960); "Homosexual Purges on at Two Universities," *Mattachine Review,* March 1960; "Michigan Campus Purge Felt With Added Fury," *Mattachine Review,* May 1960. For information on the New York bar closures, see "Here and There," *The Ladder,* May 1960.

3. ABC-TV, *Walt Disney Presents,* January 22, 1961, "Goofy's Salute to Father."

4. Those who are familiar with Warner Bros.' animated *Looney Tunes* and *Merrie Melodies* will recognize this standard cartoon scenario. For example, in "Ding Dog Daddy" (1942), one heterosexual male dog mistakenly kisses another. In response, they both spend several seconds spitting in disgust. Then the recipient of the kiss growls "Why you, why you . . . I'll break every bone in your body!" and attacks.

5. Florence Conrad, "Bergler on the Air," *The Ladder,* October 1961. The scientific community considered Edmund Bergler one of its leading researchers

into sexual deviance, and his works remain easy to find in libraries forty years later. For a sampling of his antigay theories, see Bergler's *1000 Homosexuals* (Paterson, NJ: Pageant, 1959).

6. Regarding televised comments from ONE founder Dorr Legg, see "Off the Cuff," *Variety*, March 6, 1963. Regarding the Mattachine Society of Washington and its president, Franklin Kameny: audiotape of Kameny's speech to the Columbia University Student Homophile League, 1967, and recordings of other Kameny speeches and interviews of the 1960s, in Gittings/Lahusen Tapes; interview with Barbara Gittings, January 6, 1991; correspondence and phone conversations with former Kameny protégé Jack Nichols, summer and fall 1991.

7. "The Dare of the Future," *The Ladder*, May 1962; interview with Gittings.

8. KQED-TV San Francisco first aired *The Rejected* on September 11, 1961. Historians' and KQED's attempts to locate a recording of the show have not yet succeeded.

9. John W. Reavis, Jr., "The Gay Ones," typewritten program proposal dated January 10, 1961, in MSNY papers. By the time Reavis wrote this revised proposal, the show's guests had been lined up and KQED-TV had apparently bought the idea. Reavis makes minor errors regarding the name of the Mattachine Society (he calls it the "Mattachine Committee") and regarding the cities in which the group was active. This suggests the work of an outsider just learning about the homophile movement. Also, homophile publications speak of him as they would about someone sympathetic from outside the movement.

10. "KQED (9) to Show *The Rejected*," *Mattachine Review*, September 1961: "Television Breakthrough Brings Favorable Comment," *Mattachine Review*, October 1961; "Breakthrough: When Will It Come?" *Mattachine Review*, April 1964. For sample mainstream reviews of *The Rejected*, see reprints in the October 1961 issues of *The Ladder* and *Mattachine Review*. Articles about the show appeared in *Variety*, *Life*, *TV Guide*'s California editions, and dozens of newspapers around the U.S.

11. John P. Leroy, "Blossoms on the Boob Tube," *Gay*, July 20, 1970. For general sources regarding Franklin Kameny, see note 6 above.

12. "Tapes Supplied to Other Stations in the United States in 1961 and 1962," exhibit dated April 1, 1963, in *Pacifica Foundation Hearings*, pp. 100–101; Dan Wakefield, "The Gay Crusader," *Nugget*, June 1963; Toby Marotta, *The Politics of Homosexuality* (Boston: Houghton Mifflin Company, 1981), p. 26; John D'Emilio, *Sexual Politics, Sexual Communities* (Chicago: University of Chicago Press, 1983), p. 125; interview with Randy Wicker, September 15, 1991. At the time of the WBAI show, "Randy Wicker" was the pseudonym of

Charles Hayden, Jr., whose father had asked him not to use his real name in the gay-rights movement. In 1967, he legally changed his name to Randolfe Hayden Wicker.

13. Jack O'Brien, "Jack O'Brien Says," New York *Journal-American*, July 9, 1962; "WBAI Gives Equal Time on Homosexual Issue," *Variety*, July 11, 1962; Milton Bracker, "Homosexuals Air Their Views Here," *New York Times*, July 16, 1962; Jack Gould, "Radio: Taboo is Broken," *New York Times*, July 16, 1962; "WBAI-FM Airs Problems of Homosexuals," New York *Herald-Tribune*, July 16, 1962; "Minority Listening," *Newsweek*, July 30, 1962; interview with Randy Wicker. For the serialized transcript of *Live and Let Live*, see *The Realist*, issues of August, September, and October 1962.

CHAPTER 5

1. L.E.E., "The Invisible Woman: Some Notes on Subversion," *The Ladder*, June 1965.

2. Interview with Martin and Lyon.

3. "Paul Coates Interviews," *The Ladder*, July 1962; interview with Martin and Lyon; interview with Gittings. Lyon recalled that after her first TV appearance, she returned to her office at the Glide Foundation. "The switchboard operator was going crazy. I got calls all day long from women" who had seen the show. According to Barbara Gittings, such responses were still common a decade later: for example, she received many dozens of phone calls from isolated lesbians around the country after she appeared on *The David Susskind Show* in 1972.

4. NBC-TV aired the *Eleventh Hour* episode "What Did She Mean By 'Good Luck'?" on November 13, 1963. Sources: television listings of that date in *TV Guide* and the *Philadelphia Inquirer*; Robin Richards, "Dramatic Arts," *The Ladder*, January 1964; entry for this series in Earl and Marsh; entry for this series in McNeil.

5. Reavis.

6. Hence the selection of a local chapter officer, self-employed "Terry," to appear on Paul Coates's show in 1962.

7. Interview with Martin and Lyon; informal conversations with several former DOB members from the eastern U.S. For a producer's perspective on more reasons why TV viewers rarely saw lesbians on-screen, see Reavis.

CHAPTER 6

1. Ken Worthy, *The New Homosexual Revolution* (New York: Imperial Books, 1965), p. 12. Worthy comments, "[Paar] was putting into words what has worried many TV executives for the past couple of years—there are too many homosexuals in TV." Worthy's book is one of the numerous pulp-paperback "exposés" about homosexuality published in the 1960s. Though it is hardly a scholarly volume, most of its facts check out. I particularly trust this quotation since Paar was making similar on-air cracks about "fairies" as late as 1973.

2. East Coast Homophile Organizations (ECHO) board meeting minutes, evening sessions of May 2 and July 18, 1964, in Way Archives; "That Was The Show That Wasn't," *Drum,* March 1965; Bill Greeley, "Tale of Two CBS Homo Shows," *Variety,* February 22, 1967; George Gent, "C.B.S. Reports on Homosexuals," *New York Times,* March 8, 1967.

3. ECHO board minutes, July 18, 1964; clipping from the New York *Herald-Tribune,* July 17, 1964, in "Les Crane" folder, Billy Rose Theater Collection, New York Public Library at Lincoln Center; untitled article encouraging members to write letters to *The Les Crane Show,* in the *Janus Society Newsletter,* December 1964, in Way Archives; "That Was The Show That Wasn't"; interview with Randy Wicker; George Gent, "Preminger Stops Film's Sale to TV," *New York Times,* May 10, 1965.

4. An example of the kissing/spitting gag can be found in the Fidel Castro skit, NBC-TV, *That Was the Week That Was,* January 31, 1964. Source: audio recording of that episode.

5. The radio documentary series *Homosexual: A New Minority* aired in Boston, New York, Philadelphia, San Francisco, Washington, D.C., and probably in other markets. In at least one city, Philadelphia, it was sponsored by the local Council of Churches. Sources: "Radio Series on Homosexuality," *The Ladder,* October 1965; recordings from this series in the Gittings/Lahusen Tapes.

6. "Homosexuals Picket in Nation's Capital," *The Ladder,* July 1965.

7. "Cross-Currents," *The Ladder,* September 1965.

8. The new trend in comedy from 1964 to 1967 was not a high priority for gay activists. In preparing this book, I read every television-related article in every issue of the homophile magazines *The Ladder, The Mattachine Review,* and *Drum,* and in most issues of *ONE* and *Tangents.* Only one article from that period even mentions TV humor. Nor was there any mention of it in the consulted correspondence, minutes, audiotapes, or newsletters of homophile groups from that era.

9. "Cross-Currents," *The Ladder,* September 1965; Joan Rivers on *The Hollywood Palace,* excerpted in ABC-TV, *Best of the Hollywood Palace,* November 25, 1992; interview with Gittings.

10. ABC-TV, *The Flying Nun,* January 23, 1969, "A Star is Reborn"; NBC-TV,

The Monkees, December 25, 1967, "Monkees Christmas Show"; CBS-TV, *The Munsters,* May 6, 1965, "Lily Munster, Girl Model"; CBS-TV, *The Dick Van Dyke Show,* May 26, 1965, "There's No Sale Like Wholesale." For examples of the frequent gay references on NBC-TV's *Get Smart* episodes, see two gags in "Island of the Darned" (November 26, 1966), and the "marriage policy" gag near the start of "Closely Watched Planes" (October 5, 1968).

11. S. Robert Lichter, Linda S. Lichter, Stanley Rothman, and Daniel Amundson, *Watching America* (New York: Prentice Hall Press, 1991), p. 6; S. Robert Lichter, Linda S. Lichter, and Stanley Rothman, *Prime Time* (Washington, D.C.: Regnery Publishing, 1994), p. 13; "Tangents," *ONE,* April 1965. CBS-TV originally aired the *Nurses* episode "Nurse is a Feminine Noun" on February 13, 1964. Plot summary per Bob Lamm, "The Nurses," *Journal of Popular Film and Television,* summer 1995.

CHAPTER 7

1. CBS-TV, *CBS Reports,* March 7, 1967, "The Homosexuals," recording in MTR.
2. George Gent, "C.B.S. Reports on Homosexuals," *New York Times,* March 8, 1967; C. A. Tripp, *The Homosexual Matrix,* 2nd ed. (New York: Meridian, 1987), p. 214–215; "That Was The Show That Wasn't"; Bill Greeley, "Tale of Two CBS Homo Shows," *Variety,* February 22, 1967.
3. "Madison Ave. Queens and the PTA," *The Ladder,* March 1966; Greeley; "Cross-Currents," *The Ladder,* January 1967.
4. Letter from Jack Nichols to the author, October 21, 1991; Alwood, pp. 73–74.
5. Tripp, pp. 196–197; Alwood, p. 74.
6. Susskind's view was that homosexuals were mentally ill, but deserved sympathy and tolerance rather than punishment and discrimination. Source: *Open End* (aka *The David Susskind Show*), circa February 1967, "Homosexuality," in Gittings/Lahusen Tapes. This syndicated talk series typically aired on NET stations.

CHAPTER 8

1. ABC-TV, *N.Y.P.D.,* September 5, 1967, "Shakedown."
2. Jose M. Ferrer, III, "Courage at Last—or Just Bleeps?" *Life,* April 12, 1968; NBC-TV, *Rowan and Martin's Laugh-In,* January 22, 1968, premiere; Dick Michaels, "The World is My Ashtray," *The Advocate,* June 1968. Like Gorgeous George before him, Tiny Tim made his fame by using an effeminate, seemingly gay persona. December 17, 1969, Tim made national headlines by marrying a woman, Miss Vicki, on Johnny Carson's *The Tonight Show.* The

much-hyped nuptials reportedly gave Carson his highest-rated broadcast to that date.

3. Based on my viewing roughly twenty *Laugh-In* tapes dating from 1968 to 1973. Some were complete broadcasts at MTR, and others were cut-down syndicated reruns. The episode with Carol Channing apparently first aired circa October 1969. The song "You Don't Have to be Happy to be Gay" appears on the phonograph album *Laugh-In '69* (Reprise Records, 1969).

4. Of these five shows, the only tapes I was able to locate were the *N.Y.P.D.* premiere and ABC's *Judd, for the Defense* episode "Weep the Hunter Home" (November 8, 1968). Regarding NET's *The Dwarfs*, see *Philadelphia Daughters of Bilitis Newsletter*, February 1968, in Way Archives. CBS's airing of *Advise and Consent* is mentioned in "The Issue," *Drum*, October 1967. For gay magazines' reactions to *N.Y.P.D.*, see Don Felton, "NYPD Hits Home," *The Advocate*, October 1967; Vern Niven, "Would You Believe? TV Takes an Honest Look at Homosexuality," *The Ladder*, November 1967.

5. *N.Y.P.D.*, "Shakedown." Episodes of *N.Y.P.D.* with incidental, implicitly gay characters include "The Boy Witness" (November 28, 1967) and "Night Watch" (January 21, 1969).

6. Quoted in Ronald Forsythe [pseud. of Donn Teal], "Why Can't 'We' Live Happily Ever After, Too?," *New York Times*, February 23, 1969. Crist participated in a panel discussion about homosexuality in cinema on the *Today* show of February 11, 1969 (per program description in Testing the Limits' NBC notes).

7. CBS-TV aired the *CBS Playhouse* drama "Secrets" on May 15, 1968. Sources: Bob Williams, "On the Air," *New York Post,* columns of May 16 and May 17, 1968; Ben Gross, "Some Homo Overtones in 'Secrets,' New TV Play," *New York Daily News*, May 16, 1968; Richard Engquist, letter to the editor, *New York Times*, May 26, 1968; John Marvin, "Homosexuality on TV," *QQ*, November 1972.

8. Often attributed to Rebecca West, this quotation gained currency again during the rise of the Women's Liberation Movement in the late 1960s and early 1970s.

9. ABC-TV, *N.Y.P.D.*, March 18, 1969, "Everybody Loved Him." NBC-TV aired *The Bold Ones* episode "The Lawyers: 'Shriek of Silence' " on November 30, 1969. Sources regarding this episode: *TV Guide* listings for that date; "Who Dunnit? One Guess . . .", *The Advocate*, July 8, 1970.

10. The movie industry's reduction of gay imagery to villains and victims is a central theme of Vito Russo's *The Celluloid Closet* (New York: Harper and Row, 1987). A classic example is the film *Lawrence of Arabia*, in which the hero was falsely heterosexualized but the villain remained homosexual.

11. U.S. House of Representatives, Committee on Interstate and Foreign Com-

merce, Subcommittee on Communications, *Sex and Violence on TV,* testimony of August 17, 1976. Vida's testimony is on pp. 248–251 of the transcript.

CHAPTER 9

1. "Here's What Bob Hope Said . . . ," *The Advocate,* January 6, 1971. A note identifies the article as a transcript from an audiotape of NBC's November 16, 1970 *Bob Hope Special.*
2. D'Emilio, p. 235.
3. "Cross-Currents," *The Ladder,* columns of April and June 1970; "Gays Picket ABC Station," *The Advocate,* March 1970; "r.i.p. offs," *Gay Sunshine,* August 1970.
4. Arthur Bell, *Dancing the Gay Lib Blues* (New York: Simon and Schuster, 1971), p. 31.
5. Bell, pp. 56–57. His detailed account is consistent with more fragmentary reports in other sources, including mainstream periodicals.
6. Bell, pp. 135–136; Dick Cavett and Christopher Porterfield, *Cavett* (New York: Harcourt Brace Jovanovich, 1974), p. 285. Regarding Mort Sahl's ongoing antigay tirades, see "Mort Sahl Sit-In," *Lesbian Tide,* May 1975; Ken Rothschild, "Viewpoint: Reacting to Mort Sahl's Fear of Gays," *The Blade,* March 1, 1979.
7. "CBS Producers Tell It Like It Will Be," *Variety,* March 11, 1970; Bill Davidson, "Next Week: Periateritis Nodosa," *TV Guide,* July 17, 1971; "New TV Must Be Willing to Mix Issues, Entertainment: ABC's Rule," *Variety,* May 13, 1970.
8. CBS-TV, *Medical Center,* September 23, 1970, "Undercurrent"; John Murphy, *Homosexual Liberation: A Personal View* (New York: Praeger, 1971), p. 168.
9. CBS-TV, *The Mary Tyler Moore Show,* October 31, 1970, "Toulouse-Lautrec Is One of My Favorite Artists."
10. NBC-TV, *NBC Nightly News,* November 13, 1970, quoted in the appendix to Timothy Cook, "Setting the Record Straight: The Construction of Homosexuality on Television News," a paper presented at the Outside/Inside conference of the Lesbian and Gay Studies Center, Yale University, October 1989. Per the subject index of the Vanderbilt Television News Archive, this broadcast and another report on the same story were the sole gay-themed items on *NBC Nightly News* in 1970.
11. Geoffrey Cowan, *See No Evil,* (New York, Simon and Schuster, 1979), p. 122.
12. Parker Tyler, *Screening the Sexes* (Garden City, NY: Anchor Books, 1973), pp. 189–190. The cited episode aired on NBC-TV October 19, 1970.
13. NBC-TV, *The Dean Martin Show,* December 31, 1970.

14. "Here's What Bob Hope Said . . ."; Jim Wilson, "Boycott Bob," *The Advocate,* December 9, 1970.

15. ABC aired this episode of *The Dick Cavett Show* on November 27, 1970. Sources: "Gays To Be on Cavett Show," *The Advocate,* November 25, 1970; Bell, pp. 135–137, 159–165; Donn Teal, *The Gay Militants* (New York: Stein and Day, 1971), pp. 271–272; Kay Tobin and Randy Wicker, *The Gay Crusaders* (New York: Paperback Library, 1972), pp. 192–194; Randolfe Wicker, "Threat of Zap Cows Cavett," *Gay,* November 23, 1970; Randolfe Wicker, "Dick Cavett Features Gay Activist and Mattachine Spokesmen," *Gay,* January 18, 1971. For local TV coverage of the *Harper's* zap that helped convince Cavett's staff to capitulate, see excerpt of WNEW-TV's *Metromedia News,* October 27, 1970, in the Wicker Tapes.

16. Cavett and Porterfield, p. 352; Bell, p. 165; Teal, p. 271.

17. Morgan Pinney, "Caution: Liberalism May Be Hazardous to Your Movement," *Gay Sunshine,* January 1971.

18. National Educational Television, *When This You See, Remember Me* (apparently released to NET stations on December 20, 1970), in MTR.

19. Publicity handbill transcribed in Bell, pp. 169–170.

CHAPTER 10

1. Quoted, among many other places, in Robert Andrews (ed.), *The Concise Columbia Dictionary of Quotations* (New York: Columbia University Press, 1989), p. 262.

2. Les Brown, "Update Television Morality: Bolder Themes Being Tackled," *Variety,* August 2, 1972.

3. NBC-TV, *Rowan and Martin's Laugh-In,* undated recording probably circa 1971; also, MTR recording of an episode labeled April 2, 1973 (though internal references in the show suggest a date closer to November 1972).

4. Richard Gollance, "Tab & Sympathy," *Out,* December 1973. (Not the same *Out* magazine as the one sold in the 1990s.)

5. CBS-TV, *All in the Family,* February 9, 1971, "Judging Books by Covers."

6. Quoted in Vince Waldron, *Classic Sitcoms* (New York: Macmillan, 1987), p. 185.

7. *Norman Lear Seminar* transcripts (New York: Museum of Broadcasting, 1986), pp. 67–68. I have altered the punctuation slightly to make the text easier to read.

8. CBS-TV, *All in the Family,* September 25, 1971, "Gloria Poses in the Nude." . . . Regarding Nixon's comment: Nick Thimmesch, "The Square is a Pretty Solid Shape," *McCall's,* August 1972; H. R. Haldeman, *The Haldeman*

Diaries, CD-ROM edition (Santa Monica, CA: Sony Imagesoft, 1994), entry for May 12, 1971.

9. By November 1971, *All in the Family* was near the top of the Nielsens. The lucrative merchandising tie-ins included a record album (which charted in *Cashbox* magazine's Top 100), a fan magazine, and cutout paper dolls. *All in the Family* also won four Emmys and much critical praise, making it attractive both financially and in terms of prestige. Source: "TV: Speaking About the Unspeakable," *Newsweek*, November 29, 1971.

10. ABC-TV, *Room 222*, December 3, 1971, "What Is A Man?", recording in MTR.

11. Telephone interview with Don Balluck, February 8, 1993.

12. Almost every review of this episode that I consulted, in both the gay and mainstream press, remarks that it leaves open the question of Howard's sexual orientation. After screening the episode, I agree that the ending is ambiguous.

13. ABC-TV, *Alexander: The Other Side of Dawn*, May 16, 1977, script in Annenberg Archive; CBS-TV, *Ellis Island*, November 1984, scripts in Annenberg Archive; CBS-TV, *The White Shadow*, January 27, 1979, "Just One of the Boys."

14. Harry Waters, "Blue-Collar Comedy," *Newsweek*, July 10, 1972; "The New Gay Life in TV," *Variety*, May 3, 1972.

15. "Swish Type in ABC's 'Corner Bar' Draws Heat from N.Y. Gay Alliance," *Variety*, July 12, 1972.

16. Les Brown, "Update Television Morality: Bolder Themes Being Tackled," *Variety*, August 2, 1972.

17. "The New Gay Life in TV," *Variety*, May 3, 1972.

18. Garry Marshall quoted in John Javna, *Cult TV* (New York: St. Martin's Press, 1985), p. 217. Marshall recounts the same story with greater detail, and summarizes the ABC market research, in his autobiography *Wake Me When It's Funny* (Holbrook, MA: Adams Publishing, 1995), pp. 127–128. Regarding the censored episodes of *The Odd Couple*, see untitled essay by Tony Randall in Rip Stock, *Odd Couple Mania* (New York: Ballantine, 1983), p. 20.

19. ABC-TV, *Owen Marshall, Counselor at Law*, September 14, 1972, "Words of Summer."

20. Telephone interview with Edward DeBlasio, June 3, 1997.

21. "Owen Marshall, Counselor at Law," *Variety*, September 20, 1972.

22. During my lectures, numerous gay women in the audiences have recalled that lesbian activists were enthusiastically pleased by the *Owen Marshall* episode and felt that television needed more portrayals like Meg.

23. ABC-TV, *That Certain Summer*, November 1, 1972.

24. Leo Skir, "Scott Jacoby Talks to *Gay*," *Gay*, December 11, 1972.

25. Brown, "Update Television Morality . . ."; "Schwartz on 'Progressive' TV," *Variety,* May 30, 1973.

26. Regarding *That Certain Summer's* origins, the screenwriters' interaction with ABC management, and the demands of ABC censors, see Richard Levinson and William Link, *Stay Tuned* (New York: St. Martin's Press, 1981), pp. 107–123.

27. ABC-TV, *Dan August,* January 28, 1971, "Dead Witness to a Killing."

28. Dennis Washburn, " 'Consenting Adult' About Family Crisis," *Birmingham News,* February 3, 1985.

29. Levinson and Link, pp. 131–132; "Atlanta TVer in 'Homo' Pic Shift," *Variety,* November 1, 1972.

30. "Gay Activists Weigh In with More Cons Than Pros for ABC's 'Summer,' " *Variety,* November 1, 1972.

31. "Homo Segs Draw . . ."

32. PBS, *An American Family,* January 11 to March 29, 1973.

33. Technically an *eleven*-hour exercise in voyeurism: the twelve episodes each run about fifty-five minutes.

34. Sources (in addition to the series itself): Stephanie Harrington, "An American Family Lives Its Life on TV," *New York Times,* January 7, 1973; Jean M. White, "Preview: 'An American Family,' " *Washington Post,* January 11, 1973; "PBS 'Family' Very Loud in Boston," *Variety,* February 7, 1973; Frank Rich, "The Gay Decades," *Esquire,* November 1987; Gene Seymour, "When a Family Had It All," New York *Newsday,* December 23, 1990; Amy Taubin, "America's Saddest Home Video," *Village Voice,* December 25, 1990; Lance Loud, "20 Years Louder," *American Film,* January 1991.

CHAPTER 11

1. Telephone interview with Ginny Vida, August 26, 1991.

2. Letter from Bruce Voeller to networks' broadcast-standards senior executives, excerpted in "Gays Seek Powwow with Webs," *Variety,* January 31, 1973.

3. "Gay Activists Alliance Hits 'Homosexual Humor' on Johnny Carson's Show," *Variety,* September 29, 1971; "GAA Starts Campaign Against Carson's Fag Jokes," *The Advocate,* October 27, 1971; letter from Guy Charles (GAA News and Media Relations Committee Chairperson), to Fred de Cordova, October 5, 1971, in GAA Papers.

4. Bruce Voeller, letter to the editor (and editor's footnote), *New York Times,* February 25, 1973; Nicholas von Hoffman, "Newest Cause," *Washington Post,* March 16, 1973; Worthy, p. 12; letter from Bruce Voeller to Jack Paar, quoted in "Gay Activists Rap Paar's Homo Jokes," *Variety,* January 24, 1973.

A partial videotape of GAA's *Jack Paar Tonite* appearance is in the Wicker Tapes. Regarding that broadcast, see von Hoffman, "Newest Cause"; Lige Clarke and Jack Nichols, "The Jack Paar Fiasco," *Gay,* April 9, 1973; "Politicians Make Paar Keep His Word," *Gay,* April 9, 1973.

5. Letter from Bruce Voeller to Dick Cavett, summarized and excerpted in "Gay Activists Rap . . ."
6. For mentions of Perry's and Gruber's media advocacy, see "Perry Lashes at 'Defaming' CBS Show," *The Advocate,* January 17, 1973; Randy Wicker and Martin St. John, "TV Show Sets Off Storm," *The Advocate,* March 14, 1973.
7. Levinson and Link, p. 188.
8. "Out of the Closet," *Time,* March 5, 1973; Wicker and St. John.
9. January 1973 letter from GAA to ABC, quoted in John J. O'Connor, "Pressure Groups are Increasingly Putting the Heat on TV," *New York Times,* October 6, 1974. (O'Connor mistakenly identifies the letter's source as the National Gay Task Force, which had not yet split off from GAA in early 1973.)
10. "ABC-TV Weighs a 'Welby' Change on Plea of 'Gays,' " *Variety,* February 14, 1973. The averted suicide is probably the one described in a letter from a psychiatrist, excerpted in Levinson and Link, p. 136.
11. Interview with Bill Bahlman, September 21, 1991; Wicker and St. John. For extensive video footage of a GAA zap from this era (including a similar switchboard takeover), see GAA's 1971 Manhattan Cable documentary, *Gay Activists Alliance New York Marriage License Bureau Zap,* in Wicker Tapes.
12. "Gays Call Marcus Welby 'Sick,' " *Lesbian Tide,* March 1973; Wicker and St. John.
13. "Gay Activists Win ABC Concessions," *New York Times,* February 21, 1973; Wicker and St. John; *Sex and Violence on TV,* p. 255.
14. Segal kept scrapbooks of his voluminous press coverage. He kindly gave me access to these in 1990.
15. Interview with Mark Segal, December 13, 1990; "TV Roundup: It's a Washout for Gay Activist" (unidentified article in Segal scrapbook); "A Segal Lock or How Taping Can Turn into Gay Time for Carson," *Variety,* March 14, 1973; "Tonight Show Zapped by Gay Raider," *The Advocate,* March 28, 1973; "Appointment 'Cancelled': 2 Gays Arrested at NBC-Burbank," *The Advocate,* April 11, 1973; "Of Human Bondage," *Philadelphia Magazine,* June 1973; " 'Raider' Hits Mike Douglas Show," *Gay,* June 18, 1973.
16. Randy Wicker, "The Wicker Report," *Gay,* May 7, 1973.
17. Ralph Blumenthal, "Homosexual Civil-Rights Group is Announced by Ex–City Aide," *New York Times,* October 16, 1973; Les Brown, "NBC Acts After Complaints by Homosexual Organizations," *New York Times,*

October 27, 1973; Marotta, pp. 320–321; Eric Marcus, *Making History* (New York: HarperCollins, 1992), pp. 211, 269; Charles Kaiser, *The Gay Metropolis, 1940–1996* (Boston: Houghton Mifflin Company, 1997), pp. 261–262.

18. "Gay Philadelphian Invades 'Today' Set," *Philadelphia Inquirer,* October 27, 1973; "Gay Protester Disrupts 'Today Show,'" (undated Associated Press article in Segal scrapbook); "NBC's Detente with a Homo Org After Gay Guerilla Fuss," *Variety,* October 31, 1973; Les Brown, "NBC Acts After Complaints by Homosexual Organizations," *New York Times,* October 27, 1973. The episodes of NBC-TV's *Sanford and Son* that triggered the protests were "The Piano Movers" (April 14, 1972) and "Lamont . . . Is That You?" (October 19, 1973).

CHAPTER 12

1. E. M. Forster, "Terminal Note" to *Maurice* (New York: W. W. Norton & Company, 1993), p. 255.

2. For example: Ginny Vida, "Editor's Note," *It's Time* (newsletter of the National Gay Task Force), April 1976.

3. Ron Gold, "Gays and Public Relations," *It's Time,* May 1974.

4. Gregg Kilday, "Gays Lobby for a New Media Image," *Los Angeles Times,* December 10, 1973; telephone interview with Jim Kepner, January 9, 1991; numerous documents in GMTF Records. For a more radical attendee's view of this planning meeting, see "Gay Media Task Force," *Gay Sunshine,* January 1974.

5. "Some General Principles for Motion Picture and Television Treatment of Homosexuality," mimeographed handout given to NBC executives by a coalition of gay organizations at meetings in November 1974 (in Gay Media Project Papers, PLGTF). The identical document can also be found in "Gay Media Task Force Platform," *Lesbian Tide,* January 1974.

6. Newton Deiter, "West Coast Media Group Plays Vital Role," *It's Time,* April 1976.

7. Kilday; Doug Sarff, "Gays Gain Reverse of 'Police Story' Script," *The Advocate,* January 2, 1974; Rita A. Goldberger, "Media Accepts Gay Demands," *Lesbian Tide,* January 1974.

8. Sarff; Goldberger.

9. NBC-TV, *Police Story,* February 12, 1974, "The Ripper."

10. Interview with Vida.

11. "Lesbians Zap Cavett Show," *The Advocate,* January 2, 1974.

12. "Lesbians Zap . . ."; "Flowers of Evil," *Lesbian Tide,* January 1975.

13. Per a CBS News spokesperson quoted in " 'Gay Raiders' Invade Cronkite

News Show," *New York Times,* December 12, 1973. Date of the call is mentioned in Bob Williams and Mel Juffe, "Gays Raid Cronkite's TV News," *New York Post* December 12, 1973.

14. CBS-TV, *The CBS Evening News with Walter Cronkite,* December 11, 1973, recording in the Vanderbilt Television News Archive, Vanderbilt University, Nashville, TN.

15. Joe Kennedy, "Smash! Bleep! Clean Up!: Gays Zap Network Center," *The Advocate,* April 10, 1974. A detailed, if solidly anti-NGTF, account of the protest and the related controversy can be found in an article by GAA cofounder Arthur Bell: "MASH in the Family," *Village Voice,* March 21, 1974.

16. Regarding the timing of the CBS commitment: "New C.B.S. Policy Announced," *Weekly Philadelphia Gayzette,* May 31, 1974.

CHAPTER 13

1. John Carmody, " 'Outrage'—and Outcry," *Washington Post,* October 8, 1974.

2. "Skedded 'Welby' Episode Triggers Pressures from Homosexual Org," *Variety,* August 14, 1974; O'Connor, "Pressure Groups . . ."

3. NBC-TV, *Police Woman,* November 8, 1974, "Flowers of Evil," recording in MTR; ABC-TV, *Harry O,* October 10, 1974, "Coinage of the Realm"; ABC-TV, *Marcus Welby, M.D.,* October 8, 1974, "The Outrage" (revised shooting script dated June 27, 1974, in Gay Media Project Papers, Way Archives); NBC-TV, *Born Innocent,* September 10, 1974; PBS, *Masterpiece Theatre,* "Upstairs, Downstairs: Rose's Pigeon," December 1, 1974 (first U.S. airing); ABC-TV, *The Streets of San Francisco,* October 3, 1974, "Mask of Death."

4. Montgomery, *Target: Prime Time,* pp. 80–81; Jeri Dilno, "Protest Building Over 'Welby' Episode," *Weekly Philadelphia Gayzette,* September 15, 1974; O'Connor, "Pressure Groups . . ."; Harry Langhorne, "ABC Plans to Air Marcus Welby Episode on Gay Rape," *Weekly Philadelphia Gayzette,* September 6, 1974; *Welby* script (which, judging from newspaper accounts of the script's evolution, seems to reflect the final revision).

5. O'Connor, "Pressure Groups . . ."

6. Dilno; Harry Langhorne, "ABC Offers 'Welby' to UHF Stations," *Weekly Philadelphia Gayzette,* October 4, 1974.

7. This is a common view expressed by advertising professionals. See, for example, comments from Richard Kostyra (ad executive with the renowned J. Walter Thompson agency) on ABC-TV, *Good Morning America,* October 22, 1991.

8. Untitled WPVI-TV news release, September 25, 1974 (photocopy distributed

as an insert to the *Weekly Philadelphia Gayzette*, September 27, 1974); Langhorne, "ABC Offers . . ."

9. "Mopery Episode on 'Welby' Cues Protests and Affil Defections," *Variety,* October 2, 1974; " 'Police Woman' Episode Withdrawn by NBC," *New York Times,* October 11, 1974; Les Brown, "3 Stations Reject 'Welby' Episode," *New York Times,* September 28, 1974; Montgomery, *Target: Prime Time,* pp. 83, 240; Carmody.

10. Loretta Lotman, "Media and the Message," *It's Time,* May 1975.

11. Quoted in Lichter, Lichter, and Rothman, p. 9.

12. Cecil Smith, "An Emasculated 'Flowers of Evil,' " *Los Angeles Times,* November 8, 1974.

CHAPTER 14

1. *Police Woman,* "Flowers of Evil."

2. Jeanne Cordova, "Community Plows Under 'Flowers of Evil,' " *Lesbian Tide,* January 1975.

3. " 'Police Woman' Episode Withdrawn . . ."; A. D. Murphy, "Gay Org's Protest Cues NBC's Postponement of Lesbian Episode," *Variety,* October 16, 1974; Smith, "An Emasculated 'Flowers of Evil' "; Harry Harris, "Lesbian Aspects Muted in 'Police Woman' Episode," *Philadelphia Inquirer,* November 7, 1974.

4. *Police Woman,* "Flowers of Evil" (final aired version at MTR); Don Shirley, "The Ins and Outs of 'Adult' Topics on TV," *Washington Post,* November 8, 1974; Harris; Smith, "An Emasculated 'Flowers of Evil' "; Murphy, "Gays Org's Protest . . ." Also of interest: an earlier "final draft" script of "Flowers of Evil" (then titled "The Golden Years"), dated August 21, 1974, in GMTF Records.

5. UPI article quoted in John Wiles, "Actress Asserts Lesbian Role Despite NBC Denial," *Weekly Philadelphia Gayzette,* November 8, 1974. "National Emergency Alert Network," National Gay Task Force *Action Alert,* January 31, 1975.

6. Cordova.

7. Regarding the November 15 meeting: "Top-Level NBC Meet," *The Advocate,* December 8, 1974; untitled NGTF news release dated November 15, 1974, with accompanying handouts and a list of the presented demands, at PLGTF; Kathryn Christine Montgomery, "Gay Activists and the Networks" (Ph.D. dissertation, UCLA, 1979), p. 111. The NGTF news release mistakenly lists Traviesas as a participant; per Montgomery's 1978 interview with him, he was slated to be there but deliberately did not attend out of a sense that the activists' anger was already unduly focused on him.

8. Regarding the sit-in and street protest: Les Brown, "NBC-TV Yields to Homosexuals Over Episode of 'Police Woman,'" *New York Times,* November 30, 1974; "Outraged Lesbians Zap NBC," *The Advocate,* December 18, 1974; "Community Plows Under 'Flowers of Evil' " (several articles under one title, including one by Jeanne Cordova, one by Karla Jay, and one by Gudrun Fonfa and Janie Elven), *Lesbian Tide,* January 1975; Montgomery, "Gay Activists and the Networks," pp. 109–113.

9. For ABC's agreement not to rerun "The Outrage": Gay Media Project (Philadelphia) meeting minutes, February 13, 1975, in Way Archives. For NBC's agreement not to rerun "Flowers of Evil": Brown, "NBC-TV Yields . . ."

10. Correspondence between Loretta Lotman and Newton Deiter, summer and fall 1975, in GMTF Records.

11. Letter from Ernest B. Goodman (vice president, MCA Television Limited) to Ginny Vida (media director, National Gay Task Force), December 19, 1975, in GMTF Records.

CHAPTER 15

1. Jim Wallis and Wes Michaelson, "The Plan to Save America: A Disclosure of an Alarming Political Initiative by the Evangelical Far Right," *Sojourners,* April 1976.

2. " 'Stop Immorality' Mail Campaign at NBC-TV," *Variety,* August 2, 1972; " 'Vocal' Minority as Bob Wood's Worry," *Variety,* October 17, 1973.

3. Montgomery, *Target: Prime Time,* p. 39; Levinson and Link, pp. 128–136; "Gay Activists Weigh In . . ."; "Evangelist On Warpath vs. TV," *Variety,* November 19, 1975; "Clean 'Cowboy' Still Feared," *Variety,* November 6, 1974.

4. ABC-TV, *Hot 1 Baltimore,* February 21, 1975, "George and Gordon," videotape in GMTF Records; "5 More ABC Affiliates Bolt 'Hot 1 Balt,' " *Variety,* February 5, 1975; Tom Shales, " 'HOT 1': When Less is More," *Washington Post,* February 21, 1975; "KETV and KLTV Check Out of ABC's 'Hot 1,' " *Variety,* February 26, 1975; John J. O'Connor, "When Frankness Deteriorates into Drivel," *New York Times,* March 2, 1975; Val Adams, "ABC Cool on 'Hot 1' Show," New York *Daily News,* April 24, 1975.

5. Wallis and Michaelson.

CHAPTER 16

1. Paul Molloy, "What To Do About Television Not Worth Watching," *PTA Magazine,* March 1973.

2. Bob Knight, "The New Season—What Is It?," *Variety*, September 27, 1972.

3. Joyce Brothers, "Needed: A Rating System to Guide Parents," *New York Times*, January 23, 1975.

4. " 'Vocal' Minority . . ."; "Public Not Averse to 'Hot Topic' TV," *Variety*, August 21, 1974.

5. Les Brown, "F.C.C. Chief Bids TV Adopt Joint Adult-Show Policy," *New York Times*, November 26, 1974; Larry Michie, "FCC Lays Down the Jaw on Network Sex," *Variety*, November 27, 1974; Les Brown, "TV Sex and Violence: New Move Highlights Problems," *New York Times*, November 28, 1974; Les Brown, "F.C.C. Asks Extension of TV Violence Deadline," *New York Times*, December 25, 1974.

6. Regarding adoption and vague definition of the Family Hour: "Code Board to Meet on Family TV Fare," *New York Times*, January 1, 1975; Les Brown, "ABC, Too, Adds 8–9 P.M. Family Hour," *New York Times*, January 9, 1975; Larry Michie, "TV Dilemma: What is 'Family Hour'?" *Variety*, January 15, 1975; Les Brown, "TV Designates 7–9 P.M. as 'Family Time,' " *New York Times*, April 10, 1975.

7. Cowan, pp. 144–157; Dave Kaufman, " 'Family' Restrictions Scare the 'Hell' Out of Producers," *Variety*, September 3, 1975; "Prostie on 'Barney'—With Disclaimer," *Variety*, November 19, 1975; Loretta Lotman, "Coasts United for Media Action," *It's Time*, August 1975; Sasha Gregory-Lewis, "Networks Have No Excuses Now," *The Advocate*, July 2, 1975; Gay Media Project minutes, August 28, 1975, at PLGTF.

8. Telephone interview with Danny Arnold, December 29, 1992. Arnold told *Variety*, "[ABC] approved the script. But the effeminate nature of the character was not apparent in the script. When they saw it on the screen they said 'no.' " (In Dave Kaufman, "Arnold's Complaint: Only Lear Can Get Controversy on the Air," *Variety*, December 18, 1974.)

9. Regarding *Barney Miller*: Cowan, pp. 145–149, 157. Regarding *Cabaret*: Leigh W. Rutledge, *The Gay Book of Lists* (Boston: Alyson Publications, 1987), p. 121.

10. "Gays Eye 'Family' Suit," *Variety*, June 9, 1976; *Sex and Violence on TV*, pp. 248–251.

11. Dave Kaufman, " 'Family Time' Not Intended as Children's Hour: ABC's Censor," *Variety*, October 15, 1975.

12. Robert Lindsey, "U.S. Judge Rules TV 'Family Hour' Constitutes Federal Censorship," *New York Times*, November 5, 1976; Bill Richards, " 'Family Hour': In the Networks' Court," *Washington Post*, November 5, 1976.

CHAPTER 17

1. Tom Shales, "Face It, This is the Year of the Gay on TV," *Washington Post,*
   September 30, 1976; Richard M. Levine, "How the Gay Lobby Has Changed
   Television" (second of two parts), *TV Guide,* June 6, 1981.
2. Cover story, *Newsweek,* October 25, 1976.
3. Regarding Sipple: David Gelman, "'Gays' and the Press," *Newsweek,*
   October 20, 1975; Fred Friendly, "Gays, Privacy and a Free Press," *Wash-
   ington Post,* April 8, 1990. Regarding talk shows: "David Kopay," *It's Time,*
   December 1976; *Tomorrow* summaries in Testing the Limits' NBC notes;
   Mary Lewis Coakley, *Rated X: The Moral Case Against TV,* (New Rochelle,
   NY: Arlington House, 1977), p. 219. Regarding network news: *ABC News
   Index, 1970–1985,* 2 vols., and accompanying microfiched transcripts (Wood-
   bridge, CT: Research Publications, 1990); Samuel T. Suratt, ed., *CBS News
   Index,* 1975 and 1976 vols., and accompanying microfiched transcripts (Glen
   Rock, NJ: Microfilming Corporation of America, 1976 and 1977); NBC news-
   cast summaries in Testing the Limits' NBC notes.
4. Regarding talk shows: "Gay Professionals on T.V.," *Lesbian Tide,* April 1974;
   Gay Media Project minutes, February 13, 1975, in Way Archives; Gifford Guy
   Gibson and Mary Jo Risher, *By Her Own Admission* (New York: Doubleday & Company, 1977), pp. 252–255; *Tomorrow* summaries in Testing the
   Limits' NBC notes. Regarding newscasts, see indices and transcript sources
   cited in note 3.
5. "A Sad Fad on Television," *The Phoenix Gazette,* October 4, 1976; Nicholas
   von Hoffman, "And Now, The Year of the Gay," *Washington Post,* Octo-
   ber 25, 1976. For examples of this gay would-be boyfriend plot, see CBS-TV,
   Alice, September 6, 1976, "Alice Gets a Pass"; NBC-TV, *The Practice,*
   October 22, 1976, "Helen's Beau"; ABC-TV, *Family,* September 28, 1976,
   "Rites of Friendship"; CBS-TV, *Phyllis,* November 1, 1976, "Out of the
   Closet."
6. *Snip* scripts in Annenberg Archive and in GMTF Records; videotape of the
   Snip episode "Out of the Closet and Into the Fire," in GMTF Records; Kay
   Gardella, "'Snip' Depicts Homosexual as Human, Not Stereotype," New
   York *Daily News,* June 30, 1976; Les Brown, "NBC's $6-Million 'Lay-Away
   Plan,'" *New York Times,* October 3, 1976; Jonathan Takiff, "Brenner Tallies
   111 'Tonights,'" Philadelphia *Daily News,* November 14, 1980.
7. ABC-TV, *The Nancy Walker Show,* scripts in Annenberg Archive; "Media
   Notes," *It's Time,* December 1976; CBS-TV, *All's Fair,* October 4, 1976,
   "Discovery Day," script in Annenberg Archive; syndicated TV, *Mary Hart-
   man, Mary Hartman,* miscellaneous episodes, 1976; CBS-TV, *Executive
   Suite,* December 6, 1976, "Re: The Sounds of Silence" and December 13,
   1976, "Re: What Are Patterns For?", scripts in Annenberg Archive; CBS-TV,

The American Parade, March 9, 1976, "Song of Myself," videotape in GMTF records. In the *American Parade* episode, the Whitman-Doyle relationship occupies a comparatively small portion of the show.

8. Donald E. Wildmon, *The Home Invaders,* (Wheaton, IL: Victor Books, 1985), p. 7; Coakley, p. 270; "And No One Turned to a Pillar of Salt," *Variety,* March 23, 1977; Donald Wildmon, interviewed in the Channel Four (England) documentary, *Damned in the U.S.A.,* 1991.

9. Regarding the *Good Housekeeping* poll, see M. Stanton Evans, "Anita Bryant's Right to Dissent," *Human Events,* January 21, 1978. Many thousands of news reports and features focused on Anita Bryant's antigay crusade, and dozens of these were consulted as background material for this chapter. However, much of the information can also be found in Bryant's own late-1977 memoir, *The Anita Bryant Story* (Old Tappan, NJ: Fleming H. Revell Company, 1977). Regarding her *PTL* and *700 Club* appearances, see pp. 42–43.

10. PBS, *The McNeil/Lehrer Report,* June 6, 1977; Tom Mathews, Tony Fuller, and Holly Camp, "Battle Over Gay Rights," *Newsweek,* June 6, 1977.

11. "Recruitment" rhetoric quoted in Bryant, p. 62; TV ad appears in *McNeil/Lehrer,* June 6, 1977.

12. NBC-TV, *Saturday Night Live,* April 9, 1977; Bryant, p. 36; NBC-TV, *Laugh-In '77,* September 5, 1977; CBS-TV, *The Carol Burnett Show,* November 5, 1977, script in Annenberg Archive; "Carol Burnett," Philadelphia *Gay News,* December 1977; CBS-TV, *Maude,* December 3, 1977, "The Gay Bar."

CHAPTER 18

1. "As We See It," *TV Guide,* December 17, 1977.

2. For instance, in the 1973 TV movie *Scream, Pretty Peggy,* Ted Bessell plays a queerish, cross-dressing, psychotic sculptor who is also his own insane, homicidal sister. On *The Streets of San Francisco's* "Mask of Death" (1974) a female impersonator with multiple personality disorder is a wild-eyed serial killer. In 1976, two years after *Police Woman* battled those lesbians who killed old ladies, she hunted down a young man in drag (John David Carson) who had the same hobby. Sources: NBC-TV, *The Alfred Hitchcock Hour,* February 15, 1965, "An Unlocked Window"; ABC-TV, *Scream, Pretty Peggy,* November 24, 1973; ABC-TV, *The Streets of San Francisco,* October 3, 1974, "Mask of Death"; NBC-TV, *Police Woman,* October 19, 1976, "Night of the Full Moon," summary per script in Annenberg Archive and an NBC photo caption in the files of Photofest, New York; ABC-TV, *Charlie's Angels,* February 14, 1981, "Angel on the Line," summary per TV listings and several

episode guides for this series; ABC-TV, *Starsky and Hutch,* October 15, 1977, "Death in a Different Place."

3. CBS-TV aired the *Medical Center* episode "Impasse" on October 1, 1973. Sources: *TV Guide* listing for that date; Richard Laermer, "The Televised Gay: How We're Pictured on the Tube," *The Advocate,* February 5, 1985; Ginny Vida, "The Lesbian Image in the Media," in Ginny Vida, ed., *Our Right to Love* (Englewood Cliffs, NJ: Prentice-Hall, 1978), p. 240.

4. NBC-TV broadcast the *Police Woman* episode "Trial by Prejudice" on October 12, 1976. Sources: handwritten notes in GMTF Records; plot summary in Testing the Limits' NBC notes.

5. Todd Gitlin, *Inside Prime Time* (New York: Pantheon Books, 1983), p. 261; Richard M. Levine, "How the Gay Lobby Has Changed Television" (first of two parts), *TV Guide,* May 30, 1981; ABC-TV, *Family,* November 1, 1977, "We Love You, Miss Jessup."

6. CBS-TV, *All in the Family,* September 29, 1975, "Archie the Hero"; CBS-TV, *All in the Family,* November 6, 1976, "Beverly Rides Again."

7. CBS-TV, *All in the Family,* October 9, 1977, "Cousin Liz."

8. CBS-TV, *All in the Family,* December 18, 1977, "Edith's Crisis of Faith—Part 1."

9. CBS-TV, *All in the Family,* December 25, 1977, "Edith's Crisis of Faith—Part 2."

CHAPTER 19

1. "ABC Fights for its 'Soap' Under Shower of Criticism," *Variety,* July 20, 1977.

2. Advance word on plots per Harry F. Waters, "99 and ⁴⁴⁄₁₀₀% Impure," *Newsweek,* June 13, 1977; Robert Scheer, "Censors May Wash 'Soap' of Its Taboo Sexual Topics," *New York Post,* June 29, 1977; Kay Gardella, "Will the Censor Say No Soap?" New York *Daily News,* July 10, 1977. One of the earliest public mentions of *Soap*—even before the pilot was produced—is in Sander Vanocur, " 'Soap' in ABC's Eye," *Washington Post,* November 3, 1976. The role of Jodie was already in place as "a homosexual who wants to have a sex-change operation."

3. Frank Beerman, "U.S. Catholic Hierarchy Hammers 'Soap,' " *Variety,* August 17, 1977.

4. Beerman; Les Brown, "TV: 4 Church Units Plan to Fight 'Soap,' " *New York Times,* August 31, 1977; Dwight Whitney, "How 'Soap' Survived the Uproar," *TV Guide,* November 26, 1977.

5. David MacDonald, " 'Soap' Washed Up," Philadelphia *Gay News,* July 1977.

6. Newton E. Deiter to Tom Kersey, May 17, 1977, letter in GMTF Records.

7. News release, International Union of Gay Athletes, in GMTF Records; " 'Soap'

Protest," *It's Time*, August 1977; Molly Selvin, "Somebody is Being Manipulated in the Big TV Flap Over 'Soap,'" *San Diego Union*, August 28, 1977.

8. ABC-TV, *Soap*, scripts in Annenberg Archive.

9. ABC memo to producer Paul Junger Witt, excerpted extensively in "How to Launder a TV Show: A Secret Memo," New York *Daily News*, July 10, 1977.

10. "'Soap' Protest," *It's Time*, August 1977.

11. Selvin; "Media Alert—'Soap,'" *NGTF Action Report*, August 1977; National Gay Task Force ad, *Variety*, September 7, 1977.

12. ABC-TV, *Soap*, episodes of September 13, 1977; September 20, 1977; September 27, 1977; October 4, 1977; November 8, 1977.

13. ABC-TV, *Soap*, episodes of October 4, 1977; November 22, 1977; November 29, 1977; December 6, 1977; January 10, 1978.

14. ABC-TV, *Soap*, episodes of February 21, 1978; September 14, 1978; March 20, 1980; March 27, 1980; November 12, 1980.

15. Kay Gardella, "Ritter Says His Series Doesn't Ridicule Gays," New York *Daily News*, August 1, 1977.

16. Lee Margulies, "'Hail to the Chief' Goes to a Quiet Death on ABC," *Los Angeles Times*, May 21, 1985.

17. Levine (part one).

CHAPTER 20

1. *All in the Family* episodes "Cousin Liz" and "Edith's Crisis of Faith"; CBS-TV, *WKRP in Cincinnati*, October 2, 1978, "Les on a Ledge"; *The White Shadow*, "Just One of the Boys"; ABC-TV, *Barney Miller*, September 13, 1979, "Inquisition"; ABC-TV, *Barney Miller*, January 24, 1980, "The Child Stealers"; CBS-TV, *Lou Grant*, September 17, 1979, "Cop"; *Starsky and Hutch*, "Death in a Different Place"; ABC-TV, *The Associates*, April 10, 1980, "The Censors"; ABC-TV, *A Question of Love*, November 26, 1978; NBC-TV, *Sergeant Matlovich vs. the U.S. Air Force*, August 21, 1978.

2. "1978: The Year in Review," photo caption, *It's Time*, January 1979; ABC-TV, *The Streets of San Francisco*, March 3, 1977, "Once a Con . . ."; Ginny Vida (media director, NGTF) to James Duffy (president, ABC Television), March 11, 1977, letter in GMTF Records.

3. Gibson and Risher; *A Purely Legal Matter*, script in GMTF Records; *A Question of Love* (broadcast recording).

4. *All in the Family*, "Cousin Liz"; NBC-TV, *Mulligan's Stew*, "Feet of Clay," first draft script in GMTF Records; *Family*, "We Love You, Miss Jessup"; WNET-TV New York (and possibly some other PBS stations), *Watch Your Mouth*, September 10, 1978, per plot summary in *TV Guide*; syndicated TV, *The Baxters*, October 1979, "Homosexual Teachers," per plot summaries

in UCLA Library catalog and in Don Leavitt, " 'The Baxters' Meet a Gay Teacher," *Washington Blade,* October 11, 1979.

5. ABC-TV, *The Streets of San Francisco,* February 10, 1977, "A Good Cop . . . But"; *Starsky and Hutch,* "Death in a Different Place"; CBS-TV, *Lou Grant,* September 17, 1979, "Cop"; CBS-TV, *Trapper John, M.D.,* November 11, 1981, "Straight and Narrow"; ABC-TV, *Barney Miller,* episodes: "Inquisition"; "The Child Stealers"; January 22, 1981, "Movie—Part 1."

6. *Starsky and Hutch,* "Death in a Different Place." The writing process was reconstructed by comparing the broadcast recording with notes in the GMTF Records and two versions of the script: the "work writers draft" dated April 11, 1977, in GMTF Records, and the revised final draft, dated August 22, 1977 (with revisions through August 29), in Annenberg Archive.

7. For example, on November 29, 1976, the producer of an NBC police drama wrote a scathing letter to the network's executives about an episode for which NBC wanted him to implement rewrites requested by GMTF. He said that the proposed changes had left the episode's gay bar scene "false and stilted," despite the best efforts of the episode's writer. The producer deleted the scene entirely, and recommended against the series' dealing with gay content in the future. ". . . for good or for ill," he wrote, "[NBC has] ceded at least a share of its authority in this area to an outside group." Letter in GMTF records.

8. Gitlin, pp. 260–261.

9. Cecil Smith, "Welcome Back, Komack," *Los Angeles Times,* July 19, 1976. Religious Right activists of the era picked up on Komack's comment and quoted it often. Even in the 1990s, it is still sometimes cited in tracts about the evils of gay-friendly TV shows. I first found it in the 1991 online edition of the American Life League's *Pro-Life Activist's Encyclopedia* (chapter 127, "The Media's Pro-Sodomite Bias").

10. Levine (part two).

11. ABC-TV, *Barney Miller* episodes: October 30, 1975, "Discovery"; "The Child Stealers"; "Inquisition." The "lisp" dialog is from Showtime cable, *Brothers,* July 30, 1984, pilot episode.

12. ABC-TV, *American Bandstand,* December 3, 1977, "Disco Day"; ABC-TV, *American Bandstand,* January 6, 1979, "Village People Day"; *Network Television Program Development 1979–1980,* Dancer-Fitzgerald-Sample, Inc., released ca. March 1979, p. 40; NBC-TV, *Saturday Night Live,* February 24, 1979, with host Kate Jackson. The Village People and Anita Bryant appeared in different taped segments of the same variety special, NBC's *The Sensational, Shocking, Wild, and Wacky Seventies,* aired January 4, 1980. After learning of the Village People's participation, Anita Bryant Ministries issued a written apology to its supporters.

13. "Beane's of Boston," *Variety,* May 16, 1979; "News Briefs—New York City," *The Advocate,* June 28, 1979; Lee Goldberg, *Unsold Television Pilots, 1955 through 1988,* (Jefferson, NC: McFarland, 1990), p. 291. Jeremy Lloyd, cowriter of the British *Are You Being Served?* and the *Beane's* pilot, had worked with Sues a decade earlier when they were both regulars on *Rowan and Martin's Laugh-In.* Lloyd has been quoted as saying that Sues played Mr. Humphreys in a Paul Lynde–like fashion, and was miscast (Adrian Rigelsford, Anthony Brown, and Geoff Tibballs, *Are You Being Served?: The Inside Story,* [San Francisco: KQED Books, 1995], p. 187).

14. Interview with Arnold; George Maksian, "Is Gay Sitcom Too Much for TV?" Philadelphia *Daily News,* April 8, 1980; Stuart D. Bykofsky, "Television: Touchy Subject," Philadelphia *Daily News,* July 29, 1980; "ABC Series Attacked in Christian Mailing," *The Advocate,* October 16, 1980; Kenneth R. Clark, "Preacher Unhappy Over Gay Sitcom," Philadelphia *Daily News,* December 3, 1980; "NBC Downplays Gay Angle on Fall Show," New York *Daily News,* May 4, 1981; "A Big Year for Gripes," *Washington Blade,* November 20, 1981.

15. *Network Television Program Development 1980–1981,* Dancer-Fitzgerald-Sample, Inc., released ca. March 1980, p. 10; Goldberg, p. 342.

16. Final revised shooting script for *Dynasty* pilot, in GMTF Records; *Network Television Program Development 1980–1981,* p. 38; Jostein Gripsrud, *The Dynasty Years* (London: Routledge, 1995), pp. 34–35; Joe Klein, "The Real Star of 'Dynasty': Esther Shapiro and Her Empire," *New York,* September 2, 1985.

17. *Network Television Program Development 1980–1981,* p. 31; *It Just So Happens,* final draft script in GMTF Records. A date stamp on the script's cover indicates that NBC Broadcast Standards received it June 3, 1980.

18. Goldberg, p. 342; Vincent Terrace, *The Complete Encyclopedia of Television Series, Pilots and Specials,* vol. 2 (New York: Zoetrope, 1985), p. 66.

19. Telephone interview with Gary Nardino, May 8, 1997; *Brothers* pilot episode (per Nardino, this was "exactly the Lloyd script" of 1980); Samir Hachem, "Breaking New Ground with Television's First Gay Sitcom 'Brothers'," *The Advocate,* July 24, 1984; Helen Newton, "Attention, America: *Brothers* is Coming Out of the Closet," *TV Guide,* May 10, 1986.

20. Gripsrud, p. 35; Gitlin, p. 140; Klein.

21. Allan Sloan and Anne Bagamery, "The Electronic Pulpit," *Forbes,* July 7, 1980.

22. Christopher Haun, E-mail to the author, June 5, 1997.

CHAPTER 21

1. Richard Erickson, "Jerry's Angels Tally TV Sins," San Antonio *Express-News,* June 26, 1981.

2. Ernest Holsendolph, "Religious Broadcasts Bring Rising Revenues and Create Rivalries," *New York Times,* December 2, 1979; Peter J. Schuyten, "RCA Deal on Satellite," *New York Times,* February 21, 1980 (plus correction to that article, published February 29, 1980). For a thoughtful history of Robertson's TV operation, see Stewart M. Hoover, *Mass Media Religion: The Social Sources of the Electronic Church* (Newbury Park, CA: Sage Publications, 1988), pp. 73–97.

3. Gerard Thomas Straub, *Salvation for Sale* (Buffalo, NY: Prometheus Books, 1986), p. 104; facsimile of the "Declaration" in Perry Deane Young, *God's Bullies* (New York: Holt, Rinehart, and Winston, 1982), p. 308.

4. NGTF finances per year-end financial statement mailed to the organization's members. Estimate of religious broadcasters' income per Sloan and Bagamery.

5. Razelle Frankl, *Televangelism* (Carbondale, IL: Southern Illinois University Press, 1987), pp. 114–115. In summer 1981, Frankl conducted a content analysis study of forty-eight series hosted by TV preachers. She found that ". . . opposition to homosexuality, was a specific coercive issue. While drug abuse, abortion, alcoholism, and life in the fast lane were all mentioned by the preachers, homosexuality was the most frequently cited moral issue during this period."

6. Falwell newsletter, quoted in "Fundamentalists Rev Up Lobbies," *The Advocate,* March 6, 1980; "Man of God Preaches Murder," *Washington Blade,* March 29, 1979; "FCC Rules Against Dallas Fundamentalist," *The Advocate,* May 15, 1980; Gordon Duggins, "Evangelist Robison Appeals FCC Pro-Station Ruling," Boston *Gay Community News,* May 17, 1980; Joe S. Maynor, "An Acid Test for the Fairness Doctrine," *TV Guide,* November 15, 1980; Steve Bruce, *Pray TV* (London: Routledge, 1990), pp. 47–48; David Morris, "FCC Refuses Robison Appeal," Boston *Gay Community News,* March 14, 1981.

7. Jerry Falwell, "Future-Word: An Agenda for the Eighties," in Jerry Falwell, ed., *The Fundamentalist Phenomenon* (Garden City, NY: Doubleday-Galilee, 1981), pp. 186–223.

8. Ben Stein, "Norman Lear vs. the Moral Majority: The War to Clean Up TV," *Saturday Review,* February 1981; Harry F. Waters, George Hackett, Jeff B. Copeland, and Jerry Buckley, "The New Right's TV Hit List," *Newsweek,* June 15, 1981.

9. ABC-TV, *Nightline,* May 29, 1981; Gitlin, p. 251; Tom Shales, "Television Boycott Dropped," *Washington Post,* June 30, 1981; Tom Shales, "PBS' 'Inside Story' on The Sins of Television," *Washington Post,* December 17, 1981.

10. LaHaye quoted in Stein; Gary Deeb, "Falwell: Norman Lear Sins Against the

Family," Philadelphia *Daily News,* October 28, 1981; "TV Programming Threatens Judeo-Christian Values: An Interview with Donald Wildmon, Crusader for Better TV," *Engage/Social Action,* December 1981.

11. See, for example, *Nightline,* May 29, 1981. That NBC and CBS executives joined their ABC counterparts on an ABC interview show suggests just how dire the situation must have seemed to them.

12. "NBC Downplays Gay Angle . . ."; Frank Swertlow, "TV Update: Gay Overtones in Randall Comedy Cause NBC Trouble," *TV Guide,* June 6, 1981; Gary Deeb, "Tinker May Let Sidney Out of the Closet," Philadelphia *Daily News,* August 28, 1981.

13. Kim Garfield, "Network TV Switches Channels: Tony Randall Talks About Playing a Gay Role," *The Advocate,* April 2, 1981.

14. Gary Deeb, "Tony's Back, in Gay Sitcom," Philadelphia *Daily News,* April 27, 1981.

15. NBC-TV, *Sidney Shorr: A Girl's Best Friend,* October 5, 1981.

16. Videoclip in *Nightline,* May 29, 1981.

17. Stuart D. Bykofsky, "What About Sidney? We Can't Be Shorr," Philadelphia *Daily News,* July 2, 1981; Stuart D. Bykofsky, "On TV," Philadelphia *Daily News,* July 3, 1981; Ed Bark, "What Show Needs is the Old Sidney," *Dallas Morning News,* October 28, 1981; NBC-TV, *Today,* June 2, 1981, videotape in GMTF Records; Carolyn Wyman, " 'Heartbeat' Character Reflects Change in TV's Attitude Toward Homosexuality," *New Haven Register,* December 19, 1988.

18. Bykofsky, "What About Sidney? . . ."; dialog quoted in Robert MacKenzie, "Review: Love, Sidney," *TV Guide,* December 12, 1981.

19. NBC-TV, *Love, Sidney,* spring 1983, "One is Enough."

20. NBC-TV, *Love, Sidney,* May 16, 1983, "Alison."

21. ABC-TV, *World News Tonight,* March 4, 1982; Peter J. Boyer and Betty Cuniberti, "Coalition Begins Holy War Against NBC, RCA," March 5, 1982; Shales, "PBS' 'Inside Story' . . ."; Miles Beller, "Is Wildmon's NBC Boycott a Success?" *Los Angeles Herald Examiner,* April 7, 1982.

Although some reporters cite the 1982 RCA profits as proof of the boycott's failure, the company's improved finances had more to do with RCA's 1981 losses from developing and trying to market the laser videodisc format than it had to do with any particular successes in 1982. Sources: Andrew Pollack, "RCA Rises 2.5%, Apple is Up 27.7%," *New York Times,* July 16, 1982; Philip Shenon, "Business Update: The Boycott Against RCA-NBC," *New York Times,* November 21, 1982.

CHAPTER 22

1. Urvashi Vaid, *Virtual Equality* (New York: Anchor Doubleday, 1995), p. 113.
2. For example: PBS, *Word Is Out*, October 10, 1978; ABC-TV, *ABC News Closeup*, December 18, 1979, "Homosexuals."
3. CBS-TV, *CBS Reports*, April 26, 1980, "Gay Power, Gay Politics."
4. ABC-TV, *Nightline*, September 29, 1982. Statistics on gay delegates per Virginia Apuzzo (of the Fund for Human Dignity and the National Gay Task Force), interviewed on that broadcast.
5. CBS News press release, April 11, 1980, "Emergence of Homosexual Power Chronicled in *CBS Reports*: 'Gay Power, Gay Politics,' Saturday, April 26."
6. Description of the *CBS Reports* show is based on a videotape of the documentary as broadcast. Analysis is based in part on Alfred's written complaint and CBS's official eleven-page response, both in PLGTF. The National News Council's official summary of findings appears in "Gay Complaint Against CBS Upheld in Part," *Columbia Journalism Review,* January 1981.
7. *Nightline*, September 29, 1982.
8. Hachem.
9. Several TV writers and producers interviewed for this book mentioned that series' two gay writers. The woman writer was one of the few lesbians active in AGLA. I have been unable to contact her to determine if she is "out" enough to be named here.
10. Interview with Nardino.
11. ABC-TV, *Taxi*, December 10, 1980, "Elaine's Strange Triangle."
12. Neil Feineman, "Videoland Gets Its First Real Gay Bar," *The Advocate*, April 2, 1981.
13. Telephone interview with former AGLA leader Joshua Schiowitz, April 29, 1997; David Colker, "Gay Artists Work to 'Sensitize' Media," *Los Angeles Herald Examiner*, September 19, 1983.
14. Interview with Schiowitz; Colker; "And the Winner Is . . ." (photo caption), *The Advocate*, November 11, 1982; Lichter, Lichter, Rothman, and Amundson, p. 37.
15. Colker.
16. Sexual-minority organizations change their names with bewildering regularity. In the 1980s, many groups faced the dilemma of whether to specifically mention lesbians in their name. Opponents held that the word "gay" included both men and women. They argued that saying "gay and lesbian" struck at the heart of gay unity. Proponents pointed out that in practice, "gay" groups often were male-only space, and that adding "lesbian" would explicitly state that women were welcome. More recently, similar debates have focused on the words "bisexual" and "transgendered."

17. Interview with Schiowitz; Marguerite J. Moritz, "American Television Discovers Gay Women," *Journal of Communication Inquiry,* summer 1989. For coverage of the final AGLA awards, see "Gay, Lesbian Artists Alliance Presents Media Awards," *Los Angeles Times,* April 25, 1988.

CHAPTER 23

1. Edward A. Harris, "Rock Hudson in Person," Everyday Magazine section of *The St. Louis Post-Dispatch,* October 30, 1955.
2. The main concepts in this paragraph come from Gripsrud, pp. 212–213.
3. Klein.
4. ABC-TV, *Dynasty* episodes: January 19, 1981, "The Honeymoon"; March 2, 1981, "Krystle's Lie"/"The Necklace" (2-hour special). NOTE: The writers of *Dynasty* did not begin giving the episodes descriptive titles until the second season. Instead, the first-season scripts are officially called "Dynasty I," "Dynasty II," and so on. Later, when the series was sold into syndication, titles were assigned retroactively to the first-season episodes. For ease of reference (and to simplify identification of reruns), I use these descriptive titles rather than the episode numbers.
5. Gail Shister, "Character Hasn't Gone Straight," *Philadelphia Inquirer,* March 16, 1984; Susan Stewart, "Latency Boy," Philadelphia *Daily News,* June 22, 1984; Aaron Spelling and Jefferson Graham, *Aaron Spelling: A Prime-Time Life* (New York: St. Martin's Press, 1996), p. 156; ABC-TV, *Dynasty,* February 23, 1981, "The Bordello."
6. ABC-TV, *Dynasty* episodes: February 2, 1981, "Fallon's Wedding"; "Krystle's Lie"/"The Necklace."
7. Interview with DeBlasio; Spelling and Graham, p. 156.
8. During *Soap*'s four-year run, Jodie was romantically involved with just one man: football quarterback Dennis (1977–78). After that, Jodie's romantic interests were legal assistant Carol (1978–79), his roommate Alice (a lesbian, 1979), and a detective named Maggie (1981). After an experiment with past-life regression, Jodie spends the series' final episodes stuck in the persona of an eighty-year-old straight man with a Yiddish accent. Despite Jodie's being almost exclusively heterosexual in practice, the show's dialog tags him as "gay" or "a homosexual."
9. Interview with DeBlasio. ABC-TV, *Dynasty* episodes: March 23, 1981, "The Separation"; January 20, 1982, "Sammy Jo and Steven Marry." The poetry scene presumably appears in "The Birthday Party," broadcast March 16, 1981.
10. Billy Crystal, interviewed in Mary Murphy, "I Felt a Lot of Rage," *TV Guide,* November 15, 1980. Passing references elsewhere suggest Crystal may have

discussed on TV talk shows the public harassment he experienced for playing a gay character on TV.

11. Vernon Scott, "First 'Gay' on Prime Time TV Speaks Out," *Philadelphia Daily News*, October 26, 1981. ABC-TV, *Dynasty* episodes: December 29, 1982, "The Locket"; February 16, 1983, "The Mirror."

12. Klein.

13. See documents in *Dynasty* folders, GMTF Records.

14. Esther Shapiro quoted in Klein.

15. ABC-TV, *Dynasty,* November 9, 1983, "Tender Comrades."

16. *Agnes Nixon Seminars at the Museum of Broadcasting,* (New York: Museum of Broadcasting, 1989), pp. 42–43. Transcript of a question-and-answer session held January 27, 1988.

17. ABC-TV, *All My Children,* scripts for episodes aired October through December 1983, Agnes Nixon Collection, Annenberg Archive; videotape of undated excerpts circa December 1983.

18. Gail Shister, "Her Lesbian Role is a First for the Soaps," *Philadelphia Inquirer,* November 3, 1983.

19. Hachem.

20. CBS-TV, *Scruples,* February 25–28, 1980; ABC-TV, *Paper Dolls,* May 5, 1982, per script in GMTF records; CBS-TV, *Bare Essence,* October 4–5, 1982, described in David A. Wyatt, "Gay/Lesbian/Bisexual Television Characters," 1996 (widely available on the Internet); CBS-TV, *Sins,* February 2–4, 1986.

21. ABC-TV, *The Making of a Male Model,* October 9, 1983. No recording was available. Information is based on the second draft script (titled *Male Model*) in GMTF Records. The script is accompanied by ABC censors' notes, which urge deletion of all gay content, citing its potentially offensive reliance on stereotypes.

22. CBS-TV aired the *Dallas* episode "Call Girl" on February 23, 1979. Sources: Larry Hagman and Mary Murphy, "So Long, Dallas," *TV Guide,* May 4, 1991; Bruce B. Morris, *Prime Time Network Serials* (Jefferson, N.C.: McFarland & Company), 1997, p. 78.

23. CBS-TV, *Jacqueline Susann's "Valley of the Dolls"—1981,* October 19–20, 1981. Much the same approach to lesbians, though not quite a story of wealth, appears in the 1980 TV movie *The Women's Room,* about 1970s feminism. Tovah Feldshuh very briefly appears as Iso, a lesbian whose lover leaves her to return to her husband (ABC-TV, *The Women's Room,* September 14, 1980).

24. ABC-TV, *Hotel.* Lesbian-themed episodes: November 23, 1983, "Faith, Hope and Charity"; an episode circa 1987, title unknown, described in Moritz. Gay male episodes: November 14, 1984, "Transitions"; October 2, 1985, "Rallying Cry"; January 22, 1986, "Scapegoats"; November 19, 1986, "Undercurrents"

(script and related correspondence in GMTF Records). Teen-mistaken-for-gay episode: February 1, 1984, "Mistaken Identities."

25. Box-office rankings per Art Murphy, *Art Murphy's 1982 Boxoffice Register* (Hollywood: Art Murphy's Boxoffice Register, 1990). The *20/20* ad is from ABC-TV, May 6, 1982.

CHAPTER 24

1. Vito Russo, "The Celluloid Closet" lecture at Swarthmore College, Swarthmore, PA, March 25, 1990.
2. HBO cable, *Eddie Murphy—Delirious*, October 15, 1983. NBC-TV, *Saturday Night Live* episodes: November 5, 1983; December 10, 1983.
3. Sources consulted: Compilation reel of *NBC Nightly News* reports about AIDS, in MTR. CBS-TV, *CBS Evening News:* December 10, 1982; February 26, 1983; April 15, 1983; May 18, 1983; August 6, 1983; August 30, 1983. CBS-TV, *CBS Morning News:* January 7, 1983; January 21, 1983. CBS-TV, *Morning:* May 17, 1983; May 19, 1983. CBS-TV, *Our Times with Bill Moyers,* July 26, 1983, audiotape in Tommi Avicolli Mecca Collection, Way Archives. ABC-TV, *World News Tonight* June 18, 1983. ABC-TV, *Nightline:* December 17, 1982; May 2, 1983. ABC-TV, *20/20,* May 26, 1983, "Deadly Blood." Syndicated TV, *Donahue,* July 13, 1983 (date varies by city), "AIDS," audiotape in Tommi Avicolli Mecca Collection, Way Archives.
4. Pat Buchanan, "AIDS Disease: It's Nature Striking Back," *New York Post,* May 24, 1983.
5. *Donahue,* "AIDS"; Sue Chastain, " 'Gay Plague' Has Instilled Fear of the Unknown," *Philadelphia Inquirer,* June 20, 1982.
6. Rich; interview with DeBlasio. Ed DeBlasio was in charge of *Dynasty's* dialog, originally writing it himself and later coordinating the work of staff writers and contractors. He was not involved in planning the show's story lines.
7. The earliest reference I could find to the HBO *Tales of the City* project is in George Heymont, "Future Access," *The Advocate,* September 16, 1982. HBO held the option through most of the 1980s, though the proposed thirteen-part series never came about. Sources: Betsy Sharkey, "Maupin's 'Dream of the Future, Set in the Past,' " *New York Times,* February 28, 1993; Luaine Lee, "Edgy 'Tales' Sequel Surfaces on Showtime," *Pittsburgh Post-Gazette,* June 6, 1998; John Lyttle, "No More Maupin Around," London *Independent*, September 27, 1993.
8. NBC-TV, *St. Elsewhere,* December 21, 1983, "AIDS and Comfort"; James Kinsella, *Covering the Plague* (New Brunswick, NJ: Rutgers University Press,

1989), p. 260. Per Kinsella, CNN's July 7, 1981 report on Kaposi's sarcoma marked the first time television mentioned the syndrome later known as AIDS.

9. Gerard J. Waggett, *The Soap Opera Book of Lists* (New York: Harper-Paperbacks, 1996), p. 33.

10. NBC-TV, *Celebrity*, February 12–14, 1984.

CHAPTER 25

1. Robert Lindsey, "The 'Law' According to Steven Bochco," *Boston Herald,* September 28, 1986.

2. Paul Kerr, "Drama at MTM: *Lou Grant* and *Hill Street*," in Jane Feuer, Paul Kerr, and Tise Vahimagi, eds., *MTM: "Quality Television"* (London: British Film Institute, 1984), p. 155; *St. Elsewhere* producer Bruce Paltrow, interviewed in PBS, *The MacNeil/Lehrer News Hour,* September 25, 1985; McNeil, p. 252.

3. For the history and evolution of this series, see Julie D'Acci, *Defining Women: Television and the Case of Cagney & Lacey* (Chapel Hill, NC: University of North Carolina Press, 1994). Other sources: Jay Arnold, "Nearly Doomed TV Show Rises from Ashes Minus Meg Foster," released by the Associated Press May 26, 1982; "TV Update: CBS Alters 'Cagney,' Calling It 'Too Women's Lib'," *TV Guide,* June 12, 1982.

4. CBS-TV aired the *Cagney & Lacey* episode "Conduct Unbecoming" on December 13, 1982. Sources: plot summaries in *TV Guide* and other TV listings for that date.

5. NBC-TV, *Hill Street Blues,* October 13, 1983, "Here's Adventure, Here's Romance . . ."

CHAPTER 26

1. From the headline of a *USA Today* article: Richard Laermer, "Prime Time Comes to Terms with Gay Roles in Fall Series," *USA Today,* May 30, 1984.

2. Richard Zoglin and Deborah Kaplan, "Troubles on the Home Front," *Time,* January 28, 1985.

3. In the 1983–84 season, for the first time, only *one* sitcom finished among the top fourteen Nielsen slots: CBS's *Kate and Allie* at No. 14. In 1984–85, there were three sitcoms in the top fourteen, and in 1985–86 there were seven.

4. Brandon Tartikoff on CBS-TV, *CBS Morning News,* June 1, 1984.

5. Margulies, " 'Hail to the Chief' . . ."

6. Laermer, "Prime Time Comes to Terms . . ." See also transcript of Newt

Deiter's appearance in a panel discussion about gay TV characters: syndicated TV, *Donahue*, September 18, 1984.

7. Regarding the PBS production: Alan M. Kriegsman, "Steambath: Sacrilege or Satire?" *Washington Post,* December 8, 1974. Regarding the Showtime series: Lee Winfrey, "A 'Steambath' Series Premieres on Cable," *Philadelphia Inquirer,* August 16, 1984; TV listings for *Steambath* in *TV Guide* and local newspapers.

8. Interview with Nardino.

9. ABC-TV, *The Love Boat,* November 8, 1980, "Strange Honeymoon," script in Annenberg Archive.

10. ABC-TV, *The Love Boat,* October 6, 1984, "Frat Brothers Forever" (broadcast recording); also script for that episode in Annenberg Archive.

11. "Grapevine: G(r)ay Power," *TV Guide,* September 1, 1984; NBC-TV, *Kate and Allie,* October 15, 1984, "The Landlady."

12. *Hotel,* "Transitions," summarized in Larry James Gianakos, *Television Drama Series Programming: A Comprehensive Chronicle, 1984–1986* (Metuchen, NJ: Scarecrow Press, 1992), p. 324; NBC-TV, *Night Court,* December 6, 1984, "The Blizzard." Sources for the *Hot Pursuit* episode: Alan Frutkin and Gerry Kroll, "Gays on the Tube," *The Advocate,* August 20, 1996; Stuart D. Bykofsky, "Trivial 'Pursuit' Problems Become Terminal," Philadelphia *Daily News,* December 21, 1984. (This episode may not have aired in the original network run.)

13. Gary Deeb, " 'Hill Street' Regaining Stability," *Lexington Herald-Leader,* October 25, 1984; NBC-TV, *St. Elsewhere,* November 28, 1984, "Girls Just Want to Have Fun."

14. *Ellis Island* dialog quoted in Lee Winfrey, "A TV Epic, An Actor's Farewell," *TV Week* insert of the *Philadelphia Inquirer,* November 11, 1984; overview of the show based on *Ellis Island* scripts in Annenberg Archive.

15. ABC-TV, *Consenting Adult,* February 4, 1985; Lee Margulies, " 'Consenting Adult' as Gay Son," *Los Angeles Times,* January 31, 1985; Mike Hughes, "Parent-Child Conflict No Stranger to Marlo," *Lansing State Journal.*

16. Rick Sefchik, "Generalities Flaw Film on Gays," *St. Paul Pioneer Press,* February 3, 1985; Margulies, " 'Consenting Adult' . . ."; Kim Garfield, " 'Consenting Adult' Up Close," *The Advocate,* February 5, 1985.

17. Lawrence Toppman, " 'Consenting Adult' Suffers from Predictability, Blandness," *Charlotte Observer,* February 4, 1985.

18. Nancy Pate, " 'Lesbian Nuns' Film Considered By ABC," *Lexington Herald-Leader,* July 16, 1985.

19. Richard Turner, "News Update: Gay Characters Almost Routine," *TV Guide,* April 28, 1984; Laermer, "Prime Time Comes to Terms . . ."

20. NBC-TV, *Sara* episodes from 1985: April 24 (Sara's cousin dates Marty); April 10 (Sara dates a shorter man); March 27, "27 Candles."

21. NBC-TV, *Hail to the Chief,* April 16, 1985, episode 2; Margulies, " 'Hail to the Chief' . . ."

22. Esther Shapiro quotation per Klein. ABC-TV, *Dynasty* episodes: December 5, 1984, "Krystina"; December 12, 1984, "Swept Away"; January 30, 1985, "Triangles"; March 6, 1985, "Parental Consent"; April 10, 1985, "Kidnapped"; May 15, 1985, "Royal Wedding"; October 2, 1985, "The Homecoming."

23. Forsythe.

CHAPTER 27

1. Gerald Wade, "Family Faces AIDS in NBC-TV Drama," *Omaha World Herald,* November 10, 1985.

2. Numbers were determined by looking up Nielsens for the forty-one AIDS-related comedy and drama broadcasts listed in my research database. Nielsens are per the *Philadelphia Inquirer*, which lists the ratings most weeks. *An Early Frost*'s national Nielsens were 23.3/33: just over twenty million viewers, constituting 33 percent of its time slot's viewership. In January 1995, an AIDS-related episode of NBC's *E.R.* finally topped *An Early Frost*'s ratings—and not by much.

3. Dorothy Storck, "AIDS: A Star Legitimizes It," *Philadelphia Inquirer,* July 28, 1985.

4. The *Trapper John, M.D.* episode aired November 10, 1985. Prior to that date, my research database shows one hundred twenty-one national newscasts, documentaries, and talk shows that focused on AIDS.

5. Showtime cable, *Brothers,* October 23, 1985, "The Stranger."

6. CBS-TV aired the *Trapper John, M.D.* episode "Friends and Lovers" on November 10, 1985. Sources: plot summaries in *TV Guide* and several newspapers' TV listings.

7. Rick DuBrow, "NBC Comes to Grips with AIDS in TV Movie," *Los Angeles Herald Examiner,* October 15, 1985; Jerry Buck, "Director Sought Drama on AIDS," *Lexington Herald-Leader,* November 10, 1985; Steve Sonsky, "AIDS Issue Gives TV a New Plot," *Miami Herald,* November 10, 1985; Jay Sharbutt, " 'Early Frost' a Dramatic Look at AIDS," *Los Angeles Times,* November 4, 1985.

8. Wade; Edward Guthmann, "TV's First Movie on the Dreaded AIDS," *San Francisco Chronicle,* November 10, 1985; John Kiesewetter, " 'Early Frost' Reflects Co-Author's Local Roots," *Cincinnati Enquirer,* November 11, 1985.

9. DuBrow; Barry Garron, "An Early Frost," *Kansas City Star*, November 10, 1985; Guthmann.

10. Sharbutt.

11. Moritz; Wade; Guthmann. Information about NBC's decision to move the film from its original airdate to November sweeps is per Vito Russo, quoted in Moritz.

12. Plot summary and quotation per NBC-TV, *An Early Frost*, November 11, 1985.

13. Wade.

14. Wade.

15. Sonsky; Guthmann.

CHAPTER 28

1. "Broadcasting AIDS Myths Rather Than Educating, TV Adds to the Confusion About the Risks of AIDS," *San Jose Mercury News*, December 14, 1988. The editorial asks why TV never depicts an inner-city, teenage drug user who thinks he is immune to HIV, but who gets AIDS from a needle and gives it to his girlfriend and their baby. The writer says that this scenario is far more common and more important to discuss.

2. Larry Gross, "Don't Ask, Don't Tell: Lesbian and Gay People in the Media," in Paul Martin Lester, ed., *Images that Injure* (Westport, CT: Praeger, 1996), p. 156.

3. ABC-TV aired the *Hotel* episode "Scapegoats" on January 22, 1986. Sources: production correspondence and draft materials in GMTF records; Fred Rothenberg, "AIDS Now a Hot Plot Topic on Prime Time," *Philadelphia Inquirer*, January 22, 1986; "As We See It," *TV Guide*, February 15, 1986.

4. NBC-TV, *St. Elsewhere*, episodes of January 29 and February 12, 1986; NBC-TV, *Hill Street Blues*, March 27, 1986, "Slum Enchanted Evening." NBC-TV, *L.A. Law* episodes from 1986: November 21, "The Venus Butterfly"; December 4, "Fry Me to the Moon"; December 11, "El Sid."

5. Regarding the CBS News zap, see Alwood, p. 238.

6. NBC-TV, *NBC Nightly News*, October 11, 1987, excerpt screened during a seminar about lesbian and gay TV images, Museum of Television and Radio, New York, June 16, 1994; ABC-TV, *Nightline*, October 12, 1987, "Gays and Equal Rights."

7. Mark Schwed, "Concern Over AIDS Results in Less TV Sex," *Philadelphia Inquirer*, June 29, 1987; John M. Wilson, "Putting AIDS in the Picture," *Philadelphia Inquirer*, October 18, 1987; Doug Hill, "Is TV Sex Getting Bolder?" *TV Guide*, August 8, 1987.

8. Regarding the Ray case, see Kinsella, pp. 193–203.

9. HBO cable, *HBO—On Location,* April 1987, "Sam Kinison: Breaking the Rules."

10. NBC-TV, *St. Elsewhere,* many episodes from the 1987–1988 season, including those of September 16, September 23, October 21, and October 28; CBS-TV, *Designing Women,* October 5, 1987, "Killing All the Right People"; ABC-TV, *Hooperman,* December 2, 1987, "Blues for Danny Welles."

11. Regarding her mother's illness and other background on this episode, see Lee Winfrey, "This Woman Has Four Women Speaking Her Mind Weekly on TV," *Philadelphia Inquirer,* February 13, 1989.

12. *Designing Women,* "Killing All the Right People."

13. Fox TV, *21 Jump Street,* November 8, 1987, "Honor Bound."

14. Fox TV, *21 Jump Street,* February 7, 1988, "A Big Disease with a Little Name."

15. Emile C. Netzhammer and Scott A. Shamp, "Guilt by Association: Homosexuality and AIDS on Prime-Time Television," in R. Jeffrey Ringer, ed., *Queer Words, Queer Images* (New York: New York University Press, 1994), p. 95; "AIDS Support Group Shuts Down TV Filming to Protest Episode," *San Jose Mercury News,* October 23, 1988; David Rosenthal, " 'Caller' Tries Treating AIDS One More Time," *San Jose Mercury News,* October 5, 1989; Lisa M. Krieger, "AIDSWEEK: A Reunion of ACT UP Activists," *San Francisco Examiner,* March 12, 1997; J. L. Pimsleur and Charles Burress, "New Rally Against AIDS Show," *San Francisco Chronicle,* October 26, 1988.

16. David N. Rosenthal, " 'Midnight Caller' Producers to Modify AIDS Episode," *San Jose Mercury News,* October 26, 1988; "AIDS Support Group . . ."; "Court Restricts Protesters of New TV Series," *Philadelphia Inquirer,* October 26, 1988; Marilyn Beck, "Protests Don't Upset 'Caller' Star," *San Jose Mercury News,* November 25, 1988; Pimsleur and Burress. Estimates of the number of protesters range from two hundred fifty to four hundred.

17. NBC-TV aired the *Midnight Caller* sequel episode, "Someone to Love," on November 7, 1989. Sources: Vito Russo, "Briefly Noted," *The Advocate,* September 26, 1989; Barbara Beck, "On 'Caller,' It's AIDS . . . Again," Philadelphia *Daily News,* November 7, 1989; Robert MacKenzie, "Review: Midnight Caller," *TV Guide,* March 31, 1990.

CHAPTER 29

1. ABC-TV, *The Women of Brewster Place,* second night, March 20, 1989.

2. *The Women of Brewster Place,* second night.

3. ABC-TV, *Brewster Place* promo, March 12, 1990.

4. CBS-TV, *Cage Without a Key,* March 14, 1975, described in various TV listings and in Ann Ominous, "Boob Tube Dykes," *Lesbian Tide,* May 1975;

NBC-TV, *Police Story,* January 25, 1977, "The Malflores," script in Annenberg Archive; CBS-TV, *The Jeffersons,* 1977, "Once a Friend"; NBC-TV, *Sanford Arms,* September 22, 1977, "Phil's Assertion School," script in GMTF Records.

5. NBC-TV, *Sanford,* date and title unknown; NBC-TV, *The Sophisticated Gents,* September 29 and October 1, 1981 (produced in 1979 as a series pilot); *Strike Force* premiere summarized in Bykofsky, "Violence Lives . . ." In the shows studied, the next example of a black gay character comes five years later in CBS-TV, *Sins,* February 2 to 4, 1986.

6. For example, judging from TV listings and from PBS program lists at PLGTF, most early discussions of black homosexuality on *Tony Brown's Journal* were in the context of AIDS.

7. Coretta Scott King publicly expressed her support for gay equality as early as 1983. Jesse Jackson spoke from the podium at the 1987 March on Washington, and has expressed support for the gay civil rights movement both before and since.

8. *Sins;* NBC-TV, *Hill Street Blues,* March 20, 1986, "Look Homeward, Ninja"; ABC-TV, *Hooperman,* various episodes, 1988–1989; NBC-TV, *Dear John,* February 16, 1989, "Stand By Your Man."

9. NBC-TV, *The Golden Girls,* November 10, 1986, "Isn't It Romantic?"; Moritz.

10. ABC-TV, *My Two Loves,* April 7, 1986; CBS-TV, *Second Serve,* May 13, 1986; NBC-TV, *L.A. Law,* September 13, 1986, pilot TV movie; NBC-TV, *L.A. Law,* "Those Lips, That Eye," October 3, 1986; *Taxi,* "Elaine's Strange Triangle"; CBS-TV, *WKRP in Cincinnati,* November 29, 1980, "Hotel Oceanview."

11. PBS, *Degrassi Junior High,* October 1987, "Rumor Has It."

12. *HBO Family Playhouse,* "The Truth About Alex."

13. *CBS Schoolbreak Special,* "What If I'm Gay?"; "Teen Special on Homosexuality Protested in Alabama," *Au Courant,* June 18, 1990.

14. CBS-TV, *The Twilight Zone,* February 21, 1986, "Dead Run." The gay man—along with a draft dodger, a school librarian who opposed censorship, and others—is wrongly sent to Hell by a new fundamentalist middle manager in the afterlife.

CHAPTER 30

1. Fox TV, *The Tracey Ullman Show,* April 28, 1990, "Her First Grownup."

2. NBC-TV, *Hill Street Blues,* March 13, 1986, "Jagga the Hunk."

3. NBC-TV aired the *Hill Street Blues* episodes "Wasted Weekend" and "The Cookie Crumbles" on January 13 and March 10, 1987, respectively.

Summaries per online *Hill Street Blues* episode guides by Donna LeMaster and Deborah Stevenson, confirmed against *TV Guide* listings.

4. Fox TV, *The Tracey Ullman Show* skits: May 17, 1987, "Francesca—A Girl's Life"; July 12, 1987, "Francesca's Choice"; October 11, 1987, "Francesca's First Job"; November 15, 1987, "Romantic Mommy"; May 1, 1988, "The Sleepover"; February 5, 1989, "Flesh and Desire"; April 28, 1990, "Her First Grownup."

5. Xavier Mayne [pseud. of Edward Irenaeus Prime Stevenson], *The Intersexes: A History of Simisexualism as a Problem in Social Life,* facsimile of the original 1908 edition (New York: Arno Press, 1975), p. 640. Description of *Hooperman* is based on my viewing a half dozen episodes during the original run.

6. Frank Broderick, "Tidbits," *Au Courant,* January 23, 1989; Carolyn Wyman, " 'Heartbeat' Character Reflects Change in TV's Attitude Toward Homosexuality," *New Haven Register,* December 19, 1988.

7. Wyman.

8. Lichter, Lichter, Rothman, and Amundson, p. 38.

9. ABC-TV, *Heartbeat,* April 20, 1988, "To Heal a Doctor."

10. Paraphrased from Marshall Herskovitz and Edward Zwick's introduction to the *thirtysomething* pilot script in *thirtysomething stories* (New York: Pocket Books, 1991), p. 3.

11. One of the show's detractors, quoted by Richard Kramer in his introduction to the script "Strangers" in *thirtysomething stories*, p. 291.

12. Gail Shister, "Casting Flash," *Philadelphia Inquirer,* September 10, 1988; Edward Guthmann, "Prime-Time Pillow Talk: Gay Characters Come of Age with the *thirtysomething* Generation," *The Advocate,* January 2, 1990.

13. Kramer, p. 295.

14. ABC-TV aired the *thirtysomething* episode "Trust Me" on January 3, 1989. Source: Guthmann.

15. Guthmann.

16. Guthmann.

17. ABC-TV, *thirtysomething*. Russell appears in the following episodes: "Trust Me" (January 3, 1989), "Success" (January 31, 1989—brief appearance), "Strangers" (November 7, 1989), "Pilgrims" (November 21, 1989), and "Happy New Year" (December 18, 1990).

18. Guthmann.

19. Script for this episode in *thirtysomething stories*; Jesse Green, "Day of the Locust," *Premiere,* February 1992.

20. CBS-TV, *Doctor, Doctor,* January 8, 1990, "Accentuate the Positive."

21. NBC-TV, *Hunter,* November 15, 1986, "From San Francisco with Love."

22. NBC-TV aired this *Unsub* episode in March or April 1989. No recording was

available for study. Sources: several unrelated viewers who gave me the same plot summary, and a GLAAD media release, "GLAAD Trade Ad Asks 'Where Are the Lesbian and Gay Characters This Season?' " October 1, 1990.

CHAPTER 31

1. Syndicated TV, *The Arsenio Hall Show*, circa May 1991; Otis Stuart, "Fierstein Carries the Torch," *OutWeek*, March 13, 1991. (Fierstein tells the same story in both interviews, with slightly different wording.)
2. *Action for Children's Television et al. v. Federal Communications Commission*, U.S. Court of Appeals, D.C. circuit, No. 88-1064, decided July 29, 1988. The same court reaffirmed the decision in a later case of the same name (No. 88-1916), decided May 17, 1991.
3. Regarding the initial round of staff reductions, see Gary Stern, "Network Cutbacks Mean Fewer Censors on the Job," *New York City Tribune*, February 26, 1987. During the March 2, 1989 broadcast of ABC-TV's *Nightline*, Jeff Greenfield reported, "In general, the number of censors at the three commercial broadcast networks is down by more than 50 percent in the last five years."
4. "A Mother Is Heard as Sponsors Abandon a Hit," *New York Times*, March 2, 1989; *Nightline*, March 2, 1989; Marc Gunther, "TV 'Decency' Activist's Efforts Worry Networks," *Phoenix Gazette*, June 10, 1989; "TV Sponsors Drop Programs," *The Fore Runner International*, June 1989; Barbara Beck, "Cleaning Up TV Boycott Planned," Philadelphia *Daily News*, July 18, 1989; Joe Maxwell, "Boycott Targets TV Sponsors," *Christianity Today*, August 18, 1989.
5. Marc Gunther, "Amateur Tube Censors: Last Year's Campaigns Have Lingering Effect," Philadelphia *Daily News*, January 30, 1990; "Slippery Sponsors," *GLAAD Bulletin*, March 1990; Vito Russo, "Briefly Noted," *The Advocate*, September 26, 1989; Brent Hartinger, "After Six Years, 'Band' Finally Ready to Play," *Southern Voice*, September 2, 1993.

An article by James Warren indicates that the NBC film about Hudson was still slated for production as of December 1989. The timing of this article and others about ABC's *Rock Hudson* suggests that NBC dropped its gay projects in January or February 1990. See James Warren, "When Private Lives Are Made Public on TV," *Philadelphia Inquirer*, December 31, 1989.

NBC-TV aired an edited version of HBO cable's *And The Band Played On* in 1994, more than four years after NBC dropped plans to produce the film. NBC's political concerns are evident when one compares the complete film to what NBC broadcast: the network cut almost all accusatory references to Ronald Reagan and his administration.

6. Gunther, "Amateur Tube Censors . . ."; Marc Gunther, "A Blurry Picture," *Detroit Free Press,* July 25, 1989.

7. Marc Gunther, "Nervous TV Advertisers Want a Little Less Bang for their Network Buck," *Detroit Free Press,* July 26, 1990; GLAAD/Los Angeles news release, "GLAAD Asks NBC to Reinstate 'AIDS' Episode: Cites Campaign by Anti-Gay Pressure Group," November 20, 1990; "NBC Stops Trying at 'Working It Out,' " *St. Louis Post-Dispatch,* December 11, 1990; Henry Yeager, "GLAAD Tidings" column, December 28, 1990 (downloaded from GLAAD-Net); Steve Weinstein, "Back Into the Closet," *Los Angeles Times,* April 7, 1991.

8. Weinstein; Mary Murphy, "It's an AIDS Drama—But the Main Event is Julie Andrews vs. Ann-Margret as Embattled Moms," *TV Guide,* May 18, 1991; Stuart.

9. "Hope on Anti-Gay/Lesbian Violence" and "Text of Bob Hope's Anti-Violence PSA," both in National *GLAAD Newsletter,* Winter 1989; GLAAD flyer circa 1989–1990, "Help Bob Hope Speak Out on Anti-Gay/Lesbian Violence!"; Victor F. Zonana, "Monitoring the Media, Activist Alliance Exercises Clout in Fighting Anti-Gay Images," *Los Angeles Times,* February 22, 1990.

10. CBS-TV aired *1989: A Year with Andy Rooney* on December 28, 1989. Sources for the discussion: Andrew Rooney and Stuart D. Bykofsky, "Andy Tells How He Differs from Archie," Philadelphia *Daily News,* August 26, 1980; letter from Stephen H. Miller (chair, GLAAD Media Committee) and Henry E. Scott (GLAAD Media Committee) to David Burke (president, CBS News), January 8, 1990, from a photocopy distributed at GLAAD outreach workshops in 1990; Gerry Yandel, "Gay Group Wants Andy Rooney Suspended from CBS Programs," *Atlanta Journal and Constitution,* January 26, 1990; signed, abridged version of Rooney's letter, dated January 30, 1990, faxed to GLAAD from CBS News' Northeast Bureau, from a photocopy distributed at GLAAD workshops in 1990; Michelangelo Signorile, "Gossip Watch: Zap CBS!", *OutWeek,* February 4, 1990; GLAAD news release, "Statement from GLAAD Regarding the Suspension of Andy Rooney," February 8, 1990; "Statement by David Burke, President of CBS News," released by CBS News on February 8, 1990; Jeremy Gerard, "CBS Gives Rooney a Three-Month Suspension for Remarks," *New York Times,* February 9, 1990; Chris Bull, "Andy, We Hardly Knew Ye" and Andrew A. Rooney, "Rooney's Letter to Gays," both in *The Advocate,* February 27, 1990 (distributed February 14); Jane Hall, "CBS Rescinds Suspension of Andy Rooney," *Los Angeles Times,* March 2, 1990; CBS-TV, *60 Minutes,* March 4, 1990; Arthur Unger, "Andy Rooney of *60 Minutes*," *Television Quarterly,* 1996 (undated issue, vol. 28, no. 3).

11. "GLAAD's Top 10 for '89," distributed by the Gay & Lesbian Alliance Against Defamation, circa early 1990; Rex Wockner, "Toys R Us Says It Meant No Offense to Gay Community," *Philadelphia Gay News,* February 2, 1990.

12. Cover story, *Journal of the American Family Association*, September 1990; "Bigots Hit Burgers," *GLAAD Bulletin*, November 1990; letter from Stephen H. Miller (chair, GLAAD/New York Media Committee) to Barry Gibbons (CEO, Burger King Corporation), November 8, 1990, electronic version downloaded from GLAAD-Net; Howard Rosenberg, "Burger King Bows to TV Watchdogs," *Los Angeles Times*, November 14, 1990; "Religious Group Calls Off Burger King Boycott," New York *Native*, November 19, 1990; GLAAD news release, "Burger King Ad Not Anti-Gay—Ad Policy Clarified," December 5, 1990; "Burger Chain Says 'No Offense' to Gays," *San Diego Union-Tribune*, December 10, 1990; "Rev. Wildmon Bites the Burger," *Extra!* (newsletter of the organization Fairness and Accuracy in Reporting), January 1991.

13. Jehan Agrama, "GLAAD/LA Landmarks and Successes," *GLAAD/LA Report* (fifth anniversary issue), October 1993. Per Karin Schwartz (ed.), "Items from the GLAAD Bag: Los Angeles," National *GLAAD Newsletter*, fall 1990, GLAAD/Los Angeles served as a consultant for the new NBC series *The Fanelli Boys* over the summer, before the premiere broadcast and before the GLAAD ads appeared in the trade papers. GLAAD convinced the producers to tone down some of the homophobic remarks made by the show's Italian American working class characters in several episodes, and reportedly won a partial refilming of the pilot.

14. In addition to the flagship GLAAD offices in New York and Los Angeles, there were chapters of varying sizes in Atlanta, Baltimore, Boston, Dallas, Central Florida, Houston, Orange County (California), Sacramento, San Francisco and the National Capital Area, and possibly in some other cities as well.

15. Peter Freiberg, "Longtime Activist Ellen Carton Takes Watchdog Leash," *Washington Blade,* August 30, 1991.

16. GLAAD-net was launched in 1990 through a $17,000 grant from the Paul Rapoport Foundation. Since home use of the Internet had yet to catch on, this was a Bulletin Board System (BBS) running on a small computer in the San Francisco area. It was accessible through a direct (usually long-distance) dial-up, or in "echoed" form through an informal network of local BBSs called GayCom. GLAAD-net built upon a pilot project that GLAAD/New York had conducted in 1989, in which the organization had posted newsletters and action alerts on a local gay BBS.

17. This was my general impression of the relationship between GLAAD/Atlanta and the local Queer Nation group when I attended a special joint meeting of their leaders in 1990. Joe DeRose, a busy Atlantan gay activist of that era, confirmed this for me in an E-mail dated December 28, 1998.

18. For information about gay activists' interaction with *The Arsenio Hall Show*, see: GLAAD news release, "Arsenio Hall's Failure to Respond to Gay Community's

Concern About Negative, Stereotype-Based 'Humor,'" December 16, 1990; Karin Schwartz, "GLAAD Tidings," *OutWeek,* December 18, 1990 (downloaded from GLAAD-net); Sarah Pettit, "Blurt Out," *OutWeek,* December 26, 1990; "Etcetera: Late Night with Queer Nation," *The Advocate,* January 15, 1991.

19. Signorile's "Gossip Watch" column in *OutWeek* was a weekly diatribe against the rich, famous, and closeted. For an example of his fulminations against all things Geffen, see Michelangelo Signorile, "Gossip Watch: Zap Geffen Again!", *OutWeek,* December 26, 1990.

20. Syndicated TV, the aforementioned *Arsenio Hall Show* from circa May 1991.

21. GLAAD/New York "GLAAD Tidings" column, March 1, 1991, via GLAAD-net; Joe Clark, "Star Trek: The Next Generation," *The Advocate,* August 27, 1991; Keay Davidson, "'Star Trek' Still on Cutting Edge," *St. Louis Post-Dispatch,* September 18, 1991; "Star Trek," *GLAAD/LA Reports,* November 1991. On the syndicated *700 Club* of October 24, 1991, Ted Baehr of the Christian Film and Television Commission says that he has a copy of the letter of agreement. According to Baehr, the *Trek* producers promise to present gay issues "in a positive light," but do not promise a gay role. Regarding the Gaylaxians' advocacy work for gay content on *Star Trek,* search the Internet for a document called "History of Interaction Between the Producers of *Star Trek* and the Lesbian/Gay Audience" (the URL varies as Gaylaxian web sites move around).

22. Fox TV, *Beverly Hills 90210,* July 25, 1991, "Summer Storm."

23. Regarding the NGLTF benefit: David J. Fox and Victor F. Zonana, "Guess Who's Coming to Gay-Rights Dinner," *Los Angeles Times,* August 5, 1991; Jeannine Stein, "It's Politics as Unusual at Benefit," *Los Angeles Times,* August 13, 1991.

24. For early years of Hollywood Supports, see: Green; Richard Natale, "Crucial Inroads After a Naive Start," *Los Angeles Times,* January 4, 1995; John Gallagher, "Network," *The Advocate,* August 20, 1996; Ehrenstein, pp. 174–176.

25. Dave DiMartino, Bruce Fretts, Mark Harris et al., "Power 101," *Entertainment Weekly,* October 30, 1992.

CHAPTER 32

1. Syndicated TV, *The Arsenio Hall Show,* March 30, 1993, excerpted in ABC-TV, *Day One,* January 3, 1994, "The Last Laugh."

2. Emmys per listing in McNeil.

3. NBC-TV, *L.A. Law* episodes: May 10, 1990, "Outward Bound"; November 15, 1990, "Smoke Gets in Your Thighs." Joe Windish and Karin Schwartz,

GLAAD/New York's "GLAAD Tidings" column, posted to GLAAD-net on February 15, 1991.

4. NBC-TV, *L.A. Law,* February 7, 1991, "He's a Crowd"; Fox TV, *21 Jump Street,* January 15, 1990, "Change of Heart."

5. Vicki P. McConnell, "Changing Channels," *The Advocate,* January 14, 1992; Deborah Hastings, "Gay Rights Group Hails 'L.A. Law' Lesbian Kiss," Associated Press, released February 9, 1991.

6. Most of the GLB-relevant episodes of ABC-TV's *Roseanne* were consulted. Background sources regarding the show's star, her career, her family, and the backstage battles: Tom Shales, "Roseanne Barr, Kvetch as Kvetch Can," *Washington Post,* March 7, 1987; HBO cable, *HBO—On Location,* September 19, 1987, "The Roseanne Barr Show"; Marc Gunther, "Can 'Roseanne' Stand Success?", *Philadelphia Inquirer,* August 20, 1989; Ann Trebbe, "Barr's Newest Chapter," *USA Today,* September 29, 1989; "Names in the News," Associated Press, released February 27, 1991; Marilyn Beck, "Grapevine: *Roseanne* Is Planning Plot Lines About Gays," *TV Guide,* July 27, 1991; Helen Eisenbach, "Roseanne unBarred," *QW,* June 7, 1992; Scott Hunt, "Sandra Bernhard," *Christopher Street,* December 21, 1992; Roseanne Arnold, *My Lives* (New York: Ballantine Books, 1994); Geraldine Barr and Ted Schwartz, *My Sister Roseanne* (New York: Birch Lane Press, 1994). In extracting information from the two sisters' divergent autobiographies, I have tried to stick to areas in which they agree.

7. NBC-TV, *L.A. Law* episodes: April 25, 1991, "Speak, Lawyers, for Me"; May 2, 1991, "There Goes the Judge." Other sources: "Next Season: A New Face, New Frontiers," *USA Today,* June 4, 1991; "Michele Greene, Actress in TV Lesbian Kiss, Another 'L.A. Law' Defection," Associated Press, released June 20, 1991; " 'L.A. Law' Cast Exodus Continues," *St. Petersburg Times,* June 21, 1991; Aleene MacMinn, "Pulling a Switch," July 16, 1991.

8. CBS-TV, *Northern Exposure,* July 12, 1990 (premiere).

9. Interview with Joshua Brand and John Falsey in Louis Chunovic, *The Northern Exposure Book: The Official Publication of the Television Series* (revised and updated), (New York: Citadel Press, 1995), p. 54.

10. CBS-TV, *Northern Exposure,* July 19, 1990, "Brains, Know-How and Native Intelligence."

11. CBS-TV, *Northern Exposure,* May 20, 1991, "Slow Dance."

12. NBC-TV, *L.A. Law,* December 19, 1991, "The Nut Before Christmas."

13. NBC-TV's *L.A. Law* episodes of October 22, 1992 ("L.A. Lawless") and January 7, 1993 ("Odor in the Court"), as summarized in Morris, *Prime Time Network Serials,* pp. 642, 645.

14. ABC-TV, *Roseanne,* October 15, 1991, "Tolerate Thy Neighbor."

15. Fox TV, *Melrose Place,* July 8, 1992, premiere.

16. Daniel Cerone, " 'Melrose Place' to Spotlight a Gay Character," *Philadelphia Inquirer,* October 28, 1992.

17. Various TV networks, live coverage of the Democratic National Convention, July 1992. Achtenberg's speech was on July 14.

18. "The Vision Shared: Uniting Our Family, Our Country, Our World," platform of the 1992 Republican National Convention, adopted August 17, 1992; Pat Buchanan, speech to the Republican National Convention, August 17, 1992.

19. *Murphy Brown* dialog quoted in Lichter, Lichter, and Rothman, p. 27.

20. Information about the quantity of network news coverage is based on data in the Lexis/Nexis database, in the transcript catalog of the Journal Graphics Corporation, the subject index of the Vanderbilt Television News Archive, the MTR catalog, and a list of videotapes I recorded off the air at the time.

CHAPTER 33

1. ABC-TV, *My So-Called Life,* September 22, 1994, "The Zit."

2. PBS TV, *This Old House,* February 24, 1996.

3. Quoted or summarized "Men on . . ." skits from Fox TV's *In Living Color:* April 15, 1990, "Men on Film"; April 7, 1991, "Men on Vacation"; May 12, 1991, "Men on Television"; January 26, 1992, "Men on Football." Other sources: "Reasons to be MAAD," national *GLAAD Newsletter,* winter/spring 1989; Rex Wockner, "In Living Color: Two Snaps Up!", *Philadelphia Gay News,* November 23, 1990; Essex Hemphill, "In Living Color: Toms, Coons, Mammies, Faggots and Bucks," *OutWeek,* December 26, 1990; "Two Snaps Down?", undated clipping from *The GLAAD Bulletin*; Harvey Fierstein, on the already-cited *Arsenio Hall Show* from circa May 1991. The GLAAD/San Francisco Bay Area survey was a subject of online discussion among regional GLAAD leaders in the public area of GLAAD-net in January 1993. Much of the information about general community attitudes comes from my direct observation, having discussed these characters with a large number of GLBT people in diverse contexts between 1990 and 1993.

4. Fox TV, *Roc* episodes: September 29, 1991, "Can't Help Loving That Man"; April 5, 1994, "Brothers."

5. CBS-TV, *Cutters,* undated summer 1993 episode in which the barbershop crowd and hair salon crowd clash over what magazines should be in the combined shop.

6. HBO cable, *And the Band Played On.* Other sources: Randy Shilts, *And the Band Played On* (New York: St. Martin's Press, 1987); Armistead Maupin, "A Line That Commercial TV Won't Cross," *New York Times,* January 9, 1994.

7. Telephone interview with Jordan Budde, February 10, 2000; Michelangelo Signorile, *Queer in America* (New York: Random House, 1993), pp. 251–253; Ian Spelling, "Beverly Hills' Carteris Finds Fame Has Price," *Calgary Herald*, September 12, 1992. Fox TV, *Beverly Hills 90210* episodes: July 25, 1991, "Summer Storm"; January 23, 1992, "A Competitive Edge."

8. NBC-TV, *Today*, circa June 1991, described in *Philadelphia P-FLAG Newsletter*, August 1991; ABC-TV, *20/20*, May 8, 1992, "The Only Way Out."

9. Fox TV, *Doing Time on Maple Drive*, March 16, 1992. The informal survey was my own. During speaking engagements sponsored by colleges' and universities' gay student groups, I would usually ask the audiences to indicate, by a show of hands, if they had ever seen a GLBT character on TV who reminded them of a real person they knew. Almost without exception, from 1992 to 1994, the only character anyone cited was Matt from *Doing Time on Maple Drive*.

10. Several dozen episodes of ABC-TV's *One Life to Live* gay story arc were consulted.

11. The coming-out story in "For Better or for Worse" spanned five weeks' worth of comic strips, beginning in April 1993. Some twenty newspapers refused to run the sequence. ABC-TV, *Doogie Howser, M.D.*, January 6, 1993, "Spell it M-A-N"; CBS-TV, *Picket Fences*, April 29, 1993, "Sugar and Spice"; NBC-TV, *The Mommies*, December 6, 1993, "I Got the Music in Me."

12. All nineteen episodes of ABC-TV's *My So-Called Life* were consulted. The quoted dialog is from the episode of December 1, 1994, "Pressure."

13. Winnie Holzman, interviewed on National Public Radio, *Weekend Edition*, January 22, 1995.

14. Raul appeared in about eight episodes of *ER*, ending with his deathbed scene in the episode of February 22, 1996, "The Healers."

15. NBC-TV, *Blossom*, January 31, 1994, "The Double Date"; CBS-TV, *Matt Waters*, February 7, 1996, "Who" (last show of the series).

16. HBO cable, *Dream On* episodes: June 23, 1993, "Pop Secret"; September 14, 1994, "The Courtship of Martin's Father." ABC-TV, *Grace Under Fire* episodes: December 6, 1995, "Emmett's Secret"; December 20, 1995, "Emmett, We Hardly Knew Ye."

17. ABC-TV, *Roseanne* episodes cited: November 10, 1992, "Ladies' Choice"; December 15, 1992, "It's No Place Like Home for the Holidays"; May 4, 1993, "Glengarry Glen Rosey"; January 4, 1994, "Suck Up or Shut Up."

18. NBC-TV, *Homicide: Life on the Street*, consulted episodes: January 2, 1998, "Closet Cases"; April 17, 1998, "Secrets."

19. CBS-TV, *Medical Center*, September 8 and September 15, 1975, "The Fourth Sex" (parts one and two), summary per various newspaper accounts of the

plotline; ABC-TV, *Westside Medical,* July 7, 1977, "The Mermaid" (working title: "The Freak"), script in GMTF Records.

20. CBS-TV, *Evening Shade,* January 31, 1994, "The Perfect Woman," summary per TV listings and various contemporary reviews; NBC-TV, *ER,* November 17, 1994, "ER Confidential."

21. CBS-TV, *Chicago Hope* episodes: March 13, 1995, "Informed Consent"; February 12, 1996, "Women on the Verge."

22. NBC-TV, *Carol & Company,* April 7, 1990, "Reunion"; NBC-TV, *L.A. Law,* April 25, 1991, "Speak, Lawyers, for Me"; CBS-TV, *Picket Fences,* December 11, 1992, "Pageantry."

CHAPTER 34

1. CBS-TV, *Northern Exposure,* May 18, 1992, "Cicely."

2. *The War Widow* aired in October 1976 on the anthology series *Visions.* For a summary and analysis, see Russo, *The Celluloid Closet,* pp. 225–226.

3. NBC-TV aired the *Quantum Leap* episode "Good Night, Dear Heart" on March 7, 1990. Since no recording was readily available, the summary is based on various published reviews and TV listings, in conjunction with verbal accounts I received from people who saw the show. In 1991, the Mystery Writers of America honored the "Good Night, Dear Heart" episode with its Edgar Award for Best Episode in a Television Series. Also consulted: NBC-TV, *Quantum Leap,* January 15, 1992, "Running for Honor."

4. No, the math does not *quite* work out. This episode shifts the town's founding from 1893 (given in the pilot) to 1908, out of practical necessity: otherwise, the narrator would have to be more like 125 years old. Even so, if 1992 was Cicely's hundredth birthday, she would only have been fifteen or sixteen when she and Roslyn arrived—which does not seem to be the case. It hardly matters, of course, given how well the episode works dramatically.

5. *Northern Exposure,* "Cicely."

6. CBS-TV, *Ned Blessing,* September 8, 1993, "Oscar"; Fox TV, *The Adventures of Brisco County, Jr.,* September 10, 1993, "No Man's Land."

7. The allegory for AIDS-phobia portrays members of an alien race who, as a safety precaution, want to illegally destroy a quarantine ship containing victims of a fast-spreading plague. It aired as one of the show's first episodes: syndicated TV, *Star Trek: The Next Generation,* circa December 1987, "Haven."

8. These two statements from Roddenberry were widely quoted (and misquoted) at the time. The wording used here, which matches most of the

printed accounts, was confirmed by Roddenberry's former personal assistant, Ernest C. Over, in a letter to the editor: "Star-Crossed," *Los Angeles Times*, April 18, 1993.

9. Syndicated TV, *Star Trek: The Next Generation*, May 1991, "The Host"; UPN TV, *Star Trek: Voyager*, November 25, 1998, "Infinite Regress."

10. J. Michael Straczynski in online Usenet discussions, December 13, 1993 and May 8, 1997. Episodes of the syndicated TV series *Babylon 5*: October 1995, "Divided Loyalties"; April 1997, "Racing Mars."

11. Fox TV, *The Simpsons* episodes: February 25, 1990, "The Tell-Tale Head"; November 5, 1992, "Marge Gets a Job"; October 21, 1993, "Rosebud"; February 25, 1996, "Homer the Smithers"; October 9, 1994, "Sideshow Bob Roberts"; October 29, 1992, "King Homer" segment in the special Halloween episode, "Tree House of Horror III." For an episode-by-episode analysis of allusions to Smithers's sexuality, search the Internet for a page called "Smithers' Sexuality" (which, at this writing, can be found at http://www.snpp. com/guides/smithers.sexuality.html).

12. Fox TV, *The Simpsons* episodes: October 18, 1990, "Simpson and Delilah"; February 16, 1997, "Homer's Phobia."

13. Comedy Central cable, *Out There*, December 3, 1993.

14. IKEA commercial, "Dining Room," first aired March 20, 1994. Other sources: Frank Rich, "Gay Shopping Spree," *New York Times*, April 3, 1994; Paula Spann, "ISO the Gay Consumer," *Washington Post*, May 19, 1994; Greg Gatlin, "Virgin Brings Soapbox to Hub," *Boston Herald*, August 26, 1998; Greg Johnson, "Advertisements You Won't See," *Los Angeles Times*, August 20, 1998.

CHAPTER 35

1. Armistead Maupin, *Tales of the City* (New York: Ballantine Books, 1984), p. 127. The stories originally appeared as a popular newspaper serial in San Francisco.

2. PBS-TV, *Great Performances*, June 24, 1992, *The Lost Language of Cranes;* PBS-TV, *Masterpiece Theatre*, July 19, July 26, and August 2, 1992, "Portrait of a Marriage" (3-part serialization). *Oranges Are Not the Only Fruit*, broadcast in England in 1990, was seen in the United States shortly thereafter on A&E cable in a featurized form. A number of PBS stations aired the original serialized version circa 1992.

3. Frank DeCaro, " 'Tales of the City': Why Not a Sequel?", New York *Newsday*, April 19, 1994.

4. Betsy Sharkey, "Maupin's 'Dream of the Future Set in the Past,'" *New York Times,* February 28, 1993; John Lyttle, "No More Maupin Around," London *Independent,* September 27, 1993; Armistead Maupin, "A Tale of the '70s," *TV Guide,* January 8, 1994; Armistead Maupin, "A Line That Commercial TV Won't Cross," *New York Times,* January 9, 1994; Bart Mills, "S.F.'s Wild Side, By Way of U.K.," *Philadelphia Inquirer,* January 9, 1994.

5. PBS, *American Playhouse,* "Armistead Maupin's 'Tales of the City,'" January 10, 11, and 12, 1994. PBS offered stations two different versions of the show. The summary presented here is based on the "uncensored" version. The censored version used a video-pixelation effect to obscure bare female breasts. It is rumored that one or several stations in the United States pixelated the moments of male-male kissing, but I have not been able to confirm this.

6. The earliest mention I could find of the project is in John J. O'Connor, "Top Quality Loses Out to TV Bottom Line," *Beacon Journal,* December 15, 1992. By then, the show's length and its writer had already been determined.

7. Lyttle; Mills, "S.F.'s Wild Side . . ."

8. Bart Mills, "Why Gay Isn't the Word in the States," *The Guardian,* September 22, 1993.

9. Root recounts this incident in Mills, "S.F.'s Wild Side . . ." Maupin told the same story in an interview on the Showtime cable website, June 1998.

10. Associated Press article, "TV Station Gives In, Dumps Program," in the Memphis *Commercial Appeal,* January 15, 1994.

11. Laura Linney, interviewed on the Showtime cable website, June 1998. In conjunction with its sequel *Armistead Maupin's "More Tales of the City,"* Showtime interviewed cast members about the controversy that the original miniseries had inspired in its PBS run.

12. Spring 1994 mass mailing from the American Family Association. To avoid seeming prurient themselves, AFA added censors' blocks to the photos, to cover the women's nipples. Regarding the videotape that the American Family Association sent to legislators: "American Family Association Targets 'Tales of the City,'" *Hotwire* (online newsletter of the Arts Wire computer network), March 21, 1994; Frank Rich, "The Plot Thickens at PBS," *New York Times,* April 17, 1994; "Salvos from the Religious Right: Someone Has Been Busy . . . ," *GLAAD/LA Reports,* May 1994; Showtime cable, *Ratings, Morals and Sex on TV,* June 7, 1998. The Showtime documentary includes excerpts from the AFA videotape.

13. Regarding the Georgia legislature's retaliation against *Tales of the City*: Martha Ezzard, "Would They Kill Big Bird?," *Atlanta Journal and Constitution,* October 17, 1994; "American Family Association Targets . . ." Regarding Oklahoma: Mick Hinton, "Lawmaker Objects to State TV Programming," *The*

Oklahoman, January 21, 1994; Ellen Knickmeyer, "OETA Committee to Review Program Oversight Policies," *The Oklahoman,* March 9, 1994; "American Family Association Targets 'Tales of the City.' "

14. Karen Everhart Bedford, "PBS Backs Away from Maupin Sequel, But Will Refeed First Series on Option," *Current,* April 25, 1994. The article is a thoughtful, thorough discussion about the complex practical issues behind PBS's decision not to coproduce *More Tales of the City.*

15. Tom Walter, "Funding Cut May Force End to PBS 'American Playhouse,' " Memphis *Commercial Appeal,* August 6, 1994.

16. John Carman, "Righteous Reverend Writes Again," *San Francisco Chronicle,* April 4, 1994; Jeffry Scott, "PBS Won't Finance Racy 'Tales' Sequel," *Atlanta Journal and Constitution,* April 11, 1994; John Carmody, "TV Column," *Washington Post,* April 11, 1994; "PBS Withdraws Support for 'Tales of the City' Sequel," *Pittsburgh Post-Gazette,* April 12, 1994; " 'Tales of the City' Sequel Stymied," *Chicago Tribune,* April 16, 1994; Walter.

17. Bedford; Linda Matchan, "Sequel Planned to 'Tales of City,' " *Boston Globe,* September 10, 1994; "Fund-Raising Tall Tales," *Extra!,* November 1994; "Gay-Lesbian Film and TV Projects," Hollywood Supports website, circa spring 1995.

18. Lee Winfrey, "Maupin's 'Tales' Isn't Too Racy for Showtime," *Philadelphia Inquirer TV Week,* June 7, 1998.

CHAPTER 36

1. ABC-TV, *Roseanne,* December 15, 1992, "It's No Place Like Home for the Holidays."

2. ABC-TV, *20/20,* February 18, 1994. Episode summary per ABC-TV, *Roseanne,* March 1, 1994, "Don't Ask, Don't Tell." Other sources for the *Roseanne* discussion: *Roseanne,* "It's No Place Like Home . . ."; Gunther, "Can 'Roseanne' Stand Success?"; Karen Freifeld, "Roseanne and Tom Arnold—ABC: In This Case, A Kiss Isn't Just a Kiss," *Newsday,* February 7, 1994; Joseph P. Kahn, "My 33 Minutes with Roseanne," *Boston Globe,* February 16, 1994; GLAAD/Los Angeles executive director Lee Werbel on syndicated TV, *Hard Copy,* February 11, 1994; advertisement for GLAAD, *Daily Variety,* February 14, 1994; Robert Silverman, "Harbert Tells ITVS That a TV Kiss is Still a Kiss," *Daily Variety,* February 14, 1994; GLAAD news release, "GLAAD Holds Press Conference Urging ABC to Air 'Don't Ask, Don't Tell' Episode of 'Roseanne,' " February 17, 1994; "ABC Blows Advisory Kiss to 'Roseanne' Episode," *Hollywood Reporter,* February 18, 1994; Associated Press wire story, March 9, 1994, 5:16 P.M. EST; advertisement for

GLAAD/New York outlining recent activities, in the annual *New York Pride Guide,* June 1994.

3. *21 Jump Street,* "Change of Heart"; NBC-TV, *L.A. Law,* February 7, 1991, "He's a Crowd"; CBS-TV, *Picket Fences,* April 29, 1993, "Sugar and Spice"; CBS-TV, *Trackdown: Finding the Goodbar Killer,* October 15, 1983; CBS-TV, *Guyana Tragedy: The Story of Jim Jones,* April 15 and 16, 1980; CBS-TV, *Picket Fences,* February 12, 1993, "Be My Valentine."

4. According to Armistead Maupin (who worked with actor William Campbell on *Tales of the City*), Jack Coleman and Campbell filmed a Steven/Luke kiss for *Dynasty* in the mid 1980s, but it was never broadcast. See Maupin, "A Line That Commercial TV Won't Cross." Regarding the other shows: Aaron Spelling and Jefferson Graham, *Aaron Spelling: A Prime-Time Life,* (New York: St. Martin's Press, 1996), p. 156; Gunther, "Amateur Tube Censors . . ."; *The Women of Brewster Place,* March 20, 1989; Phil Kloer, "TV Review: 'And the Band Played On,' " *Atlanta Journal and Constitution,* September 9, 1993; Gail Shister, "No Kissing for Gay 'Melrose' Character: Fox Chief Fears Ad Losses," *Philadelphia Inquirer,* July 15, 1994; Joseph Hanania, "Resurgence of Gay Roles on Television," *Los Angeles Times,* November 3, 1994.

5. Fox TV, *The Simpsons,* October 18, 1990, "Simpson and Delilah."

6. Marlo Thomas, interviewed on Fox TV, *Behind the Laughs,* May 27, 1998; Gitlin, pp. 183–184; NBC-TV, *Star Trek,* November 22, 1968, "Plato's Stepchildren."

7. Syndicated TV, *Star Trek: Deep Space Nine,* October 1995 (date varied by city), "Rejoined."

8. *Roseanne,* "Don't Ask, Don't Tell"; NBC-TV, *Friends,* October 31, 1996, "The One with the Flashback"; ABC-TV, *Ellen,* April 30, 1997, "The Puppy Episode."

9. Rena Dictor LeBlanc, " 'My Two Loves': A TV Movie Confronts a Woman's Bisexuality," *Philadelphia Inquirer,* April 4, 1986; Shirley Eder, "They Cut the Mariette-Lynn Kiss, But Not the Message," *Detroit Free Press,* April 12, 1986; ABC-TV, *My Two Loves,* April 7, 1986; *L.A. Law,* "He's a Crowd."

10. Matt Roush, "Flirting With Kiss of Death," *USA Today,* April 29, 1993; *Picket Fences,* "Sugar and Spice;" *Picket Fences,* "Be My Valentine."

11. GLAAD/SFBA *Media Watch,* March 11, 1994; John Koch, "HBO's 'Leiter' a Tender Love Story," *Boston Globe,* March 7, 1994; Matt Roush, "Hearts Young and Gay: Tales of Teen Sex, Homosexuality," *USA Today,* March 7, 1994; Maria Koklanaris, " 'Coming Out' Flops: Teacher Admits Error in Using Lesbian Film," *Washington Times,* May 13, 1994.

12. MTV cable, *Singled Out,* June 28, 1996, special one-time lesbian and gay edition.

13. Summary of *The Real World*'s summer 1994 wedding episode per Hanania.

14. GLAAD news release, "GLAAD Places Full Page Ad in Response to Fox's

Reported Threat to Censor Part of Season Finale of Melrose Place," May 10, 1994; Fox TV, *Melrose Place,* May 18, 1994, "Till Death Do Us Part."

15. Gail Shister, "No Kissing for Gay 'Melrose' Character," *Philadelphia Inquirer,* July 15, 1994; Stephen Seplow, "Gays on TV," *Philadelphia Inquirer,* October 17, 1994.

16. Front cover, *The Advocate,* December 27, 1994.

17. Spelling and Graham, pp. 156–157.

CHAPTER 37

1. Comedy Central cable, *Out There,* December 3, 1993.

2. Front covers of the following magazines: *New York,* May 10, 1993; *Newsweek,* June 21, 1993; *Vanity Fair,* August 1993.

3. Text from an extended headline to Alexis Jetter, "Goodbye to the Last Taboo," *Vogue,* July 1993.

4. Montgomery, *Target: Prime Time,* p. 64.

5. Karin Schwartz (GLAAD/New York's deputy director for Public Affairs), "Lesbian Invisibility," National *GLAAD Newsletter,* fall 1990.

6. "Grapevine," *TV Guide,* November 9, 1991; GLAAD news release, "GLAAD Meets with NBC Over Reports Network is Quashing Gay Characters," November 20, 1991.

7. ABC-TV, *20/20,* October 23, 1992, "Women Who Love Women."

8. CBS-TV, *Overkill: The Aileen Wuornos Story,* November 17, 1992; CBS-TV, *Nash Bridges,* February 7, 1997, "Knockout."

9. Various episodes of NBC-TV's *Sisters* (1995 and 1996), NBC-TV's *Friends* (especially 1994 to 1996), and ABC-TV's *NYPD Blue* (1997). Specific episodes: ABC-TV, *Civil Wars,* December 2, 1992, "A Bus Named Desire"; Fox TV, *Herman's Head,* September 20, 1992, "Sperm 'n Herman"; *Roseanne,* "It's No Place Like Home . . ."

10. *All's Fair,* "Discovery Day" script; NBC-TV, *Dear John,* September 20, 1991, "Kirk's Ex-Wife." For detailed information about Diandra and Ruth's guest appearances on *Hearts Afire,* see the well-researched "Hearts Afire Episode Guide" by Melissa Pollak (1997), widely available on the Internet.

11. NBC-TV, *Friends,* September 29, 1994, "The One With the Sonogram at the End." (In this one episode—Carol's first appearance—she is played by Anita Barone. Jane Sibbett assumed the role that November.)

12. NBC-TV, *Friends* episodes: May 11, 1995, "The One With the Birth"; September 28, 1995, "The One With the Breast Milk"; January 18, 1996, "The One With the Lesbian Wedding."

13. Phil Kloer, "Sitcom Jokes Putting Spotlight on Lesbians," *Atlanta Journal and Constitution,* January 18, 1995; CBS-TV, *Cybill,* January 2, 1995, "Virgin,

Mother, Crone"; CBS-TV, *Women of the House,* January 4, 1995, "Miss Sugar-baker Goes to Washington."

14. Michael McWilliams, "Ellen's next step," *The Detroit News,* October 23, 1996; Karen Ocamb, "Cybill Shepherd: The LN Interview," *The Lesbian News,* January 1998.

15. NBC-TV, *Serving in Silence: The Colonel Margarethe Cammermeyer Story,* February 6, 1995.

CHAPTER 38

1. NBC-TV, *The Golden Girls,* January 12, 1991, "Sister of the Bride."

2. Rex Wockner's syndicated column, "Quote Unquote," released April 29, 1997.

3. *All's Fair* dialog per Coakley, p. 37.

4. For a thumbnail summary of the Arizona case (in which a minister, not a judge, performed the marriage), see Leigh W. Rutledge, *The Gay Decades* (New York: Plume, 1992), pp. 73, 78. NBC aired the *Sirota's Court* episode "Court Fear" in late 1976 or early 1977. Summary per script in GMTF Records. Since Montgomery summarizes this plotline in *Target: Prime Time* (p. 93), the episode apparently did air.

5. Jesse Helms quotation per Peter Applebome, "Pit Bull Politician," *New York Times,* October 28, 1990.

6. *The Golden Girls,* "Sister of the Bride."

7. Syndicated TV, *Donahue,* May 1991 (date varied by market), broadcast of a gay male wedding. Responses from Carson et al. are per "Wedding Bells . . . On Donahue," *GLAAD Rag,* June 1991.

8. *Roc,* "Can't Help Loving That Man."

9. "New Emphasis on Gay Themes," *TV Guide,* August 17, 1991; Devon Clayton, "Dear John Gets the Queer Story Straight," *The Advocate,* September 24, 1991; NBC-TV, *Dear John,* September 20, 1991, "Kirk's Ex-wife."

10. NBC-TV aired the *L.A. Law* episode "Do the Spike Thing" on October 31, 1991—summary per "NBC's 'L.A. Law' Has Pro-Homosexual Themes," *Journal of the American Family Association,* November 1992, compared against several unofficial episode guides for the series. NBC-TV, *Seinfeld,* January 8, 1992, "The Subway."

11. CBS-TV, *Northern Exposure,* May 2, 1994, "I Feel the Earth Move"; " 'Exposure' pulled by 2 CBS affils," *Daily Variety,* May 2, 1994; GLAAD news release, "Nestlé Corporation Withdraws Sponsorship on *Northern Exposure* Gay Wedding," May 2, 1994.

12. ABC-TV, *Roseanne,* December 12, 1995, "December Bride"; Peter Johnson, "A Later Altar Time for 'Roseanne' Gay Wedding," *USA Today,* Decem-

ber 11, 1995; Biddle; theories about Roseanne's motives for including shocking content in her shows that season are per comments posted to fan-based Internet discussion groups and websites.

13. Conversation among Roseanne, Martin Mull, and Fred Willard on syndicated TV, the *Roseanne* talk show, 1998.

14. NBC-TV, *Friends,* January 18, 1996, "The One With the Lesbian Wedding"; "TV Stations Ditch 'Friends' Episode," released by the Associated Press on January 18, 1996; "Hearts Young and Gay," *USA Today,* January 18, 1996; Richard Stewart, "Port Arthur Station is Un-Friend-ly," *Houston Chronicle,* January 19, 1996; David W. Dunlap, "Gay Images, Once Kept Out, Are Out Big Time," *New York Times,* January 21, 1996; transcript of syndicated radio show *This Way Out,* January 22, 1996; "The Ratings," *Entertainment Weekly,* February 2, 1996.

15. C-SPAN cable, *National Campaign to Protect Marriage Rally,* February 10, 1996.

16. ABC-TV, *Spin City,* October 29, 1996, "Grand Illusion"; ABC-TV, *The Practice,* December 20, 1997, "The Civil Right"; ABC-TV, *Ellen,* July 22, 1998, "Vows."

17. CBS-TV, *Picket Fences,* April 24, 1996, "Bye-Bye, Bey-Bey."

CHAPTER 39

1. GLAAD news release, "GLAAD Urges Support of Television's Gay and Lesbian Characters," November 15, 1995.

2. Where much of this book has focused on individual episodes of shows, this chapter provides capsule summaries of lengthy story arcs. Citing every relevant episode in the endnotes is not practical here, except where specific broadcasts are quoted or summarized in detail.

3. NBC-TV, *Seinfeld,* February 11, 1993, "The Outing."

4. NBC-TV, *Seinfeld,* September 18, 1991, "The Note."

5. NBC-TV, *Seinfeld,* February 9, 1995, "The Beard."

6. Fox TV, *The Critic,* April 30, 1995, "Sherman of Arabia."

7. Fox TV, *The Simpsons,* February 16, 1997, "Homer's Phobia." (Title is often given erroneously as "Homer Phobia." Correct title per copyright registration record.)

8. Comedy Central cable, *South Park,* September 3, 1997, "Big Gay Al's Big Gay Boat Ride."

9. NBC-TV, *ER,* February 6, 1997, "Who's Appy Now?"

10. ABC-TV, *NYPD Blue,* October 14, 1997, "Three Girls and a Baby."

11. ABC-TV, *NYPD Blue,* December 16, 1997, "Remembrance of Humps Past,"

summary per write-ups in *Entertainment Weekly*'s TV listings and in Dennis Kytasaari, "*NYPD Blue:* An Episode Guide," available online at www.epguides.com.

12. ABC-TV, *Relativity,* January 11, 1997, "The Day the Earth Moved."

13. "Will Steamy Sex Leave Some Leery of 'Relativity'?", New York *Daily News,* January 8, 1997.

14. ABC-TV, *Spin City,* September 17, 1996, pilot episode.

15. ABC-TV, *Spin City* episodes: October 29, 1996, "Grand Illusion"; October 8, 1996, "Pride and Prejudice."

16. CBS-TV, *Touched by an Angel,* December 22, 1996, "The Violin Lesson."

CHAPTER 40

1. "Sound Bites," *Entertainment Weekly,* October 17, 1997.

2. Syndicated TV, *The Rosie O'Donnell Show,* September 25, 1996; Ginia Bellafante and Jeffrey Ressner, "Looking for an Out," *Time* magazine online edition, October 7, 1996; A.J. Jacobs and Dan Snierson, "Out?", *Entertainment Weekly,* October 4, 1996; ABC-TV, *Ellen,* October 2, 1996, "Splitsville, Man"; NBC-TV, *NewsRadio,* October 30, 1996, "Halloween."

3. Ellen DeGeneres's acceptance speech for the Creative Integrity Award, Los Angeles Gay and Lesbian Center, March 10, 1998, as webcast by GLOradio/PlanetOut Broadcasting; Channel Four (England), *The Real Ellen Story,* April 25, 1998; ABC-TV, *Primetime Live,* May 6, 1998, "Ellen: Uncensored."

4. The biography is Kathy Tracy and Jeff Rovin's *Ellen DeGeneres Up Close.* (New York: Pocket Books, 1994). Regarding the 1996 outing, see, Rex Wockner, "Ellen Outed," released to gay newspapers and radio shows February 6, 1996.

5. Quotations from Joyce Millman's article are from a reprint in the *San Diego Union-Tribune,* April 1, 1995, retitled " 'Ellen': Is She or Isn't She?"

6. CNN cable, *Larry King Live,* May 12, 1998, interview with Ellen DeGeneres; Jacobs and Snierson; Frederic M. Biddle, "Gays in Prime Time," *Boston Globe,* December 24, 1995.

7. Jacobs and Snierson; *The Real Ellen Story.*

8. Jacobs and Snierson.

9. ABC-TV, *Ellen* episodes: November 15, 1995, "Salad Days"; February 28, 1996, "Two Ring Circus."

10. DeGeneres's acceptance speech, Creative Integrity Award; *The Real Ellen Story;* "1995–96 Rankings: Nielsen Rankings," *Akron Beacon Journal,* May 30, 1996.

11. Tom Gliatto et al., "Tube," *People Weekly,* May 5, 1997; *Ellen* producers Jonathan Stark, Tracy Nelson, and Mark Driscoll interviewed in *The Real*

Ellen Story; Jennifer Bowles, "TV's 'Ellen' is Coming Out of Closet," released by the Associated Press March 7, 1997.

12. Kevin Chen, "Reuters/Variety Entertainment Summary," released by Reuters news service June 10, 1996.

13. *Larry King Live,* May 12, 1998; *The Real Ellen Story.*

14. "Ellen," *Entertainment Weekly,* September 13, 1996.

15. Jacobs and Snierson; "Lifetime Buys 'Ellen' Repeats," *Tampa Tribune,* September 8, 1996; "Dramatic Returns: Rerun Prices at a Glance," *Entertainment Weekly,* October 17, 1997.

16. Valerie Kuklenski, "About Being Out," released by UPI September 13, 1996; Lisa de Moraes, " 'Ellen' Asked But Won't Tell on Lesbianism," *Hollywood Reporter,* September 13, 1996; *The Real Ellen Story*; Daniel Howard Cerone, *"Ellen* May be Telling, Even Though Not Asked," *TV Guide,* September 28, 1996.

17. Alan Bash, "Ad Buyers Ponder Rumored 'Ellen' Twist," *USA Today,* September 17, 1996; Skip Wollenberg, "Is Madison Avenue Ready for a Lesbian 'Ellen'?", *Fort Worth Star-Telegram,* September 19, 1996; Jacobs and Snierson.

18. Lou Sheldon, interviewed in *The Real Ellen Story*; Pat Robertson on Fox TV, *Fox News Sunday,* quoted in "Verbatim," *Time,* September 30, 1997; "Ellen Next Skeleton in Disney Closet?", *AFA Journal* online edition, October 1996; Jacobs and Snierson.

19. Heather Joslyn, "The Cathode Closet," Baltimore *City Paper* online edition, September 24, 1996.

20. This is a prime example of how intertwined the publicity from the opposing camps became. The quotation was found on a GLAAD website in fall 1996, in its posting of an AFA Action Alert, that was, in turn, quoting (accurately, it turned out) a GLAAD spokesperson.

21. E-mailed alert from the Philadelphia chapter of Parents and Friends of Lesbians and Gays, October 4, 1996.

22. DiPasquale's statement is from *The Real Ellen Story.*

23. ABC-TV, *Ellen,* September 18, 1996, "Give Me Equity or Give Me Death."

24. ABC-TV, *Ellen,* October 2, 1996, "Splitsville, Man."

25. Julie Pecenco, "The 'Ellen' Clues List," Internet document originally posted at http://web.syr.edu/~jnpecenc/clues.txt during the 1996–1997 television season. Pecenco took detailed, accurate notes from recordings of every *Ellen* episode that season, and compiled this summary of lesbigay innuendo and allusions. I have relied on it only for shows I could not locate on tape.

26. Stuart Miller, "Alphabet Hopes 'Practice' Pays," *Variety,* January 20, 1997.

27. Jefferson Graham, "ABC Has 7 New Plots to Improve Its Ratings," *USA Today,* January 10, 1997; "Spotlights," *Toronto Star,* January 13, 1997.

28. ABC-TV, *Ellen*, February 2, 1997, "Ellen Unplugged."

29. My initial sources for this were fans' accounts on the Internet. Peter Johnson later reported the incident in his "Inside TV" column in *USA Today*, January 27, 1997. Savel and DeGeneres confirm the incident in *The Real Ellen Story*.

30. "UltimateTV Daily News," UltimateTV web site, February 17, 1997; Peter Johnson, "Inside TV: Out of the Closet," *USA Today*, February 20, 1997.

31. Bowles; Shelly Lyons, " 'Ellen's' Out, So What's Next?," ultimatetv.com web article posted June 2, 1997.

32. *The Real Ellen Story.*

33. Front cover, *Time*, April 14, 1997.

34. Tom Gliatto et al., "Outward Bound," *People Weekly*, May 5, 1997.

35. Reverend Falwell's famous comment at a 1997 legislative conference was a reference to an earlier speaker's remarks. Falwell alluded to the episode in which "Ellen Morgan, played by Ellen DeGeneres—some have said 'DeGenerate'—announces her lesbianism." He was more famous than the man he was quoting, so reporters made it sound as though Falwell originated the barb. (Neither of them had done that: the comment had been circulating in antigay activist circles for months, and DeGeneres had heard similar taunts from early childhood onward.)

36. Syndicated TV, *Geraldo*, interview with Jerry Falwell, April 1997.

37. ABC-TV, *Roseanne*, March 4, 1997, "Roseanne-Feld"; NBC-TV, *Suddenly Susan*, April 27, 1997, "A Boy Like That" (preceded by several episodes that included gay references); ABC-TV, *NYPD Blue*, April 15, 1997, "A Wrenching Experience" and other episodes that season; Fox TV, *Married . . . With Children*, April 28, 1997, "Lez Be Friends"; USA cable, *Breaking the Surface: The Greg Louganis Story*, March 19, 1997; CBS-TV, *Dr. Quinn, Medicine Woman*, April 5, 1997, "The Body Electric"; ABC-TV, *Step by Step*, March 14, 1997, "Road Trip."

38. ABC-TV, *20/20*, April 25, 1997; ABC-TV, *Primetime Live*, April 30, 1997; syndicated TV, *The Oprah Winfrey Show*, April 30, 1997.

39. Frank Rich, "Disney's Homosynergy," *New York Times*, May 4, 1997; National Gay and Lesbian Task Force news release, " 'Ellen' Misses the Boat," April 10, 1997; "ABC Advertising Won't Let Women's Cruise Commercial Dock," *GLAADalert*, April 11, 1997; Ellen Gray, "ABC's Dilemma: Whose 'Ellen' Is It, Anyway?," Philadelphia *Daily News*, April 14, 1997.

40. Ellen Coming-Out House Party kit, Human Rights Campaign, 1997; Carolyn Lochhead, "Toasting 'Ellen' at Home," *San Francisco Chronicle*, April 14, 1997; Megan Rosenfeld, "The 'Ellen' Coming-Out Club," *Washington Post*, April 24, 1997; "GLAAD Works With Locals to Bring Birmingham Bounced 'Ellen' Episode," *GLAADalert*, April 11, 1997.

41. Bruce Fretts, "A Second Opinion," *Entertainment Weekly*, December 26, 1997.

42. *Ellen*, "The Puppy Episode."

43. Bowles.

44. One of several fan letters read aloud by Kathy Najimy in introducing Ellen DeGeneres at the Los Angeles Gay and Lesbian Center's Creative Achievement Award ceremony. See note 3.

45. Stefani G. Kopenec, "To Them, Disney's Become Devil's Worship," Philadelphia *Daily News*, June 19, 1997.

46. Tim Doyle, interviewed on Showtime cable, *Ratings, Morals and Sex on TV*, June 7, 1998.

47. CNN cable, interview with Jeremy Piven, aired May 12, 1998.

48. Tim Doyle, quoted in Greg Braxton, "Barr Savoring Attention She's Getting for Lesbian Portrayals," *Wichita Eagle*, November 20, 1997.

49. ABC-TV, *Ellen* episodes: November 12, 1997, "Public Display of Affection"; November 26, 1997, "Like a Virgin"; January 28, 1998, "Escape from L.A."

50. For this discussion, I compared the content ratings as they appeared in *TV Guide* listings for the period from April 1997 (the month Ellen came out) to July 1998 (when *Ellen* went off the air). I focused on four ABC sitcoms (*Ellen, Spin City, The Drew Carey Show*, and, from its September premiere, *Dharma and Greg*) and two popular NBC sitcoms (*Friends* and *Mad About You*). In some cases, an episode's content rating was not announced in time for publication; in these cases, I relied on the listing for the episode's first network rerun. Specific episodes cited in the analysis are ABC-TV, *Spin City*, April 29, 1997, "Bone Free"; ABC-TV, *Spin City*, December 10, 1997, "They Shoot Horses, Don't They?"; NBC-TV, *Mad About You*, November 25, 1997, "Le Sex Show"; and NBC-TV, *Friends*, March 26, 1998, "The One with the Free Porno."

51. David Bauder, "DeGeneres Accuses ABC of Censorship," released by Associated Press on October 8, 1997; Bill Carter, "Star of 'Ellen' Threatens to Quit Over Advisory," *New York Times*, October 9, 1997.

52. Videotape of first ABC-TV airing of the *Spin City* episode "Kiss Me, Stupid," February 11, 1997; ABC-TV, *Primetime Live*, May 6, 1998, "Ellen: Uncensored." The *Primetime* broadcast also includes a recording of the cited *Drew Carey* promo.

53. Carter; Scott Williams, "It Ain't Goldilocks: Who Will Be Sleeping in 'Ellen's' Beds?," Philadelphia *Daily News*, October 15, 1997; *Ellen*, "Like a Virgin."

54. ABC-TV, *Ellen*, November 19, 1997, "Emma."

55. DeGeneres's acceptance speech, Creative Integrity Award.

56. ABC-TV, *Ellen*, February 18, 1998, "Neighbors." For another high-concept

episode, see ABC-TV, *Ellen*, February 25, 1998, "It's a Gay, Gay, Gay, Gay World."

57. NBC-TV, *Just Shoot Me*, January 29, 1998, "Pass the Salt"; Comedy Central cable, *South Park*, February 11, 1998, "Tom's Rhinoplasty."

58. ABC-TV, *Ellen*, May 13, 1998, "Ellen: A Hollywood Tribute."

59. Quotation is from *Larry King Live*, May 12, 1998.

60. "People in the News," released by Associated Press, December 8, 1997; DeGeneres's acceptance speech, Creative Integrity Award.

CONCLUSION

1. Quote is per Jefferson Graham, "Man Trouble and More in Store for 'Will & Grace,' " *USA Today*, September 1, 1999.

2. Most *Will & Grace* episodes from the premiere through February 2000 were consulted. The NBC protest episode is "Acting Out," aired February 22, 2000. Other sources: Robert Bianco, "Network's Fall Debuts Aim to Fill Bottom Line," *USA Today*, July 21, 1998; John Carman, " 'Will's' Gay Lead Plays it Chaste," *San Francisco Chronicle*, July 22, 1998; Eric Mink, " 'Ellen' Led the Way—New Sitcom 'Will' Follow," New York *Daily News*, August 27, 1998; Jefferson Graham, "Man Trouble and More in Store for 'Will & Grace,' " *USA Today*, September 1, 1999.

3. Fox TV, *That '70s Show*, December 6, 1998, "Eric's Buddy."

4. Most of the Jack-related episodes of WB's *Dawson's Creek* were consulted, including the two that deal most directly with the start of his coming-out process: February 10, 1999, "To Be or Not To Be . . ."; February 17, 1999, ". . . That Is the Question." Kevin Williamson quotation per Frank DeCaro, "In with the Out Crowd," *TV Guide*, May 1, 1999.

5. About a dozen episodes of NBC-TV's *Veronica's Closet*, dated 1997 to 1999, were consulted.

6. Fox TV, *Party of Five* episodes: April 28, 1999, "Fragile"; May 5, 1999, "I'll Show You Mine"; May 12, 1999, "Haunted."

7. Fox TV, *Ally McBeal* episodes: November 23, 1998, "You Never Can Tell"; November 1, 1999, "Buried Pleasures."

8. NBC-TV, *Homicide: Life on the Street*, January 2, 1998, "Closet Cases."

9. NBC-TV, *Homicide: Life on the Street*, April 17, 1998, "Secrets."

10. Dave Walter, ed., *Today Then* (Helena, MT: American & World Geographic, 1992).

11. Syndicated radio, *This Way Out*, January 22, 1996, per transcript on the show's website.

12. Vito Russo, *The Celluloid Closet*, p. 292.

ACKNOWLEDGMENTS

This book owes an enormous debt to my partner, Ed Ferry. Not only was he supremely patient and supportive when I would disappear into my writing room for days on end or run off to other cities to do research, but he also contributed countless insights, facts, reference materials, and critiques.

Alternate Channels would never have existed without the example and inspiration of my role model: the late Vito Russo, a longtime gay activist and a very sweet man, who wrote the landmark book *The Celluloid Closet*. Although our approach to this subject matter is rather different, Vito's lecture style and political slant on media criticism have influenced my work tremendously. His words of encouragement about this project during the final year of his life meant a great deal to me.

I am grateful to those who read parts of the manuscript as it was in development, and offered frank criticisms and suggestions. In particular, Maran Fulvi and Greg Robinson went above and beyond the call of friendship, and spent many hours helping me to sharpen and focus some highly problematic chapters. I also offer special thanks to the following people who helped to revise the text: Peter Borland (who edited the book for Ballantine), David Ament, Lloyd Bowman, Douglas Brunk, Christopher Connelly, Glenn Finnan, Gwynne Jenkins, Robin Gutkin, Jim Kiley-Zufelt, Alan Lutton, Jennifer Maguire, James B. Moran, Gary Morreale, William J. Murphy III, Eric Peterson, David Serlin, Julie Stewart, Rich Wandel, and Sloan Wiesen. In a similar vein, as the publication deadline approached, Roy Conard, Glenn Finnan,

David Jacobs, and Dan McDougall took time out of their busy schedules to sit in my living room, watch video clips, and brainstorm ideas for
some of the later chapters. Thank you all.

The gracious, wonderful, and politically savvy Barbara Gittings and
Kay Tobin Lahusen, pioneers of East Coast gay civil rights organizing,
have been a source of enthusiasm, solid information, political analysis,
and good cheer ever since I first interviewed them in 1991. They kindly
put me in touch with other key activists of the 1950s, 1960s, and 1970s,
and lent me their unique reel-to-reel audio tapes of mid–twentieth-
century broadcasts and homophile conferences. I am pleased and
proud to know them.

Many people involved in the events described in this book gave of
their time to answer questions in person, by phone, or in writing. Some
came from the world of television, such as Danny Arnold, Don Balluck,
Jordan Budde, Ed DeBlasio, Christopher Haun, Richard Heffner, and
Gary Nardino. Others have been gay media activists or panelists on
notable broadcasts, such as Bill Bahlman, Joe DeRose, Newton Deiter,
Barbara Harwood, Jim Kepner, Phyllis Lyon, Del Martin, Tommi Avicolli Mecca, Jack Nichols, Joshua Schiowitz, Mark Segal, Ginny Vida,
and Randy Wicker.

Without the efforts of the following, this would have been a very
different—and less interesting—book: my agent, Faith Hornby Hamlin
of the Sanford Greenberger Agency; Rita Addessa, executive director of the Philadelphia Lesbian & Gay Task Force; Margaret Berry,
general counsel, Peter L. Stein, executive producer, and Red Dana,
audience services, at KQED-TV, San Francisco; Sharon Black, former
curator of the Annenberg Television Script Archive, and her colleagues
at the Annenberg Library, University of Pennsylvania; Mimi Bowling
and the staff of the Rare Book and Manuscripts Division, New York
Public Library; Steve Campellone, my successor at the William Way
GLBT Library/Archives; Geraldine DuClow, curator of the Theatre
Collection, and many others at the Free Library of Philadelphia;
Sandra Elgear and her colleagues at the Testing The Limits video
collective; Douglas Haller, former archivist of the Lesbian & Gay Library/
Archives of Philadelphia (now the William Way GLBT Library/
Archives); Maggie Heineman; Al Kielwasser, whose gay-focused online

newsletter *MEDIAlert!* was a tremendously useful resource; the brilliant historian John Loughery, who offered both encouragement and sound advice; Brenda J. Marston, curator of the Human Sexuality Collection, and her colleagues in the Division of Rare and Manuscript Collections, Kroch Library, Cornell University; Carol Mortimer, her successor Michael Biocco, and his successor Jason Lin, whose weekly online postings of gay-relevant TV listings alerted me to dozens of shows; Cathy Renna of the Gay & Lesbian Alliance Against Defamation; Bob Schoenberg; historian Marc Stein, who granted me access to as-yet unpublished materials; Bill Walker, archivist of the Gay and Lesbian Historical Society of Northern California; Rich Wandel, archivist, National Museum and Archive of Lesbian and Gay History, New York Gay and Lesbian Community Services Center; numerous participants in the ILink computer network's GayIssues Conference, 1992 to 1994; instructors and students in the Women's Studies program at Mankato State University, who let me sit in on several relevant classes during my February 1997 lecture visit there; World of Wonder Productions, who kindly sent me a copy of their documentary *The Real Ellen Story* long before it was released in the United States; and the staff of the following repositories: the Lesbian Herstory Archives, Brooklyn, NY; the Museum of Television and Radio, New York; the Billy Rose Theatre Collection, New York Public Library.

Throughout the writing process, I frequently received tips from—as a friend of mine calls them—my "spies": people who provided detailed information about shows and/or gave me access to their videotapes and transcripts. These include Allan Altman, Edward Alwood, Doreva Belfiore, Bruce Bernstein, Allan Bérubé, K. Robert Binder, Allen Capsuto, Rona and Leon Capsuto, Wayne Clawans, Barbara Cohen, Laura Cohen, Steven J. Cohen, Sarah Cole, Frank Darmstadt, Audrey De Lisle, Stephen Demos, Charles Eliason, Sheryl Erez, Steve Fabiani, Roy Fritz, Maran Fulvi, Oscar García-Vera, Reggie Garrison, Barbara Gindhart, Fco. Javier Marín Gracia, Maureen Guthman, Douglas Haller, Stephanie Hamersky, Sharon Jackson, Sharon Jaeger, Melissa James, Ruth Klein, John Michael Koroly, Gina Kozik-Rosabal, Marla Leech, Bill Mann, Geoffrey Maugham, Steve Mayo, Sue Molyneaux, Leonard Niedermayer, Patricia Partridge, Ralph Passante,

Tracey Rich, Mark Rosen, Nels Sandberg, Myke Thomas, Stephen Tropiano, and Steve Wigod.

Finally, this book was shaped by the audiences every place I lectured on this topic between 1989 and 1999. They pointed me toward countless specific broadcasts, and asked difficult questions that challenged some of my basic assumptions about the relationship between sexual minorities and the media. Their eager interest in this material made the writing process far more enjoyable, and the end product more accurate.

Index

About the Author

Steven Capsuto received his B.A. from Rutgers University-New Brunswick in 1986 with concentrations in U.S. history and mass media and journalism. He served as director of the Gay, Lesbian, Bisexual & Transgendered Library/Archives of Philadelphia from 1990 to 1998, and currently manages its archival and rare books collections. He is also a past board member of the library/archives' parent organization, the GLBT Community Center of Philadelphia (now the William Way Center). Since 1989, Mr. Capsuto has toured the country with his lecture "Alternate Channels: Lesbian and Gay Images on Network TV." He and his partner live in eastern Pennsylvania.